SUSTAINING ECONOMIC GROWTH IN ASIA

JÉRÉMIE COHEN-SETTON
THOMAS HELBLING
ADAM S. POSEN
CHANGYONG RHEE
editors

SUSTAINING ECONOMIC GROWTH IN ASIA

JÉRÉMIE COHEN-SETTON
THOMAS HELBLING
ADAM S. POSEN
CHANGYONG RHEE
editors

Peterson Institute for International Economics
Korean Ministry of Strategy and Finance
Bank of Korea
International Monetary Fund

Washington, DC
December 2018

Jérémie Cohen-Setton is research fellow at the Peterson Institute for International Economics.

Thomas Helbling is a division chief in the International Monetary Fund's Asia and Pacific Department, covering Australia and New Zealand.

Adam S. Posen is the president of the Peterson Institute for International Economics.

Changyong Rhee is the director of the Asia and Pacific Department at the International Monetary Fund.

**PETERSON INSTITUTE FOR
INTERNATIONAL ECONOMICS**
1750 Massachusetts Avenue, NW
Washington, DC 20036-1903
1+202.328.9000   www.piie.com

Adam S. Posen, *President*
Steven R. Weisman, *Vice President for
Publications and Communications*

*Cover Photo by © CJ Nattanai—Fotolia
Printing by Ironmark*

Printed in the United States of America
20   19   18   5   4   3   2   1

**Library of Congress
Cataloging-in-Publication Data**
Names: Cohen-Setton, Jérémie, editor. | Helbling, Thomas, editor. | Posen, Adam S., editor. | Changyong Rhee, editor. Title: Sustaining economic growth in Asia / Jérémie Cohen-Setton, Thomas Helbling, Adam S. Posen, editors. Description: Washington, DC : Peterson Institute for International Economics, 2018. | Includes bibliographical references and index.
Identifiers: LCCN 2018006494 (print) | LCCN 2018007715 (ebook) | ISBN 9780881327342 (ebook) | ISBN 9780881327335
Subjects: LCSH: Economic development—Asia. | Asia—Economic conditions—21st century. | Business cycles—Asia. | Stagnation (Economics) Classification: LCC HC412 (ebook) | LCC HC412 .S883 2018 (print) | DDC 338.95—dc23
LC record available at https://na01.safelinks.protection.outlook.com/?url=https%3A%2F%2Flccn.loc.gov%2F2018006494&data=02%7C01%7Csluetjen%40piie.com%7Cc11425f8858e4c30ab4108d57 5356fb7%7C55339d36654f44c1a1df1ed0983fad cd%7C1%7C0%7C636543794751849480&sdata= oUSLWYOGvpfumicnf8BDAFVnhRr8bo5CskA6-A%2BquahQ%3D&reserved=0

This publication has been subjected to a prepublication peer review intended to ensure analytical quality. The views expressed are those of the authors. This publication is part of the overall program of the Peterson Institute for International Economics, as endorsed by its Board of Directors, but it does not necessarily reflect the views of individual members of the Board or of the Institute's staff or management.

The Peterson Institute for International Economics is a private nonpartisan, nonprofit institution for rigorous, intellectually open, and indepth study and discussion of international economic policy. Its purpose is to identify and analyze important issues to make globalization beneficial and sustainable for the people of the United States and the world, and then to develop and communicate practical new approaches for dealing with them. Its work is funded by a highly diverse group of philanthropic foundations, private corporations, and interested individuals, as well as income on its capital fund. About 35 percent of the Institute's resources were provided by contributors from outside the United States. A list of all financial supporters is posted at https://piie.com/sites/default/files/supporters.pdf.

Contents

Preface   vii

1   **Introduction: Toward a New Long-Term Growth Model for Asia**   1
Jérémie Cohen-Setton, Thomas Helbling, Adam S. Posen, and Changyong Rhee

2   **Secular Stagnation: History and Reality**   9
Joel Mokyr

3   **Is Asia at Risk of Growing Old before Becoming Rich?**   33
Serkan Arslanalp, Jaewoo Lee, Minsuk Kim, Umang Rawat, Jacqueline Pia Rothfels, Jochen Markus Schmittmann, and Qianqian Zhang

4   **Invention, Productivity, and the Evolution of East Asia's Innovation Systems**   73
Lee Branstetter and Namho Kwon
Comment: Jong-Wha Lee

5   **Secular Stagnation and Asia: International Transmission and Policy Spillovers**   103
Olivier Jeanne

6   **Getting Out of Secular Stagnation: Turning Japanese May Be a Good Thing Now**   129
Adam S. Posen

7   Secular Stagnation and the Labor Market in Japan   139
    Kyoji Fukao
    Comment: Jonathan Woetzel

8   Declining Potential Growth in Korea   165
    Dongchul Cho and Kyooho Kwon

9   A New Macroeconomic Policy Framework for Prudence   181
    and Higher-Quality Growth in China
    Ma Jun

10 Do India's Exports Reflect the New Normal?   193
    Prachi Mishra and Siddhartha Nath
    Comment: Kenneth Kang

11 How Has Indonesia Fared in the Age of Secular Stagnation? 235
    Mitali Das
    Comment: Muhamad Chatib Basri

12 Twenty-Five Years of Global Imbalances   269
    Maurice Obstfeld

13 Monetary and Exchange Rate Policies for Sustained   285
    Growth in Asia
    Joseph E. Gagnon and Philip Turner

14 Monetary Policy in the New Mediocre   315
    Rania Al-Mashat, Kevin Clinton, Benjamin Hunt,
    Zoltan Jakab, Douglas Laxton, Hou Wang, and
    Jiaxiong Yao

15 Avoiding a New Mediocre in Asia: What Can Fiscal   343
    Policy Do?
    Ana Corbacho, Dirk Muir, Masahiro Nozaki, and Edda Zoli

16 Global Imbalances and the Trade Slowdown: Implications   387
    for Asia
    Caroline Freund
    Comment: Davin Chor

17 Toward a "New" Asian Model   407
    Subir Gokarn

    Index   413

Preface

Asia largely avoided the worst of the global financial crisis of 2008–10 and remains one of the most dynamic regions of the world economy. Yet, signs of secular stagnation in the form of depressed levels of economic growth and low interest rates are now appearing in emerging Asia, not just Japan. Demographic trends and declining openness to trade in the advanced economies mean that Asian policymakers must prepare now to prevent such stagnation taking hold.

In this volume, scholars affiliated with the International Monetary Fund (IMF), the Peterson Institute for International Economics (PIIE), and other institutions around the world explore the relevance and implications of the secular stagnation hypothesis in Asia. The volume contains research focused by subject area (demographics, innovation, imbalances, spillovers, trade, and fiscal and monetary policies) and by country (China, South Korea, India, Indonesia, and Japan). This two-pronged comparative approach yields a compelling and multifaceted case for getting ahead of developments.

A major finding of this book is that in a secular stagnation environment, the highly successful Asian growth model of the past few decades is unlikely to remain the blueprint for future growth or for further convergence among emerging and developing economies in the region. Instead, economic integration within the region is likely to become the critical source for steady demand and productivity improvements. This regional opening should be accompanied by structural reforms aimed at offsetting some of the predictable forces of demographic change to keep the growth engine powerful. Adaptation of macroeconomic frameworks to be ready to undertake aggressive stimulus when necessary will be needed in Asia as well.

The Bank of Korea and the Korean Ministry of Strategy and Finance sponsored and hosted a conference in Seoul in September 2017, where the earlier versions of the research included in this volume were initially presented. We would like to express our sincere gratitude to economists from the Bank of Korea, IMF, PIIE, and the other organizations who have contributed their research to this ambitious project. We would also like to especially thank the IMF Asia and Pacific Department's Thomas Helbling and PIIE's Jérémie Cohen-Setton, who jointly managed and coordinated the project. The IMF's Nadine Dubost and Medha Madhu Nair and PIIE's Madona Devasahayam, Egor Gornostay, Susann Luetjen, and Steven R. Weisman together made possible the publication of this volume, with full documentation disclosure. Finally, we would like to acknowledge the generous financial support for the whole project by the Korean Ministry of Strategy and Finance. We believe that this highly forward-looking book will be a valuable resource for analysts, investors, and policymakers in Asia and beyond.

***

The Peterson Institute for International Economics is a private nonpartisan, nonprofit institution for rigorous, intellectually open, and indepth study and discussion of international economic policy. Its purpose is to identify and analyze important issues to making globalization beneficial and sustainable for the people of the United States and the world and then to develop and communicate practical new approaches for dealing with them.

The Institute's work is funded by a highly diverse group of philanthropic foundations, private corporations, and interested individuals, as well as income on its capital fund. About 35 percent of the Institute resources in our latest fiscal year were provided by contributors from outside the United States. A list of all our financial supporters for the preceding year is posted at www.piie.com/supporters.cfm.

The Executive Committee of the Institute's Board of Directors bears overall responsibility for the Institute's direction, gives general guidance and approval to its research program, and evaluates its performance in pursuit of its mission. The Institute's President is responsible for the identification of topics that are likely to become important over the medium term (one to three years) that should be addressed by Institute scholars. This rolling agenda is set in close consultation with the Institute's research staff, Board of Directors, and other stakeholders.

The President makes the final decision to publish any individual Institute study, following independent internal and external review of the work. Interested readers may access the data and computations underlying Institute publications for research and replication by searching titles at www.piie.com. The Institute hopes that its research and other activities will contribute to building a stronger foundation for international economic policy around the world. We invite readers of these publications to let us know how they think we can best accomplish this objective.

***

The International Monetary Fund's Asia and Pacific Department is one of the IMF's five area, or regional, departments. It is responsible for advising member countries in the Asia Pacific Region on macroeconomic policies and the financial sector, putting together, when needed, financial arrangements to support economic reform programs, and capacity building, mainly through its regional technical assistance centers. To accomplish its mission, the Department seeks to engage in policy debates in the Asia-Pacific and to distill lessons from the experience in the region. In this mission, it collaborates with experts from and outside region.

ADAM S. POSEN
President
Peterson Institute for
International Economics

CHANGYONG RHEE
Asia and Pacific Department Director
International Monetary Fund

Introduction: Toward a New Long-Term Growth Model for Asia

JÉRÉMIE COHEN-SETTON, THOMAS HELBLING,
ADAM S. POSEN, AND CHANGYONG RHEE

There is a false sense of security among many Asian economic policymakers regarding their own and the region's growth prospects. This is to some degree understandable, because Asia overall has continued to enjoy high rates of economic growth since the global financial crisis in 2008–10. In fact, the region has become the main driver of global economic activity, accounting for some two-thirds of global growth. In contrast, economic recovery from the crisis in advanced economies outside Asia has entailed a decade of mostly subpar growth and persistent labor market slack, despite sustained loose monetary policy. This experience has motivated the revival of Alvin Hansen's secular stagnation hypothesis by Lawrence Summers (2013) and others, as well as more structural explanations (notably Gordon 2016), for the lasting downshift in trend productivity growth at the technological frontier. Given the continued contrast in growth rates and ample room for most countries to continue catch-up growth, the secular stagnation hypothesis usually is not associated with Asia, except for Japan with its aging population and high per capita income.

Nevertheless, the danger from secular stagnation to Asian economies of an extended and difficult-to-exit growth slowdown, as has arguably beset

Jérémie Cohen-Setton is research fellow at the Peterson Institute for International Economics. Thomas Helbling is a division chief in the International Monetary Fund's Asia and Pacific Department, covering Australia and New Zealand. Adam S. Posen is the president of the Peterson Institute for International Economics. Changyong Rhee is the director of the Asia and Pacific Department at the International Monetary Fund. The views expressed in this chapter are those of the authors and do not necessarily represent the views of the IMF, its Executive Board, or its management.

the G-7 economies, is real and approaching. This threat is not just the result of the difficulties experienced through trade and financial linkages with the advanced economies, their low growth and inflation, and the resultant very low interest rates. When considering the broader macroeconomic picture, several of the symptoms associated with secular stagnation are already prominent in several Asian economies. Growth, for example, while strong in cross-national comparison, has remained below the rates recorded before the global financial crisis in Asia as well as the West. More troublingly, average productivity growth has declined relative to precrisis rates in many countries in the region, as it has elsewhere. Rapid population aging and lower population growth are already shaping the demographics in many countries of the region; turning points toward rising dependency ratios and shrinking workforces will soon be a reality well beyond Japan. Inflation has been below target for an unusually long period in several countries in the region, while interest rates, nominal and real, have declined to very low levels in many economies, even in countries with still high real growth. Therefore, risks of nominal policy interest rates reaching the effective lower bound after a large shock and related problems of macroeconomic adjustment might be likely rather than tail risks.

For this reason, the Asia and Pacific Department of the International Monetary Fund (IMF) and the Peterson Institute for International Economics launched a joint research project to explore the relevance of the secular stagnation hypothesis for Asia and the policy implications. The papers published in this volume were presented at a conference organized jointly with the Korean Ministry of Strategy and Finance and the Bank of Korea in September 2017. The project combined research organized by economic themes and by countries. For the country case studies, the project distinguishes three groups of countries in Asia. The first category consists of Japan, a country in which symptoms of secular stagnation have already been present for some years. The second group includes Korea and other middle-income economies in which the reversal of the demographic dividend is imminent and which are already exhibiting some of the features of secular stagnation but not yet to an extent that would support wide recognition of the problem. In these transitionally threatened economies, fundamentals point to increasing risks of stagnation over the next few years but also some advance warning, meaning time to prepare and change policy. Finally, in many of the emerging and lower-income economies in Asia, the exposure to secular stagnation is primarily through international spillovers to date, but these spillovers are likely to last and to constrain growth and policy in an ongoing way.

Summary of Contributions to This Volume

In chapter 2 Joel Mokyr reminds us that secular stagnation was the rule rather than the exception until 1800. Negative demographic feedbacks, predatory rent-seeking institutions, and limitations on the accumulation of human knowledge made growth imperceptibly slow. Today, the economy is facing headwinds, but progress made in a year no longer melts away subsequently. A first headwind is the risk of growing old before becoming rich in parts of Asia. In chapter 3, Serkan Arslanalp et al. find that rapid aging is now set to create a demographic tax on growth that could subtract ½ to 1 percentage point from annual GDP growth over the next three decades in countries such as China and Japan. A second headwind is the slowdown in R&D productivity growth. Based on the experience of Japan, South Korea, and Taiwan, Lee Branstetter and Namho Kwon argue in chapter 4 that these countries' innovation systems have become a drag on productivity growth because of their pro-incremental and pro-incumbent biases.

Headwinds for the region are not only domestic. In fact, the concomitance of low growth and inflation in a large set of countries at different stages of development suggests a role for contagion. In chapter 5 Olivier Jeanne explores several possible channels of contagion but finds that post-crisis total factor productivity growth is surprisingly orthogonal to most measures of international economic integration. There is, however, evidence that the transmission of secular stagnation to emerging economies has been delayed, with rebalancing in current accounts happening against the backdrop of domestic credit booms.

When economists want to draw lessons from recent historical experience, they study Japan's two lost decades. The problem, writes Adam S. Posen in chapter 6, is that Japan had only one lost decade, not two. Since 2002, its per capita GDP growth and productivity growth have been decent. And its difficulty in generating inflation is not Japan specific. Explaining the empirical puzzles of the 21st century requires a more general rethinking of our understanding of macroeconomics, where factors other than just expectations can influence inflation. In chapter 7 Kyoji Fukao illustrates the importance of changes in workforce composition such as the increase in nonregular employment in the Japanese labor market to explain both inflation and productivity developments.

In chapter 8 Dongchul Cho and Kyooho Kwon observe that developments in South Korea seem to mimic those of Japan with a 20-year lag. They project that potential output growth will fall further, given demographic trends and capital deepening, and call for bold structural reforms to raise TFP and to lower the risks of Korea experiencing the deflation pressures Japan has faced. In China, writes Ma Jun in chapter 9, the slow down in economic growth will be driven by demographics, environmental costs, and changing consumer preferences. Altogether, these factors are expected to slow annual growth by 2 percentage points in the coming decade. While ongoing technological innovations and reforms can partially cushion this deceleration, a further slowdown in growth appears inevitable over the medium term. This trend, together with the growing financial risks due to a high macro leverage ratio, calls urgently for a new macroeconomic management framework that is less growth-centric but focuses more on macro and financial stability.

In chapter 10 Prachi Mishra and Siddhartha Nath write that India's merchandise exports have undergone a quiet revolution with new-age engineering, electronic, and pharmaceutical exports gradually replacing India's traditional exports of leather, textiles, gems, and jewelry. But structural rigidities are still holding back diversification and thus make India vulnerable to global risks. The contrast with Indonesia is striking as it has progressively turned inward. This retrenchment, writes Mitali Das in chapter 11, has insulated Indonesia against the vicissitudes of global developments but at the price of a reduction in productivity-enhancing spillovers. In fact, potential output growth has declined in recent years despite strong demographic tailwinds and steady capital accumulation.

In reviewing the past 25 years of global imbalances, Maurice Obstfeld emphasizes in chapter 12 that excessive imbalances declined after the global financial crisis but are still present. Monocausal explanations for excessive global imbalances rarely apply. Instead, such imbalances usually reflect global forces and multiple distortions in many countries, notably diverse financial sector distortions. Notwithstanding the need for collective action, excess surplus countries still face little that would force them to adjust—outside of the threat of protectionist responses—whereas most deficit countries face the risk that lenders will withdraw. Reducing global imbalances should be a collective effort based on a shared appreciation of the roles individual countries need to play.

In chapter 13 Joseph Gagnon and Philip Turner study the implications of a slowdown in growth for monetary policy. A first implication is the importance of keeping core inflation at or above 2 percent. A second implication is that central banks should not shy away from using balance sheet policies. The view that central banks should stick to setting the overnight rate is unhistorical. If anything, balance sheet policies have more potential today than before given the increased size and importance of domestic Asian bond markets in influencing financial conditions. Rania Al-Mashat et al. make the case in chapter 14 for a risk avoidance approach to monetary policy that heavily penalizes large deviations of the target variables (output and inflation) from their preferred values. In a world of secular stagnation where the probability of entering low-inflation traps is higher, a prudent approach to a recessionary shock from a weak starting point is to take a more aggressive stance than usual. The authors of both chapters 13 and 14 argue that financial stability worries do not in general justify keeping the policy rate higher than warranted by macroeconomic conditions.

In chapter 15 Ana Corbacho et al. analyze the implications of subdued growth and rapid aging for fiscal sustainability and discuss options for fiscal policy to support growth potential. Left unchecked, age-related spending would be an overwhelming force driving up public debt in many countries in the region. A reversal of the favorable interest rate–growth differential that helped keep debt ratios in check in recent times would put debt dynamics at even further risk. This being said, model-based simulations show that many countries in Asia have scope to anchor drivers of growth potential by redirecting budgets to infrastructure, human capital, and R&D.

In chapter 16 Caroline Freund studies the relationship between global imbalances and trade. In the 1990s and early 2000s, increased borrowing from abroad allowed high-demand countries to import more than if they were constrained by their exports, stimulating trade growth. The relationship between trade imbalances and trade flows is especially strong for the United States and East Asia. In recent years, moderating imbalances have been associated with slowing trade growth, especially in the United States and East Asia. Going forward, even as global growth picks up, the new weaker relationship between trade and income may remain in place if global imbalances remain constrained.

In chapter 17 Subir Gokarn writes that the "Asian model" as we have come to recognize it is obsolete. Countries in the region have to recognize this and reorient their strategies for sustaining growth. Changing demand patterns in the advanced economies clearly indicate that these markets will become less and less important sources of demand for Asian products. But the key element of the "old" Asian model—the promotion of efficiency and competitiveness up the supply chain—provides the basis for a "new" model where the focus would be on meeting the needs of the growing markets in the region itself. Whether the "new" Asian model is a move toward mediocrity or renewed excellence depends on how effectively the countries in the region recognize and act on the opportunities and respond to the challenges.

Agreeing on the Need for a Forward-Looking Policy

There was broad agreement among conference participants that forward-looking adaptation of policy frameworks is needed to sustain growth in Asia for the medium term. So, even though the conference took place against the backdrop of an improved global outlook compared with the time when the research program was conceived, and the global expansion has continued in the months since, the best tradition of Asian economic policymaking to plan with a long time horizon was affirmed. In particular, the profound challenges from the impending demographic transitions in many Asian economies to rapidly aging populations and lower population growth resonated with participants. The demographic dividend has already started to reverse in many countries in the region, including in China, the engine of growth for the region and the world in the past two decades.

Recent experience in Japan and in Western Europe suggests that aging and lower population growth could reduce growth in per capita incomes and productivity, not just aggregate growth in output and investment. There are strong hypotheses suggested by Japan and Western Europe as well that there might even be negative feedback loops from demographics to technical progress: Lower rates of innovation in the frontier economies and eroding intellectual property rights could interact with aging to slow diffusion of progress within and across countries (Posen 2012); aging could change the structure of household demand toward less capital-intensive services, providing yet another reason for lower investment, thus limiting positive productivity spillovers; structural reforms are needed to strengthen domestic innovation capacity and productivity in service sectors.

The reversal of the demographic dividend would therefore likely result in more than just persistent even if small declines in aggregate demand. So, even absent macroeconomic imbalances, which arguably made the problems more acute in the G-7 economies, Asian policymakers are right to be concerned about the negative impact of the demographic transition on productivity and medium-term growth. The conference participants emphasized that the transition reinforced the need to change the Asian growth paradigm.

Similarly, the international dimension of the challenges facing Asia for sustaining growth go well beyond the cyclical and direct immediate spillovers from insufficient demand and low growth in advanced economies since the global financial crisis. After a decade of very low growth since the global financial crisis, external demand growth from advanced economies outside Asia is unlikely to return to providing the momentum it had before the global financial crisis. An implication is that manufacturing exports are unlikely to be the motor for growth and development that they were over the past few decades. This development intensifies the phenomenon of "premature deindustrialization" identified by Dani Rodrik (2016). Moreover, the trade tensions taking shape between the United States and many of its largest trading partners in Asia and elsewhere are further eroding the room for export-led growth. Even if these conflicts are resolved or at least stepped down, legitimate doubts about the wisdom of relying on access to advanced economies' markets for large-scale exports will remain. If so, the highly successful Asian growth model of the past few decades is unlikely to remain the blueprint for future growth and convergence in emerging and developing economies in the region.

A third major theme is that macroeconomic policy frameworks in Asia had to be prepared for the possibility of policy rates hitting the lower bound on nominal interest rates after contractionary or deflationary shocks, even if the source of shock or of the low level of interest rates going in was external, and the domestic macroeconomy appeared well-balanced. This means that in the case of a downturn, there is a need for determined aggressive macroeconomic policy responses, given higher risks of protracted adjustment to shocks. Many conference participants were concerned about the risks to financial stability from such policy responses, noting the possible limited effectiveness of prudential policies to offset those side effects.

This scenario is relevant for Asian policymakers, even if not induced by their own economies' actions. Admittedly, there is no easy answer to the tradeoff between demand stimulus and financial stability, though to some degree the risks from financial side effects can be exaggerated during recovery phases. As argued in Summers (2013), such a situation presents the risk not only of more severe downturns but also of getting stuck in a trap of extended need for still lower rates and substantial fiscal stimulus. Just as for their counterparts in the advanced economies, the risk of getting trapped in secular stagnation with only monetary policy to get the economy out is that it will be ineffective as well as distortionary. Thus, it is important that Asian policymakers get ahead of the curve to build fiscal space ahead of such situations and be prepared to use that fiscal space in productive as well as stimulative ways (such as ready infrastructure projects). The failure of US and European policymakers to do so, and apparent benefits with hindsight of such aggressive fiscal action in Japan, is an object lesson.

Asia remains the most vibrant, the most diverse, and the largest economic region of the world economy. Its citizens' economic well-being remains largely in the hands of their own markets and governments. The economic policymakers of the region could take solace from their economies' relatively good performance compared with their counterparts in other parts of the world, even as their growth rates of income and productivity have slowed. They could even blame those slowdowns on the spillovers from the advanced economies' own crises and policy mistakes. That, however, would be a mistaken approach. Significant unfavorable demographic trends, a less open and slower-growing rest of the world to trade with, and ongoing risks of falling into stagnation from persistently low levels of nominal interest rates and growth in the major economies combine to demand a new growth model for Asia.

The broad outlines of such a model for sustaining growth are applicable for all Asian economies and should be put in place without undue delay.

- Undertake a structural reform agenda—including making better use of the female labor force, promoting innovation and technological diffusion internally, and encouraging productivity gains in service sectors—that can robustly offset some of the predictable forces of demographic change.

- Pursue international economic integration within the Asian region, and openness to South-South trade and investment more broadly, to maintain the benefits for productivity and steady demand that go with export competition.

- Prepare macroeconomic frameworks to be ready to undertake aggressive stabilizing stimulus when needed in the likely-to-persist global low interest rate environment. This preparation requires a recognition both of the risks of excessively anti-inflationary monetary policy and of the need to build up fiscal space in advance of problems.

References

Gordon, Robert J. 2016. *The Rise and Fall of American Growth: The U.S. Standard of Living since the Civil War.* Princeton, NJ: Princeton University Press.

Posen, Adam S. 2012. What the Return of 19th Century Economics Means for 21st Century Geopolitics. Lecture, Chatham House, London, January 17. Available at www.chathamhouse.org/sites/default/files/public/Meetings/Meeting%20Transcripts/170112aposen.pdf (accessed on September 7, 2018).

Rodrik, Dani. 2016. Premature Deindustrialization. *Journal of Economic Growth* 21, no. 1: 1–33.

Summers, Lawrence H. 2013. Remarks at the IMF Fourteenth Annual Research Conference in Honor of Stanley Fischer, Washington, DC, November 8. Available at http://larrysummers.com/imf-fourteenth-annual-research-conference-in-honor-of-stanley-fischer/ (accessed on September 7, 2018).

2

Secular Stagnation: History and Reality

JOEL MOKYR

Should we be concerned with "secular stagnation," the decline of long-term economic growth (Summers 2016)? Modern economic growth, or as Deirdre McCloskey has termed it "the Great Enrichment," has been a relatively recent phenomenon. If recorded human history is approximately 6,000 years long, sustained growth that doubled income every generation or so has been experienced only for at most 3 percent of human history, with the remaining 97 percent characterized by stagnant economies. No one before the Industrial Revolution complained about secular stagnation—practically nobody imagined that economic growth and continuous progress in the material conditions of life were at all possible. Whatever progress made in one year would have melted away subsequently, and a random individual born on this planet at the time of Napoleon would not have been significantly richer than a random individual born at the time of Nebuchadnezzar.[1] In that sense, secular stagnation would have been a return to normal.

Joel Mokyr is Robert H. Strotz Professor of Arts and Sciences and Professor of Economics and History at Northwestern University and Sackler Professor (by special appointment) at the Eitan Berglas School of Economics, Tel Aviv University. He is indebted to Ashish Aggarwal for research assistance, Jérémie Cohen-Setton and Deirdre McCloskey for helpful comments, and Madona Devasahayam for outstanding editing. The Balzan Foundation and Northwestern's Center for Economic History provided financial support.

1. For powerful, if somewhat overstated, descriptions of this absence of growth, see Clark (2007) and Galor (2011). There were some exceptions to the rule of stagnation in northwest Europe and Italy, where growth had already raised living standards significantly by 1800, but even that growth had been slow and uneven, and it affected a tiny part of humanity.

But what was normal for most of human history is not normal in the 20th and 21st centuries. Growth has been the norm in the more recent past, despite two world wars, a wave of totalitarian regimes, repeated genocide, a nuclear arms race, and other assorted disasters. In what follows, I explain how the modern era was different from everything that came before, which will give us a unique perspective to assess the chances of past conditions returning. Needless to say, all such assessments need to be phrased in the conditional and subjunctive modes, since the entire point of this chapter is to argue that we are still in the midst of a phase transition in economic history, and hence all bets are off. But some scenarios can still be assigned a low probability.

The Malthusian Curse

The most widely cited explanation for why growth could not take place in the past is population dynamics. The idea was famously enunciated by Thomas Malthus and has since carried his name, although it was perhaps most eloquently expressed by H. G. Wells (1923, 68): Humanity "spent the great gifts of science as rapidly as it got them in a mere insensate multiplication of the common life." Every economist knows the argument. Under some fairly reasonable assumptions, any rise in income per capita or productivity, whether derived from the "great gifts of science" or any other source, will lead to a decline in deaths and a rise in births, and as population growth sets in, diminishing returns to a fixed factor such as land or more generally the environment will set in, and income will decline (Clark 2007, Galor 2011, Ashraf and Galor 2011). This kind of demographic negative feedback explains why in the very long run any improvement in the human condition was quite ineffectual, and the only indicator of technological progress in the very long run is population size (Kremer 1993).

Whether the classical "iron law" is a good description of historical reality remains to be seen; some parts of it have been confirmed using historical data (Kelly and Ó Gráda 2012, 2014), but it is also clear that the stark implications of the fundamentalist Malthusian position are a simplification of history (Voigtländer and Voth 2012, 2013). Either way, there is a general consensus that the Malthusian model had ceased to be a good description of the world at just about the time of the writing of Malthus's famous book, and that the stagnation it implied no longer held in the second half of the 18th century, when demographic growth took off in most parts of Europe.

The three basic assumptions that the Malthusian theory rested on have been undone in modern times. The first is that birth rates rise with income: On both global and intranational levels, the correlation is reversed. The richer a nation, or a person, the lower their fertility tends to be, although it is far from obvious that there is a causal connection (Black et al. 2013). Four major explanations have been proposed for this correlation, all of them the direct consequence of some form of economic modernization: the wide availability of inexpensive means of effective fertility control; the desire to have higher-quality children at the expense of quantity; the many substitutes that have emerged for children in their various economic and social functions; and the decline of religion in much of the secular and humanistic West. In the richest part of the world, Europe, fertility rates are now below replacement levels in *every* nation (except in France), and in North America, both the United States and Canada are now in the same situation.

The second assumption of the Malthusian story, that mortality rates will decline with income, is less clearly refuted. Rich countries or people still have lower mortality rates. But that curve is flattening out, and for a large range of incomes a negative correlation between income and mortality rates is not observable.[2] Malthusian "positive checks" (famines, epidemics, and wars that would have reduced the population if income was too low) have by and large disappeared from most of the world, and when famines occurred in the 20th century, they tended to be entirely man-made and *not* the result of overpopulation (Ó Gráda 2015, Alfani and Ó Gráda 2017).[3] Spikes in mortality that in the preindustrial past were correlated with poor harvests and/or the outbreaks of epidemics and have been seen as Malthusian responses to population pressure have more or less disappeared in most of the world.

The third leg of the Malthusian model is that overpopulation presses income down through diminishing returns from land and natural resources. The responses to population growth have always been a subject of debate; scholars have argued that population growth basically triggered technological responses that adapted to the labor-land ratio through the intensification of agriculture (Boserup 1965, 1981) or even that population growth led to a high rate of technological progress simply because the likelihood of a technological genius appearing in a larger population is higher (Simon 2001, Kremer 1993). Yet the main argument for diminishing returns that

---

2. Simple regressions of mortality rates on log GDP per capita for 168 nations still show a significant negative coefficient. However, once we limit the sample to the top 60 countries, the significance vanishes and the adjusted R-square is essentially zero (author's calculations; all data from CIA World Factbook, www.cia.gov/library/publications/resources/the-world-factbook/index.html).

3. The evidence for the existence of Malthusian checks in which disasters occur as a result of overpopulation is scant. Nineteenth century writers believed that the Irish Famine was a clear-cut example, but the evidence for overpopulation as a clear cause of the famine is far from persuasive (Mokyr 1985).

Malthusians or neo-Malthusians have relied upon is the finiteness of nonreproducible resources. As the shares of land and natural resources in national income have declined, the assumption that a permanently "fixed" factor in the economy limits the growth of per capita income is weakened by the enormous land- and resource-augmenting technological progress in the past century.[4]

Rent-Seeking and Predation

Perhaps the least noticed reason why incomes before the Industrial Revolution were more or less stagnant is that most economies were "extractive" in the nomenclature popularized by Acemoglu and Robinson (2012) and found themselves in a "natural state" (North, Wallis, and Weingast 2009). In these states, dominant elites extracted rents from the rest of the population. The institutional weakness of these societies was not so much the absence of a "rule of law" as the rule of *bad* law, a legal system that was biased toward the politically powerful and favored a rapacious rent-seeking minority. The absence of any concept of "equality before the law" in most societies meant that greedy strongmen, above all of course the rulers, could easily expropriate the wealth of successful individuals. This risk remained a constraint on the incentives of would-be entrepreneurs.[5] Only in areas where the political influence of successful merchants, industrialists, and financiers could protect them from such expropriations did entrepreneurs feel comparatively safe from the threat of expropriation or confiscatory fiscal extraction. There were many such places in Europe, to be sure, but rent-seeking remained pervasive in the age of mercantilism and was clearly an obstacle to economic growth (Ekelund and Tollison 1981) even when property rights became more secure.

---

4. The most striking land-augmenting inventions were fertilizers and pesticides, the most dramatic of which by all accounts was the Haber-Bosch nitrogen-fixing process. According to Vaclav Smil (2001, 204), by the end of the 20th century at least 2.4 billion people were alive because the proteins in their bodies could be synthesized from amino acids whose nitrogen originated in this invention.

5. A notorious example was the French merchant and entrepreneur Jacques Cœur (1395–1456), an immensely rich and powerful merchant who basically monopolized France's Mediterranean trade and was wealthy enough to bankroll many of Charles VII's triumphs in the final stages of the Hundred Years' War against England. His wealth and power attracted the greed and envy of many, including eventually the king. Cœur was arrested and tried on what historians have deemed were trumped-up charges; his possessions were confiscated and distributed among the king and his cronies. Two centuries later, a similar fate befell Nicolas Fouquet (1615–1680), the fabulously wealthy tax collector who had enriched himself during the ministry of Mazarin during Louis XIV's minority. He was arrested in 1661 by Louis XIV and imprisoned for life, and the king's servants stripped his sumptuous chateau.

Such legal protections were insufficient, however. Many of Europe's most successful pre–Industrial Revolution economies were located in relatively small political entities, some of which were classic city-states. Such entities became rich because they were able to set up city governments that protected merchants' properties (Gelderblom 2013). Many urban areas were able to raise living standards above the subsistence levels that Malthusian fundamentalists believe constrained living standards. In the highly fragmented and violent Europe before the Enlightenment, however, such wealth attracted strong but poor foreign predators as honey attracts flies. The wealthy towns of northern Italy were ravaged in the early 16th century by Spanish and French soldiers (not to mention *condottieri* from a variety of origins), and most of them did not recover. German trading towns such as Augsburg, Magdeburg, Frankfurt an der Oder, Stralsund, and Prague, among many others, were mercilessly looted and sacked by the mercenary armies that roamed Germany during the Thirty Years' War. Since none of those armies could provide their supplies, they imposed enormous extortions on the territories they moved through.[6] As a recent essay (Béaur and Chevet 2017) points out, not only the war itself but also the actions of the military had devastating effects on the countryside. Soldiers looted all around them, which discouraged farmers from cropping land and raising animals too exposed to danger. The authors note that this was especially disastrous in France during the wars of religion (1572–98) and the wars of the Fronde (1648–52) (Béaur and Chevet 2017, 85). The deadweight losses of such actions were thus enormous. Cities that were spared had to invest heavily on fortifications, such as Hamburg, or they paid off the soldiers to prevent looting.

The most striking example of what could best be called negative institutional feedback is provided by the Low Countries, a region of Europe that successfully broke through the Malthusian barrier to provide its citizens with a standard of living considerably higher than the subsistence level implied by the iron law. Yet powerful neighbors threatened their prosperity: France and above all, but after 1648, England just as much. The wealthy medieval towns of Ghent, Bruges, and Courtray had to repeatedly fend off French invaders in the Middle Ages; the Burgundian rulers of the 15th century allowed these towns to return to prosperity, which was overshadowed by the meteoric rise of Antwerp in the 16th century. But after 1555 these provinces were part of Spain, and Spain was a violent and pred-

---

6. These extortions, known as *Kontributions* or *Brandschatzung*, were confiscatory taxation and extortion imposed on local towns and countrysides. Armies often chose itineraries that led through the most prosperous areas. See, for instance, Guthrie (2003, 30–31).

atory master. By 1585 (the notorious sack of Antwerp), much of Flanders and Brabant's prosperity had declined and the southern Netherlands entered two centuries of sustained stagnation. In their place, of course, came the northern Netherlands, which was more favorably located (as they could fend off invading armies by flooding the lands). Yet it, too, had to spend inordinate amounts on defense, which by the 18th century contributed to the economic stagnation of the United Provinces. Britain's success in the Industrial Revolution was at least in part due to the fact that no hostile ruler after William the Conqueror had successfully invaded it or could even threaten to do so credibly.

Part of the reason why growth was so vulnerable in the pre–Industrial Revolution era is that most growth was "Smithian" in nature, that is, it was fueled by gains from trade and specialization. Such growth tended to be vulnerable to political shocks, including the use of state-sponsored pirates (known as privateers) and economic embargoes of various kinds. Mercantilist protectionist policies, whose primary purpose was political rather than economic, diverted trade flows and even distorted consumption patterns in the long run (Nye 2007).

In short, through much of history, both internal rent-seekers and predatory foreigners were attracted to the riches that economic success had allowed local populations to accumulate. In so doing, they were of course killing the goose that laid the golden egg, but especially during war, when the future was discounted heavily, such expropriation was often resorted to. A high rate of discount—as would occur during war—could turn a stationary bandit into a roving one. As a result, even when economic growth occurred, it was often undone by its own success in a dialectic way.

This negative feedback has sharply declined in modern democratic economies. Between 1750 and 1850 much of mercantilist rent-seeking disappeared in Britain (Mokyr 2009, 423–27) and declined elsewhere. In most developed Western democracies, rent-seeking today is at historically low levels, but it has far from disappeared worldwide. For example, in countries like Venezuela, Nigeria, and Russia, governments have degenerated into modern kleptocracies, where massive theft and corruption by ruling elites have condemned large economies to economic stagnation or worse. Yet on the whole in many of the advanced and successful countries rent-seeking has been kept within limits, and corruption does not reach levels at which it seriously threatens entrepreneurship and economic progress. It is not surprising that many of these countries rank well on the corruption indices compiled by Transparency International and the World Bank. Not all rent-seeking takes the form of corruption, of course, and no simple index of rent-seeking exists.[7] These indices are quite strongly correlated, and one could conceptualize some principal component that would combine the six into some "quality of institutions" variable.[8] It is fair to state that the quality of these institutions in some of the most economically successful economies such as Denmark, Canada, and Singapore is higher than it has ever been in history. At the same time, the threat of economic nationalism and notions of "fair" trade (a euphemism for protectionism) seem indestructible weeds in the garden of trade.

Technology and Knowledge

Many past economies experienced some technological progress, including many in which growth was so slow that one would surely refer to them as suffering from secular stagnation. Inventions did occur, and in some cases they were game-changing (think of the mechanical clock and the moveable-font printing press invented in the late Middle Ages). The medieval economy, far from being technologically backward or even stagnant, was actually quite dynamic in many areas, including agriculture, manufacturing, civil engineering, shipbuilding, and metallurgy. Yet these breakthroughs usually had only a small and temporary impact on economic well-being. One may wonder why none of these advances translated into any form of sustained technological progress and productivity growth.

The effectiveness of sustained technological progress depends largely on the *epistemic base* of the invention, namely the extent to which it is understood why and how the new technique works (Mokyr 2002, 31–32). Technological progress occurred through much of history, but there was something deeply different in the innovations during and after the Industrial Revolution. Before 1750, the vast bulk of inventions had occurred through serendipity, experience, continuous trial and error, and the gradual accumulation of small incremental improvements. The techniques worked, but those who employed them did not understand how and why they did so. Blacksmiths made steel, brewers brewed beer, and farmers fertilized their fields, but nobody had much of an idea of the chemical and biological processes at work. The nature of combustion, one of the most elementary techniques used throughout manufacturing, was not under-

---

7. The World Bank indices are Voice and Accountability, Political Stability and Absence of Violence, Government Effectiveness, Regulatory Quality, Rule of Law, and Control of Corruption. See http://info.worldbank.org/governance/wgi/index.aspx#home.

8. The pairwise correlation coefficients of three of the measures that are closest to rent-seeking are especially high: between "control of corruption" and "government effectiveness": $R = .909$; between "control of corruption" and "rule of law": $R = .962$; and between "government effectiveness" and "rule of law": $R = .940$ (author's calculations).

stood until the late 18th century. Even during the Industrial Revolution itself, some of the great breakthroughs—especially those in the mechanical parts of the cotton industry—were purely the result of mechanical intuition and tinkering rather than any profound understanding of the underlying physics or biology. It was possible to discover new products and techniques that worked better when their underlying natural rules were not known, but without such knowledge it was much harder to debug, improve, and adapt a technique and to keep raising productivity. Hence most inventions were one-off events followed by slow, artisan-driven improvements that eventually petered out. At times such incremental improvements substantially increased productivity, as was the case in the British watch industry in the 18th century (Kelly and Ó Gráda 2016). In other cases, a minimum epistemic base was required before a technological advance could be realized, as was the case with electricity and nitrogen-fixing.

The problem with premodern technology, then, was that even the very best natural philosophers (as scientists were known then) did not know enough to give farmers, brewers, shipbuilders, blacksmiths, physicians, and all other fabricants much sound advice on why their techniques worked, and hence they could not tell them how to make the techniques work better, nor could they suggest to would-be inventors what would work and what would not. As a result, even when a technique clearly worked, it was often used inappropriately. The great transition of the Industrial Revolution was not the growth of invention as such but its changing nature. What made it "modern" is the gradual widening epistemic base of technology.[9] Some of it came from the autonomous growth of science, often inspired by practical problems. After many centuries of experience-based steelmaking, in 1786 three French followers of Lavoisier wrote a pioneering paper proposing the chemical composition of steel.[10] But its quaint terminology may have made it "incomprehensible except to those who already knew how to make steel" (Harris 1998, 220). It took decades for their findings to actually be of use to steelmakers (Wertime 1961). Water power had been known since antiquity

---

9. Lin (1995) points out that the difference between Chinese and modern Western technology was that both Chinese and pre-1700 Western technological progress were experience-based and advanced through learning by doing and trial and error. The growth of what he calls knowledge-based technological change changed the historical balance in favor of the West. This was already realized in the 18th century. Condorcet, in his famous 1795 essay on human progress, argued that although "isolated nations long influenced by despotism and superstition" (he means in all likelihood Asia) had been the origin of many important new technologies in textiles, ceramics, and metal, they were being surpassed by Europe in his age because there is nothing these countries did that "announces the presence of genius—all improvements there appear as the slow and painstaking work of a long routine" (Condorcet 1796, 51).

10. The famous paper was by Vandermonde, Berthollet, and Monge (1786).

yet advanced painstakingly slowly, through trial and error until about 1700. Its accelerated improvement was due to a combination of better experimental techniques and the systematic use of formal science in its analysis (Reynolds 1983, 204–65; Wootton 2015, 486–89). Gaslighting, one of the paradigmatic inventions of the Industrial Revolution, was supported by the development of the concepts, materials, experience, and apparatus of pneumatic chemistry (Tomory 2012, 13–36). The same was true of fertilizer. Farmers had been fertilizing fields for millennia, but nobody knew why and how fertilizers made crops grow more abundant. Once that became known through the emergence of organic chemistry in Germany in the 1830s and 1840s, farmers could apply chemical manures as needed for specific crops.[11]

By no means does this suggest that the modus operandi of a technique was fully understood when it was first developed—but in many cases some minimum had to be in place. Once operational, however, the technique stimulated scientists to develop the underlying science and widen the epistemic base endogenously to allow for further improvements. The classic example remains the steam engine, the invention of which in the early 18th century motivated scientists to develop the theory of thermodynamics (i.e., the physics of steam power) over a century later. The old gag that science owes more to the steam engine than the other way around, however, remains one of those oft-repeated half-truths that confuse as much as they enlighten. Some formal scientific understanding mattered in the invention of the steam engine. Torricelli's discovery of atmospheric pressure in 1643 spawned the first atmospheric steam engines in the early 18th century. Then in 1765 James Watt revolutionized the steam engine by adding a separate condenser. Long before the birth of thermodynamics, Watt had learned from the Scottish chemist William Cullen that in a vacuum water would boil at much lower, even tepid, temperatures, releasing steam that would ruin the vacuum in a cylinder. That piece of knowledge was essential to Watt's realization that he needed a separate condenser (Hills 1989, 53).[12]

---

11. Another example is hydrostatics needed for ship design, with which 18th century scientists struggled mightily. Isaac Newton's theory on hydrostatics, known later as impact theory, was embraced by many contemporaries, but it turned out to be unsatisfactory and was corrected by Leonhard Euler and the Bernoullis, who designed a theory that could deal with the physical state variables in the whole domain of fluid. See Nowacki (2008).

12. Another paradigmatic example of how practical invention stimulated the underlying science rather than the reverse can be found in the evolution of aerodynamics. The formal theory of aerodynamics was laid out in 1918 by Ludwig Prandtl, 15 years after Kitty Hawk (Constant 1980, 105; Vincenti 1990, 120–25). Even then, the ancient method of trial and error was still widely used in airplane design. The search for the best use of flush riveting in holding together the body of the plane or the best way to design landing gear remained highly experimental (Vincenti 1990, 170–99; Vincenti 2000).

When did the connection between propositional knowledge (knowledge of "what") and prescriptive knowledge (knowledge of "how") begin to get more powerful? It clearly did not erupt suddenly in 1500 and medieval natural philosophers and inventors, as already noted, were far from the benighted ignoramuses that subsequent writers have tried to make them seem (Hannam 2011). Yet the notion that useful knowledge was primarily meant, as Francis Bacon famously wrote, to be "a rich storehouse for the glory of the creator and the relief of man's estate" fully took hold only in the 16th and 17th centuries. To be sure, much of natural philosophy remained cloaked in mysticism and the occult, but by the late 17th century more and more scientists emerged following the model of John T. Desaguliers in England and Antoine Parent in France, who applied their knowledge of physics and mathematics to solving practical problems in mining and watermills.

The Great Enrichment could sustain itself because between 1700 and 1850 the epistemic base of many areas in technology widened continuously, in part through cumulative progress in science and in part as a response to challenges and stimuli from the practical world. In the 19th century we see an ever-increasing input of formal knowledge in the origins and—even more so—the subsequent development of new techniques.

Where a social and informational chasm separated those who knew things and those who made things, it was much harder to mutually reinforce artisanal and formal knowledge and a stationary state of little or no growth would ensue. Scholars in the Greek ancient world were still committed to *banausia*, a sense of contempt for practical knowledge, a contempt that the Romans shed to a great extent, at least for a while, as exemplified by the practical work of writers such as Cato the Elder, Vitruvius, and Varro. In this (late Republican) period, Macmullen (2017, 15) notes, "Mediterranean civilization could be thus raised to new levels of tangible comfort, health, and handsomeness upon the basis of knowledge necessarily shared between the ruling classes and labor, with master craftsmen to bridge the gap between the two." Unfortunately, this cultural trait did not last, and Rome did not generate a sustainable process of technological progress. Similarly, in China the gap was becoming more formidable during the rule of the Ming and Qing dynasties. For example, Needham pointed to the fact that the real work in Chinese engineering was "always done by illiterate or semi-literate artisans and master craftsmen who could never rise across that sharp gap which separated them from the 'white collar literati'" (Needham 1969, 27). In Enlightenment Europe this chasm closed considerably in many areas. There was a widely shared conviction that artisans and scientists could benefit from each other, and in much of Western Europe places and forums where natural philosophers and mathematicians could interact with engineers and industrialists came into being (Stewart 1992, Mokyr 2009). Zilsel (1942) pointed to artisans and craftsmen as a major source of information for philosophers and the explicit acknowledgment of their role by many of the leading scientists of the age.[13] In the two centuries before 1700, the social distance between "pure" natural philosophy and its application slowly but irresistibly shrank in Western Europe.

Secular Stagnation?

If the three factors described above accounted for a substantial part of secular stagnation in the past, they provide us with a way to reassess the likelihood of secular stagnation as a normal condition in the foreseeable future. As far as the specter of a Malthusian curse is concerned, the notion that the human race is facing some risk of overpopulation (still popularized by Paul Ehrlich's *Population Bomb,* first published in 1968, followed unrepentantly in 1990 by his *Population Explosion*) has been thoroughly discredited. Even without the huge increase in effective and available natural resources due to technological progress, this doomster prediction is doomed itself by the astonishing slowdown in fertility rates worldwide. Fertility rates in developing economies in Asia and Latin America are mostly hovering around replacement. Fertility is declining in the most populated economies in Asia and is approaching or has fallen below replacement levels. In Indonesia and Bangladesh, for instance, fertility rates today are down to 2.11 and 2.17 births per woman, from 5.7 and 6.7 in 1960, respectively (CIA 2017, World Bank 2017), while fertility in both China and Iran is now significantly below replacement levels. The region where Malthusian pressures may remain a serious limitation to growth is Africa. African fertility rates have remained stubbornly high, and the resource base in most of the continent is being eroded by overuse and mismanagement. For the rest of the world, the demographic transition, whatever its exact microeconomic foundations, is steering toward zero population growth now predicted for some point in the 21st century.

Indeed, it is no small irony that if demography is any concern today, it is that zero or negative population growth, coupled with the continuing rise in the average age in most economies, is seen as a source of secular stagnation (Hansen 1939). Globally, the old-age dependency ratio is expected to rise from 13 percent in 2015 to 38 percent by the end of the 21st century.[14]

---

13. For a more recent restatement of Zilsel's ideas, see, for instance, Roberts and Schaffer (2007).

14. "The New Old," *Economist,* July 8, 2017, 3. The median age in the United States has increased from 28.1 in 1970 to 37.6 in 2015 (Statista 2017) and is projected to rise to 41 by

But the notion that somehow an aging population will lead to declining aggregate demand seems unpersuasive. For one thing, assuming retirement rates do not change much, a rising dependency rate means that the growth of aggregate demand will exceed that of aggregate supply, as rising numbers of nonworking persons will still consume. Second, the notion that somehow slow or zero population growth slows down investment seems weak. It will more likely change the composition of investment, for example, toward medical care, tourism, and home services for the elderly. New technologies can and will substitute capital for labor in a range of such activities. Moreover, faced with the inevitable crushing expenses of medical care and pensions, governments will have to increase spending, offsetting any shortfall in aggregate demand. The negative effects of aging on GDP growth would be felt more if most of the population over 65 retired from the labor force. Such a decline would count as "stagnation" only because we do not count the leisure of the golden age as output.

However, the 65 years cutoff is a relic of the 19th century, when life expectancy was much shorter. Increased labor force participation by those in the 65–80 age bracket may hold one of the keys to future growth just as increased female participation did in the 1960s and 1970s. Modern medical technology has extended the number of years the post-65 cohort can remain productive, and future technological progress suggests that this will continue to improve.[15] The more those in the 65–80 bracket can be deployed productively, the more concerns about the economic effects of aging will be mitigated. More than anything else, however, the concern is with declining GNP growth, which fails to capture the huge gain in economic welfare accruing to people who do not wish to work beyond retirement, because of better access to entertainment, better medical technology, greater independence, and (hopefully) some measure of economic

---

2050. This is relatively moderate compared with projected rises in median age in other industrialized countries: In Germany it will rise from 38 in 2010 to 51 in 2050, in China from 35 to 46, and in South Korea from 38 to 53 (Pew Research Center 2014, chapter 2).

15. Research suggests that in repetitive work, productivity declines with age, but in knowledge-based jobs age makes no difference in performance and in jobs that require "social skills" productivity rises with age ("The New Old," *Economist*, July 8, 2017, 6). As automation and the increased use of artificial intelligence replace repetitive work but not the kind of work that requires knowledge or social skills, labor market bias against workers over 50 may be doomed. Elderly workers will be increasingly able to participate in the "gig economy" by, for instance, driving Uber cars, letting rooms through Airbnb, or providing babysitting services through such sites as sitters.com. Technology also allows the elderly to cope with many of the handicaps of old age, including on-demand services and smart appliances. As the generation that is comfortable with smart phones and computers enters their 60s and 70s, such technologies will become easier to implement.

security if inflation can be kept under control and old-age insurance markets adapt.

If there is any substance to Malthusian-driven stagnation for our near future, it might be that the finite resource is not land or even natural resources, but the overall limited capability of the planet to carry a *richer* population rather than a *bigger* one. Even if population growth is no longer a factor, it may be argued that rising income per capita on a global scale is self-limiting because it exhausts the finite resources that the world can produce—which include maintaining a stationary temperature distribution. While some extreme environmentalist groups may be opposed to economic growth in any form, their resistance is not based on any economic principle and will remain a fringe movement. After all, growth can be natural-resource-using (as it was in the first centuries of the Industrial Revolution when fossil fuel and iron consumption increased by a huge factor), but it can also be resource-saving, if it takes the form of renewable energy investment, public transportation, recycling of materials, and such. In other words, resource considerations may still steer the growth vehicle but are unlikely to become the brakes. Whether or not such resource-augmenting technological progress will actually happen remains to be seen; in terms of both demography and technological change, the times we live in have no parallel in the past, and so history may be a poor guide to the future.

Politics and growth-hostile institutional change are more of a concern. It should be obvious that in the present world order, a war of predation against small but wealthy nations is rather unlikely even if they have powerful but poor neighbors. Singapore is at first glance uncomfortably hemmed in between two larger and poorer neighbors, Indonesia and Malaysia. Its income per capita exceeds that of Malaysia by a factor of 3.2 and that of Indonesia by a factor of 7.4, yet its population is tiny compared with either. All the same, the likelihood of a predatory war against it is very low. Indeed, the last time such a predatory war took place was Saddam Hussein's invasion of Kuwait in August 1990, which ended disastrously for him. The international order, through formal multinational institutions such as the North Atlantic Treaty Organization (NATO) and the United Nations (UN) as well as informal institutions such as US-led coalitions, will not tolerate such predatory attacks, and potential predators know this full well. Rather than full-scale roving-bandit raids, however, there is a danger that medium-sized but poor nations could engage in the future in nuclear blackmail.

The issue of *internal* rent-seeking is far more complex, and, as already noted, stagnation driven by paralyzing levels of corruption and ineffective governance can indeed threaten future growth in many countries. One of the hardest questions to predict is whether modern countries that have been able to confine cronyism, nepotism, and rent-seeking to tolerable levels will become more corrupt over time, or whether corrupt countries will slowly engage in institutional reform and eventually reduce corruption to manageable levels. When highly corrupt nations interact closely with nations with better institutions, or join supranational organizations with them, one would hope that some reforms would take place. Romania and Bulgaria joined the European Union in 2007; since then Romania's governance indicators have improved somewhat but Bulgaria's not as much.[16] Data for Greece, which joined in 1981, do not go all the way back to the time of joining, but the trend of its scores since 1996 is quite discouraging. In China, the campaign against corruption in the past decade seems to have led to major improvements in the three most crucial governance indicators: in "control of corruption" China moved from the 37th percentile in 2006 to the 49th percentile in 2016, in "government effectiveness" from the 57th to the 68th percentile, and in "rule of law" from 31st to 46th percentile. Greater integration with the world economy may thus have had salutary effects on institutional quality—yet this has not turned China into a more democratic and open polity. The score on the "voice and accountability" indicator remains very low and declined from the 8th percentile in 2005 to the 5th in 2015.

Whether and how the rise of authoritarian regimes in the 21st century will actually affect governance quality is far from clear. In some cases a highly authoritarian regime can turn countries away from corruption if the autocrat—one thinks above all of Singapore's Lee Kuan Yew—has himself or herself high ethical standards. There is no easy way to predict whether the new autocratic regimes established in some countries will be more like Lee or more like the egregiously corrupt and erratic Nicolae Ceauşescu. Clearly location is correlated with the kind of cultural foundations that help determine the quality of governance. The three Baltic nations, all former Soviet republics, have European-level scores on their governance indicators, while the Central Asian republics score abysmally on almost all of them.[17]

Yet history suggests some room for optimism. Countries can change their political structure fairly quickly if there is a profound cultural-ideological change such as the European Enlightenment of the 18th century.

---

16. World Bank, Worldwide Governance Indicators, http://info.worldbank.org/governance/wgi/index.aspx#reports.

17. At the same time, idiosyncratic and contingent factors can override both geography and history. Consider the sharp contrast between neighboring Poland and Belarus: In 2010, Belarus scored in the 27.14 and 15.17 percentiles on "control of corruption" and "rule of law," while Poland scored 70.00 and 68.25, respectively. By 2015, the gap between the two countries had declined somewhat.

As already noted, "old corruption" declined in Britain after 1750, under the leadership of William Pitt the Younger and Edward Burke (Mokyr 2009, 424–27). By 1850, rent-seeking in Britain had been reduced to a minimum. The same occurred in Prussia, the Low Countries, Scandinavia, and Switzerland. There can be little question that the countries affected most by the Enlightenment and its spread after the French Revolution (and their overseas offshoots) are still the ones that tend to score the best on the World Bank and Transparency International corruption indices in our time.

The one concern that may arise is that bad institutions will support resistance to innovation, as incumbents will try to block innovations using a variety of political and rhetorical devices, from concerns about employment opportunities being eroded because of automation to imaginary fears about "frankenfoods." Such fears are a real concern (Mokyr 1998, 2008; Juma 2016). A good case in point is transgenic crops. As Juma (2016) notes, the use of such crops not only increases agricultural productivity but is also environmentally responsible, as it reduces the use of pesticides and fertilizers. Yet opposition to transgenic crops led to the formulation of the infamous Cartagena Protocol on Biosafety, adopted in 2000. The main thrust of this emblematic manifestation of resistance to such crops, known as the "precautionary principle," was to reverse the burden of proof: The originator of the biological innovation had to show it was harmless before it could be marketed—basically an impossible task. As Juma stresses, those who are averse to loss or risk make the logical error of assuming that the status quo is risk-free. Yet it remains to be seen if such resistance will be more effective now than it has been in the past. International competition will make resistance costly, since nations that refuse to adopt the best techniques clearly will be outcompeted by others. The fear of being left behind in the technological race may outweigh the concern about possible adverse effects of new techniques.

All in all, in our age bad governance and rent-seeking are unlikely to stifle long-term economic growth worldwide. This is not to say that endemic corruption and poor institutions do not impede or even stifle economic growth in any single country or even large segments of continents. Global competition between nations has at times induced nations to reform their institutions, but these reforms seem especially prevalent after violent conflict such as the Stein-Hardenberg reforms in Prussia after 1806, the abolition of serfdom in Russia after the Crimean War, or the reintroduction of liberal democracy in Italy and Germany after 1945. The problem, as always, is that the decision makers in high-corruption nations are normally people who benefit from rent-seeking and whose power depends on it; they are unlikely to voluntarily support reforms unless they feel they have to. Yet the overthrow of such venal dictators as Ceaușescu, Yanukovych, and Mubarak shows that corrupt regimes can be deposed even if they are not invariably replaced by better regimes.

Finally, our knowledge of nature in the past century provides us with far better ways of developing and improving technologies. Modern science has penetrated to the atomic and subatomic levels as well as to remote outer space with ever more powerful tools. That is not to say that we fully "understand" why and how nature operates or that we ever will, only that we have a much better grip on regularities and patterns that can be exploited and harnessed to our needs. The basic reason is quite simple: We have far better tools and techniques to observe and analyze natural phenomena and patterns, and those who need to know have far better access to the rapidly expanding body of useful knowledge.

To put it differently, against the widespread concern that innovation is getting increasingly difficult because the "low-hanging fruits" have already been picked in the past century, it can be argued that science provides us with taller and taller ladders. But that is not the entire story. Technology and science coevolve in a powerful positive feedback relationship. Science advances when it has better tools. Seventeenth century science in Europe blossomed in large part because it produced new instruments, most famously the telescope, the microscope, and the vacuum pump. In the 20th century, one of the unsung heroes of science was x-ray crystallography, first proposed by the German theoretical physicist Max von Laue (1879–1960) and realized by William Henry Bragg (1862–1942) with his son, William Lawrence Bragg (1890–1971). The technique has been instrumental in discovering the structure and function of many biological molecules, including vitamins, drugs, and proteins. Its most famous application was Rosalind Franklin's work in 1953, which led to the discovery of the structure of the DNA molecule, but its use has been instrumental in 29 Nobel Prize–winning projects (International Union of Crystallography 2017).

In the past 50 years the toolkits that scientists and researchers in any area have at their disposal have improved and expanded at an undreamed-of rate. Old tools like microscopes and telescopes have been improved beyond imagination, to the point where the developers of the Betzig-Hell super-resolved fluorescent microscope—Eric Betzig, William Moerner, and Stefan Hell—were awarded the Nobel Prize for chemistry. The telescope, similarly, underwent such radical improvements that the much-touted James Webb Space Telescope, to be launched in 2021, will be able to study the origins of galaxies and search for planetary systems in the universe in ways unimaginable before. Every laboratory in the world today uses equipment that is vastly superior to what was available in the late 20th century. Research in a plethora of fields was enriched in the past half-century by two "general-purpose scientific instruments," computers and lasers. The impact of computers on science has gone much beyond simple calculations and statistical analysis: A new era of data science has arrived, in which models are replaced by colossal mega-data-crunching machines, which detect patterns that the human mind could not have dreamed up or fathomed. Such deep learning models engage in data mining in artificial neural networks. Rather than dealing with models, such regularities and correlations are detected by powerful computers even if they are "so twisty that the human brain can neither recall nor predict them" (Weinberger 2017, 12). Here the slogan might well be: Who needs causation as long as we have correlation? In some sense, there is nothing new here: There was always an inductive method in science, in which scientists collected data on plants, shells, and rocks and looked for regularities without fully understanding the underlying laws. The difference may be just in scale, but in these matters scale is everything. Much as the much-touted James Webb is to Galileo's first telescope, the huge data banks of mega crunchers are to Carl Linnaeus's notebooks.

But computers can do more than crunch data: They also simulate, and by doing so, they can solve fiendishly complex equations and allow scientists to study physiological processes and design new materials *in silico* and simulate natural processes that hitherto defied human attempts. Such simulations have spawned entirely new "computational" fields of research, in which simulation and large data processing are strongly complementary in areas of high complexity.

Much like computers, lasers have been used very widely in industry and medicine, but their power as a scientific tool may be just as significant in the long run. Among its many applications, one of the most important is laser-induced breakdown spectroscopy (LIBS) (Thakur and Singh 2007). It is applied in remote material assessment in nuclear power stations; geological analysis in space exploration; diagnostics of archaeological objects; metal diffusion in solar cells; biomedical applications to analyze biological samples like bones, tissues, and fluids; and detection of excess or deficiency of minerals and toxic elements in bodies. Light radar (Lidar) is a related laser-based surveying technique that creates highly detailed three-dimensional images used in geology, seismology, remote sensing, and atmospheric physics. Lasers are also a mechanical tool that can ablate (remove) materials for analysis. Among many other uses, laser interferometers have been used to detect the gravitational waves Einstein postulated, one of the holiest grails in modern physics, and awarded the Nobel Prize in physics in 2017.

In addition to improving the tools of actually conducting research, the modern age has revolutionized *access* to the existing pool of scientific knowledge. As the body of scientific knowledge is increasing continuously, the question of *access* looms ever larger. The reason access is important is well understood: The only way to define "what is known" (social knowledge) is as the union of all scientific knowledge known to individuals. As scientific knowledge has expanded since 1500, an inevitable process of specialization has taken place. Scientists know more and more about less, and there are fewer and fewer "polymaths."[18] The "burden of knowledge" is increasing, and the amount that scientists working at the frontier have to learn is growing (Jones 2009). Often the relevant knowledge is quite remote from one's own specialization and requires access, and access requires an access technology. Inventors need to have access to best-practice science on the frontier to push the envelope and make sure they take technology as far as it can possibly be taken conditional on the largest epistemic base. Moreover, they need to know what already exists so as to avoid reinventing an expensive wheel. Finally, many inventions recombine existing devices, in which disparate elements are put together in new ways, in Matt Ridley's famous formulation, "ideas having sex." Hence, the people working at the frontier need to know what others know. It is no accident that the age of Enlightenment, during which the Industrial Revolution shifted into high gear, was also the age of the encyclopedia, which organized existing knowledge and made it accessible. Many "handbooks" and "technical compendia" were compiled by groups of experts, and they were disseminated through cheap print editions and local libraries with the explicit purpose of making useful knowledge accessible.[19] It is thus obvious that cheap and fast access to existing knowledge is enormously valuable in modern research and underlines the significance of the internet to continued progress.

The race between storage-and-search techniques and the growth of scientific content in the last few years seems so far to have been won by the former. Anyone engaged in research can access vast banks of knowledge and data. Cloud technology is just getting started. Moreover, search

---

18. Indeed, there are two separate books entitled *The Last Man Who Knew Everything*. One of them (Findlen 2004) places the title on the Jesuit scholar Athanasius Kircher (1601–80), a German-born polymath of prodigious scholarly productivity who wrote important books on topics as different as natural history, mathematics, geology, and the history of ancient Egypt. The other book (Robinson 2007) is about Thomas Young (1773–1829), a physician who established the wave theory of light, discovered a formula for the elasticity of materials, and helped decipher the Rosetta Stone.

19. A good example is Temple Croker's three-volume *Complete Dictionary of Arts and Sciences* (1764–66), which explicitly promised its readers that in it "the whole circle of human learning is explained and the difficulties in the acquisition of every Art, whether liberal or mechanical, are removed in the most easy and familiar manner." In close to 2,000 pages, the collection contained detailed essays on diverse topics such as architecture, botany, and hydrostatics.

and storage costs have fallen faster in the past decades than ever before.[20] As Ridley (2010) has remarked, "The cross-fertilization of ideas between, say, Asia and Europe, that once took years, decades, or centuries, can now happen in minutes." Needless to say, a large part of the information stored is not in any way scientific, and even much of the scientific information includes more chaff than wheat and requires verification and validation. While access may become easier, validation may become increasingly more costly as the volume of data keeps expanding. That said, the internet and the easy and cheap access to scientific literature and public databases are now a part of our academic infrastructure. This means that any process of economic growth based on further expanding the epistemic base of technology will continue apace at least at the rate that we have experienced in the past decades.

As a consequence of the exponential growth of knowledge, the nature of scientific research is changing: Jones (2009) observes that "burden of knowledge" effects make innovation more difficult and require more collaborators. Training people to the point they can make important contributions takes more time, so that "ever increasing effort may be needed to sustain long-run growth" (p. 310). Yet Jones also notes that improved methods of knowledge transmission may mitigate the negative effects of the growing burden of knowledge. The emergence of virtual reality as an educational tool may, in fact, do exactly that. He also notes that if sufficiently new technological opportunities emerge, "the output of innovators may become sufficient, despite a rising educational burden, to sustain growth without increasing effort." Ever more powerful research tools will in all likelihood raise the efficiency of capital in the production of new knowledge.

Bloom et al. (2017), in a careful empirical paper, find that productivity in the generation of ideas has been falling across the board in a slew of existing industries. At first glance, this finding seems worrisome, suggesting that if we are to avoid secular stagnation and maintain a constant rate of productivity growth, we will need to allocate more and more researchers to the research and development (R&D) sector. Part of the problem, as Bloom et al. recognize, is that in individual sectors diminishing returns to research may set in but this may not be true for the economy as a whole as new product lines are developed all the time. They deal with this by looking at total factor productivity (TFP) growth in the economy as a whole and find that it has actually slowed as the research effort has increased.

---

20. According to one estimate (Goldman 2013), in 1981 a Macintosh storage drive cost approximately $700,000 per gigabyte. In July 2013, a Western Digital My Book external hard drive cost $0.06 per gigabyte. The cost of flash memory, introduced in 2003, was $8,000 per gigabyte, which fell to $0.94 in 2013 and about $0.40 in 2016.

Equating TFP growth based on GDP statistics with idea growth or technological progress, however, is of course hazardous. Oddly, Bloom et al. do not note that the number of patents, a measure of output of R&D, has been increasing economywide at a rate much faster than TFP. Whether the authors will turn out to be correct or not, it is of course the *total* "output of ideas" that matters for future economic performance, not the output per unit of input. As Bloom et al. stress, ideas are nonrivalrous and so as long as we produce more of them (and their quality does not decline) secular stagnation will not become the rule. Resources allocated to R&D in the past may have been considerably below optimal, and the increase in R&D may have led to a decline in the *marginal* product of labor in R&D that was socially optimal. It may also be true that what they observe is a race between the growing difficulty of coming up with new ideas and the growing capability of equipment and instruments to create them.

Finally, of course, the flow of new ideas may increase even if the productivity in generating them somehow declines. As the economy gets richer and as robotization and artificial intelligence (AI) replace even highly trained knowledge workers, the economy can afford to keep increasing the proportion of the labor force engaged in the R&D sector and thus keep the output of new ideas from declining. What is even more tantalizing, of course, is whether AI itself can generate some new ideas, which at some point in the future could reverse the trends found by Bloom et al.

So far I have discussed the movement of the technological frontier or best practice techniques. But what about the process of catching up by technological followers? European history suggests that technological followers do quite well. Some of the smaller European economies such as the Netherlands, Switzerland, and Ireland have been able to take advantage of inventions made elsewhere and enjoy high standards of living. It is no secret what makes for successful adoption: a high level of sophisticated human capital that can absorb, operate, and exploit the techniques designed by others (and pay the patent royalties if need be), and institutions that make such adoption easy and smooth, including law and order, low political risk, low levels of corruption and red tape, and openness to new ideas. These make all the difference between a Switzerland and an Afghanistan.

Conclusion

Secular stagnation was a defining feature of most of recorded history and has turned into sustained growth only in recent centuries. However, if the technological frontier does not keep moving ahead, modern economies will indeed not be able to avoid the secular stagnation that Alvin Hansen feared. An examination of what drove the technological frontier in the past suggests that the likelihood of reverting to a world of stasis in the foreseeable future is not high. All the same, one could have legitimate concerns whether open institutions that are favorable to growth can keep pace with technological capabilities. Maintaining a high level of innovation will imply ever-improving tools and equipment, which could change the nature of research in ways that we cannot imagine.

References

Acemoglu, Daron, and James Robinson. 2012. *Why Nations Fail: The Origins of Power, Prosperity, and Poverty*. New York: Crown.

Alfani, Guido, and Cormac Ó Gráda. 2017. Famines in Europe: An Overview. In *Famine in European History*, ed. Guido Alfani and Cormac Ó Gráda. Cambridge: Cambridge University Press.

Ashraf, Quamrul, and Oded Galor. 2011. Dynamics and Stagnation in the Malthusian Epoch. *American Economic Review* 101 (August): 2003–41.

Béaur, Gérard, and Jean-Michel Chevet. 2017. France. In *Famine in European History*, ed. Guido Alfani and Cormac Ó Gráda. Cambridge: Cambridge University Press.

Black, Dan A., Natalia Kolesnikova, Seth G. Sanders, and Lowell J. Taylor. 2013. Are Children 'Normal'? *Review of Economics and Statistics* 95, no. 1: 21–33.

Bloom, Nicholas, Charles I. Jones, John Van Reenen, and Michael Webb. 2017. Are Ideas Harder to Find? Unpublished working paper. Stanford University.

Boserup, Ester. 1965. *The Conditions of Agricultural Growth*. Chicago: Aldine.

Boserup, Ester. 1981. *Population and Technological Change*. Chicago: University of Chicago Press.

Boussingault, J. B. 1821. On the Presence of Silicia Platina and Its Presence in Steel. *Repertory of Arts, Manufactures and Agriculture*, 2nd series, volume 39: 366–73.

CIA (Central Intelligence Agency). 2017. Country Comparison: Total Fertility Rate. *The World Factbook*. Available at www.cia.gov/library/publications/the-world-factbook/rankorder/2127rank.html.

Clark, Gregory. 2007. *A Farewell to Alms*. Princeton, NJ: Princeton University Press.

Condorcet, Marie J. A. N. C. 1796. *Outlines of an Historical View on the Progress of Human Mind*. Philadelphia: Lang and Ustick.

Constant, Edward W. 1980. *The Origins of the Turbojet Revolution*. Baltimore: Johns Hopkins Press.

Croker, Temple Henry. 1764–66. *The Complete Dictionary of Arts and Sciences*. London: Printed for the authors.

Ekelund, Robert B., Jr., and Robert D. Tollison. 1981. *Mercantilism as a Rent-Seeking Society*. College Station: Texas A&M University Press.

Findlen, Paula, ed. 2004. *Athanasius Kircher: The Last Man Who Knew Everything*. New York: Routledge.

Galor, Oded. 2011. *Unified Growth Theory*. Princeton, NJ: Princeton University Press.

Gelderblom, Oscar. 2013. *Cities of Commerce: The Institutional Foundations of International Trade in the Low Countries, 1250–1650*. Princeton, NJ: Princeton University Press.

Goldman, Cooper. 2013. *What's the True Cost of Big Data?* Available at www.gooddata.com/blog/whats-true-cost-big-data.

Guthrie William P. 2003. *The Later Thirty Years War: From the Battle of Wittstock to the Treaty of Westphalia*. Westport, CT: Greenwood Press.

Hannam, James. 2011. *The Genesis of Science: How the Christian Middle Ages Launched the Scientific Revolution.* Washington: Regnery Publishing.

Hansen, Alvin H. 1939. Economic Progress and Declining Population Growth. *American Economic Review* XXIX (March): 1-15.

Harris, John R. 1998. *Industrial Espionage and Technology Transfer: Britain and France in the Eighteenth Century.* Aldershot: Ashgate.

Hills, Richard L. 1989. *Power from Steam: A History of the Stationary Steam Engine.* Cambridge: Cambridge University Press.

International Union of Crystallography. 2017. *Nobel Prize winners associated with crystallography.* Available at www. iucr.org/people/nobel-prize.

Jones, Benjamin F. 2009. The Burden of Knowledge and the Death of the Renaissance Man: Is Innovation Getting Harder? *Review of Economic Studies* 76, no. 1: 282-317.

Juma, Calestous. 2016. *Innovation and Its Enemies: Why People Resist New Technologies.* New York: Oxford University Press.

Kelly, Morgan, and Cormac Ó Gráda. 2012. The Preventive Check in Medieval and Pre-industrial England. *Journal of Economic History* 72, no. 4: 1015-35.

Kelly, Morgan, and Cormac Ó Gráda. 2014. Living Standards and Mortality since the Middle Ages. *Economic History Review* 67, no. 2: 358-81.

Kelly, Morgan, and Cormac Ó Gráda. 2016. Adam Smith, Watch Prices, and the Industrial Revolution. *Quarterly Journal of Economics* 131, no. 4: 1727-52.

Kremer, Michael. 1993. Population Growth and Technological Change: One Million BC to 1990. *Quarterly Journal of Economics* 108, no. 4 (August): 681-716.

Lin, Justin Yifu. 1995. The Needham Puzzle: Why the Industrial Revolution Did Not Originate in China. *Economic Development and Cultural Change* 43, no. 2: 269-92.

Macmullen, Ramsay. 2017. The Darkening of the West: A Note. Unpublished manuscript. Yale University.

Mokyr, Joel. 1985. *Why Ireland Starved.* London: Allen and Unwin.

Mokyr, Joel. 1998. The Political Economy of Technological Change: Resistance and Innovation in Economic History. In *Technological Revolutions in Europe,* ed. Maxine Berg and Kristin Bruland. Cheltenham, UK: Edward Elgar Publishers.

Mokyr, Joel. 1999 [2008]. Innovation and Its Enemies: The Economic and Political Roots of Technological Inertia. In *A Not so Dismal Science,* ed. Mancur Olson and Satu Kähkönen. Oxford: Oxford University Press. [Reprinted in Magnus Henrekson and Robin Douhan, eds., *The Political Economy of Entrepreneurship,* volume 2. Cheltenham, UK: Edward Elgar.]

Mokyr, Joel. 2002. *The Gifts of Athena.* Princeton, NJ: Princeton University Press.

Mokyr, Joel. 2009. *The Enlightened Economy.* New York and London: Yale University Press.

Needham, Joseph. 1969. *The Grand Titration.* Toronto: University of Toronto Press.

North, Douglass C., John J. Wallis, and Barry Weingast. 2009. *Violence and Social Orders: A Conceptual Framework for Interpreting Recorded Human History.* Cambridge: Cambridge University Press.

Nowacki, Horst. 2008. Leonhard Euler and the Theory of Ships. *Journal of Ship Research* 52, no. 4: 274-90.

Nye, John. 2007. *War, Wine, and Taxes: The Political Economy of Anglo-French Trade, 1689-1900.* Princeton, NJ: Princeton University Press.

Ó Gráda, Cormac. 2015. *Eating People Is Wrong, and Other Essays on Famine, Its Past, and Its Future.* Princeton, NJ: Princeton University Press.

Pew Research Center. 2014. *Attitudes about Aging: A Global Perspective.* Available at www.pewglobal.org/2014/01/30/attitudes-about-aging-a-global-perspective.

Reynolds, Terry S. 1983. *Stronger Than a Hundred Men: A History of the Vertical Water Wheel*. Baltimore: Johns Hopkins University Press.

Ridley, Matt. 2010. *When Ideas Have Sex*. Available at http://designmind.frogdesign.com/articles/and-now-the-good-news/when-ideas-have-sex.html (accessed on December 27, 2014).

Roberts, Lissa, and Simon Schaffer. 2007. Preface. In *The Mindful Hand: Inquiry and Invention from the Late Renaissance to Early Industrialization*, ed. Lissa Roberts, Simon Schaffer, and Peter Dear. Amsterdam: Royal Netherlands Academy of Arts and Sciences.

Robinson, Andrew. 2007. *The Last Man Who Knew Everything: Thomas Young, the Anonymous Genius Who Proved Newton Wrong and Deciphered the Rosetta Stone, among Other Surprising Feats*. Penguin.

Simon, Julian L. 2001. *The Great Breakthrough and Its Cause* (edited by Timur Kuran). Ann Arbor: University of Michigan Press.

Smil, Vaclav. 2001. *Enriching the Earth*. Cambridge, MA: MIT Press.

Statista. 2017. Median age of the resident population of the United States from 1960 to 2015. Available at www.statista.com/statistics/241494/median-age-of-the-us-population/.

Stewart, Larry. 1992. *The Rise of Public Science*. Cambridge: Cambridge University Press.

Summers, Lawrence H. 2016. The Age of Secular Stagnation: What It Is and What to Do About It. *Foreign Affairs* 95: 2–9.

Thakur, S. N., and J. P. Singh. 2007. Fundamentals of Laser-Induced Breakdown Spectroscopy. In *Laser-Induced Breakdown Spectroscopy*, ed. J. P. Singh and S. N. Thakur. Amsterdam: Elsevier.

Tomory, Leslie. 2012. *Progressive Enlightenment: The Origins of the Gaslight Industry, 1780–1820*. Cambridge, MA: MIT Press.

Vandermonde, Alexandre-Théophile, Claude Berthollet, and Gaspard Monge. 1786. *Mémoire sur le fer considéré dans ses différens états métalliques*. Paris: Académie Royale des Sciences.

Vincenti, Walter. 1990. *What Engineers Know and How They Know It*. Baltimore: Johns Hopkins University Press.

Vincenti, Walter. 2000. Real-World Variation-Selection in the Evolution of Technological Form: Historical Examples. In *Technological Innovation as an Evolutionary Process*, ed. John Ziman. Cambridge: Cambridge University Press.

Voigtländer, Nico, and Hans-Joachim Voth. 2012. The Three Horsemen of Riches: Plague, War, and Urbanization in Early Modern Europe. *Review of Economic Studies* 80: 774–811.

Voigtländer, Nico, and Hans-Joachim Voth. 2013. How the West "Invented" Fertility Restriction. *American Economic Review* 103, no. 6: 2227–64.

Weinberger, David. 2017. *Alien Knowledge: When Machines Justify Knowledge*. Available at https://backchannel.com/our-machines-now-have-knowledge-well-never-understand-857a479dcc0e.

Wells, H. G. 1923. *Men Like Gods*. London: Cassell.

Wertime, Theodore A. 1961. *The Coming of the Age of Steel*. Leyden: Brill.

Wootton, David. 2015. *The Invention of Science: A New History of the Scientific Revolution*. London: Allen Lane.

World Bank. 2017. Fertility Rates, Total. Available at http://data.worldbank.org/indicator/SP.DYN.TFRT.IN.

Zilsel, Edgar. 1942. The Sociological Roots of Science. *American Journal of Sociology* 47, no. 4: 544–60.

3

Is Asia at Risk of Growing Old before Becoming Rich?

SERKAN ARSLANALP, JAEWOO LEE, MINSUK KIM,
UMANG RAWAT, JACQUELINE PIA ROTHFELS,
JOCHEN MARKUS SCHMITTMANN, AND
QIANQIAN ZHANG

Asia benefited significantly from demographic trends in recent decades. Many parts of the region, particularly East Asia, reaped a "demographic dividend," as the number of workers grew faster than the number of dependents, providing a strong tailwind for growth.

This dividend is about to end for many Asian economies. The change will have important implications for labor markets, investment and saving decisions, and public budgets.

This chapter examines the implications of projected demographic changes in major Asian economies over the coming decades by looking at the implications for growth, external balances, and financial markets in the region.[1] It presents policy options to address some of the unique challenges arising from Asia's demographic transition.

Serkan Arslanalp is deputy division chief, Jaewoo Lee is an advisor, Minsuk Kim, Umang Rawat, and Jochen Markus Schmittmann are economists, and Qianqian Zhang is a research assistant at the International Monetary Fund (IMF). Jacqueline Pia Rothfels is an economist at the German Ministry of Finance. All authors were in the IMF's Asia and Pacific Department when the chapter was written. The chapter draws on chapter 2 of the 2017 IMF Asia and Pacific Regional Economic Outlook (IMF 2017), which includes additional analysis on Japan's experience with adverse demographic trends in recent decades and fiscal implications of aging for Asia, along with details on the data, methodology, and results. The views expressed in this chapter are those of the authors and do not necessarily represent the views of the IMF, its Executive Board, or its management.

1. The chapter analyzes developments in the 13 largest Asian economies: Australia, China, Hong Kong, India, Indonesia, Japan, Korea, Malaysia, New Zealand, the Philippines, Singapore, Thailand, and Vietnam.

Figure 3.1 Fertility, life expectancy, and population growth in Asia, 1950–2050

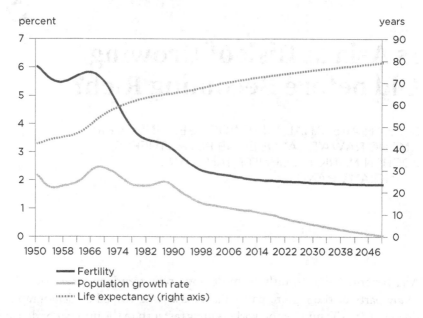

Source: IMF Staff estimates based on United Nations, *World Population Prospects: 2015 Revision* (medium-fertility scenario).

Demographic Trends in Asia

Asia is undergoing a demographic transition marked by slowing population growth and aging. The change mainly reflects declining fertility rates since the late 1960s and to a lesser extent rising life expectancy (figure 3.1). The population growth rate, already negative in Japan, is projected to fall to zero for Asia by 2050. The share of the working-age population is projected to decline over coming decades. The share of the population 65 and older will increase rapidly, reaching almost 2.5 times the current level by 2050. East Asia is projected to be the world's fastest-aging region in coming decades, with its old-age dependency ratio roughly tripling by 2050.[2]

The demographic outlook varies across Asia. Broadly following the findings of the World Bank (2015), three broad groups of countries can be distinguished (table 3.1):

---

2. Population projections in this chapter are based on the United Nations' *World Population Prospects: 2015 Revision* (medium-fertility scenario with unchanged net migration flows). Projections of the various fertility scenarios do not differ much until 2030, but uncertainty increases with the projection horizon, primarily because of different assumptions about future fertility rates (World Bank 2015).

Table 3.1 Demographic classification of Asia

Economy	Demographic characteristics in 2015	Projected demographic characteristics in 2030
Australia	Late-dividend	Late-dividend
China	Post-dividend	Post-dividend
Hong Kong	Post-dividend	Post-dividend
India	Early-dividend	Early-dividend
Indonesia	Early-dividend	Late-dividend
Japan	Post-dividend	Post-dividend
Korea	Post-dividend	Post-dividend
Malaysia	Late-dividend	Late-dividend
New Zealand	Late-dividend	Late-dividend
Philippines	Early-dividend	Early-dividend
Singapore	Late-dividend	Post-dividend
Thailand	Post-dividend	Post-dividend
Vietnam	Late-dividend	Late-dividend

Note: Post-dividend is defined as a total fertility rate 30 years prior below 2.1 and a shrinking working-age population share over the next 15 years or a shrinking absolute working-age population. Late-dividend is defined as a total fertility rate 30 years prior above 2.1 and a shrinking working-age population share over the next 15 years. Early-dividend is defined as an increasing working-age population share over the next 15 years.

Source: IMF Staff estimates based on United Nations, *World Population Prospects: 2015 Revision* (medium-fertility scenario).

- In post-dividend economies, the size of the working-age population is shrinking both absolutely and in terms of its share of the total population. This group includes China, Hong Kong, Japan, Korea, and Thailand. These economies are projected to age rapidly and reach some of the highest old-age dependency ratios globally by 2050.[3] Japan has the world's highest old-age dependency ratio (43 percent at the end of 2015). It will rise to 71 percent by the end of 2050. Singapore is projected to transition to post-dividend status by 2030 (table 3.2).

- In late-dividend economies, the working-age population is declining as a share of total population but is still growing in absolute numbers. This group includes Malaysia and Vietnam (two moderately aging emerging markets) as well as Australia and New Zealand (advanced economies that experienced a demographic transition earlier than other countries

---

3. China began relaxing its one-child policy in 2013; since 2016 it has allowed all couples to have two children. Demographers expect a positive but limited impact of the policy change on fertility (Basten and Jiang 2015). The 2015 UN population projections see the fertility rate gradually rising from 1.5 children per woman in 2010 to 1.7 by 2030 (UN 2015).

Table 3.2 Old-age dependency ratios in Asia, 2000–50 (percent)

Country	2000	2005	2010	2015	2020	2025	2030	2035	2040	2045	2050
Japan	25.2	29.9	36.0	43.3	48.3	50.6	53.1	57.0	63.8	68.1	70.9
Hong Kong	15.3	16.5	17.2	20.6	26.5	35.1	43.7	50.1	55.6	60.4	64.6
Korea	10.2	12.7	15.0	18.0	22.2	29.4	37.6	46.1	54.4	60.7	65.8
Singapore	10.3	11.3	12.2	16.1	21.4	28.6	36.5	43.7	51.1	57.2	61.6
Thailand	9.5	11.0	12.4	14.6	18.4	23.4	29.2	35.8	42.3	48.2	52.5
New Zealand	18.0	18.1	19.6	22.9	26.3	30.2	34.9	38.0	40.6	40.5	40.7
China	9.7	10.4	11.1	13.1	17.1	20.4	25.3	32.7	39.6	43.0	46.7
Australia	18.5	19.2	20.0	22.7	25.3	28.3	31.3	32.8	34.8	35.3	37.3
Vietnam	10.4	9.9	9.4	9.6	11.7	14.8	18.3	21.8	25.6	29.5	34.1
Malaysia	6.1	6.7	7.2	8.4	10.0	12.2	14.5	16.7	18.7	21.0	25.3
Indonesia	7.3	7.4	7.5	7.7	8.6	10.4	12.4	14.7	17.0	19.2	21.3
India	7.2	7.7	8.0	8.6	9.8	11.1	12.5	14.0	15.8	17.8	20.5
Philippines	5.5	5.8	6.7	7.2	8.0	9.1	10.3	11.5	12.5	13.5	14.5

Note: The old-age dependency ratio indicates the size of the population 65 years of age and older as a share of the working-age population (15–64 years old).

Source: IMF Staff calculations and projections based on United Nations, *World Population Prospects: 2015 Revision* (medium-fertility scenario).

in the region but maintain higher fertility rates than most East Asian economies and have substantial immigration). Immigration has also kept Singapore in this category, despite one of the lowest fertility rates in the region.

■ In early-dividend economies, the share of the working-age population will rise both as a share of the total population and in absolute terms over the next 15 years. This group includes India, Indonesia, and the Philippines. These countries have some of the youngest populations in the region and will see their working-age populations increase substantially in coming decades. Fertility rates are projected to remain above the replacement rate of 2.1 for India and Indonesia until 2030 and beyond 2030 for the Philippines. Indonesia is projected to transition to late-dividend status by 2030.

Migration is an important factor in the demographic evolution of some Asian economies. As migrants tend to be of working age, migrant flows can slow the demographic transition in recipient countries. Immigration has been sizable in Australia, Hong Kong, New Zealand, and Singapore. Continued immigration in these economies is projected to substantially slow the decline in the size of the working-age population.

Emigration of working-age people is substantial in the Philippines, but the impact on the working-age population is small relative to the population size. In China, Japan, Korea, and the other member countries of the Association of Southeast Asian Nations (ASEAN), net migration is relatively small.

The population of Asia is not the oldest in the world—Europe holds that distinction—but the speed of aging in Asia is remarkable. Figure 3.2 displays the number of years it takes for the old-age dependency ratio to increase from 15 percent to 20 percent. This transition took 26 years in Europe and more than 50 years in the United States. In Asia, only Australia and New Zealand aged at similar speeds. For China, Japan, Korea, Singapore, Thailand, and Vietnam, the same transition has taken (or will take) less than 10 years.

The rapid speed of aging has two implications. First, countries in Asia will have less time to adapt policies to their older population than many advanced economies had. Second, some countries in Asia are getting old before becoming rich; they are therefore likely to face the high fiscal costs of aging and demographic headwinds to growth at relatively low per capita income levels. Figure 3.3 shows per capita income at purchasing power parity relative to the United States at the historical or projected peak of the share of the working-age population in each country. Except for Australia and Japan, per capita income in major Asian countries is at significantly

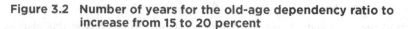

Figure 3.2 Number of years for the old-age dependency ratio to increase from 15 to 20 percent

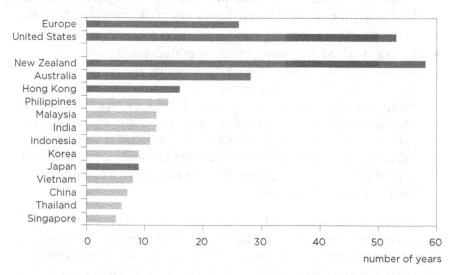

Note: The old-age dependency ratio indicates the population 65 years and older as a share of the working-age population (15–64 years). Data shown in darker shading reflect historical data, while economies in lighter shading reflect projections.

Source: IMF Staff calculations based on United Nations, *World Population Prospects: 2015 Revision* (medium-fertility scenario).

lower levels than reached by mature advanced economies at the same stage of the aging cycle. This trend underscores the need to sustain high growth rates in these economies.

Asia's demographic evolution has important global implications, because of the region's contribution to global growth, current account balances, and capital flows, as well as relative wage levels and competitiveness. Figure 3.4 presents absolute changes in the working-age population for different demographic country groups in Asia and the rest of the world. Between 1970 and 2010, Asia contributed more to the growth of the global working-age population than the rest of the world combined.

This situation is changing. Over the coming decades, rapidly aging East Asian economies are projected to see their working-age populations drop substantially. The largest absolute decline will be in China, where the working-age population will fall by 170 million over the next 35 years. Substantial absolute declines are also projected for Japan, Korea, and Thailand. In contrast, Africa will account for most of the growth in the global working-age population (IMF 2015a).

Figure 3.3 Per capita income level at the peak of working-age population share (based on purchasing power parity; in percent of US per capita income at each country's peak year)

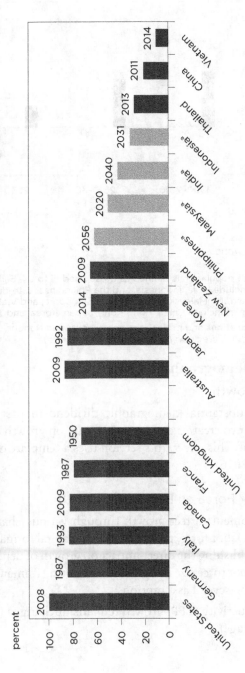

a. Based on IMF Staff projection. For Malaysia, the income level relative to the United States is calculated from the April 2017 *World Economic Outlook* projection for 2020. For India, Indonesia, and the Philippines, the income levels are calculated by applying the projected purchasing power parity per capita income growth rate in 2022, starting from 2023 and up to the year in which the working-age population share is projected to peak.

Note: For the countries shown in the figure, the working-age population (15–64 years) share of the total population has peaked, or is projected to reach the peak, in the year indicated in parentheses.

Sources: IMF, *World Economic Outlook* database; IMF Staff calculations based on United Nations, *World Population Prospects: 2015 Revision* (medium-fertility scenario).

Figure 3.4   Change in working-age population in Asia and the rest of the world

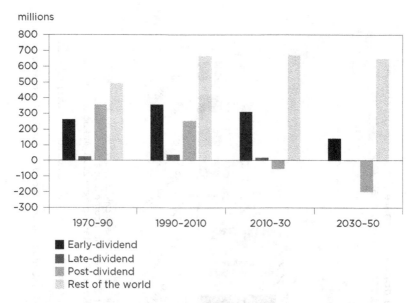

millions

Note: The working-age population is defined as those aged 15 to 64. Early-dividend economies include India, Indonesia, and the Philippines. Late-dividend economies include Australia, Malaysia, New Zealand, Singapore, and Vietnam. Post-dividend economies include China, Hong Kong, Japan, Korea, and Thailand.

Source: IMF Staff calculations and projections based on United Nations, *World Population Prospects: 2015 Revision* (medium-fertility scenario).

Implications of Demographic Trends

Implications for Growth

Asia has enjoyed a substantial demographic dividend in past decades. Rapid aging is now set to create a demographic "tax" on growth in several economies. To quantify this effect, this section uses a template devised by Amaglobeli and Shi (2016).

Impact of the Labor Force on Economic Growth

Demographic developments affect growth through various channels, including the size of the labor force, productivity, and capital formation. The analysis begins by establishing the direct impact on growth of demography-induced changes in labor force size in a growth accounting framework. This baseline impact rests on several assumptions:

- Total factor productivity (TFP) growth remains unchanged (based on the historical average).

- Age- and gender-specific labor force participation rates (and employment rates) remain unchanged.
- The capital-to-effective-labor ratio remains constant.[4]

Long-term output is estimated using a production function approach with capital and labor as inputs. The function is defined in logarithmic terms as follows:

$$\log(Y_t) = \log(TFP_t) + (1-\beta) \times \log(K_t) + \beta \times \log \sum_{j=1}^{J} N_t^j \times LFP_t^j \times E_t^j \times w_t^j \quad (3.1)$$

where t is time; Y is real output; TFP is total factor productivity; K is the stock of capital; β is the share of labor in output; j is the age-gender cohort; N is the number of individuals in each cohort; LFP and E denote cohort-specific labor force participation and employment rates, respectively; and w is the weight factor used to adjust for the difference between the number of employees and the effective units of labor supplied.

Population projections affect output in this framework through aggregate labor and capital. To establish the baseline impact of demographic change, we compare estimated output based on the United Nations' medium-fertility scenario (which includes migration) with a hypothetical status quo scenario that assumes constant population size and age structure. Separately, we also consider the UN zero-migration scenario, to assess the impact of migration.

Figure 3.5, panel a, shows the average annual growth impact from 2020 to 2050 relative to the status quo. It reveals the following:

- Demographic trends will create strong headwinds for post-dividend countries. In Japan the impact of aging could reduce the average annual growth rate by almost 1 percentage point. The growth impact for China, Hong Kong, Korea, and Thailand could be 0.5–0.75 percentage point.[5] For Singapore, which transitions from late- to post-dividend status by 2030, the estimated overall impact is almost zero.

- Early- and late-dividend countries could still enjoy a substantial annual demographic dividend, ranging from 0.5 percentage points for New Zealand to almost 1.5 percentage points for the Philippines. Reaping

---

4. This assumption means that investment adjusts over time to the labor force, where labor is expressed in efficiency units (i.e., incorporating TFP). If, for example, the capital stock is 300 percent of GDP and the effective labor force growth declines by 1 percentage point, the investment ratio will fall by 3 percentage points of GDP. As some substitution between capital and labor is likely, this assumption creates an upper bound on the growth impact.

5. The drag on growth is broadly stable for Japan over the next three decades, near 1.0 percentage point in each decade. In contrast, the drag for China rises over time, from 0.4 percentage point in the first decade to about 1.1 percentage points in the last decade.

Figure 3.5 Baseline growth impact of demographic trends in Asia

a. Impact on real GDP growth

percentage points; average, 2020–50

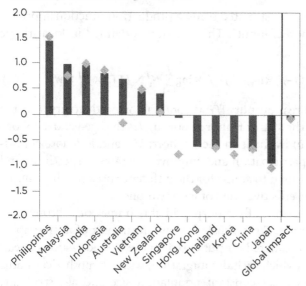

b. Impact on real GDP per capita growth

percentage points; average, 2020–50

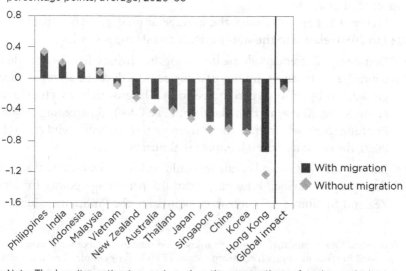

■ With migration
◆ Without migration

Note: The baseline estimates are based on the assumptions of unchanged labor force participation by age-gender cohort, constant capital-to-labor ratio, and total factor productivity growth unchanged from historical average. Migration projections follow historical trends. Global impact indicates the purchasing power parity-weighted average as a percent of global GDP.

Sources: IMF Staff projections based on Amaglobeli and Shi (2016); United Nations, *World Population Prospects: 2015 Revision* (medium-fertility scenario); and Penn World Tables 9.0.

the demographic dividend is not automatic, however. It depends on good policies to raise productivity and create a sufficient number of good quality jobs for the growing working-age population, as Bloom, Canning, and Fink (2010) show.[6]

- Inward migration can prolong the demographic dividend or soften the impact of rapid aging. In Australia, Hong Kong, New Zealand, and Singapore, the impact of continued immigration on the workforce could add 0.5–1 percentage point to average annual growth.[7] The impact of net emigration from Indonesia, the Philippines, and Vietnam is small, because of the small size of emigration as a share of population in these countries.

- Migration can reduce but cannot reverse the negative impact of aging on growth. Australia, for example, would need to receive immigration equal to approximately 23 percent of the actual workforce to maintain the same dependency ratio by 2030. For Singapore the figure would be 51 percent.

Figure 3.5, panel b, shows the growth impact on a per capita basis. The country ordering changes slightly. The drag from demographics is smaller for Japan but larger for Hong Kong and Singapore, because the positive impact of immigration is partially eliminated.

We next relax several assumptions in this stylized exercise—in particular the assumptions of unchanged TFP growth and labor force participation rates—and discuss why we keep the capital-to-effective-labor ratio assumption.

Impact of Aging on Total Factor Productivity

The first assumption in the baseline estimates is unchanged TFP growth. But age groups differ in their productivity, because of factors such as accumulation of experience, depreciation of knowledge, and age-related differences in physical and mental capabilities.

---

6. Long-term demographic projections are uncertain. Compared with the United Nations' medium-fertility scenario, average annual growth is about 0.2 percentage point higher in the high-fertility scenario and about 0.2 percentage point lower in the low-fertility scenario.

7. This effect is driven only by an increase in the size of the workforce. In addition, Jaumotte, Koloskova, and Saxena (2016) estimate that a 1 percentage point increase in the share of migrants in the working-age population can raise GDP per capita over the long term by up to 2 percent, by increasing labor productivity and, to a lesser extent, boosting investment. This second-round effect is not shown in panel a of figure 3.5. The long-term UN assumptions on net migration rates for these countries range from 2.5 percent in New Zealand to 6 percent in Australia.

Figure 3.6 Share of older workers in working-age population in Asia

population aged 55–64 in percent of working-age population

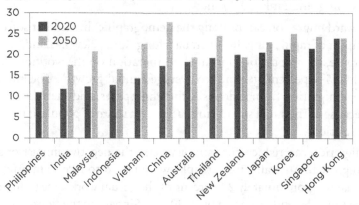

Note: The working-age population is defined as those aged 15 to 64.

Sources: IMF Staff estimates based on United Nations, *World Population Prospects: 2015 Revision* (medium-fertility scenario); and Penn World Tables 9.0.

Several studies find evidence of a decline in worker productivity and innovation starting between ages 50 and 60 (Feyrer 2007; Aiyar, Ebeke, and Shao 2016; and Börsch-Supan and Weiss 2016). In contrast, Acemoglu and Restrepo (2017) find no robust negative impact of aging on productivity, based on cross-country regressions linking aging to GDP per capita growth. They argue that their result may reflect the more rapid adoption of automation technologies in countries that are aging more rapidly.

Figure 3.6 shows that in most Asian countries, the share of older workers (55–65) in the workforce is projected to increase substantially by 2050. The largest increases are projected for China, Malaysia, and Vietnam.

The impact of aging may differ across professions. Veen (2008) argues that productivity of workers in physically demanding professions (construction, factory work) declines at older ages, whereas productivity in other professions (law, management, medicine) may increase with age.

Figure 3.7 applies Veen's taxonomy to selected Asian economies. Countries with lower per capita income, such as Thailand and Vietnam, tend to have larger shares of their workforce in professions in which productivity tends to decline with age. This finding underscores the importance of structural transformation to prepare for an aging workforce.

We estimate the effect of workforce aging (measured by the share of workers 55–65 in the workforce) on productivity following the approach in

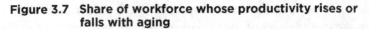

Figure 3.7 Share of workforce whose productivity rises or falls with aging

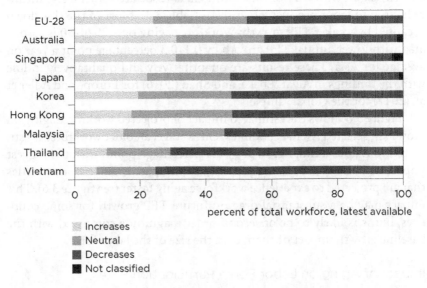

percent of total workforce, latest available

- Increases
- Neutral
- Decreases
- Not classified

Note: Category productivity "increases" with age includes managers and professionals; Category "neutral" includes clerical support workers and services and sales workers; Category "decreases" includes technicians, skilled agricultural, forestry and fishery workers, craft and related trades workers, plant and machine operators and assemblers, elementary occupations and armed forces occupations.

Sources: Veen (2008); International Labor Organization; IMF Staff calculations.

Aiyar, Ebeke, and Shao (2016) and Adler et al. (2017).[8] The baseline model fits the growth in real output per worker on the share of workers 55 and older and the combined youth and old-age dependency ratios, with decade (10 years) and country fixed effects. The model takes the following form:

$$\Delta logYW_{it} = \theta_1 w55_{it} + \theta_2 DR_{it} + u_i + \eta_t + \varepsilon_{it} \qquad (3.2)$$

where i indicates the country, t the decade, YW real output per worker, $w55$ the share of the workforce aged 55–64, DR the dependency ratio, u_i the country fixed effect, η_t the decade fixed effect, and ε_{it} the error term. Correcting for various econometric pitfalls—such as reverse causality—the approach measures the impact of workforce aging on output per worker. To address the endogeneity issue, the model also instruments the workforce share variable and the dependency ratio with lagged birth rates (of 10, 20, 30, and 40 years), as in Jaimovich and Siu (2009).

---

8. The two studies use the same approach, regressing either TFP or TFP growth on demographic variables and testing whether workforce aging is associated with a permanent loss in productivity or a slowdown in productivity growth as a result of less innovation.

For a sample of Asian and European countries, the results show that an increase in the share of older workers is associated with a significant reduction in labor productivity growth (table 3.3). Most of the slowdown is caused by weaker TFP growth: Workforce aging over 2020–50 is associated with lower annual TFP growth by 0.1–0.3 percentage point a year on average for Asia. These results are quantitatively and qualitatively in line with the findings in Aiyar, Ebeke, and Shao (2016) for Europe and Adler et al. (2017) for the global sample.

Figure 3.8 shows the estimated impact of projected workforce aging on growth in selected Asian economies. On average, an older workforce is estimated to reduce annual growth by 0.1 percentage point, with the biggest impact in China (0.3 percentage point). The impact is higher for countries that are projected to experience workforce aging faster (see figure 3.6). This impact may be a substantial drag on future TFP growth for some countries, but it is likely to be of second-order magnitude compared with the baseline growth impact of changes in the size of the labor force.

Impact of Aging on Labor Force Participation Rates

The second assumption in the baseline estimates is constant age- and gender-specific labor force participation rates (LFPRs). LFPRs change over time and can be affected by policies. For example, increases in life expectancy could encourage older people to stay in the workforce. In fact, the effective retirement age has increased in most Organization for Economic Cooperation and Development (OECD) countries, although the increases have been modest compared with increases in life expectancy (Bloom, Canning, and Fink 2010). Alternatively, the decline in fertility rates could encourage more women to participate in the labor force (Bloom et al. 2007). In most Asian economies, there is scope for greater female labor force participation, although unleashing the full potential of female employment requires a comprehensive set of policies (Steinberg and Nakane 2012, Elborgh-Woytek et al. 2013, Kinoshita and Guo 2015). In contrast, LFPRs tend to decline for younger workers as countries develop and average years of schooling increase.

Figure 3.9 displays the changes in LFPRs for working-age populations in Asian economies between 1990 and 2015. It shows that LFPRs remained remarkably stable over this period, despite shifts for age-gender subgroups.[9]

---

9. Female LFPRs increased in the region's advanced economies but declined in China, India, Thailand, and Vietnam; male LFPRs declined in most countries. LFPRs for workers 15–24 declined in all countries by up to a third, reflecting longer schooling. LFPRs for workers 55–64 increased in most countries, most notably Australia, New Zealand, and Singapore.

Table 3.3 Panel regression: Demographics and labor productivity[a]

Dependent variables	Change in real output per worker	Change in real capital stock per worker	Change in human capital per worker	Change in TFP (model based) per worker[b]	Change in TFP (from PWT 9.0) per worker
Workforce share aged 55–64	−0.612***	0.187***	−0.0589***	−0.740***	−0.502***
	(−5.309)	(−4.144)	(−2.896)	(−4.714)	(−5.643)
Dependency ratio	−0.122	−0.105	0.0382	−0.0549	0.279**
	(−0.695)	(−1.532)	(−1.232)	(−0.229)	(−2.057)
Observations	571	571	571	571	571
Number of countries	33	33	33	33	33

PWT 9.0 = Penn World Tables 9.0; TFP = total factor productivity

a. All regressions include both country and time effects.

b. Following a Cobb-Douglas function, the model takes the form of log (real output) = $\dfrac{a}{1-a}\log\left(\dfrac{real\ capital\ stock\ per\ worker}{real\ output\ per\ worker}\right)$ + log (human capital per worker) + log (TFP per worker).

Note: t-statistics in parentheses; *** p<0.01, ** p<0.05, * p<0.1.

Source: IMF Staff estimates.

Figure 3.8 Impact of aging on total factor productivity

percentage point impact on real GDP growth; average over 2020–50

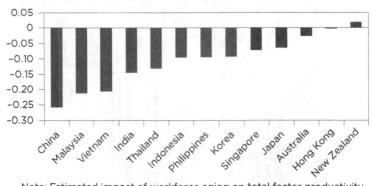

Note: Estimated impact of workforce aging on total factor productivity growth follows Aiyar, Ebeke, and Shao (2016) based on a sample of Asian and European economies.

Sources: IMF Staff estimates based on United Nations, *World Population Prospects: 2015 Revision* (medium-fertility scenario) and Penn World Tables 9.0.

Figure 3.9 Labor force participation rates ages 15–64 in 1990 and 2015

percent of population between ages 15–64 years

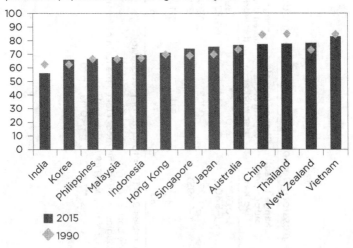

■ 2015
◆ 1990

Source: IMF Staff calculations based on International Labor Organization figures.

Figure 3.10 Baseline growth impact of demographic trends and higher labor force participation

percentage point impact on real GDP growth; average over 2020–50

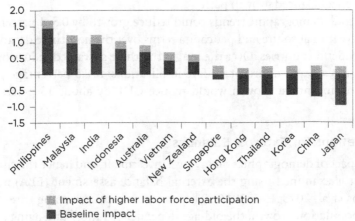

■ Impact of higher labor force participation
■ Baseline impact

Note: The rising labor force participation rates scenario is based on the experience of Japan from 1990 to 2015.

Source: IMF (2017).

Within the region, LFPRs increased the most in Japan, the world's oldest country, rising by almost 6 percentage points since 1990.

What if the LFPR of other Asian economies were to rise by as much as it did in Japan? Figure 3.10 shows the impact of such a scenario on growth. Annual GDP growth rises 0.2–0.3 percentage point, offsetting the lower TFP growth that results from workforce aging. Such changes in the LFPR are unlikely to counter the baseline growth effects induced by changes in the overall labor force, however.[10]

Impact of Aging on Investment

The third assumption in the baseline impact estimates is a constant capital-to-effective-labor ratio. Workforce aging is associated with higher capital per worker (accounting for TFP), but economically the effect is small (table 3.3). There is no statistically significant relationship between the old-age de-

---

10. The impact on growth for small changes in LFPRs is close to linear. A more ambitious scenario, in which the employment gender gap is eliminated, could add 0.25 percentage point to annual GDP growth for Japan and up to 1 percentage point for India by 2050 (Elborgh-Woytek et al. 2013, Cuberes and Teignier 2016, Khera 2016). Gonzales et al. (2015) show that reducing a broader measure of gender inequality in education, political empowerment, the LFPR, and health could lower income inequality and boost growth: A 10 percentage point reduction in the gender inequality index is associated with almost 1 percentage point higher per capita GDP growth.

pendency ratio and capital per worker. Taken together, these results suggest that a constant capital-to-labor ratio assumption is reasonable, especially for thinking about the next three decades, when countries would presumably be on a balanced growth path.

Overall, demographic trends could reduce growth by 0.5–1 percentage point a year in absolute and per capita terms over the next three decades in post-dividend countries. Over the long term, these sustained reductions in growth rates have important welfare implications: A 0.5 percentage point reduction in annual growth would reduce GDP by about 15 percent by 2050.

Implications for External Balances

The impact of demographics on savings, investment, and hence the current account is examined using the external balance assessment (EBA) model (Phillips et al. 2013, IMF 2016). The impact is captured using three variables: population growth, the old-age dependency ratio,[11] and aging speed (defined as the expected change in old-age dependency in 20 years) (see IMF 2017 for details).[12]

Demographic trends affect savings, investment, and the current account balance in the following ways:

- *Savings.* Countries with larger shares of dependent populations generally have lower savings.[13] Therefore, both higher population growth (a proxy for higher youth dependency) and higher old-age dependency are linked with lower savings (table 3.4). Faster aging implies a higher probability of survival and therefore a greater need for life-cycle savings.[14]

---

11. Following the EBA model, the working-age population is defined as people 30–64, which captures the prime-age population. As 15-year-olds are not routinely in the employed population, the prime-age population is considered a better choice for examining savings-investment relationships. Accordingly, the old-age dependency ratio indicates people 65 and over as a share of the prime-age population.

12. In the EBA model, population growth is a proxy for the fertility rate or youth dependency ratio. Aging speed is a measure of the "probability of survival" or longevity, reflecting the prospects of population aging; old-age dependency captures the outcome of population aging so far (IMF 2017).

13. Grigoli, Herman, and Schmidt-Hebbel (2014) provide a comprehensive survey of saving determinants. They find that both youth and old-age dependency lower savings in both the theoretical and the empirical literature.

14. As people expect to live longer, they are induced to save more, counterbalancing the effects of higher old-age dependency (Li, Zhang, and Zhang 2007). The impact of aging on saving behavior is subject to model uncertainty, depending on whether this forward-looking element is accounted for.

Table 3.4 Expected impact of demographic variables on current account

Variable	Savings	Investment	Current account balance
Youth dependency	↓	↑	↓
Old-age dependency	↓	↓	Ambiguous
Aging speed	↑	↓	↑

Source: Authors' illustration.

- *Investment.* As population growth increases, the capital-to-labor ratio falls, raising the return on capital and boosting investment.[15] Rising old-age dependency works in the opposite direction, as it leads to a higher capital-to-labor ratio. To the extent that it reflects expectations of a larger future population of older people and lower future aggregate demand, aging speed also results in lower investment.

- *Current account balance.* Population growth, aging speed, and rising old-age dependency are expected to have negative, positive, and ambiguous impacts, respectively, on the current account.

A large body of literature investigates the macroeconomic impact of population aging on savings and investment. Based on a sample of Asian countries from the early 1950s to the 1990s, Higgins and Williamson (1997) find that countries with relatively young populations are capital importers, whereas countries with relatively old populations are capital exporters. Higgins (1998) finds similar results based on a larger sample of 100 countries. Chinn and Ito (2007); Gruber and Kamin (2007); and Legg, Prasad, and Robinson (2007) find large and empirically significant impacts of demographics on the current account, with higher old-age dependency reducing the current account balance. Eichengreen and Fifer (2002) find the demographic impact on savings and investment to be roughly similar, based on a larger sample of 90 countries spanning 1980–94.

The significance of the negative impact of youth dependency on the current account is less robust in the empirical literature. Jaumotte and Sodsriwiboon (2010) find that the population growth rate has a negative effect on the current account balance. Much of this literature misses the impact of longevity on current account balances. Research that explicitly captures this channel includes Li, Zhang, and Zhang (2007) and Barnes,

---

15. The impact of population growth (or youth dependency) on investment is less certain than on savings. Some studies (e.g., Higgins 1998) find a positive effect; others (e.g., Williamson 2001, Bosworth and Chodorow-Reich 2007) find a negative effect.

Lawson, and Radziwill (2010), who find that increased longevity is associated with higher savings.

Empirical results based on the EBA model support our priors on the effect of population growth and aging speed. Higher population growth leads to lower current account balance (as in Jaumotte and Sodsriwiboon 2010), but the effect is not empirically significant. Aging speed is strongly associated with higher current account balances, reflecting aging-related precautionary savings (as in Li, Zhang, and Zhang 2007 and Barnes, Lawson, and Radziwill 2010). Higher old-age dependency is positively associated with the current account balance when aging speed is higher than the world average.

What changes in regional current accounts does the EBA model predict as a result of demographic transition in the coming decade?[16] By 2020 Australia, Japan, and New Zealand will have higher old-age dependency ratios than the (GDP-weighted) world average. By 2030 Hong Kong, Korea, and Singapore will also have higher old-age dependency ratios than the world average.[17] Several economies in the region—most notably Hong Kong, Japan, Korea, and Singapore (advanced economies) and China, Thailand, and Vietnam (emerging markets)—will experience very rapid aging until 2030 (IMF 2017). In contrast, some advanced economies (Australia and New Zealand) will have lower speeds of aging than the world average.

Over 2020–30, the EBA model suggests that, all else equal, demographic trends are likely to exert upward pressure on current account balances in surplus countries, such as Thailand, Korea, and Japan given the increase in their aging speeds between 2020 and 2030 (figure 3.11). Among deficit countries, demographic trends are likely to exert downward pressure, particularly in New Zealand, given its falling aging speed. Overall, demographics are projected to materially increase current account balances in only a few economies in Asia. The total impact of demographics on global imbalances is limited.

What will be the effect on capital flows? All else equal, demographic factors are likely to strengthen the current dynamics of capital flows. Over 2020–30, changes in the current account as a result of demographic trends are likely to be positively correlated with 2015 current account balances

---

16. The rest of this section focuses on old-age dependency and aging speed as the main drivers of the current account because changes in population growth between 2020 and 2030 are expected to be relatively small. The contribution of population growth to changes in current account is less than 0.1 percent of GDP for the sample period.

17. Demographic variables are expressed relative to the (GDP-weighted) world average, reflecting the fact that countries need to be at different stages of the demographic transition in order for it to have an impact on their external positions.

Figure 3.11 Demographic impact on current account

percent of GDP, change from 2020 to 2030

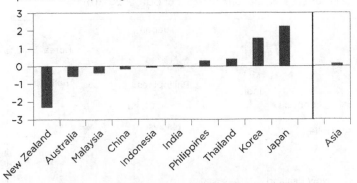

Note: Current account norms (based on demographic variables only) are adjusted for multilateral consistency. Asia impact indicates the sum of projected changes in Asia's current accounts as a percent of world GDP. Hong Kong, Singapore, and Vietnam are not shown as they are not included in the sample for the external balance assessment model.

Sources: United Nations, *World Population Prospects: 2015 Revision* (medium-fertility scenario); IMF, *World Economic Outlook*; and IMF Staff projections.

(figure 3.12): Countries with current account surpluses are expected to remain capital exporters, and countries in deficit are expected to remain capital importers.

These results are based on a partial equilibrium analysis, which takes the values of other macroeconomic variables in the EBA model (the future expected growth rate, the level of relative productivity, relative output gap, relative fiscal balance) as fixed. The broader impact of demographics may be smaller or larger than the estimated partial effect, depending on how aging interacts with these variables.[18]

Implications for Financial Markets

The changes in savings and investment associated with aging can also have implications for domestic financial markets. A panel regression was conducted to examine the potential impact of demographic trends on domestic interest rates, equity returns, and real estate prices in the region (IMF 2017). The results suggest that both rising old-age dependency in post-dividend

---

18. For example, aging may affect fiscal balance through higher pension and healthcare spending. As public health spending is included as a control variable in the EBA, the estimates (figure 3.11) account for this channel based on health spending projections (Amaglobeli and Shi 2016). The estimates do not account for the role of generosity of pension systems, which could be an important factor behind private saving behavior.

Figure 3.12 Changes in current account induced by demographics and current account balances in 2015

change in current account norm (percent of GDP, 2020–30)

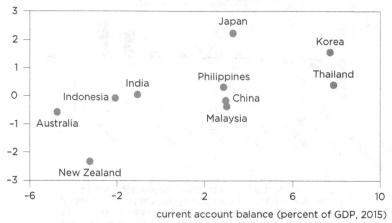

current account balance (percent of GDP, 2015)

Note: Current account norms (based on demographic variables only) are adjusted for multilateral consistency.

Sources: United Nations, *World Population Prospects: 2015 Revision* (medium-fertility scenario); IMF, *World Economic Outlook*; and IMF Staff estimates.

countries and falling youth dependency in early-dividend countries are likely to put downward pressure on domestic real interest rates. The impact of these factors diminishes with financial openness.

Impact on Interest Rates

The decline in long-term interest rates is a global phenomenon. Long-term bond yields have declined significantly in Europe and the United States. A similar trend is observed in Asia, particularly Korea and Australia, where the decline has been nearly as large (figure 3.13). Besides reflecting better-anchored inflation expectations, these declines reflect a significant decline in world real interest rates, which drifted down from about 4 percent in the late 1990s to about zero in 2013 (figure 3.14).

The decline in real interest rates reflected the decline in the natural rate of interest (the interest rate that is consistent with full employment and inflation at the central bank's target). The estimated natural rates of interest in Europe, the United Kingdom, and the United States declined dramatically after the start of the global financial crisis (Lubik and Matthes 2015; Rachel and Smith 2015; Holston, Laubach, and Williams 2016). Natural rates have fallen in Australia, Japan, and Korea while remaining broadly stable and relatively high in emerging economies that have not yet come under aging pressures. Natural rates in China have fallen but remain high relative to advanced Asian economies (figure 3.15).

Figure 3.13   Change in 10-year government yield in selected countries

percentage points; end-2016 compared with 2000–07 average

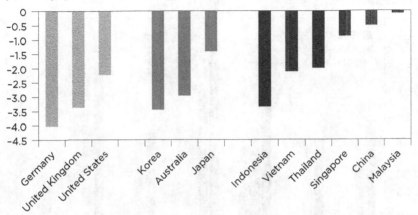

Sources: Haver Analytics; Bloomberg LP; CEIC Asia database; IMF Staff calculations.

Figure 3.14   World real interest rates, 1985–2013

percent

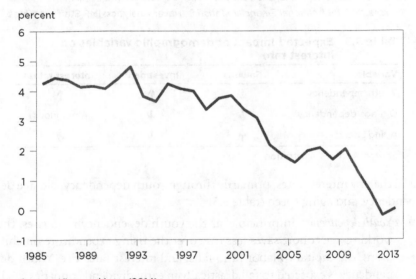

Source: King and Low (2014).

Demographic changes have been hailed as important drivers of the secular decline in interest rates.[19] In closed economies, they can affect savings

---

19. Other drivers of the secular decline in natural interest rates can be a slowdown in trend productivity growth, shifts in saving and investment preferences (rising inequality), precautionary saving in emerging markets, a fall in the relative price of capital goods, and a preference away from public investment (Rachel and Smith 2015). This section focuses on real

Figure 3.15 Real neutral interest rates in selected countries

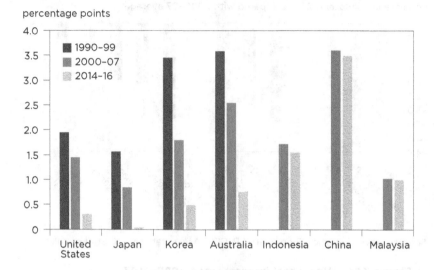

percentage points

Note: For Indonesia, China, and Malaysia, 1990–99 data are not available.

Sources: IMF, *International Financial Statistics*; Haver Analytics; IMF Staff estimates.

Table 3.5 Expected impact of demographic variables on interest rate

Variable	Savings	Investment	Interest rates
Youth dependency	↓	↑	↑
Old-age dependency	↓	↓	Ambiguous
Aging Speed	↑	↓	↓

Source: Authors' illustration.

and thereby interest rates, primarily through youth dependency, old-age dependency, and aging speed (table 3.5):[20]

- *Youth dependency.* In principle, as the youth dependency ratio rises, the working-age cohort saves less (to cover the rising expenditure on children), the capital-to-labor ratio falls, and interest rates rise. Youth dependency is expected to fall drastically in early-dividend countries, such as the Philippines and India (figure 3.16, panel a).

---

interest rates. Low interest rates may also reflect low steady-state inflation as a result of similar demographic pressures that weaken growth and drive up savings.

20. The previous section was based on the EBA model, which uses population growth as a proxy for youth dependency. As youth dependency is a more direct measure of population dynamics (and a complement to the old-age dependency ratio), we use it in this section.

Figure 3.16a   Selected Asia: Youth dependency ratios

percentage points, change between 2020 and 2030

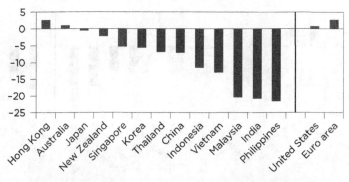

Note: Youth dependency ratio indicates the size of the population 14 years of age and younger as a share of the prime working-age population (30–64 years old).

Sources: United Nations, *World Population Prospects: 2015 Revision* (medium-fertility scenario); IMF, *World Economic Outlook*; IMF Staff projections.

Figure 3.16b   Selected Asia: Old-age dependency ratios

percentage points, change between 2020 and 2030

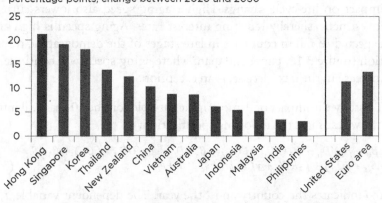

Note: Old-age dependency ratio indicates the size of the population 65 years of age and over as a share of the prime working-age population (30–64 years old).
Sources: United Nations, *World Population Prospects: 2015 Revision* (medium-fertility scenario); IMF, *World Economic Outlook*; IMF Staff projections.

■   *Old-age dependency.* As old-age dependency rises, savings fall. As the labor force shrinks, the capital-to-labor ratio rises and investment falls. The impact of old-age dependency on interest rates is therefore theoretically uncertain. Old-age dependency is expected to rise relatively quickly in Hong Kong, Singapore, and Korea (figure 3.16, panel b).

Figure 3.16c   Selected Asia: Aging speed

percentage points, change between 2020 and 2030

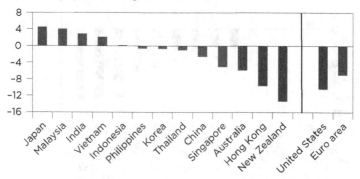

Note: Aging speed is the projected change in the old-age dependency ratio over the next 20 years. Old-age dependency ratio indicates the size of the population 65 and older as a share of the prime working-age population (30–64 years old).

Sources: United Nations, *World Population Prospects: 2015 Revision* (medium-fertility scenario); IMF, *World Economic Outlook*; IMF Staff projections.

■ *Aging speed.* Higher aging speed implies a higher probability of survival, which, if not matched by later retirement, is likely to have a positive impact on life-cycle savings. Higher aging speed also lowers current investment, thereby reducing interest rates. Aging speed is high and expected to fall in countries in late stages of the demographic transition (figure 3.16, panel c). Japan, where aging speed will continue to increase in the next decade, is an exception.

To study the impact of demographic variables on the 10-year real interest rate, we estimate the following specification:

$$r_{it} = \beta_0 + \beta_1\, YD_{it} + \beta_2\, (YD_{it} * CO_{it}) + \beta_3\, OD_{it} + \beta_4\, (OD_{it} * CO_{it}) + \beta_5\, AS_{it} + \beta_6\, (AS_{it} * CO_{it}) + \beta_7 RW_t + \gamma Controls_{it} + u_i + \varepsilon_{it} \tag{3.3}$$

where i indicates the country and t the year. The dependent variable, r, is the 10-year real interest rate. Among the explanatory variables, YD and OD denote the youth dependency ratio (the ratio of the population under 30 to the population 30–64) and the old-age dependency ratio (the ratio of the population over 64 to the population 30–64), respectively, to account for the effects of changes in fertility and aging population on interest rates. AS denotes the aging speed. These variables are separately interacted with the capital openness index (CO) to analyze how the openness of the economy affects the impact of demographic variables on interest rates. RW denotes the world interest rate. The 10-year real interest rates and world interest rate data come from IMF (2014), King and Low (2014), and the IMF *World*

Economic Outlook. The control variables include the ratio of a country's per capita GDP to that of the United States, growth in labor productivity, and the cyclically adjusted primary balance.

The empirical estimates support our priors for the effect of youth dependency and aging speed on interest rates. Higher old-age dependency is found to reduce interest rates. These results are consistent with the results presented in the previous section on the saving and investment balance.

The effects of demographic factors are not wholly channeled domestically in open economies. As one moves to an economy with an open capital account, the savings-investment balance—and hence interest rates—are at least partly determined by global saving and investment. In the extreme case of perfect capital mobility, arbitrage in financial markets should equalize interest rates across borders, and demographic factors of each country should not have an impact on domestic interest rates (unless they are large enough to contribute to global demographic trends).

We test this hypothesis by imposing restrictions on equation (3.3), such that $\beta_1 = -\beta_2$, $\beta_3 = -\beta_4$, and $\beta_5 = -\beta_6$. The results hold. Hence we run a restricted model:

$$r_{it} = \alpha_0 + \alpha_1 YD_{it}(1 - CO_{it}) + \alpha_2 OD_{it}(1 - CO_{it}) + \alpha_3 AS_{it}(1 - CO_{it}) + \alpha_4 RW_t + \gamma Controls_{it} + u_i + \varepsilon_{it}. \tag{3.3a}$$

The impact of domestic demographic factors on interest rates tends to diminish as a country becomes more open. In our analysis based on the restricted model (table 3.6), the impact of demographic variables (youth dependency, old-age dependency, and aging speed) all become zero as an economy becomes perfectly open (based on the Chinn-Ito index). Youth dependency, old-age dependency, and aging speed are expressed as ratios. A 1 percentage point increase in youth dependency increases the interest rate by 8.26 basis points when the economy is fully closed; there is no impact in the case of a fully open economy. Hence in estimating the demographically induced changes in real interest rates over 2020–30, interest rates in Japan, Hong Kong, New Zealand, and Singapore with full capital mobility are decoupled from their domestic demographic trends.

In countries that are not perfectly open, the old-age dependency effect is important for mature economies, and the youth dependency effect dominates for economies that are relatively young. Increasing old-age dependency is expected to decrease interest rates, especially in post-dividend countries, such as China, Korea, and Thailand. Declining youth dependency is expected to decrease interest rates, especially in early-dividend countries, such as India, Indonesia, and the Philippines, where fertility rates are projected to decline.

Table 3.6 Panel regression: Demographics and long-term interest rates

Dependent variables	10-year real interest rate (15–64)
Youth dependency ratio * (1 – capital openness)	8.26*** (1.29)
Old-age dependency ratio * (1 – capital openness)	–16.16*** (5.51)
Aging speed * (1 – capital openness)	–29.26*** (9.87)
World interest rate	0.84*** (0.11)
Ratio of GDP per capita to that of the US	2.43* (1.39)
Cyclically adjusted primary balance	0.00 (0.04)
Growth in labor productivity	0.07 (0.06)
Observations	740
Number of groups	42

*** $p<0.01$, ** $p<0.05$, * $p<0.1$.

Note: Standard errors in parentheses. P denotes the p-value as the probability of obtaining a result equal to or more extreme than that observed. The regression controls for the country fixed effect.

Source: IMF Staff estimates.

A slower pace of aging can be expected to push up interest rates. They are expected to increase most in China and Australia, as the aging speeds in these countries fall, reducing savings and, consequently, raising interest rates. Aging speed is projected to increase in currently young countries, such as India and Malaysia, driving down their interest rates.

The results suggest that demographic trends could push interest rates down by about 1–2 percentage points in the next decade, all else equal (figures 3.17 and 3.18).[21,22] The impact depends on three factors: the degree of openness, the state of aging, and the speed of aging. For countries that are fully open, demographic factors do not have a direct effect on domestic long-term interest rates. For post-dividend countries (Korea and Thailand),

---

21. Given the low-frequency variation in demographic variables, annual real interest rates may introduce substantial noise to any relationship with a demographic structure. To account for this problem, we also considered three- and five-year rates for nonoverlapping periods, as explained in IMF (2017). Such multiperiod rates emphasize the low-frequency variation in real interest rates. The results are broadly similar to the results for the baseline scenario.

22. Rachel and Smith (2015) find that demographic factors, public investment, and a global savings glut explain about 2 (out of 4.5) percentage points of the decline in global neutral rates between 1980 and 2015.

Figure 3.17 Selected Asia: Impact of demographics on 10-year real interest rates

percentage points, cumulative change between 2020 and 2030

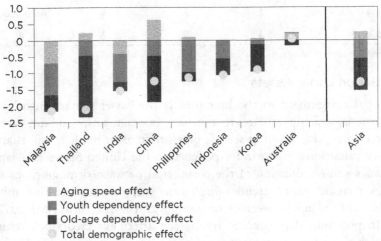

Note: The figure for Asia reflects the nominal GDP-weighted average.
Source: IMF Staff projections.

Figure 3.18 Selected Asia: Impact of demographics on 10-year real interest rates, by country

percentage points, cumulative change between 2020 and 2030

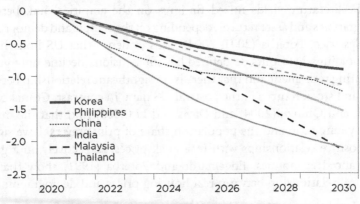

Source: IMF Staff projections.

rising old-age dependency is expected to depress interest rates. For early-dividend countries (India and the Philippines), falling youth dependency is projected to reduce interest rates. As the speed of aging slows in some cases, the aging speed effect will attenuate the decline in interest rates.

Table 3.7 Expected impact of demographic variables on asset returns

Variable	Interest rate	Risk appetite	Equity premium	Stock returns
Youth dependency	↑	↑	↓	Ambiguous
Old-age dependency	↓	↓	↑	Ambiguous
Aging speed	↓	↑	↓	↓

Source: Authors' illustration.

Impact on Other Assets

A popular argument in the literature is the "asset market meltdown" hypothesis, which postulates that as baby boomers retire and draw down their savings, the resulting sell-off pressure in asset markets will sharply reduce valuations. Historical experience in the United States and Japan provides some indication of the correlation between demographics and postwar stock market trends. But recent empirical studies find mixed evidence of the link between demographics and asset returns (IMF 2017).

In principle, demographic trends can affect expected stock returns through their impact on interest rates and risk premiums (table 3.7).[23] In particular, a decline in youth dependency, or an increase in old-age dependency, is expected to lead to a fall in interest rates, as discussed in the previous section (table 3.6). At the same time, these trends also reduce the lifetime investment horizon, lower the preference for risky assets, and raise the equity risk premium.[24] The expected impact of dependency ratios on stock returns is thus conceptually ambiguous.

The literature yields mixed findings on the empirical link between demographics and asset returns, depending on the sample and demographic variables used. Poterba (2001, 2004) finds evidence that US households' asset holdings held outside defined-benefit pensions decline only gradually during retirement and that there is no significant relationship between aging and stock returns in the postwar US data. In contrast, Geanakoplos, Magill, and Quinzii (2004) and Davis and Li (2003) find that the middle age to young ratio and the population share of prime savers have significant positive relationships with real stock prices, respectively, in a group of advanced economies. Engelhardt and Poterba (1991) show that the empirical relationship between real housing prices and demographic vari-

---

23. By definition, expected stock returns are equal to the sum of the risk-free rate and the equity risk premium.

24. If the correlation between labor income and stock returns is sufficiently low, a labor income stream acts as a substitute for risk-free bond holdings, implying that investors should hold a declining share of stocks in their portfolio as they get older (Jagannathan and Kocherlakota 1996).

Table 3.8 Panel regression: Demographics and asset returns

Dependent variables	Percent growth in stock return	Percent growth in real property price
Youth dependency ratio	67.28*** (23.66)	-11.32*** (3.96)
Youth dependency ratio * capital openness	-31.01** (14.22)	0.67 (4.00)
Old-age dependency ratio	-32.69 (82.26)	-53.18* (31.77)
Old-age dependency ratio * capital openness	138.26* (75.02)	-5.37 (26.99)
Aging speed	315.31* (163.18)	-100.95*** (34.05)
Aging speed * capital openness	-317.04** (142.92)	60.79* (31.86)
World interest rate	-1.18 (2.17)	-1.48*** (0.53)
Growth in labor productivity	4.75*** (0.98)	0.3 (0.20)
Observations	406	716
Number of groups	14	56

*** $p<0.01$, ** $p<0.05$, * $p<0.1$.

Note: Standard errors in parentheses. P denotes the p-value as the probability of obtaining a result equal to or more extreme than that observed. The regression controls for the country fixed effect.

Source: IMF Staff estimates.

ables that Mankiw and Weil (1989) find for the United States does not hold for Canada. Takáts (2010) finds that an increase in the change of old-age dependency lowers real housing price growth by about 66 basis points in a group of 22 advanced economies.

We find that lower youth (or higher old-age) dependency is associated with lower stock returns (i.e., the interest rate channel dominates), but the relationships are not statistically strong (table 3.8). Moreover, as with interest rates, the impact of domestic demographic factors is partially offset in more financially open countries.

For real estate, the relationship with demographic variables is even more difficult to identify, because of the asset's dual role as a durable good. Conceptually, a fall in interest rates, triggered by a fall in youth dependency (or a rise in old-age dependency), would raise housing prices. At the same time, these trends are expected to reduce demand for housing, as they are associated with declines in household formation.[25] Empirically, we

25. Furthermore, because the housing stock responds with lags, subsequent downward price adjustments may mask an initial price increase caused by a positive demand shock (Poterba

find weak links between these variables and real estate prices. The degree of openness plays an insignificant role, likely reflecting the local nature of housing markets.

Policy Implications of Demographic Trends

For early-dividend countries in Asia (India, Indonesia, and the Philippines), the main policy challenge is to harness the demographic dividend where possible, as discussed in Bloom, Canning, and Sevilla (2003), and mitigate any adverse spillovers from aging in the rest of Asia.

For Asian countries in the late- or post-dividend stages, adapting to aging could be especially challenging, because of relatively low per capita income levels. In light of this phenomenon, policies aimed at protecting vulnerable older people and prolonging strong growth take on particular urgency in Asia. These challenges call for adapting macroeconomic policies early, before aging sets in. Specific structural reforms can also help, especially in the areas of labor markets, pension systems, and retirement systems. These policies could be supplemented by productivity-enhancing reforms (e.g., research and development and education), as discussed in chapter 3 of the IMF's *Regional Economic Outlook: Asia and Pacific* (IMF 2017).

Macroeconomic Policies

Japan's experience shows that it is important to adapt macroeconomic policies before aging sets in. Fiscal policy may include introducing a credible medium-term fiscal framework to secure debt sustainability, shifting the burden of taxes from labor to consumption, and revamping the social safety net.[26] Monetary policy may involve studying how monetary transmission may change with aging. If, for example, monetary transmission works more through asset prices and household wealth than through corporate borrowing costs, the interest rate sensitivity of output and inflation may decline (Miles 2002, Bean 2004). To the extent that aging leads to declines in the natural interest rate, regular assessment of the neutral monetary stance by central banks is needed to avoid a potential tightening bias. Prolonged low interest rates may also call for a strong macroprudential framework to mitigate related financial stability risks.

1984, Lindh and Malmberg 2008). Moreover, higher demand for housing could manifest itself more prominently through the rental rate, which may not always move together with housing prices (Hamilton 1991).

26. At the same time, with a credible medium-term fiscal framework, fiscal policy can be used more actively in the short run, given its higher potency in a low interest rate environment, including to support aging-related structural reforms.

Structural Reforms

Labor Market Reforms

Labor market reforms aimed at tackling labor shortages and workforce aging can help offset some of the adverse growth effects of aging discussed in the chapter. Measures include the following:

- *Increase labor force participation, especially for women and older people.* Expanding the availability of childcare facilities, removing fiscal disincentives against older peoples' labor participation, and promoting flexible employment can be especially effective at raising labor participation by women and older people (Elborgh-Woytek et al. 2013, Kinoshita and Guo 2015, Olivetti and Petrongolo 2017). Moving from a seniority-based to a performance-based wage system can incentivize firms to relax retirement age requirements while reducing labor market duality, which can segment the labor market into permanent and transitory jobs (Dao et al. 2014).

- *Attract foreign workers, including through guest worker programs that target specific skills.* Foreign workers could address labor shortages and have a generally positive impact on receiving countries (Ganelli and Miake 2015; Jaumotte, Koloskova, and Saxena 2016). The experiences of Australia, Hong Kong, New Zealand, and Singapore show that immigration can prolong the demographic dividend or soften the negative impact of rapid aging.[27]

- *Promote active labor market policies.* Making affordable health care available for older workers (who are disproportionately affected by health risks) and facilitating the upgrading of human capital of and retraining workers can moderate the negative effect that workforce aging can have on productivity growth (Aiyar, Ebeke, and Shao 2016).

Pension System Reforms

Given the rapid aging and related fiscal costs in Asia, as well as the region's relatively low pension coverage (World Bank 2016), strengthening pension systems should be a high priority. Policy measures could include the following:

- *Create automatic adjustment mechanisms that link changes in the retirement age (or benefits) to life expectancy,* in order to help depoliticize pension

---

27. IMF research finds that key to harnessing the long-term gains of foreign workers are actions that facilitate their integration into the labor market, including language training and job search assistance, better recognition of migrants' skills through the recognition of credentials, and lower barriers to entrepreneurship (IMF 2017).

reform and contain pension costs (Arbatli et al. 2016). Many European countries have introduced such rules; their use has been limited in Asia outside of Japan.

- *Encourage voluntary saving* (e.g., tax deductions for long-term retirement saving), to help relieve long-term fiscal burdens.

- *Increase pension coverage, by providing minimum pension guarantees.* This reform could provide a safety net for the vulnerable, mitigate the impact of entitlement reforms, and reduce incentives for precautionary savings (Zaidi, Grech, and Fuchs 2006).

- *Reform the management of public pension funds.* Asia is home to some of the largest public pension funds in the world (OECD 2016). Reducing home bias—along the lines of the recent Government Pension Investment Fund reforms in Japan that increased allocation to foreign assets—could help raise the returns on these funds and secure more sustainable resources for aging societies.

Retirement System Reforms

New financial products that help older people dissave their postretirement savings (e.g., reverse mortgages) or insure against longevity risks (e.g., annuities) could reduce the need for precautionary savings. The diverse demographic trends in Asia could also offer rich opportunities for cross-border risk-sharing and financial integration.[28] For example, savings in late- or post-dividend countries seeking higher returns could be used to finance the large infrastructure gaps in early-dividend Asian countries (Ding, Lam, and Peiris 2014). Increasing the availability of "safe assets"—such as long-term government bonds or inflation-linked securities—can be especially attractive for pension funds and insurance companies (Groome, Blancher, and Ramlogan 2006).

Summary of Findings and Policy Recommendations

This chapter reports five main findings:

- *Trends.* Asia is aging rapidly. The speed of aging is especially remarkable compared with the historical experience in Europe and the United States. Parts of Asia risk becoming old before becoming rich. Until recently, Asia had the largest share of the world's working-age people.

---

28. Financial integration in Asia remains low, especially given its high degree of trade integration. About 60 percent of Asia's exports and imports go to, or originate from, elsewhere within the region; only 20–30 percent of cross-border portfolio investment and bank claims are intraregional (IMF 2015b).

In the coming decades, it will remove hundreds of millions of working-age people from that population.

- *Growth.* Asia has enjoyed a substantial demographic dividend in past decades. But rapid aging is now set to create a demographic tax on growth. Demographic trends could shave 0.5–1 percentage point from annual GDP growth over the next three decades in post-dividend countries such as China and Japan. In contrast, they could add 1 percentage point to annual GDP growth in early-dividend countries, such as India and Indonesia, if the transition is well managed. Overall, demographics are likely to be slightly negative for Asian growth. They could reduce annual global growth over the next three decades by 0.1 percentage point (0.2 percentage point if early-dividend countries are unable to reap the demographic dividend). If past trends continue, immigration could play an important role in softening the impact of aging or prolonging the demographic dividend in Australia, Hong Kong, New Zealand, and Singapore.

- *Inflation.* Where structural excess savings and low investment because of demographic changes lead to such a low real neutral interest rate that monetary policy is no longer able to act as a stimulus, the economy may operate below potential, keeping inflation under the central bank's target. Asia could fall into a period of "secular stagnation" at a lower income level than in advanced economies and with less effective policy buffers.

- *External flow balance.* The diversity of demographic trends in the region creates opportunities for capital flows and cross-border risk sharing, as savings from surplus countries can be used to meet capital needs in economies with younger populations. Projections based on the IMF's EBA model suggest that surpluses of some Asian economies are projected to increase over the next decade as a result of demographic change. The impact is material only for a small set of countries, however, and the overall effect on global imbalances is likely to be limited (about 0.1 percent of global GDP over the next decade).

- *Financial markets.* Demographic trends are likely to put downward pressure on real interest rates and asset returns for most major countries in Asia. These effects are likely to be less important for economies that are financially open. For them, changes in the world interest rate—which may also be driven by global aging trends—will likely matter more.

Three main policy implications emerge from these findings:

- *Adapting to aging may be especially challenging for Asia,* where aging is taking place at relatively low per capita income levels. Policies aimed at protecting vulnerable older people and prolonging strong growth take on particular urgency there.

■ *It is important to adapt macroeconomic policies before aging sets in.* Policies may include securing debt sustainability and monitoring potential changes in monetary transmission related to aging.

■ *Structural reforms can help address these challenges.* They may include labor market reforms (promotion of labor force participation of women and older people, guest worker programs, and active labor market policies); pension reforms (automatic adjustment mechanisms and minimum pension guarantees); and retirement system reforms (new financial products to reduce precautionary saving and increase the availability of "safe assets"). These policies could be supplemented by specific productivity-enhancing reforms (e.g., research and development and education), as discussed in the IMF's *Regional Economic Outlook* (IMF 2017).

References

Acemoglu, D., and P. Restrepo. 2017. *Secular Stagnation? The Effect of Aging on Economic Growth in the Age of Automation.* NBER Working Paper 23077. Cambridge, MA: National Bureau of Economic Research.

Adler, G., R. Duval, D. Furceri, S.K. Çelik, K. Koloskova, and M. Poplawski-Ribeiro. 2017. *Gone with the Headwinds: Global Productivity.* IMF Staff Discussion Note SDN/17/04. Washington: International Monetary Fund.

Aiyar, S., C. Ebeke, and X. Shao. 2016. *The Impact of Workforce Aging on European Productivity.* IMF Working Paper 16/238. Washington: International Monetary Fund.

Amaglobeli, D., and W. Shi. 2016. *How to Assess Fiscal Implications of Demographic Shifts: A Granular Approach.* Fiscal Affairs Department How to Note 2/2016. Washington: International Monetary Fund.

Arbatli, E., C. Feher, J. Ree, I. Saito, and M. Soto. 2016. *Automatic Adjustment Mechanisms in Asian Pension Systems?* IMF Working Paper 16/242. Washington: International Monetary Fund.

Barnes, S., J. Lawson, and A. Radziwill. 2010. *Current Account Imbalances in the Euro Area: A Comparative Perspective.* Economics Department Working Paper ECO/WKP(2010)82. Paris: Organization for Economic Cooperation and Development.

Basten, S., and Q. Jiang. 2015. Fertility in China: An Uncertain Future. *Population Studies* 69 (Supplement1): 97–105.

Bean, C. 2004. Global Demographic Change: Some Implications for Central Banks. Paper presented at the Federal Reserve Bank of Kansas City Annual Symposium, Jackson Hole, WY.

Bloom, D.E., D. Canning, and G. Fink. 2010. Implications of Population Ageing for Economic Growth. *Oxford Review of Economic Policy* 26, no. 4: 583–612.

Bloom, D.E., D. Canning, G. Fink, and J.E. Finlay. 2007. *Fertility, Female Labor Participation, and the Demographic Dividend.* NBER Working Paper 13583. Cambridge, MA: National Bureau of Economic Research.

Bloom, D.E., D. Canning, and J. Sevilla. 2003. The Demographic Dividend: A New Perspective on the Economic Consequences of Population Change. *Population Matter Series.* Santa Monica, CA: RAND.

Börsch-Supan, A., and M. Weiss. 2016. Productivity and Age: Evidence from Work Teams at the Assembly Line. *Journal of the Economics of Ageing* 7: 30–42.

Bosworth, B., and G. Chodorow-Reich. 2007. *Saving and Demographic Change: The Global Dimension*. Working Paper. Chestnut Hill, MA: Center for Retirement Research, Boston College.

Chinn, M.D., and H. Ito. 2007. Trade Account Balances, Financial Development and Institutions: Assaying the World Saving Glut. *Journal of International Money and Finance* 26, no. 4: 546–69.

Cuberes, D., and M. Teignier. 2016. Aggregate Costs of Gender Gaps in the Labor Market: A Quantitative Estimate. *Journal of Human Capital* 10, no. 1: 1–32.

Dao, M., D. Furceri, J. Hwang, M. Kim, and T.-J. Kim. 2014. *Strategies for Reforming Korea's Labor Market to Foster Growth*. IMF Working Paper 14/137. Washington: International Monetary Fund.

Davis, E. P., and C. Li. 2003. *Demographics and Financial Asset Prices in the Major Industrial Economies*. Brunel University Public Discussion Paper 03-07. London: Brunel University.

Ding, D., W. Lam, and S. Peiris. 2014. *Future of Asia's Finance: How Can It Meet Challenges of Demographic Change and Infrastructure Needs?* IMF Working Paper 14/126. Washington: International Monetary Fund.

Eichengreen, B., and M. Fifer. 2002. The Implications of Ageing for the Balance of Payments between North and South. In *The Economics of Ageing Societies*, ed. Horst Siebert, 81–105. Tubingen, the Netherlands: Mohr.

Elborgh-Woytek, K., M. Newiak, K. Kochhar, S. Fabrizio, K. Kpodar, P. Wingender, B. Clements, and G. Schwartz. 2013. *Women, Work, and the Economy: Macroeconomic Gains from Gender Equity*. IMF Staff Discussion Note SDN/13/10. Washington: International Monetary Fund.

Engelhardt, G. V., and J. Poterba. 1991. House Prices and Demographic Change: Canadian Evidence. *Regional Science and Urban Economics* 21, no. 4: 539–46.

Feyrer, J. 2007. Demographics and Productivity. *Review of Economics and Statistics* 89, no. 1: 100–109.

Ganelli, G., and N. Miake. 2015. *Foreign Help Wanted: Easing Japan's Labor Shortages*. IMF Working Paper 15/181. Washington: International Monetary Fund.

Geanakoplos, J., M. Magill, and M. Quinzii. 2004. Demography and the Long-run Predictability of the Stock Market. Cowles Foundation Discussion Papers, No. 1380R. New Haven, CT: Cowles Foundation for Research in Economics, Yale University.

Gonzales C., S. Jain-Chandra, K, Kochhar, M. Newiak, and T. Zeinullayev. 2015. *Catalyst for Change: Empowering Women and Tackling Income Inequality*. IMF Staff Discussion Note SDN/15/20. Washington: International Monetary Fund.

Grigoli, F., A. Herman, and K. Schmidt-Hebbel. 2014. *World Saving*. IMF Working Paper 14/204. Washington: International Monetary Fund.

Groome, W. T., N. Blancher, and P. Ramlogan. 2006. Aging and Financial Markets. *Finance and Development* 43 (September).

Gruber, J.W., and S. B. Kamin. 2007. Explaining the Global Pattern of Current Account Imbalances. *Journal of International Money and Finance* 26, no. 4: 500–22.

Hamilton, B.W. 1991. The Baby Boom, the Baby Bust, and the Housing Market: A Second Look. *Regional Science and Urban Economics* 21, no. 4: 547–52.

Higgins, M. 1998. Demography, National Savings, and International Capital Flows. *International Economic Review* 39, no. 2: 343–69.

Higgins, M., and J.G. Williamson. 1997. Age Structure Dynamics in Asia and Dependency on Foreign Capital. *Population and Development Review* 23, no. 2: 261–93.

Holston, K., T. Laubach, and J. Williams. 2016. *Measuring the Natural Rate of Interest: International Trends and Determinants*. Federal Reserve Bank of San Francisco Working Paper 2016-11.

IMF (International Monetary Fund). 2014. Perspectives on Global Real Interest Rates. In *World Economic Outlook* (April). Washington.

IMF (International Monetary Fund). 2015a. *Regional Economic Outlook: Sub-Saharan Africa: Navigating Headwinds*. Washington.

IMF (International Monetary Fund). 2015b. *Regional Economic Outlook: Asia and Pacific: Stabilizing and Outperforming Other Regions*. Washington.

IMF (International Monetary Fund). 2016. *Methodological Note on EBA-Lite*. IMF Policy Paper. Washington.

IMF (International Monetary Fund). 2017. *Regional Economic Outlook: Asia and Pacific: Preparing for Choppy Seas*. Washington.

Jagannathan, R., and N.R. Kocherlakota. 1996. Why Should Older People Invest Less in Stocks than Younger People? *Federal Reserve Bank of Minneapolis Quarterly Review* 20: 11-23.

Jaimovich, N., and Henry Siu. 2009. The Young, the Old, and the Restless: Demographics and Business Cycle Volatility. *American Economic Review* 99, no. 3: 804-26.

Jaumotte, F., K. Koloskova, and S. Saxena. 2016. *Impact of Migration on Income Levels in Advanced Economies*. Spillover Note. Washington: International Monetary Fund.

Jaumotte, F., and P. Sodsriwiboon. 2010. *Current Account Imbalances in the Southern Euro Area*. IMF Working Paper WP/10/139. Washington: International Monetary Fund.

Khera, P. 2016. *Macroeconomic Impacts of Gender Inequality and Informality in India*. IMF Working Paper 16/16. Washington: International Monetary Fund.

King, M., and D. Low. 2014. *Measuring the "World" Real Interest Rate*. NBER Working Paper 19887. Cambridge, MA: National Bureau of Economic Research.

Kinoshita, Y., and F. Guo. 2015. *What Can Boost Female Labor Force Participation in Asia?* IMF Working Paper 15/56. Washington: International Monetary Fund.

Legg, A., N. Prasad, and T. Robinson. 2007. *Global Imbalances and the Global Saving Glut: A Panel Data Assessment*. Research Discussion Paper 2007-11. Sydney: Reserve Bank of Australia.

Li, H., J. Zhang, and J. Zhang. 2007. Effects of Longevity and Dependency Rates on Saving and Growth: Evidence from a Panel of Cross Countries. *Journal of Development Economics* 84: 138-54.

Lindh, T., and B. Malmberg. 2008. Demography and Housing Demand: What Can We Learn from Residential Construction Data? *Journal of Population Economics* 21, no. 3: 521-39.

Lubik, T., and C. Matthes. 2015. *Calculating the Natural Rate of Interest: A Comparison of Two Alternative Approaches*. Economic Brief EB15-10. Federal Reserve Bank of Richmond.

Mankiw, N. G., and D. N. Weil. 1989. The Baby Boom, the Baby Bust, and the Housing Market. *Regional Science and Urban Economics* 19: 235-58.

Miles, D. 2002. Should Monetary Policy Be Different in a Greyer World? In *Ageing, Financial Markets and Monetary Policy*, ed. Alan Auerbach and Hermann Heinz. Heidelberg: Springer.

OECD (Organization for Economic Cooperation and Development). 2016. *Annual Survey of Large Pension Funds and Public Pension Reserve Funds*. Paris.

Olivetti, C., and B. Petrongolo. 2017. The Economic Consequences of Family Policies: Lessons from a Century of Legislation in High-Income Countries. *Journal of Economic Perspectives* 31, no. 1.

Phillips, S., L. Catao, L. Ricci, R. Bems, M. Das, J. Di Giovanni, D.F. Unsal, M. Castillo, J. Lee, J. Rodriguez, and M. Vargas. 2013. *The External Balance Assessment (EBA) Methodology*. IMF Working Paper 13/272. Washington: International Monetary Fund.

Poterba, J.M. 1984. Tax Subsidies to Owner-Occupied Housing: An Asset-Market Approach. *Quarterly Journal of Economics* 99, no. 4: 729–52.

Poterba, J.M. 2001. Demographic Structure and Asset Returns. *Review of Economics and Statistics* 83 (November): 565–84.

Poterba, J.M. 2004. Portfolio Risk and Self-Directed Retirement Saving Programs. *Economic Journal* 114 (March): C26–C51.

Rachel, L., and T. Smith. 2015. *Secular Drivers of the Global Real Interest Rate.* Staff Working Paper 571. London: Bank of England.

Steinberg, C., and M. Nakane. 2012. *Can Women Save Japan?* IMF Working Paper 12/248. Washington: International Monetary Fund.

Takáts, E. 2010. *Ageing and Asset Prices.* BIS Working Paper No. 318 (August). Basel: Bank for International Settlements.

UN (United Nations). 2015. *World Population Prospects: 2015 Revision.* Department of Economic and Social Affairs Population Division. New York. Available at https://esa.un.org/unpd/wpp/publications/files/key_findings_wpp_2015.pdf.

Veen, S. 2008. *Demographischer Wandel, alternde Belegschaften und Betriebsproduktivität.* Munich: Rainer Hampp Verlag.

Williamson, J. G. 2001. Demographic Shocks and Global Factor Flows. In *Seismic Shifts: The Economic Impact of Demographic Change,* ed. J.N. Little and R.K. Triest. Conference Series 46. Boston: Federal Reserve Bank.

World Bank. 2015. *Global Monitoring Report 2015/16: Development Goals in an Era of Demographic Change.* Washington.

World Bank. 2016. *East Asia and Pacific Regional Report: Live Long and Prosper: Aging in East Asia and Pacific.* Washington.

World Bank. 2017. *Doing Business 2017: Equal Opportunity for All.* Washington.

Yoon, J-W., J. Kim, and J. Lee. 2014. *Impact of Demographic Changes on Inflation and the Macroeconomy.* IMF Working Paper 14/210. Washington: International Monetary Fund.

Zaidi, A., A. Grech, and M. Fuchs. 2006. *Pension Policy in EU25 and Its Possible Impact on Elderly Poverty.* CASE Paper 116. London: Centre for Analysis of Social Exclusion, London School of Economics and Political Science.

4

Invention, Productivity, and the Evolution of East Asia's Innovation Systems

LEE G. BRANSTETTER AND NAMHO KWON

Japan's rapid growth from the 1950s through the early 1970s had many drivers, but most impressive was its rapid productivity growth (Denison and Chung 1976). Economic growth slowed in all advanced economies in the 1970s, but Japan grew more rapidly than the other rich Western economies, and its measured productivity growth remained higher than theirs. In the 1970s and early 1980s, Japan's industrial structure quickly shifted from resource- and labor-intensive manufacturing toward knowledge- and technology-intensive industries. Japanese manufacturers of steel, autos, industrial machines, and, increasingly, electronics began displacing long-established Western manufacturers worldwide. Japan's research and development (R&D) intensity and the number of patents held by Japanese firms at home and abroad surged.

By the early 1980s, Japanese firms, long derided as "copycat" imitators of Western technology, managed to outengineer their Western rivals in a range of iconic industries.[1] By the late 1980s, prestigious bodies like the US National Research Council were glumly concluding that Japanese firms were ahead of their American rivals in 25 out of 34 "critical" areas of tech-

Lee G. Branstetter is nonresident senior fellow at the Peterson Institute for International Economics and professor of economics and public policy at Carnegie Mellon University. Namho Kwon is an associate fellow at the Korea Institute of Public Finance. The authors thank their discussant, Jong-Wha Lee, for insightful comments and suggestions. We also acknowledge the helpful input of Jérémie Cohen-Setton, Kyoji Fukao, Ken Kang, and Adam Posen. This paper builds on research funded by the National Science Foundation (SciSIP grant 136170) and the Carnegie Mellon Portugal Program. However, the views expressed in this chapter are those of the authors, and we take responsibility for all errors and omissions.

1. Mansfield (1988a, 1988b, 1988c) documented the high productivity of Japan's corporate R&D spending.

nology (National Research Council 1992), and in 1987, the president of the US Semiconductor Research Corporation conceded, "We may never match Japan's R&D efficiency."

By the end of the 1980s, South Korea and Taiwan appeared to be following in Japan's footsteps. At the beginning of that decade, both nations were regarded as low-wage manufacturers of labor-intensive goods. By its end, both were rapidly increasing their patenting in the United States (Branstetter and Kwon 2018), and their export mix was quickly shifting toward labor- and knowledge-intensive goods. Analysts began predicting that the innovation leadership in electronics and information technology was in the early stages of a permanent shift to East Asia.

The degree to which those prophecies of innovation leadership remain unfulfilled suggests that the East Asian approach to R&D, pioneered by Japan and adopted by South Korea and Taiwan, had both strengths and weaknesses (Okimoto and Rohlen 1988). This system was arguably better than the American system at applied research, hardware, miniaturization, process equipment and technology, product variety, and process engineering, whereas the American system was stronger in basic research, software, creating new products, high-technology systems, and creation of new industries.[2] It was perhaps natural that engineers and firms in late-developing states would focus their efforts on a technological frontier largely defined by prior foreign invention, rather than on fundamental innovation (Gerschenkron 1962).

Once Japan and its former colonies reached the technological frontier, and lost their longstanding cost advantages, however, the firms based in these economies had to shift from an innovation system appropriate for their "catch-up" periods to one that could generate its independent frontier innovations. This chapter argues that the policies pursued during the high growth eras of these economies may well have contributed to the difficulties their firms have experienced in this transition. In Japan, South Korea, and Taiwan, the evidence suggests that public policy choices during their years of rapid growth concentrated R&D in particular activities, industries, and firms. And these choices have slowed the ability of these countries to adapt to current circumstances, imposing a drag on growth.[3] Other nations in the region seeking to follow in the footsteps of these economies should learn from these policy missteps. (See box 4.1.)

---

2. Okimoto and Saxonhouse (1987) viewed these differences as reflecting intelligent adaptation to the circumstances in which Japanese firms found themselves in the postwar era, and some of the observations in their essay anticipate the arguments in this chapter.

3. Nelson (1992) influenced our thinking about the evolution of these economies' innovation systems.

Box 4.1 Radical innovation, pro-incumbent/pro-incremental bias, and the decline in innovation productivity

Healthy innovation systems need radical and incremental approaches, and transformative innovations require incremental inventions to reach their full potential (Helpman and Trajtenberg 1998a, 1998b). Most innovative activity in any economy at any time is incremental (Harhoff, Scherer, and Vopel 2003). But incremental invention generally runs into diminishing returns. A fundamentally new idea brought into the marketplace can create a new technological paradigm, raising the returns on the applied R&D investment, which refines this fundamental new idea and implements it in multiple contexts (Evenson and Kislev 1976).

Radical technological breakthroughs are fueled by rapid entry of a large number of new firms offering competing business and product models (Klepper 1996). Eventually, a few of these entrants hit upon business and product models that succeed commercially. A small number of especially successful entrants then invest in cost-reducing, process R&D to cement their success (Cohen and Klepper 1996).

Often this success stifles further radical experimentation and leads to a shakeout, leaving just a few players and product models and designs. At this point, technological change in the industry slows substantially, and the focus of innovation shifts from radical experimentation with new designs to incremental improvements of existing designs. The historical development of a number of major industries—autos, tires, televisions, lasers, and semiconductors—has been consistent with this theory (Klepper 2010, Buenstorf and Klepper 2009).

In all cases, rapid progress to practical and usable designs and business models requires rapid entry of many new firms. Economic research highlights the importance of labor mobility into and among these new firms. One common pattern in nearly all new industries is the early emergence of an important set of leading firms, which "seed" the industry with a large number of "spinoffs." At an early stage in a new industry, a small number of firms establish themselves as market leaders and attract talented pioneers who want to make their fortunes in this new domain. Eventually, managers disagree over which new business models and product designs to pursue. Disaffected managers then leave to start their own firms, which can take a new industry in new directions (Buenstorf and Klepper 2009).

(box continues)

Box 4.1 Radical innovation, pro-incumbent/pro-incremental bias, and the decline in innovation productivity *(continued)*

Empirical evidence and theory also suggest that established incumbents often resist investment in experiments that render existing business models obsolete, highlighting the importance of making capital available to newcomers and fostering competition. Christensen (1997), for example, points out that successful incumbents face a double bind when seeking to engage in radical innovation. They typically arrive at their position after years, even decades, of successful refinement of existing products and business practices but are then ill equipped to succeed in a radically different approach to the same product class or service.

New industry creation in the 21st century is more science-based and more closely connected to frontier university research than in the past, thereby highlighting the importance of labor mobility and connections between the academic and industry sectors. The development of successful products based on these discoveries often requires "human bridges"—entrepreneurial faculty and graduate students conversant in the new technology who can partner with experienced managers and engineers to embed the new ideas in successful firms and products (Agrawal and Henderson 2003; Zucker, Darby, and Brewer 1998).

In the United States, strong protection of intellectual property rights and the willingness of American courts to levy significant damages or even issue injunctions when inventions are infringed by financially stronger manufacturers have strengthened the potential for innovation (Hochberg. Serrano, and Ziedonis 2018; Jaffe and Lerner 2004). Strong intellectual property rights also enable holders of patents to bargain with contract manufacturers and other business partners without fear of expropriation (Hall and Ziedonis 2001). These protections raise the chances of success by loosening the historical requirement that firms excel in both product and process innovation. America's open capital markets allow new startups to offer outsized returns to investors willing to take high risks, further upping the odds of success. The historically open US market for consumer and industrial goods enables new innovators to compete with established sellers. In America's fluid labor markets for top managers and engineers, past association with an ambitious startup—even if it fails—is viewed as a useful career experience. By contrast, the repeated downsizing and chronic competitive woes of traditional American manufacturers in more technologically quiescent industries have lessened the appeal of spending an entire career as an engineer or manager in an established firm. For talented young American managers and engineers, the balance of risks and rewards tilts toward smaller firms in technologically dynamic sectors.

Japan

Human Capital

In a world of globalized supply chains, where it is commonplace for components of even the most sophisticated manufactured products to be assembled in low-wage developing countries, it is easy to forget what a novelty Japan was in the early postwar era. It had been the first and only nonwestern nation to acquire modern manufacturing capabilities on a significant scale in the years prior to World War II. In the postwar era, it continued to grow with surprising vigor, rapidly becoming the first nonwestern nation to join the Organization for Economic Cooperation and Development (OECD). These achievements were, in part, the result of Japan's exceptionally successful, decades-long strategy of investing in the acquisition of both general human capital and specific technical capabilities.

The strategy took shape after Japan's Meiji Restoration of 1868, when the new imperial state created a modern educational system and brought Western expertise into its leading firms and government ministries.[4] The government subsidized study abroad for thousands of Japanese students and imported foreign instructors, consultants, and experts. Jones (1980) describes how, in these early years, half of the Ministry of Education's budget and two-thirds of the national public works budget was spent on foreign experts. As Japan's educational system expanded, these expensive foreigners were quickly replaced with qualified locals. Japan exported its educational system and philosophy to its colonies, Taiwan and Korea, which benefited from the investment.

All three economies committed themselves to educational excellence in the postwar era. By the mid-1960s, Japanese students were outscoring Europeans and Americans on international standardized tests of mathematics and science. By the 1980s, Japan graduated more than twice as many engineers per capita as the United States, and its ordinary workers had dramatically more competence in science and math than their American counterparts (Rohlen 1983). Today, standardized tests of science and mathematics skills suggest that the average levels of skill mastery and the fraction of students scoring one standard deviation above the OECD average are extremely high in Japan, South Korea, and Taiwan (Hanushek and Woessman 2015). In chapter 7, Kyoji Fukao documents the almost embarrassing degree to which the basic skills of the average Japanese worker exceed those of his or her American counterpart.

---

4. Branstetter (2017) also highlights the importance of Japan's early investment in education. This section draws on that earlier study.

This investment in human capital enabled these nations to converge technologically with the West. In fact, Romalis (2004) shows that standard models of international trade can largely explain the rise of East Asian nations as exporters of knowledge-intensive goods once this human capital investment is taken into account. But this national human capital strategy had its limits. Japanese universities did well in providing a basic engineering education to technical graduates, but they underperformed in graduate education, which was relatively underfunded and institutionally neglected. In the early 1980s, the United States spent six times as much as Japan on doctoral-level training and generated six times as many PhD graduates in the sciences and engineering (Okimoto and Saxonhouse 1987).

In the United States, many graduate students found employment in industries where the top corporate R&D labs were effectively led by PhD recipients. In Japan, in contrast, advanced training for corporate R&D personnel took place mostly within the larger, technology-intensive firms. While this very different approach to training an industrial R&D workforce clearly did not prevent leading Japanese firms from quickly reaching the technology frontier, it reduced labor mobility across firms and made it more difficult for high-tech startups in Japan to acquire highly skilled researchers, strengthening the pro-incumbent bias of the Japanese innovation system (see box 4.1). Japanese academic culture and bureaucratic practices further constrained basic research funding from reaching the most promising young scientists. Academic salaries lagged behind advances in scientific productivity.

The connection between academic research and frontier innovation in the United States has already been the subject of a large literature (Mansfield 1991; Rosenberg and Nelson 1994; Zucker, Darby, and Brewer 1998). The research demonstrates that nations lacking universities in which faculty and graduate students are pursuing frontier science lose out in the global competition for venture capital investment and radical new inventions. Conversely, American universities excelling in global science lie at the core of innovation ecosystems that attract abundant inflows of early-stage venture capital investment. In Japan—and in South Korea and Taiwan—human capital policy choices strengthened incremental research capabilities while constraining more fundamental research capabilities.

Intellectual Property

Prewar Japan imported the patent system of Bismarck-era Germany in the 19th century, which remained the basis of Japanese intellectual property policy throughout the 20th century. The Japanese system, like the German one, provided limited intellectual property protection for even modest, incremental inventions. However, until the late 1990s, it did not protect fundamental innovations as well as the German system did (Ordover 1991).

Until the 1990s Japanese firms could include only one claim per patent application, and Japanese courts had no "doctrine of equivalents," under which minor variations on a patented invention could be ruled as violating the original patent. So, to protect their inventions, firms were required to file a large number of patent applications describing all the features and possible permutations of their patents. Even a well-financed large firm would often fail to effectively prevent rivals from using a closely related technology, since Japanese courts interpreted claims broadly when determining whether an invention was sufficiently novel to merit a patent application, but they interpreted them narrowly when determining patent infringement (Sakakibara and Branstetter 2001). Japan also required that patent applications be published before patents were granted, and, through the early 1990s, it allowed interested parties to contest the granting of a patent prior to issue. Finally, until the 1990s, Japanese courts almost never awarded large damages to inventors whose intellectual property had been infringed.

Small firms with brilliant ideas but limited financial resources were especially disadvantaged under this patent system. Even for larger firms, the weakness and narrowness of the Japanese patent system undermined its usefulness as a mechanism for appropriating the returns to R&D. Instead, firms in postwar Japan tended to rely on their manufacturing capabilities, brand names, and quickness to market as the primary mechanisms for appropriating the returns to R&D investment. This, in turn, reinforced the Japanese tendency to focus on incremental innovation, process engineering, and inventions that were close to commercialization.[5]

Exchange Rates

Japan began reintegrating into the postwar global economy with a high level of human capital, impressive manufacturing skills, and—given the extent of wartime devastation—much lower factor costs than Western rivals. Japan's economy quickly recovered, but low inflation, rapid productivity convergence, and participation in the postwar system of fixed exchange rates and limited capital flows kept Japan's cost of production relatively low when measured in Western currencies, especially the US dollar (Ito 1992). Despite episodic protectionism, Japan generally found open Western markets for its ever-expanding range of export goods. As

---

5. Branstetter (2017) also stressed the role of relatively weak, narrow patents in shaping the Japanese style of innovation focused on relatively incremental invention.

Japan's real and nominal exchange rates increasingly failed to fully reflect its degree of productivity convergence with the Western world, Japanese firms found that if they could close the quality gap with their Western rivals, they would often outcompete them in the marketplace, thanks to their cost advantage.

A long period under an undervalued exchange rate moved Japanese firms away from fundamental innovation and toward incremental innovation. As Japanese firms invested in incremental improvements in manufacturing efficiency and quality, a consistently favorable exchange rate reinforced the competitiveness of that production base. Even after the collapse of the Bretton Woods system in the early 1970s, concerns about the impact of yen appreciation led the Japanese government to limit exchange rate appreciation at every opportunity, while depreciation was generally welcomed. In real terms, the yen remained much cheaper in the 1970s and 1980s than it was for much of the 1990s.

Labor Market Institutions

An extensive literature exists on the "lifetime employment" system that developed in postwar Japan. While some Western analyses sought to connect the emergence of this system to traditional Japanese cultural values and practices, in reality the system was a postwar arrangement designed to buy labor peace and protect firms' investments in worker skills. Prewar labor markets were characterized by high labor turnover and mass layoffs during downturns and recessions. The imperial government ruthlessly suppressed efforts to form labor unions. When Japan was occupied by the New Deal administration of Harry Truman, strong protections for labor were hard-wired into the postwar legal regime and union organizers—many of them radicalized by long prison terms and harsh treatment—were set free. Japan's labor movement sought to make up for lost time, and Japanese postwar industrialists viewed frequent strikes and work stoppages as a threat to their prosperity in a growing economy. Since they could no longer rely on the secret police to suppress union organizers, they started bargaining with them. Industrialists also realized that Japan's industrial structure was changing rapidly, educational institutions were not keeping up with these changes, and effective adaptation would necessitate extensive investment in workers' skills—but firms needed some mechanism to ensure that workers trained at the expense of company A would not just "jump ship" and put those skills to work for company B.

The bargain hammered out between industrialists and the Japanese labor movement in the 1950s resulted in what became known in English as the lifetime employment system (Ito 1992). This system applied only to full-time, male employees in Japan's largest companies and covered them through an early retirement age, forcing many of them to seek secondary employment after they were "retired" as early as in their 50s. Still, the system guaranteed blue- and white-collar employees employment security, a labor representative's presence on the corporate management team, and profit sharing for all rank-and-file workers, not just senior executives. In return, though, workers were expected to complete their entire career in the firm in which they started. Firms generally promoted from within, wages depended heavily on tenure within the firm, and any worker who moved from one firm to another had to start at the bottom of the wage scale.

While this system helped insure workers against economic shocks, it also drastically limited the flow of workers across firms and industries. Furthermore, only the top firms really honored the system, which concentrated Japan's top talent in the leading enterprises and drastically limited the appeal of startups and new entrants. Any Japanese executive at a leading firm who left to join a (risky) startup had to start all over at the bottom of the wage scale in the (likely) event that the startup failed. The evolution of Japanese labor market institutions thus left the nation with a pronounced pro-incumbent bias. As Kyoji Fukao documents in chapter 7 of this volume, even in today's Japan, striking productivity gaps remain between large and small firms, and Fukao concludes that Japan's advanced human capital remains disproportionately concentrated in large firms.

Financial Markets

Japan's industrial evolution required access not just to skilled workers but also to capital. An extensive literature describes the evolution of Japan's highly regulated postwar capital markets (Hoshi and Patrick 2000, Hoshi and Kashyap 2001) from wartime capital controls and industrial planning. Postwar regulatory barriers sharply limited the issuance of stocks and bonds into the 1980s.

For most firms, it was simply not practical to obtain significant external financing through direct sales of equity or bonds to investors. Instead, Japan's postwar financial system was dominated by a highly regulated banking cartel. This cartel operated under deposit and commercial lending rates that were set by government fiat rather than the supply and demand of financial capital. To access sufficient external finance in Japan's booming postwar economy, most large Japanese manufacturing firms forged a close connection with one of the main commercial banks.

This system provided large amounts of financial capital to a limited set of "insider" firms at reasonably low interest rates (Hoshi, Kashyap, and Scharfstein 1991; Hoshi and Kashyap 2001). New firms outside this system were at a significant disadvantage in the postwar race for external finance. Stringent regulation of the stock and bond markets effectively precluded the rise of robust venture capital markets or junk bond markets, which would have incentivized investment in risky projects by offering high interest rates to investors with sufficiently high-risk tolerance. Financial deregulation in Japan proceeded in stages. Important moves in the early 1980s enabled blue chip manufacturers to decouple from their historical bank relationships and issue direct stock and equity. But other important stages of the financial deregulation process were delayed until the 1990s and 2000s, by which time the Japanese economy had been stuck in slow growth for more than a decade (Hoshi and Patrick 2000). While this may have been unintended, the historical evolution of Japan's financial market policies tended to reinforce the pro-incumbent bias in its innovation system.

Competition

Japan's postwar development is often mischaracterized as "export-led." In fact, Japan did not start running consistent and significant current account surpluses until the 1970s, and these surpluses remained limited in size relative to GDP until the first half of the 1980s. Instead, Japanese growth was driven predominantly by domestic sources of demand.

One of the first legal changes the Japanese government instituted when it regained full sovereignty from its American occupiers was to substantially weaken the Anti-Monopoly Law it inherited from the New Deal government of Harry Truman (Eads and Yamamura 1987, Uekusa 1987, Weinstein 1995). The Japanese government regularly created legal cartels when industries experienced cyclical downturns, with the government itself playing the role of cartel enforcer (Uekusa 1987, Weinstein 1995). The market was effectively divided up on the basis of pre-recession market shares, a policy that—to the extent that it worked—benefitted established incumbents.

The postwar Japanese distribution system was, by contrast, fragmented and dominated by small-scale, "mom and pop" style stores. These small establishments could not resist efforts by much larger manufacturers to tie them into exclusive dealing contracts. Foreign consumer goods sellers in the 1980s regularly cited the difficulty of breaking into the Japanese retail/distribution system as one of the most important barriers to their expansion in the Japanese market (Flath 2002). Of course, this barrier was even greater for small, startup Japanese firms trying to enter or expand into the market for consumer goods.

Strong alliances between traditional business partners in Japan also impeded entry of both foreign and domestic firms. So-called keiretsu networks dominated the market for industrial goods, at least in key sectors like automobiles. In Japan's complicated systems of interfirm alliances

(Gerlach 1992), would-be entrants had no recourse given the relatively weak antitrust law and practice.

Finally, in much of Japan's service economy, heavy-handed government regulation strictly restricted entry and competition well into the 1980s. This was true in banking, securities trading, insurance, construction, telecommunications, intercity freight transportation, and airlines. As elsewhere in the industrialized world, regulatory capture limited competition and ensured rents for incumbents, at the expense of consumers and would-be entrants. All of these factors tended to reinforce the pro-incumbent bias in the Japanese innovation system.

Decline in Japanese Industrial Research Productivity

Figure 4.1 shows the differing industrial R&D productivity trends for firms in the electronics sector and other manufacturing firms. The figure graphs the estimated coefficients on year dummy variables obtained by regression of a "patent production function," as described in equation (3) in Branstetter and Nakamura (2003):

$$n_{it} = \beta r_{it} + \sum_t \gamma_t T_t + \sum_c \delta_c D_{ic} + \varepsilon_{it}$$

where, n_{it} is innovation, r_{it} is the firm's own R&D investment, the Ds are dummy variables to control for differences in the propensity to generate new knowledge across technological fields (indicated by the subscript c), the Ts are year dummies, and ε is an error term. Branstetter and Nakamura proxy innovation with patents and present the patterns sketched out by their year dummies as a statistical description of trends in the productivity of industrial R&D. The results reproduced in figure 4.1 report the coefficients of time dummies obtained from a version of equation (3) that incorporates firm-level fixed effects. Results are estimated separately for firms in the electronics sector and other manufacturing firms. Measured R&D productivity of other Japanese firms rose sharply through the 1980s, then gradually declined through the late 1990s. R&D productivity in the electronics sector continued to increase through the mid-1990s, but began to reverse in the late 1990s.[6] These results are qualitatively robust to the use of data on Japanese patent applications, to the weighting of US patent grants by forward citations, and to the use of firm fixed effects.

These developments were linked to important structural changes in the nature of private sector R&D in Japan (Branstetter and Nakamura 2003).

---

6. Several other scholars have also highlighted adverse shifts in the relative performance of the Japanese innovation system since the early 1990s (Goto 2000, Goto and Odagiri 2003, Nagaoka 2007).

Figure 4.1 Trends in Japanese R&D productivity

R&D productivity increase relative to base year (1981)

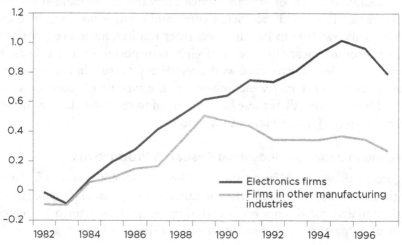

Source: Branstetter and Nakamura (2003).

As Japanese firms reached the natural limits of an R&D strategy that was focused on adapting foreign technology—a focus on process and incremental innovation and convergence with a technology frontier rather than an effort to go beyond it—they were forced to change their approach to R&D. They had to build larger central R&D laboratories with more ambitious agendas and focus on more fundamental, science-based research. Unfortunately, the Japanese innovation system was itself still insufficiently developed to make this new emphasis successful and, at least initially, the structural changes within Japanese firms were unable to forestall a decline, or, at best, a stagnation, in research productivity.

In the early 1990s, Japanese stock and real estate markets plunged, inducing a significant and persistent macroeconomic slowdown. Five years into the decade, the internet revolution was well under way in the United States, but Japanese firms were conspicuously absent from the group of firms—many of them new entrants—that were introducing fundamental new innovations in IT. Even in less technologically dynamic sectors like autos, Japanese firms seemed to be losing ground in the 1990s.

By the mid-1990s industrialists and policymakers in Japan increasingly recognized these shortcomings. The so-called Science and Technology Basic Law, implemented in late 1995, clearly articulated the need for fundamental reform of the nation's innovation system. Since the passage of this law, Japan has not only strengthened its intellectual property system (Sakakibara and Branstetter 2001) but also fundamentally reformed its national university system (Amano and Poole 2005) and developed a venture capital market. The so-called big bang financial liberalization of the mid-1990s (key components of which were not fully completed until the 2000s) also included ways to make it easier for innovative firms to motivate employees with stock options. An effort was also made to make Japan's product markets more open to competition. Restrictions on large-scale retailers in Japan, which had kept the balance of power between manufacturers and distributors in favor of the former, were significantly relaxed in the 1990s, and the importance of keiretsu linkages between suppliers and assemblers in key industries declined. Unfortunately, these reforms have neither accelerated Japanese productivity growth at the macro level nor revived the fortunes of Japan's once-vaunted electronics industry.[7]

South Korea

Korea spent roughly the first half of the 20th century as a colony of the Japanese Empire. Shortly after achieving its independence, it was devastated by civil war. Economic upheaval and political turmoil followed in the wake of this bloody conflict. The South Korean economic miracle really dates from the military coup that brought General Park Chung-hee to power in the early 1960s. For better and for worse, General Park left a stamp on Korea's political economy that endures to this day (Yi 2006).

Legacy of Park Chung-hee

The democratic constitution that occupying authorities imposed on postwar Japan tightly constrained the scale and direction of industrial policy (Calder 1988). A free press, open elections, and the requirement that government policy be based on laws passed by the Diet meant that Japanese industrial policymakers had to stay in line with popular opinion.

In striking contrast, General Park faced few constraints on his exercise of authority. He was not answerable to a constitution, an opposition, or a free press. Park was not limited by bureaucratic infighting because all bureaucracies were directly answerable to him. One of Park's first economic policy moves was to nationalize Korea's banks—a move that would have been unthinkable in postwar Japan—making its financial markets an arm of state policy. The general thus quickly acquired a degree of authority over the allocation of resources in the Korean economy of which Japan's industrial policy bureaucrats could have only dreamed. He did not hesitate to use it (Clifford 1997).

---

7. For an in-depth analysis of the loss of competitiveness of Japan's IT sector, see Arora, Branstetter, and Drev (2013).

The breathtakingly rapid growth of Korea during this period—even more rapid than that of Japan—attests to the fact that the policy mix pursued during this period had many positive elements. But one of the most important legacies of this period was the rise of the chaebols—Korea's industrial conglomerates (Joh 2014). Park used his command over Korea's resources to build up globally competitive national champions. Low-cost capital, scarce foreign exchange, and industrial licenses were awarded to conglomerates headed by business leaders who became his close allies (Clifford 1997). Of course, Park's favoritism tilted the playing field against all other players and left South Korea with a degree of industrial concentration that was arguably the highest in the industrialized world.

In the late 1990s, when the financial crisis hit, Korean public opinion turned against the chaebols; their "reckless" borrowing and investing was partly blamed for the crisis.[8] Influential commentators criticized the concentration of economic power within the large groups and the collusive ties between these groups and several successive South Korean governments. The gradual political liberalization and democratization of South Korea encouraged politicians to reform the chaebols (Haggard, Lim, and Kim 2003). Since the crisis of 1997, nearly every South Korean president has promised to check the power of the chaebol and encourage entrepreneurship, but the results have been disappointing. Figures 4.2 and 4.3 depict the concentration of US patent grants and R&D spending, respectively, across Korean firms. A shockingly high share of both is concentrated in a single chaebol—the Samsung Group.

South Koreans refer to their nation, somewhat ruefully, as the Republic of Samsung (Pesek 2015). In addition to dominating patenting and R&D expenditure in South Korea, the Samsung Group accounts for a high fraction of South Korean exports and represents a disproportionate fraction of the value of the South Korean stock exchange.[9] Former president Lee Myung-bak pardoned the group's former chairman, Lee Kun-hee, who was convicted of financial wrongdoing and tax evasion. The justification was that Samsung was so important to the South Korean economy that it

---

8. The five largest chaebols—Samsung, LG, Daewoo, Hyundai, and SK—accounted for 20 percent of all outstanding debt and 75 percent of all new borrowing in 1998 (*Economist*, 1999, "Survey of South Korea," originally appeared June 3, 1995 issue, pp. 10–17).

9. The Samsung Group accounts for more than one-fifth of the value of the South Korean stock exchange. See Steven Borowiec and Paresh Dave, "South Koreans live in 'the Republic of Samsung,' where the Galaxy Note 7 crisis feels personal," *Los Angeles Times*, October 11, 2016, www.latimes.com/business/technology/la-fi-tn-samsung-note-7-korea-20161011-snap-story.html; Zahra Ullah, "How Samsung dominates South Korea's economy," CNN.com, February 17, 2017, http://money.cnn.com/2017/02/17/technology/samsung-south-korea-daily-life/index.html.

Figure 4.2 Concentration of US patent grants to South Korean firms

share of patents awarded to each group of firm(s)

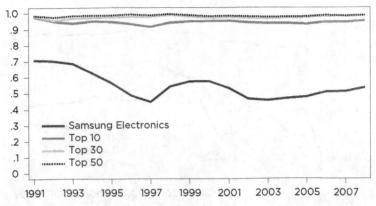

Note: This figure measures the fraction of total US patent grants awarded to South Korean inventors that are accounted for by Samsung Electronics and by firms affiliated with the top 10, top 30, and top 50 chaebols. Patents are assigned a date based on year of application. South Korean patent data also indicate a significant concentration of patenting in the portfolios of these chaebols. Samsung Electronics alone accounts for more than 50 percent of all US patent grants received by South Korean firms.

Source: US Patent and Trademark Office.

would be destabilizing to jail the head of the firm, even if he were guilty of crimes. Lee Kun-hee has since transferred effective control of Samsung to his son, Lee Jae-yong. The younger Lee was recently convicted of bribing Lee Myung-bak's successor (and General Park's daughter), Park Gyeun-hye, who was the first South Korean president to be impeached and removed from office. However, that sentence was suspended in February 2018, and many observers expect the younger Lee will escape the legal consequences of his crime. The tangled state of South Korean politics attests to the extreme degree of pro-incumbent bias that Park's industrial policies generated.

Policies and Pro-Incremental Bias in South Korea

Once Park took over, the Korean educational system expanded in reach and quality even more rapidly than did the educational system of its former colonial master. Younger Koreans are now among the most highly educated people in the industrial world, and Korean students regularly outperform Japanese students on the sorts of internationally comparable standardized tests in which Japanese students regularly outperform Americans (OECD 2016).

Figure 4.3 Concentration of R&D spending among South Korean firms

share of R&D by each group of firm(s)

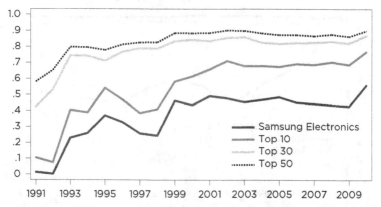

Note: This figure uses data on total R&D expenditure, as reported by the publicly traded firms listed on South Korean equity markets, to calculate the fraction of annual expenditure accounted for by Samsung Electronics and the top 10, top 30, and top 50 chaebols. In 2010, Samsung Electronics accounted for more than 50 percent of total R&D expenditure reported by these firms.

Source: Korean Listed Companies Association (KLCA).

But South Korea's educational system also has some of the same weaknesses as Japan's. Like their Japanese counterparts, South Korea's elite universities are better known for the intensive competition for admission than for the quality of research or even instruction. The same institutional neglect of graduate education, lack of research funding, unwillingness of the education ministry or the universities to concentrate research resources in the hands of innovative scholars rather than senior scholars, and indifference to immigrants have historically limited the research capabilities of South Korean universities.[10] While leading chaebols can set up R&D facilities in Silicon Valley, the relative weakness of Korean universities drastically limits the access of South Korean startups to world-class faculty entrepreneurs and graduate students capable of translating laboratory breakthroughs into new products and services.

South Korea inherited the Japanese patent system and, even after independence, the evolution of the Korean system followed that of Japan's. After a long period of weak and narrow protection with indifferent enforcement by courts, reforms in the 1980s led to stronger patents and enforcement, and patent practices began converging with Western standards in

10. Only one university from South Korea is on the list of "Top 200 Universities in the World," www.4icu.org/top-universities-world.

the 1990s (La Croix and Kawaura 1996). Nevertheless, the persistence of weak protection during Korea's high growth period may have reinforced a pro-incremental bias in Korea, as it did in Japan.

Prior to the mid-1980s, South Korean firms received few domestic patents and almost none from international patent agencies like the US Patent and Trademark Office. After the mid-1980s, the number of international patents granted to South Korean firms exploded, seemingly marking a surprisingly sudden transition by South Korean firms from imitators to innovators. Several scholars argue that this patent explosion can be explained by the domestic patent reform, which increased the incentives for R&D. However, our research (Branstetter and Kwon 2018) suggests a different interpretation. Firm-level patenting and R&D data reveal little immediate growth in chemicals and pharmaceutical patenting, even though domestic patent law strengthened the most in these industries. In contrast, R&D and patenting rapidly expanded in exporting firms for which foreign markets were more important than the domestic market potentially affected by the change in Korean patent law.

Branstetter and Kwon (2018) also point out that the relative exchange rates of the yen and the won sharply changed in the mid-1980s. The yen appreciated sharply against the US dollar after 1985. The won, still pegged to the dollar, effectively depreciated sharply against the yen. Korea-based producers suddenly gained a large cost advantage over Japanese rivals. By investing in process engineering and other efforts to close the quality gap vis-à-vis Japanese firms, they stood to outsell their rivals in the United States and Western Europe. It was the tantalizing prospect of outselling Japanese firms in the world's largest markets, rather than marginally better patent protection in the small South Korean market, that induced a South Korean R&D and patenting explosion.

South Korea underpriced Japanese rivals in the 1980s the same way Japanese firms undercut American and European rivals in the 1970s and early 1980s. With cheaper factor costs and a favorable exchange rate, South Korean firms could do to Japan what Japan had done to the industrial West. Throughout the 1990s, low-cost Korean producers of commodity semiconductor products like DRAM chips were edging out their Japanese rivals in global markets.[11] By the end of the decade, Korean firms were decisively in the lead, and the once vaunted Japanese semiconductor industry was a shadow of its former self (Cho, Kim, and Rhee 1998). Japanese firms whose R&D investment strategies had been predicated on their retaining a

---

11. In 1993, Samsung produced more DRAM chips than any other firm. In the same year, Hyundai and LG (formerly Lucky GoldStar) ranked ninth and tenth on the list of top global DRAM producers (Cho, Kim, and Rhee 1998).

cost advantage vis-à-vis foreign competitors were increasingly "squeezed" between the rising quality and manufacturing capability of lower-cost Asian nations, like South Korea, and the persistently superior product innovation capabilities of their American rivals (Lee 2013).

The strength of the Korean won ebbed and flowed over the next two decades. The financial crisis of 1997–98 led to a collapse in the value of the won, a long period of relative won weakness, and a revival of South Korean firms' innovation strategies built around relatively low production costs, scale, and strength in process engineering. However, as Chinese manufacturing capabilities grew, Korean production sites found it increasingly difficult to compete on price with those based in a country at a fundamentally lower level of economic development. In the 2000s, Korean firms felt the same kind of "squeeze" as they had put on their Japanese rivals in the prior decade (Lee 2013).

This chapter's discussant, Jong-Wha Lee, notes that a highly competitive exchange rate could help a late-developing country transition from "pure imitator" to "incremental innovator." But South Korean firms are now struggling to move from incremental innovation to more fundamental innovation. They remain important exporters of consumer electronics goods and electronic components, but are rarely the source of major product innovations. Firms located in other countries are leading the development of artificial intelligence (AI) and machine learning technologies. Similarly, South Korea remains a successful exporter of autos, but the major innovations in that sector, like self-driving cars and electric vehicles, are being pioneered elsewhere.

Samsung's prominence in the global smartphone industry is perhaps emblematic of the strengths and weaknesses of South Korea's innovation system. Shortly after the introduction of the iPhone, a revolutionary innovation by Apple, Samsung introduced a very similar product based on the Android operating system and web platform created by Google. Samsung's products were so similar that Apple launched a global round of patent infringement lawsuits. In the end, these lawsuits did not result in damage judgments large enough to displace Samsung from the market,[12] and Samsung's lower-priced products have sold in large volumes around the world, boosting Samsung's profits.[13]

---

12. Seth Fiegerman, "Supreme Court sides with Samsung in Apple patent case," CNN.com, December 6, 2016, http://money.cnn.com/2016/12/06/technology/samsung-apple-supreme-court/index.html.

13. Lance Whitney, "Samsung selling more of its cheaper smartphones," Cnet.com, November 2, 2015, www.cnet.com/news/samsung-selling-more-phones-at-cheaper-prices-says-new-research.

Samsung's global market share remains high in terms of handsets sold, but its share of global profits earned from smartphones declined over the three years ending in 2016.[14] Other Asia-based electronics firms began manufacturing even cheaper smartphones, also based on the open Android system. These lower-cost firms took market share away from Samsung, which had to respond by cutting prices, since it was offering little in the way of product innovation that lower-cost Asian rivals could not quickly and closely match.[15] The real innovation that made Samsung phones so attractive—the Android platform—was not Samsung's innovation, but Google's, which maximized its revenues by offering the platform to as many manufacturers as possible, including low-cost Chinese producers like Huawei, Oppo, and Xiaomi. The other major revenue driver for Samsung is manufacture of commodity components like DRAM chips. South Korea's innovative strengths thus appear to be concentrated on the "incremental" side of the innovation spectrum and overwhelmingly concentrated in a small number of chaebols whose future is uncertain (IMF 2014). South Korean policy choices may have reinforced these pro-incremental and pro-incumbent biases.

Taiwan

Like Korea, Taiwan was a colony of the Japanese Empire from 1895 until the defeat of Imperial Japan in 1945. While brutal, exploitative, and authoritarian in many ways, Japanese colonial rule was markedly less harsh in Taiwan than in Korea. The Japanese left Taiwan with the physical and institutional infrastructure of a modern economy. When it was ceded to Chiang Kai-shek's Republic of China by the Allied Powers at the end of World War II, it was the richest province in his nation by a large margin. Initially welcomed by the Taiwanese, Chiang's army and provincial government quickly demonstrated a remarkable combination of corruption, brutality, and incompetence. A popular uprising against mainland authority in 1947 was brutally suppressed, and when Chiang Kai-shek relocated his Nationalist government to Taiwan in 1949, he presided over an authoritarian regime characterized by martial law, systematic oppression of any

---

14. Samsung's share of global smartphone shipments decreased after 2013. However, the share was still over 20 percent in 2016 (data from Statista.com, www.statista.com/statistics/271492/global-market-share-held-by-leading-smartphone-vendors/).

15. The market shares of Chinese phone makers such as Huawei, Xiaomi, Oppo, and Vivo have been increasing. See Scott Cendrowski, "How China's Smartphone 'Big Four' Are Fighting for Global Customers," *Fortune*, January 25, 2017, http://fortune.com/2017/01/24/china-smartphones-oppo-vivo-huawei-xiaomi.

political dissent, and concentration of economic policymaking authority in his own hands.

Taiwan's experience was similar to South Korea's in several ways. Taiwan inherited an educational system that downplayed research and graduate education and an intellectual property system that offered, at best, narrow protection that was weakly enforced. The much lower factor prices in Taiwan fostered process-oriented, cost-reducing, and incremental R&D. The sharp appreciation of the Japanese yen in the mid-1980s gifted Taiwanese producers with the opportunity to undercut their traditional Japanese rivals in the world's most important export markets. Just as the South Koreans, Taiwanese firms responded to this opportunity with a surge of investment in R&D, a surge in international patents, and an export boom.

However, the direction in which the Chiang dynasty moved Taiwan differed in important ways from that of Park's South Korea. First, Chiang Kai-shek's economic planners came to believe that the devastating bouts of inflation that wracked the Chinese mainland were one of the chief reasons his Nationalist Party lost the Chinese civil war to the Communists. To avoid repeating this fatal error, the technocrats in charge of monetary and financial policy adopted the so-called high interest rate policy (Wade 1990). This policy increased saving because it rewarded Taiwanese savers for placing funds in the financial system. Because all firms, even large ones favored by the government-run banking system, paid relatively high interest rates, the financial playing field was never tilted toward favored conglomerates to the same extent as it was in South Korea.

Taiwanese authorities also tolerated the "gray market" for capital that leaked out of the formal banking system to fund highly profitable enterprises that could not secure formal bank loans. In fact, the authorities used the interest rates charged in this gray market as a benchmark for setting official interest rates. Smaller firms outside favored corporate groups and sectors had much easier access to capital than was possible in South Korea. While some degree of official favoritism existed, the government of Taiwan was not nearly as attached to the idea of building national champions as was the government of South Korea, and Taiwan's level of industrial concentration was much lower. As the Taiwanese economy matured, it came to host a fairly robust domestic venture capital market, in which local firms were able to find sufficient financing to enter even reasonably complex industries. The pro-incumbent bias that was so overwhelming in South Korea was not as significant in Taiwan.

Taiwan's industrial structure was different also because of the entrepreneurial character of Taiwanese managers, and the greater openness and flexibility of Taiwanese markets for electronic products, labor, and capital. The Taiwanese electronics industry, which eventually became the mainstay of Taiwanese manufacturing, is characterized by a very high degree of entry and exit (Aw, Chen, and Roberts 2001). The extensive government involvement in Taiwan also helped differentiate the industrial structure. In Japan, government subsidization of R&D was quite limited; firms were left to fend for themselves. Only larger enterprises had the private resources to make large, risky investments in adopting and modifying (or creating) technology and to construct the mechanisms to appropriate the returns from such investments. In Taiwan, the state bore a considerable fraction of the fixed costs of technology adoption and refinement and provided the results to local firms on favorable terms. These efforts had a strong industry focus and, to some extent, a pro-incremental bias.

It is perhaps inevitable that an economy like Taiwan, which is substantially smaller in geographic size and population than South Korea, would be less diversified than its larger neighbor. South Korea is a significant global player in capital-intensive sectors such as autos, shipbuilding, and steel, as well as electronics. In contrast, Taiwan's exports and industrial structure are more concentrated in electronics and information technology (IT). The promotion of the electronics industry has been a key priority of the Taiwanese government for decades. The Industrial Technology Research Institute (ITRI), established in 1973 to increase national R&D capacity, accounted for roughly 25 percent of the government's total R&D expenditures by 1987—a research budget of some US$215 million (Wade 1990, 98).

In 1974, the Electronic Research and Service Organization (ERSO) was established under ITRI to recruit foreign partners to develop and commercialize semiconductor fabrication technology. The government was heavily involved in the 1986 formation of the highly successful Taiwan Semiconductor Manufacturing Corporation (TSMC), initially a joint venture between Philips and several domestic public and private firms. ERSO was deeply involved in international technology transfer through the 1980s, often identifying key foreign technologies itself, then sublicensing them to local firms (Wade 1990, 103–107).[16] Thus, the Taiwanese government was very successful in directing and subsidizing substantial international technology transfer in this industry.[17] Given the special

---

16. This practice of sublicensing could mean that our plant-level data fail to capture all "effective" foreign technology purchases.

17. In contrast, the Japanese government began the postwar period with a policy of *limiting* foreign technology purchases (Wakasugi 1997). As the Japanese economy developed and the potential benefits of technology imports became clear to government authorities, these limits were progressively relaxed. Wakasugi (1997) has argued that the government allowed

Figure 4.4 Concentration of US patent grants to Taiwanese firms in electronics hardware, 1981–2014

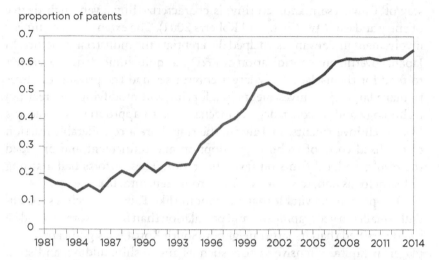

Note: This graph uses data from the US Patent and Trademark Office to calculate the share of patents awarded to Taiwanese inventors that are in patent classes associated with electronics and IT hardware. Software-related patents are omitted. Since the late 1990s, patents in these classes have accounted for more than 60 percent of the total. Taiwanese patents and data on Taiwanese R&D spending also point to a strong concentration of activity in the electronics industry.

Source: Branstetter and Chen (2006).

favors showered on electronics, it is not surprising that, as Taiwan's industrial structure shifted from labor-intensive goods to more knowledge-intensive goods, it became increasingly concentrated in that sector. Figure 4.4 illustrates the high concentration of Taiwanese firms' US patents in classes associated with electronics hardware.

ITRI/ERSO was not the only source of Taiwanese government largesse for electronics relative to other industries. Taiwanese industrial planners sought to build an electronics-based industrial park south of the capital, Taipei, in Hsinchu, that would become the island's answer to Silicon Valley. First proposed in 1976, the park was initially opened in 1980 and grew rapidly over the next two decades. The government made massive investments in infrastructure, offered special financing to new firms moving into the park, and even constructed American-style schools for families of expatriate Taiwanese it hoped to lure back to Taiwan from the United States.

only "favored" firms to bid for foreign technology to prevent competition among potential Japanese purchasers from driving up the price of the license. This may have lowered the price of foreign technology for these firms, but it effectively *increased* the price (to infinity) for the firms that were not favored, and, in Wakasugi's view, it is unlikely that this intervention was welfare-enhancing.

Taiwan's drive to build the Hsinchu Science Park kicked into high gear just as rising living standards and a shift to democracy were making Taiwan more attractive to expatriates seeking career advancement. As American high-tech companies began to offshore their manufacturing to Asia, Taiwanese expatriate engineers facing weak career prospects (or layoffs) in the United States were increasingly inclined to move "home" to Hsinchu. By the mid-1990s, social scientists and international investors were hailing the success of the park.[18]

The limitations of Hsinchu's success, and of the more general nexus of policies that nurtured Taiwan's high-tech industries, however, have become more apparent over the years. Relatively small firms that historically relied on ITRI/ERSO to do the "heavy lifting" of identifying key foreign technologies and underwriting assimilative R&D were naturally focused on implementing and refining technologies developed by others, rather than breaking new ground. The new firms taking shape in Hsinchu were more focused on the efficient contract manufacturing of Silicon Valley designs than creating "breakthrough" new products. Like a "helicopter parent" who does too much to position their children for success, the institutions and policies designed to nurture Taiwan's high-tech sector may have inadvertently undermined the incentives for these firms to develop within themselves more fundamental capabilities for research. The industry that took root in Hsinchu was focused on hardware, not software, and incremental, rather than transformative, R&D.

Despite government fears of excessive economic dependence on mainland China, Taiwanese electronics firms could not resist the attraction of China's low costs and apparently limitless skilled labor. The controversial Chen Shui-bian administration in Taiwan liberalized cross-straits investment, and a tidal wave of investment ensued. Branstetter et al. (2017) analyze the impact of this relocation of manufacturing on the R&D of Taiwanese firms in the technological domains related to the products and components that were offshored. They find a statistically robust negative effect. Taiwan's trade flows to and from China first rose sharply, then fell substantially as an increasingly large fraction of the entire value chain moved to China.

Taiwan's leading contract manufacturing firms have managed to stay one step ahead of their "indigenous" Chinese competitors on the mainland, but the Taiwanese economy has slowed sharply since the go-go 1990s, incomes have stagnated, and the facts on the ground no longer support the notion that Hsinchu Science Park is going to match Silicon Valley. As was the case in Japan and South Korea, it seems likely that Taiwanese govern-

---

18. See Saxenian and Hsu (2001) for a typical positive assessment of the venture.

ment policies reinforced and deepened the pro-incremental bias in Taiwan's innovation system. While these policies did not leave Taiwan with the same pro-incumbent bias as its larger neighbors, they appear to have concentrated Taiwanese activity in sectors that no longer hold the most significant technological opportunities. Like Japan and South Korea, Taiwan seems increasingly squeezed between Silicon Valley and China. American firms continue to generate fundamental innovations Taiwan cannot match. China continues to offer a mix of lower costs and rising skills that Taiwanese manufactures cannot resist. For Taiwan, the increasingly tight economic embrace of the Chinese mainland raises existential political questions about the future of the island as a de facto independent state.

Conclusion

Japan, South Korea, and Taiwan have successfully climbed the development ladder, yet, when measured by their own past performance, one cannot help but be struck by the degree to which they have each fallen short of what might have been reasonably expected a decade or two ago. Compared with the United States, Japan's overall total factor productivity has actually *declined* substantially over the past 20 years, even as it has become a much more R&D-intensive economy than the United States (IMF 2017). Despite emerging as the most R&D-intensive nation in the OECD, South Korea's level of productivity relative to the United States has essentially remained the same over the past 20 years—stuck at around 60 percent of the US aggregate TFP level.

The three countries have suffered, to varying degrees, from declining R&D productivity because the national innovation systems designed for their high growth periods are no longer as effective in their maturing economies. The pro-incremental and pro-incumbent biases that government policies created or reinforced in these countries have made it difficult to change these innovation systems. Other nations in the region, including China, seeking to emulate the success of these three nations should avoid reinforcing the same kinds of biases in their own emerging innovation systems. The costs of not doing so appear to be high. Once these biases penetrate the fabric of an economy's innovation system, they are difficult to eliminate.

References

Agrawal, A., and R. Henderson. 2003. Putting Patents in Context: Exploring Knowledge Transfer from MIT. *Management Science* 48, no. 1: 44–60.

Amano, I., and G. Poole. 2005. The Japanese University in Crisis. *Higher Education* 50: 685–711.

Arora, A., L. Branstetter, and M. Drev. 2013. Going Soft: How the Rise of Software-Based Innovation Led to the Decline of Japan's IT Industry and the Resurgence of Silicon Valley. *Review of Economics and Statistics* 95, no. 3: 757–75.

Aw, B., X. Chen, and M. Roberts. 2001. Firm-Level Evidence on Productivity Differentials, Turnover, and Exports in Taiwanese Manufacturing. *Journal of Development Economics* 66: 51–86.

Branstetter, L. 2017. Intellectual Property Rights, Innovation, and Development: Is Asia Different? *Millennial Asia* 8, no 4: 5–25.

Branstetter, L., and J.-R. Chen. 2006. The Impact of Technology Transfer and R&D on Productivity Growth in Taiwanese Industry: Microeconometric Analysis Using Plant and Firm-Level Data. *Journal of the Japanese and International Economies* 20, no. 2: 177–92.

Branstetter, L., and N. Kwon. 2018. *South Korea's Transition from Imitator to Innovator: The Role of External Demand Shocks.* Forthcoming in *Journal of the Japanese and International Economies.*

Branstetter, L., and Y. Nakamura. 2003. Has Japan's Innovative Capacity Declined? In *Structural Impediments to Growth in Japan*, ed. A. Kashyap, J. Corbett, M. Blomström, and F. Hayashi. University of Chicago Press and National Bureau of Economic Research.

Branstetter, L., J. Chen, B. Glennon, C. Yang, and N. Zolas. 2017. *Does Offshoring Manufacturing Harm Innovation in the Home Country? Evidence from Taiwan and China.* Working Paper (July). Carnegie Mellon University.

Buenstorf, G., and S. Klepper. 2009. *Heritage and Agglomeration: The Akron Tire Cluster Revisited. Economic Journal* 119, no. 537: 705–33.

Calder, K. 1988. *Crisis and Compensation: Public Policy and Political Stability in Japan.* Princeton, NJ: Princeton University Press.

Cho, D. S., D. J. Kim, and D. K. Rhee. 1998. Latecomer Strategies: Evidence from the Semiconductor Industry in Japan and Korea. *Organization Science* 9, no. 4: 489–505.

Christensen, C. 1997. *The Innovator's Dilemma: When New Technology Causes Great Companies to Fail.* Cambridge, MA: Harvard University Press.

Clifford, M. 1997. *Troubled Tiger: Businessmen, Bureaucrats, and Generals in South Korea.* New York: Routledge.

Cohen, W., and S. Klepper. 1996. Firm Size and the Nature of Innovation within Industries: The Case of Process and Product R&D. *Review of Economics and Statistics* 78, no. 2: 232–43.

Denison, E., and W. Chung. 1976. *How Japan's Economy Grew So Fast.* Washington: Brookings Institution.

Eads, G., and K. Yamamura. 1987. The Future of Industrial Policy. In *The Political Economy of Japan, Volume 1: The Domestic Transformation,* ed. K. Yamamura and Y. Yasukichi. Stanford, CA: Stanford University Press.

Evenson, R., and Y. Kislev. 1976. A Stochastic Model of Applied Research. *Journal of Political Economy* 84: 265–82.

Flath, D. 2002. *Distribution Keiretsu, FDI, and Important Penetration in Japan.* Working Paper. Columbia University.

Gerlach, M. 1992. *Alliance Capitalism: The Social Organization of Japanese Business.* Berkeley, CA: University of California Press.

Gerschenkron, A. 1962. *Economic Backwardness in Historical Perspective: A Book of Essays.* Cambridge, MA: Harvard University Press.

Goto, A. 2000. Japan's National Innovation System: Current Status and Problems. *Oxford Review of Economic Policy* 16, no. 2: 103–13.

Goto, A. and H. Odagiri, eds. 2003. *Science-Based Industries.* Tokyo: NTT Publishing.

Haggard, S., W. Lim, and E. Kim, eds. 2003. *Economic Crisis and Corporate Restructuring in Korea: Reforming the Chaebol.* Cambridge: Cambridge University Press.

Hall, B., and R. Ziedonis. 2001. The Patent Paradox Revisited: An Empirical Study of Patenting in the U.S. Semiconductor Industry, 1979–1995. *RAND Journal of Economics* 32, no. 1: 101–28.

Hanushek, E., and L. Woessman. 2015. *The Knowledge Capital of Nations: Education and the Economics of Growth.* Cambridge, MA: MIT Press.

Harhoff, D., F. Scherer, and K. Vopel. 2003. Citations, Family Size, Opposition, and the Value of Patent Rights. *Research Policy* 32, no. 8: 1343–63.

Helpman, E., and M. Trajtenberg. 1998a. A Time to Sow and a Time to Reap. In *General Purpose Technologies and Economic Growth*, ed. E. Helpman. Cambridge, MA: MIT Press.

Helpman, E., and M. Trajtenberg. 1998b. The Diffusion of General Purpose Technologies. In *General Purpose Technologies and Economic Growth*, ed. E. Helpman. Cambridge, MA: MIT Press.

Hochberg, Y., C. Serrano, and R. Ziedonis. 2018. Patent Collateral, Investor Lending, and the Market for Venture Lending. *Journal of Financial Economics* (forthcoming).

Hoshi, T., and A. Kashyap. 2001. *Corporate Finance and Governance in Japan: The Road to the Future.* Cambridge, MA: MIT Press.

Hoshi, T., A. Kashyap, and D. Scharfstein. 1991. Corporate Structure, Liquidity, and Investment: Evidence from Japanese Industrial Groups. *Quarterly Journal of Economics* 106: 33–36.

Hoshi, T., and Patrick, H., eds. 2000. *Crisis and Change in the Japanese Financial System.* Boston, MA: Kluwer.

IMF (International Monetary Fund). 2014. *Article IV Consultation: South Korea.* IMF Country Report No. 14/101. Washington.

IMF (International Monetary Fund). 2017. The "New Mediocre" and the Outlook for Productivity in Asia. In *Regional Economic Outlook: Asia and Pacific, April 2017: Preparing for Choppy Seas.* Washington.

Ito, T. 1992. *The Japanese Economy.* Cambridge, MA: MIT Press.

Jaffe, A., and J. Lerner. 2004. *Innovation and Its Discontents.* Princeton, NJ: Princeton University Press.

Joh, S. W. 2014. Chaebols as South Korean Entrepreneurship. In *Handbook of East Asian Entrepreneurship*: 157–68.

Jones, H. 1980. *Live Machines: Hired Foreigners and Meiji Japan.* Vancouver: University of British Columbia Press.

Klepper, S. 1996. Entry, Exit, Growth, and Innovation over the Product Life Cycle. *American Economic Review* 86, no. 3: 562–83.

Klepper, S. 2010. The Origin and Growth of Industry Clusters: The Making of Silicon Valley and Detroit. *Journal of Urban Economics* 67, no. 1: 15–32.

La Croix, S., and A. Kawaura. 1996. Product Patent Reform and Its Impact on Korea's Pharmaceutical Industry. *International Economic Journal* 10, no. 1: 109–24.

Lee, K. 2013. *Schumpeterian Analysis of Economic Catch-Up: Path-Creation and the Middle Income Trap.* New York: Cambridge University Press.

Mansfield, E. 1988a. Industrial Innovation in Japan and the United States. *Science* 241: 1769–74.

Mansfield, E. 1988b. Industrial R&D in Japan and the United States: A Comparative Study. *American Economic Review* 78, no. 2: 223–28.

Mansfield, E. 1988c. The Speed and Cost of Industrial Innovation in Japan and the United States: External vs. Internal Technology. *Management Science* 34, no. 10: 1157–68.

Mansfield, E. 1991. Academic Research and Industrial Innovation. *Research Policy* 20, no. 1: 1–12.

Nagaoka, S. 2007. Assessing the R&D Management of a Firm in Terms of Speed and Science Linkage: Evidence from U.S. Patents. *Journal of Economics, Management, and Strategy* 16, no. 1: 129–56.

National Research Council. 1992. *Japan's Growing Technological Capability: Implications for the U.S. Economy.* Washington: National Academy Press.

Nelson, R. 1992. National Innovation Systems: A Retrospective on a Study. *Industrial and Corporate Change* 1, no. 2: 347–74.

OECD (Organization for Economic Cooperation and Development). 2016. Korea. In *Education at a Glance 2016: OECD Indicators.* Paris: OECD Publishing.

Okimoto, D. I., and T. P. Rohlen. 1988. *Inside the Japanese System: Readings on Contemporary Society and Political Economy.* Stanford, CA: Stanford University Press.

Okimoto, D., and G. Saxonhouse. 1987. Technology and the Future of the Economy. In *The Political Economy of Japan, Volume 1: The Domestic Transformation*, ed. K. Yamamura and Y. Yasukichi. Stanford, CA: Stanford University Press.

Ordover, J. A. 1991. A Patent System for Both Diffusion and Exclusion. *Journal of Economic Perspectives* 5, no. 1: 43–60.

Pesek, W. 2015. Life in the Republic of Samsung. *Barron's Online*, December 3. Available at www.barrons.com/articles/life-in-the-republic-of-samsung-1449106291.

Rohlen, T. 1983. *Japan's High Schools.* Berkeley, CA: University of California Press.

Romalis, J. 2004. Factor Proportions and the Structure of Commodity Trade. *American Economic Review* 94, no. 1: 67–97.

Rosenberg, N., and R. Nelson. 1994. American Universities and Technical Advance in Industry. *Research Policy* 23, no. 3: 323–48.

Sakakibara, M., and L. Branstetter. 2001. Do Stronger Patents Induce More Innovation? Evidence from the 1988 Japanese Patent Law Reforms. *RAND Journal of Economics* 32, no. 1: 77–100.

Saxenian, A., and J. Hsu. 2001. The Silicon Valley-Hsinchu Connection: Technical Communities and Industrial Upgrading. *Industrial and Corporate Change* 10, no. 4.

Uekusa, M. 1987. Industrial Organization: The 1970s to the Present. In *The Political Economy of Japan, Volume 1: The Domestic Transformation*, ed. K. Yamamura and Y. Yasukichi. Stanford, CA: Stanford University Press.

Wade, R. 1990. *Governing the Market: Economic Theory and the Role of Government in East Asian Industrialization.* Princeton, NJ: Princeton University Press.

Wakasugi, R. 1997. Technology Importation in Japan. In *Innovation in Japan*, ed. A. Goto and H. Odagiri. Oxford: Clarendon Press.

Weinstein, D. 1995. Evaluating Administrative Guidance and Cartels in Japan, 1957–1988. *Journal of the Japanese and International Economies* 9: 200–23.

Yi, P. C., ed. 2006. *Developmental Dictatorship and the Park Chung-hee Era: The Shaping of Modernity in the Republic of Korea.* Homa & Sekey Books.

Zucker, L., M. Darby, and M. Brewer. 1998. Intellectual Capital and the Birth of U.S. Biotechnology Enterprises. *American Economic Review* 88: 290–306.

Comment

Jong-Wha Lee

Lee Branstetter and Namho Kwon introduce the concepts of "pro-incremental" and "pro-incumbent" biases in the innovation systems of three East Asian economies—Japan, South Korea, and Taiwan—using case studies. However, their illustration is limited on how incremental and incumbent innovation affects research productivity, research input, and output differently than radical innovation. The determinants of these two different types of innovation are also unclear. Further discussion would be useful to support their main arguments on the role of pro-incremental and pro-incumbent innovation.

The chapter also does not provide robust evidence on the role of pro-incremental and pro-incumbent innovation in declining research productivity. In this regard, Branstetter and Kwon use firm-level data on patenting and R&D spending in Japan in the 1990s as evidence. The decline in research productivity in Japan, however, might have been caused by other factors both domestic and global. Productivity growth in Japan and many other East Asian economies has been impeded by many more important country-specific factors. They include slower convergence in productivity, limited innovative capability, low productivity growth in the services sector, low efficiency in resource allocation between small and large enterprises and between manufacturing and service sectors—mainly due to inefficiencies in labor and financial markets—and low quality of institutions (i.e., government regulation, intellectual property protection, corporate governance, and policy uncertainty). Thus, it is important to identify the exact extent to which pro-incremental and pro-incumbent biases, rather than other factors, cause diminishing returns to R&D investment. Furthermore, the decline in productivity growth might be attributable to global factors such as the absence of revolutionary invention and slow diffusion of new technologies across industries and firms globally in recent decades.

Some studies point out that declining productivity growth is not unique to East Asian economies. For example, Bloom et al. (2017) show that despite the increase in the effective number of researchers, research productivity has continuously declined in the United States since the 1940s. Also, given that research productivity is different from total factor productivity (TFP), it would be helpful to discuss whether research produc-

Jong-Wha Lee is a professor of economics and director of the Asiatic Research Institute at Korea University. He was chief economist and head of the Office of Regional Economic Integration at the Asian Development Bank and an economist at the International Monetary Fund.

tivity has declined more rapidly in East Asian economies compared with the United States or Western Europe. One should also note that it is natural for economies like those in East Asia—which successfully transformed themselves from imitators to innovators—to create pro-incremental and pro-incumbent biases in the early stages of development and then build up innovative capabilities with the accumulation of knowledge.

Branstetter and Kwon explain how policies, such as human capital policy, intellectual property policy, and exchange rate policy in the three East Asian economies reinforced pro-incumbent and pro-incremental biases in their innovation systems, contributing to a slowdown in R&D productivity. On exchange rate policy, lack of evidence makes it hard to believe their argument that an undervalued exchange rate policy turned Japanese and Korean firms away from fundamental innovation and toward incremental innovation. The "export-oriented policy" did indeed support export firms, which are seen to be more innovative than domestic ones. This policy was also effective in pushing the pace of change in comparative advantage, from labor-intensive manufacturing to more capital-intensive and then to technology-intensive industries. These East Asian countries switched to more market-based flexible exchange rate systems a few decades ago. Therefore, more discussion is needed on the role of exchange rate policy in creating pro-incremental and pro-incumbent biases.

For East Asian economies, technological progress is most critical to maintaining strong growth. Branstetter and Kwon suggest reforming outdated policies and emulating the Israeli or Silicon Valley model as an alternative. These economies should make the effort to build innovative capabilities on their own because the role of government in promoting technological innovation, especially fundamental, radical innovation, is not always clear. To do so, policies should be prioritized to tackle country-specific factors impeding productivity growth. For instance, in South Korea, the government can nurture research capabilities by upgrading the quality of tertiary education and human capital in science and technology and increasing investment in basic research. The government should also develop the venture capital industry and startups, improve resource allocation across enterprises and sectors, and reduce political instability and policy uncertainty.

References

Lee, Jong-Wha. 2016. Korea's economic growth and catch-up: Implications for China. *China & World Economy* 24, no. 5: 71–97.

Bloom, Nicholas, Charles I. Jones, John Van Reenen, and Michael Webb. 2017. *Are ideas getting harder to find?* NBER Working Paper 23782. Cambridge, MA: National Bureau of Economic Research.

5

Secular Stagnation and Asia: International Transmission and Policy Spillovers

OLIVIER JEANNE

Depressed economic growth and interest rates are the two main symptoms of secular stagnation. Low interest rates can have problematic side effects, such as liquidity traps or unsustainable booms in credit and asset prices. The relationship between these symptoms and their underlying causes are a matter of debate. If secular stagnation were a health condition, it would more likely be called a syndrome than a disease.[1]

To extend the medical metaphor, this chapter explores the contagion of secular stagnation across countries. The symptoms of secular stagnation have not been limited to a particular group of countries. Many countries at different stages of economic development and in different regions have displayed these symptoms. The concomitance of the symptoms could reflect domestic factors that would have appeared independently in many countries, but it may suggest that some form of international transmission or contagion has been at work, raising the question of the mechanisms and processes by which secular stagnation can spread from a country to its neighbors.

In a globally integrated economy it is not difficult to imagine channels of international transmission of secular stagnation. In a financially integrated world a surplus of savings in one part should depress interest rates

Olivier Jeanne is senior fellow at the Peterson Institute for International Economics and professor of economics at Johns Hopkins University. He thanks the conference participants and in particular the chapter's discussant, Heenam Choi, for their insightful comments, as well as Medha Nair for her research assistance.

1. A syndrome is a set of correlated symptoms that may or may not be associated with a well-defined disease.

globally. A country attempting to resist lowering its interest rate would be doing so at the cost of currency appreciation. In a world integrated via trade a negative demand shock in one part of the world may reduce growth in the rest of the world. Textbook macroeconomic theory does not say much about spillovers in productivity growth, but channels of transmission related to international finance and international trade can explain such spillovers.

This chapter first provides a quick review of the literature on secular stagnation. It then tries to better understand the channels by which low productivity growth can spill over across countries. In principle this spillover can occur through several channels, related to finance or trade. For example, if efficient financial intermediation is important for firms to finance productivity-enhancing expenditures, then an internationally contagious banking crisis could depress productivity growth in many countries at the same time. Or if learning-by-exporting is important for firms to adopt more efficient foreign technologies, then a slowdown in international trade could explain a general decrease in productivity growth.

The chapter then investigates how the other symptom of secular stagnation—low interest rates—was transmitted across countries. A simple open-economy model is presented to set a benchmark for what one should look for in the data. The model features a country that is an "innocent bystander" affected by secular stagnation in the rest of the world. Secular stagnation abroad takes the form of lower real interest rates and lower demand in the rest of the world. The model shows that the domestic response must involve a fall in the domestic real rate of interest and net capital inflows. These spillovers are part of the natural adjustment process of the domestic economy to secular stagnation abroad and should not a priori be resisted. However, they may have problematic side effects, such as drawing monetary policy closer to the zero lower bound or increasing domestic credit. The chapter then looks for these side effects in the data for emerging-market economies as a whole and for the Asian region, taking the global financial crisis as a watershed event.

Although secular stagnation is by definition a protracted phenomenon, the crisis was an important step in its diffusion. Furthermore it is an event in which the direction of transmission is not ambiguous: The impulse originated in the advanced economies at the epicenter of the banking crisis and was transmitted to the rest of the world.[2] This chapter is an attempt to learn something about the transmission of secular stagnation from differ-

---

2. This is not to say that secular stagnation is in general transmitted from advanced economies to the rest of the world. For example, many have argued that China has been an important source of excess saving in the global economy.

ences in the way the global financial crisis affected countries depending on their circumstances and policies.

Literature

The literature on secular stagnation has been growing since Lawrence Summers popularized the concept in 2013. A large part of this literature considers this topic in a closed-economy context—see, for example, Andrews, Criscuolo, and Gal (2016) or IMF (2017a) for recent discussions of internal factors of stagnation such as the information technology revolution, population aging, slowing human capital accumulation, or fading structural reform efforts. These factors may exercise their effects concomitantly, which could explain why the symptoms of secular stagnation have affected many countries at the same time without its being the result of contagion. This chapter is related more to the literature that considers international transmission of secular stagnation in an open economy. One part of that literature has focused on the financial channels by which excess saving in some countries can depress the real interest rate in others. That literature is mostly theoretical. Eggertsson et al. (2016) and Caballero, Farhi, and Gourinchas (2015) study global equilibria in which negative spillovers can spread secular stagnation worldwide.[3] In the model of Caballero, Farhi, and Gourinchas (2015) secular stagnation results from a shortage of safe assets. Corsetti et al. (2017) build on the model of Eggertsson et al. (2016) to study the behavior of exchange rates and capital flows in a global liquidity trap.

On the empirical side there is a large literature on the channels of contagion during the global financial crisis. This literature has found it surprisingly difficult to relate the strength of contagion to conventional measures of economic openness. Rose and Spiegel (2011) considered a wide range of indicators in the precrisis data that might predict the cross-country incidence of the Great Recession and generally found no significant link between these indicators and a variety of financial and real manifestations of the 2008 crisis. Lane and Milesi-Ferretti (2011) find similar results. Kalemli-Ozcan, Papaioannou, and Perri (2013) find that economies with stronger financial ties to the United States were more affected by the global financial crisis but establish this result only for developed economies. Hausmann-Guil, van Wincoop, and Zhang (2016) present a model of self-fulfilling crises to explain that integration did matter for contagion beyond some threshold.

There is a large literature on the determinants of productivity growth and some involve international transactions. I am not aware of any studies

---

3. Earlier papers had studied the international propagation of liquidity traps; see, for example, Fujiwara et al. (2013), Devereux and Yetman (2014), Cook and Devereux (2013), and Acharya and Bengui (2016).

Table 5.1 Sample of Asian countries

Advanced		Emerging-market and developing	
AUS	Australia	BGD	Bangladesh
HKG	Hong Kong	CHN	China: Mainland
JPN	Japan	IND	India
KOR	Korea	IDN	Indonesia
NZL	New Zealand	LAO	Laos
SGP	Singapore	MYS	Malaysia
TWN	Taiwan	MNG	Mongolia
		MMR	Myanmar
		NPL	Nepal
		PNG	Papua New Guinea
		PHL	Philippines
		LKA	Sri Lanka
		THA	Thailand
		VNM	Vietnam

Note: This table reports the Asian countries in the sample used in this chapter. It includes the countries under the surveillance of the Asia and Pacific Department of the International Monetary Fund (IMF), excluding those with a population of less than 1 million as well as Cambodia and Timor Leste, for which data were insufficient.

Source: IMF, *World Economic Outlook*.

that have harnessed the theoretical insights from that literature to explore the international transmission of secular stagnation. I discuss the relevant literature in the next section. Adler et al. (2017) also discuss these channels and present empirical evidence.

Productivity Spillovers

The main feature of secular stagnation is a persistent fall in productivity growth. Total factor productivity (TFP) growth fell at about the same time in countries with very different levels of economic development (see table 5.1 for the sample of Asian countries). This concomitance is not just a feature of the last ten years: De Gregorio (2017) shows that the TFP growth of emerging-market economies has been correlated with that of advanced economies since the 1960s, suggesting the existence of spillovers from advanced to less developed economies. However, there is no well-established theory of international spillovers in productivity growth. This section first discusses the theoretical channels through which secular stagnation in the rest of the world could affect productivity growth in a country and then looks for evidence on these spillovers in the data.

Theory

Development economists distinguish between advanced economies that are at the world technology frontier and less advanced economies that are catching up to this frontier. *Innovation* determines productivity growth at the frontier, while away from the frontier it is determined by the *diffusion* of the technologies and processes that are used at the frontier. Technopessimists such as Gordon (2016) or Fernald (2015) attribute secular stagnation to a slowdown in productivity growth caused by a natural exhaustion of economies' innovative potential. This view does not explain why productivity growth also slowed down in countries that are catching up to the frontier by adopting existing technologies rather than by innovating. Moreover, it does not explain why productivity growth in these countries slowed during the global financial crisis.

One possible explanation for the general slowdown in productivity growth is that financial frictions may have spilled over across countries. Financial frictions can bias business investment toward more liquid, low-risk/low-return projects, which may in turn slow technological progress embodied in new capital goods or resulting from risky investments. For example, Caballero, Hoshi, and Kashyap's (2008) model shows how banking problems in Japan may have persistently depressed Japanese productivity growth. Anzoategui et al. (2016) propose a model in which an increase in demand for liquidity, as observed during the crisis, decreases investment and productivity growth. In a financially integrated world, lower productivity growth could be transmitted across countries through financial channels. This is a plausible channel of transmission for the global financial crisis, where global banks seem to have played a significant role in the transmission of the crisis from advanced to emerging-market economies (Cetorelli and Goldberg 2011).

Secular stagnation could also be diffused via international trade in goods and services. Economic researchers have often noted the simultaneous slowing of productivity growth and of trade integration after the global financial crisis (IMF 2016). According to the learning-by-exporting hypothesis, export participation improves productivity. A firm's expected profits from process or product innovation rise with the size of the final market so that increased exports allow firms to bear higher fixed costs of research and development (Rodrik 1988, Yeaple 2005). Alternatively, trade flows might facilitate international knowledge spillovers and thus contribute to the adoption of new technologies (Coe and Helpman 1995). If this is true, the fact that many advanced economies reduced their demand for imports after the global financial crisis could result in lower productivity growth in the rest of the world.

Finally, the spillovers could result from the fact that productivity is endogenous to demand—consistent with the hysteresis view that cyclical changes in demand have a permanent impact on output. For example, Benigno and Fornaro (2017) present a model in which low demand leads to low productivity growth because firms spend less on productivity-enhancing activities. A fall in global demand could thus lead to a generalized decrease in productivity growth even in a model where there is no learning-by-exporting.

Evidence

Several branches of empirical literature are relevant to quantify the theoretical mechanisms discussed above, but they have not been systematically harnessed to analyze the international transmission of secular stagnation. There is a large empirical literature on the link between exporting and productivity growth based on firm-level evidence.[4] Whereas Keller's (2004) review of the literature concluded that there is little evidence of a strong learning-by-exporting effect, recent research was more supportive of such effects (see Bustos 2011, De Loecker 2007, Lileeva and Trefler 2010). One problem with applying this research to the analysis of secular stagnation is that the results from studies based on firm-level data are often difficult to translate to the aggregate level.[5]

One line of literature investigates the financial channels of contagion during the global financial crisis and in the global financial cycle, but it does not make the link to productivity (Hausmann-Guil, van Wincoop, and Zhang 2016). Another line of literature has investigated how productivity is determined by the efficiency of factor allocation and in particular the quality of financial intermediation. For example, Adler et al. (2017) report that TFP growth fell more in companies with weaker balance sheets prior to the global financial crisis than in their counterparts with stronger balance sheets. But to the best of my knowledge this literature has not quantified the extent to which secular stagnation is transmitted internationally through financial channels.

The remainder of this section investigates the channels of international

---

4. There is an older literature based on cross-country macroeconomic evidence; see, for example, Frankel and Romer (1999).

5. Many studies estimate the impact on an individual firm of a binary decision to start exporting, which is difficult to translate into an estimate of the impact of the aggregate volume of exports on productivity. Studies based on the difference-in-difference methodology do not easily lend themselves to estimating aggregate effects.

Table 5.2 Change in total factor productivity (TFP) growth and economic integration

Variable	(1)	(2)	(3)
Exports/GDP (10^{-2})	−0.614 (0.831)	−1.395 (1.184)	−1.309 (0.905)
De jure financial openness	−1.808** (0.704)		
De facto financial integration (10^{-2})		0.006 (0.083)	
De facto banking integration (10^{-2})			0.015 (0.134)
Constant	1.499*** (0.506)	0.785* (0.463)	0.667 (0.405)
R-squared	0.108	0.033	0.039
Number of observations	81	82	77

Note: The dependent variable is the change in TFP growth between 2000–07 and 2008–14 in percentage points. Trade openness is measured as the ratio of exports to GDP in 2007 in percentage points. De jure financial openness is the Chinn-Ito index of financial openness for 2007. De facto financial integration is the ratio of foreign assets plus liabilities to GDP in 2007 in percentage points. De facto banking integration is the ratio of "other investments" assets plus liabilities to GDP in 2007 in percentage points. See appendix 5A for sources. Standard errors are in parentheses. *, **, and *** indicate statistical significance at the 10, 5, and 1 percent levels, respectively.

transmission for productivity growth with simple cross-country regressions. My main identification assumption is that in the global financial crisis the spillovers went from the advanced economies that were at the epicenter of the banking crisis to the rest of the world. The theories discussed above have different implications for which countries should have been most affected by the crisis. For example, if the main channel of transmission is financial, one should expect the countries that are more financially integrated to be more affected by the crisis. If the most important channel is trade, then countries that are most integrated with world trade should be affected the most. What do the data show?

Table 5.2 presents the results of three cross-country regressions of the change in the TFP growth rate associated with the global financial crisis on measures of financial and trade integration. The country sample includes all the countries for which data are available, excluding the countries at the center of the global financial system (the United States, the euro area, Japan, the United Kingdom, and Switzerland). Precrisis measures of economic integration are used to reduce the endogeneity bias in the explanatory variables.

Trade integration is measured by the ratio of exports to GDP in 2007 (a standard measure in the literature). Financial openness is more difficult to measure and three different indicators are used, corresponding to the three columns of the table. The first measure is the Chinn-Ito (2008) index of de jure financial openness. This index is based on binary variables that codify the tabulation of restrictions on cross-border financial transactions reported in the International Monetary Fund's *Annual Report on Exchange Arrangements and Exchange Restrictions* (AREAER). The other indicators are measures of de facto financial integration. The explanatory variable used in the second column of the table is the ratio of the sum of total foreign assets plus total foreign liabilities to GDP based on the data in Lane and Milesi-Ferretti (2017)—a measure that has often been used in the literature. The last measure is similar to the second one but is limited to the "other investments" category in foreign assets and liabilities in an attempt to capture international banking integration. All the indicators of financial integration are taken in 2007, the year before the crisis erupted.

Several observations can be made from the regression results in table 5.2. First, trade integration has a negative impact on TFP growth in all three specifications and the point estimates are economically significant. For example, the coefficient reported in the second column implies that, other things equal, having a 10 percent larger exports-to-GDP ratio in 2007 lowered postcrisis TFP growth by about 0.14 percent per year. However, this relationship is not statistically significant in any of the regressions.

Second, the impact of de jure financial integration is statistically significant whereas the impact of de facto integration is not. The impact of de jure financial openness seems to be large. Based on my estimates, increasing de jure financial openness from the Chinese to the US level is associated with a 1.8 percent reduction in TFP growth after the crisis. However, this effect seems too large to be interpreted as reflecting causality from financial openness to productivity growth and it is difficult to understand given that the main channel through which de jure openness should matter is by fostering de facto integration, and I find that de facto integration itself has no impact on productivity growth.

To summarize, postcrisis TFP growth seems orthogonal to most measures of international economic integration (with the exception of de jure financial openness). The weakness of the relationship between postcrisis TFP growth and economic openness is robust to changes in the regression specification. I tried many variants of the regressions reported in table 5.2. For example, I looked at the impact on productivity growth of a decrease in the demand for each country's exports, where demand was measured based on postcrisis growth in the country's regional export markets. The country sample was changed in different ways, for example, by excluding oil exporters or including only emerging-market and developing economies. Extreme observations were excluded. I used growth in GDP per capita (instead of TFP), which yielded several more years of data after the crisis. Standard growth regressions were tried controlling for the initial level of GDP per capita. Details of these regressions are not reported here for the sake of brevity, but the important point is that they did not substantially revise the general conclusion that there seems to be little relationship between post-crisis TFP growth and measures of economic openness.

The results presented here are perhaps not surprising from the point of view of the empirical literature that finds no robust relationship between economic openness and the decline in growth during the Great Recession (Kalemli-Ozcan, Papaioannou, and Perri 2013; Kamin and DeMarco 2012; Hausmann-Guil, van Wincoop, and Zhang 2016; IMF 2013; Lane and Milesi-Ferretti 2011). The main difference between these studies and the regressions presented here is that I look at TFP growth rather than GDP growth, and I look at it over a longer period after the crisis. Nevertheless my results are puzzling for the view that international spillovers are important in explaining why secular stagnation affected so many countries at about the same time.

Macroeconomic Spillovers: A Model

The rest of the chapter takes productivity as exogenous and focuses on the macroeconomic spillovers in the transmission of secular stagnation across countries. This section presents a model of how a small open economy responds to secular stagnation abroad. Foreign secular stagnation is represented as the combination of two developments: a decrease in the foreign real rate of interest and a decrease in foreign demand for the country's exports. The question is whether these developments can bring foreign stagnation home and through which channels.

The model is written in real terms and is intended to capture the long run. It predicts the behavior of the real interest rate, the real exchange rate, and capital flows. The real interest rate predicted by the model can be interpreted as the "natural" rate of interest—the level of the real interest rate that ensures full employment. Modern macroeconomic theory holds that the main function of monetary policy is to keep the real rate of interest close to the natural level so as to stabilize both employment and inflation.

The model is simple and does not capture all the international spillovers of interest. In particular, it takes domestic growth as given and so does not have anything to say about spillovers in productivity growth. The model focuses on the rebalancing of trade and financial flows that must take place in response to foreign secular stagnation. Some features missing from the model are discussed later in the section.

The main findings of the model are that in response to foreign secular stagnation:

- the domestic natural rate of interest falls by the same amount as the foreign rate in the long run, but less so initially;
- there is a net capital inflow and an increase in domestic demand in the short run (which is reversed in the long run); and
- restrictions to capital mobility may reduce the response of the domestic interest rate but amplify that of the real exchange rate.

The model is in continuous time and can be summarized by the following three equations:

$$\begin{cases} \dot{a}_t = x(q_t, y_t^*) + r_t^* a_t \\ \dot{a}_t = \sigma[\bar{a}(r_t^*) - a_t] \\ r_t = r_t^* + \dot{q}_t / q_t \end{cases}$$

The main variables are the net foreign assets a_t, the net trade balance x_t, the real exchange rate q_t, and the domestic and foreign real rates of interest r_t and r_t^*. The derivative of a variable is denoted with a dot.

The first equation is the balance-of-payments equation: the rate of increase in net foreign assets a_t is equal to the trade balance x_t plus the return on foreign assets. The trade balance is an increasing function of the real exchange rate q_t and of foreign demand y_t^*. The real exchange rate is defined in such a way that an increase in q corresponds to a real depreciation. A real depreciation shifts domestic and foreign spending toward the home good.

The second equation describes the dynamics of foreign assets. Foreign assets converge toward a desired level $\bar{a}$, which is a function of the return on these assets. The desired stock of net foreign wealth is an increasing function of the interest rate. This is a shortcut to capture the foreign asset dynamics resulting from open-economy models with overlapping generations such as Coeurdacier, Guibaud, and Jin (2015) or Eggertsson et al. (2016) (although the dynamics of net foreign assets are more complicated in these models).

The third equation is interest parity. The domestic real rate of interest is equal to the foreign rate plus the rate of real exchange rate depreciation. As a starting point perfect financial integration is assumed, implying that interest parity holds between domestic and foreign bonds.

The model assumes full employment so that r_t is the natural rate of interest. Foreign secular stagnation takes the form of decreases in the foreign real rate of interest, r_t^*, and in foreign demand for the country's exports, y_t^*. The question of interest is how capital flows, the real interest rate, and the real exchange rate must respond to ensure full employment at home.

Let us summarize a few key properties of the model, starting with the long run. I assume that foreign variables converge toward long-run values denoted with bars:

$$\lim_{t \to +\infty} r_t^* = \bar{r}^* \text{ and } \lim_{t \to +\infty} y_t^* = \bar{y}^*.$$

In the long run the country's foreign assets converge to $\bar{a}(\bar{r}^*)$. It then follows from the balance-of-payments equation that the real exchange rate is constant and satisfies

$$x(\bar{q}, \bar{y}^*) + \bar{r}^* \bar{a}(\bar{r}^*) = 0.$$

Secular stagnation reduces the foreign interest rate $\bar{r}^*$ and demand $\bar{y}^*$ in the long run. It follows that $\bar{q}$ increases, that is, there is a real depreciation in the long run. The real exchange rate must depreciate to offset lower foreign demand as well as the lower domestic demand coming from the decrease in foreign assets.

The real exchange rate is constant in the long run so that interest parity implies

$$\bar{r} = \bar{r}^*.$$

That is, the domestic interest rate decreases by the same amount as the foreign interest rate in the long run. This is an implication of perfect financial integration.

The transition dynamics are different. Assume that foreign secular stagnation is "announced" at time $t = 0$ in an equilibrium where the initial foreign assets are equal to zero ($a_0 = 0$). Then,

$$\sigma \bar{a}(r_0^*) = x(q_0, y_0^*).$$

The impact of foreign secular stagnation (lower r_0^* and y_0^*) on the real exchange rate is ambiguous in the short run. On one hand, the lower foreign demand y_0^* should be offset by a real depreciation (an increase in q_0). On the other hand, the lower foreign interest rate r_0^* leads to capital inflows that have an expansionary effect on the domestic economy. The real exchange rate depreciates only if the impact of lower foreign demand dominates that of higher domestic demand. In general the real exchange rate depreciates less in the short run than in the long run,

$$q_0 < \bar{q}.$$

This implies that the real exchange rate must depreciate over time ($\frac{\dot{q}_t}{q_t} > 0$) so that by interest parity

$$r_0 > r_0^*.$$

In the short run the domestic rate of interest decreases by less than the foreign rate—the interest rate pass-through is less than one-for-one.

It is important to observe that foreign secular stagnation must lead initially to a boom in capital inflows and an expansion in domestic demand. These spillovers are part and parcel of the adjustment process to secular stagnation abroad. Low foreign interest rates are expansionary and domestic demand must increase to offset the fall in foreign demand.

However, this adjustment process may have problematic side effects. The first one comes from the zero bound on the nominal interest rate. The analysis has been in real terms so far but it is not difficult to introduce monetary policy. The home central bank determines the nominal interest rate i, which is equal to the real interest rate plus inflation

$$i_t = r_t + \pi.$$

Let us assume that inflation is equal to the inflation target, π, which is exogenously determined. In general nothing guarantees that the natural rate of interest should be positive. If the inflation target is too low, the implied nominal interest rate may hit the zero lower bound. Then the economy falls into a liquidity trap with some unemployment.

The second side effect is related to the booms in capital inflows and domestic demand. These developments may lead to excessive growth in domestic credit and asset prices. The associated risks could in principle be kept in check by using macroprudential policy, but not all countries have the appropriate policy instruments and frameworks in place.

So far the analysis here has assumed perfect financial integration, but the analysis can easily be extended to the case where the arbitrage between foreign and domestic bonds is limited by financial frictions, risk premia, or capital controls. For that, one simply needs to replace r_t^* by $r_t^* + \tau_t$ in the model, where the wedge τ_t could be interpreted as a risk premium or a tax on capital inflows. Then it is easy to see that the country can insulate its interest rate from foreign secular stagnation by increasing τ_t as the foreign interest rate r_t^* goes down. This policy can prevent the country from falling into a liquidity trap. However, it could be viewed as mercantilist as it requires the real exchange rate to depreciate earlier and by a larger amount as the country keeps foreign capital out. The real interest rate can be insulated at the cost of a larger response in the real exchange rate.

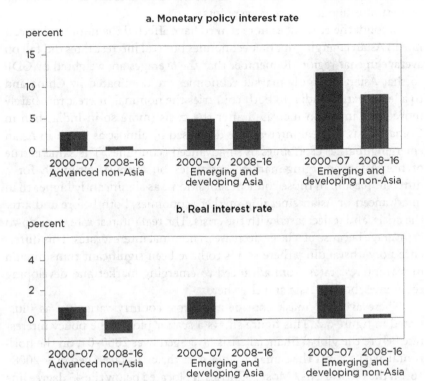

a. Monetary policy interest rate

percent

2000–07 2008–16
Advanced non-Asia

2000–07 2008–16
Emerging and
developing Asia

2000–07 2008–16
Emerging and
developing non-Asia

b. Real interest rate

percent

2000–07 2008–16
Advanced non-Asia

2000–07 2008–16
Emerging and
developing Asia

2000–07 2008–16
Emerging and
developing non-Asia

Note: The figure compares the level of the interest rate before the crisis
(2000–07) and after the crisis (2008–16). Country classification is from the IMF
World Economic Outlook and averages are GDP-weighted.

Source: IMF, *International Financial Statistics.*

Interest Rates

Having established a theoretical benchmark for the macroeconomic spillovers associated with secular stagnation, this section looks at interest rates
in the data.

Figure 5.1 compares the levels of interest rates before the global financial crisis (2000–07) and after the crisis (2008–16). The upper and lower
panels, respectively, show the nominal policy rate and the real interest rate.
The figure compares non-Asian advanced economies with emerging-market
and developing economies, both in Asia (middle bars) and outside Asia
(right bars).

The figure shows several interesting facts. First, the zero bound constraint on the nominal interest rate has not prevented advanced economies
from lowering the real interest rate into negative territory after the crisis as

they have maintained positive levels of inflation. In those economies the real interest rate has decreased by about the same amount as the nominal interest rate (about 2 percentage points).

Second, the crisis does not seem to have affected the nominal interest rate in Asian emerging-market economies but real interest rates did fall on average in that region. Remember that the averages are weighted by GDP so that Asian emerging-market economies are dominated by China and to a lesser extent India. In both countries the nominal interest rate barely moved but inflation increased after the crisis (more so in India than in China). Thus the real interest rate decreased by almost as much in Asian emerging-market economies as in advanced economies. The same is true of non-Asian emerging-market economies on average, although for a different reason. In those countries inflation was significantly higher than in advanced or Asian emerging-market economies, both before and after the crisis, and it decreased with the crisis. The real interest rate went down on average because of a large decrease in nominal interest rates. This difference notwithstanding, there seems to have been significant transmission in real interest rates from advanced to emerging-market and developing economies, both in Asia and elsewhere.

These averages mask considerable cross-country variation, as illustrated in figure 5.2. This figure shows a scatter plot of the policy interest rate before the global financial crisis (averaged over 2000–07, on the horizontal axis) against the same variable after the crisis (averaged over 2008–16, on the vertical axis). Most countries are located below the 45 degree line because their policy rates were reduced after the crisis. The figure differentiates between advanced economies and emerging-market and developing economies and labels only Asian economies.

Figure 5.2 shows that advanced and emerging-market economies have had quite different experiences with the zero lower bound. Most advanced economies are situated in the lower left side of the figure. These countries lowered their interest rates after the crisis, and many of them were constrained by the zero lower bound because their rates were already relatively low before the crisis. In Asia this group includes Japan (which was already at the lower bound before the crisis), Korea, Singapore, Hong Kong, and to a lesser extent Taiwan. Australia and New Zealand stayed away from the zero bound because they maintained higher real interest rates than their Asian advanced counterparts.

Most emerging-market economies also reduced their policy interest rates but they were much less likely to come close to the zero bound because they started from higher levels. Asian exceptions include Thailand.

Figure 5.2   Interest rates before and after the global financial crisis, by country, 2000-16

2008-16 (percent)

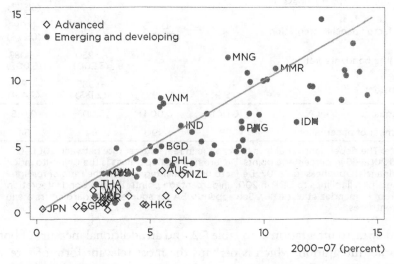

Note: The figure does not include countries that had a precrisis interest rate in excess of 15 percent. Most countries are located below the 45 degree line because their policy rate was reduced after the crisis. See table 5.1 for country key.

Source: IMF, *International Financial Statistics.*

Bulgaria is the only emerging-market economy to have a policy rate below 0.5 percent in 2016.[6]

Emerging-market economies had higher nominal interest rates in part because of higher inflation, but this is not the only reason. They also had higher *real* interest rates before the crisis. This is a silver lining of limited financial integration: keeping real interest rates high leaves more room for reducing them if necessary.

The magnitude of the fall in interest rates is very different across countries. The model presented in the previous section suggests that less financially integrated countries might be able to insulate their interest rate from foreign secular stagnation. Is this observed in the data?

One can investigate this question with cross-country regressions of the change in interest rate associated with the global financial crisis on countries' levels of financial openness. The results of four regressions are reported in table 5.3. The changes in the real interest rates that followed the global financial crisis were regressed on the same measures of de jure

6. Bulgaria has a currency board with the euro. No other emerging-market economy had a policy rate below 0.5 percent in any year after 2008.

Table 5.3 Change in real interest rate and financial integration

Variable	(1)	(2)	(3)	(4)
De jure financial openness	-0.967 (2.368)			4.396 (5.577)
De facto financial integration		-0.146 (0.234)		-0.083 (0.278)
De jure bond integration			-2.250 (3.200)	-5.083 (5.007)
Constant	-2.12 (1.519)	-1.915 (1.099)	-1.985 (2.133)	-2.903 (2.481)
R-squared	0.001	0.004	0.008	0.018
Number of observations	98	99	64	64

Note: The dependent variable is the change in real interest rate between 2000–07 and 2008–16 in percentage points. De jure financial openness is the Chinn-Ito index of financial openness for 2007. De facto financial integration is the ratio of foreign assets plus liabilities to GDP in 2007 in percentage points. De jure bond integration is from Fernandez et al. (2016). See appendix 5A for sources. Standard errors are in parentheses.

and de facto integration as in table 5.2, and an additional measure of bond market integration, which is perhaps the most relevant form of integration for interest rate parity. The last measure is taken from the database constructed by Fernandez et al. (2016). The country sample is the same as in table 5.2.

The upshot from the table is that none of the financial openness indicators explains the cross-country differences in interest rate transmission. The absence of explanatory power is robust to many changes in the regression specification. For example, it remains true if the dependent variable is the nominal (instead of real) interest rate, if the restrictions are to money market flows rather than bond flows, and if de facto integration is measured for banking specifically. It also remains true if one restricts the regression to emerging-market and developing economies. In other words, cross-country differences in interest rate transmission seem unrelated to countries' openness to financial flows.

In particular it does not seem that countries were willing or able to insulate themselves from foreign secular stagnation through capital controls. This finding may disappoint proponents of capital flow management. However, note that capital flow management is meant to buffer economies against relatively high-frequency variation in capital flows, not to insulate interest rates against persistent pressure from foreign secular stagnation.

To conclude, this analysis finds that secular stagnation affected nominal or real interest rates in a wide range of countries irrespective of their financial openness. The implications of lower interest rates were different for countries at different levels of economic and financial development. In more advanced economies the main adverse effect was to bring policy rates close to the zero bound constraint. Affected countries include Korea, Hong Kong, Taiwan, and Singapore in Asia. This problem generally did not affect emerging-market and developing economies, although Thailand is borderline in this regard. There is no evidence that emerging-market economies have insulated themselves against foreign secular stagnation by restricting their financial openness.

Credit

Real interest rates have gone down in emerging-market and developing economies. What was the impact on credit conditions? Rebalancing the economy from foreign to domestic demand is a natural adjustment to foreign secular stagnation, as shown in the model presented earlier. This rebalancing could be accompanied by an increase in domestic credit. At the same time, this expansion is problematic if it is excessive and leads to a boom-bust cycle. The buildup of excessive credit features prominently in discussions about financial crises. Importantly, from a policy perspective, large credit expansions have been found to be a reliable early warning indicator of banking crises or severe distress. Some models, such as Eggertsson and Krugman (2012), explain secular stagnation in advanced economies by the deleveraging in the private nonfinancial sector that took place after the crisis. An excessive expansion of credit in emerging-market and developing economies might generate concerns about a delayed transmission of secular stagnation from advanced economies.

I look into this question by using the credit gap measures produced by the Bank for International Settlements (BIS). BIS measures the credit-to-GDP gap as the deviation of the credit-to-GDP ratio from its long-run trend. This measure takes account of all sources of credit to the private nonfinancial sector, rather than just bank credit. Drehmann (2013) finds that total credit developments predict the risk of systemic crises better than indicators based solely on bank credit.

Figure 5.3 shows the credit gap in advanced and emerging-market economies between 2000 and 2016. Advanced economies witnessed a sharp expansion of credit, followed by a sharp restriction after the global financial crisis. By contrast, the credit gap expanded continuously in emerging-market and developing economies. The magnitude of this development reflects primarily the expansion of credit in China (the credit gap of emerging-market economies is heavily influenced by China because the average is GDP-weighted). But the credit gap did not expand just in China. In Asia, Hong Kong, Singapore, and to a lesser extent Thailand, Indonesia, and Malaysia also experienced large increases in their credit gaps.

Why do some countries have credit booms while others do not? I found no significant cross-country correlation between credit booms and

Figure 5.3 Credit gap, 2000–16

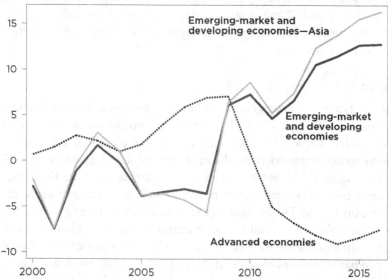

percent

- Emerging-market and developing economies—Asia
- Emerging-market and developing economies
- Advanced economies

Note: The figure shows the credit gaps as measured by the Bank for International Settlements. Country classification is from the IMF's *World Economic Outlook* (see table 5.1 for Asian countries). Averages are GDP-weighted.

Sources: IMF, *World Economic Outlook*; Bank for International Settlements.

low real or nominal interest rates in the data (the regression results are not reported here). In the case of China the expansion in credit was driven by administrative measures rather than lower market interest rates. As shown in figure 5.4 the intensity of macroprudential measures significantly increased after the crisis in emerging-market economies and especially in Asia. Macroprudential policy thus appropriately leaned against the wind but without fully containing the underlying pressure. Anecdotal evidence suggests, in the case of China, that macroprudential restrictions often moved the credit growth pressure from one area of the economy to another without having serious effects on total credit.

The model presented earlier suggests that domestic financial developments may be related to the rebalancing of the economy toward domestic demand associated with a decrease in the current account balance, i.e., an increase in net capital inflows. Indeed, one variable that is clearly correlated with credit is the current account balance. Figure 5.5 plots the change in the credit gap between 2007 and 2016, on the vertical axis, against the change in the current account balance over the same period, on the horizontal axis. All variables are in share of GDP. There is very significant negative correlation between the two variables.

Figure 5.4 Intensity of macroprudential policies, 2000–13

intensity

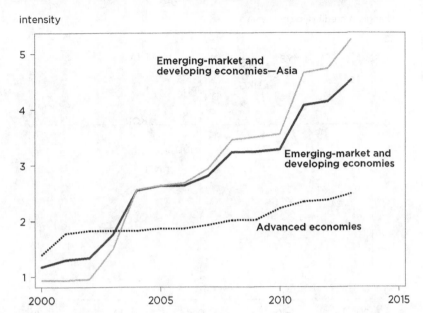

Note: The figure shows the intensity of macroprudential policy as measured by Cerrutti, Claessens, and Laeven (2015). Country classification is from the IMF's *World Economic Outlook* (see table 5.1 for Asian countries). Averages are GDP-weighted.
Source: Cerrutti, Claessens, and Laeven (2015); IMF, *World Economic Outlook*.

On average the countries that had credit booms also saw an increase in net capital inflows (or a decrease in net capital outflows). The line of best fit implies that a 1 percent increase in net capital inflows is associated with a 3.7 percent increase in the credit gap. Several Asian emerging-market economies are in the upper-left quadrant of the figure—countries that had both a decrease in the current account balance and an increase in domestic credit.

One might interpret this correlation as a manifestation of the global financial cycle, with credit booms being financed by capital inflow surges.[7] But there are several reasons why this is probably not the main explanation for the correlation observed in figure 5.5. First, the current account balance measures net capital outflows, not the much larger gross capital flows that analysts have focused on in recent discussions of the global financial cycle. Second, the figure focuses on a relatively long period (nine years), which is the appropriate frequency to study secular stagnation but probably too long for the global financial cycle. Third, several countries close to the

---

7. Studies on the correlation between capital inflows and credit include Magud, Reinhart, and Vesperoni (2014) and Avdjiev et al. (2017).

Figure 5.5 Current account balance and credit gap, 2007-16

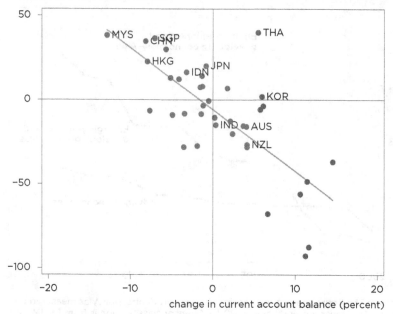

change in credit gap (percent)

change in current account balance (percent)

Note: See table 5.1 for country key.
Sources: IMF, *World Economic Outlook*; Bank for International Settlements.

regression line were not severely affected by the global financial cycle. For example, it is clear in the case of China that the decrease in its current account balance and the concomitant increase in domestic credit are not the result of a surge in capital inflows. Rather, the Chinese authorities had to compensate for the decrease in foreign demand by raising domestic demand, which they did through a credit stimulus.

An interpretation of figure 5.5 that is more in line with the model presented earlier is that changes in credit reflect demand rebalancing that followed the global financial crisis. The crisis was followed by a contraction in current account surpluses and deficits. The countries in the upper-left quadrant of the plot are countries that, like China, had to stimulate domestic demand in order to offset the reduction in foreign demand. The countries in the lower-right quadrant of the plot are advanced economies that, like the United States, had to reduce their current account deficits and their domestic demand after the crisis (in Asia this group includes Australia and New Zealand). The main takeaway from the figure is that changes in domestic demand were strongly correlated with changes in domestic credit during that period.

Whether the credit growth observed in emerging-market economies such as China is sustainable is a source of concern for the international community. In its latest Article IV consultations with China the IMF observes that among the 43 cases of credit booms in which the credit-to-GDP ratio increased by more than 30 percentage points over a five-year period, only five cases ended without a major growth slowdown or a financial crisis (IMF 2017b). The IMF staff recommend deep reforms to transition from the current growth model that relies on credit-fed investment toward less credit-intensive growth. This suggests that the international transmission of secular stagnation may go beyond what has been observed so far since the global financial crisis. The demand rebalancing that took place after the global financial crisis may have come at the cost of financial developments that plant the seeds of secular stagnation in the future.

Conclusion

This analysis revolved around two symptoms of secular stagnation, low productivity growth and low interest rates. Productivity growth and interest rates have decreased everywhere since the early 1990s, with the global financial crisis marking a watershed in these developments. During the crisis, spillovers went from the advanced economies that were at the epicenter of the banking crisis to the rest of the world. Thus this chapter uses the global financial crisis as a "natural experiment" that can shed light on the mechanisms of international transmission of secular stagnation.

Productivity growth has decreased in advanced economies as well as countries that are far from the technology frontier. This is puzzling because the determinants of growth should not be the same in the former and in the latter. The chapter discussed several channels involving trade and financial flows by which low productivity growth could spill over from advanced to developing economies. However, the analysis of the data in this chapter does not support the importance of these channels, and the reason why TFP growth fell in so many countries at about the same time remains a mystery. I doubt that much more information can be obtained from the type of cross-country regressions presented in this chapter and believe that more efforts should be put into extracting information from firm-level evidence, along the lines of Adler et al. (2017).

Nominal interest rates hit the zero lower bound in most advanced economies at the time of the global financial crisis, whereas they did not seem to change very much in the rest of the world. However, this analysis found that *real* interest rates decreased by the same amount in emerging-market economies as in advanced economies. There is no evidence that countries that were more closed financially were willing or able to insulate their interest rates from foreign secular stagnation.

Low interest rate environments can have a number of adverse effects. One is to push the economy into a liquidity trap where monetary policy loses a lot of its traction. Another potential problem is the emergence of unsustainable booms in capital inflows, credit, and asset prices. To some degree credit and asset price increases should be expected as they are part of the natural process of adjustment to foreign secular stagnation. But these developments, if excessive and left unchecked, can also lead to costly financial crises down the road.

Asian advanced economies behaved similarly to advanced economies elsewhere. They had relatively low levels of inflation and nominal interest rates before the crisis and were pulled toward liquidity traps at the time of the crisis. Leaving Japan aside, nominal interest rates fell closest to zero in Hong Kong and Singapore, followed by Korea and Taiwan. Australia and New Zealand were somewhat less affected because these countries had higher real and nominal interest rates before the crisis.

Emerging-market and developing economies generally remained at a safe distance from liquidity traps (with Thailand perhaps an exception in Asia). These countries were protected not so much by lower levels of international financial integration as by the fact that they had higher levels of nominal interest rates before the crisis. This is due in part to higher inflation than in advanced economies but also to higher *real* interest rates. Thus what could be construed as a cost of low financial integration (a higher cost of capital) became somewhat of a blessing in an environment of global secular stagnation.

As for the other potential cost of low interest rates—the risk of unsustainable credit booms—evidence shows that the credit boom that turned to a bust in advanced economies was replaced by a credit boom of even greater magnitude in emerging-market economies. Excessive expansion of credit generates concerns of a delayed transmission of secular stagnation from advanced economies. Global secular stagnation could enter a new phase if the emerging-market credit boom turned into a bust.

Appendix 5A Data Sources

Interest Rates. The source for the nominal interest rate is the IMF *International Financial Statistics*. The central bank interest rate is the minimum of the discount rate and the central bank policy rate when one or the other is available. In selected economies where neither rate was available (Argentina, the Czech Republic, Malaysia, Mexico, Poland, and Russia), the minimum of the money market rate and the treasury bill rate was used.

The real exchange rate was derived by subtracting the inflation rate (measured as the annual change in the consumer price index from the IMF *World Economic Outlook*).

Productivity. Total factor productivity (TFP) is from the Penn World Tables version 9.0 (Feenstra, Inklaar, and Timmer 2015). I used TFP at constant national prices (RTFPNA), which is the recommended measure to compare productivity growth over time in a given country. This variable is normalized to 1 in 2005 for all countries. To obtain the TFP levels reported in figure 5.1 RTFPNA is multiplied by the value of CTFP in 2005 (CTFP measures the productivity level across countries in each year).

Credit. The source is credit-to-GDP gap statistics from the Bank for International Settlements. See Dembiermont, Drehmann, and Muksakunratana (2013).

Financial Openness. The Chinn-Ito index of financial openness is described in Chinn and Ito (2008). This index is based on the binary dummy variables that codify the tabulation of restrictions on cross-border financial transactions reported in the IMF's *Annual Report on Exchange Arrangements and Exchange Restrictions*. The measure of bond market integration is from Fernandez et al. (2016). The data to construct de facto measures of international financial integration come from the External Wealth of Nations dataset, constructed by Lane and Milesi-Ferretti (2007).

References

Acharya, Sushant, and Julien Bengui. 2016. Liquidity Traps, Capital Flows and Currency Wars. University of Montreal. Photocopy.

Adler, Gustavo, Romain Duval, Davide Furceri, K. Sinem, Ksenia Koloskova, and Marcos Poplawski-Ribeiro. 2017. *Gone with the Headwinds: Global Productivity*. IMF Staff Discussion Note 17/04. Washington: International Monetary Fund.

Andrews, Dan, Chiara Criscuolo, and Peter N. Gal. 2016. *The Best versus the Rest: The Global Productivity Slowdown, Divergence across Firms and the Role of Public Policy*. OECD Productivity Working Paper 5. Paris: Organization for Economic Cooperation and Development.

Anzoategui, Diego, Diego Comin, Mark Gertler, and Joseba Martinez. 2016. *Endogenous Technology Adoption and R&D as Sources of Business Cycle Persistence*. NBER Working Paper 22005. Cambridge, MA: National Bureau of Economic Research.

Avdjiev, Stefan, Bryan Hardy, Sebnem Kalemli-Ozcan, and Luis Servén. 2017. *Gross Capital Inflows to Banks, Corporates and Sovereigns*. NBER Working Paper 23116. Cambridge, MA: National Bureau of Economic Research.

Benigno, Gianluca, and Luca Fornaro. 2017. *Stagnation Traps*. ECB Working Paper 2038. Frankfurt: European Central Bank.

Bustos, Paula. 2011. Trade Liberalization, Exports and Technology Upgrading: Evidence on the Impact of MERCOSUR on Argentinean Firms. *American Economic Review* 101, no. 1: 304–40.

Caballero, Ricardo J., Emmanuel Farhi, and Pierre-Olivier Gourinchas. 2015. *Global Imbalances and Currency Wars at the ZLB*. NBER Working Paper 21670. Cambridge, MA: National Bureau of Economic Research.

Caballero, Ricardo J., Takeo Hoshi, and Anil K Kashyap. 2008. Zombie Lending and Depressed Restructuring in Japan. *American Economic Review* 98, no. 5: 1943–77.

Cerrutti, Eugenio, Stijn Claessens, and Luc Laeven. 2015. *The Use and Effectiveness of Macroprudential Policies: New Evidence*. IMF Working Paper 15/21. Washington: International Monetary Fund.

Cetorelli, Nicola, and Linda S. Goldberg. 2011. Global Banks and International Shock Transmission: Evidence from the Crisis. *IMF Economic Review* 59: 41–6. Washington: International Monetary Fund.

Chinn, Menzie D., and Hiro Ito. 2008. A New Measure of Financial Openness. *Journal of Comparative Policy Analysis* 10, no. 3: 309–22.

Coe, David T., and Elhanan Helpman. 1995. International R&D Spillovers. *European Economic Review* 39, no. 5: 859–87.

Coeurdacier, Nicolas, Stéphane Guibaud, and Keyu Jin. 2015. Credit Constraints and Growth in a Global Economy. *American Economic Review* 105, no. 9: 2838–81.

Cook, David, and Michael B. Devereux. 2013. Sharing the Burden: Monetary and Fiscal Responses to a World Liquidity Trap. *American Economic Journal: Macroeconomics* 5, no. 3: 190–228.

Corsetti, Giancarlo, Eleonora Mavroeidi, Gregory Thwaites, and Martin Wolf. 2017. Step Away from the Zero Lower Bound: Small Open Economies in a World of Secular Stagnation. Cambridge University. Photocopy.

De Gregorio, José. 2017. Productivity in Emerging-Market Economies: Slowdown or Stagnation? Paper presented at conference on the Policy Implications of Sustained Low Productivity Growth, Peterson Institute for International Economics, Washington, November 9.

De Loecker, Jan. 2007. Do Exports Generate Higher Productivity? Evidence from Slovenia. *Journal of International Economics* 73: 69–98.

Dembiermont, Christian, Mathias Drehmann, and Siriporn Muksakunratana. 2013. How much does the private sector really borrow? A new database for total credit to the private non-financial sector. *BIS Quarterly Review* (March): 65–81. Basel: Bank for International Settlements.

Devereux, Michael B., and James Yetman. 2014. Capital Controls, Global Liquidity Traps, and the International Policy Trilemma. *Scandinavian Journal of Economics* 116, no. 1: 158–89.

Drehmann, Mathias. 2013. Total Credit as an Early Warning Indicator for Systemic Banking Crises. *BIS Quarterly Review* (June): 41–45. Basel: Bank for International Settlements.

Eggertsson, Gauti B., and Paul Krugman. 2012. Debt, Deleveraging, and the Liquidity Trap: A Fisher-Minsky-Koo Approach. *Quarterly Journal of Economics* 127, no. 3: 1469–513.

Eggertsson, Gauti B., Neil R. Mehrotra, Sanjay R. Singh, and Lawrence H. Summers. 2016. A Contagious Malady? Open Economy Dimensions of Secular Stagnation. *IMF Economic Review* 64, no. 4: 581–634.

Feenstra, Robert C., Robert Inklaar, and Marcel P. Timmer. 2015. The Next Generation of the Penn World Table. *American Economic Review* 105, no. 10: 3150–82.

Fernald, John G. 2015. Productivity and Potential Output Before, During, and After the Great Recession. *NBER Macroeconomics Annual* 29, no. 1: 1–51. Cambridge, MA: National Bureau of Economic Research.

Fernandez, Andrés, Michael W. Klein, Alessandro Rebucci, Martin Schindler, and Martin Uribe. 2016. Capital Control Measures: A New Dataset. *IMF Economic Review* 64, no. 3: 548–74. Washington: International Monetary Fund.

Frankel, Jeffrey, and David Romer. 1999. Does Trade Cause Growth? *American Economic Review* 89, no. 3: 380–99.

Fujiwara, Ippei, Tomoyuki Nakajima, Nao Sudo, and Yuki Teranishi. 2013. Global Liquidity Trap. *Journal of Monetary Economics* 60, no. 3: 936–49.

Gordon, Robert J. 2016. *The Rise and Fall of American Growth: The US Standard of Living since the Civil War*. Princeton, NJ: Princeton University Press.

Hausmann-Guil, Guillermo, Eric van Wincoop, and Gang Zhang. 2016. The Great Recession: Divide between Integrated and Less Integrated Countries. *IMF Economic Review* 64, no. 1: 134–76. Washington: International Monetary Fund.

IMF (International Monetary Fund). 2013. Dancing Together? Spillovers, Common Shocks, and the Role of Financial and Trade Linkages. Chapter 3 in *World Economic Outlook* (October). Washington.

IMF (International Monetary Fund). 2016. Global Trade: What's Behind the Slowdown? Chapter 2 in *World Economic Outlook* (October). Washington.

IMF (International Monetary Fund). 2017a. Asia at Risk of Growing Old before Becoming Rich? In *Regional Economic Outlook, Asia and Pacific* (April). Washington.

IMF (International Monetary Fund). 2017b. *People's Republic of China*. IMF Country Reports 17/247 and 17/248. Washington.

Kalemli-Ozcan, Sebnem, Elias Papaioannou, and Fabrizio Perri. 2013. Global Banks and Crisis Transmission. *Journal of International Economics* 89, no. 2: 495–510.

Kamin, Steven B., and Laurie Pounder DeMarco. 2012. How did a domestic housing slump turn into a global financial crisis? *Journal of International Money and Finance* 31, no. 1: 10–41.

Keller, Wolfgang. 2004. International Technology Diffusion. *Journal of Economic Literature* 42, no. 3 (September): 752–82.

Lane, Philip R., and Gian Maria Milesi-Ferretti. 2007. The External Wealth of Nations Mark II: Revised and Extended Estimates of Foreign Assets and Liabilities, 1970–2004. *Journal of International Economics* 73, no. 2: 223–50.

Lane, Philip R., and Gian Maria Milesi-Ferretti. 2011. The Cross-Country Incidence of the Global Crisis. *IMF Economic Review* 59, no. 1: 77–110. Washington: International Monetary Fund.

Lane, Philip R., and Gian Maria Milesi-Ferretti. 2017. *International Financial Integration in the Aftermath of the Global Financial Crisis*. IMF Working Paper 17/115. Washington: International Monetary Fund.

Lileeva, A., and D. Trefler. 2010. Improved Access to Foreign Markets Raises Plant-level Productivity ... For Some Plants. *Quarterly Journal of Economics* 125, no. 3: 1051–99.

Magud, Nicolas E., Carmen M. Reinhart, and Esteban R. Vesperoni. 2014. Capital Inflows, Exchange Rate Flexibility and Credit Booms. *Review of Development Economics* 18, no. 3: 415–30.

Rodrik, Dani. 1988. *Closing the Technology Gap: Does Trade Liberalization Really Help?* NBER Working Paper 2654. Cambridge, MA: National Bureau of Economic Research.

Rose, Andrew K., and Mark M. Spiegel. 2011. Cross-Country Causes and Consequences of the Crisis: An Update. *European Economic Review* 55, no. 3: 309–24.

Yeaple, Stephen Ross. 2005. A Simple Model of Firm Heterogeneity, International Trade, and Wages. *Journal of international Economics* 65, no. 1: 1–20.

6

Getting Out of Secular Stagnation: Turning Japanese May Be a Good Thing Now

ADAM S. POSEN

Economists used to play a game asking which country was turning Japanese. Back in 2003, I wrote a paper playing off this game, where I assessed whether Germany might fall into a Japan-like trap of persistent low growth (Posen 2003). Today, the fear of suffering Japan's fate persists for advanced economies, including those in Asia (see chapter 8 by Dongchul Cho and Kyooho Kwon in this volume). But the analogy is mistaken. Rather than focusing on the risk of turning Japanese in the late 1990s sense, it would be better for countries in Asia to learn how Japan got itself off the growth floor from 2003 to 2018. It is true that both productivity growth and labor force growth have slowed in most of the advanced economies and an increasing number of emerging markets, even in Asia.

There is a popular but incorrect characterization of Japan as having suffered two lost decades. Japan lost one decade, where the effect of an asset price collapse was prolonged and deepened by a set of idiosyncratic Japan-specific factors, many of which were due to policy (Posen 2010, Kuttner and Posen 2002). The lost decade ended with the Koizumi administration and the cleanup of the country's banks in late 2002/early 2003. Since then, per capita GDP growth in Japan has actually been quite good, especially in comparison to the rest of the G-7 nations, even leaving aside the global financial crisis. Productivity growth has been decent. If anything, the macroeconomic challenges that Japan faced in failing to increase inflation and to

Adam S. Posen is the president of the Peterson Institute for International Economics.

reduce government debt have been faced simultaneously by other countries and so are no longer Japan-specific. The puzzling failure of inflation to increase, despite best-practice aggressive monetary policy, remains troubling but should not obscure the progress in the real economy.

Japan's growth and productivity performance stands out against demographic decline at home and increasing stagnation and even crisis among many of its trading partners. The eventual cleanup of the financial system and reversal of mistaken contractionary macroeconomic policies were necessary to end the decline (Posen 2010). But they are not sufficient to explain the long and resilient subsequent recovery. Instead, Japan took major steps to address the sources of secular stagnation that were open to domestic amelioration: using the fiscal room still available to smooth exogenous shocks like the Fukushima natural disasters and the spillovers from the global financial crisis; partially offsetting the demographic-driven shrinkage of the labor force by increasing female labor force participation and employment flexibility; and in recent years, under Prime Minister Shinzō Abe, pursuing greater economic integration with the world, notably via the Comprehensive and Progressive Agreement for Trans-Pacific Partnership (CPTPP) and EU-Japan trade agreements. These steps were taken slowly and did not fulfill all the promises of Abenomics, let alone the free market fantasies of some Western commentators. These three initiatives, however, when accelerated by Abe, did materially improve Japan's real economic performance and resilience. As such, this three-part framework—fiscal stabilization, labor market reform, and trade integration—provides a useful model for emerging Asia today.

Reconsidering the Japanese experience along these lines raises three questions. First, has recent underperformance in Japan been a puzzle for modern macroeconomics? In other words, since Abenomics has basically done many of the things that we were all calling for—including aggressive monetary stimulus with a forward-looking positive inflation target—why has it not resulted in consistently positive inflation near the target? I believe that this can in part be explained by the overemphasis on a credibility-centered view of macroeconomic policy (Posen 2012) and by a failure to properly account for the effects of nonmonetary factors on inflation.

Second, does the apparent failure to raise the inflation rate in Japan matter for economic performance? My sense is that it does, but much less significantly than many of us initially thought. Despite consistently failing to reach its inflation target, Japan never fell into the much feared deflation spirals that the United States, for example, experienced in the 1930s. For this reason, the growth and welfare costs of low inflation are much lower than we initially believed, although they are not negligible.

Third, how should we think about the political economy in a context where the punishments for bad policies and the rewards for good policies are, if not completely muted, at least substantially delayed? How should we think about the political economy of reform if inadequate monetary policies do not translate into deflation spirals and if long-term interest rates do not go up against the backdrop of unsustainable fiscal policies? In Posen (2003), I argued that the pressure provided by European regional integration saved Germany from itself. If anything, this lesson applies more to Asia today than to Europe then.

Fiscal Room and Expectation-Centered View of Macro Policies

It is often said that Abenomics has generated a series of weird and hard to rationalize economic facts. Monetary policy appears unable to offset the impact of fiscal shocks (e.g., as in 2014 with the rise in the consumption tax). Inflation and imports appear to be insensitive to the long and sustained depreciation of the yen. If not dead, the Phillips curve is at least dormant. And most stunningly of all, Japan continues to rack up public debt and its long-term interest rates do not rise. The discrepancy between many economists' predictions and essential observations reflects two shortcomings of our standard models. First, too much emphasis is put on forward-looking expectations. Second, not enough emphasis is put on the short- and medium-term impacts of nonmonetary factors on inflation and output.

Take fiscal policy, where our academic models assume that, at the long-run horizon, all debts must be paid off completely somehow and that implies some Ricardian equivalence affecting today's behavior of savers. In this world, the impact of an increase in the consumption tax should have been particularly small given Japan's large stock of public debt. After all, these debts would have to be repaid at some point by this or near future generations of consumers. To the extent that this generation cares about future generations, changing the particular time profile for repaying this liability should not have a large economic impact. Unfortunately, the tax hikes of 1997 and 2014, among others, did have a large recessionary impact. Yet those of us who discounted the importance of this notion of perfect foresight were not surprised (Kuttner and Posen 2002).

In the spirit of the view that inflation is "always and everywhere a monetary phenomenon" (Friedman 1963), market monetarists also argued that the Abe 2014 consumption tax hike should have had no negative impact as long as the fiscal shock could be fully offset by monetary policy. In this view, the negative impact of the value-added tax hike on output and inflation reflected a failure by the Bank of Japan (BoJ) to provide enough monetary stimulus. At this point, it is, however, worth remembering that since the bank's new leadership took over in April 2013, the BoJ has done pretty much everything that the likes of Paul Krugman, Ben Bernanke, Lars Svensson, and I asked them to do a decade earlier.

The BoJ has announced a positive inflation target. It has bought long-term rather than short-term bonds. It has let the exchange rate go. It has coordinated with the government when fiscal expansion occurred. Some would even say that it has compromised its independence, which I think is inaccurate but should be inflationary as a market perception. In any case, this is what the liquidity trap literature recommended (Krugman 1998). Despite this, we have not seen huge inflation, and the contraction in growth due to the consumption tax increase was not offset.

Remember, the fact that we are not seeing major moves in interest rates in response to much higher public debt levels is not specific to Japan. We are not just disproving Reinhart and Rogoff's (2010) mythical 90 percent debt-to-GDP ratio as a tipping point for government debt sustainability but also learning that our simple framework for distinguishing permanent and temporary tax policy impacts is inadequate. This is not to say that even Japan's net debt (currently at 160 percent of GDP) is in any sense on a sustainable path, given demographics and healthcare commitments. It is to say that some measures of financial repression and monetary financing are clearly more effective at calming individual behavior than one would have been led to believe by much of the economics profession in recent years.

Arguably, what governments spend or tax, and when they do it, may matter more than debt levels. Governments in emerging Asia have long been predisposed to being fiscally conservative for good reason. The history of their counterparts among the economies of Latin America and Eastern and Southern Europe serves as a warning against budgetary laxity. Japan's experience, however, is an equally valid caution against abjuring fiscal stabilization too blindly. There are shocks, often financial, that are too sizable and panic inducing to be dealt with by monetary policy alone. When Japan resolutely refused to use the fiscal means it had in the 1990s and early 2000s, it made matters far worse (Posen 1998, 2010). Of course, the problems caused by premature austerity starting in 2010 for most of the European Union, including the United Kingdom, and to a lesser degree the United States are self-evident. While evidence on labor market hysteresis is mixed, it is clear that the negative effects of persistent downturns on investment and politics are asymmetrically larger than the costs of extended booms. Part of Japan's success since 2003 has been a more flexible fiscal response when needed.

Determining available fiscal room is challenging both analytically and politically. Even robust clear analysis will not always restrain political desire for wasteful procyclical fiscal policies (as exemplified by the US fiscal stance of 2018–19). Temporary targeted stimulus programs linked to a clear shock are different, however, and seem to be recognized as such by markets and households. The first important thing is to try to keep fiscal policy on a broadly sustainable trend in terms of limits on primary deficits so that there is room to aid. The second key measure is to have savers who maintain faith in domestic currency–denominated assets, if not excessive home bias. On both these counts, much of emerging Asia shares the attributes that enable Japan to maintain fiscal stabilization capacity even today: high household saving rates, local institutions and vehicles for safety depositing those savings, monetary (a.k.a. price) stability, common support for public investment projects, and the ability to collect taxes when necessary. Given these widespread attributes, it would be wise for Asian governments to advance their fiscal conservatism to allow for stabilization policy against negative shocks, as Japan has rightly done.

Reemphasizing the Role of Demographic and Structural Factors in Growth

The view that the BoJ has not done enough to raise inflation expectations is just not convincing. An alternative hypothesis is that our standard models have simply a too naïve view of the inflation process. In particular, they fail to recognize that nonmonetary factors have a major influence on inflation in the short and medium runs. Once we account for these factors and recognize that they have over the past decade all been disinflationary, then the difficulty faced by Japan and its spread to other advanced economies become less puzzling.

Take recent labor market changes, notably the addition of many female workers and workers working flexible hours rather than traditional full-time Japanese employment patterns (see chapter 7 by Kyoji Fukao in this volume). People generally fail to comprehend the scale of these rapid changes in Japan. "Womenomics," as the policy of incentives to bring more women into the workforce has been dubbed, has raised female labor force participation by over 3 percentage points in about five years. This means that more than 1.5 million women have rejoined a shrinking workforce of about 60 million. Many of these women have joined the workforce on a part-time or flexible basis, but we know from the Nordic experience that this is one way of retaining women in the workforce, so it should not be discounted.

Such a large structural shock is disinflationary, if not deflationary, in the short run. First, in the absence of an increase in labor demand, increases in the supply of labor decrease wages and thus prices. Already in Germany in 2003, it was clear that the Hartz IV labor market reform had this side effect. Second, and often less understood, it is deflationary because of how it changes the composition of the labor force. Bringing more women into the labor force means bringing in people who are paid less than comparable male workers because of both differentials in seniority and unfair treatment. An increase in part-time workers also has a similar effect on the aggregate. We do not yet have a specific quantification of this effect for Japan, but a recent decomposition by Daly, Hobijn, and Pyle (2016) for the United States suggests that these composition effects actually account for the main drag on wage growth between 2010 and 2016. Over these years, the United States has seen large outflows of baby boomers from the labor force, large inflows of new entrants into the labor force, and large flows of workers from part-time to full-time jobs. As the retiring baby boomers typically earn above the median, these margins pull down median earnings growth. The effects are much larger in Japan given the scale of the changes.

From a productivity point of view, the increase in female labor is hopeful because the most productive women are the first to come back into the workforce. These women are presumably displacing or competing with some men who are underqualified for the jobs they hold (even if sexism dampens this effect). So it is a positive supply shock, with an additional deflationary effect on aggregate wages.

There is a tendency to take demographics as destiny. This view is related in spirit as well as substance to the idea of the middle-income trap. Both compel policymakers to be realistic about the inability to sustain high GDP growth rates as economies age and develop. In chapter 8 in this volume, Cho and Kwon make a strong case of this sort for Japan, Korea, and China in sequence. It is better as well as quite feasible to treat these factors like a golf handicap—one cannot expect to putt or drive in one's 50s as one did in one's 20s, let alone score the same as a touring pro. A golfer can, however, continue to work on her or his swing, get the right clubs, and work to improve even if their handicaps do not go all the way to zero. Not only is the game still worth playing but also expectations can be beaten.

The transformation of the Japanese labor supply has been tremendous through a combination of female labor force participation increases, greater flexibility in work hours, and contracting and informal acceptance of more migrant workers. This has all been achieved with little fiscal effect in terms of changes to benefits and taxes and with no social dislocation of note. The result has been a postponement of labor force shrinkage by more than five years and improved productivity to boot. Though Japan and Korea were and remain laggards in gender equality in employment, all of emerging Asia can offset the effects of aging by better utilizing female labor supply. Enhancements to labor market flexibility, particularly for young people—if their employment remains in the formal sector of the economy—can serve a similar goal.

Unlike during the 1990s, many of the observed phenomena in Japan today—low wage growth, low exchange rate pass-through to inflation, a barely visible short-run Phillips curve, low long-term interest rates despite debt accumulation, low response of imports to depreciation, among others—are simultaneously occurring worldwide. The depreciation of the yen between 2013 and 2016 from ¥79 to ¥120 against the dollar without appreciable inflation has raised issues to do with exchange rate pass-through and the trade balance. But this issue of diminished exchange rate pass-through is hardly specific to Japan. For economies at the upper end of the international division of labor, this is the result of global supply chains, network effects, and trade in services. Like Japan, the United Kingdom showed a lack of sustained inflation passthrough following a 25 percent depreciation of the sterling in 2008.

Integration of production is certainly not enough to fully explain the limited net export improvement following a depreciation, especially in societies where household consumption of imported goods remains high and where the manufacturing share of GDP is declining. But if this is a puzzle, it is a more interesting and deeper puzzle than just one about understanding Japan.

Even the absence of large balance sheet effects (Koo 2003) as an engine for investment is not specific to Japan. The situation in the United States and some Western European countries is similar. There is no question that the resolution of the banking crisis in 2003 undertaken by Heizo Takenaka, then minister of financial services, which included recapitalization and consolidation of the banking sector, was a necessary condition to get Japan out of its lost decade. But it must be reckoned that while fixing a banking crisis prevents bad outcomes, it does not seem to be sufficient to stimulate good outcomes. Clean balance sheets across the Japanese economy seem to have brought less benefit in terms of growth and investment than we expected. Demand had to come from abroad, as did supply-enhancing competition and efficiencies.

Can Regional Integration Prevent Domestic Stagnation Traps?

In Posen (2003) I argued that for an advanced economy to perpetually stagnate, its political economy must have four syndromes: (1) incomplete financial liberalization where nonperforming banks are not allowed to fail despite deregulation; (2) uncoordinated deflationary macroeconomic policy; (3) financially and politically passive citizens; and (4) a lack of openness to trade or capital flows or foreign ideas.

What made Japan different was that obvious economic underperformance, fed by regulatory neglect and deflationary policies (not to mention overt corruption), would not and did not turn into public outcry. Government and established interests had eluded most pressures for change. Passivity was reinforced by the closed nature of much of Japan's economy and society, as reflected by its discouragement of immigration and the virtual absence of regional security or trade integration.

Germany, in contrast, was spared from this passivity by its long-standing openness and commitment to international economic integration. If anything, it was forced to be more open, it was forced to be more responsive, it was forced to better coordinate monetary and fiscal policies by the European Central Bank, albeit against its will.

That then raises the question of whether there is now enough openness and integration in Asia to forestall falling into the trap of repressing savings, in which an economy's savers cannot force accountability either by exiting the system (taking capital out) or by voicing complaints effectively. It also raises the question whether aging groups will push for deflation and protectionism. I agree with Subir Gokarn (see chapter 17 in this volume) that much of emerging Asia isn't there yet. But a new Asian growth impetus focused on regional integration makes economic sense. From a political economy point of view, integration would also be beneficial as it would help generate external pressure against the status quo, which is still missing in many Asian economies. The CPTPP, Regional Comprehensive Economic Partnership, and other plurilateral trade arrangements, as well as decentralized efforts to increase intraregional trade and investment, will pay off along multiple dimensions—as Japan is belatedly but now decidedly experiencing.

References

Daly, Mary C., Bart Hobijn, and Benjamin Pyle. 2016. *What's Up with Wage Growth?* FRBSF Economic Letter 2016-07 (March 7). San Francisco, CA: Federal Reserve Bank of San Francisco.

Friedman, Milton. 1963. *Inflation: Causes and Consequences.* Bombay: Asian Publishing House.

Koo, Richard. 2003. *Balance Sheet Recession: Japan's Struggle with Uncharted Economics and Its Global Implications.* Hoboken, NJ: Wiley and Sons.

Krugman, Paul. 1998. *It's Baaack: Japan's Slump and the Return of the Liquidity Trap.* Brookings Papers on Economic Activity 29, no. 2: 137–206. Washington: Economic Studies Program, Brookings Institution.

Kuttner, Kenneth N., and Adam S. Posen. 2002. Fiscal Policy Effectiveness in Japan. *Journal of the Japanese and International Economies* 16, no. 4 (December): 536–58.

Posen, Adam S. 1998. *Restoring Japan's Economic Growth.* Washington: Institute for International Economics.

Posen, Adam S. 2003. *Is Germany Turning Japanese?* Working Paper 03-2. Washington: Institute for International Economics.

Posen, Adam S. 2010. *The Realities and Relevance of Japan's Great Recession: Neither Ran Nor Rashomon.* PIIE Working Paper 10-7. Washington: Peterson Institute for International Economics.

Posen, Adam S. 2012. *Comments on "Methods of Policy Accommodation at the Interest-Rate Lower Bound" by Michael Woodford.* FRBKC Economic Policy Symposium on the Changing Policy Landscape, Jackson Hole, WY, August 31. Available at www.kansascityfed.org/publicat/sympos/2012/posen.pdf.

Reinhart, C. M., and K. S. Rogoff. 2010. Growth in a Time of Debt. *American Economic Review* 100: 573–78.

7

Secular Stagnation and the Labor Market in Japan

KYOJI FUKAO

Japan has been suffering from secular stagnation since the economic bubble burst in 1989–90. Its labor productivity stopped catching up with that of the United States around 1990 (figure 7.1). In fact, labor productivity (measured in purchasing power parity [PPP]) in Japan today is much lower than in other major OECD countries except South Korea (figure 7.2). This chapter examines the structural causes of Japan's secular stagnation, focusing on labor market issues.

A number of studies have attempted to identify the causes of Japan's secular stagnation. Most scholars seem to agree that there are two major structural causes of the stagnation, and they are related to each other: insufficient final demand (excess saving problem) and slow total factor productivity (TFP) growth.[1] When TFP growth is slow, fixed capital formation becomes sluggish, which reduces final demand. On the other hand, when there is excess supply, firms are reluctant to invest in intangibles, which reduces TFP growth.

Based on this diagnosis, in early 2013 the Japanese government embarked on so-called Abenomics, which consists of three arrows: aggressive monetary easing, fiscal stimulus, and a growth strategy (structural reforms) to tackle the twin problems of insufficient demand and slow TFP growth

Kyoji Fukao is professor at the Institute of Economic Research, Hitotsubashi University, and president of the Institute of Developing Economies, Japan External Trade Organization.

1. For a more general discussion of these structural causes, see Fukao (2013) and Fukao et al. (2016b).

Figure 7.1 Labor productivity in Japan and the United States, 1947–2012

US dollars in 2012 prices per hour worked

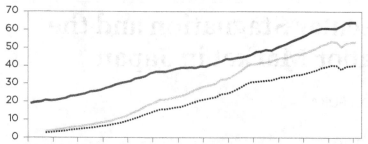

1947 1952 1957 1962 1967 1972 1977 1982 1987 1992 1997 2002 2007 2012

— United States, gross value added per hour worked, US dollars in 2012 prices

Japan, gross value added per hour worked, converted into US dollars in 2012 prices by market exchange rate of 2012 (79.8 yen/dollar)

······ Japan, gross value added per hour worked, converted into US dollars in 2012 prices by 2012 PPP (106.0 yen/dollar)

PPP = purchasing power parity
Source: OECD Statistics, https://stats.oecd.org.

Figure 7.2 Labor productivity in major OECD countries, 2014

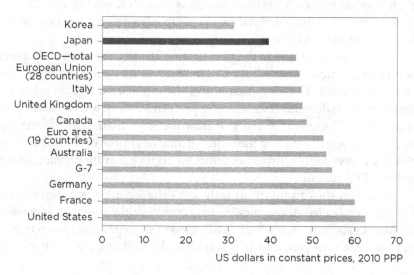

US dollars in constant prices, 2010 PPP

PPP = purchasing power parity
Source: OECD Statistics, https://stats.oecd.org.

Figure 7.3   Total factor productivity of Japan's macroeconomy, 1995–2015

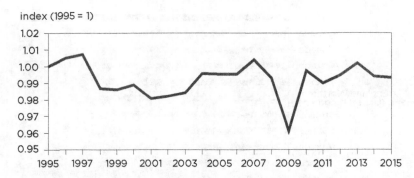

index (1995 = 1)

Source: Conference Board, Total Economy Database: Growth Accounting and Total Factor Productivity, 1995–2015 (adjusted version).

simultaneously. The first two arrows seem to have resolved the problem of insufficient demand to some extent. The recovery of major economies such as the United States and China has helped gradually shrink the GDP gap, which the Cabinet Office estimated had declined to minus 0.4 percent by the fourth quarter of 2016. Japan's labor market has also been tightening, with the ratio of job openings to applicants reaching 1.45 in March 2017, the highest since November 1990.

Major structural reforms of the third arrow are (1) stimulating private investment in targeted sectors such as medical services, renewable energy, and agriculture; (2) promoting female labor participation; (3) pushing for the Trans-Pacific Partnership (TPP); and (4) deregulating targeted sectors, such as healthcare, agriculture, and energy. Despite these reforms, the TFP of Japan's macroeconomy has hardly changed since 2013 (figure 7.3), and private investment has not accelerated.

The disappointing results of the structural reforms prompted the Japanese government in October 2015 to introduce Abenomics 2.0, labeled "All 100 Million Playing an Active Role" [Ichi-Oku Sou-Katsuyaku], which consists of four pillars: (1) a strong economy (continuation of active monetary and fiscal stimulus); (2) support for child rearing; (3) improvement of the social security system; and (4) introduction of an "equal work, equal pay" rule. The government also introduced life-work balance policies in an attempt to reduce overtime work. These reforms focus more on labor market and social policy issues than did the first round of reforms. This change seems to partly reflect the new strategy of the ruling parties, the Liberal Democratic Party and Komeito, to incorporate traditional policies of the opposition party, the Democratic Party. At the same time, it also

Figure 7.4 Literacy proficiency among 16–65-year-olds, major OECD countries, 2011–12

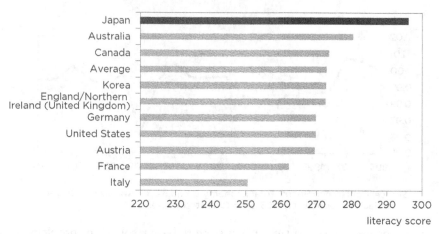

Source: OECD (2016a).

Figure 7.5 Literacy proficiency by country and gender, 2011–12

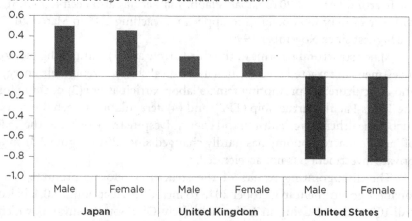

Note: The average and the standard deviation are calculated from all the microdata of about 10,000 adults (both males and females) in the three countries.
Source: Kawaguchi (2017).

reflects the widespread view in Japan that labor market issues are the key to Japan's revitalization.

The OECD's Survey of Adult Skills (PIAAC) ranks Japan at the top among OECD countries in terms of adult proficiency in key information-processing skills such as literacy, numeracy, and problem solving in technology-rich environments (figures 7.4 and 7.5 show results on literacy).

Figure 7.6   Use of literacy proficiencies at work, by country and gender, 2011–12

deviation from average divided by standard deviation

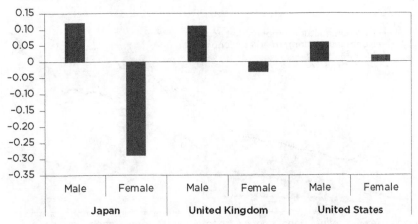

Note: Based on the item response theory (OECD 2013), Kawaguchi estimated these scores from responses to questions on use of literacy proficiency at work. The average and the standard deviation are calculated from all the microdata of about 10,000 adults (both males and females) in the three countries.

Source: Kawaguchi (2017).

Japan's problem is that it does not fully utilize its labor, especially female workers, whose proficiency is barely utilized at work (figure 7.6).

Greater utilization of workers' proficiency would raise Japan's productivity and labor efficiency. Since one of the main causes of insufficient demand in Japan is the stagnation of capital formation, which is partly caused by the shrinking working-age population and low TFP growth, labor market reforms will also contribute to relieving Japan's two structural problems.

This chapter analyzes two key issues in Japan's labor market—nonregular employment and productivity and wage gaps between large and small firms (dual labor market problem)—and derives policy implications.

Japan's Nonregular Employment Problem

The share of nonregular employees in total workers has increased substantially since the end of the 1980s.[2] In the nonmanufacturing sector (in both the nonmarket and market economies),[3] the share of nonregular employees

---

2. In Japan, a regular employee "is generally considered as an employee who is hired directly by his/her employer without a predetermined period of employment, and works for scheduled hours.... Consequently, a 'nonregular employee' is an employee who does not meet one of the conditions for regular employment" (Asao 2011).

3. Nonmarket economy comprises general government and nonprofit institutions of education, medical services, and other services.

Figure 7.7   Share of nonregular employees in total workers, by sector, 1970–2012

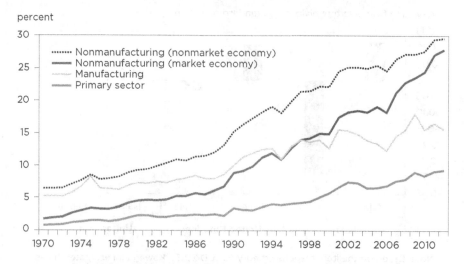

percent

Legend:
- Nonmanufacturing (nonmarket economy)
- Nonmanufacturing (market economy)
- Manufacturing
- Primary sector

Source: Japan Industrial Productivity Database 2015, Hitotsubashi University and Research Institute of Economy, Trade and Industry (RIETI).

is around 30 percent (figure 7.7). The wage gap between nonregular and regular employees is large (figure 7.8). Wages of regular workers increase as they get older and accumulate experience in the workplace.

Labor economists have argued that two factors are behind this upward slope of the age-wage profile. First, as workers accumulate human capital, their marginal contribution to production increases, which raises their wages. Second, to enhance worker loyalty and incentivize them, firms defer compensation until workers are older. Japanese firms provide active on-the-job training and some off-the-job training for regular employees (Fukao et al. 2009) but not much for nonregular employees. This may be why the age-wage profile of regular employees in Japan is steeper than that in other developed countries (Fukao et al. 2006).

If the upward slope of the age-wage profile is mainly caused by an increase in the marginal productivity of regular employees through the accumulation of human capital, then the wage gap between regular and nonregular workers in figure 7.8 can be regarded as representing the difference in labor quality between the two, meaning that the recent increase in nonregular workers has important implications. Using the Japan Industrial Productivity (JIP) Database,[4] one can estimate the impact of the increase

4. The database is available at www.rieti.go.jp/en/database/jip.html.

Figure 7.8 Wage level as a percent of the average wage of regular employees, June 2015

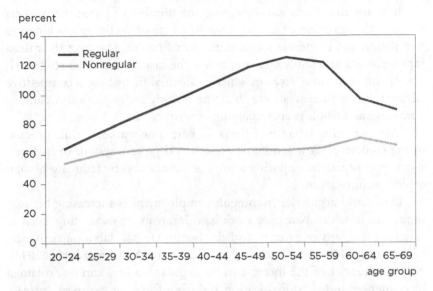

percent

Legend:
— Regular
— Nonregular

y-axis: 0, 20, 40, 60, 80, 100, 120, 140

x-axis (age group): 20-24 25-29 30-34 35-39 40-44 45-49 50-54 55-59 60-64 65-69

Source: OECD (2017). The original data are from Ministry of Health, Labour, and Welfare, *Basic Survey on Wage Structure 2015.* Overtime payments and bonuses are not included.

in nonregular employees on Japan's labor quality through counterfactual simulation. If the share of nonregular employees in total workers had not increased since 1988, the average quality of Japanese labor would have been 8 percent higher than it is now.[5]

To examine the relationship between the wage profile and the marginal productivity of employees, Fukao et al. (2006) estimated both the marginal productivity and wage rate of part-time employees compared with those of regular employees, using employer-employee matched data at the factory level. We found that the productivity gap between part-time and regular employees is larger than the wage gap. This finding means that firms pay a premium to part-time workers to obtain flexibility of employment. We also found that although there is some deferred compensation, the major

---

5. Suppose that Japan is on the kind of balanced growth path assumed in standard neoclassical growth models. An 8 percent improvement in labor quality will raise Japan's real GDP by 8 percent. Since the labor income share in Japan is about two-thirds, 5.3 percentage points of the increase in GDP will be due to the increase in (quality-adjusted) labor input and 2.7 percentage points will be due to the increase in capital input induced by the labor input increase.

part of regular employees' wage increase with age reflects increases in their marginal productivity with age.[6]

It seems that firms are increasing the number of part-time workers to maintain flexibility of employment in an era of declining working-age population and economic stagnation. Most firms don't expect their need for employees to steadily increase, as was the case during the high-growth era. At the same time, areas in which individual firms have a competitive advantage over their rivals are changing quickly and Japan's comparative advantage as a whole is also changing over time.[7]

The increasing reliance of firms on part-time workers, while rational in the context of slow economic growth and Japan's system of high job security, may also be imposing a huge economic loss by reducing human capital accumulation.

One could argue that nonregular employment is increasing because industries in which part-time work is widespread are expanding, such as care for the elderly or eateries, and also because female labor participation is increasing. However, according to Asano, Ito, and Kawaguchi (2013), only one-quarter of the increase in nonregular workers can be explained by changes in industry distribution and labor force composition. Instead, nonregular employment is rising because new labor market entrants, male workers of younger cohorts, and female workers of all cohorts are increasingly taking up part-time employment, suggesting that long-term employment relationships have declined in importance. As shown in figure 7.9a, the share of nonregular employees is particularly high among young male workers, even among university graduates (Hamaaki et al. 2012). Moreover, most female workers are nonregular employees (figure 7.9b), as are most older male workers.

Slow economic growth and increasing international competition are discouraging firms from employing most of their workers as regular employees under Japan's traditional lifetime employment system. These workers accumulate less human capital because most of them are part-time workers.

---

6. The Japanese employment system for regular workers is also changing. Using microdata from the *Basic Survey on Wage Structure*, Hamaaki et al. (2012) found that the age-wage profile has become flatter in recent years.

7. Matsuura, Sato, and Wakasugi (2011) constructed a theoretical model in which trade liberalization encourages firms to reduce the number of products, which raises uncertainty about the demand firms face. This change will increase firms' demand for temporary workers. They empirically test their model using microdata for Japanese manufacturing plants and find moderate support for the model's predictions.

Figure 7.9 **Labor force participation rate, by age and employment status, 2013**

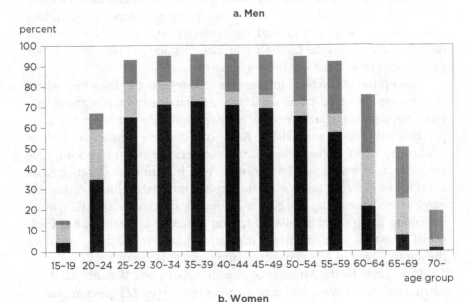

a. Men

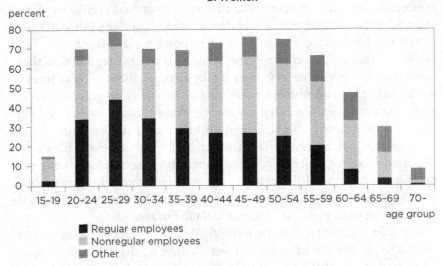

b. Women

Regular employees
Nonregular employees
Other

Source: International Labor Organization, *Labour Force Survey.*

Simply prohibiting nonregular employment is not an appropriate policy response. Such a policy would substantially misallocate workers among firms.[8] On the other hand, reducing the job security of regular workers and

8. See Fukao and Kwon (2006).

improving the social security net would also not be an appropriate policy response, since it risks substantially slowing down skill accumulation among workers, given that training of workers in Japan greatly depends on the lifetime employment system. Instead, Japan needs to enhance (1) labor market flexibility and (2) human capital accumulation among workers who do not participate in the lifetime employment system.

One option would be to increase "limited regular employment," where workers are employed based on job-specific labor contracts without lifetime employment guarantees but receive high compensation for their professional skills (Tsuru 2017). A job card system, which would allow workers to prove their skills and work experience, would also improve reallocation of workers and accumulation of human capital. Yet another avenue would be to replace the system of internal training of regular employees with training and education outside firms, which would require reforming Japan's professional education system at universities and vocational schools. Other important measures include regulations to reduce the unfair wage gap between regular and nonregular employees.

In a survey by the Ministry of Health, Labour and Welfare (MHLW), when asked why they worked as nonregular employees, 22.8 percent of male nonregular workers answered that they could not find regular employment, while 5.6 percent replied that they wanted to balance work with their family responsibilities, 15.6 percent of respondents answered that they could not find regular employment, while 35.9 percent replied that they wanted a job compatible with their family circumstances, such as housework, child care, and nursing in the case of female nonregular workers.[9] Reducing nonregular employment among women would require making regular employment compatible with workers' family circumstances.

Life-work balance is also important to resolve Japan's low fertility rate. The average age at which a Japanese woman first marries has risen especially among educated full-time female workers, who tend to postpone getting married and raising families because of the demands of regular employment (Sakamoto and Kitamura 2008, Brinton 2015).

It is important to note that the rigidity of Japan's labor market is related to Japan's low inflation problem. Reflecting the increasingly tight labor market, wages of nonregular workers have started rising considerably (at an annual rate of about 2 percent). However, regular workers have seen very limited wage increases (Bank of Japan 2017, chart 28). This difference is likely due to the following facts: First, labor unions, which are composed of regular workers, tend to prioritize job security over wage increases. Second,

---

9. *General Survey on Diversified Types of Employment 2014* conducted by the Ministry of Health, Labour and Welfare (MHLW).

because of deferred compensation, workers do not change their jobs even when their wages are temporarily lower than at other firms, Third, since labor unions oppose wage cuts and it is difficult for firms to fire regular workers, wage setting for regular workers is like a long-term leasing contract for durable machines with a fixed fee. Firms' decisions on wage rates of regular workers crucially depend on their expectations of future inflation. And since inflation expectations are still low in Japan, firms are reluctant to raise the wage rates of regular workers.

Productivity and Wage Gaps between Large and Small Firms

Japan's market economy has been characterized by large differences in labor productivity and wage rates between large firms and small and medium enterprises (SMEs) since the interwar period (the so-called dual economy [Nakamura 1983]). Oi and Idson (1999) found that firm-size wage differences in Japan are greater than in the United States. Labor productivity differences between small and large firms in Japan are also larger than in most other OECD countries (figure 7.10).

These differences have widened since the 1990s, especially in the manufacturing sector (Fukao 2013),[10] where the TFP growth of large firms has actually accelerated, while SMEs have lagged behind (Fukao and Kwon 2006). One possible explanation is that SMEs have not kept up with the information and communication technology (ICT) revolution and internationalization (Fukao et al. 2016a; Ito, Deseatnicov, and Fukao 2016).

Another potential explanation of the slowdown of SMEs' TFP growth is the decline in technology spillovers from large firms (Belderbos et al. 2013). In the manufacturing sector, large assemblers, which produce final goods, have conducted intensive research and development (R&D) to create new products. Meanwhile, SMEs have tended to supply parts and components to these assemblers. Supplier relationships between large assemblers and SMEs have usually been stable and tight, and SMEs likely benefited from spillovers from assemblers. Moreover, R&D intensity of SMEs is much lower than that of larger firms in Japan. In fact, this gap is much larger in Japan than in other OECD countries (figure 7.11). However, since the 1990s Japan's leading export industries, such as the electronic and automotive industries, have increasingly relocated production abroad. Because of this and other factors such as restructuring at large assemblers, buyer-supplier rela-

---

10. Andrews, Criscuolo, and Gal (2015) report that TFP differences between frontier firms, which tend to be large and internationalized, and nonfrontier firms have been widening in many OECD countries since the 2000s. However, since their data do not cover the 1990s, one cannot judge whether such widening in TFP differences started in the 1990s like Japan or not.

Figure 7.10 Labor productivity differences: Firms with 20–49 workers/firms with more than 250 workers, 2013

value added

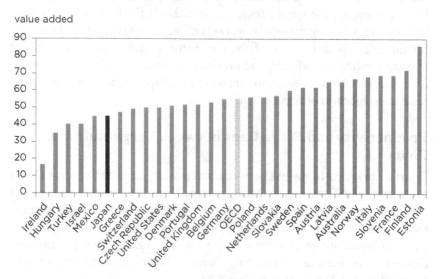

OECD = Organization for Economic Cooperation and Development

Note: Value added per person employed in 2013 in firms with 20–49 workers relative to that in firms with more than 250 workers = 100.

Source: OECD (2016b).

tionships in these industries in Japan have become more open (Paprzycki 2004, Ikeuchi et al. 2015).

Despite the importance of the widening productivity gap between large and small firms, analysis of the "dual economy" in the nonmanufacturing sector has been limited. Previous studies have also not sufficiently studied differences in labor input, such as workers' education level, sex, age, and employment status, between different firm-size groups. Against this background, Fukao et al. (2014) examined these issues by splitting KLEMS-type data of the market economy by firm size and industry. This section summarizes the results and discusses the policy implications.

For control totals, Fukao et al. (2014) used the JIP Database (KLEMS data on Japan). It is implicitly assumed that prices of outputs and intermediate inputs do not differ across different firm-size groups. To split data by firm size, we employed the *Corporate Enterprise Annual Statistics* from the Ministry of Finance. These statistics provide data on value added, capital stock, number of workers, and total labor cost by firm size within each industry (the financial industry is not covered). Statistics by firm size are available only in terms of paid-in capital. Using the microdata underlying these statistics, we created a matrix of the distribution of workers for each industry by amount of paid-in capital and by number of workers. Using these

Figure 7.11 Business R&D and government support for business R&D, by firm size, 2013

percent

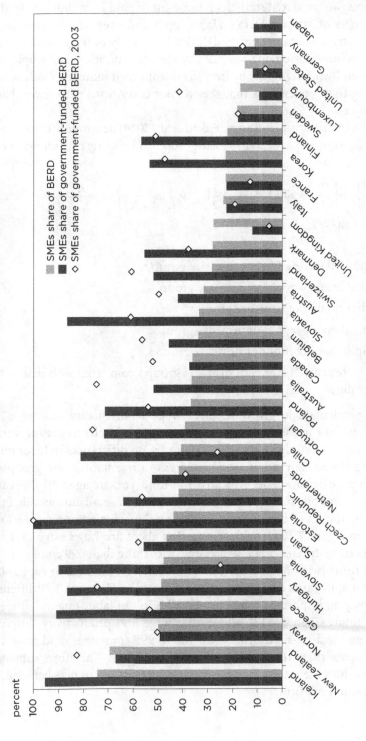

■ SMEs share of BERD
■ SMEs share of government-funded BERD
◇ SMEs share of government-funded BERD, 2003

SMEs = small and medium enterprises; BERD = business enterprise research and development

Source: OECD Science, Technology and Industry (STI) Scoreboard 2015, http://dx.doi.org/10.1787/sti_scoreboard-2015-en.

matrices, we converted statistics by amount of paid-in capital into statistics by number of workers. Data on labor input and wage rates by firm size and by industry are obtained from MHLW's *Basic Survey on Wage Structure*, which provides information on wage rates by age, sex, education, and employment status and working hours by firm size within each industry. One caveat regarding these statistics is that they do not cover firms with fewer than 10 employees.

For each year and industry, Fukao et al. (2014) decompose labor productivity differences between firm-size group s and s' using the following equation:

$$\ln\left(\frac{V_s}{H_s}\right) - \ln\left(\frac{V_{s'}}{H_{s'}}\right) = \ln(q_s) - \ln(q_{s'}) + \frac{1}{2}(v_s + v_{s'})\left(\ln\left(\frac{K_s}{q_s H_s}\right) - \ln\left(\frac{K_{s'}}{q_{s'} H_{s'}}\right)\right) + \ln(RTFP_{s,s'})$$

where

V_s: Nominal value added of firm-size group s,

H_s: Total hours worked in firm-size group s,

q_s: Labor quality of firm-size group s,

v_s: Cost share of capital in firm-size group s,

K_s: Capital service input of firm-size group s,

$RTFP_{s,s'}$: Relative TFP level of firm-size group s compared with that of firm-size group s'.

To calculate Jorgenson-Griliches-type labor quality indices, q_s, our study uses the industry average wage premium of each category of workers. Therefore, the study assumes that there are no differences in labor quality among the same type of workers across different firm-size groups—for instance, male university-educated full-time workers aged 30–34 years in large automobile firms and their counterparts in small automobile firms.

The results of our analyses for the total market economy are summarized in figure 7.12a, which shows that there are huge wage and labor productivity differences between large (with more than 999 employees) and small firms (with fewer than 100 employees). Differences in capital-labor ratios mainly cause labor productivity differences. However, TFP differences also play an important role. The contribution of labor quality differences is declining. Figure 7.12b shows that wage and productivity differences between medium-sized firms (with 100 to 999 employees) and small firms (with fewer than 100 employees) are not so large. Therefore, subsequent figures show the results for wage and productivity differences between large firms and small firms.

Figure 7.12 Wage and productivity differences, total market economy, 1975–2010

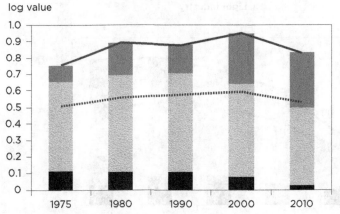

a. Firms with more than 999 employees/firms with up to 99 employees

log value

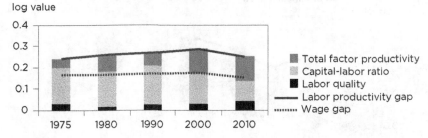

b. Firms with 100 to 999 employees/firms with up to 99 employees

log value

■ Total factor productivity
■ Capital-labor ratio
■ Labor quality
— Labor productivity gap
········ Wage gap

Source: Fukao et al. (2014).

In the manufacturing sector, differences in both labor productivity and wages have increased (figure 7.13). Widening TFP differences substantially contributed to the increase in labor productivity differences.

The results for the nonmanufacturing sector are shown in figure 7.14. In wholesale and retail, both TFP and wage differences are declining. On the other hand, in construction as well as transportation, communication, utilities, and real estate, TFP differences increased from 1975 to 2010.

One of the most interesting findings of the above analysis is that while wage differences are quite large, differences in labor quality based on the Jorgenson-Griliches approach are not. Figure 7.15 decomposes the labor quality gap in the total market sector between large firms (with more than 999 employees) and small firms (with fewer than 100 employees) in terms of worker characteristics. Labor quality of large firms based on the Jorgenson-Griliches approach is higher than that of small firms mainly because of

Figure 7.13 Wage and productivity differences: Firms with more than 999 employees/firms with up to 99 employees, by manufacturing sector, 1975–2010

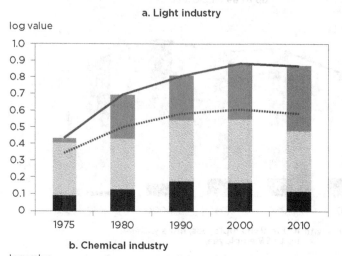

a. Light industry

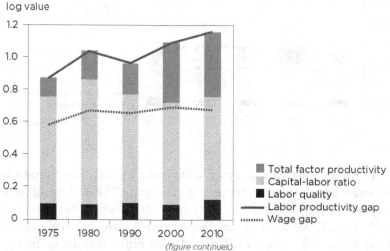

b. Chemical industry

Total factor productivity
Capital-labor ratio
Labor quality
Labor productivity gap
Wage gap

(figure continues)

differences in education. The labor quality gap has declined over time and was 7 percent in 2010. The decline was mainly caused by the increase in nonregular employees in large firms (in figure 7.15, this factor is included in "employment status").

It is important to note that although the wage gap between the two firm groups is more than 50 percent (figure 7.12a), measured labor quality explains only 7 percentage points of this gap in 2010. Rebick (1993) reports that in the United States, about one-third of firm-size wage differences are explained by labor characteristics, such as education, experience, etc., while

Figure 7.13 Wage and productivity differences: Firms with more than 999 employees/firms with up to 99 employees, by manufacturing sector, 1975–2010 *(continued)*

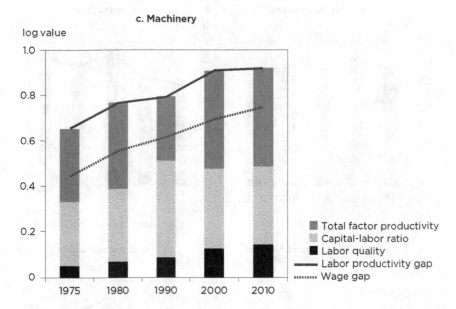

c. Machinery

Source: Fukao et al. (2014).

in Japan it is only one-tenth. Our result for Japan is roughly consistent with Rebick's finding.

What causes firm-size wage differences that worker characteristics cannot explain? One possible explanation is that since labor mobility across firms is limited in Japan, workers of large firms enjoy rents as a result of belonging to larger, more productive firms. However, since most large firms remain large and do not go bankrupt, it is difficult to understand why employees at large firms can continue to enjoy windfalls in the form of high wages. Two other explanations seem more plausible. The first is differences in on-the-job and off-the-job training. As shown in figure 7.16, large firms in Japan tend to provide much more job training to workers than SMEs. Using microdata on labor turnover and resulting wage changes, Genda (1996) finds that firm-size differences in job training contribute much more to firm-size wage differences than unmeasured ability differences. The second explanation is that, in Japan, graduates of top-ranked universities are much more likely than other graduates to get a job at a large firm (Higuchi 1994). This suggests that there might be a large gap in innate ability across workers in different firm-size groups that is difficult to measure using the Jorgenson-Griliches approach.

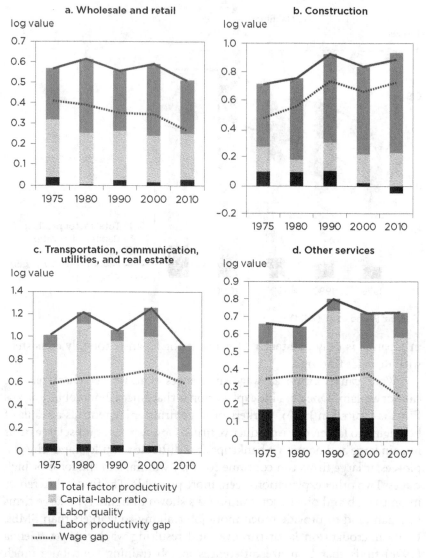

Figure 7.14   Wage and productivity differences: Firms with more than 999 employees/firms with up to 99 employees, by nonmanufacturing sector, 1975–2010

a. Wholesale and retail

b. Construction

c. Transportation, communication, utilities, and real estate

d. Other services

■ Total factor productivity
▨ Capital-labor ratio
■ Labor quality
— Labor productivity gap
········ Wage gap

Source: Fukao et al. (2014).

Firm-size wage differences that are not explained by the standard Jorgenson-Griliches approach account for about 45 percentage points (the 52 percent in figure 7.12a minus the 7 percent in figure 7.15). If we assume that all of this gap is due to labor quality differences, the TFP of firms with more than 999 employees relative to firms with fewer than

Figure 7.15 Decomposition of the labor quality gap: Total market sector, firms with more than 999 employees/firms with up to 99 employees, 1975–2010

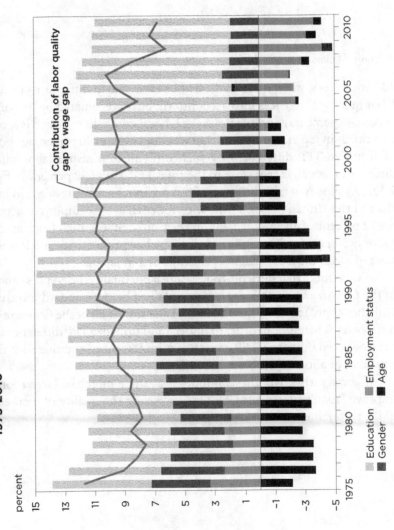

Source: Fukao et al. (2014).

Figure 7.16 Off-the-job training expenses (including opportunity costs) by firm size, total market sector, 1975–2010

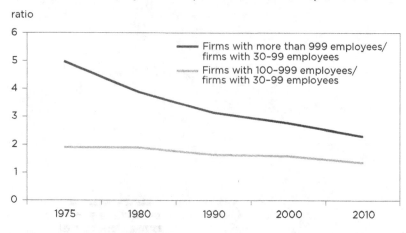

Source: Fukao et al. (2014).

100 employees, when measured without taking such difficult-to-measure labor quality differences into account, will be overestimated by this difference of 45 percentage points times the labor income share, which is around two-thirds in Japan. This means that we could explain 30 percentage points of firm-size TFP differences by such difficult-to-measure labor quality differences, which is very close to the total TFP gap of 32 percent in figure 7.12a. As shown in table 7.1, small firms are much more prevalent in Japan than in the United States. Firms with fewer than 999 employees account for 72 percent of all employment. In the United States, such firms account for only 55 percent. This indicates that the low productivity and low wage rates of SMEs are a particularly pressing issue in Japan.

If we assume that difficult-to-measure labor quality differences cause all of the firm-size wage differences not explained by the standard Jorgenson-Griliches approach, then this factor explains almost all of the firm-size TFP differences. Therefore, in order to understand firm-size TFP differences and the slowdown in Japan's TFP growth, it is important to examine such firm-size labor quality differences in more detail.

If correct, this hypothesis implies that there might be large room to improve Japan's macro-level TFP by improving the quality of workers in SMEs through education and training.

Table 7.1 Number of employees by firm size, all industries, Japan and United States, 2001 and 2006

Firm size (number of employees)	Japan 2001		Japan 2006		United States 2001		United States 2006	
	Number of employees	Percent of total	Number of employees	Percent of total	Number of employees	Percent of total	Number of employees	Percent of total
1 to 4	1,486,150	4	1,574,110	5	5,866,666	5	6,262,490	5
5 to 9	2,176,265	7	1,993,335	6	6,844,090	6	7,274,534	6
10 to 19	2,954,728	9	2,736,690	9	8,369,988	7	8,794,210	7
20 to 49	4,442,234	13	4,188,269	13	11,767,978	10	12,260,057	10
50 to 99	3,300,383	10	3,166,835	10	8,442,216	7	8,868,873	7
100 to 249	4,177,981	13	4,144,598	13	9,813,665	9	10,497,066	9
250 to 499	2,832,588	9	2,794,966	9	6,258,633	5	6,762,233	6
500 to 999	2,528,727	8	2,573,958	8	5,866,407	5	6,063,319	5
1,000+	9,274,478	28	8,935,484	28	51,128,895	45	52,125,133	44
Total	33,173,534	100	32,108,245	100	114,358,538	100	118,907,915	100

Source: Fukao et al. (2016a). Original data are from the Establishment and Enterprise Census for Japan and the Business Dynamics Statistics for the United States.

References

Andrews, Dan, Chiara Criscuolo, and Peter Gal. 2015. *Frontier Firms, Technology Diffusion and Public Policy: Micro Evidence from OECD Countries*. The Future of Productivity: Main Background Papers. Paris: Organization for Economic Cooperation and Development.

Asano, Hirokatsu, Takahiro Ito, and Daiji Kawaguchi. 2013. Why Has the Fraction of Nonstandard Workers Increased? A Case Study of Japan. *Scottish Journal of Political Economy* 60, no. 4: 360–89.

Asao, Yutaka. 2011. Overview of Non-Regular Employment in Japan. In *Non-Regular Employment–Issues and Challenges Common to the Major Developed Countries*. JILPT Report, no. 10: 1–43. 2011 JILPT Seminar on Non-regular Employment. Tokyo: Japan Institute for Labour Policy and Training.

Bank of Japan. 2017. *Outlook for Economic Activity and Prices, July 2017*. Tokyo.

Belderbos, René, Kenta Ikeuchi, Kyoji Fukao, YoungGak Kim, and Hyeog Ug Kwon. 2013. *Plant Productivity Dynamics and Private and Public R&D Spillovers: Technological, Geographic and Relational Proximity*. CEI Working Paper Series, no. 2013-05. Center for Economic Institutions, Institute of Economic Research, Hitotsubashi University.

Brinton, Mary C. 2015. Japanese Low Fertility and the Low Labor Force Participation of Married Women: The Role of Rigid Labor Markets and Workplace Norms. *Perspectives from Around the World*, no. 56. Tokyo: Research Institute of Economy, Trade and Industry.

Fukao, Kyoji. 2013. Explaining Japan's Unproductive Two Decades. *Asian Economic Policy Review* 8, no. 2 (December): 193–213.

Fukao, Kyoji, and Hyeog Ug Kwon. 2006. Why Did Japan's TFP Growth Slow Down in the Lost Decade? An Empirical Analysis Based on Firm-Level Data of Manufacturing Firms. *Japanese Economic Review* 57, no. 2: 195–228.

Fukao, Kyoji, Ryo Kambayashi, Daiji Kawaguchi, Hyeog Ug Kwon, YoungGak Kim, and Izumi Yokoyama. 2006. Deferred Compensation: Evidence from Employer-Employee Matched Data from Japan. *Hi-Stat Discussion Paper Series*, no. 187. Institute of Economic Research, Hitotsubashi University.

Fukao, Kyoji, Tsutomu Miyagawa, Kentaro Mukai, Yukio Shinoda, and Konomi Tonogi. 2009. Intangible Investment in Japan: Measurement and Contribution to Economic Growth. *Review of Income and Wealth* 55, no. 3: 717–36.

Fukao, Kyoji, Tatsuji Makino, Kenta Ikeuchi, Hyeog Ug Kwon, and YoungGak Kim. 2014. Productivity and Wage Differences by Firm Size [in Japanese]. *Japanese Journal of Labour Studies*, no. 649: 14–29.

Fukao, Kyoji, Kenta Ikeuchi, YoungGak Kim, and Hyeog Ug Kwon. 2016a. Why Was Japan Left Behind in the ICT Revolution? *Telecommunications Policy* 40, no. 5: 432–49.

Fukao, Kyoji, Kenta Ikeuchi, HyeogUg Kwon, YoungGak Kim, Tatsuji Makino, and Miho Takizawa. 2016b. The Structural Causes of Japan's Lost Decades. In *The World Economy, Growth or Stagnation?* ed. Dale W. Jorgenson, Kyoji Fukao, and Marcel P. Timmer. Cambridge: Cambridge University Press.

Genda, Yuji. 1996. "Ability" or "Training": Ability Difference Hypothesis on Firm-Size Wage Differences [in Japanese]. *Japanese Journal of Labour Studies*, no. 430: 17–29.

Hamaaki, Junya, Masahiro Hori, Saeko Maeda, and Keiko Murata. 2012. Changes in the Japanese Employment System in the Two Lost Decades. *Industrial and Labor Relations Review* 65, no. 4: 810–46.

Higuchi, Yoshio. 1994. University Education and Income Distribution [in Japanese]. In *Income and Wealth Distribution in Japan*, ed. Tsuneo Ishikawa. Tokyo: University of Tokyo Press.

Ikeuchi, Kenta, Kyoji Fukao, Hiromichi Goko, YoungGak Kim, and Hyeog Ug Kwon. 2015. *Empirical Analysis on the Openness of Buyer-Supplier Relationships and Productivity in the Japanese Automobile Parts Industry*. RIETI Discussion Paper Series 15-J-017 [in Japanese]. Tokyo: Research Institute of Economy, Trade and Industry.

Ito, Koji, Ivan Deseatnicov, and Kyoji Fukao. 2016. Do Exporters' and Non-exporters' Factor Inputs Differ? A Study Based on Employer-Employee Matched Data for Japan. Presentation prepared for the joint meeting of the Working Party on Industry Analysis (WPIA) and the Working Party on Globalisation of Industry (WPGI), OECD, Paris, October 10–11.

Kawaguchi, Daiji. 2017. Gender Gap in Skill Use in Japan: Findings from Japan-US-UK Comparison Based on PIAAC. In *Current Trends in Economics (Gendai Keizaigaku no Choryu)*, ed. Masako Ii, Chiaki Hara, Kaoru Hosono, and Hitoshi Matsushima. Tokyo: Toyo Keizai Shinpo Sha [in Japanese].

Matsuura, Toshiyuki, Hitoshi Sato, and Ryuhei Wakasugi. 2011. *Temporary Workers, Permanent Workers, and International Trade: Evidence from Japanese Firm-Level Data*. RIETI Discussion Paper Series, no. 11-E-30. Tokyo: Research Institute of Economy, Trade and Industry.

Nakamura, Takafusa. 1983. *Economic Growth in Prewar Japan*. New Haven, CT: Yale University Press. (Originally published in Japanese as *Senzenki Nihon Keizai Seicho no Bunseki [An Analysis of Economic Growth in Prewar Japan]*, Tokyo: Iwanami Shoten, 1971).

OECD (Organization for Economic Cooperation and Development). 2013. *Technical Report of the Survey of Adult Skills*. Paris.

OECD (Organization for Economic Cooperation and Development). 2016a. *Skills Matter: Further Results from the Survey of Adult Skills*. OECD Skills Studies. Paris: OECD Publishing.

OECD (Organization for Economic Cooperation and Development). 2016b. *Entrepreneurship at a Glance 2016*. Paris: OECD Publishing. Available at http://dx.doi.org/10.1787/entrepreneur_aag-2016-en.

OECD (Organization for Economic Cooperation and Development). 2017. *2017 OECD Economic Survey of Japan*. Paris.

Oi, Walter, and Todd Idson. 1999. Firm Size and Wages. In *Handbook of Labor Economics* 3, no. 3, ed. O. Ashenfelter and D. Card. Elsevier.

Paprzycki, Ralph. 2004. *Interfirm Networks in the Japanese Electronics Industry*. Sheffield Centre for Japanese Studies/Routledge Series. London: Routledge.

Rebick, Marcus E. 1993. The Persistence of Firm-Size Earnings Differences and Labor Market Segmentation in Japan. *Journal of the Japanese and International Economies* 7, no. 2: 132–56.

Sakamoto, Kazuyasu, and Yukinobu Kitamura. 2008. Marriage Behavior from the Perspective of Intergenerational Relationships. *Japanese Economy* 34, no. 4 (Winter): 76–122.

Tsuru, Kotaro. 2017. Reforming the Regular Employment System: Toward a New Norm of Job-Specific Employment Contracts. *Social Science Japan Journal* 20, no. 1: 59–72.

Comment

Jonathan Woetzel

Kyoji Fukao makes an important contribution to our understanding of Japan's economic stagnation. He outlines the problem in terms of weak labor productivity—much lower today than in other major OECD countries except South Korea—and offers a solution through his examination of two recent labor market changes: rising nonregular employment and an expanding wage gap between large and small firms. He builds a compelling case that declining labor quality is a critical reason behind Japan's worsening productivity performance and argues that education and training would go a long way in improving Japan's economic situation. Education and training should help, but significantly improving Japan's productivity performance is no small feat. The labor productivity gap between Japan and the United States has been widening across most industries since 2000. At the current pace, it is expected to grow from 29 percent in 2010 to 37 percent by 2025, according to our research at the McKinsey Global Institute (MGI). As a result, other measures will need to be considered in conjunction with those Fukao recommends in his chapter.

Fukao first analyzes the rapid rise of nonregular employment in Japan since the end of the 1980s. He defines a regular employee as anyone hired directly by an employer, without a predetermined period of employment, and who works for scheduled hours, while a nonregular employee is anyone who does not meet one of these conditions. In figure 7.7, he shows that nontraditional employment in the nonmanufacturing market economy has grown from around 5 percent in 1980 to a little under 30 percent in 2012. But he also identifies a large wage gap between nonregular and regular employees, especially in mid to late career years, as regular workers tend to earn more as they gain more experience (figure 7.8). Regular workers also receive training, which builds human capital, but nonregular workers typically don't and therefore accumulate less human capital.

Fukao surmises that in an environment of slow economic growth and increasing international competition, firms have become reluctant to invest in employing more regular employees under Japan's traditional lifetime employment system. While such firm behavior is rational in the face of slow economic growth and Japan's system of high job security, Fukao shows that this behavior has resulted in a "huge economic loss by reducing human capital accumulation." The drop in regular employment—and con-

Jonathan Woetzel is director of the McKinsey Global Institute and a senior partner in McKinsey & Company's Shanghai office.

current rise in nonregular employment—has led to a decline in the quality of Japanese labor. Fukao provides a neat calculation of this effect. Using the Japan Industrial Productivity (JIP) Database, he calculates that if the share of nonregular workers in total workers had not increased since 1988, the average quality of Japanese labor would have been 8 percent higher today.

To address the labor quality problem, Fukao suggests not to do away with labor market flexibility but to invest in the human capital of nonregular employees. Some of his options include establishing a job card system, where workers can prove their skills and work experience, and potentially moving training and education from within firms to universities and vocational schools. On this score, more research needs to be done to uncover the best way to train a growing nonregular workforce. One answer may be to require firms to provide benefits to nonregular workers after a period of time, even as they make regular workers less tenured. The ultimate solution, though, is competition to ensure that firms less willing to innovate and thus retain talented workers no longer dominate the workplace.

On the second labor market change, Fukao argues that the widening productivity and wage gap between large and small firms may also be a labor quality issue. Using level accounting, Fukao finds large differences in total factor productivity (TFP) between the two groups that cannot be explained by standard approaches. He argues that the difference in fact may be caused by hard-to-measure differences in labor quality. If that indeed is the case, he believes training and education may significantly improve Japan's macro-level TFP and boost economic growth more broadly.

While Fukao has put the spotlight on an underappreciated aspect of the Japanese economy, more work needs to be done on the implications of labor quality issues for policy and companies, as well as on the right mix of additional measures for accelerating Japanese productivity. Our research at MGI identifies a number of important trends worth taking into account. Japan's advanced manufacturing industries have relied on the domestic market while losing ground globally, which has implications for weak productivity. Japanese companies overall have significantly underinvested in organizational capabilities and talent for commercializing innovation globally compared with the United States and a range of European economies. At the same time, there is a distinct lack of women in senior leadership roles (a point that Fukao also makes in his chapter). Finally, Japan has fallen behind the United States, United Kingdom, Germany, and France in enterprise creation and growth.

These developments suggest that accelerating productivity in Japan may require a wider array of policies and measures than those addressing labor quality. The private sector can accelerate productivity growth by adopting best practices and new technologies to increase value added. Steps to adopt best practices include going global, building best-in-class capabilities across the entire value chain, and continuing to digitize. Steps to adopt new technologies include harnessing the power of big data, leveraging technology to create and commercialize new products and services, and deploying advanced technologies in manufacturing processes. If Japan takes these steps, we calculate that it could increase value added by up to 28 percent above the current trajectory.

Government policies that encourage entrepreneurship and global competitiveness are crucial to aid companies in their transformation. But as Fukao points out in his chapter, so too are policies that unlock new talent sources and encourage education. We find policies to unlock new talent sources could include encouraging more women to enter the workforce, providing seniors with flexible work arrangements to stay in the workforce, and rethinking immigration policies. Policies to encourage education could include building on top of the strong outcomes on hard skills (e.g., math and science), instilling the innovative and global mindset needed in a 21st century economy, and creating a true education-to-employment pipeline to identify where labor will be needed and match labor supply with demand. The payoff from these measures could be large. Accelerating productivity growth would fundamentally change Japan's economic trajectory over the next decade.

8

Declining Potential Growth in Korea

DONGCHUL CHO AND KYOOHO KWON

Since the global financial crisis in 2008, "secular stagnation" has become a catchword for the economic conditions of advanced countries (see Summers 2014, among many others). Recovery from the crisis has been slow, and inflation has remained low, despite unprecedentedly aggressive monetary policies. Asia has maintained relatively rapid growth, but the pace has been slower than it was before the crisis. Japan is struggling to escape from a deflation trap, and China is suffering from the aftereffects of the overinvestment it pushed to counter the negative shocks from the global financial crisis.

The economic performance of Korea, the third-largest economy in East Asia, has been weak. The average rate of growth over the past five years was less than 3 percent, the lowest since the 1960s. The unfavorable global environment undoubtedly affected Korea, but its growth rate has been on a secular decline since the 1990s, well before the global crisis. The weakening of its growth momentum has raised concerns that Korea may be following in Japan's footsteps, that "lost decades" may lie ahead. What factors underlie

Dongchul Cho is a member of the Monetary Policy Board of the Bank of Korea. Kyooho Kwon is a fellow at the Korea Development Institute. The views expressed are those of the authors and do not necessarily reflect the views of the Bank of Korea or the Korea Development Institute. The authors are grateful to Shinwook Woo for research assistance.

Figure 8.9 and table 8.2 in this chapter were produced using simulations of the overlapping generations model from Kwon (2017b) published by the Korea Development Institute (KDI) Journal of Economic Policy. The authors employed a Fortran code for their model that may be difficult to use to replicate the authors' results without their assistance. Accordingly, this chapter does not provide the Fortran code as part of the normal replication package required by PIIE. PIIE does not assume responsibility for the calculations underlying figure 8.9 and table 8.2 in this chapter. Anyone seeking further information should contact the authors at dccho@bok.or.kr and kwonkh@kdi.re.kr.

the secular decline of Korea's growth? What policies are needed to reverse, or at least mitigate, the trend?

This chapter addresses these questions. The first section presents the results of growth accounting and speculates on the likely path of the Korean economy based on recent empirical evidence on total factor productivity (TFP). The second section touches on the possibility of Korea's "Japanization," by comparing Korea of today with Japan two decades ago. The third section examines the decline in the natural interest rate (a result of the decline in potential growth rate) and its implications for monetary policy. The last section summarizes the chapter's main results.

Korea's Growth Trend

Growth Accounting

Figure 8.1 shows annual growth rates in Korea and the global economy for the period between 1980 and 2017. The positive correlation between the two series suggests that Korea's slow growth in recent years is attributable to some extent to the stagnation of the global economy. Korea's growth has been on a secular decline since the 1990s, however, whereas global growth accelerated. The deterioration in external conditions alone can thus not explain the recent slowdown of the Korean economy.

A standard growth accounting exercise provides a starting point for understanding the secular decline in Korea's growth. According to Kwon (2017a), all three components of growth accounting (labor, capital, and TFP) decelerated, for various reasons (table 8.1). An extremely low fertility rate led to a continuing decrease in the absolute number of workers entering the labor market, causing the pace of labor force expansion to decelerate and the age profile to become older (figure 8.2).[1] The capital accumulation rate also slowed, as the capital-to-output ratio approached the ratios in advanced countries or a steady-state level, after a decades-long capital deepening process (figure 8.3). Increases in TFP also slowed, perhaps because the technology gap between Korea and the global frontier narrowed.

The decline in Korea's potential growth is likely to continue for the next two decades. The size of the working-age population began to decline in 2017; given the current age structure, the pace of this decline is projected to accelerate.[2] The shrinking of the working-age population will eventually reduce the aggregate labor force (although the rise in female participation

---

1. Korea's fertility rate has been about 1.3 since 2000, lower than the rate in Japan and Germany.

2. It is sometimes argued that massive immigration or reunification with North Korea could substantially change the demographic projections for Korea. This chapter does not consider such scenarios.

Figure 8.1 Real GDP growth trends in Korea and the world, 1980-2017

percent, year on year

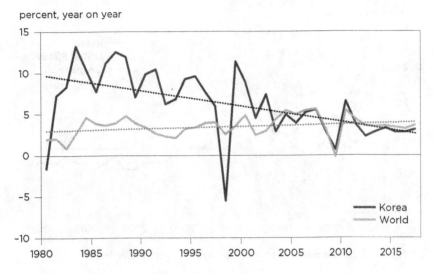

Sources: Bank of Korea; IMF Staff calculations.

Table 8.1 Growth accounting of Korea

Period	GDP (A+B+C)	Capital (A)	Employment (B)	Total factor productivity (C)
1981–1990	9.4	4.1	1.7	3.6
1991–2000	6.7	3.8	1.0	1.9
2001–2005	4.7	2.1	1.0	1.5
2006–2010	4.1	1.8	0.5	1.8
2011–2015	3.0	1.4	1.0	0.5
2016–2020	1.7+?	1.1	0.6	?
2021–2025	1.3+??	1.0	0.3	??
2026–2030	0.7+???	0.8	−0.1	???
2031–2035	0.2+????	0.6	−0.4	????
2036–2040	0.0+?????	0.5	−0.5	?????

Source: Kwon (2017a).

rate can mitigate the downward trend for a while).[3] Inasmuch as growth in output slows as a result of labor contraction, the pace of aggregate capital accumulation will also decline, assuming that Korea's capital-to-output

---

3. The projection in table 8.1 takes this factor into account.

Figure 8.2 Fertility rates in Korea and select countries, 1980–2015

children per woman

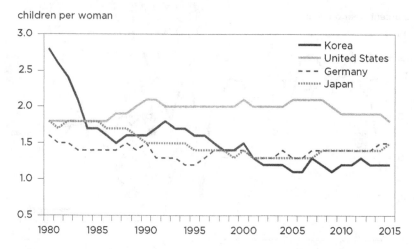

Source: Organization for Economic Cooperation and Development.

Figure 8.3 Capital-to-output ratios in Korea and selected countries, 1970–2015

ratio

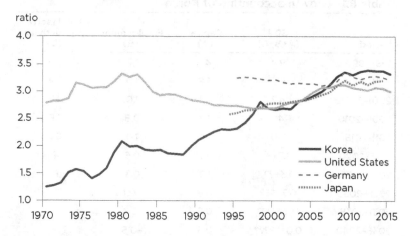

Source: Organization for Economic Cooperation and Development.

ratio has reached a steady-state level. This argument can be concisely explained using the standard growth accounting formula:

$$\Delta Y/Y = \Delta A/A + \alpha \Delta L/L + (1 - \alpha)\Delta K/K,$$

where Y, A, L, K, and α denote output, technology, labor, capital, and the labor income share, respectively. A steady-state output-to-capital ratio implies that $\Delta K/K = \Delta Y/Y$, simplifying the formula to

$$\Delta Y/Y = (1/\alpha)\,\Delta A/A + \Delta L/L \text{ or } \Delta y/y = (1/\alpha)\,\Delta A/A,$$

where y denotes income per labor. If demography exogenously drives L and the capital-to-output ratio remains unchanged, Korea's growth rate will decrease in line with the contraction of the labor force, unless TFP improves sufficiently rapidly.

Efficiency of Resource Allocation

Given demographic trends and the capital-deepening process, progress in TFP will become the only source of growth for Korea. However, TFP progress declined until recently, and its prospects do not seem rosy. Many factors could affect TFP progress, but few are likely to work in Korea's favor. The literature cites various factors that can boost TFP, including the narrowing of the technology (or income) gap with respect to the frontier, a young demographic structure, and the establishment of institutions to ensure efficient resource allocation. Korea's technology gap will narrow as long as Korea's per capita income converges to those of advanced countries.[4] Korea's population will age over the next several decades, hampering TFP progress.[5] The improvement of institutions to achieve more efficient resource allocation may be the key factor that Korea should rely on.

Recent empirical results on the efficiency of Korea's resource allocation using microdata are not encouraging. Kwon and Kim (2014) find that labor mobility in response to industry-specific demand shocks has fallen significantly in the manufacturing sector. The finding implies that declining industries do not flexibly lay workers off and rising industries do not hire sufficient numbers of workers. Instead, in response to demand shocks, firms adjust their investment and the wages of incumbent workers. Kwon and Kim present evidence that low mobility is attributable largely to excessive protections for regular workers, who impose the burdens of employment adjustment on nonregular workers. This dual labor market structure not only hinders resource allocation efficiency but also intensifies social conflicts between the two groups of workers.

---

4. Since Barro (1991) and Mankiw, Romer, and Weil (1992), the convergence argument—that lower-income countries tend to grow faster than higher-income countries, conditional on their fundamentals—has become a standard notion in the empirical growth literature.

5. The negative effects of population aging on TFP have been found over a wide range of data. For European countries, for example, Aiyar, Ebeke, and Shao (2016) project that the current age structure could lead to a reduction in TFP growth by an average of 0.2 percentage points every year over the next two decades. Using prefectural data from Japan for 1990–2007, Liu and Westelius (2016) find that aging of the working-age population has had a significant negative impact on TFP.

The efficiency of financial markets has been eroded by the continued supply of credits to "zombie" firms—firms that would be unable to survive without preferential financial support from either the government or financial institutions. Based on their empirical results for Japan, Caballero, Hoshi, and Kashyap (2008) argue that the increase in bank lending to zombies was a major cause of the chronic recession in the 1990s after the bursting of the economic bubble. Jeong (2014) finds that the portion of credit to zombies in Korea increased after the global financial crisis, thanks to wide-ranging public support, such as credit guarantees, loans through public financial institutions, and other programs. Based on cross-section regression results, he contends that zombies hinder investment and employment by sound firms in the same industries.

Korea's product markets are among the most heavily regulated in the Organization for Economic Cooperation and Development (OECD)—and entry barriers are being heightened to protect incumbent and "weak" firms.[6] Applying the methodology of Hsieh and Klenow (2009) and Oberfield (2013) to data on about 50,000 establishments in the manufacturing sector, Oh (2017) finds that product market efficiency has been declining since the mid-2000s. The deviation of the actual from the "optimal" level of production for each firm indicates that distortion by firm size (overproduction in small firms and underproduction in large firms) is especially serious.

These and other research results consistently suggest that the efficiency of resource allocation in Korea has not been improving in recent years. Although these findings are sobering, they may imply that there is room for improving Korea's TFP. The question is how to implement reforms to enhance efficiency, which will inevitably provoke resistance from vested interest groups.

Is Korea at Risk of "Japanization"?

The weakening dynamism of the Korean economy invokes concerns that Korea may be heading for a prolonged recession accompanied by deflation pressures, as Japan did in the 1990s. Some fundamentals in Korea are similar to those in Japan 20 years ago. As Cho and Kwon (2014) noted, Korea's demography is following Japan's in almost every dimension, with a lag of about 20 years. The population of Korea is projected to decrease beginning around 2030 (Japan's population began decreasing in 2010). The old-age dependency ratio in Korea will also follow that of Japan (figure 8.4).

---

6. Korea ranked 30th out of 33 member countries on the 2013 Product Market Regulation Index of the OECD (2014).

Figure 8.4 Demographics in Korea and Japan

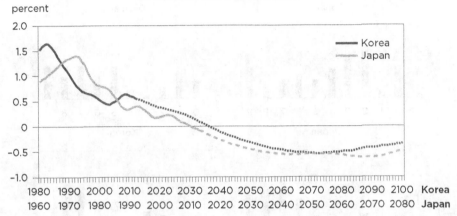

a. Total population growth rates

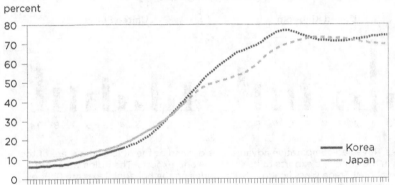

b. Aged dependency ratios

Source: Kwon (2017a).

It is not only in demography that Korea resembles Japan. As a result of efforts to emulate its neighbor's success, the economic structure of Korea has become similar to that of Japan in many respects. At the heart of both economies are export-oriented manufacturing industries such as electronics, automobiles, and shipbuilding—all of which are included in industry 7 of figure 8.5. Korea caught up with Japan in some of these industries over the past two to three decades but is now being fiercely pursued by China. Jung (2017) examines the competition and catch-up processes of Japan, Korea, and China in the export market, arguing that the pace of China's catching-up with Korea is accelerating.

Figure 8.5 Revealed comparative advantages of Korea and select countries (ratio)

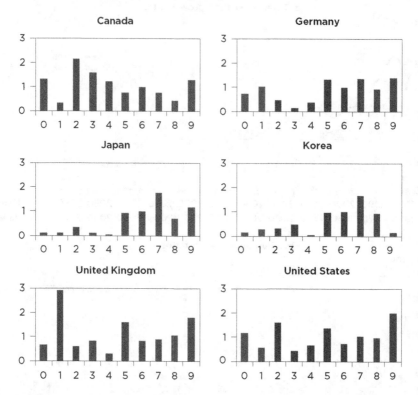

Notes: Revealed comparative advantage is defined as the ratio of the share of the item in the country's exports to its share in world exports. The 1-digit Standard International Trade Classification (SITC) codes on the horizontal axis are 0: Food and live animals, 1: Beverages and tobacco, 2: Crude materials, inedible, except fuels, 3: Mineral fuels, lubricants and related materials, 4: Animal and vegetable oils, fats and waxes, 5: Chemicals and related products, n.e.s., 6: Manufactured goods classified chiefly by material, 7: Machinery and transport equipment, 8: Miscellaneous manufactured articles, and 9: Commodities and transactions not classified elsewhere in the SITC.

Source: UN Comtrade Database.

Korea's per capita income also trails Japan's by 20 years. Figure 8.6, panel a, overlaps the trend of Korea's nominal GDP growth rate with that of Japan with a 20-year lag. The two series are almost indistinguishable. After a similar pace of rapid growth for several decades, in 2010 Korea attained per capita income of about $30,000—the level Japan reached in 1990.

Insofar as demography, industrial structure, and per capita income are the crucial determinants of a country's social and economic landscape, it seems natural to study Japan's history in order to draw a picture of Korea's future. An issue of interest is whether Korea will fall into chronic deflation,

Figure 8.6 Trends in nominal GDP growth rates in Korea and Japan

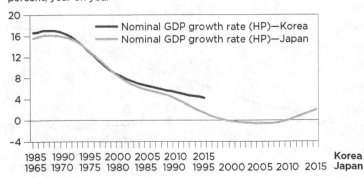

a. Up to 2010 for Korea

percent, year on year

Nominal GDP growth rate (HP)—Korea
Nominal GDP growth rate (HP)—Japan

1985	1990	1995	2000	2005	2010	**Korea**
1965	1970	1975	1980	1985	1990	**Japan**

b. Up to 2016 for Korea

percent, year on year

Nominal GDP growth rate (HP)—Korea
Nominal GDP growth rate (HP)—Japan

1985	1990	1995	2000	2005	2010	2015				**Korea**
1965	1970	1975	1980	1985	1990	1995	2000	2005	2010	2015 **Japan**

HP = Hodrick-Prescott filter
Sources: Bank of Korea; Cabinet Office of Japan (reproduced from Cho and Kwon 2014).

as Japan did. Panel b of figure 8.6, which extends the Korean data to 2016, appears to send a relieving signal. Unlike in panel a, Korea's trend growth in nominal GDP began deviating from that of Japan in the 2010s, implying that Korea is not replicating Japan's deflation. Korea's inflation rate has fallen to a worrisome level since 2013, but the pace of disinflation has been slower than Japan faced after the bursting of its bubble in the 1990s.

The divergence between the two economies in terms of inflation/deflation seems to stem from a difference in their real estate markets. Entering the 1990s, Japan's real estate market was in a bubble, the bursting of which triggered a deflationary spiral that was too abrupt for the Bank of Japan to

Figure 8.7 Real estate prices and consumer price index in Korea and Japan

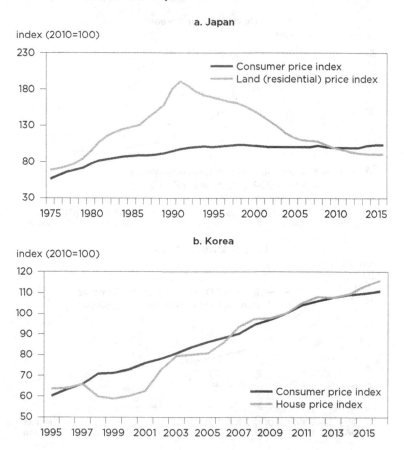

a. Japan

index (2010=100)

- Consumer price index
- Land (residential) price index

b. Korea

index (2010=100)

- Consumer price index
- House price index

Sources: Statistics Korea; Kookmin Bank.

counteract.[7] In contrast, housing prices in Korea have risen roughly in accordance with general prices over the past two decades (figure 8.7).[8] Perhaps for this reason, Korea has not experienced any major corrections in asset prices, and the Bank of Korea has had sufficient time to adjust its policy stance to disinflationary pressures.[9]

---

7. For the debate on Japan's monetary policy in the 1990s, see Hayami (2000), Kuttner and Posen (2001), and Ito and Mishkin (2004), among many others.

8. Cho (2017) extracts the market's capital gains expectations from the data on the unique rental system of Korea, called *chonsei*, which cannot be assessed as "excessive" compared with macroeconomic variables such as inflation and interest rates.

9. Cho (2017) compares Korea's monetary policy with Japan's, arguing that the Bank of Korea responded passively to inflation/deflation pressures.

Figure 8.8 Nominal and real interest rates (3-year government bond)

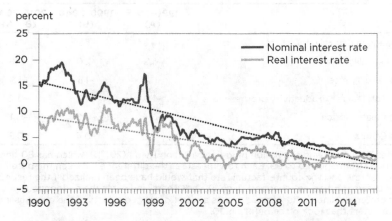

percent

Note: The real interest rate is computed by subtracting the year-on-year consumer price index (CPI) inflation rate from the nominal rate. For the period of 1990Q1–1995Q4, the 3-year government bond rate is not available and thus the rate for 3-year bonds issued by the Industrial Bank of Korea (under government guarantee) is used.

Sources: Statistics Korea; Kookmin Bank.

Declining Natural Interest Rate and Monetary Policy

There is no a priori reason to believe that Korea should follow Japan into deflation, but the changes in real sector fundamentals carry important implications for monetary policy.[10] The decline in the "natural interest rate," for example, could greatly complicate monetary policy by increasing the probability that the nominal interest rate hits the zero lower bound.

In the context of the recent debate on secular stagnation, the literature on the effects of fundamental variables on the natural interest rate is growing (see Laubach and Williams 2003 and Eggertsson, Mehrotra, and Robbins 2017, among others). This sort of study may be more relevant to Korea (a country experiencing drastic structural changes) than to relatively stable advanced countries. Korea's nominal interest rate declined from double-digit levels in the 1990s to low single digits in the 2010s; long-term rates are now similar to rates in the United States (figure 8.8). The real interest rate in Korea fell by more than 5 percentage points between 1990

---

10. The effect of population aging on inflation is not as clear as its negative impact on growth, because aging should reduce both aggregate demand and aggregate supply at the same time. The empirical results are mixed. IMF researchers Yoon, Kim, and Lee (2014) and Liu and Westelius (2016) present evidence from various data sets that aging operates as a disinflationary factor. Using a larger data set, Juselius and Takáts (2015), of the Bank for International Settlements, find that population aging is inflationary.

Table 8.2 Changes in simulated real natural interest rate (percentage points)

	1990–2015 (A)	1990–2040 (B)	2015–2040 (B – A)
Change in natural interest rate	–4.3	–5.9	–1.6
(1) Mortality rate	–1.2	–2.0	–0.8
(2) Fertility rate	–0.5	–1.8	–1.3
(3) Total factor productivity progress rate	–1.0	–1.2	–0.2
(4) Relative price	–0.4	–0.5	–0.1
(5) Others	–1.2	–0.4	+0.8

Note: The underlying simulation model is based on Kwon (2017b), which has 80 generations from ages 20 to 99. Each row measures the difference between the baseline interest rate and the counterfactual rate that would have been realized if the respective parameter had not changed since 1990. "Others" indicates the endogenously generated decline in the interest rate as a result of lagged effects of the changes in parameters that took place before 1990.

Source: Kwon (2017b).

and 2015; over the same period, it dropped by about 1–2 percentage points in advanced countries (Williams 2017).

To assess how much of the decline in (real) interest rates is attributable to changes in real sector fundamentals, we conducted experiments similar to those in Eggertsson, Mehrotra, and Robbins (2017) by using the overlapping generations model of Kwon (2017b) for Korea.[11] Table 8.2 summarizes the effects of the counterfactual scenarios that the mortality rate, fertility rate, rate of TFP progress, and relative price of capital goods have not changed since 1990. Of the 4.3 percentage point decline in the natural interest rate generated by the model between 1990 and 2015, 3.1 percentage points are attributed to changes in these fundamental variables: 1.2 percentage points to the lower mortality rate, 1.0 percentage points to the TFP slowdown, 0.5 percentage point to the reduced fertility rate, and 0.4 percentage point to the lower price of capital goods. The remaining 1.2 percentage point decline reflects the prolonged effects of changes in fundamentals that occurred before 1990. It takes an extremely long time before the effects of demographic changes are fully realized (figure 8.9). The effect of the fertility rate, for example, begins to show up after 10 years; it attains its maximum only after almost half a century. Changes in the fertility rate since 1990 lowered the real interest rate by 0.5 percentage point through 2015; an additional impact of 1.3 percentage points is expected to kick in by 2040. Similarly, the

---

11. This model is composed of 80 overlapping generations from ages 20 to 99 in any calendar year, reflecting all demographic changes of the past and the projected future. As there is no money in the model, the marginal productivity of capital determines the (real) interest rate (see Kwon 2017b for details).

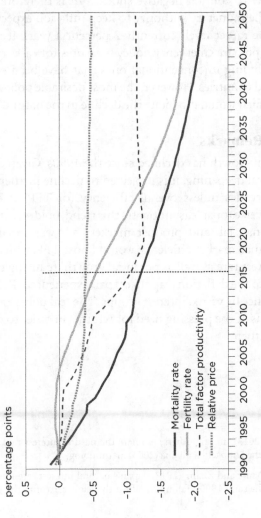

Figure 8.9   Effects on real natural interest rate of changes in fundamental variables

percentage points

Mortality rate
Fertility rate
Total factor productivity
Relative price

Note: The underlying simulation model is based on Kwon (2017b), which has 80 generations from ages 20 to 99. Each row measures the difference between the baseline interest rate and the counterfactual rate that would have been realized if the respective parameter had not changed since 1990.

Source: Kwon (2017b).

decrease in the mortality rate can bring about another 0.8 percentage point of decline in the real interest rate over the next two decades. The simulation results in table 8.2 indicate that the natural interest rate will decline by 1.6 percentage points between 2015 and 2040.

A 1.6 percentage point change is sizable, considering the current level of the natural interest rate, measured in terms of the overnight interbank call rate—the target rate of monetary policy in Korea. Estimates differ substantially depending on model specifications and econometric methodologies, but most studies on Korea's natural interest rate find that it has fallen below 1 percent.[12] Korea's natural interest rate may well fall below zero in the not so distant future, as it has in Japan. The probability of the nominal interest rate hitting the zero lower bound will increase, squeezing the monetary policy buffer to counter negative shocks.[13] It is therefore increasingly important for the monetary authority to keep inflation expectations from falling below the target level (currently 2 percent a year). It is also advisable that Korea prepare emergency policy measures for cases of large negative shocks, including unconventional ones that have been experimented with in advanced countries. However, the most desirable policy would be to increase TFP, which would moderate the decline in the natural interest rate.

Concluding Remarks

Korea's potential growth has declined since the 1990s. Given demographic trends and capital deepening, it is projected to decline further for the next two to three decades unless overall efficiency (or TFP) is substantially enhanced. To reverse (or at least mitigate) this trend, bold structural reforms in the labor, financial, and product markets are warranted. Successful reforms to enhance market efficiency would boost TFP, which could raise the natural interest rate as well as potential growth, reducing the danger of Korea falling into the deflation trap that Japan experienced. Reforms always confront resistance by vested interest groups. The real policy task may be to convince Koreans of the pressing need for reforms in order to gain political momentum for them.

---

12. Kim and Park (2013), among others, estimate the natural interest rate of Korea using various versions of the Laubach-Williams (2003) methodology.

13. According to Wynne and Zhang (2017), Japan's natural interest rate fluctuated around zero beginning in the early 1990s, falling significantly below zero after the global financial crisis.

References

Aiyar, Shekhar, Christian Ebeke, and Xiaobo Shao. 2016. *The Impact of Workforce Aging on European Productivity*. IMF Working Paper WP/16/238. Washington: International Monetary Fund.

Barro, Robert. 1991. Economic Growth in a Cross Section of Countries. *Quarterly Journal of Economics* (May): 407–43.

Caballero, Ricardo J., Takeo Hoshi, and Anil K. Kashyap. 2008. Zombie Lending and Depressed Restructuring in Japan. *American Economic Review* 98, no. 5: 1943–77.

Cho, Dongchul. 2017. Is Korea's Monetary Policy Following in the Footsteps of Japan? In *Japanization: Causes and Remedies*, ed. Takatoshi Ito, Dongchul Cho, and Andrew Mason. Cheltenham, UK: Edward Elgar Publishing.

Cho, Dongchul, and Kyooho Kwon. 2014. Japan of 20 Years Ago and Korea of Today: Aging and Declining Dynamism [in Korean]. In *Economic Dynamism of Korea: With a Focus on a Comparison with Japan*, ed. Dongchul Cho. KDI Research Monograph 2014-03. Sejong City: Korea Development Institute.

Eggertsson, Gauti B., Neil R. Mehrotra, and Jacob A. Robbins. 2017. *A Model of Secular Stagnation: Theory and Quantitative Evaluation*. NBER Working Paper 23093. Cambridge, MA: National Bureau of Economic Research.

Hayami, Masaru. 2000. Price Stability and Monetary Policy. Speech presented to the Research Institute of Japan, Tokyo, March 21.

Hsieh, C., and P. Klenow. 2009. Misallocation and Manufacturing TFP in China and India. *Quarterly Journal of Economics* 124, no. 4: 1403–48.

Ito, T., and F. S. Mishkin. 2004. Monetary Policy in Japan: Problems and Solutions. Photocopy. Graduate School of Business, *Columbia* University, New York.

Jeong, Daehee. 2014. Adverse Effects of Zombie Firms: The Case of Korea [In Korean]. In *Economic Dynamism of Korea: With a Focus on a Comparison with Japan*, ed. Dongchul Cho. KDI Research Monograph 2014-03. Sejong City: Korea Development Institute.

Jung, Kyu-Chul. 2017. Export Dynamics of Japan, Korea, and China. In *Japanization: Causes and Remedies*, ed. Takatoshi Ito, Dongchul Cho, and Andrew Mason. Cheltenham, UK: Edward Elgar Publishing.

Juselius, Mikael, and Előd Takáts. 2015. *Can Demography Affect Inflation and Monetary Policy?* BIS Working Paper 485. Basel: Bank for International Settlements.

Kim, Minsu, and Yang Su Park. 2013. Estimating the Neutral Real Interest Rate (NRIR) and Analyzing Factors of Its Fluctuation in Korea [in Korean]. *Economic Analysis* (Bank of Korea) 14: 47–86.

Kuttner, Kenneth N., and Adam S. Posen. 2001. The Great Recession: Lessons for Macroeconomic Policy from Japan. *Brookings Papers on Economic Activity* 2001, no. 2: 93–185.

Kwon, Hyuk-Wook, and Daeil Kim. 2014. An Analysis of Korea's Labor Market Efficiency in Human Resource Allocations [in Korean]. In *Economic Dynamism of Korea: With a Focus on a Comparison with Japan*, ed. Dongchul Cho. KDI Research Monograph 2014-03. Sejong City: Korea Development Institute.

Kwon, Kyooho. 2017a. GDP Growth from the Perspective of Demographic Change: Will Aging Korea Become Another Japan? In *Japanization: Causes and Remedies*, ed. Takatoshi Ito, Dongchul Cho, and Andrew Mason. Cheltenham, UK: Edward Elgar Publishing.

Kwon, Kyooho. 2017b. Korea's Demographic Transition and Long-Term Growth Projection Based on an Overlapping Generations Model. *KDI Journal of Economic Policy* 39, no. 2: 25–51. Sejong City: Korea Development Institute.

Laubach, Thomas, and John C. Williams. 2003. Measuring the Natural Rate of Interest. *Review of Economics and Statistics* 85, no. 4: 1063–70.

Liu, Yihan, and Niklas Westelius. 2016. *The Impact of Demographics on Productivity and Inflation in Japan*. IMF Working Paper WP/16/237. Washington: International Monetary Fund.

Mankiw, N.G., David Romer, and David N. Weil. 1992. A Contribution to the Empirics of Economic Growth. *Quarterly Journal of Economics* (May): 407-37.

Oberfield, Ezra. 2013. Productivity and Misallocation during a Crisis: Evidence from the Chilean Crisis of 1982. *Review of Economic Dynamics* 16, no. 1: 100-19.

OECD (Organization for Economic Cooperation and Development). 2014. Product Market Regulation Database. Paris. Available at www.oecd.org/economy/pmr.

Oh, Jiyoon. 2017. Misallocation in the Manufacturing Sector of Korea: A Micro Data Analysis. In *Japanization: Causes and Remedies*, ed. Takatoshi Ito, Dongchul Cho, and Andrew Mason. Cheltenham, UK: Edward Elgar Publishing.

Summers, Lawrence H. 2014. U.S. Economic Prospects: Secular Stagnation, Hysteresis, and the Zero Lower Bound. *Business Economics* 49, no. 2: 65-73.

Williams, John C. 2017. Three Questions on R-Star. *FRBSF Economic Letter*. San Francisco: Federal Reserve Bank of San Francisco.

Yoon, Jong-Won, Jinil Kim, and Jungjin Lee. 2014. *Impact of Demographic Changes on Inflation and the Macroeconomy*. IMF Working Paper WP/14/210. Washington: International Monetary Fund.

Wynne, Mark A., and Ren Zhang. 2017. *Estimating the Natural Rate of Interest in an Open Economy*. Working Paper 316. Dallas: Federal Reserve Bank of Dallas, Globalization and Monetary Policy Institute.

9

A New Macroeconomic Policy Framework for Prudence and Higher-Quality Growth in China

MA JUN

China's economic growth potential will slow in the coming decade for structural reasons that cannot easily be reversed. Technological innovation and reforms can cushion the deceleration, but it calls for a macroeconomic management framework that is more consistent with a slower, quality-driven growth model.

Reining in the buildup of macroeconomic leverage (measured by the M2/GDP ratio) will be key. There is a consensus that high and growing macroeconomic leverage has been the main cause for rising financial sector risks. According to the Bank for International Settlements, China's nonfinancial credit-to-GDP ratio stood at 256.8 percent in the third quarter of 2017, the highest ratio among the Group of Twenty (G-20) economies. This ratio grew at an annual average pace of 11 percentage points over the past decade, the highest rate among G-20 countries. China's leadership has emphasized that prevention of financial sector risks is its top priority.

The targeting or pursuit of an aggressive GDP growth rate has contributed to the excessive growth of monetary aggregates and thus the rapid buildup in leverage. In 2009–10, the period after the global financial crisis, for example, the government targeted a GDP growth rate of 8 percent. It achieved 9.4 percent in 2009 and 10.6 percent in 2010. M2 growth accelerated to 27.7 percent in 2009, 11.2 percentage points higher than the annual

Ma Jun is director of the Center for Finance and Development, Tsinghua National Institute of Financial Research, and member of the People's Bank of China Monetary Policy Committee. The author thanks Wang Lisheng, Zhu Shouqing, He Xiaobei, Qi Xing, Yang Xiaohai, and Wang Tianyu for their contributions to this research and Changyong Rhee and Alfred Schipke of the IMF for arranging the author's presentation at the conference.

average M2 growth during 2000–08. During 2011–16, the M2/GDP ratio continued to rise by 6.9 percentage points a year, as the government aimed for GDP growth of around 7 percent.

Structural Reasons for Growth Deceleration

Three key structural factors will continue to decelerate the Chinese economy in the coming decade or decades: demographics, environmental costs, and a shift in consumer preferences from goods to services. All of them are difficult or impossible to reverse.

Demographics: Rapid Decline in the Labor Force

Thanks to the one-child policy introduced in the 1970s, China's total fertility rate dropped from 4.8 percent in the early part of that decade to 1.7 percent in 2016 (Ministry of Health and Family Planning 2016). The policy has led to a significant decline in the labor force (population aged 15–64) since 2013 (figure 9.1).

According to the author's demographic model,[1] which accounts for the effect of the two-child policy introduced in 2016, the decline in China's labor force will accelerate from 1.8 million in 2017 to 10 million in 2028, equivalent to 1.1 percent of the labor force that year. Given a baseline labor share of 50 percent in the production function, in the production function, the acceleration in the decline in the labor force will lead to a drop in economic growth of about 0.5 percentage point in 2028 from the 2017 rate.[2] (This estimate does not account for the fact that the rapid aging of the population may result in additional deceleration in growth via a lower saving rate.)

Environmental Costs

China's traditional growth model, led by investment and heavy manufacturing, resulted in serious environmental degradation. This deterioration is beginning to limit potential growth and may threaten social stability.

Most of the environmental costs China is facing arise from air and water pollution, soil contamination, and CO_2 emissions. Future generations will bear these costs, the benefits of which were reaped by people who enjoyed very high income and wealth growth in the past several decades. Remediation costs in China during 2000–10 accounted for 6.5 percent of GDP for air, 2.1 percent for water, and 1.1 percent for land pollution/degradation, according

---

1. The author's demographic model is available on the PIIE website at https://piie.com/bookstore/sustaining-economic-growth-asia.

2. According to the literature, the labor share in the production function in China is about 50 percent (see Cai and Lu 2013, among many others).

Figure 9.1 Actual and projected labor force participation in China, 2000–50

population aged 15-64 (100 million)   population growth (percent)

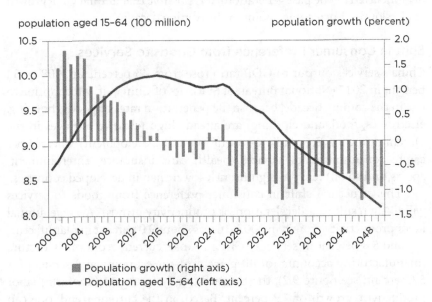

■ Population growth (right axis)
— Population aged 15-64 (left axis)

Sources: National Bureau of Statistics of China and author's demographic model.

to estimates by the RAND Corporation (Crane and Mao 2015). Water pollution and land contamination costs are likely to rise. According to Zhuang Guotai, deputy director general of the Ministry of Environment, the remediation costs for land contamination will be far greater than the costs for air and water pollution and could amount to many trillions of renminbi.[3]

These costs will significantly increase the costs of producing goods and services. For example, carbon prices may rise by a factor of 10 to 15 in the coming decade, according to the World Bank (2017), reaching $50 to $100 a ton by 2030.

Higher input costs should lead to lower profitability and thus less production and lower economic growth. Our dynamic CGE model shows that China's annual GDP growth may slow 0.5 percentage point during the energy transition in 2017–2030 assuming clean energy is 30 percent more expensive than dirty energy.[4] Rising water and food costs may have a similar

---

3. See He Gwangwei, "The Soil Pollution Crisis in China: A Cleanup Presents Daunting Challenge," Yale Environment 360, July 14, 2014, https://e360.yale.edu/features/the_soil_pollution_crisis_in_china_a_cleanup_presents_daunting_challenge.

4. The author employed the GEMPACK software to calculate this estimate of GDP growth slowdown during the energy transition period. Replicating this estimate may be difficult without the author's assistance. Accordingly, this chapter does not provide the GEMPACK code as part of the normal replication package required by PIIE. PIIE does not assume

impact. After accounting for these environment-related costs (essentially a debt incurred by the past generation), it is possible that annual GDP growth could slow by 1 percentage point in the coming decade.

Shift in Consumer Preference from Goods to Services

China's services output-to-GDP ratio rose from 43 percent in 2008 to 52 percent in 2017 (National Bureau of Statistics of China). It will continue to rise in the coming decade, because the penetration rates of goods (housing, electronics, food, and clothing) are already high (close to averages in the Organization for Economic Cooperation and Development) whereas per capita consumption of services (health care, insurance, entertainment, sports, and so on) remains significantly lower than in developed countries.

This structural shift in consumer preference from goods to services will likely result in a deceleration of productivity growth. Average annual labor productivity growth in 2007–16 was about 9.0 percent in manufacturing and 5.8 percent in services.[5] Given China's current economic structure (manufacturing accounts for 40 percent of the economy and services for 52 percent; see figure 9.2), these figures imply aggregate (nonfarm) labor productivity growth of 7.2 percent. Based on the current trend, one can expect a 10 percentage point rise in the share of the services sector over the coming decade (and a decline in the share of the manufacturing sector). This structural change implies aggregate (nonfarm) labor productivity growth of roughly 6.9 percent in 10 years. All else held constant, a decline of 0.3 percentage point (from 7.2 to 6.9 percent) in annual labor productivity growth reduces annual economic growth by roughly 0.3 percentage points in a decade.

Inevitability of a Growth Slowdown

The headwinds from these structural changes are difficult to reverse. In addition, China's economic growth is facing other challenges, including very high macroeconomic leverage, which means the country is no longer positioned to borrow at the pace it had. Urbanization is also slowing, which means that growth driven by infrastructure and property investment may lose steam.

Fortunately, the growth slowdown may not necessarily translate into severe unemployment, as the number of people seeking jobs will shrink as well. According to the author's demographic model, the labor force will

---

responsibility for the calculations underlying this estimate. Anyone seeking further information should contact the author at maj@pbcsf.tsinghua.edu.cn.

5. "Manufacturing" is used as shorthand for "manufacturing, construction, and mining."

Figure 9.2 Services and manufacturing sectors in China as percent of GDP, 1990–2017

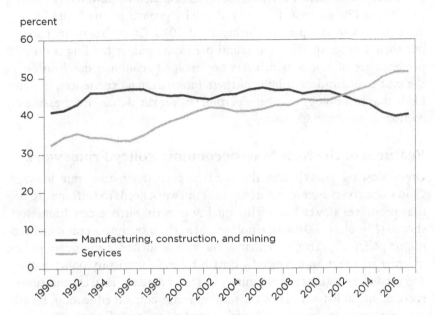

percent

Manufacturing, construction, and mining
Services

Source: National Bureau of Statistics of China.

decline by 11 million people, obviating the need to create net new jobs by 2028.[6]

Measures Already Taken to Offset Deceleration Pressures

The Chinese government has launched a number of initiatives to offset some of these factors and boost growth potential. The most notable effort is the promotion of technological innovation. Central and local governments have promoted technological innovation and the development of new business models through measures such as tax deductions and exemptions; increased government expenditure on research and development; the establishment of more than 3,000 high-tech startup incubators; encouragement of the transformation of scientific products for commercial use; and the creation of one-stop services for patent examination, verification, and protection. Many Chinese high-tech companies, especially internet and e-commerce businesses, were listed on stock exchanges in the past few years. In power, engineering, mining, high-speed rail, and construction, China has become a technology exporter.

6. Rural labor migration is projected at about 8 million people in 2028, almost the same as the net reduction in the urban labor force that year.

Acceleration of technology development may not be enough to offset the economic deceleration caused by structural factors, however. According to Gordon (2016), total factor productivity growth in the United States averaged less than 1 percent during 1980–2010. China has many patents, but their average quality is low, and per capita patent holding is only 10 percent that of Korea, which has not escaped economic deceleration in the past two decades. In light of these international experiences, it seems likely that technology may only partially offset the downward pressure on economic growth in China.

Features of the New Macroeconomic Policy Framework

Given slowing growth and the need to curb macroeconomic leverage, China's macroeconomic management framework needs to shift toward one that promotes slower but higher-quality growth. Such a new framework should (1) replace GDP with employment as the most important macroeconomic policy objective; (2) enhance the independence of monetary policy, in order to avoid dominance by dovish tones in monetary policymaking; and (3) make sure that the planning of fiscal and quasi-fiscal expenditures—such as unfunded mandates for local governments on education, healthcare, environment, poverty alleviation, and so on, as well as the launching or support of economic/high-tech development zones—is consistent with macroeconomic and financial stability objectives, in order to avoid further expansion of local government debt.

China's macroeconomic management system centers on achieving growth targets. It has the following key features:

- The central government sets 1-, 5-, and 10-year growth targets. Provincial and lower-level governments also set their own targets for growth, which are typically higher than the national target (e.g., if the central government targets 6.5 percent, the provincial government targets 7.5 percent and the city- or county-level government possibly 8.5 percent). Promotion of local government officials (such as party chiefs and mayors) depends largely on achievement of local-level GDP growth targets.

- Various ministries and bureaus (including those in charge of industrial development, infrastructure, and social services) set targets for sectoral growth. Once aggregated, they are typically more ambitious than the national growth target. Based on these sectoral targets, the central government issues mandates for local governments (such as achieving targets for poverty reduction, environmental protection, education, health care, elder care), many of which are not funded or only partially funded by national budgets. Most of these mandates have been funded by local government financial vehicles or public-private partnership projects that borrowed from banks or the bond market. They are a key reason why local government debt surged over the past decade.

- China sought to spur regional development by launching many development zones. The central and provincial governments launched about 5,000 such zones (economic development, high-tech, free trade, and so on). City, county, and township governments also established numerous development zones. No official statistics exist on their number, but there are likely many thousands, if not tens of thousands. Infrastructure investment demand in the 5,000 development zones at or above provincial levels could amount to nearly RMB50 trillion, or 60 percent of China's GDP in 2017.

- Historically, the State Council set monetary growth targets, based on negotiations among key ministries. M2 grew at a pace that was about 3 percentage points higher than nominal GDP over the past two decades. The main reason for the excessively high M2 growth was that most parties influencing policymaking were beneficiaries of rapid monetary expansion and none of them cared about its eventual macroeconomic consequences, such as inflation and financial risks. The central bank, where professionals are most concerned about macroeconomic stability, has limited influence in this process.

These features suggest that the current macroeconomic management framework may be prone to overheating, as a result of untenable promises on deliverables (as reflected in the large unfunded mandates for local governments), excessive incentives for achieving higher GDP growth through overborrowing, and limited restraints on monetary expansion. When the economy enjoyed strong underlying growth potential (of about 10.5 percent in the 2000s) and financial leverage was still modest, such features did not pose a major threat to macroeconomic and financial stability. In the "new normal" phase, which may see growth slow and room for leverage shrink, the old macroeconomic management model becomes unsustainable.

This growth-centered macroeconomic management model needs to be replaced with a quality-centered one that focuses on macroeconomic prudence and financial stability. The decline in growth potential and labor force makes this transition feasible, as there is no more need to maintain strong growth for job creation. The need to contain macroeconomic leverage makes the transition imperative. The new approach needs to focus on several areas.

Abandoning the GDP Growth Target

China has long used GDP growth targets to boost investment and economic growth. In the 12th Five-Year Plan, the government set the goal of doubling the country's real GDP and household income by 2020 from 2010 levels.

The drawbacks of this kind of target-setting have become increasingly evident. The main problem is that local governments top up the national growth target by setting higher targets and then resort to heavy borrowing to achieve them, pushing up local government debt and hence the leverage ratio of the overall economy.

In addition to boosting local government debt and macroeconomic leverage, the overemphasis on GDP growth performance caused overcapacity, environmental degradation, and statistical fraud. As many local governments lack sufficient revenues to fund their infrastructure investments, they resorted to multiple sources of debt financing, including loans, bonds, and shadow banking products. When they failed to meet their GDP targets, some local governments manipulated their statistics, as evidenced by the fraud reported in Liaoning, Tianjin, and Inner Mongolia.[7]

China should scrap the national GDP growth target and replace it with an unemployment rate target as the most important macroeconomic policy objective. Doing so would reduce the political pressure on local governments to borrow. GDP growth forecasts (instead of targets) should still be used as a guide for budgetary activities. They could be issued by the central bank, the National Development and Reform Commission, or the Ministry of Finance.

Enhancing Monetary Policy Independence

The State Council, rather than the central bank, makes all key monetary policy decisions in China, including adjustments to the benchmark interest rates and reserve requirement ratios. As the State Council makes decisions largely by consensus, the system often reflects the collective opinions of ministries in charge of economic development and policymaking, as well as the views of local governments, which are less concerned than national policymakers about the macroeconomic spillover of such policies. The views of the central bank—the agency mandated to maintain macroeconomic and financial stability—carry limited weight. This system has a natural bias toward excessive monetary expansion.

---

7. Yawen Chen and Ryan Woo, "Another Chinese city admits 'fake' economic data," Reuters, January 16, 2018, www.reuters.com/article/us-china-economy-data/another-chinese-city-admits-fake-economic-data-idUSKBN1F60I1.

The central bank should be given more independence in monetary policy making, transitioning away from M2 growth targeting toward interest rate targeting. To do so, when authorities announce the official policy rate (to replace the benchmark lending and deposit rates) as the intermediate target for monetary policy, the central bank should be given key decision-making power. This arrangement would better ensure macroeconomic and financial stability as a top priority of monetary and macroprudential policies.

Creating a Macroeconomic Stability Screening Mechanism to Cut Unrealistic Public Policy Mandates

To avoid further expansion of local government debt, especially implicit debt, it is important to make sure that the planning of quasi-fiscal expenditures (such as unfunded mandates for local governments on education, health care, environment, poverty reduction, and so on) is consistent with macroeconomic and financial stability objectives. A "macroeconomic stability screening mechanism" should be established for all major macroeconomic policies by quantifying their fiscal and monetary implications. For example, many targets set for poverty reduction, pollution reduction, and improvements in health care, education, and infrastructure require significant fiscal resources. If not included in the official fiscal budget, these mandates most likely result in local government quasi-fiscal debt. If they do not pass the macroeconomic stability screening, which sets a limit on total government borrowing (including targets of budgetary fiscal deficit and quasi-fiscal deficit), such mandates should not be included in the government's work plan.

Abolishing Some Development Zones

Some development zones have contributed to rapid regional economic growth and technological innovation. But many are heavily indebted, because they borrow excessively for expenditures on infrastructure investment without credible plans for repayment.

The current policy of "one county, one zone" is inappropriate, because many counties lack the natural resources, workers, talent, and locational comparative advantages to attract private investment and land purchase in large-scale infrastructure development. As many as two-thirds of China's 5,000 development zones (at and above the provincial level) lack the growth potential initially foreseen or claimed. Continuing to advance large-scale development zones broadly would exacerbate the local government debt problem and increase macroeconomic leverage. The central government should therefore consider abolishing many of these development zones and refraining from launching new ones.

Enhancing the Transparency of the Quasi-Fiscal Debt of Local Governments

In 2013 the Third Plenary Session of the 18th Chinese Communist Party Congress decided that central and local governments would henceforth publish their government balance sheets, in order to enhance the transparency and responsibility of local government operations. Progress has been slow, with many local governments compiling but not publishing their balance sheets.

The rapid increase in local government quasi-fiscal debt in the past five years has underscored the importance and urgency of implementing this reform. A mandatory requirement for disclosure of local government balance sheets, including local financing vehicle debts, which represent contingent or implicit liabilities of the local governments, is critical to deter irresponsible and excessive borrowing by local governments. Publishing information on quasi-fiscal borrowing gives the general public, local residents, members of the local people's congress, the media, banks, the debt market, and third-party service providers such as rating companies important information with which to assess local government debt risks. Public opinion and pressure from all these parties for local governments to be prudent could be very powerful.

The authorities could take the following steps to implement the decision:

- The Ministry of Finance should create a standardized template for local government balance sheets, with clear definitions of contingent and implicit liabilities of local governments. For example, debts incurred by companies that are majority owned by local governments and for developing infrastructure projects whose cash flows are insufficient to cover debt repayments should be treated as implicit or contingent government liabilities, regardless of whether the local government issued an official guarantee.[8]

- The Ministry of Finance could select a few provinces and cities as pilot programs for launching this reform.

- Once sufficient experience is gained, this practice should be quickly replicated in the rest of the country.

---

8. The author was an advisor to the "balance sheeting working group" of a provincial-local government a few years ago and was involved in many technical discussions on definitions, scope, and valuations of local government balance sheet items. His experience suggests that these issues are not as problematic as many people perceive.

Conclusion

Unlike countries that face secular stagnation, China is facing a slowdown in economic growth driven by three unavoidable structural issues: demographics, environmental costs, and changing consumer preferences. Ongoing technological innovations and reforms can partially cushion the deceleration, but a further slowdown in growth is inevitable over the medium term.

This trend, together with the growing financial risks caused by a high macroeconomic leverage ratio, calls for a new macroeconomic management framework. Key to sustainable, high-quality, and environment-friendly growth in China is adoption of a framework that is less growth-centric and focuses more on macroeconomic and financial stability. To put such a new framework in place, policymakers should consider the following actions:

- Make employment, rather than GDP, the most important macroeconomic policy objective.

- Enhance the independence of monetary policy, in order to avoid the dominance of dovish tones in monetary policymaking.

- Make sure the planning of fiscal and quasi-fiscal expenditures is consistent with macroeconomic and financial stability objectives, in order to avoid further expansion of local government debt, especially implicit debt.

- Abolish unqualified development zones.

- Enhance the transparency of quasi-fiscal borrowing by local governments.

Even at somewhat lower rates, China's growth will still be among the highest in the world in the coming decade—and the declining size of its labor force will allow it to tolerate a more moderate GDP growth rate without causing serious unemployment. Hence there is no convincing reason to be obsessed about reaching an annual GDP growth target. By reducing the probability of financial crises and large disruptions to growth, the new macroeconomic management framework described in this chapter should help China better achieve its sustainable development objectives in the medium and long terms.

References

Cai, Fang, and Yang Lu. 2013. Population Change and Resulting Slowdown in Potential GDP Growth in China. *China & World Economy* 21, no. 2: 1–14.

Crane, Keith, and Zhimin Mao. 2015. *Costs of Selected Policies to Address Air Pollution in China*. Santa Monica, CA: RAND Corporation.

Gordon, Robert J. 2016. *The Rise and Fall of American Growth: The U.S. Standard of Living since the Civil War*. Princeton, NJ: Princeton University Press.

Ministry of Health and Family Planning. 2016. *Statistics on China's Health and Family Planning Development*. Beijing.

World Bank. 2017. *Guidance Note on Shadow Price of Carbon in Economic Analysis*. Washington. Available at http://pubdocs.worldbank.org/en/911381516303509498/2017-Shadow-Price-of-Carbon-Guidance-Note-FINAL-CLEARED.pdf.

10

Do India's Exports Reflect the New Normal?

PRACHI MISHRA AND SIDDHARTHA NATH

India's merchandise exports underwent a quiet revolution over the last two decades, with exports of engineering goods, electronics, and pharmaceuticals gradually replacing India's traditional exports of leather, textiles, gems, and jewelry. This chapter uses sectoral and firm-level data to examine what drives India's exports. It answers the following questions: How has India fared since the global financial crisis? Is India a closed economy? Has it been insulated from global shocks? The first two sections examine how open India's economy is and how the composition of its exports has changed. The next two sections analyze the determinants of India's exports (global growth, the real effective exchange rate, supply bottlenecks) at the aggregate and firm levels. The last section summarizes the chapter's conclusions and identifies their policy implications.

How Open Is India's Economy?

Since the global financial crisis, low economic growth has been recognized as the "new normal" or "new mediocre," especially in advanced economies. The new mediocre has been attributed to both demand and supply factors—inadequate aggregate demand and a slowdown in productivity growth. Although demand recently rose in advanced economies, underlying potential

Prachi Mishra is deputy division chief in the Western Hemisphere Department at the International Monetary Fund. Siddhartha Nath is research officer at the Reserve Bank of India. They would like to thank Medha Madhu Nair for excellent research assistance. The views expressed in this chapter are those of the authors and do not necessarily represent the views of the IMF, its Executive Board, or its management, nor the views of the institutions to which they belong.

Figure 10.1a   India's exports and imports, 2000–16

percent of GDP

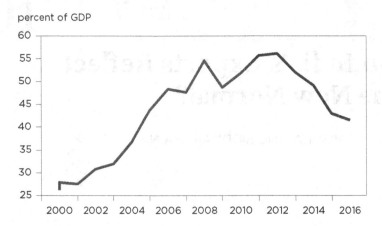

Source: Ministry of Statistics and Program Implementation, Government of India.

growth is significantly lower than in emerging-market economies, reflecting unfavorable demographics and soft productivity growth.

The new mediocre has coincided with a slowdown in trade growth relative to overall global growth. China, India, and Indonesia have continued to enjoy relatively higher growth since the global financial crisis, in contrast to Japan and Korea. Their success reflects supportive macroeconomic policies and strong convergence dynamics.

India's financial integration with the rest of the world is increasingly appreciated and visible. Capital inflows and outflows are rising, and asset prices in India are increasingly correlated with their global counterparts. But India's integration into the global real economy continues to be underappreciated, particularly on the export front. The conventional wisdom is that India remains a largely closed economy, in which exports are of only marginal significance. This line of thinking is often used to suggest that India is insulated from global growth and/or protectionist shocks.

Over the last two decades, India's tradable sector grew rapidly. Total trade (the sum of exports and imports as a percent of GDP) rose from 27 percent in 2000 to 56 percent in 2012, before slowing during the deglobalization of recent years (figure 10.1a). Increased integration and exposure to global markets forced supply chain efficiencies and resulted in the technological transfer and productivity growth that comes with them. But the growth and productivity benefits of global integration also made India's economy more vulnerable to global growth and protectionist shocks—more than is commonly assumed.

Measuring India's exposure on the export side is a function of how

Figure 10.1b Share of India's exports in GDP, 2000-16

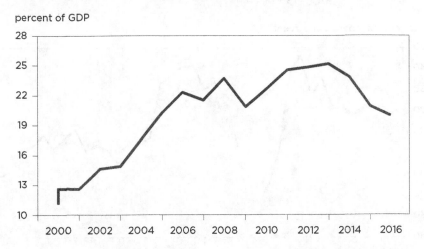

percent of GDP

Source: Ministry of Statistics and Program Implementation, Government of India.

exports have grown as a share of GDP and how sensitive they are to changes in partner-country growth. The larger the share of exports in GDP and the more elastic/cyclical they are to changes in global economic conditions, the more vulnerable the economy is.

India's exports as a share of GDP more than doubled between 2000 and 2013, rising from 12 percent to 25 percent. This share declined in recent years (figure 10.1b), broadly mirroring changes in emerging markets (figure 10.1c). Despite the slowdown, however, India's exports still represented almost 20 percent of GDP in 2017. This share is almost twice what it was 15 years ago and almost as large as in Indonesia.

Complementing this openness is the fact that until recently, India's export basket had become progressively more sensitive to global growth. Although the relationship between growth in the advanced economies and exports in India has softened in recent years, elasticity to partner-country growth remains high (Aziz and Chinoy 2012, Rangarajan and Mishra 2013). It is the primary driver of export volumes, eclipsing the role of the exchange rate and supply bottlenecks.

The growing role of exports in India's growth process can be appreciated by recognizing the contribution of slowing exports to slowing headline GDP growth (figure 10.2). India's much-celebrated 9 percent growth in the 2000s came largely as a result of surging export growth, as global growth rose and India plugged into the global export market. Exports underpinned India's 8.8 percent GDP annual growth in 2003–07 (nearly 18 percent a year in real terms).

In contrast, over 2012–16, export growth slowed to just 2.6 percent a

Figure 10.1c   Exports of goods and services (current US dollars), 2006–15

year-on-year change in percent

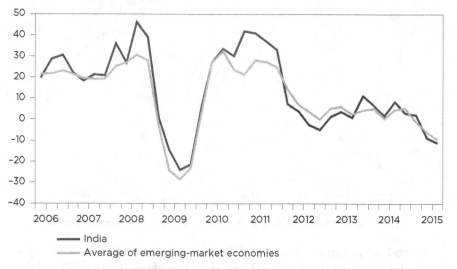

— India
--- Average of emerging-market economies

Note: The average for emerging markets is an export-weighted average.
Source: IMF, Balance of Payments Statistics Database.

Figure 10.2   Role of exports in India's growth slowdown

percent year on year

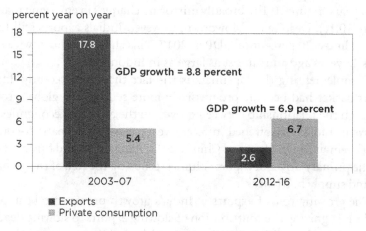

■ Exports
▨ Private consumption

Source: Ministry of Statistics and Program Implementation, Government of India.

Figure 10.3 Role of exports in slowing growth

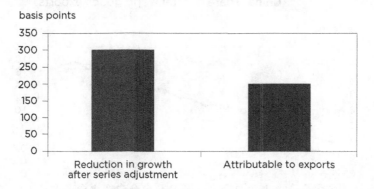

basis points

Source: Authors' calculations.

year in real terms. With exports constituting 20 percent of GDP, a 15 percentage point slowdown in exports—after adjusting for their import content—would shave off more than 2 percentage points from headline GDP growth.

GDP growth in India averaged 6.9 percent over 2012–16, down from 8.8 percent in 2003–07. The slowdown in exports explains virtually all of the slowdown in GDP growth over the two periods.

A change in the GDP methodology renders comparison between the two periods tricky, because there appears to be a level shift up in GDP growth under the new series. For the two years in which the series overlap, the new GDP series is about 110 basis points higher on average than the old series. If one bumps up the old GDP series by 110 basis points to facilitate a more apples-to-apples comparison, the slowdown in growth is closer to 3 percentage points, with exports accounting for two-thirds of the slowdown (assuming that the markup to GDP growth in the old series is not accompanied by a commensurate markup in export growth). This assumption appears reasonable, because the methodological changes to GDP appear to have affected mainly consumption and investment, not exports. In the two years in which the data overlap, export growth is virtually identical across the two series.

These results indicate that exports have been a critical driver of India's slowdown, accounting for about two-thirds of India's GDP slowdown over the last decade (figure 10.3). India did not escape the deglobalization blues that afflicted the world since the global financial crisis.

If global growth remains sluggish, export growth will be tepid. Either one needs to reevaluate potential growth in India (is 7 percent growth today equivalent to 9 percent growth when global growth was surging in the mid-2000s?) or India will have to increase its share of global exports, which was flat in recent years (see figure 10.4), or India needs to find other sources of domestic growth to offset the loss from external demand. Something will have to give.

Figure 10.4 Evolution of global export share of India versus China (share of total world goods exports)

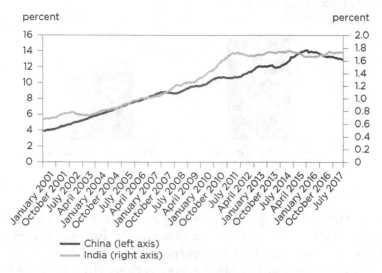

Source: World Trade Organization.

Changing Composition of India's Exports

India's export sector has undergone two revolutions. The first was the surge in services exports. In 2003 service exports constituted 30 percent of the total export basket. Just four years later, they jumped to 40 percent of the basket, reflecting the global software and business process outsourcing (BPO) revolution. Services exports then plateaued over the last decade (figure 10.5).

The second revolution occurred in manufacturing (figure 10.6). In 2003 textiles, leather, and gems/jewelry—India's traditional exports—constituted nearly 60 percent of the merchandise export basket (excluding petroleum). By 2015 they accounted for just 40 percent of the basket. In contrast, exports of engineering goods (such as auto parts and capital goods) grew at an average annual pace of almost 20 percent for 13 years. Their share of the manufacturing export basket rose from 20 percent in 2003 to around 35 percent in 2015. India thus moved up the value chain, with exports increasing in sophistication and value addition. By 2015, for example, engineering goods, electronics, and pharmaceuticals/chemicals constituted almost 60 percent of the merchandise goods basket (excluding oil). (All of this growth occurred in capital-intensive sectors, not in sectors that would have created jobs in a country with a favorable demographic dividend.)

The changed composition of exports has a crucial bearing on the extent to which global demand affects Indian exports, because sector elasticities

Figure 10.5 Share of services in export basket (excluding oil), 2003–15

percent of total

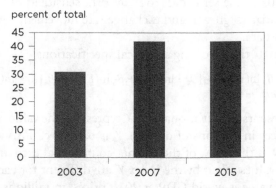

Source: Authors' calculations.

Figure 10.6 Sectoral change in manufacturing exports, 2003–15

change in share of indicated manufacturing products as a percent of total merchandise exports in percentage points

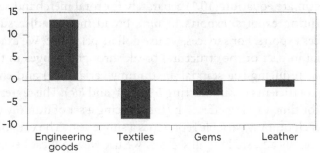

Sources: Ministry of Commerce, Government of India; JP Morgan Research.

to global growth are very heterogeneous. India's new exports (engineering goods, pharmaceuticals, software services) typically have far higher elasticity to global growth than its traditional exports of leather, textiles, gems, and jewelry—a hypothesis tested in this chapter. As in countries of the Association of Southeast Asian Nations (ASEAN), the export basket in India has become more cyclical and more sensitive to global business cycles, surging in good times and contracting in a down cycle. The volatility of global growth transmits more directly and acutely into India given this changed composition of exports.

Macroeconomic Analysis: How Sensitive Are Exports to Changes in Trading Partners' Growth and Exchange Rates?

This section uses time-series data to analyze the sensitivity of India's exports to trading partners' growth and exchange rate movements. Appendix 10A describes the data.

We estimate the following empirical specification:

$$\ln(X_t) = \alpha + \beta_1 \ln(Y_t) + \beta_2 \{D_t * \ln(Y_t)\} + \beta_3 \ln(ER_t) + \beta_4 \{D_t * \ln(ER_t)\} + \gamma Z_t + \delta T_t + \omega D_t + \epsilon_{it} \tag{10.1}$$

where t represents time (the quarter), X_t represents the value of real exports (in 2010 prices in millions of dollars), Y_t is partner country GDP (2010 = 100), and ER_t is the index of the partner country real exchange rate (2010 = 100). The values taken by the index Y_t are different for each sector. For services, the value is world GDP at 2010 prices, in millions of dollars. D_t is a dummy variable indicating the structural break, which we identify by applying the Quandt-Andrews test in each regression separately. Z_t denotes additional time-varying controls, such as the number of stalled projects (a proxy for domestic supply constraint) and volatility in the rupee-to-dollar exchange rate.

We estimate equation (10.1) separately for total merchandise exports, manufacturing exports, exports in nine broad merchandise subsectors, and services exports. For services, we use dollars per rupee. We examine the differential impact of the structural break through changes in the intercept (by introducing the standalone dummy variable D_t) and changes in the slope coefficients (by interacting D_t with Y_t and ER_t). The regression also controls for time-varying effects, by introducing a set of dummy variables, T_t where each dummy variable represents a single year. The variables X_t and Y_t are seasonally adjusted for all sectors. We use Newey-West heteroskedasticity and autocorrelation-adjusted standard errors in all the regressions.

The coefficient β_1 measures the elasticity of India's exports with respect to partner country GDP in the pre–structural break sample period. It shows the percentage by which India's real exports change if the partner countries grow by 1 percent. The coefficient β_2 measures the differential effect of partner country demand on Indian exports after the structural break. β_3 measures the percentage change in India's real exports from a 1 percent appreciation in the real effective exchange rate in the pre–structural break period. β_4 measures the differential effect of real exchange rates on Indian exports after the structural break.

The empirical models yield several main findings:

- The elasticity of India's exports to partner country GDP is positive and statistically significant. A 1 percent growth in partner country GDP

Table 10.1 Determinants of India's merchandise and services exports

Variable	(1) Total merchandise exports	(2) Manufactured items	(3) Services exports
Log of partner GDP	2.8*** (0.2)	2.3*** (0.1)	1.6*** (0.5)
Log of partner GDP * Structural break dummy	-2.5*** (0.2)	-1.4*** (0.2)	-0.8 (0.7)
Log of partner exchange rate	-1.3*** (0.2)	-0.8 (0.9)	2.5*** (0.5)
Log of partner exchange rate * Structural break dummy	1.7*** (0.3)	1.9 (2.3)	-2.7*** (0.6)
Log of number of stalled projects	0.1** (0.0)	0.1 (0.1)	
Volatility of dollar/rupee exchange rate	79.1* (41.4)	72.0 (70.0)	71.3 (59.7)
Structural break dummy	3.0** (1.3)	-2.3 (11.1)	-6.2 (4.8)

Model properties

Sample period	2002Q4 to 2016Q3		
Number of observations	56	56	56
Structural break date	2005Q1	2005Q1	2005Q4
Max Wald-F: Quandt-Andrews test for structural break	59.8***	48.4***	77.0***

Dependent variable: Log of exports (2010 prices) in US dollars.

Notes: Manufacturing exports exclude the exports of petroleum products, gems and jewelry, and primary products like agricultural items, ores, and minerals. Numbers in parentheses represent standard errors. *, **, and *** indicate statistical significance at 10, 5, and 1 percent, respectively.

Sources: CEIC database; World Bank, *World Development Indicators*; Centre for Monitoring the Indian Economy (CMIE) Capex database.

was associated with a 2.8 percent rise in India's merchandise exports before 2005. The elasticity was 2.3 percent for manufacturing exports and 1.6 percent for services exports (table 10.1).

■ There is evidence of a sharp structural break in the effect of partner country output on Indian exports around 2005, well before the global financial crisis (see table 10.1). Partner country income elasticity falls sharply after the structural break, declining by 2.5 percentage points, reducing the effective elasticity to almost zero after 2005. The elasticity of manufactured goods remained high, at 1 percent, and statistically significant after 2005. In contrast, for services exports, there is no significant evidence for changes in elasticity with respect to partner growth after the structural break.

- There is significant variation in partner income elasticities across manu-facturing sectors,[1] both before and after the structural break (table 10.2). Engineering and electronics reported the highest elasticities before 2005, followed by chemicals, pharmaceuticals, and leather and textiles. The fall in elasticity after 2005 was very sharp for electronics and en-gineering goods. Despite the decline, engineering and pharmaceuticals reported the highest income elasticities after 2005. There was no change in the elasticity of leather and textiles after the structural break.

- There is little evidence that an appreciating rupee hurts Indian exports. The weak relationship between exports and exchange rates is not sur-prising, as it is very hard to separate out the effect of exchange rates on trade (Engel 2009). The estimation of exports–exchange rate equations is plagued by concerns about reverse causality and omitted variables, which are hard to address with macroeconomic data. Moreover, several papers show that the aggregation of heterogeneous firms or sectors can result in aggregation bias in the estimation of the elasticity of exports to exchange rate changes (see, e.g., Dekle, Jeong, and Ryoo 2009; Imbs and Méjean 2009). We examine the implications of such heterogeneity at the firm level in the next section.

- In the leather, textiles, and chemical products subsectors, appreciation of the rupee was associated with a fall in real exports, mostly in recent years. In all other cases, the elasticity both before and after the struc-tural break was either very insignificant or (counterintuitively) positive.

- The volume of stalled projects and volatility in the exchange rate do not seem to affect Indian exports adversely (tables 10.1 and 10.2). There is no evidence for nonlinearity in the estimates of elasticity for partner GDP and exchange rates (see appendix table 10A.1 at the end of the chapter). The partner income elasticity of Indian exports declined. It remained substantial for manufactured items, however, particularly leather, textiles, and engineering goods. In contrast, exchange rate movements did not seem to have a significant effect on exports.

Firm-Level Analysis: How Do Exporting Firms React to Exchange Rate Changes?

How can one explain the low aggregate elasticity of exports to exchange rate movements in India? Is there heterogeneity across exporting firms in the responses to exchange rate movements? If so, could it explain low aggregate elasticities?

---

1. Break dates vary widely. They are 2005 for engineering and pharmaceuticals, 2008–09 for electronics, and 2013–14 for leather, textiles, and chemicals.

Table 10.2 Determinants of India's merchandise and services exports, by sector

Variable	(1) Total merchandise exports	(2) Manufacturing exports	(2.1) Leather and textiles	(2.2) Engineering	(2.3) Chemical products	(2.4) Pharmaceutical products	(2.5) Electronics	(3) Services
Log of partner GDP	2.8*** (0.2)	2.3*** (0.1)	2.0*** (0.7)	5.5*** (0.3)	2.3*** (0.7)	2.2*** (0.2)	2.8*** (0.6)	1.6*** (0.5)
Log of partner GDP * Structural break dummy	-2.5*** (0.2)	-1.4*** (0.2)	-1.1 (1.0)	-4.2*** (0.7)	-1.2* (0.7)	-1.0*** (0.0)	-4.0*** (1.1)	-0.8 (0.7)
Log of partner exchange rate	-1.3*** (0.2)	-0.8 (0.9)	0.6 (0.6)	-0.7 (1.8)	0.6 (0.8)	5.2*** (0.7)	2.2** (1.1)	2.5*** (0.5)
Log of partner exchange Rate * Structural break dummy	1.7*** (0.3)	1.9 (2.3)	-3.3*** (0.6)	2.3 (2.2)	-2.7*** (0.8)	-6.7*** (0.9)	-0.1 (2.1)	-2.7*** (0.6)
Log of number of stalled projects	0.1** (0.0)	0.1 (0.1)	-0.2 (0.1)	0.0 (0.1)	-0.1 (0.2)	0.0 (0.0)	0.2*** (0.0)	
Volatility of dollar/rupee exchange rate	79.1* (41.4)	72.0 (70.0)	-18.1 (67.4)	93.5 (118.5)	47.6 (33.6)	3.5 (25.0)	120.1* (64.8)	71.3 (59.7)
Structural break dummy	3.0** (1.3)	-2.3 (11.1)	20.7*** (4.5)	7.9 (10.7)	18.0*** (4.6)	34.9*** (4.4)	19.2 (11.9)	-6.2 (4.8)
Model properties								
Sample period				2002Q4 to 2016Q3				
Number of observations	56	56	56	56	56	56	56	56
Structural break date	2005Q1	2005Q1	2013Q4	2005Q1	2014Q1	2005Q1	2008Q2	2005Q4
Max Wald-F: Quandt-Andrews test for structural break	59.8***	48.4***	176.0***	45.6***	79.4***	91.6***	73.7***	77.0***

Dependent variable: Log of exports (2010 prices) in US dollars.

Note: *, **, and *** indicate statistical significance at 10, 5, and 1 percent, respectively. Numbers in parentheses represent standard errors.

Source: Authors' calculations.

This section draws on the literature (see, e.g., Berman, Martin, and Mayer 2012) and granular firm-level data for India in order to answer these questions.

We estimate the following specification:

$$\ln(F_{it}) = \alpha + \beta \ln(ER_t) + \gamma X_t + s_i + \delta t + \epsilon_{it} \qquad (10.2)$$

where firms are indexed by i; time is indexed by t; F_{it} is a firm-level outcome that includes the value of exports, imported raw materials, total sales (domestic and foreign), total costs, and profits; ER_t is the average annual exchange rate; and X_t are additional time-varying controls, which include world GDP growth (to measure external demand conditions) and the volume of stalled projects (as a proxy for domestic supply constraints). All regressions include firm fixed effects (s_i) and therefore use variation within firms over time to identify the responses to exchange rate movements. The regressions also control for a time trend (t).[2] Standard errors are clustered at the firm level.

The main findings from the empirical analysis include the following:

- There is little evidence that appreciation of the exchange rate reduced the value of exports. In fact, the elasticity of exports with respect to the exchange rate was positive after 2009 and in the smaller sample of firms; an appreciation of the exchange rate was associated with a higher value of average exports at the firm level. The long-run effect was also positive and stronger than the short-run effect (table 10.3).[3]

- The value of imported intermediates rises sharply in response to an appreciation of the rupee (table 10.4). The finding is robust across several specifications. A 1 percent increase in the real effective exchange rate (REER) was associated with a 0.4 percent increase in the value of imported intermediates. The magnitude of the effect was much larger after 2009, for the balanced panel of firms, and in the long run.

- The effect of appreciation of the rupee varied across sectors. There is some evidence that exports of firms in sectors with *high* domestic value added (top 25th percentile) declined following appreciation of the

---

2. Time dummies cannot be included, because the main variable of interest (the exchange rate) varies only over time.

3. The long-run effect is estimated by introducing a lagged dependent variable in the model (columns 10–15 in table 10.3). It is calculated as $\frac{\beta}{1-\theta}$, where β is the coefficient on the exchange rate and θ the coefficient on lagged exports. The dynamic effects shown in table 10.1 are robust to using a generalized method of moments (GMM) estimator (which addresses concerns about bias arising from introducing a lagged dependent variable in a panel data model with fixed effects). The smaller sample of firms is a "balanced" panel with the same set of firms over the entire period.

rupee. The value of imported intermediate inputs rose more significantly in sectors with *low* domestic value added (or high foreign value-added) content. Exports of firms in these sectors did not decline following an appreciation of the rupee (table 10.5). This result is not surprising, as greater reliance on foreign inputs is analytically analogous to a lower pass-through, which would dampen the competitiveness effect of changes in the exchange rate (see, e.g., Ahmed, Appendino, and Ruta 2015).

- Consistent with the firm-level evidence, the market share of exports by several sectors with high domestic value-added content (e.g., readymade garments, other textiles, minerals, copper and copper products, trading) declined with the strengthening of the rupee (figure 10.7). Sectors with high foreign value-added content (e.g., drugs and pharmaceuticals, other chemical products, and gems and jewelry) increased their market shares with the strengthening of the rupee (figure 10.8).

- Total sales (domestic and foreign) increased following an appreciation of the rupee. Total costs also increased, perhaps because of increased spending on foreign inputs (tables 10.6 and 10.7).

- Profits showed no significant relationship with exchange rate movements. There is no evidence that profitability declined at the firm level following an appreciation of the rupee (table 10.8).

- Expenditure on wages and salaries is positively associated with a strengthening of the rupee (table 10.9).

- Firms did not seem to adjust their investments in response to exchange rate fluctuations (table 10.10).

These findings suggest that following a strengthening of the rupee, firms import more intermediate inputs, export more, increase overall sales, and pay higher wages and salaries. They do not adjust their investments, and their profits do not change significantly. The adjustments on all these margins are significantly higher for firms in which the imported intermediate content of exports is higher.

Table 10.3   Firm outcomes and exchange rates: Value of exports (millions of rupees)

Variable	[1] REER	[2] NEER	[3] US$/Rs	[4] REER	[5] NEER	[6] US$/Rs
	Full sample			Post-2009 sample		
Exchange rate (one-year lag, in logs)	−0.349 [0.260]	−0.14 [0.197]	−0.005 [0.13]	1.364^ [0.85]	1.131^ [0.70]	0.499^ [0.31]
World growth (one-year lag)	0.020*** [0.006]	0.016*** [0.004]	0.014*** [0.004]	−0.02 [0.020]	−0.007 [0.013]	0.004 [0.007]
Volume of stalled projects (one-year lag, in logs)	−0.225*** [0.046]	−0.260*** [0.040]	−0.266*** [0.042]	−0.205 [0.171]	−0.329^ [0.201]	−0.306^ [0.193]
Value of exports (one-year lag, in logs)						
Time trend	0.186*** [0.01]	0.184*** [0.017]	0.192*** [0.015]	0.169*** [0.045]	0.278*** [0.088]	0.226*** [0.062]
Long-run effect						
Number of observations	27,899	27,899	27,899	15,379	15,379	15,379
Number of firms	6,561	6,561	6,561	5,247	5,247	5,247

Variable	[7] REER	[8] NEER	[9] US\$/Rs	[10] REER	[11] NEER	[12] US\$/Rs	[13] REER	[14] NEER	[15] US\$/Rs
	Balanced panel of firms			Dynamic effects			Dynamic effects: Post-2009		
Exchange rate (one-year lag, in logs)	0.863*** [0.282]	0.890*** [0.207]	0.674*** [0.131]	0.334 [0.72]	2.197*** [0.589]	0.869*** [0.228]	1.415^ [0.91]	1.173^ [0.760]	0.518^ [0.335]
World growth (one-year lag)	-0.002 [0.007]	0.003 [0.005]	0.006 [0.004]	0.016 [0.015]	-0.012 [0.010]	0.008^ [0.005]	-0.012 [0.022]	0.002 [0.014]	0.013^ [0.008]
Volume of stalled projects (one-year lag, in logs)	-0.253*** [0.049]	-0.207*** [0.041]	-0.163*** [0.041]	-0.313** [0.136]	-0.537*** [0.085]	-0.337*** [0.047]	-0.21 [0.169]	-0.339^ [0.205]	-0.315^ [0.196]
Value of exports (one-year lag, in logs)				0.325*** [0.019]	0.325*** [0.019]	0.325*** [0.019]	0.227*** [0.027]	0.227*** [0.027]	0.227*** [0.027]
Time trend	0.175*** [0.015]	0.220*** [0.018]	0.189*** [0.015]	0.161*** [0.037]	0.366*** [0.061]	0.219*** [0.026]	0.130*** [0.045]	0.243*** [0.094]	0.188*** [0.065]
Long-run effect				0.504	3.255	1.287	1.831	1.517	0.670
Number of observations	10,304	10,304	10,304	20,645	20,645	20,645	13,666	13,666	13,666
Number of firms	1,288	1,288	1,288	5,486	5,486	5,486	4,743	4,743	4,743

Dependent variable: Value of exports (in logs).

REER = real effective exchange rate; NEER = nominal effective exchange rate

Note: All regressions include firm fixed effects. Standard errors are clustered at the firm level. An increase in all measures of the exchange rate denotes an appreciation. ***, **, *, and ^ denote statistical significance at 1, 5, 10, and 15 percent levels, respectively.

Source: Authors' calculations.

Table 10.4   **Firm outcomes and exchange rates: Value of imported raw materials**
(millions of rupees)

Variable	[1] REER	[2] NEER	[3] US$/Rs	[4] REER	[5] NEER	[6] US$/Rs
	Full sample			Post-2009 sample		
Exchange rate (one-year lag, in logs)	0.452 [0.316]	0.611*** [0.234]	0.524*** [0.154]	2.084* [1.099]	1.727* [0.911]	0.763* [0.402]
World growth (one-year lag)	0.017** [0.007]	0.018*** [0.005]	0.019*** [0.005]	-0.02 [0.025]	-0.001 [0.016]	0.016* [0.009]
Volume of stalled projects (one-year lag, in logs)	-0.149** [0.058]	-0.122** [0.049]	-0.083* [0.050]	0.134 [0.224]	-0.055 [0.271]	-0.019 [0.260]
Time trend	0.109*** [0.018]	0.137*** [0.021]	0.115*** [0.018]	0.015 [0.058]	0.181ˆ [0.119]	0.101 [0.084]
Long-run effect						
Number of observations	19,427	19,427	19,427	10,777	10,777	10,777
Number of firms	4,524	4,524	4,524	3,578	3,578	3,578

Variable	[7]	[8]	[9]	[10]	[11]	[12]	[13]	[14]	[15]
	REER	NEER	US$/Rs	REER	NEER	US$/Rs	REER	NEER	US$/Rs
	Balanced panel of firms			Dynamic effects			Dynamic effects: Post-2009		
Exchange rate (one-year lag, in logs)	1.166*** [0.358]	1.063*** [0.264]	0.766*** [0.171]	0.405 [0.983]	3.345*** [0.737]	1.326*** [0.282]	2.859** [1.112]	2.369** [0.921]	1.046** [0.407]
World growth (one-year lag)	-0.003 [0.008]	0.005 [0.006]	0.008^ [0.005]	0.02 [0.020]	-0.024** [0.012]	0.006 [0.006]	-0.040^ [0.026]	-0.014 [0.016]	0.009 [0.009]
Volume of stalled projects (one-year lag, in logs)	-0.148** [0.071]	-0.074 [0.061]	-0.02 [0.060]	-0.138 [0.182]	-0.503*** [0.107]	-0.199*** [0.060]	0.12 [0.230]	-0.139 [0.280]	-0.091 [0.268]
Time trend	0.095*** [0.022]	0.145*** [0.026]	0.107*** [0.022]	0.081^ [0.050]	0.401*** [0.076]	0.177*** [0.032]	0.013 [0.060]	0.240** [0.122]	0.131^ [0.087]
Long-run effect				0.497	4.099	1.611	3.009	2.494	1.101
Number of observations	8,643	8,643	8,643	14,308	14,308	14,308	9,530	9,530	9,530
Number of firms	1,173	1,173	1,173	3,723	3,723	3,723	3,192	3,192	3,192

Dependent variable: Value of imported raw materials (in logs).

REER = real effective exchange rate; NEER = nominal effective exchange rate

Note: All regressions include firm fixed effects. Standard errors are clustered at the firm level. An increase in all measures of the exchange rate denotes an appreciation. ***, **, *, and ^ denote statistical significance at 1, 5, 10, and 15 percent levels, respectively.

Source: Authors' calculations.

Table 10.5 Firm outcomes and exchange rates: By domestic value added (millions of rupees)

Variable	Dependent variable: Value of exports (in logs)					
	[1]	[2]	[3]	[4]	[5]	[6]
	REER	NEER	US$/Rs	REER	NEER	US$/Rs
	High domestic value added			Low domestic value added		
Exchange rate (one-year lag, in logs)	−0.874** [0.398]	−0.497* [0.296]	−0.227 [0.194]	0.575 [0.714]	0.696 [0.541]	0.578^ [0.359]
World growth (one-year lag)	0.026*** [0.009]	0.017*** [0.006]	0.014** [0.006]	−0.01 [0.015]	−0.008 [0.011]	−0.006 [0.010]
Volume of stalled projects (one-year lag, in logs)	−0.189*** [0.070]	−0.272*** [0.060]	−0.298*** [0.063]	−0.515*** [0.123]	−0.477*** [0.106]	−0.434*** [0.111]
Time trend	0.202*** [0.023]	0.187*** [0.025]	0.210*** [0.023]	0.261*** [0.040]	0.292*** [0.046]	0.266*** [0.040]
Number of observations	12,204	12,204	12,204	3,638	3,638	3,638
Number of firms	2,942	2,942	2,942	788	788	788

Variable	Dependent variable: Value of imported raw materials (in logs)					
	[7]	[8]	[9]	[10]	[11]	[12]
	REER	NEER	US$/Rs	REER	NEER	US$/Rs
	High domestic value added			Low domestic value added		
Exchange rate (one-year lag, in logs)	0.423 [0.497]	0.574^ [0.367]	0.489** [0.239]	1.015 [0.725]	0.939* [0.551]	0.698* [0.367]
World growth (one-year lag)	0.012 [0.011]	0.013* [0.008]	0.014** [0.007]	0.003 [0.016]	0.009 [0.011]	0.012 [0.010]
Volume of stalled projects (one-year lag, in logs)	−0.097 [0.088]	−0.073 [0.073]	−0.036 [0.074]	−0.109 [0.129]	−0.03 [0.109]	0.026 [0.112]
Time trend	0.120*** [0.027]	0.146*** [0.032]	0.125*** [0.027]	0.116*** [0.042]	0.154*** [0.048]	0.117*** [0.041]
Number of observations	8,418	8,418	8,418	3,067	3,067	3,067
Number of firms	2,010	2,010	2,010	677	677	677

REER = real effective exchange rate; NEER = nominal effective exchange rate

Note: All regressions include firm fixed effects. Standard errors are clustered at the firm level. An increase in all measures of the exchange rate denotes an appreciation. Domestic value added (DVA) content is based on an ICRIER study submitted to the Ministry of Finance. High DVA industries are defined as those with DVA content greater than the 25th percentile. ***, **, *, and ^ denote statistical significance at 1, 5, 10, and 15 percent levels, respectively.

Source: Authors' calculations.

Figure 10.7 Market share of exports over time: Selected sectors with high domestic value added, 2007–14

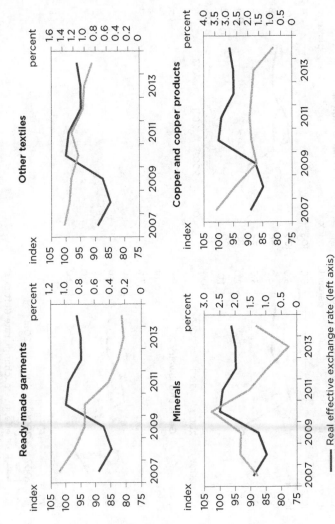

Real effective exchange rate (left axis)
Market share (percent of total exports, right axis)

Sources: Ministry of Statistics and Program Implementation, Government of India; authors' calculations.

Figure 10.8   Market share of exports over time: Selected sectors with high foreign value added

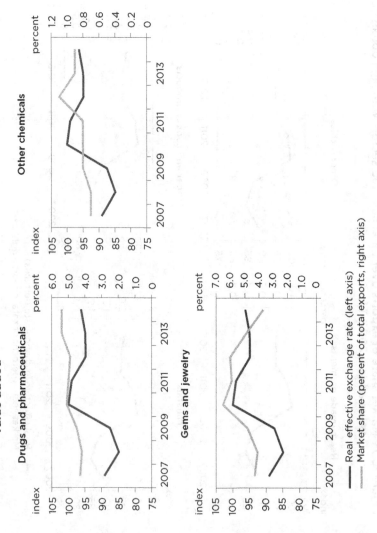

Drugs and pharmaceuticals

Other chemicals

Gems and jewelry

—— Real effective exchange rate (left axis)

⋯⋯ Market share (percent of total exports, right axis)

Sources: Ministry of Statistics and Program Implementation, Government of India; authors' calculations.

Table 10.6 Firm outcomes and exchange rates: Total sales (millions of rupees)

Variable	[1]	[2]	[3]	[4]	[5]	[6]
	REER	NEER	US$/Rs	REER	NEER	US$/Rs
	Full sample			Post-2009 sample		
Exchange rate (one-year lag, in logs)	0.675*** [0.136]	0.586*** [0.104]	0.402*** [0.069]	0.748** [0.372]	0.620** [0.308]	0.274** [0.136]
World growth (one-year lag)	0.002 [0.003]	0.006*** [0.002]	0.009*** [0.002]	-0.006 [0.009]	0.001 [0.005]	0.007** [0.003]
Volume of stalled projects (one-year lag, in logs)	-0.077*** [0.023]	-0.021 [0.020]	0.014 [0.021]	0.242*** [0.084]	0.174* [0.097]	0.187** [0.094]
Total sales (one-year lag, in logs)						
Time trend	0.119*** [0.008]	0.142*** [0.009]	0.118*** [0.008]	0.029 [0.022]	0.089** [0.041]	0.060** [0.030]
Number of observations	27,542	27,542	27,542	15,186	15,186	15,186
Number of firms	6,488	6,488	6,488	5,186	5,186	5,186

(continues on next page)

213

Table 10.6 Firm outcomes and exchange rates: Total sales (millions of rupees) *(continued)*

Variable	[7] REER	[8] NEER	[9] US$/Rs	[10] REER	[11] NEER	[12] US$/Rs	[13] REER	[14] NEER	[15] US$/Rs
	Balanced panel of firms			Dynamic effects			Dynamic effects: Post-2009		
Exchange rate (one-year lag, in logs)	1.262*** [0.142]	1.025*** [0.107]	0.679*** [0.068]	0.045 [0.309]	0.244 [0.254]	0.099 [0.100]	0.395 [0.381]	0.328 [0.315]	0.145 [0.139]
World growth (one-year lag)	-0.013*** [0.003]	-0.003 [0.002]	0.001 [0.002]	0.019*** [0.006]	0.017*** [0.004]	0.019*** [0.002]	0.01 [0.009]	0.014** [0.006]	0.017*** [0.003]
Volume of stalled projects (one-year lag, in logs)	-0.106*** [0.024]	-0.017 [0.019]	0.038** [0.018]	0.056 [0.058]	0.032 [0.038]	0.054** [0.022]	0.06 [0.079]	0.025 [0.093]	0.031 [0.090]
Total sales (one-year lag, in logs)				0.455*** [0.027]	0.454*** [0.027]	0.454*** [0.027]	0.416*** [0.037]	0.416*** [0.037]	0.416*** [0.037]
Time trend	0.119*** [0.007]	0.164*** [0.009]	0.124*** [0.007]	0.021 [0.017]	0.043^ [0.027]	0.027** [0.012]	0.019 [0.020]	0.05 [0.041]	0.035 [0.029]
Number of observations	10,242	10,242	10,242	20,375	20,375	20,375	13,493	13,493	13,493
Number of firms	1,286	1,286	1,286	5,427	5,427	5,427	4,692	4,692	4,692

Dependent variable: Total sales (in logs).

REER = real effective exchange rate; NEER = nominal effective exchange rate

Note: All regressions include firm fixed effects. An increase in all measures of the exchange rate denotes an appreciation. Standard errors are clustered at the firm level. ***, **, *, and ^ denote statistical significance at 1, 5, 10, and 15 percent levels, respectively.

Source: Authors' calculations.

Table 10.7 Firm outcomes and exchange rates: Total expenses (millions of rupees)

Variable	[1] REER	[2] NEER	[3] US$/Rs	[4] REER	[5] NEER	[6] US$/Rs
	Full sample			Post-2009 sample		
Exchange rate (one-year lag, in logs)	0.761*** [0.114]	0.685*** [0.086]	0.490*** [0.056]	1.287*** [0.314]	1.066*** [0.260]	0.471*** [0.115]
World growth (one-year lag)	-0.001 [0.003]	0.004** [0.002]	0.006*** [0.002]	-0.017** [0.007]	-0.005 [0.004]	0.005** [0.002]
Volume of stalled projects (one-year lag, in logs)	-0.125*** [0.020]	-0.063*** [0.016]	-0.021 [0.017]	0.192*** [0.068]	0.076 [0.080]	0.097 [0.077]
Total expenses (one-year lag, in logs)						
Time trend	0.141*** [0.006]	0.167*** [0.007]	0.140*** [0.006]	0.051*** [0.018]	0.154*** [0.034]	0.104*** [0.025]
Number of observations	27,891	27,891	27,891	15,375	15,375	15,375
Number of firms	6,558	6,558	6,558	5,245	5,245	5,245

(continues on next page)

Table 10.7 Firm outcomes and exchange rates: Total expenses (millions of rupees) (continued)

Variable	[7]	[8]	[9]	[10]	[11]	[12]	[13]	[14]	[15]
	REER	NEER	US$/Rs	REER	NEER	US$/Rs	REER	NEER	US$/Rs
	Balanced panel of firms			Dynamic effects			Dynamic effects: Post-2009		
Exchange rate (one-year lag, in logs)	1.180*** [0.113]	0.978*** [0.086]	0.660*** [0.055]	0.09 [0.253]	0.756*** [0.214]	0.300*** [0.084]	0.670** [0.332]	0.555** [0.275]	0.245** [0.121]
World growth (one-year lag)	-0.009*** [0.003]	0.00 [0.002]	0.003** [0.002]	0.019*** [0.005]	0.009** [0.004]	0.016*** [0.002]	0.005 [0.008]	0.011** [0.005]	0.016*** [0.003]
Volume of stalled projects (one-year lag, in logs)	-0.123*** [0.019]	-0.041*** [0.016]	0.011 [0.016]	0.016 [0.047]	-0.066** [0.032]	0.003 [0.018]	0.056 [0.061]	-0.004 [0.073]	0.007 [0.070]
Total expenses (one-year lag, in logs)				0.471*** [0.021]	0.469*** [0.021]	0.469*** [0.021]	0.413*** [0.028]	0.413*** [0.028]	0.413*** [0.028]
Time trend	0.132*** [0.006]	0.175*** [0.008]	0.137*** [0.006]	0.039*** [0.013]	0.111*** [0.023]	0.060*** [0.011]	0.030* [0.016]	0.083** [0.034]	0.057** [0.023]
Number of observations	10,304	10,304	10,304	20,639	20,639	20,639	13,663	13,663	13,663
Number of firms	1,288	1,288	1,288	5,483	5,483	5,483	4,741	4,741	4,741

Dependent variable: Total expenses (in logs).

REER = real effective exchange rate; NEER = nominal effective exchange rate

Note: All regressions include firm fixed effects. Standard errors are clustered at the firm level. An increase in all measures of the exchange rate denotes an appreciation. ***, **, *, and ^ denote statistical significance at 1, 5, 10, and 15 percent levels, respectively.

Source: Authors' calculations.

Table 10.8 Firm outcomes and exchange rates: Profits (millions of rupees)

Variable	Full sample			Post-2009 sample			Balanced panel of firms		
	REER	NEER	US$/Rs	REER	NEER	US$/Rs	REER	NEER	US$/Rs
Exchange rate (one-year lag, in logs)	0.093 [0.431]	-0.074 [0.316]	-0.124 [0.209]	-0.703 [1.797]	-0.583 [1.489]	-0.257 [0.658]	0.824^ [0.531]	0.427 [0.381]	0.187 [0.249]
World growth (one-year lag)	-0.003 [0.009]	-0.001 [0.006]	0.00 [0.006]	0.025 [0.042]	0.019 [0.026]	0.013 [0.014]	-0.021* [0.011]	-0.012^ [0.008]	-0.01 [0.008]
Volume of stalled projects (one-year lag, in logs)	0.221*** [0.083]	0.235*** [0.069]	0.228*** [0.069]	-0.273 [0.347]	-0.209 [0.429]	-0.221 [0.410]	0.07 [0.107]	0.147* [0.088]	0.173** [0.086]
Time trend	0.02 [0.026]	0.015 [0.030]	0.016 [0.026]	0.137^ [0.091]	0.081 [0.194]	0.108 [0.135]	0.051^ [0.033]	0.063^ [0.039]	0.042 [0.033]
Number of observations	14,635	14,635	14,635	8,041	8,041	8,041	6,142	6,142	6,142
Number of firms	4,802	4,802	4,802	3,552	3,552	3,552	1,213	1,213	1,213

Dependent variable: Profits (in logs).

REER = real effective exchange rate; NEER = nominal effective exchange rate

Note: All regressions include firm fixed effects. Standard errors are clustered at the firm level. An increase in all measures of the exchange rate denotes an appreciation. Firms with negative profits are dropped from the regressions. ***, **, *, and ^ denote statistical significance at 1, 5, 10, and 15 percent levels, respectively.

Source: Authors' calculations.

217

Table 10.9   Firm outcomes and exchange rates: Salaries and wage expenses (millions of rupees)

Variable	[1]	[2]	[3]	[4]	[5]	[6]
	REER	NEER	US$/Rs	REER	NEER	US$/Rs
	Full sample			Post-2009 sample		
Exchange rate (one-year lag, in logs)	1.008*** [0.107]	0.851*** [0.081]	0.573*** [0.052]	0.597** [0.288]	0.495** [0.239]	0.218** [0.105]
World growth (one-year lag)	-0.014*** [0.002]	-0.007*** [0.002]	-0.004** [0.002]	-0.008 [0.007]	-0.003 [0.004]	0.002 [0.002]
Volume of stalled projects (one-year lag, in logs)	-0.158*** [0.018]	-0.074*** [0.015]	-0.022 [0.016]	0.199*** [0.062]	0.145** [0.074]	0.155** [0.071]
Value of exports (one-year lag, in logs)						
Time trend	0.170*** [0.006]	0.202*** [0.007]	0.167*** [0.006]	0.070*** [0.016]	0.117*** [0.031]	0.094*** [0.022]
Number of observations	27,708	27,708	27,708	15,277	15,277	15,277
Number of firms	6,502	6,502	6,502	5,208	5,208	5,208

Variable	[7] REER	[8] NEER	[9] US$/Rs	[10] REER	[11] NEER	[12] US$/Rs	[13] REER	[14] NEER	[15] US$/Rs
	Balanced panel of firms			Dynamic effects			Dynamic effects: post-2009		
Exchange rate (one-year lag, in logs)	1.287*** [0.108]	1.034*** [0.082]	0.673*** [0.052]	-0.304 [0.245]	0.358* [0.201]	0.173** [0.077]	0.254 [0.310]	0.211 [0.257]	0.093 [0.113]
World growth (one-year lag)	-0.021*** [0.003]	-0.011*** [0.002]	-0.007*** [0.002]	0.020*** [0.005]	0.008*** [0.003]	0.011*** [0.002]	0.003 [0.007]	0.006 [0.005]	0.008*** [0.003]
Volume of stalled projects (one-year lag, in logs)	-0.127*** [0.019]	-0.035** [0.015]	0.021 [0.015]	0.059 [0.046]	-0.042 [0.029]	-0.012 [0.016]	0.132** [0.056]	0.109^ [0.069]	0.114* [0.066]
Value of exports (one-year lag, in logs)				0.553*** [0.023]	0.553*** [0.023]	0.553*** [0.023]	0.458*** [0.034]	0.458*** [0.034]	0.458*** [0.034]
Time trend	0.152*** [0.005]	0.197*** [0.007]	0.156*** [0.005]	0.027** [0.012]	0.078*** [0.022]	0.056*** [0.010]	0.018 [0.014]	0.038 [0.032]	0.028 [0.022]
Number of observations	10,295	10,295	10,295	20,521	20,521	20,521	13,588	13,588	13,588
Number of firms	1,288	1,288	1,288	5,444	5,444	5,444	4,713	4,713	4,713

Dependent variable: Value of salaries and wage expenses (in logs).

REER = real effective exchange rate; NEER = nominal effective exchange rate

Note: All regressions include firm fixed effects. Standard errors are clustered at the firm level. An increase in all measures of the exchange rate denotes an appreciation. ***, **, *, and ^ denote statistical significance at 1, 5, 10, and 15 percent levels, respectively.

Source: Authors' calculations.

Table 10.10 **Firm outcomes and exchange rates: Investment** (millions of rupees)

Variable	[1]	[2]	[3]	[4]	[5]	[6]
	REER	NEER	US$/Rs	REER	NEER	US$/Rs
	Full sample			Post-2009 sample		
Exchange rate (one-year lag, in logs)	-2.294 [2.729]	2.262 [2.216]	1.136 [0.847]	1.957 [3.709]	1.622 [3.073]	0.716 [1.357]
World growth (one-year lag)	0.080^ [0.056]	-0.001 [0.037]	0.015 [0.019]	-0.029 [0.088]	-0.011 [0.055]	0.005 [0.031]
Volume of stalled projects (one-year lag, in logs)	0.59 [0.525]	-0.117 [0.357]	0.065 [0.195]	1.080* [0.590]	0.903 [0.772]	0.936 [0.730]
Value of exports (one-year lag, in logs)						
Time trend	-0.134 [0.145]	0.201 [0.243]	0.071 [0.104]	-0.271* [0.159]	-0.115 [0.384]	-0.19 [0.259]
Number of observations	17,866	17,866	17,866	12,099	12,099	12,099
Number of firms	5,182	5,182	5,182	4,420	4,420	4,420

Variable	[7]	[8]	[9]	[10]	[11]	[12]	[13]	[14]	[15]
	REER	NEER	US$/Rs	REER	NEER	US$/Rs	REER	NEER	US$/Rs
	Balanced panel of firms			Dynamic effects			Dynamic effects: Post-2009		
Exchange rate (one-year lag, in logs)	-3.774 [2.999]	1.645 [2.630]	1.003 [1.004]	-2.197 [2.361]	3.281 [2.600]	1.791* [1.020]	2.489 [3.264]	2.063 [2.705]	0.911 [1.195]
World growth (one-year lag)	0.094^ [0.061]	-0.008 [0.042]	0.001 [0.020]	0.069^ [0.048]	-0.033 [0.048]	-0.015 [0.027]	-0.066 [0.078]	-0.043 [0.049]	-0.023 [0.028]
Volume of stalled projects (one-year lag, in logs)	1.118* [0.598]	0.227 [0.440]	0.33 [0.233]	0.356 [0.442]	-0.434 [0.346]	-0.175 [0.165]	1.148** [0.524]	0.923 [0.657]	0.965^ [0.623]
Value of exports (one-year lag, in logs)				-0.225*** [0.052]	-0.225*** [0.052]	-0.225*** [0.052]	-0.234*** [0.065]	-0.234*** [0.065]	-0.234*** [0.065]
Time trend	-0.292* [0.166]	0.05 [0.298]	-0.025 [0.127]	-0.044 [0.121]	0.387^ [0.268]	0.211** [0.105]	-0.237^ [0.137]	-0.038 [0.323]	-0.134 [0.216]
Number of observations	8,017	8,017	8,017	11,778	11,778	11,778	9,673	9,673	9,673
Number of firms	1,286	1,286	1,286	3,750	3,750	3,750	3,443	3,443	3,443

Dependent variable: Value of investment (in logs).

REER = real effective exchange rate; NEER = nominal effective exchange rate

Note: All regressions include firm fixed effects. Standard errors are clustered at the firm level. An increase in all measures of the exchange rate denotes an appreciation. ***, **, *, and ^ denote statistical significance at 1, 5, 10, and 15 percent levels, respectively.

Source: Authors' calculations.

221

Conclusions and Policy Implications

India's merchandise exports underwent a quiet revolution over the last two decades, with engineering, electronic, and pharmaceutical exports gradually replacing India's traditional exports of leather, textiles, and gems and jewelry. Sectoral data reveal that changes in partner country growth drive export volumes, with new exports exhibiting the highest elasticities.

A structural break occurred around 2005—well before the global financial crisis and the subsequent deglobalization. Partner country growth elasticities fell sharply after 2005, but they remained significant, especially for engineering, textiles, and leather. In contrast, changes in the exchange rate and supply-side constraints did not affect India's export volumes significantly.

Analysis based on firm-level data produces broadly similar results. Sectors with higher imported intermediate input content (such as pharmaceuticals) exhibited a sharper increase in the value of imported intermediates and a weaker response of exports to appreciation of the exchange rate. In sectors with low foreign value added (such as textiles), the response of exports to exchange rate movements was larger.

How can India increase its exports in the new global normal, especially if the exchange rate is unlikely to be a helpful tool? If exports are less likely to power growth and investment, where will growth come from? In this new global environment—flush with manufacturing capacity—it may take a brave entrepreneur to invest in a new manufacturing facility in India.

The answer to the first question may rest on four pillars:

- building and improving infrastructure,
- raising human capital, with emphasis on vocational and on-the-job training,
- simplifying business regulation and taxation, and
- improving access to finance.

A related question is whether India should encourage or focus on particular industries. Creating a conducive business environment, strengthening the four pillars, and leaving it to Indian entrepreneurs to choose the "right" industry seems to be a better solution (Ministry of Finance 2012, Rajan 2016).

As for the new source of growth, public and private investments in physical and human infrastructure, where India still stares at a large deficit, may be needed. Where will the fiscal space needed to finance them come from? Asset sales remain one sustainable option in the medium term. Private investment in infrastructure will require getting rid of the debt overhang on public sector banks and private sector balance sheets (Acharya, Mishra, and Prabhala 2017). Doing so will require—in one form or other—creative destruction of capital, the political economy of which is daunting.

Boosting supply in India is critical. As the French economist Jean-Baptiste Say once said, supply creates its own demand. Doubling down on investment in physical and human capital would generate demand while addressing a key bottleneck in the economy and improving productivity. The network of infrastructure connecting many of the major industrial, agricultural, and cultural centers of India (the golden quadrilateral) boosted asset prices; rural and urban demand; and, most of all, firm productivity and competitiveness. This kind of policy must be the response to deglobalization.

India has benefited enormously from global integration. But integration has increased its exposure to global risks. The sooner policymakers accept and prepare for this reality, the sooner they can lay the ground for a new set of growth drivers in the current global environment.

References

Acharya, Viral, Prachi Mishra, and N. R. Prabhala. 2017. The Anatomy of India's Credit Cycle. Photocopy. Reserve Bank of India.

Ahmed, Swarnali, Maximiliano Appendino, and Michele Ruta. 2015. *Global Value Chains and the Exchange Rate Elasticity of Exports*. IMF Working Paper 15/252. Washington: International Monetary Fund.

Aziz, Jahangir, and Sajjid Chinoy. 2012. *India: More Open Than You Think*. JP Morgan Note.

Berman, Nicolas, Philippe Martin, and Thierry Mayer. 2012. How Do Different Exporters React to Exchange Rate Changes? *Quarterly Journal of Economics* 127, no. 1: 437–92.

Dekle, Robert, Hyeok Jeong, and Heajin Ryoo. 2009. *A Re-Examination of the Exchange Rate Disconnect Puzzle: Evidence from Firm Level Data*. Los Angeles: University of Southern California.

Engel, Charles. 2009. *Exchange Rate Policies*. Staff Paper. Dallas: Federal Reserve Bank of Dallas.

Imbs, Jean, and Isabelle Méjean. 2009. *Elasticity Optimism*. CEPR Discussion Paper 7177. London: Centre for Economic Policy Research.

Ministry of Finance. 2012. Seizing the Demographic Dividend. In *Economy Survey*. New Delhi: Government of India.

Rajan, Raghuram. 2016. India in the Global Economy. Ramnath Goenka Lecture, March 13.

Rangarajan, C., and Prachi Mishra. 2013. India's External Sector: Do We Need to Worry? *Economic and Political Weekly* 48, no. 7: 52–59.

Appendix 10A Data

Macroeconomic Data

We use quarterly data from calendar year 2002Q4 to 2016Q3 in our empirical models. The data on merchandise and services exports are from the CEIC database. They are available monthly. We derive the quarterly exports figures from the monthly information available for October 2002–September 2016. For merchandise exports, disaggregated data are for the "principal commodity groups," which cover more than 92 percent of all merchandise exports. Based on these groups, we identify 11 broad sectors: agriculture, ores and minerals, chemicals, pharmaceuticals, electronics, engineering goods, leather and textiles, metal and metal products, miscellaneous manufactured items, gems and jewelry, and petroleum products. We classify the following as manufactured items: chemicals, pharmaceuticals, electronics, engineering goods, leather and textiles, metal and metal products, and miscellaneous manufactured items (products such as paper and print-related items, ceramics and glassware, wood and wood products, plastic and rubber products, handicrafts, and other unclassified manufactured items).

The data on merchandise and services exports are available in millions of dollars (the value of exports). The database does not contain information on volumes. We therefore deflate nominal exports' to obtain real exports (in millions of dollars). We deflate exports of chemicals, pharmaceuticals, electronics, engineering goods, leather and textiles, and miscellaneous manufactured items by the US Producer Price Index. We deflate services exports by the US Consumer Price Index (CPI). We deflate the remaining sectors (petroleum products, gems and jewelry, agricultural goods, and metal and metal products) by the UK Brent (international crude price), international gold prices, the Food and Agriculture Organization's Food Price Index, and the Commodity Research Bureau (CRB) Metal Price Index, respectively. For ease of comparison, we normalize all price indexes to the year 2010. After deflating sectoral exports, we sum them to derive the series on manufactured items. Total merchandise exports include manufactured items as well as exports of sectors that are not classified as manufacturing sectors.

The quarterly dataset also includes information on the following:

- GDP of India's export partners
- the exchange rate of the rupee vis-à-vis trading partners' currencies
- domestic supply constraints (proxied by the number of stalled projects in a sector)
- the volatility of the dollar/rupee exchange rate.

Quarterly GDP data in current prices come from the CEIC. They cover about 105 of India's export partners, representing more than 92 percent of

India's exports. We use the weighted-average index of real GDP of India's export partners. We first deflate the GDP series for each country by the US CPI. We then normalize the real GDP of each country to the year 2010 and combine the country-specific real GDP indexes (2010 = 100) to a composite weighted-average index called Partner Country GDP Index (2010 = 100), in which we use each country's share in the value of India's exports as weights. As the export share of partner countries varies significantly across sectors, we construct this index separately for each sector and also for total merchandise and manufactured items. We create a separate export-weighted partner country GDP series for each sector, using sector-specific export shares. Because bilateral data on trade in services are not available, we use the world real GDP (in millions of dollars) to estimate partner income elasticity for services.

We also construct an index for the real exchange rate. Specifically, we construct a partner country export-weighted real exchange rate for each sector, using sector-specific export shares as weights. (By construction, a higher value of the exchange rate indicates an appreciation of the rupee against the partner country's currency.) We first convert the rupee/partner country nominal exchange rate to a real exchange rate by multiplying with the ratio of India's consumer price index (2010 = 100) to the partner country's consumer price index (2010 = 100). We use annual country CPI data from the World Bank's *World Development Indicators*. We normalize the real exchange rates of the rupee vis-à-vis each country's domestic currency to the year 2010. As the export shares of countries vary across sectors, we construct this index separately for each sector and also for total manufactured items.

For total merchandise exports, we use the index of the exports' weighted real effective exchange rate for the rupee based on 36 partner countries, published by the Reserve Bank of India. For the services sector, for which export shares are not available, we use the nominal dollar/rupee exchange rate, published by the Reserve Bank of India.

We compile quarterly series on the number of stalled projects based on the Capex database, collected by the Centre for Monitoring the Indian Economy (CMIE). We measure exchange rate volatility by the standard deviation of daily exchange rates each quarter. Daily exchange rates are from the CEIC database.

Firm-Level Data

We compile an annual firm-level panel dataset that spans 2007–14, based on the Prowess database, collected by the CMIE. It covers about 6,500 publicly listed exporting firms across 143 industries whose export earnings represent roughly 40 percent of total exports (based on the 2013 balance of payments). The dataset includes information on the value of exports of goods and services, the value of imported raw materials, total costs, and total sales (all in millions of rupees) at the firm level. It does not contain information on quantities of exports or imports, unit values, or the destination of exports. The firm-level database is merged with data on average annual exchange rates based on three measures (the real effective exchange rate, the nominal effective exchange rate, and the dollar-to-rupee exchange rate) and the domestic value-added content.

Table 10A.1 Determinants of India's manufacturing and services exports: Check for nonlinearity

	(1)	(2)	(3)	(4)	(5)	(6)	(7)	(8)
	Manufacturing exports				Services exports			
Variable	Linear model	Nonlinearity in partner GDP	Nonlinearity in exchange rate	(2) + (3)	Linear model	Nonlinearity in partner GDP	Nonlinearity in exchange rate	(6) + (7)
	Dependent variable: Log of exports (2010 prices) in US dollars							
Log of partner GDP	2.3***	2.3***	2.3***	2.3***	1.6*	3.0***	1.2	2.7***
Log of partner GDP * High partner growth		0.2		0.2		-0.4		-0.3
Log of partner exchange rate	-0.8	-0.9	-0.8	-0.9	2.5*	3.6***	2.3	3.4***
Log of partner exchange rate * High rupee appreciation			-0.7	-0.3			0.1	0.1
Log of number of stalled projects	0.1	0.2	0.1	0.1				
Volatility of dollar/rupee exchange rate	72.0	82.6	65.1	77.9	71.3	56.8	54.7	44.6
Structural break dummy * Log of partner GDP	-1.4**	-1.5*	-1.4**	-1.5**	-0.8	-2.2	-0.6	-2.1*
Structural break dummy * Log of partner GDP * High partner growth	0.0	0.0		0.0		0.1***		0.1*
Structural break dummy * Log of partner exchange rate	1.9	2.4	1.9	2.4	-2.7**	-3.8***	-2.6	-3.7***
Structural break dummy * Log of partner exchange rate * High rupee appreciation	0.0		0.0	0.0			0.0	0.0

(continues on next page)

Table 10A.1 Determinants of India's manufacturing and services exports: Check for nonlinearity (*continued*)

	(1)	(2)	(3)	(4)	(5)	(6)	(7)	(8)
	Manufacturing exports				Services exports			
Variable	Linear model	Nonlinearity in partner GDP	Nonlinearity in exchange rate	(2) + (3)	Linear model	Nonlinearity in partner GDP	Nonlinearity in exchange rate	(6) + (7)
	Dependent variable: Log of exports (2010 prices) in US dollars							
Dummy variables:								
Structural break	-2.3	-4.7	-2.4	-4.1	-6.2	-4.5	-7.0	-4.7
High partner growth		-0.8		-0.9		1.7		1.1
High rupee appreciation			3.0	1.2			0.5	0.5
Sample period				**2002Q4 to 2016Q3**				
Observations	56	56	56	56	56	56	56	56
Structural break date		**2005Q1**				**2005Q4**		
Maximum Wald-F stat: Quandt-Andrews test		48.4***				97.0***		
Durbin-Watson d-statistic	2.8	2.6	2.6	2.6	1.9	2.1	2.1	2.1
Ljung-Box Q-stat for first order autocorrelation	8.5***	4.9***	5.4**	5.2**	0.0	0.2	0.2	0.1

Notes: *, **, and *** indicate statistical significance at 10, 5, and 1 percent, respectively. High partner growth is a dummy variable that assumes a value equal to 1 when the quarter-over-quarter change in partner GDP is more than 2 percent. High rupee appreciation is a dummy variable that assumes a value equal to 1 when the quarter-over-quarter change in partner exchange rate is more than 2 percent. Regression uses heteroskedasticity-consistent robust standard errors.

Source: Authors' calculations.

Comment

Kenneth Kang

Prachi Mishra and Siddhartha Nath use macro-level evidence supported by sectoral and firm-level analysis to examine the drivers of India's exports. They highlight how India's exports have undergone a "quiet revolution" over the past two decades as their composition has shifted from traditional goods to new engineering, electronics, and pharmaceutical products.

Not surprising is the fact that external demand has been the main driver. The negligible role of the exchange rate and relative prices is surprising. The authors' findings raise important implications for exports as a source of growth should weak demand from the advanced economies persist. My comments focus on how their findings relate with other research, including at the International Monetary Fund (IMF), and what can be done to address this "new mediocre" risk for India's exports.

The IMF has analyzed the export performance of India and other emerging markets. Its results on the role of trading partner demand are similar to those described in the chapter. It finds that weak investment accounted for three-quarters of the global trade slowdown after the global financial crisis (IMF 2016). IMF research using both macro and industry-level data finds export elasticities similar to those described in their chapter, as well as declines after 2005. However, the decline in export elasticities brings them closer to their long-run average of 1, rather than the values of almost zero found in the chapter. The decline in demand elasticity comes mainly from the electronics sector, where elasticity is negative; for other sectors, they remain significantly positive and closer to 1.

The result that exchange rate changes do not affect exports is somewhat surprising. The chapter confirms the more standard result that appreciation hurts exporters in higher domestic value sectors, suggesting that India's growing participation in global supply chains may explain the weaker link between exports and the exchange rate. The weak link between the exchange rate and exports suggests that relative price signals in India may be distorted and be holding back the efficient reallocation of resources. If this is the case, identifying the distortion and crafting policies for addressing them can help India's exports become more competitive and responsive to external demand.

Kenneth Kang is the deputy director of the Asia and Pacific Department at the International Monetary Fund. The views expressed are those of the author and do not necessarily represent the views of the IMF, its Executive Board, or its management.

Figure 10C.1 Most-favored nation (MFN) applied tariff rates

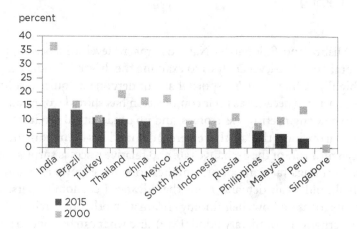

percent

Note: For countries where 2015 data are not available, 2013 or 2014 data are used.

Source: World Bank, *World Integrated Trade Solution* database.

One obvious distortion is India's relatively high tariff barriers (figure 10C.1). Emerging-market and developing economies have made significant progress in reducing average tariff rates, cutting them by almost two-thirds over the past 35 years. India also made significant progress, lowering its applied tariff rates from about 37 percent in 2000 to less than 15 percent in 2015. India's tariffs are still higher than most emerging-market economies and other countries in Asia, especially China, with which India is competing. There is room to reduce tariff and nontariff barriers, especially in the food, agriculture, and manufacturing sectors.

Another barrier is India's limited role in global value chains. The value of India's intermediate goods exports increased steadily through 2008; since then it has plateaued (figure 10C.2). India's share of foreign value added in total merchandising exports has stagnated at less than 25 percent, similar to the trend in other countries but still below China and Indonesia. Further integration into global value chains would both enhance the responsiveness to external demand and expand access to technology and foreign direct investment (FDI).

At the same time, given India's large economy and population, there is significant scope to strengthen domestic supply linkages. The July 2017 rollout of the nationwide goods and services tax (which applies a single, uniform indirect tax on the supply of goods and services across India's 29 states and 7 union territories) is an important step in promoting national integration and could have important trade effects given the size of India's

Figure 10C.2   Merchandise exports of India, 2000-14

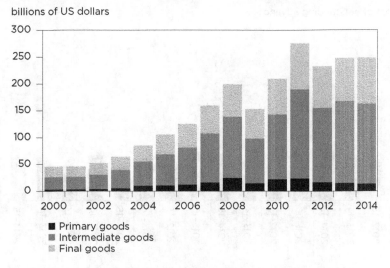

billions of US dollars

■ Primary goods
■ Intermediate goods
▨ Final goods

Note: Export values based on Broad Economic Categories classification system in order to classify all of the trade goods by production stage. "Primary goods" are materials to be used for food and beverages and in industrial supplies. "Intermediate goods" are trade goods that represent the intermediate input along the path toward becoming the final product. These goods are manufactured goods (processed or assembled) that are produced from primary goods but are not yet final products. "Final goods" are defined here as goods used by the producer (as the intermediate input) and goods consumed by households and the government.

Sources: Research Institute of Economy, Trade and Industry (REITI) database; Yes Bank.

states (if India's most populous state, Uttar Pradesh, were a separate country, it would be the fifth largest country in the world by population, just after Brazil). Leemput and Wiencek (2017) find that internal trade barriers in India account for up to 40 percent of total trade barriers on average but vary substantially by state. According to them, reducing trade barriers across Indian states could lead to real GDP gains of more than 4 percent.

India's competitiveness may also be a factor behind weak export response. India's nominal effective exchange rate has steadily declined since the global financial crisis, especially against Indonesia and China. In real effective terms, however, India's exchange rate appreciated by more than 20 percent since 2008, more so than that of Brazil or Russia. This appreciation largely reflects India's higher average rate of inflation, highlighting the need to keep inflation under control and pursue reforms to enhance competitiveness. The legacy of the credit bubble of the mid-2000s in the corporate and banking sectors may be holding back credit allocation. Credit growth and real investment are closely correlated. It is perhaps not coincidental that

Figure 10C.3   Banks' nonperforming and restructured assets, 2012–16

percent of outstanding advances

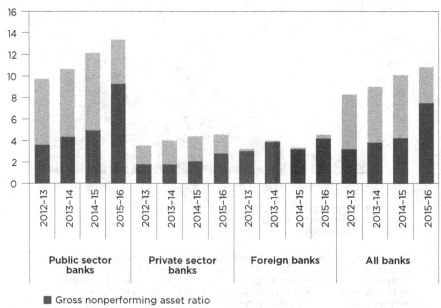

Sources: Reserve Bank of India; IMF Staff estimates.

the post-2005 decline in exports elasticity coincides with the peak of the credit and investment bubble. Nonfinancial corporate debt in India is low (about 50 percent of GDP) compared with other emerging-market countries (among which it averages 90 percent). But the level of nonperforming loans is high, at about 12 percent for all banks—significantly higher for public banks—and rising (figure 10C.3). Nonperforming loans are concentrated in metals and mining, construction and engineering, and transportation and infrastructure—sectors closely tied with exports. High corporate leverage and nonperforming loans may be hindering efficient resource allocation, preventing the exit of nonviable zombie firms, the entry of new firms, and the growth of productive ones. Forthcoming research by the IMF finds that the misallocation of resources in India is much greater than in the United States and that it varies widely across Indian states. Credit availability is one of the key drivers of resource misallocation in India, suggesting that removing structural rigidities in key input markets and improving credit allocation across firms would help reduce distortions and boost competitiveness.

India is an open economy with a young and growing population subject to spillovers from stagnation elsewhere, particularly through trade and investment. The chapter highlights the need for India and other countries to address structural rigidities holding back export growth and diversification. The priorities should be on getting prices right in order to reallocate resources more efficiently and enhance export competitiveness.

References

IMF (International Monetary Fund). 2016. *World Economic Outlook* (Fall). Washington.

Van Leemput, Eva, and Ellen A. Wiencek. 2017. *The Effect of the GST on Indian Growth.* IFDP Notes (March 24). Washington: Board of Governors of the Federal Reserve System.

11

How Has Indonesia Fared in the Age of Secular Stagnation?

MITALI DAS

This chapter analyzes the implications of secular stagnation in advanced economies for macroeconomic dynamics and policy tradeoffs in Indonesia, one of the world's largest emerging-market economies. The first section describes secular stagnation. The second section presents a retrospective analysis of the impact of secular stagnation on Indonesia. It reviews the channels through which secular stagnation can spill over to growth, describes the evolution of trade and financial exposure in Indonesia to advanced economies, and decomposes the contributions of domestic and external factors to Indonesia's output dynamics. The last section presents a prospective analysis, discussing the policies that can limit the impact of secular stagnation on potential growth. It begins with a decomposition of the contributors to the potential growth rate, then considers an illustrative scenario analysis by which potential growth may evolve under policies that raise total factor productivity (TFP) growth to its precrisis trend. It concludes that, although greater insularity has allowed Indonesia to enjoy more stable growth, to achieve its

Mitali Das is deputy division chief of the Strategy, Policy and Review Department of the International Monetary Fund. She thanks Luis Breuer, Jérémie Cohen-Setton, Thomas Helbling, Ken Kang, and Adam Posen for their overall guidance on this chapter and Agnes Isnawangsih, Yinqiu Liu, Toh Seng Guan, Medha Nair, Ranil Salgado, Jongsoon Shin, and participants at the Peterson Institute for International Economics conference on "The New Mediocre and Asia" held in May 2017 and the conference on "Prospects and Challenges for Sustained Growth in Asia" organized by the Bank of Korea, the Korean Ministry of Strategy and Finance, the International Monetary Fund, and the Peterson Institute for International Economics in Seoul on September 7–8, 2017, for their helpful comments. Special thanks to M. Chatib Basri, whose insights and discussion of this chapter improved both its contents and presentation, and to Egor Gornostay, for his outstanding assistance with the empirical section. The views expressed in this chapter are those of the author and do not necessarily represent the views of the IMF, its Executive Board, or its management. Any remaining errors are the author's.

ambitious growth objectives and generate good-quality jobs for its expanding labor force, Indonesia will require higher investment and technological innovations that may be best facilitated by greater global integration.

Why Does Stagnation Matter?

In advanced economies, the long-lasting slowdown in output growth, along with underemployment, disinflation dynamics, and negative market-clearing real interest rates, have raised questions about whether these economies are in secular stagnation. At the heart of this debate are questions about whether weak growth reflects transitory factors associated with the financial crisis, deeper structural factors, or transitory factors that have become permanent from the scarring effects of hysteresis. Competing explanations have emerged, ascribing secular stagnation to deficiencies in aggregate demand;[1] the debt supercycle (Rogoff 2016); a global savings glut;[2] and structural supply-side weaknesses, as put forward most prominently by Gordon (2016).

There is little consensus about whether advanced economies are in secular stagnation or what its proximate causes are. Still less is known about secular stagnation in emerging markets. Increasingly, however, following successive markdowns of actual and potential growth rates in emerging markets (IMF 2015b), commentators have noted that macroeconomic dynamics in these economies are unlikely to have decoupled from those of advanced economies amid the deep trade and financial linkages between them. This decoupling has raised questions about how strongly secular stagnation has transmitted from advanced to emerging economies, what the likely transmission channels are, and how quantitatively significant the impact on output dynamics has been.

These questions are important for at least two reasons. First, emerging markets represent a significant and growing fraction of the global economy. In 1980 they accounted for about 36 percent of global GDP and 43 percent of global GDP growth; by 2010–15 they accounted for 56 percent of global GDP and 79 percent of global growth.[3] Consequently, stagnation—or even a temporary slowdown—in emerging markets presents a serious risk that

---

1. Lawrence Summers, "Why Stagnation Might Prove to Be the New Normal," *Financial Times*, December 15, 2013, http://larrysummers.com/commentary/financial-times-columns/why-stagnation-might-prove-to-be-the-new-normal; Lawrence Summers, "Reflections on the New 'Secular Stagnation Hypothesis,'" VoxEU, October 30, 2014, https://voxeu.org/article/larry-summers-secular-stagnation.

2. Ben Bernanke, Why Are Interest Rates So Low? Brookings Institution Blog, March 30, 2015, www.brookings.edu/blog/ben-bernanke/2015/03/30/why-are-interest-rates-so-low/.

3. IMF, *World Economic Outlook* June 2017 database, measured in purchasing power parity (PPP) terms and PPP weights, respectively.

could reinforce the weak growth dynamics in advanced economies and raise the likelihood of a global deflationary spiral.

Second, these questions are important for emerging markets themselves, many of which have seen a sharp deceleration in trend growth since the global financial crisis, despite strong countercyclical stimulus and, in some cases, favorable demographics (IMF 2015b). This deceleration has occurred at much lower levels of income per capita than in richer economies (IMF 2017). If the slowdown in advanced economies proves permanent, emerging economies reliant on export-led growth may need significant structural adjustments to offset the weaker growth from a slowdown in external demand. For economies that face significant domestic headwinds, a durable external slowdown could be the catalyst that precipitates a crisis.

The implications of these global changes could be significant for policy frameworks in emerging markets. Following the financial crisis, advanced economies deployed a range of conventional and unconventional policies to counter the protracted demand slump, with mixed results domestically and large and often disruptive implications globally (IMF 2015b, Fischer 2015). Emerging-market policy responses to these spillovers were by and large countercyclical, including nominal exchange rate adjustment, some use of foreign exchange reserves, and capital flow management measures (Sahay et al. 2014). In part, these responses reflected a perception that the volume and volatility of capital flows spurred by unconventional monetary policy were transitory ahead of an imminent normalization, requiring effective stabilization policies but not deeper structural responses.

To the extent that the slowdown in advanced economies is now perceived as durable, emerging markets will need to adapt policy frameworks accordingly. They will need to tailor their responses to country-specific considerations, making changes to traditional policy frameworks (fiscal, monetary, and prudential) and adopting deeper reforms to institutions. Some may need to reorient the structure of their economies so that growth is more reliably linked to domestic factors. To limit their exposure to lower volumes and higher volatility of capital flows, they may need to create prudential buffers that raise resilience to external shocks and reduce their dependence on external financing. Boosting competitiveness, limiting dependence on external demand, and raising potential growth may require changes in the regulation of product and factor markets, educational reforms, improvement in technological know-how, and other measures. Reorienting from external to domestic demand will require institutional changes that improve the business climate and speed the process of structural transformation.

Retrospective Analysis: Spillovers of Secular Stagnation to Output Dynamics in Indonesia

In the years since the Asian financial crisis, Indonesia retrenched from the global economy in terms of both trade and financial integration. This retrenchment reflected a complex set of factors, including a large domestic base and favorable demographics, which enabled strong growth without high reliance on exports, as well as a strengthening of populist forces that explicitly favor inward-looking policies and protectionism (Basri and Patunru 2012).

A perhaps unanticipated consequence of its rising insularity has been the remarkable stability of output growth. Indonesia was among the few emerging markets that did not suffer from the recessionary impact of the global financial crisis (Blanchard, Das, and Faruqee 2010). More recently, Indonesia's inward-looking stance may have limited the transmission of secular stagnation from advanced economies.

The benefits of high levels of growth and low growth volatility from rising insularity could be ephemeral, however. Since the global financial crisis, the potential growth rate of output in Indonesia has been falling, driven entirely by lower TFP growth. The causes of slowing TFP growth can be wide-ranging, including both domestic and external factors. But it is likely that they at least partly reflect the ongoing decline in Indonesia's trade and financial engagement with the global economy, including a rise in protectionism, which may have limited more efficient resource allocation, the development of the domestic financial sector, and the transfer of technology, technological know-how, and best practices—the well-known productivity-raising benefits of trade and financial integration.

Output Dynamics in Indonesia: Stylized Facts

After a period of high growth in 2005–08—marked by a commodity boom, cheap global credit, and strong performance in trading partners—growth in Indonesia decelerated (figure 11.1). Because this slowdown occurred contemporaneously with secular stagnation in advanced economies, it is tempting to conclude that the two are linked.

The historical evidence, however, suggests that Indonesia's output dynamics evolved distinctly from global output dynamics. Between 2004 and 2009, the growth rate of real GDP rose steadily in Indonesia, averaging 5.7 percent. In contrast, the growth rate declined steadily in the United States, where it averaged 1.4 percent (figure 11.2).[4] The divergence of growth

---

4. The growth rate in the United States is taken as a proxy for the growth rate of the global economy.

Figure 11.1 Real GDP growth rates, 1990-2016

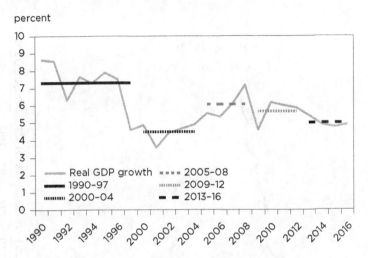

Sources: IMF, *World Economic Outlook* database; author's calculations.

paths is reflected in a correlation of –0.73. Although the growth rates in Indonesia and the United States have moved together more closely since the financial crisis, the change may reflect responses to common global shocks rather than greater synchronicity of Indonesia and global output dynamics.[5]

One fact that is consistent with the insularity of Indonesia's output dynamics from global output dynamics is the remarkably low volatility of its real output growth. The stability of Indonesia's output growth in 2000-16 stands out among both its regional peers and emerging markets more generally (figures 11.3a and 11.3b). It is especially notable given the profound changes that took place in the global economy in this period, including the steep rise and subsequent sharp decline in commodity prices, the severity of recessions in many of Indonesia's trading partners following the financial crisis, and the large swings in capital flows, including the taper tantrum, which was especially significant for Indonesia.

This stability of output in Indonesia is unsurprising once one takes account of the structure and evolution of its economy. Domestic demand is higher than in most of its peers, reducing the country's vulnerability to the vicissitudes of external demand. Fueled by a large and growing population, domestic demand averaged 97 percent of GDP in 2000-16, with the

---

5. As predicted by theory (see Cesa-Bianchi, Imbs, and Saleheen 2016), in response to common global shocks, business cycle synchronization increases when financial integration declines.

Figure 11.2 Real GDP growth rates in Indonesia and the United States, 2000Q1–2017Q1

percent

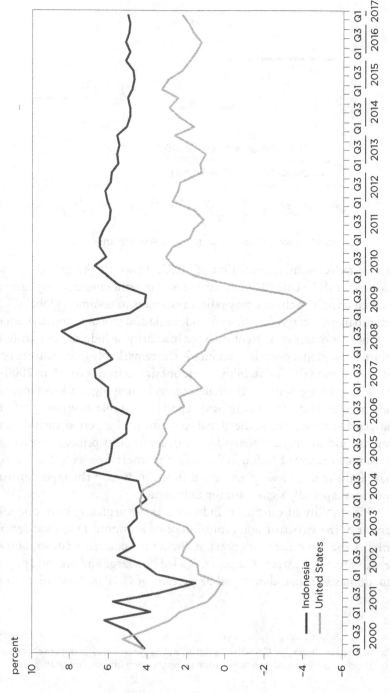

Sources: IMF, *World Economic Outlook* database; author's calculations.

Figure 11.3a Real GDP growth relative to ASEAN-4, 2000–16

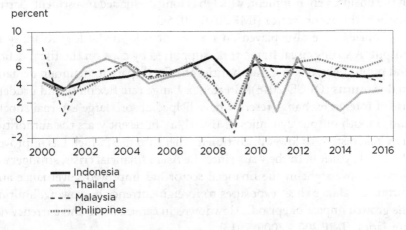

percent

- Indonesia
- Thailand
- - - Malaysia
- .... Philippines

ASEAN = Association of Southeast Asian Nations
Sources: IMF, *World Economic Outlook* database; author's calculations.

Figure 11.3b Real GDP volatility, 2000–16

percent

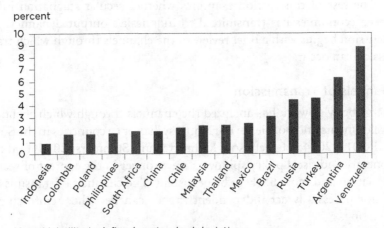

Note: Volatility is defined as standard deviation.
Sources: IMF, *World Economic Outlook* database; author's calculations.

large domestic base accounting for two-thirds of consumption.[6] External demand is a relatively small contributor to aggregate demand, and both the export basket and export destinations are diversified (as discussed below).[7]

---

6. IMF, *World Economic Outlook* June 2017 database.

7. Basri and Rahardja (2010) cite the composition of Indonesia's export basket (particularly its concentration in primary commodity exports) as a key reason for the stability of export demand during the global financial crisis.

The declining importance of external demand may also reflect weaknesses in the business environment, which has long dissuaded investment, particularly in the export sector (IMF 2010, 2015a).

Policies have also played an important role in the low volatility of output. A strong fiscal framework, supported by caps on the fiscal deficit and public debt, has given authorities the fiscal space to maintain demand in downturns (OECD 2016). Greater exchange rate flexibility and prudent use of foreign exchange reserves have helped absorb large external shocks and smooth output dynamics (IMF 2014a). In recent years the authorities have taken steps to lower distortionary fuel subsidies, which has improved the fiscal position. In the years since the Asian financial crisis, stronger supervisory oversight in the financial sector has improved governance and curtailed balance sheet exposures to foreign currency borrowing, limiting the growth impact of episodic slowdowns in capital flows and currency depreciation (IMF 2007, 2009, 2013).

Will the stability of output dynamics continue in the new economic environment? How will secular stagnation in advanced economies affect the growth of output in Indonesia? What role will policies play?

The rest of this section examines whether secular stagnation in advanced economies has transmitted to Indonesia's output dynamics. The discussion begins with a brief review of the channels through which transmission can occur.

Channels of Transmission

A large body of work has analyzed the channels through which economic developments and policies in the North spill over to countries in the South (IMF 2013, 2014c). Eggertsson, Mehrotra, and Summers (2016) find that monetary and fiscal policy spillovers are stronger in the context of secular stagnation and more likely to be persistent. The channels of transmission do not necessarily act independently; they can be either reinforcing or offsetting.

Trade Channel

Trade linkages are a direct source of transmission of the spillovers of secular stagnation. Deceleration of demand in advanced economies lowers import demand from emerging markets. Indeed, the global trade slowdown is commonly viewed as symptomatic of secular stagnation in advanced economies (IMF 2016a). The impact of weaker external demand from advanced economies can be amplified if it is accompanied by highly accommodative monetary policy in advanced economies, leading to larger capital outflows to emerging markets and an appreciation of their nominal exchange rates.

Exposure to China may also affect trade-related spillovers of secular stagnation to Asian economies.[8] Slowing external demand from advanced economies has affected China. Given its role as a hub in the regional supply chain, the impact of secular stagnation in advanced economies may be transmitted even to economies with low trade links to advanced economies, through their links to China. China has recently begun to rebalance its economy from investment toward consumption. Because the import intensity of investment is significantly higher than that of consumption (Kang and Liao 2016), exporters of investment goods (such as firms in the euro area) may have been affected negatively whereas exporters of consumption goods (many of which are in Asia) may have benefited.

The trade-related spillovers of secular stagnation will vary across countries, reflecting how high their exposure is to demand from advanced economies, how strong their trade links are with China, and how significant external demand is in overall domestic demand.[9]

Financial Channel

Financial linkages are a second source of transmission, directly or indirectly. Emerging markets' financial linkages to advanced economies include the net inflows of foreign capital that supply credit and finance investment in their financial, nonfinancial, and official sectors and their stocks of external assets and liabilities.

Financial spillovers of secular stagnation can come from the weakness in demand in advanced economies, which generally leads to lower exchange rates abroad as a result of weaker demand for exports (Eggertsson, Mehrotra, and Summers 2016). Weaker exchange rates may benefit trade, but they can have large and deleterious balance sheet effects and adverse growth consequences when the foreign currency exposure of external liabilities is high (Eichengreen, Hausmann, and Panizza 2007).[10] Both the size of the external balance sheet and its foreign currency denomination are important: For a

---

8. Basri and Rahardja (2010) note that the impact of the global crisis on the Indonesian economy was relatively limited in part because of the strong demand from China and India, in particular for primary commodity exports. As natural resources account for the majority of Indonesia's exports, the composition of exports stabilized external demand.

9. External demand in countries that are more exposed to the sectors slowing most sharply in advanced economies (such as construction and manufacturing) may be more affected than exporters of consumption goods (IMF 2016a).

10. By contrast, external assets denominated in foreign currency would improve in local currency value. For a net creditor, the net impact of a depreciation on the external balance may be to raise the value of the net international investment position (NIIP). For a net debtor (like Indonesia), the negative revaluation of liabilities would likely exceed the positive revaluation of assets, leading to a lower NIIP.

given scale of the external balance sheet, the exchange rate impacts will be larger the greater is foreign currency exposure. For a given foreign currency exposure, the impact will be larger the bigger the external balance sheet.

Financial linkages also have the potential for self-fulfilling prophecies to transmit secular stagnation from advanced to emerging-market economies, which can occur if financial markets expect a permanent slowdown in advanced economies to reduce the growth prospects of emerging markets, resulting in lower capital inflows to emerging markets, an increase in the risk premium for new lending, or both. The financial spillovers of secular stagnation may have highly heterogenous impacts across emerging markets depending on the foreign currency exposure of external balance sheets, dependence on external credit, and fundamentals that affect the risk premium (Blanchard, Das, and Faruqee 2010).

How Exposed Is Indonesia to Secular Stagnation in Advanced Economies?

This section compares Indonesia with a large group of emerging-market countries, including regional peers in ASEAN-4 (Malaysia, Thailand, and the Philippines). As historical perspective is also useful, it examines the evolution of these exposures from the Asian financial crisis to today.

Trade-Related Exposure

Three indicators can shed light on Indonesia's trade-based exposure to secular stagnation: the size of the external sector in relation to the overall economy, the diversity of exposure to exports and imports across regions, and the contribution of net exports to output growth.

The size of Indonesia's external sector as a share of the economy has steadily declined since the early 2000s (figure 11.4a).[11] Exports were 40 percent and imports 32 percent of GDP in 2000; both had declined to less than 20 percent by 2016. Except for a short-lived uptick in 2003–05, these declines were steady through the domestic business cycles, the commodity price boom before the financial crisis, the commodity price bust starting in 2013, and the expansion of global value chains in Asia since the early 2000s.[12]

---

11. The change is not just a reflection of the rapid expansion of the economy. Growth rates of exports and imports have been on a trend decline (in both nominal and real terms) since the global financial crisis; in 2016 they registered negative growth rates.

12. These trends suggest that deeper structural factors lie behind the rise in insularity. By some accounts, they reflect long-standing institutional weaknesses in the regulatory framework, the legal and judiciary system, and tax administration, which have dissuaded private investors, particularly in export sectors (IMF 2005).

Figure 11.4a   Evolution of Indonesia's external sector, 2000-16

percent of GDP

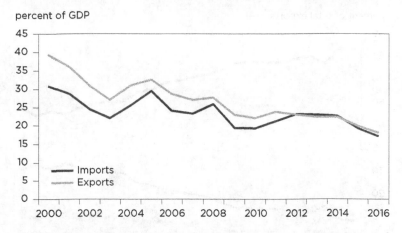

Sources: IMF, *World Economic Outlook* database; author's calculations.

Figure 11.4b   Average openness (exports + imports), 2000-16

percent of GDP

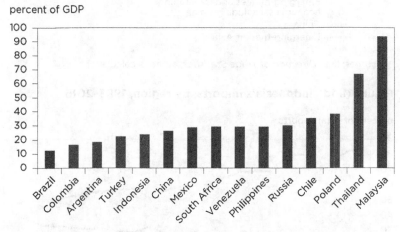

Sources: IMF, *World Economic Outlook* database; author's calculations.

Figure 11.4b illustrates how these trends compare with average openness among emerging-market peers. The data reveal two facts. First, there is tremendous heterogeneity in external exposure across emerging economies. Second, although Indonesia is more closed than all its regional peers, it is more exposed than other large economies, including Brazil and Turkey.

A natural question is whether the extent of Indonesia's declining external exposure is heterogenous across its trading partners. To shed light on this question, figures 11.4c and 11.4d show the evolution of Indonesia's export and import shares by region. All of the decline in Indonesia's external

Figure 11.4c   Indonesia's exports, by region, 1993–2016

percent of total exports

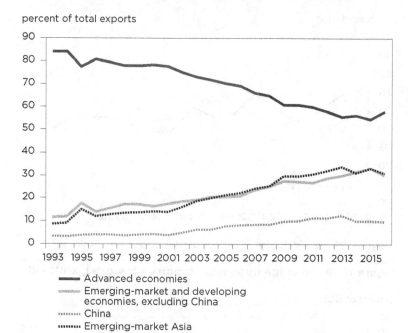

Advanced economies
Emerging-market and developing economies, excluding China
China
Emerging-market Asia

Sources: IMF, *Direction of Trade Statistics*; author's calculations.

Figure 11.4d   Indonesia's imports, by region, 1993–2016

percent of total imports

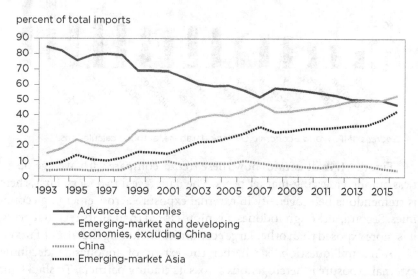

Advanced economies
Emerging-market and developing economies, excluding China
China
Emerging-market Asia

Sources: IMF, *Direction of Trade Statistics*; author's calculations.

Figure 11.4e Contributions to Indonesia's real GDP growth, 2001–16

percent change, year over year

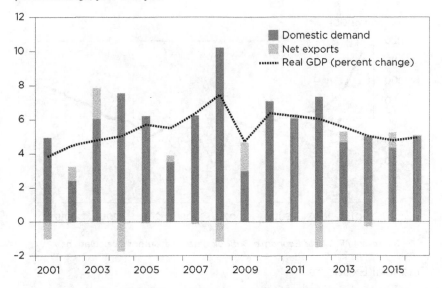

Sources: IMF, *World Economic Outlook* database; author's calculations.

sector exposure resulted from reduced trade with advanced economies. Between 2000 and 2016, the share of Indonesia's exports to advanced economies declined by about 25 percentage points, and the share of imports from advanced economies declined by 45 percentage points. The region that absorbed those declining shares from advanced economies was predominantly emerging Asia, where exports rose by about 20 percentage points and imports by about 30 percentage points.[13]

The compositional evolution of its trading partners indicates that Indonesia is likely to have been significantly insulated from weaker export demand. Not only did exposure to advanced economies decline, Indonesia's exports to these economies as a percent of GDP was modest, averaging about 6 percent in 2000–16.[14]

The data in figure 11.4e indicate that Indonesia has moderate to low exposure to external demand from advanced economies. As a share of the economy, the external sector has declined, and its contributions to output growth have been small (figure 11.4e).

---

13. China did not drive the rise in trade with emerging Asia, as shown in figures 11.4c and 11.4d.

14. IMF, *World Economic Outlook* June 2017 database.

Figure 11.5a Indonesia's financial integration with the global economy (external assets + external liabilities), 2001–16

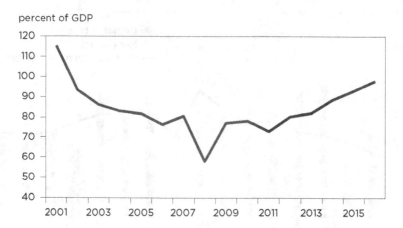

percent of GDP

Sources: IMF, *World Economic Outlook* database; author's calculations.

Financial Exposure

Both stock and flow indicators shed light on the channels through which secular stagnation abroad can transmit to the domestic economy. A key stock indicator is the size and (currency) composition of its external balance sheet. The main flow indicators are the volume and volatility of nonofficial international capital flows, which supply credit and finance investment to the domestic economy.

In the years between the Asian financial crisis and the global financial crisis, Indonesia steadily reduced its financial integration with the global economy, as reflected in the declining sum of external assets and external liabilities (figure 11.5a). By this measure, financial integration fell from 118 percent of GDP in 2001 to 80 percent of GDP in 2007.[15] This evolution lies in marked contrast with one of the major trends of the last quarter century in the world economy (as well as in newly industrialized Asian economies and developing Asia), which has seen record cross-border transactions and a concomitant rise in financial integration (Obstfeld 2015).

One reason for the low and declining exposure to external liabilities is a regulatory environment that has impeded foreign direct investment (FDI). On the FDI Regulatory Restrictiveness Index of the Organization for Economic Cooperation and Development (OECD), Indonesia has among

---

15. The trough of the sum of foreign assets and liabilities in ratio to GDP is 42 percent in 2008. However, the 2008 level may well be sui generis, reflecting large valuation effects from both the steep depreciation of the rupiah and the large drops in asset prices.

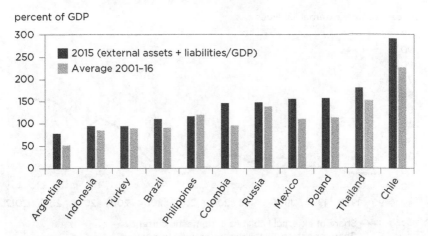

Figure 11.5b   Global financial integration across emerging markets, 2015 and average 2001–16

percent of GDP

Legend:
- 2015 (external assets + liabilities/GDP)
- Average 2001–16

Sources: IMF, *World Economic Outlook* database; author's calculations.

the strictest limitations in the ASEAN-9 (Cambodia, Indonesia, Laos, Malaysia, Myanmar, the Philippines, Singapore, Thailand, and Vietnam), including outright bans on foreign participation in certain sectors.

Another factor is the rapid decline in foreign currency liabilities by banks and nonfinancial corporates, amid tighter supervision, intended to address the corporate governance problems that proved so damaging in 1997. Debt liabilities declined from 90 percent of GDP in 2000 to less than 30 percent of GDP in 2013.[16] Since the global financial crisis, Indonesia's financial integration has reversed course, climbing to about 93 percent of GDP in 2015, a level last seen in 2002. External assets and liabilities increased by about the same amount.[17]

Nevertheless, as of 2015, Indonesia remained one of the least financially integrated economies among emerging-market peers (figure 11.5b). External assets and liabilities each lie well in excess of 100 percent of GDP in the Philippines and Thailand.

A few years after the Asian financial crisis, the foreign currency denomination of external liabilities declined steadily in Indonesia (figure 11.5c). On the eve of the Asian financial crisis, 83 percent of foreign liabilities were denominated in foreign currency. By 2012 this figure had fallen to

---

16. IMF, *External Wealth of Nations* Database.

17. The increase in external assets reflects an increase in outward FDI and other investment (including lending to foreign financial institutions and banks). Portfolio investment and some increase in inward FDI have driven external liabilities.

Figure 11.5c Foreign currency exposure of Indonesia's external balance sheet, 1990–2012

percent of total external liabilities

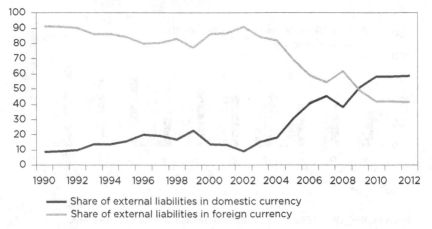

━━━ Share of external liabilities in domestic currency
━━━ Share of external liabilities in foreign currency

Source: Bénétrix, Lane, and Shambaugh (2015).

about 42 percent (Bénétrix, Lane, and Shambaugh 2015).[18] The combination of a small external balance sheet and moderate foreign currency exposure limits the financial channel of transmitting secular stagnation from advanced economies to Indonesia (see figures 11.5b and 11.5c).

Some flow indicators support these conclusions. Despite some episodic retrenchment, most notably during the taper tantrum of 2013, exposure to capital flow volatility net and gross international capital flows to Indonesia have been steady since the global financial crisis (IMF 2016b). Since the early 2000s, the volatility of Indonesia's net nonofficial inflows has been similar to that of its emerging-market peers, and it compares favorably with regional peers (figure 11.5d). Research indicates that the adverse impact of global financing shocks is stronger for emerging markets prone to higher capital flow volatility (IMF 2014c). This finding suggests that vicissitudes in the supply of foreign capital are not a strong source of growth spillovers for Indonesia. There is also no evidence that the cost of external financing has changed (figure 11.5e). There is thus little evidence of financial market self-fulfilling prophecies. With low to moderate financial linkages with the rest of the world and steadily falling foreign currency denomination of external liabilities, Indonesia is not heavily exposed to financial-related spillovers from advanced economies.

---

18. Indonesia is not unique in this respect. The decline in "original sin" (as Eichengreen, Hausmann, and Panizza [2007] call the foreign currency exposure of liabilities) has been observed in emerging markets across the world.

Figure 11.5d   Volatility of the supply of foreign capital (net nonofficial inflows), 2000–15

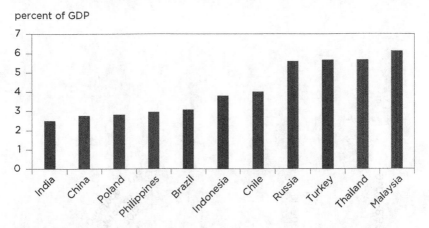

percent of GDP

Sources: IMF, *Balance of Payments* database; author's calculations.

Decomposition of Domestic and External Contributions to Growth

The analysis in this section is based on a vector auto-regression (VAR) analysis, using quarterly data from the first quarter of 1999 to the fourth quarter of 2016. The VAR is limited to 10 variables (4 external and 6 domestic factors), in order to limit the number of estimable parameters relative to the number of observations. All variables enter the VAR with four lags.

External factors include US real GDP growth (a proxy for advanced economy demand shocks); US inflation (a proxy for advanced economy supply shocks, once US growth is controlled for); and the one-year US Treasury bond rate (to capture the advanced economy monetary policy stance). The VAR includes the real growth rate in China, given China's growing significance in the region. Domestic factors include the real output growth rate in Indonesia, domestic consumer price inflation, the rate of real exchange rate appreciation versus the US dollar, the Emerging Market Bond Index (EMBI) spread (to proxy external financing conditions), the percentage change in terms of trade (capturing factors other than changes in external demand or financing conditions), and the short-term interest rate. Terms of trade are arguably either a domestic or an external factor; results were not sensitive to this choice.[19] All growth rates and inflation rates are measured in year-over-year terms.

---

19. In the estimation of the VAR, the key restriction is that shocks to the external block are assumed to be exogenous to shocks to the internal block. The external variables thus

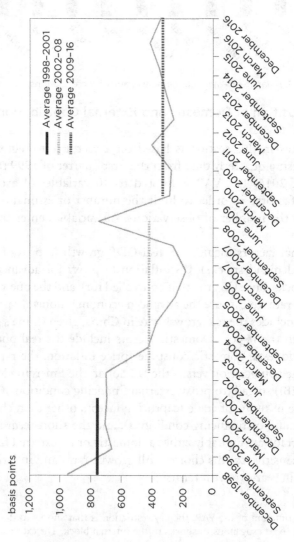

Figure 11.5e Indonesia's Emerging Market Bond Index (EMBI) spread, 1998–2016

basis points

Average 1998–2001
Average 2002–08
Average 2009–16

Sources: JP Morgan; author's calculations.

Table 11.1 Correlation between domestic real GDP growth in Indonesia and domestic and global factors

Variable	2000–16	2009–16
US real GDP growth	–0.06	0.41
US inflation	0.36	0.72
One-year US Treasury bond rate	–0.05	–0.36
China's real GDP growth	0.29	0.51
Inflation in Indonesia	–0.07	–0.07
Terms-of-trade growth	0.07	0.28
Emerging Market Bond Index spread	–0.42	–0.31
Real effective exchange rate change (increase is depreciation)	–0.27	0.35
Monetary policy in Indonesia	–0.40	–0.45

Sources: Author's calculations using data from IMF *World Economic Outlook* database, JP Morgan, and US Treasury.

Table 11.1 displays the correlations between domestic real GDP growth in Indonesia and external and domestic factors over the entire period (2000–16) and the period after the global financial crisis (2009–16). The correlation between real GDP growth in the United States and Indonesia was negligible over the entire period (consistent with figure 11.2) but strengthened considerably after the global financial crisis. This finding provides prima facie evidence that secular stagnation in advanced economies may have been transmitted to domestic output dynamics since the global financial crisis.

The VAR estimates are used to compute what fraction of Indonesia's real GDP growth (relative to its estimated average growth over the sample period) can be attributed to external versus domestic factors. The results show that domestic factors explain more than three-fourths of the deviation of Indonesia's growth from the estimated sample mean between 1999 and the end of 2002 (figure 11.6). The contribution of external factors to deviations from average growth started rising intermittently in 2003, making positive contributions for most quarters in 2006 through the first quarter of 2009. External factors strongly dominated growth dynamics during the

---

do not respond to the internal variables contemporaneously. Within the external factors, identification of the shocks is based on a recursive scheme: US growth affects all variables within a quarter, whereas shocks to other variables can affect US growth only with a lag of at least one quarter. US inflation shocks may affect all variables other than US growth within a quarter; the one-year US Treasury rate is placed last in the recursive ordering, implying that it responds contemporaneously to all external factors but not to any of the domestic shocks. Within the internal block, shocks are not explicitly ordered. These assumptions follow closely the VAR exercise in IMF (2014a).

Figure 11.6 Contribution of domestic and global factors to Indonesia's real GDP growth deviations, 1999Q1–2016Q4

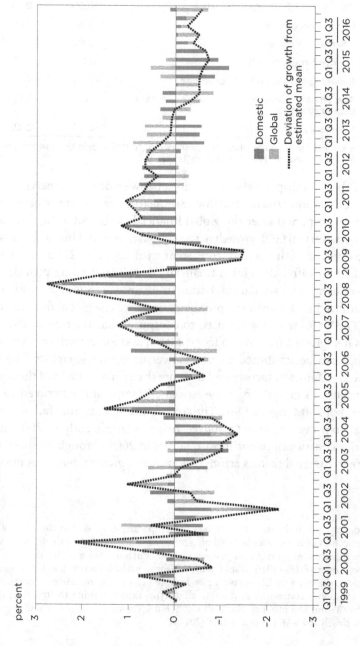

Sources: IMF, *World Economic Outlook* database; author's calculations.

global financial crisis, with domestic factors reemerging as important late in the second quarter of 2012.

Both domestic and external factors played roles in output dynamics after 2012. The contribution of external factors was predominantly negative; domestic factors somewhat offset their impact.

The VAR results are consistent with the hypothesis that secular stagnation in advanced economies was transmitted to Indonesia. However, the quantitative impact of the drag from external factors was not historically large. After late 2013, it was strong enough to partially or even fully offset the strength of domestic factors. That it did so despite fairly low and declining linkages between Indonesia and the global economy points to the complexity of spillovers, including possibly reinforcing channels and indirect transmission through regional trade partners.

It is impossible to know how secular stagnation would have affected Indonesia in the counterfactual scenario in which its international trade and financial linkages were strong and rising. A reasonable (albeit qualified) conclusion from the results presented here is that the impact would have been larger.

Prospective Analysis: Countering the Headwinds from Secular Stagnation

Assessing the medium-term path of output is critical for the conduct of monetary, fiscal, and structural policies. To the extent that demand weakness in advanced economies is temporary, countercyclical stabilization policies may suffice in addressing the short-term deceleration of domestic growth. If the decline represents a longer-term structural change in the growth rate of advanced economies, different policies may be needed in Indonesia.

Possible Output Dynamics in Indonesia: Stylized Facts

Potential growth in Indonesia has been on a downward trend since the global financial crisis, a period that broadly coincides with the slowdown in advanced economies (figure 11.7). The potential growth rate rose from about 4.0 percent in 2000 to 5.7 percent in 2008. It edged down to 5.4 percent in 2009–16 and is projected to trend down farther over the medium term.[20]

This trend is not unique to Indonesia. The IMF (2015b) finds that the potential growth rate declined by about 2 percentage points in emerging markets after the global financial crisis. From that perspective, the declining trend in Indonesia is mild.

---

20. IMF, *World Economic Outlook* June 2017 database.

Figure 11.7 Potential output growth rate in Indonesia, actual and forecast, 2000–22

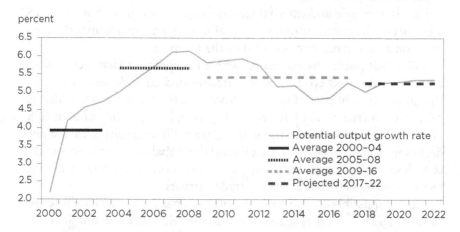

Sources: IMF, *World Economic Outlook* database; author's calculations.

Identifying the sources of lower potential growth in Indonesia is a first step in identifying policy implications. To the extent that lower potential growth rates emerged from lower factor accumulation—including human and physical capital—policy measures may need to target raising the supply of labor, reducing rigidity in hiring and firing policies, and addressing other domestic impediments to investment, including regulation, red tape, and the business environment. If they arose from declining TFP, deeper structural issues may be at play.

Decomposition of the growth rate of potential output into growth rates of factor inputs and growth rates of TFP reveals the importance of TFP (figure 11.8).[21] Before the global financial crisis, acceleration of TFP lay behind the increase in potential growth rates. More than half of the increase in the growth rate of potential output—from about 5 percent in 2001–04 to 6 percent in 2006–08—reflected the increase in employment, possibly in part due to weak employment growth in preceding years due to a base effect. Weak employment growth in 2001–04 (reflected in the low contribution of labor input in 2001–04) in turn reflects the very slow decline in unemployment after the Asian financial crisis, in part the result of weak investment and a poor investment climate (IMF 2005). The contribution of capital accumulation also increased between 2001–04 and 2006–08.

---

21. The decomposition is of potential growth rate into the actual capital growth rate and the potential employment growth rate reflecting the working-age population, as described in IMF (2014c).

**Figure 11.8 Decomposition of Indonesia's potential growth rate,
2001–14**

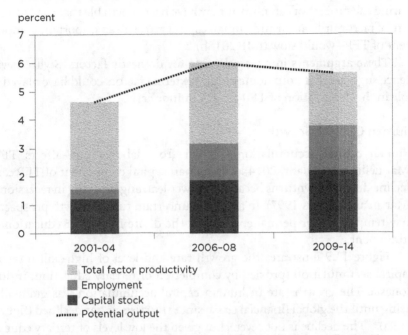

percent

Sources: World Bank, *World Development Indicators* database; IMF, *World Economic Outlook* database; author's calculations.

The decline in potential output growth rate since the global financial crisis is attributable largely to the decline in the growth of TFP. The contribution of employment and capital growth helped offset some of the decline in TFP growth, thanks partly to the modest stimulus Indonesia implemented as external demand softened in 2009. For emerging markets as a whole, TFP has been found to account for the entire postcrisis decline in potential growth rates (see Cubeddu et al. 2014, IMF 2015b).

Sources of Changes in Total Factor Productivity

A prominent supply-side explanation for secular stagnation, associated with Gordon (2016), is that the slowdown in technological innovation accounts for low growth in advanced economies. Because advanced economies are at the technological frontier, and technological spillovers across borders have been found to raise TFP and growth (see, e.g., Coe and Helpman 1995, Amman and Virmani 2015), a slowdown in TFP growth in advanced economies could transmit to lower TFP growth and lower potential growth in emerging markets. Lower trade and financial spillovers, for instance, could limit the diffusion of technology, technological know-how, and best practices.

Declining TFP growth may also be a result of convergence to the technological frontier. After more than a decade of rapid factor accumulation during the process of catch-up, it may have been inevitable that the growth rate of factor utilization and human capital growth—an important component of TFP—would slow (IMF 2015b).[22]

These arguments imply a role only for domestic factors. Stylized evidence suggests that both domestic and external factors could have played a role in the deceleration of TFP growth in Indonesia.

Human Capital Growth

Human capital accumulation—distinct from labor input—affects TFP (Manuelli and Seshadri 2014). The human capital component of TFP can decline during downturns because of lower learning by doing in recessions (Martin and Rogers 1997). In addition, uncertain future growth prospects may temporarily or permanently lower the desire for higher educational attainment.

Figure 11.9 illustrates the growth rate and level of high-skill human capital accumulation (proxied by completion of tertiary education) in Indonesia. The growth rate of human capital accumulation was gradually rising until the global financial crisis; since the crisis, it has declined (figure 11.9a).[23] The decline is not severe, but given the low levels of tertiary education in Indonesia (figure 11.9b), a slowdown in human capital accumulation could present bottlenecks for high-value-added employment.

Trade Restrictions

Restrictions on trade (such as import tariffs) result in inefficient allocation of the factors of trade, reducing TFP. A large body of empirical work corroborates this theoretical prediction (e.g., Caselli, Esquivel, and Lefort 1996; Hall and Jones 1999).

Data from the World Bank's *Temporary Trade Barriers* database show a steady increase in protectionism in Indonesia. The rise in protectionism is evident in both average tariff rates and nontariff barriers (Basri and Patunru 2012). Protectionist measures were on a downward trend before the global financial crisis but rose sharply thereafter (figure 11.10). They have since edged down but remain high relative to the precrisis years.

---

22. In traditional growth decomposition, TFP traditionally accounts for factor utilization—such as hours worked, capacity utilization, and the quality of labor and capital inputs, as distinct from the volume of labor and capital inputs—rather than labor or capital inputs.

23. Data on human capital accumulation are from the Barro-Lee dataset, which go only through 2010.

Figure 11.9a   Indonesian students with higher education, 2002–16

percent change, year over year

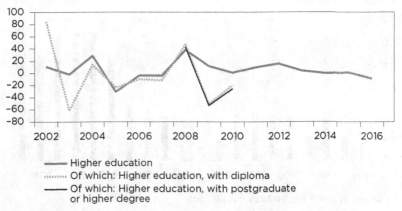

——— Higher education
·········· Of which: Higher education, with diploma
——— Of which: Higher education, with postgraduate
         or higher degree

Sources: Central Statistics Bureau; author's calculations.

Figure 11.9b   Share of Indonesia's population with tertiary education, 1988–2010

percent of population

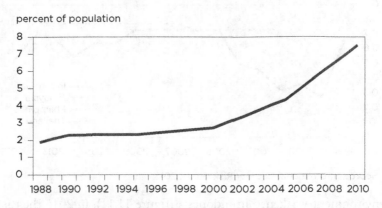

Source: Barro and Lee database, www.barrolee.com.

Institutions

The quality of institutions—such as labor regulations, the legal and judicial system, and accountability—can play a key role in a country's ability to adopt superior technologies, and thus raise TFP, income, and living standards (McGuiness 2007, Acemoglu 2008).

Indonesia ranks poorly on several measures of the ease of doing business (World Bank 2017). International financial institutions have noted structural impediments, including a weak investment climate, complex regulations, and shallow financial markets (IMF 2016b). After improvements between the Asian financial crisis and global financial crisis, the regulato-

Figure 11.10 Temporary trade restrictions on Indonesian imports, 1996–2015

percent of total imports

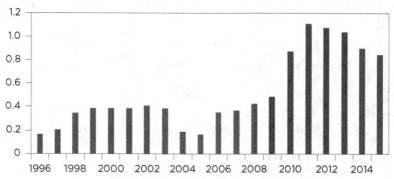

Sources: World Bank; author's calculations.

Figure 11.11 Regulatory quality in Indonesia, Malaysia, the Philippines, and Thailand, 1996–2015

index (1 = highest; 0 = weakest)

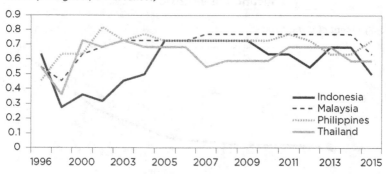

Source: International Country Risk Guide, 2015.

ry environment weakened in Indonesia (figure 11.11). In 2015 the ease of doing business was somewhat lower than in regional peers. The declining path of regulatory quality may have contributed to lower TFP growth.

Baseline and Alternative Paths for Potential Output Growth Rates

To identify the role for policies if the deceleration in TFP continues to present headwinds to the growth rate of potential output, this section considers the evolution of potential growth through a scenario analysis, assuming a path for each of its components (labor, capital accumulation, and TFP). The scenarios are illustrative only, given the high uncertainty of the projections on which they are based.

Figure 11.12a Growth rate of the working-age population in Indonesia, 1955-2065

percent, 5-year intervals

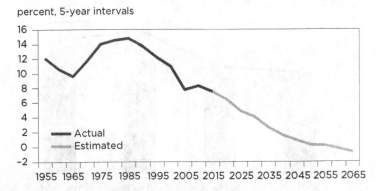

Sources: UN Population Division; author's calculations.

Figure 11.12b Labor force participation rates, Indonesia vs. EU-28 and OECD, 2006-13

percent

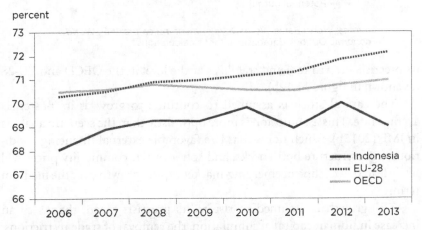

EU-28 = 28 member countries of the European Union; OECD = Organization for Economic Cooperation and Development

Sources: World Bank, *World Development Indicators*; IMF, *World Economic Outlook* database; OECD Statistics; author's calculations.

The future paths for labor are derived from demographic projections and assumptions about labor force participation rates. Indonesia has the opportunity to reap large demographic dividends, given the projected increase in the working-age population through 2060 (figure 11.12a). However, labor force participation rates, which were rising steadily before the financial crisis, have been volatile since 2010, registering negative average growth rate in 2010-13 (figure 11.12b). Taking the working-age projections as given, the scenario analysis assumes that the labor force participation rate reverts to

Figure 11.13 Illustrative scenario analysis

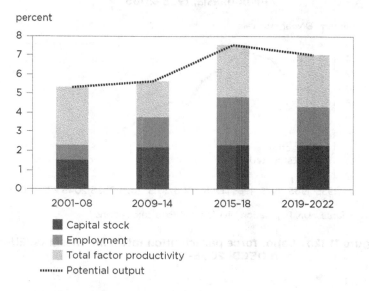

percent

Sources: World Bank, *World Development Indicators*; IMF, *World Economic Outlook* database; author's calculations.

its precrisis growth rate and stabilizes at the level in the OECD and EU-28 (as shown in figure 11.12b).

The capital stock is assumed to continue to grow at its postcrisis average rate. This assumption is more optimistic than the scenario analysis in IMF (2015b), which notes that less favorable external financing conditions, infrastructure bottlenecks, and softer or flat commodity prices will likely lead to a decline in emerging-market capital growth over the medium term.

TFP growth is assumed to rise to its precrisis mean, thanks to an increase in human capital accumulation, the removal of trade restrictions, greater foreign participation in industry through FDI, and a better business climate (achieved by simplifying regulations and increasing financial depth).

Under this scenario, medium-term potential growth in Indonesia increases from about 6 percent under the baseline to 7 percent (figure 11.13). Potential growth could evolve differently for several reasons, such as an upward revision to the forecast of commodity prices (which could spur investment and capital growth), a more rapid easing of barriers to FDI inflows (which could raise TFP), or a downward revision to global growth.

Conclusion

In the years after the Asian financial crisis, Indonesia's engagement with the global economy weakened in terms of both trade and financial integration. This retrenchment was extremely unusual, among both regional peers and emerging markets more generally. The low exposure to global economic and financial developments, a large and strengthening domestic base, a strong fiscal framework, and prudence in managing international capital movements insulated Indonesia significantly from the vicissitudes of global developments, reflected in remarkably stable output growth. Its inward-looking stance limited the transmission of secular stagnation from advanced economies to the domestic economy.

Policies will need to calibrate the tradeoff between the potential stability gains of retrenching from a slowing world economy and the long-term costs that an increasingly inward-looking stance may entail, however.

Low exposure to global developments has also limited the diffusion of technological advances and productivity-enhancing spillovers of global economic integration. Potential output growth declined in recent years, despite strong demographic tailwinds and steady capital accumulation, as a result of lower TFP growth. The slowdown in human capital accumulation, the rise in protectionism, and some weakening of the regulatory environment may have contributed to the TFP growth slowdown. Structural supply-side policies that enhance productivity may help Indonesia raise potential growth and weather the negative impulse from a slowing world economy.

References

Acemoglu, Daron. 2008. *Introduction to Modern Economic Growth*. Princeton, NJ: Princeton University Press.

Amman, E., and S. Virmani. 2015. Foreign Direct Investment and Reverse Technology Spillovers: The Effect on Total Factor Productivity. *OECD Journal: Economic Studies*. Available at www.oecd.org/eco/growth/Foreign-direct-investment-and-reverse-technology-spillovers-The-effect-on-total-factor-productivity-OECD-Journal-Economic-Studies-2014.pdf.

Basri, M. Chatib, and A. Patunru. 2012. How to Keep Trade Policy Open: The Case of Indonesia. *Bulletin of Indonesian Economic Studies* 48, no. 2.

Basri, M. Chatib, and S. Rahardja. 2010. The Indonesian Economy amidst the Global Crisis: Good Policy and Good Luck. *ASEAN Economic Bulletin* 27, no. 1: 77–97.

Bénétrix, Agustin S., Philip R. Lane, and Jay C. Shambaugh. 2015. International Currency Exposures, Valuation Effects and the Global Financial Crisis. *Journal of International Economics* 96: 98–109.

Blanchard, Olivier J., Mitali Das, and Hamid Faruqee. 2010. The Initial Impact of the Crisis on Emerging Market Countries. *Brookings Papers on Economic Activity* (Spring): 263–307. Available at www.brookings.edu/wpcontent/uploads/2010/03/2010a_bpea_blanchard.pdf.

Caselli, F., G. Esquivel, and F. Lefort. 1996. Reopening the Convergence Debate: A New Look at Cross-Country Growth Empirics. *Journal of Economic Growth* 1, no. 3: 363–89. Available at https://link.springer.com/article/10.1007/BF00141044.

Cesa-Bianchi, A., J. Imbs, and J. Saleheen. 2016. *Finance and Synchronization*. London: Centre for Economic Policy Research. Available at www.cepr.org/active/publications/discussion_papers/dp.php?dpno=11037.

Coe, David T., and Elhanan Helpman. 1995. International R&D Spillovers. *European Economic Review* 39, no. 5: 859–87.

Cubeddu, L., A. Culiuc, G. Fayad, Y. Gao, K. Kochhar, A. Kyobe, C. Oner, R. Perrelli, S. Sanya, E. Tsouta, and Z. Zhang. 2014. *Emerging Markets in Transition*. IMF Staff Discussion Note 14/06. Washington: International Monetary Fund. Available at www.imf.org/external/pubs/ft/sdn/2014/sdn1406.pdf.

Eggertsson, G., N. Mehrotra, and L. Summers. 2016. Secular Stagnation in the Open Economy. *American Economic Review* 106, no. 5: 503–507.

Eichengreen, B., R. Hausmann, and U. Panizza. 2007. Currency Mismatches, Debt Intolerance and Original Sin: Why They Are Not the Same and Why It Matters. In *Capital Controls and Capital Flows in Emerging Economies: Policies, Practices and Consequences*, ed. Sebastian Edwards. Chicago: University of Chicago.

Fischer, S. 2015. Monetary Policy in the United States and in Developing Countries. Speech at the Crockett Governors' Roundtable 2015 for African Central Bankers, University of Oxford, Oxford, UK, June 30.

Gordon, Robert. 2016. *The Rise and Fall of American Growth: The U.S. Standard of Living Since the Civil War*. Princeton, NJ: Princeton University Press.

Hall, Robert E., and C. I. Jones. 1999. Why Do Some Countries Produce So Much More Output Per Worker than Others? *Quarterly Journal of Economics* 114, no. 1: 3–116.

IMF (International Monetary Fund). 2005. *Indonesia: 2005 Article IV Consultation and Third Post-Program Monitoring Discussions*. IMF Country Report 05/326. Washington. Available at www.imf.org/external/pubs/ft/scr/2005/cr05326.pdf.

IMF (International Monetary Fund). 2007. *Indonesia: 2007 Article IV Consultation and Third Post-Program Monitoring Discussions*. IMF Country Report No. 07/272. Washington. Available at www.imf.org/external/pubs/ft/scr/2007/cr07272.pdf.

IMF (International Monetary Fund). 2009. *Indonesia: 2009 Article IV Consultation and Third Post-Program Monitoring Discussions*. IMF Country Report No. 09/230. Washington. Available at www.imf.org/external/pubs/ft/scr/2009/cr09230.pdf.

IMF (International Monetary Fund). 2010. *Indonesia: 2010 Article IV Consultation*. IMF Country Report 10/284. Washington. Available at www.imf.org/external/pubs/ft/scr/2010/cr10284.pdf.

IMF (International Monetary Fund). 2013. *2013 Spillover Report*. IMF Multilateral Policy Issues Report. Washington. Available at www.imf.org/external/np/pp/eng/2013/070213.pdf.

IMF (International Monetary Fund). 2014a. On the Receiving End? External Conditions and Emerging Market Growth Before, During and After the Global Financial Crisis. In *World Economic Outlook*, April. Washington. Available at www.imf.org/~/media/Websites/IMF/imported-flagship-issues/external/pubs/ft/weo/2014/01/pdf/_c4pdf.ashx.

IMF (International Monetary Fund). 2014b. *2014 Pilot External Sector Report*. Multilateral Policy Issues Report. Washington. Available at www.imf.org/external/np/pp/eng/2014/062614.pdf.

IMF (International Monetary Fund). 2014c. *2014 Spillover Report*. IMF Multilateral Policy Issues Report. Washington. Available at www.imf.org/external/np/pp/eng/2014/062514.pdf.

IMF (International Monetary Fund). 2015a. *Indonesia: 2015 Article IV Consultation*. IMF Country Report 16/81. Washington. Available at www.imf.org/external/pubs/ft/scr/2016/cr1681.pdf.

IMF (International Monetary Fund). 2015b. Where Are We Headed? Perspectives on Potential Output. In *World Economic Outlook*, April. Washington. Available at www.imf.org/~/media/Websites/IMF/imported-flagship-issues/external/pubs/ft/weo/2015/01/pdf/_c3pdf.ashx.

IMF (International Monetary Fund). 2016a. Global Trade: What's Behind the Slowdown? In *World Economic Outlook*, October. Washington. Available at www.imf.org/~/media/Websites/IMF/imported-flagship-issues/external/pubs/ft/weo/2016/02/pdf/_c2pdf.ashx+&cd=1&hl=en&ct=clnk&gl=us.

IMF (International Monetary Fund). 2016b. *Indonesia: 2016 Article IV Consultation*. IMF Country Report 17/37. Washington. Available at www.imf.org/~/media/Files/Publications/CR/2017/cr1737.ashx.

IMF (International Monetary Fund). 2017. *Indonesia: 2017 Article IV Consultation*. IMF Country Report No. 18/32. Washington. Available at www.imf.org/~/media/Files/Publications/CR/2018/cr1832.ashx.

Kang, J., and C. Liao. 2016. *Chinese Imports: What's behind the Slowdown?* IMF Working Paper WP/16/106. Washington. Available at www.imf.org/external/pubs/ft/wp/2016/wp16106.pdf.

Manuelli, R., and A. Seshadri. 2014. Human Capital and the Wealth of Nations. *American Economic Review* 104, no. 9: 2736–62.

Martin, Phillip, and Carol A. Rogers. 1997. Stabilization Policy, Learning by Doing and Economic Growth. *Oxford Economic Papers* 49, no. 2: 152–66.

McGuiness, Anne. 2007. *Institutions and Total Factor Productivity Convergence*. Working Paper 9/RT/07. Dublin: Bank of Ireland.

Obstfeld, M. 2015. *Trilemmas and Tradeoffs: Living with Financial Globalization*. BIS Working Paper 480. Basel: Bank for International Settlements. Available at www.bis.org/publ/work480.htm.

OECD (Organization for Economic Cooperation and Development). 2016. *Economic Survey of Indonesia 2016*. Paris. Available at www.oecd.org/eco/surveys/economic-survey-indonesia.htm.

Rogoff, Kenneth. 2016. Debt Supercycle, Not Secular Stagnation. In *Progress and Confusion: The State of Macroeconomic Policy*, ed. Olivier Blanchard, Raghuram Rajan, Kenneth Rogoff, and Lawrence Summers. Cambridge, MA: MIT Press.

Sahay, R., V. Arora, T. Arvanitis, H. Faruqee, P. N'Diaye, and T. Mancini-Griffoli. 2014. Emerging Market Volatility: Lessons from the Taper Tantrum. Staff Discussion Note SDN/14/09. Washington: International Monetary Fund.

World Bank. 2017. *Doing Business 2017: Indonesia*. Washington. Available at www.doingbusiness.org/~/media/wbg/doingbusiness/documents/profiles/country/idn.pdf.

Comment

Muhamad Chatib Basri

Mitali Das' excellent chapter dissects Indonesia's economic growth since the Asian financial crisis. Her analysis is commendable, and I agree with her findings. To sharpen the analysis, I offer several comments.

First, Basri and Rahardja (2011) indicate that an outward-looking strategy has been the source of Indonesia's economic growth. Exports have a large effect in supporting economic growth, despite being less stable than domestic demand. Therefore, a strategy that safeguards a balance between the domestic economy and an outward-looking strategy must be part of the development strategy. An outward-looking strategy brings the risk of growth volatility, however. An important question in the chapter is how to adopt an outward-looking strategy without destabilizing economic growth.

Basri and Rahardja (2011) show a positive correlation between the concentration of exports in products and markets with export volatility: The higher the export concentration of markets and products, the higher the level of export volatility. This finding suggests that export diversification helps reduce export volatility. Medium- and high-tech export manufactures have a negative relationship with export volatility. The higher concentration in medium- and high-tech manufacturing makes export volatility lower. This finding supports the argument that overdependence on a single export has a risk of higher export volatility. This argument is particularly true for Indonesia. Export diversification is as important as human capital accumulation and open trade regime.

Second, the chapter does not discuss the terms of trade. Indonesia is a producer of energy and commodities such as coal and palm oil. The prices of oil and these commodities are strongly correlated (World Bank 2015), because when oil prices rise, the demand for nonoil energy substitutes rises. Deterioration in the terms of trade will have a negative impact on household consumption, exports, and economic growth. A decrease in commodity and energy prices will also lead to a reduction in government revenue. The government's fiscal expansion capacity is thus limited, especially in Indonesia, where the budget deficit is legally limited to 3 percent of GDP.

Improvement in the terms of trade has had a positive impact on Indonesia's economy. One of the explanations for the relatively strong growth of the economy between 2002 and 2012 was the commodity super-

Muhamad Chatib Basri, former minister of finance of Indonesia, is chairman of the Advisory Board of the Mandiri Institute and chairman of Indonesia Infrastructure Finance. He teaches at the Department of Economics, University of Indonesia, and is cofounder of Creco Research Institute, a Jakarta-based economic consulting firm.

cycle. The reverse was true after 2013, when the energy price began to collapse.

If Indonesia wants to boost economic growth and reduce its boom-bust cycle, the growth strategy should target manufacturing, especially exports. Services exports also play an important role, because exports of tourism, design, and workers' remittances are likely to have direct links with private consumption.

Third, I agree with Das that structural supply-side policies will help Indonesia increase productivity. But one cannot ignore the importance of demand-side issues, especially in the short term. Private consumption accounts for about 50 percent of GDP in Indonesia. Improving purchasing power is an important tool for boosting economic growth. The administration of President Joko Widodo has emphasized supply-side policies by building infrastructure. It also engaged in deregulation. Despite these measures, economic growth hovered around 5 percent in the last three years and may stay there for a few years. The Bank of Indonesia cut interest rates by 300 basis points between January 2016 and September 2017, but annual credit growth remained stuck at 7 to 8 percent, much lower than the 18–20 percent Indonesia enjoyed in the past. Undisbursed loans are steadily rising. This suggests that in the short term, boosting demand is very important.

If demand for goods and services is weak, what can the government do to encourage firms to resume borrowing and expand production? If there is no demand, what is the point in expanding?

Basri, Fitrania, and Zahro (2016) show that consumption encourages investment after one quarter but that an increase in investment does not significantly increase consumption. Supply-side policies and interest rate cuts do not necessarily produce demand, at least in the short term.

What are the implications for policy? The government needs to launch a fiscal stimulus that targets the lower middle class. It is very important to stimulate domestic consumption through direct cash and conditional cash transfer programs, as Indonesia did during the global financial crisis and taper tantrum, because doing so boosts aggregate demand in the short term.

Fourth, I support Das' suggestion that Indonesia focus on increasing productivity by improving the quality of human capital and opening up the economy. In the short term, it can do so by attracting foreign direct investment and incentivizing foreign investors to provide training or build R&D departments by offering tax deductions. The Indonesian government's policy of providing scholarship and sending the best students to the best universities in the world should be continued.

References

Basri, M. Chatib, Namira Fitrania, and Shirin Zahro. 2016. *Causality between Investment and Private Consumption in Indonesia*. Jakarta: Creco Research.

Basri, M. Chatib, and Sjamsu Rahardja. 2011. Should Indonesia Say Goodbye to Strategy Facilitating Export? In *Managing Openness: Trade and Outward-Oriented Growth After the Crisis*, ed. Mona Haddad and Ben Shepherd. Washington: World Bank.

World Bank. 2015. *Commodity Markets Outlook*, July. Washington.

12

Twenty-Five Years of Global Imbalances

MAURICE OBSTFELD

The modern floating exchange rate era that began in 1973 falls into two stages. The first, which ended in the mid-1990s, was a period of adjustment to the new international monetary regime. Financial markets underwent liberalization, internationally as well as domestically, and international trade expanded, while central bankers learned how to manage inflation in a world of national fiat currencies. The period's end is marked by the foundation of the World Trade Organization (WTO) and the 1994–95 Mexican crisis, which Michel Camdessus, the managing director of the International Monetary Fund (IMF) at the time, labeled "the first 21st century crisis."

The second 21st century crisis arrived even before the 21st century did, in the form of the 1997–98 Asian crisis. The Asian crisis was notable in that several of its victims succumbed despite the absence of garden-variety macroeconomic imbalances—such as big public deficits—that IMF economists and others viewed as red flags. This facet of the crisis certainly influenced academic thinking (witness the celebrated Kaminsky and Reinhart 1999 analysis of twin banking and currency crises), but it also pointed to the dawn of a new, second stage of the post-1973 era.

Maurice Obstfeld is director of the Research Department at the International Monetary Fund. This chapter is based on remarks made at the conference on "Prospects and Challenges for Sustained Growth in Asia" organized by the Bank of Korea, the Korean Ministry of Strategy and Finance, the International Monetary Fund, and the Peterson Institute for International Economics in Seoul on September 7–8, 2017. The author is grateful for suggestions and assistance from Gustavo Adler, Eugenio Cerutti, Luis Cubeddu, Thomas Helbling, and Haonan Zhou. The views expressed in this chapter are those of the author and do not necessarily represent the views of the IMF, its Executive Board, or its management. All errors and interpretations are the author's alone.

That stage, covering roughly the last 25 years, is characterized by hyper-financialization, greater exchange rate flexibility on the part of many emerging-market economies, and a decisive shift of Asian growth leadership from Japan to China, especially after China's accession to the WTO. Subramanian and Kessler (2013) characterize developments in international trade, including rapidly expanding global value chains, as "hyperglobalization." The forces unleashed after the mid-1990s led to the global financial crisis of 2008–09, a crisis with long-lived repercussions that are still being felt.

One notable feature of the second period of floating was a significant widening of global current account imbalances, which roughly tripled in the decade after 1995 and remained higher, albeit at lower levels than the peak they reached before the global financial crisis (figure 12.1). That global imbalances had the potential to widen is not surprising, given financial market development, including further financial opening, after the mid-1990s. Controversy remains, however, over both the causes of these imbalances and their potential causal role in the global financial crisis. On one side is the view, expressed by US Treasury Secretary Henry Paulson as he was leaving office in 2009, that global imbalances originating in the emerging markets were the root cause of the global crisis.[1] Others (such as Obstfeld and Rogoff 2009) have argued that this view deflects too much blame from other critical factors.

The debate raises at least four questions, which this chapter tries to answer:

- Why did global imbalances expand after the mid-1990s?

- What circumstances and concomitant factors provide clues about the origins of the global financial crisis?

- If one accepts that a monocausal story about the global financial crisis based on global imbalances is inaccurate, how should one view the potential threats from excessive global imbalances today?

- What policy implications follow?

Rise of Global Imbalances

A prominent feature of the expansion of global imbalances after the mid-1990s was the growing US deficit (see figure 12.1). In a justly famous speech, Bernanke (2005) argued for "locating the principal causes of the US current account deficit outside the country's borders." In his telling, in

---

1. See Krishna Guha, "Paulson says crisis sown by imbalance," *Financial Times*, January 1, 2009, www.ft.com/content/ff671f66-d838-11dd-bcc0-000077b07658.

Figure 12.1 Global current account balances and reserve purchases, 1990-2017

percent of world GDP

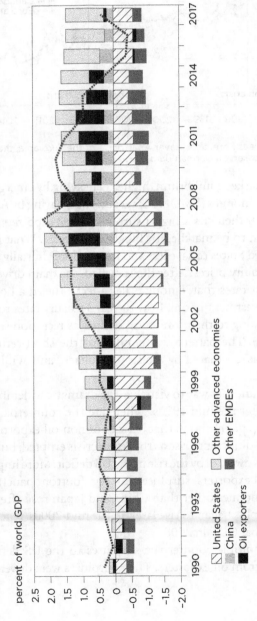

EMDEs = emerging-market and developing economies

Note: "Oil exporters" follows WEO classification and includes Norway. Bars represent regional current account balances, the dotted line total reserve purchases.

Source: IMF, *World Economic Outlook.*

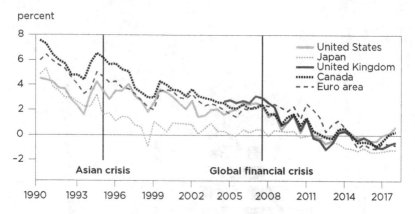

Figure 12.2 Real 10-year bond yield in advanced economies, 1990–2018

Sources: Consensus Forecasts; Haver Analytics. For the euro area, the period before 2003 is based on German data.

a global capital market equilibrium, higher net saving by emerging-market and developing economies (EMDEs)—precautionary saving by Asian emerging economies after their crisis, bigger surpluses of oil exporters as the price of oil rose—needed to be matched by bigger US deficits. What mechanism induced the United States to save less and invest more? Initially responsible was a run-up in equity prices. After they crashed, the main driver became a fall in real interest rates that, among other effects, fueled a housing price and residential investment boom. Real 10-year Treasury rates rose after the Asian crisis, returning to their long-term decline as recession set in during 2001 (figure 12.2). The pattern was similar for the short-term "natural" policy rates (r^*), as calculated by Holston, Laubach, and Williams (2017) (see figure 12.3).

Figure 12.4 is another way to visualize the dramatic widening of the US external deficit after the mid-1990s. Where are the counterpart widening surpluses? The top panel shows that deficits of non-oil-exporting EMDEs (including China) did start to rise as the Asian crisis erupted, but the extent of the increase was dwarfed by the rise in the US deficit. More important was the increase in oil exporters' surpluses. In Asia (bottom panel), surpluses of East Asian economies other than China and Japan rose after the Asian crisis. China's surplus began to rise later, in the mid-2000s, reaching about 0.6 percent of global GDP in 2008.

There were multiple counterpart surpluses to the US deficit; one of the biggest came from oil exporters. Their surpluses were driven by steeply

Figure 12.3 Natural rate of interest (r^*) in advanced economies, 1990–2016

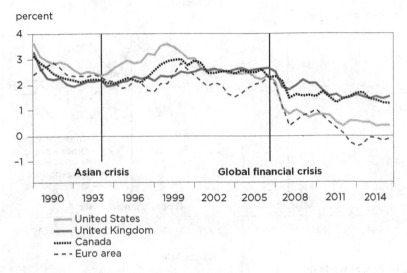

percent

Asian crisis   Global financial crisis

—— United States
—— United Kingdom
······ Canada
– – – Euro area

Source: Holston, Laubach, and Williams (2017).

rising global oil prices, however (figure 12.5).[2] As US real activity, financial conditions, and domestic oil production are critical determinants of conditions in the world oil market, it seems implausible that changes in oil prices emanated entirely from outside US borders to influence its current account. Instead, the US deficit reflected domestic as well as global forces—global forces coming from other advanced economies, not just EMDEs—all of which helped set the stage for the global financial crisis.

Background to the Global Financial Crisis

Common factors drove oil prices, oil surpluses, and bigger current account deficits in several advanced economies. They included very loose global financial conditions, enabled by generally accommodative monetary policies, as well as financial deregulation and innovation, and a global reach for yield and safety that contributed to widespread housing market booms.

One component of this constellation, though likely not the most important one, was the accumulation of foreign reserves by EMDEs, which Bernanke (2005) noted (figure 12.1). During 1998–2008, intervention

2. In the early 2000s, measured world surpluses surged above world deficits; a substantial global discrepancy—a "missing deficit"—emerged. Missing deficits tend to be positively correlated with oil prices. The discrepancy could be related to some countries understating the cost of oil imports.

Figure 12.4 Current account balances, 1991–2017

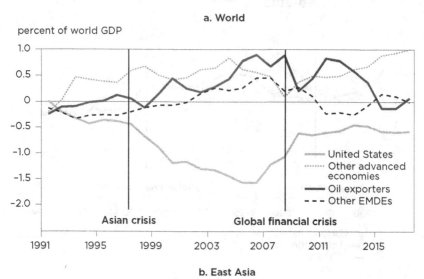

a. World

percent of world GDP

Asian crisis   Global financial crisis

Legend:
- United States
- Other advanced economies
- Oil exporters
- - - Other EMDEs

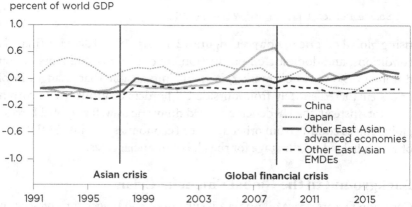

b. East Asia

percent of world GDP

Asian crisis   Global financial crisis

Legend:
- China
- Japan
- Other East Asian advanced economies
- - - Other East Asian EMDEs

EMDEs = emerging-market and developing economies
Source: IMF, *World Economic Outlook.*

tended to be associated with wider surpluses for countries purchasing foreign exchange. But the US housing bubble also drew fuel from European banks' purchases of asset-backed securities, as Bernanke et al. (2011) and Bayoumi (2017) document. Perceiving low sovereign and no currency risk within a permissive regulatory environment, banks in France, Germany, and other European countries recycled global funding into peripheral economies in the euro area, such as Spain, Ireland, Portugal, and Greece, financing housing or sovereign debt bubbles and big external deficits (Hale and Obstfeld 2016). Similar dynamics played out in the Baltics.

Figure 12.5 World oil price and oil exporters' current account, 1991–2017

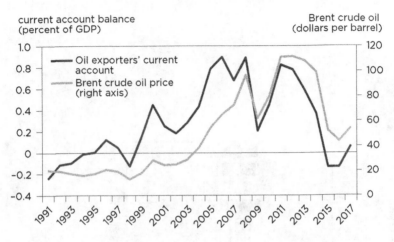

Source: IMF, *World Economic Outlook*; Haver Analytics; IMF Staff calculations.

A symptom of global financial ease during the 2000s, coupled with ongoing deregulation and innovation, was an explosion of two-way capital flows across borders. Figure 12.6 shows the pattern of *gross* international financing corresponding to the *net* international financing needs illustrated in figure 12.1. Starting in the mid-1990s, gross flows began to expand markedly, reaching unprecedented proportions on the eve of the global financial crisis. Tellingly, the vertical axis scale needed to chart gross flows in figure 12.6 is a full order of magnitude greater than the scale needed in figure 12.1: The bare minimum capital flows needed to finance current account imbalances would have been only a tenth of the flows that actually took place.

In theory, gross two-way flows fulfill economic functions beyond the financing of current account imbalances, notably, asset swaps that enable international portfolio diversification and risk sharing. No known economic or financial model can easily rationalize gross flows that were persistently such a big share of global GDP in the run-up to the crisis, however.

Much of the asset churning was likely driven by tax avoidance strategies or regulatory arbitrage, exemplified by the surge in European purchases of US mortgage-related assets (see, e.g., Acharya and Schnabl 2010). These developments were a symptom of the financial distortions that ultimately helped power the US current account deficit.

Following their sharp expansion starting in the mid-1990s, gross external positions leveled off after the finanical crisis, at least in the aggregate (see figure 12.7). An increasing fraction of gross external positions now seems to represent foreign direct investment (FDI), although as Lane and

Figure 12.6 Global gross financial flows, 1990–2017

percent of world GDP

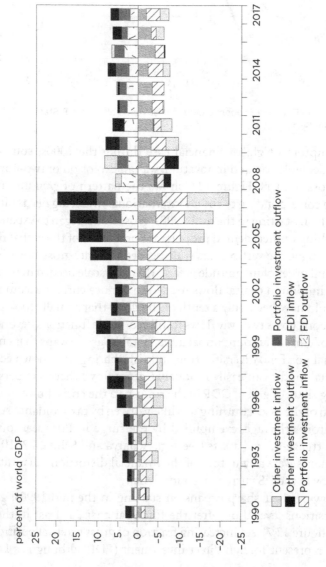

FDI = foreign direct investment

Source: IMF, *Balance of Payments Statistics.*

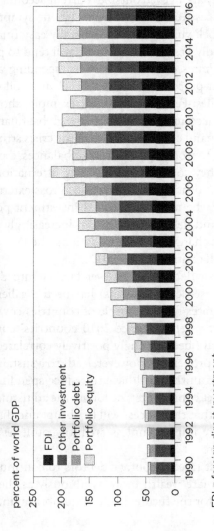

Figure 12.7 Global investment liabilities stock, 1990–2016

percent of world GDP

- FDI
- Other investment
- Portfolio debt
- Portfolio equity

FDI = foreign direct investment

Source: IMF, International Investment Position, *World Economic Outlook.*

Miles-Ferretti (2018) document, much of this so-called FDI reflects not risk sharing or greenfield investment but claims on offshore financial centers, driven by tax minimization strategies.

Risks from Excess Global Imbalances

Twenty-first century crises have largely been balance sheet crises, driven more by predetermined vulnerabilities (currency and maturity risk) than by the risk that the flow of financing for the current account deficit dries up. The very large gross flows in figure 12.6 represent potentially fragile balance sheet positions that could threaten financial stability, with severe macroeconomic consequences.

Why, then, worry about even outsized current account imbalances? One reason is that an excessive flow deficit may be one symptom of an underlying buildup of stock vulnerabilities. Generally easy financial conditions (including lax or badly designed regulation) will tend to promote leverage, which in turn facilitates divergence between spending and income. The eventual adjustment process can be costlier when it follows bigger imbalances. Lane and Milesi-Ferretti (2015), for example, show how countries with bigger current account deficits before the global financial crisis tended to suffer greater demand compression when the crisis struck.

Another reason to worry about excess imbalances, especially if they are persistent, is that they could imply widening international disparities in net external wealth. Although the growth of gross external positions has leveled off for now, the net international investment positions of international creditors and debtors have grown increasingly divergent (figure 12.8). Absent future changes in asset valuations, the IMF projects that this divergence trend will continue (IMF 2017).

The tendency for debtors to go ever farther into debt (while creditors accumulate those debts as assets) has been a salient phenomenon, as figure 12.9 illustrates for the sample of countries covered in the IMF's annual *External Sector Reports*. Since 2010 countries' cumulative current account balances have been strongly positively correlated with initial net foreign assets. That propensity, however, leads to a sustainability problem. Eventually, debtor countries will have to reduce spending to reflect their intertemporal budget constraints; the longer the adjustment is postponed, the more likely it is that the process will be abrupt and disruptive, creating a global deflationary impulse unless creditor countries just as abruptly decide to spend more.

Low real interest rates encourage debtors to continue borrowing and creditors to accumulate wealth more assiduously as they seek to ensure adequate resources for the future. Higher equilibrium interest rates could

Figure 12.8   Net international investment positions, 2002–17

percent of world GDP

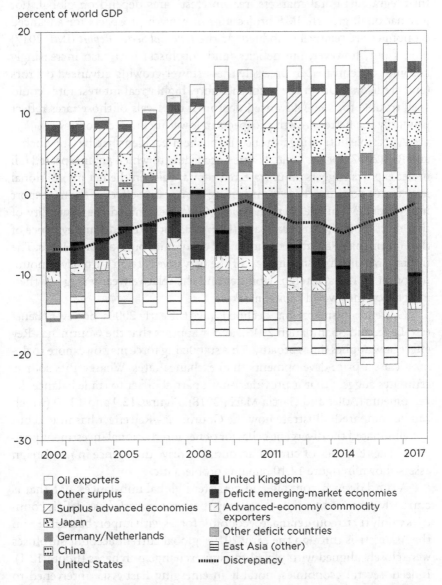

Legend:
- Oil exporters
- Other surplus
- Surplus advanced economies
- Japan
- Germany/Netherlands
- China
- United States
- United Kingdom
- Deficit emerging-market economies
- Advanced-economy commodity exporters
- Other deficit countries
- East Asia (other)
- ▪▪▪▪▪ Discrepancy

Surplus advanced economies = Korea, Hong Kong, Singapore, Sweden, Switzerland, and Taiwan; Advanced-economy commodity exporters: Australia, Canada, and New Zealand; Deficit emerging-market economies = Brazil, India, Indonesia, Mexico, South Africa, and Turkey; Oil exporters = *World Economic Outlook* definition plus Norway.

Source: IMF, *World Economic Outlook*; IMF Staff calculations.

create problems if they rise more than underlying economic growth rates. In integrated capital markets, real interest rates depend on global, not just national, growth. IMF projections of growth prospects for advanced economies are relatively subdued. As the *External Sector Report* (IMF 2017) points out, however, big deficits (and surpluses) have also increasingly become concentrated in precisely these slower-growing advanced debtors (and creditors). Down the road, therefore, higher real interest rates could spell trouble for some advanced debtors if the levels of those rates reflect primarily the better growth prospects in lower-income economies.

A possible mitigating factor could be the effect identified by Gourinchas and Rey (2007) for the United States, according to which an unexpected fall in net exports triggers an unexpected capital gain on the net international investment position, thereby mitigating the negative effect of the net export innovation. When the *World Economic Outlook* examined the generality of this effect more than a decade ago (IMF 2005), it detected some evidence of the Gourinchas-Rey effect for advanced economies but not for EMDEs. The finding was unsurprising in view of the pervasive foreign currency denomination of EMDEs' foreign liabilities and the relatively early stage of their integration into world capital markets.

Currency mismatch has declined since the early 2000s, however (Bénétrix, Lane, and Shambaugh 2015), and it appears that the Gourinchas-Rey effect now applies more broadly. This stabilizing force may owe more to domestic asset price developments than exchange rates. Whatever its source, estimates suggest that it provides only a partial offset to trade balance developments (Adler and Garcia-Macia 2018). Figures 12.9 and 12.10 (which can be compared) illustrate how the Gourinchas-Rey effect has muted but not eliminated the divergent behavior of net international investment positions. The tendency of current accounts to drive divergence in net foreign assets shown in figure 12.10 remains problematic.

A third danger from big and persistent global imbalances, one that is currently prominent, is that they may spark trade warfare as deficit countries vainly try to counter macroeconomic forces with import barriers. From the Asian crisis through the early 2010s, global current account surpluses were closely aligned with global foreign exchange purchases (figure 12.1). Indeed, several economies, notably in emerging East Asia, intervened to maintain their currencies at undervalued levels, as did some important oil exporters. Charges of currency manipulation and trade tensions resulted.[3]

---

3. In the cases of oil exporters with exchange rate pegs (e.g., Saudi Arabia), causality clearly ran from the price of oil through the current account to reserve accumulation. In Asian economies—notably China, with its capital control regime—intervention likely had some causal impact on the current account, to different degrees in different economies.

Figure 12.9 Current account behavior has led net international investment positions to diverge

change in international investment positions (2017–2010)
excluding valuation changes, percent of GDP

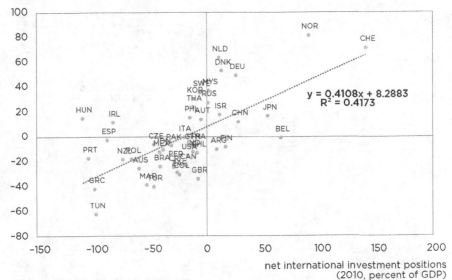

net international investment positions
(2010, percent of GDP)

Note: Vertical axis measures cumulated nominal current accounts between 2010 and 2017, adjusted to reflect the path of nominal income growth.
Source: IMF, *World Economic Outlook;* IMF Staff calculations.

In more recent years, however, global imbalances owe little to foreign exchange intervention by EMDEs, as IMF (2017) observes and figure 12.1 shows. This change is consistent with the greater concentration of imbalances within the advanced economy group noted above. Although discussion of currency manipulation is much more muted than it was a few years ago, it can be expected to return to the fore if the US dollar strengthens in response to Federal Reserve tightening and procyclical fiscal expansion in the United States. Because of those US macroeconomic prospects, the IMF now projects a bigger US current account deficit in coming years, notwithstanding the US administration's avowed aim of trimming deficits through trade policies. That tension will doubtless be a source of future trade frictions between the United States and the rest of the world. Those frictions may in turn take a toll on global economic growth.

Figure 12.10 Valuation effects have moderated but not eliminated the tendency for net international investment positions to diverge

change in net international investment positions (2017–2010)
including valuation changes, percent of GDP

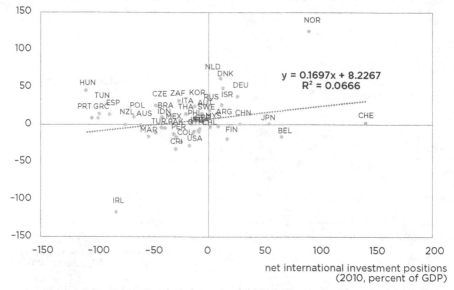

$$y = 0.1697x + 8.2267$$
$$R^2 = 0.0666$$

net international investment positions
(2010, percent of GDP)

Source: IMF, *World Economic Outlook*; IMF Staff calculations.

Policy Implications

This analysis yields four main implications for policy:

- Excess global imbalances usually reflect global forces and multiple distortions in many countries, including diverse financial sector distortions. Monocausal explanations rarely apply. Reducing global imbalances should therefore be a collective effort based on a shared appreciation of the roles individual countries need to play. To promote that objective, the IMF monitors external excess imbalances annually and makes its findings public through the *External Sector Report*.

- Notwithstanding the need for collective action, excess surplus countries still face little that would force them to adjust (outside of the threat of protectionist responses). In contrast, most deficit countries face the risk that lenders will withdraw. The trend of diverging net international investment positions thus looks unsustainable. Its end is likely to originate with external debtors.

- That endgame could be messy. Gross capital flows far exceed the minimal needs of current account financing. These flows can give rise to balance sheet vulnerabilities, underlining the need for continuing international financial cooperation (within the Basel Committee, the Financial Stability Board, and other international forums) to address cross-border financial stability risks. Similar cooperation to address socially costly tax minimization strategies and money laundering is richly warranted.

■ Economic theory suggests that trade restrictions will do little to alter global current account imbalances, which are primarily macroeconomic phenomena. But protectionism can do great harm to global growth. Stronger multilateral dispute resolution within the rules-based system is the right way to deal with the range of policies that distort trade and tilt the playing field.

References

Acharya, V., and P. Schnabl. 2010. Do Global Banks Spread Global Imbalances? Asset-Backed Commercial Paper During the Financial Crisis of 2007-09. *IMF Economic Review* 58, no. 1: 37-73.

Adler, G., and D. Garcia-Macia. 2018. *The Stabilizing Role of Net Foreign Asset Returns.* IMF Working Paper WP/18/79 (March). Washington: International Monetary Fund.

Bayoumi, T. 2017. *Unfinished Business: The Unexplored Causes of the Financial Crisis and the Lessons Yet to Be Learned.* New Haven, CT: Yale University Press.

Bénétrix, A., P. Lane, and J. Shambaugh. 2015. International Currency Exposures, Valuation Effects, and the Global Financial Crisis. *Journal of International Economics* 96, no. S1: S98–S109.

Bernanke, B. 2005. The Global Saving Glut and the U.S. Current Account Deficit. Sandridge Lecture to the Virginia Association of Economists, Richmond, VA, March 10.

Bernanke, B., C. Bertaut, L. DeMarco, and S. Kamin. 2011. International Capital Flows and the Returns to Safe Assets in the United States, 2003-2007. *Financial Stability Review* (Banque de France) 15: 13-26.

Gourinchas, P.-O., and H. Rey. 2007. International Financial Adjustment. *Journal of Political Economy* 114, no. 4: 665-703.

Hale, G., and M. Obstfeld. 2016. The Euro and the Geography of International Debt Flows. *Journal of the European Economic Association* 14, no. 1: 115-44.

Holston, K., T. Laubach, and J. Williams. 2017. Measuring the Natural Rate of Interest: International Trends and Determinants. *Journal of International Economics* 108, no. S1: S59-S75.

IMF (International Monetary Fund). 2005. Globalization and External Imbalances. In *World Economic Outlook* (April). Washington.

IMF (International Monetary Fund). 2017. *External Sector Report* (July). Washington.

Kaminsky, G., and C. Reinhart. 1999. The Twin Crises: The Causes of Banking and Balance-of-Payments Problems. *American Economic Review* 89, no. 3: 473-500.

Lane, P. and G. Milesi-Ferretti. 2015. Global Imbalances and External Adjustment After the Crisis. In *Global Liquidity, Spillovers to Emerging Markets and Policy Responses*, ed. C. Raddatz, D. Saravia, and J. Ventura. Santiago: Central Bank of Chile.

Lane, P., and G. Milesi-Ferretti. 2018. The External Wealth of Nations Revisited: International Financial Integration in the Aftermath of the Global Financial Crisis. *IMF Economic Review* 66, no. 1: 189-222.

Obstfeld, M., and K. Rogoff. 2009. Global Imbalances and the Financial Crisis: Products of Common Causes. In *Asia and the Global Financial Crisis*, ed. R. Glick and M. Spiegel, 131–172. Federal Reserve Bank of San Francisco.

Subramanian, Arvind, and Martin Kessler. 2013. *The Hyperglobalization of Trade and Its Future*. PIIE Working Paper 13-6 (July). Washington: Peterson Institute for International Economics.

13

Monetary and Exchange Rate Policies for Sustained Growth in Asia

JOSEPH E. GAGNON AND PHILIP TURNER

The more advanced economies in Asia are experiencing slower growth rates. Structural reforms are the most important policies for keeping growth rates up, but this chapter takes the growth slowdown as given and focuses on implications for monetary policy. The key policy implication is the importance of keeping core inflation at or above 2 percent to avoid prolonged periods of economic slack.

Flexible inflation targeting has provided a successful and adaptable framework for monetary policy worldwide.[1] It is hard to overstate the importance for monetary policy of keeping inflation within the central bank's policy mandate. Such mandates typically specify some target for average inflation in the medium term, either a single number or some range. In our view, such a target should be no less than, and possibly greater than, 2 percent.

Forecasts at the time of writing (January 2018) suggest strong global growth in 2018. The threat of deflation has faded in most countries. But with inflation expectations still comparatively low, monetary policy should react promptly to any significant negative shocks to growth or to inter-

Joseph E. Gagnon is senior fellow at the Peterson Institute for International Economics. Philip Turner is visiting lecturer at the University of Basel and former deputy head of the Monetary and Economic Department at the Bank for International Settlements. This chapter reflects the views of the authors and should not be interpreted as reflecting the views of the Institute or the Bank or any members of the boards or staffs of those institutions.

1. Graeme Wheeler, "Reflections on 25 years of inflation targeting," speech at Reserve Bank of New Zealand and International Journal of Central Banking conference, Wellington, December 1, 2014.

national financial markets (e.g., a new taper tantrum). In Thailand, core inflation remains well below 2 percent and there is a case for additional monetary ease already.

Japan failed to keep inflation above zero after a severe financial crisis and suffered two decades of excess unemployment and forgone output. The longer inflation is allowed to remain below target, the harder it is to raise inflation to target. When inflation expectations settle at low levels, central banks have less scope to use conventional monetary policy to stabilize cyclical fluctuations. Central banks, however, can still expand their balance sheets (so-called unconventional policy) when the conventional policy rate is near zero.

We rebut three possible criticisms of our advice.

First, it is argued that monetary policy has only a weak impact on inflation as reflected in declining estimates of the slope of the Phillips curve. We suggest that the Phillips curve slope is nonlinear in both the output gap and the level of inflation. When inflation is close to zero, a negative output gap has very little effect on inflation because of downward rigidities in nominal wages and prices. But a positive output gap is expected to have a significant effect, and this effect is likely to grow as the gap becomes larger.

Second, it is argued that central banks should stick to setting the overnight rate and should avoid the so-called unconventional balance sheet policies of the kind implemented by the Federal Reserve, European Central Bank (ECB), Bank of Japan (BOJ), and Bank of England. This view is unhistorical. Central banks have used their balance sheets to advance their objectives since their inception more than 300 years ago. In Asia, the accumulation of foreign exchange reserves and related policies to stabilize financial markets and control any excess liquidity in domestic banks were major planks of monetary policy in the years during and after the Asian financial crisis. What is new is that the substantial development of domestic financial markets in emerging-market economies has widened the possibilities for balance sheet policies. Because bond markets have become more important in monetary policy transmission in Asia, and because the liquidity of such bond markets can be especially fragile when global markets are disturbed, balance sheet policies should be on the policy agenda. This would be reinforced if weak growth and low inflation were to push the policy rate to zero.

Third, it is argued that easy monetary policy encourages risky behavior in financial markets. We argue that the evidence for such an effect is very weak. Moreover, ultra-low inflation and persistent negative output gaps themselves raise risks to financial stability. Prudential regulatory policies are far more potent at preserving financial stability than monetary policy. Regulatory policy includes tools such as bank capital and liquidity requirements; rules on currency and maturity mismatches in banks; limits to

Figure 13.1 Growth rate of real per capita GDP, 1985–2016, five-year moving average (percent)

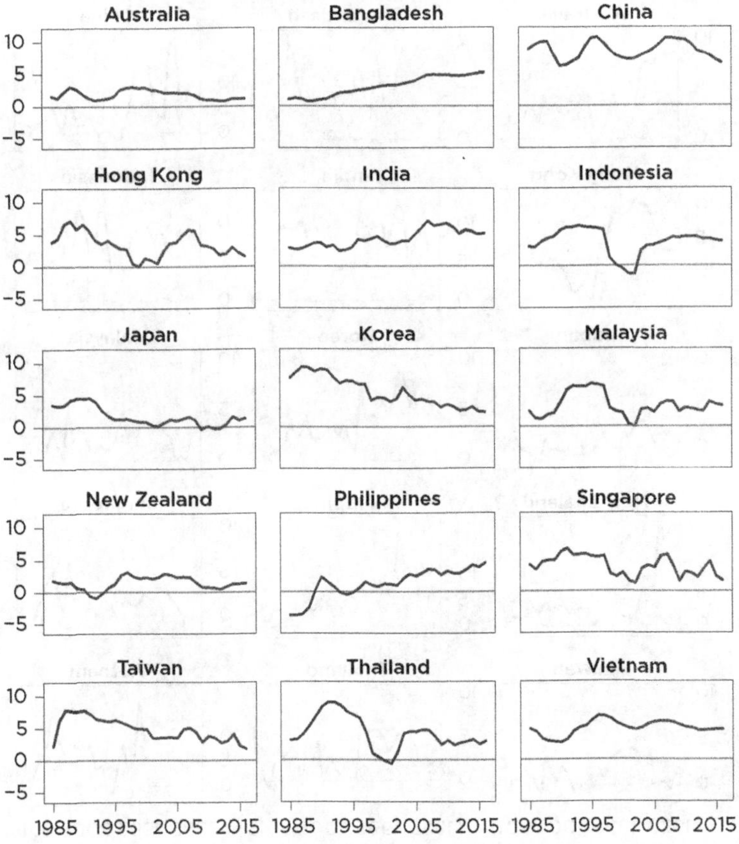

Source: IMF World Economic Outlook database.

interest rate exposures; and enhanced stress tests to make sure the balance sheets of financial intermediaries are resilient to any eventual tightening of monetary policy. New macroprudential policy tools (such as loan-to-value and debt-to-income ratios for house mortgages) give the central bank new ways of limiting risks to financial stability arising from low interest rates.

Macroeconomic Developments in Asia

Figure 13.1 displays five-year moving averages of the growth rate of real per capita GDP for the 15 largest economies (based on 2016 GDP at market exchange rates) in the Asia-Pacific region. Many economies appear to be growing more slowly over time. However, for some economies there is no clear trend in the growth rate, and for a few economies growth seems to be increasing.

Figure 13.2 CPI inflation rates in Asia, 1985–2016
(percent per year)

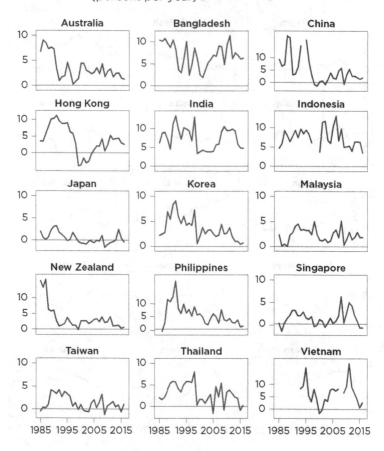

CPI = consumer price index
Note: Observations above 20 percent have been dropped.
Source: IMF, World Economic Outlook database.

The main policy option to raise an economy's growth rate regardless of its relative income level is structural reform that opens up protected sectors to competition and encourages investments in human and physical capital and research and development (R&D). However, structural reform is the topic of other chapters in this volume. This chapter focuses on implications for monetary policy, which can help to avoid prolonged underemployment of resources and to sustain investment. Monetary policy can thus help an economy achieve its long-run potential growth rate.

Figure 13.2 displays inflation rates in the Asia-15 economies. In every case, inflation in 2016 was below its historic average, often by a considerable amount. In 2016, inflation was below 5 percent in 14 of the 15 economies; below 3 percent in 12 economies; below 2 percent in 8 economies; below 1 percent in 5 economies; and below 0 percent in 2 economies.

In most of the economies with inflation below 1 percent in 2016—Singapore, Japan, Thailand, New Zealand, and Korea—GDP growth slowed markedly over time. In these economies, there was probably a gap between actual and potential GDP growth at some point either before or when inflation was declining. As we discuss in the next section, a key priority for monetary policy in Asia should be keeping inflation from falling persistently below 2 percent and possibly even targeting a rate slightly higher than 2 percent.

Dangers of Ultra-Low Inflation

It is a widely acknowledged human failing that we learn more readily from our own mistakes than from the mistakes of others. A similar truth holds at the level of national economic policies. The United States and the euro area did not fully absorb the lessons of real estate bubbles and banking crises in the Nordic countries, the United Kingdom, and Japan in the early 1990s and in developing Asia in the late 1990s. This failure doomed them to suffer their own crises in 2008.

In our view, many Asian policymakers are not sufficiently concerned about the likely persistence and economic costs of ultra-low inflation. All their lives, inflation has been a problem only when it was too high, and they take satisfaction in having conquered it. Yet both economic research and the experiences of some advanced economies suggest that inflation can get stuck below target for extended periods and that allowing ultra-low inflation to persist has serious costs.

Lessons from Japan

The bursting of the equity and real estate price bubbles in 1990–91 devastated the Japanese financial system but it was not until 2000 that the authorities developed systematic policies to deal with insolvent banks.[2] Since 1993, nominal GDP growth and core consumer price index (CPI) inflation in Japan have fluctuated around zero[3] (see figure 13.3). Real GDP growth slowed after 1993. The severe impairment of financial inter-

---

2. Nakaso (2001) provides an authoritative account of how it took years for the authorities in Japan to develop policies to deal with this financial crisis.

3. In the four quarters following each increase in the consumption tax, the inflation rate shown in figure 13.3 was adjusted downward by the change in inflation in the first quarter minus the change in inflation in the fifth quarter divided by two. The consumption tax was increased in 1997Q2 and 2014Q2.

Figure 13.3 Macroeconomic developments in Japan, 1954Q1–2017Q1

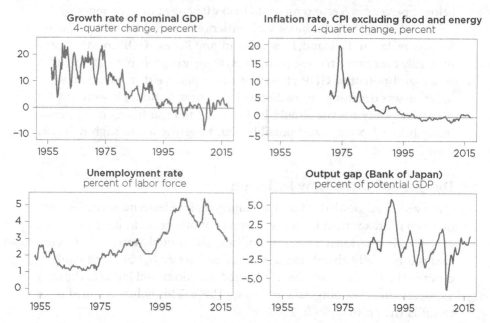

CPI = consumer price index

Note: Inflation has been adjusted to remove the effects of increases in the consumption tax.

Sources: Bank of Japan, Haver Analytics, and authors' calculations.

mediation during much of the 1990s, slower growth of the working-age population, and convergence toward per capita income levels of the most advanced economies would have slowed real growth regardless of monetary policy or inflation.

However, ultra-low inflation makes it harder to reduce the real value of debts, and banks find it difficult to improve their balance sheets when nominal GDP is stagnant. In any event, the level of output does appear to have been below potential on average since the advent of ultra-low inflation. The BOJ's estimate of the output gap has fallen from an average of 1.7 percent before 1993 to –1.0 percent since 1993 (see figure 13.3). This estimate probably understates the economy's true underperformance. The unemployment rate has risen from an average of 1.9 percent before 1993 to 4.1 percent since then. Even if the natural rate of unemployment is now close to 3 percent, as appears likely, Okun's law suggests that an average excess unemployment rate of 1 percent implies a shortfall in GDP of 2 percent.[4] Cumulated over more than 20 years, this shortfall represents an

---

4. Note that the BOJ estimates that output is slightly above potential in 2017 with an unemployment rate slightly below 3 percent.

enormous loss of goods and services that could have been consumed or invested in Japan.

In 1993—well after the bubbles had burst—the BOJ's policy interest rate was above 3 percent. Adam Posen (1998) provided one of the earliest critiques of Japanese macroeconomic policy after the bubbles. He argued for coordinated monetary and fiscal expansion to return output to potential and avoid deflation. Soon thereafter, the BOJ began to take more aggressive monetary policy measures (the zero interest rate policy in 1999 and quantitative targeting in 2001) but it reversed direction before deflation was fully conquered. A faster, stronger, and more sustained response to deflation in the early 1990s would have been warranted and might have maintained inflation near 2 percent in the subsequent decades (Ahearne et al. 2002). Twenty years of zero inflation, however, have changed the expectations of firms and workers in Japan. Raising inflation back to 2 percent is much harder now, as evidenced by the limited success of the BOJ's massive quantitative easing policy since 2013 (Ball et al. 2016, 48–50). Surveys of professional forecasters reveal that long-term inflation expectations in Japan were very slow to decline and remained above actual inflation for most of the 1990s and 2000s.[5] Getting expectations to rise will also take time and is likely to require a sustained increase in actual inflation. A key lesson for Asian economies is not to allow inflation and inflation expectations to become entrenched below 2 percent.

Economic Costs of Ultra-low Inflation

One important cost of ultra-low inflation is that relative prices become more difficult to change. When inflation is positive and prices and wages are rising on average, firms can adjust relative prices in response to shifts in tastes, technology, and competitive conditions by increasing some prices at a faster rate and others at a slower rate. When overall inflation is zero, adjustments in relative prices require firms to reduce some prices in nominal terms. If there is resistance to cutting prices, the economy needs to run below its full-employment level to force some wages and prices down to keep the average inflation rate near zero (Akerlof, Dickens, and Perry 1996; Benigno and Ricci 2011). Studies find evidence of such downward rigidities in wages in many countries (Dickens et al. 2007; Fallick, Lettau, and Wascher 2016). Once nominal wages begin to decline, the fear of a deflationary spiral can lead households and firms to cut spending, adding further downward pressure to an already weak economy.

Akerlof, Dickens, and Perry estimated that an overall inflation rate of

---

5. *Consensus Forecasts*, various issues.

at least 2 percent is needed to avoid the bulk of the economic cost of downward nominal wage rigidity.[6] In comments published with the Akerlof, Dickens, and Perry paper, Robert Gordon and Greg Mankiw suggested that downward nominal wage rigidity might become less apparent as people become used to low inflation or in the event of severe economic distress. However, Fallick, Lettau, and Wascher show that these conjectures did not prove correct in the aftermath of the Great Recession in the United States.

Another reason to prefer a positive inflation rate is that price indexes do not fully control for quality improvements and the welfare benefits of new goods. These omissions bias published inflation measures up by as much as 1 percent per year, so that a reported inflation rate of 1 percent may reflect constant true prices (Bank of Canada 2013).

Ultra-low Inflation, Interest Rates, and Monetary Policy

Because economic equilibrium depends on the real rate of interest over both short and long horizons, an environment of low expected inflation must be accompanied by low nominal rates of interest. Moreover, recent studies document a decline in the equilibrium real rate of interest in many advanced economies (Holston, Laubach, and Williams 2016; Williams 2017). Figure 13.4 shows that the real short-term interest rate has trended down in many of the Asia-15 economies. In 2016 it was below its historical average in these economies except India and Vietnam.

In most economies in the Asia-Pacific region with active and open bond markets, long-term interest rates have declined since 2000, a period in which long-term inflation expectations are likely to have been fairly stable. As figure 13.5 shows, this has mirrored the movement in average long-term rates in advanced economies. Since the mid-2000s local-currency bond markets of many Asian emerging-market economies have thus become part of this expanding global market (Obstfeld 2015). But note that the long-term rates of emerging Asian economies on average rose more sharply than rates in advanced economies in the two periods of bond market turbulence—in 2008 and during and after the 2013 taper tantrum.

As King and Low (2014) have concluded, given the high correlation between bond yields of different countries (emerging as well as advanced economies), "it therefore is quite reasonable to talk about a 'world' interest rate." The real long-term rate has been declining for about 30 years. Observations for the most recent years using a principal-components estimate based on 10-year government bonds of three major markets show that the world real long-term interest rate has been hovering around zero

---

6. Wyplosz (2001) also argues for optimal rates of inflation above 2 percent in major European economies.

Figure 13.4 Real short-term interest rates in Asia, 1985–2016
(percent)

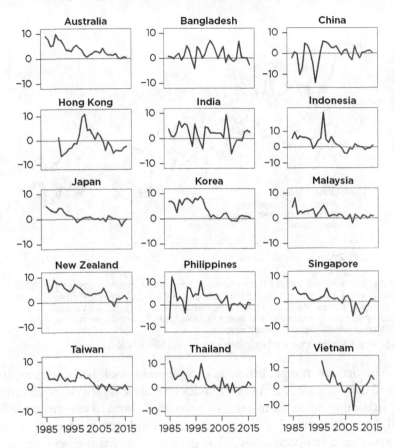

Note: Real interest rate is three-month Treasury bill rate (or closest equivalent) minus current consumer price index (CPI) inflation rate.

Sources: Haver Analytics and IMF *International Financial Statistics* and *World Economic Outlook* databases.

since mid-2011 (graph 2 in Hördahl, Sobrun, and Turner 2016). Rachel and Smith (2015) attribute about two-thirds of the long-run decline to secular factors shaping desired saving and investment rates in the global economy. They argue that the likely persistence of these factors suggests that the underlying global neutral real rate will settle at around 1 percent in the medium to long run.[7] If this prognosis is correct, central banks will again grapple with the zero lower bound for the policy rate.

---

7. Laubach and Williams (2015) also estimate a long-run equilibrium real rate of around 1 percent for the United States. They attribute the decline in the long-run equilibrium real rate mainly to the decline in the growth rate of potential output.

Figure 13.5 Long-term bond yields: Emerging Asia and selected advanced economies, January 2001 through July 2017

Note: Vertical lines denote the collapse of Lehman Brothers in September 2008 and the taper tantrum in July 2013. Emerging Asia is the unweighted average of Indonesia, Korea, Malaysia, Philippines, Taiwan, and Thailand. Advanced economies are the unweighted average of Australia, Canada, euro area, New Zealand, Sweden, and United Kingdom.

Sources: Bank for International Settlements and Haver Analytics.

The decline in equilibrium rates of interest took both markets and central banks by surprise. Because policy rates have lagged the equilibrium rate in coming down, there has been a secular downward pressure on inflation. To some degree this downward trend in inflation has been welcome. However, in a few economies it has gone too far. Asian economies with slowing trend growth rates are at risk of getting trapped in harmful deflation, as in the case of Japan since the early 1990s.

With a low inflation rate and a low equilibrium real interest rate, the nominal policy interest rate will be close to zero in the future. The difficulty of setting the policy rate much below zero greatly reduces the scope for countercyclical monetary policy, at least using the conventional policy tool. Ball et al. (2016) show for the United States that the zero bound is likely to constrain conventional monetary policy in all but the mildest of recessions as long as inflation and inflation expectations remain near 2 percent. Although fiscal policy can, in principle, play an important role in macroeconomic stabilization when monetary policy faces the zero bound, the experience of the major advanced economies in the aftermath of the global financial crisis demonstrates that political and institutional barriers to effective fiscal policy can be substantial.

The case of Korea is instructive (see figure 13.6). From 2000 through 2008, Korea's short-term interest rate averaged 4.3 percent and core inflation averaged 2.8 percent, implying a real interest rate of 1.5 percent. To stabilize the Korean economy during the global financial crisis, the Bank of Korea cut short-term interest rates by more than 3 percentage points.

Since 2009, the short-term interest rate has averaged 2.2 percent and the core inflation rate also averaged 2.2 percent, implying a real interest rate of 0.0 percent. Currently, core inflation is 1.4 percent. If inflation were to settle in at 1 percent and the equilibrium real interest rate is now 0 percent, then the "new normal" policy rate would be 1 percent. In the event of a negative shock to the Korean economy, the Bank of Korea would not be able to lower the policy rate by as much as it did in 2009. Without the help of fiscal policy or unconventional monetary policy (discussed below) Korea would be subject to longer recessions and slower recoveries. To reduce this risk, the Bank of Korea should set its policy stance to ensure that inflation returns at least to its target rate of 2 percent and seriously consider a slightly higher target, say 3 percent, which had been the target only two years ago.

Figure 13.7 shows that Thailand is at risk of falling into sustained deflation. With the policy rate at 1.5 percent, the Bank of Thailand would not be able to deliver the 2 percentage point easing of conventional policy that it did during the global financial crisis. Moreover, policy seems to be too tight as the real interest rate is higher than in Korea and core inflation is falling further below target. In the latest Article IV consultation, IMF staff recommended further monetary ease. Thai authorities preferred to preserve space for future policy action, arguing that inflation expectations are well anchored and lower interest rates could raise risks to financial stability. However, as seen in Japan in the 1990s, measures of expectations typically lag rather than lead actual inflation trends. In addition, research suggests that preserving policy space is the wrong strategy for an economy at risk of deflation. In such circumstances, an inflation surprise to the downside is harder to deal with than a surprise to the upside. Therefore, a central bank should be more aggressive than otherwise in easing policy as it approaches the zero lower bound to avoid the danger of the liquidity trap (Reifschneider and Williams 2000).

We also note that Singapore and Taiwan are currently at the zero lower bound. Any additional monetary ease in these economies must come in the form of unconventional monetary policies, which we discuss in the next section.

Figure 13.6   Korean monetary policy since the Asian financial crisis, 2000Q1–2017Q2

percent

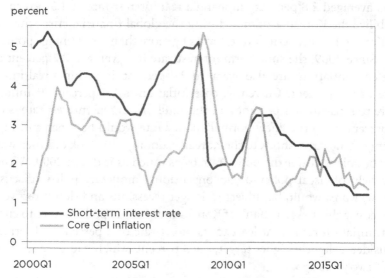

CPI = consumer price index

Source: Haver Analytics. Interest rate is the call money rate. Inflation is the four-quarter change in the CPI excluding agriculture and oil.

Figure 13.7   Thai monetary policy since the Asian financial crisis, 2000Q1–2017Q2

percent

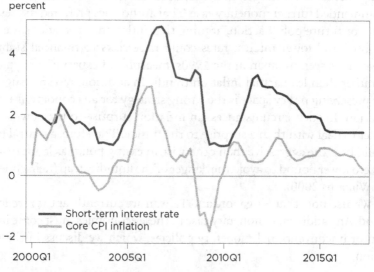

CPI = consumer price index

Source: Haver Analytics. Interest rate is the call money rate. Inflation is the four-quarter change in the CPI excluding food and energy.

Risks from Global Bond Markets: The "Taper Tantrum"

Central banks in Asia facing subpar growth and below-target inflation are vulnerable to shocks from global bond markets that could suddenly tighten domestic financing conditions. The increased importance of domestic bond markets in monetary policy transmission (Mohanty 2014) means that central banks in Asia may have to make greater use of their balance sheets than when credit was supplied exclusively by banks at rates linked to the short-term interest rate set by the central bank.

Central banks need to be ready for external shocks to the world real interest rate. As described above, there are sound reasons to believe that the equilibrium real interest rate has declined secularly. Yet part of the decline observed since 2011 is cyclical and reflects central bank purchase of bonds. The unexpected depth and length of the recession in advanced economies after the global financial crisis (and the associated pessimism about the future) has depressed the world long-term rate. If growth-friendly policies succeed in closing the global output gap and end the trend decline in inflation, investment rates would probably rise and precautionary savings fall. We cannot know how suddenly global long-term rates would rise. The taper tantrum of 2013 showed that expectations of monetary policy tightening in the United States could have a large effect on Asian bond markets even when domestic conditions in Asia do not change (see figure 13.5).

The taper tantrum demonstrated how externally driven swings in local bond market liquidity in emerging markets can affect local financial conditions in a dramatic way. Monetary policy, notably central bank balance sheet policies, may need to offset these shocks. During the taper tantrum, the average of yields on local-currency government bonds in the more open Asian markets rose sharply—from 3.2 percent in April 2013 to 4.4 percent by January 2014—and market volatility spiked higher. In some emerging markets, currencies fell sharply just as bond prices declined, although exchange rate movements in the Asia-15 economies were mixed and mostly rather small.

The bond markets in most emerging markets are of recent birth, and market liquidity is vulnerable to swings in foreign investor sentiment. In many countries, the domestic investor base is narrow, dominated by banks or state-run pension funds. Because the intrinsic liquidity of the markets for government bonds in many emerging markets is still comparatively low, some foreign investors tend to rely on intermediary instruments (bond funds, synthetic exchange traded funds [ETFs], etc.) that promise daily liquidity. When market sentiment changes, this liquidity illusion can be shattered, leading to very heavy sales: Shek, Shim, and Shin (2015) have shown that investor flows into and out of emerging-market funds tend to cluster much more than for advanced-economy bond flows.

As discussed further later in the chapter, the central bank can use its balance sheet to keep the markets for local financial assets operating in the face of a market liquidity shock. This can forestall any self-feeding price movements that could produce a sharp and unwarranted tightening of financial conditions. A particularly bold policy move along these lines was the decision of the Hong Kong Monetary Authority in 1998 to buy 7 percent of domestic equities to thwart a joint speculative attack on its currency peg and stock market (Bayoumi and Gagnon 2018). This policy worked because of the credibility of the central bank's commitment to free financial markets in normal times. In the aftermath of the global financial crisis, several central banks in the emerging markets undertook to lend against (or even buy) financial assets, private as well as public (BIS 2009). Some offered to indemnify asset holders for any eventual losses from continuing to hold government bonds or other paper. Such policies aimed at countering temporary bouts of extreme market illiquidity.

Is Low Inflation beyond the Control of Central Banks?

The Phillips Curve Is Dormant, Not Dead

Many observers have noted that very large increases in unemployment rates during the Great Recession had only small effects on inflation in advanced economies. However, it does not follow that inflation is beyond the control of central banks. Rather, the very low trend rates of inflation coupled with downward nominal wage and price rigidity have put economies in a region where the Phillips curve is flat. But the slope is likely to increase as economies exceed potential by a significant amount. And the slope is likely to be higher in general when inflation is significantly above zero.

This subsection examines the evidence on inflation and the output gap in the United States, which has the longest available series of these data. The first column in table 13.1 presents an estimate of an expectations-augmented Phillips curve (equation 13.1). The dependent variable is the four-quarter percent change in the GDP deflator minus the value of inflation that had been predicted eight quarters ago for the following four quarters.[8] The gap is the difference between the Congressional Budget Office's estimate of the natural rate and the actual unemployment rate. The infla-

---

8. The predicted value is from a survey of professional economic forecasters and is provided by Haver Analytics. The inflation forecast of four quarters earlier should have incorporated the effects of the gap of four quarters earlier, leaving no systematic prediction error if forecasters are efficient. An alternative specification based on the contemporaneous output gap and forecasted inflation with a four-quarter lag had a lower R^2 (0.12) and a much smaller coefficient on the gap of 0.46.

Table 13.1 Phillips curves regressions on US GDP deflator

Inflation – Expected Inflation = α + β Gap + γ Gap*(Inflation Dummy)

Expectations measure	Survey	Survey	Lag	Lag	Lag
Emp Gap	1.16*** (0.25)		1.00*** (0.12)	1.15*** (0.13)	
Cap Util Gap		0.53*** (0.08)			0.45*** (0.05)
Emp Gap (Inf<3)	-0.96*** (0.22)		-0.98*** (0.16)	-1.01*** (0.14)	
Cap Util Gap (Inf<3)		-0.56*** (0.09)			-0.45*** (0.07)
Constant	0.32 (0.29)	-0.38** (0.17)	-0.02 (0.17)	0.16 (0.17)	-0.41*** (0.14)
R-squared	0.58	0.58	0.47	0.56	0.60
Observations	182	182	271	199	199
Sample	1972Q2– 2017Q3	1972Q2– 2017Q3	1950Q1– 2017Q3	1968Q1– 2017Q3	1968Q1– 2017Q3

Note: ***, **, and * denote 1, 5, and 10 percent significance levels, respectively. Newey-West standard errors with three lags are in parentheses.

Sources: Haver Analytics and authors' calculations. See text for description of variables.

tion dummy equals zero when inflation is above 3 percent and one when inflation is below 3 percent.

$$\text{Inflation}(t) - \text{Expected Inflation}(t-8) = \hspace{2cm} (13.1)$$
$$\alpha + \beta \, \text{Gap}(t-4) + \gamma \, \text{Gap}(t-4)*(\text{Inflation Dummy}(t-4))$$

The results show that the gap has a large and strongly significant effect when inflation is above 3 percent, but the effect largely disappears when inflation is below 3 percent. This simple model can explain nearly 60 percent of the overall variance of inflation, as shown by the R^2 statistic. The second column displays results using an alternative measure of the output gap: the Federal Reserve's index of capacity utilization in manufacturing, mining, and utilities minus its average value since 1967. The effect on inflation of a 1 percentage point gap in capacity utilization is about half as large as that of a 1 percentage point employment gap, but the explanatory power is essentially identical. As with the employment gap, the effect of the capacity utilization gap declines sharply when inflation is very low.

The remaining columns of table 13.1 display results using a lagged three-year moving average of inflation as a measure of inflation expectations (equation 13.2). The regression shown in column 3 has a much longer sample, back to 1950, and a somewhat lower R^2 than column 1. But the coefficients on the employment gap are reasonably close to those in column

1. Column 4 displays the same regression starting in 1968. The coefficients are almost identical to those in column 1. The final column displays a regression using lagged inflation and capacity utilization. It obtains results similar to those of column 2.

$$\text{Inflation}(t) - 3\text{-year Ave. Inflation}(t{-}4) = \tag{13.2}$$
$$\alpha + \beta \text{ Gap}(t{-}4) + \gamma \text{ Gap}(t{-}4)^*(\text{Inflation Dummy}(t{-}4))$$

To check whether the Phillips curve slope may have changed over time, we also ran the regressions of table 13.1 starting in 1992Q1, just after US inflation fell below 3 percent on a sustained basis. There are only nine quarters with inflation above 3 percent in this subsample (2004Q4–2006Q3 and 2007Q1), yet we obtain estimates of the gap coefficients that are almost identical to those shown in columns 1 and 2 and moderately smaller than those in columns 3 to 5.

Figure 13.8 displays the inflation surprises (left-hand sides of equations 13.1 and 13.2) and employment gaps (right-hand sides of both equations), where the sample is split between lagged inflation above and below 3 percent. Similar results (not shown) are obtained using capacity utilization. The greater slope in the high inflation regime is apparent for both measures of expectations. It also appears that the slope may steepen for the most positive values of the output gap. However, adding the interacted value of the output gap and a dummy when the output gap is above its mean value yields a significant coefficient (at the 10 percent level) in only the first of the five regressions shown in table 13.1.

Scope for Unconventional Monetary Policy

Central banks can ease policy and achieve their objectives even at the zero bound. It would be absurd to assume that—irrespective of circumstances—the only legitimate policy tool for a central bank is the overnight rate in interbank markets. The analysis by Reddy (2017) supports this policy conclusion. The following paragraphs suggest some possibilities. What would work best will depend on country circumstances (including political constraints) and on macroeconomic conditions.

To a small extent, central banks can reduce policy rates below zero. Switzerland has pushed short-term interest rates more deeply negative than any other economy, at –0.75 percent. It may be possible to go more negative, but there is a risk that at some point banks and firms might begin to store large volumes of paper currency. In addition, banks in any economy with negative policy rates have not passed the negative rates through to household deposits. This lack of pass-through to household deposits limits the effectiveness of negative policy rates and hurts bank profitability.

Figure 13.8 US Phillips curves for GDP inflation and employment gap, 1955Q1–2017Q1

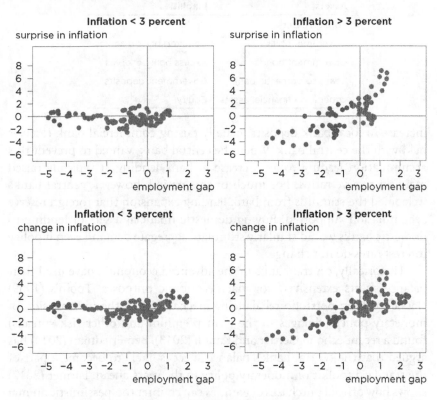

Source: Haver Analytics and authors' calculations.

Another channel for easing policy at the zero bound is to provide forward guidance to markets that the policy rate will remain near zero for several years. The credibility of such a commitment almost surely declines with the horizon of the commitment, as central bank governors and policy board members cannot legally restrict their own future actions, let alone those of their successors. But forward guidance does appear to have worked over horizons of two to three years (Campbell et al. 2012).

Probably the most general avenue for easing policy at the zero bound is the active use of the central bank's own balance sheet. Table 13.2 represents a stylized central bank balance sheet to show just how many tools a central bank has at its disposal. In almost all emerging-market economies in Asia, the central bank balance sheet is very large. A major driver of this expansion was the huge accumulation of foreign exchange reserves after the Asian financial crisis (discussed in the next section). One consequence of foreign exchange accumulation for the domestic financial system was an

Table 13.2 A central bank balance sheet

Assets	Liabilities
Foreign assets	Cash
Government bills	Required bank reserves
Government bonds	Excess bank reserves
Loans to domestic banks	Government deposits
Other local financial assets	Equity

increase in local bank deposits, usually raising commercial bank reserves held with the central bank. When the central bank wanted to prevent this accumulation leading to an increase in bank lending, it typically raised required reserve ratios. For much of this period, however, central banks welcomed the stimulus from bank lending expansion that foreign reserve accumulation supported. Buying domestic financial assets or lending to domestic banks would similarly stimulate aggregate demand even if policy interest rates do not change.

Historically, central banks in the advanced economies have used their balance sheets extensively for macroeconomic purposes. Tobin's (1969) classic work on portfolio rebalancing mechanisms in the transmission of monetary policy (changes in the term premium and other risk spreads) found a recent echo in Gertler and Karadi (2013). Ben Friedman (2014) has argued that the central bank's balance sheet is likely to become a part of the standard toolkit of monetary policy in the years ahead. Farmer (2017) shows how official purchases of equities can counter too-pessimistic animal spirits in markets, and so sustain business investment.

Table 13.3 shows the scope for quantitative easing (QE) in the Asia-15 economies. Among these economies, only Japan is currently engaged in QE, as reflected in the very large size of the BOJ's balance sheet. Many other Asian economies have large central bank balance sheets, primarily reflecting large stockpiles of foreign exchange reserves. We discuss exchange rate and intervention policy in the final section below.

All of these economies have at least some scope for central banks to conduct QE through purchases of government bonds. Three advanced economies (the euro area, Japan, and the United Kingdom) have also subsidized lending to the banking system. The Bank of England estimates that its Funding for Lending scheme has had a macroeconomic impact equivalent to a reduction in the policy rate of 0.75 to 1.50 percent (Bank of England 2014). The column labeled broad money in table 13.3 gives an approximate size of the domestic banking system through which subsidized central bank credit could operate.

Table 13.3 Scope for quantitative easing, December 2016 (percent of 2016Q4 GDP, seasonally adjusted annual rate)

Country	Central bank liabilities	General government gross debt	Broad money[a]	Equity market capitalization
Australia	10	41	112	100
Bangladesh[b]	n.a.	33	55	16
China	45	44	202	66
Hong Kong[c]	60	0	232	560
India[d]	21	70	82	69
Indonesia	8	28	38	45
Japan	88	239	236	104
Korea	28	38	201	92
Malaysia	35	56	128	131
New Zealand[e]	10	29	99	n.a.
Philippines	30	35	62	80
Singapore	37	112	137	221
Taiwan	87	36	238	157
Thailand	46	42	124	103
Vietnam[b]	n.a.	61	n.a.	3

n.a. = not available

a. M3 where available, otherwise M2.
b. Based on 2016 annual GDP.
c. Data exclude assets denominated in foreign currency and shares of mainland companies.
d. Broad money based on April 2017 to avoid effects of demonetization in late 2016.
e. Central government debt.

Sources: Haver Analytics, Hong Kong Monetary Authority, and International Monetary Fund *World Economic Outlook* database.

Perhaps the most untapped channel for QE is equity purchases. The BOJ is buying about 1 percent of domestic equities per year, but this pace could be increased considerably. In some economies, equities represent a much larger potential market for central banks than government bonds.

A vast literature documents the powerful effects of QE on long-term bond yields in the euro area, Japan, the United Kingdom, and the United States (Gagnon 2016). Though more difficult to prove, there is evidence that QE has stimulated economic activity and inflation. The Federal Reserve purchased long-term bonds equivalent to nearly 25 percent of GDP in successive rounds from 2008 through 2014. Staff estimate that these purchases had a macroeconomic effect roughly equal to that of a 250 basis point cut in the federal funds rate (Engen, Laubach, and Reifschneider 2015). Wu and Xia (2015) estimate a shadow federal funds rate to capture the macroeconomic impact of QE. They find that as of 2014, QE had reduced the shadow federal funds rate by 200 to 300 basis points. A similar estimate by Lombardi and Zhu (2014) places more weight on the Federal Reserve's balance sheet and implies a shadow federal funds rate of minus 400 basis points by 2011.

In some circumstances, however, governance considerations may in practice limit the large-scale use of the central bank's balance sheet. This can be the case in jurisdictions where full instrument independence of the central bank is not securely established. Central banks must avoid the traps of fiscal and financial dominance; they need to be sure they are free to decide to sell the assets they have purchased if monetary policy so requires. Governments with large debts to refinance may resist higher bond yields. While no central bank will want to provoke financial market volatility, worries about destabilizing bond or equity markets should not prevent central banks from gradually tightening monetary policy when inflation is expected to remain above their targets. The warning of Shirakawa (2015) that markets must not be misled into believing the policy regime has become a "put-option type of monetary policy" is well taken.

Should Risks to Financial Stability Constrain Monetary Policy?[9]

Some central banks feel in a quandary. They worry that a prolonged period of very low interest rates could create risks for financial stability—a reasonable worry since monetary policy works in part by changing financial risk exposures. Lower interest rates reduce the debt service burdens of borrowers and may help keep them solvent. And lower rates typically increase asset prices, raising the value of collateral held by firms and households, thus making them seem better credit risks in the eyes of potential lenders. Debt-to-income ratios can be expected to rise if the decline in interest rates persists, as some recent research suggests (Laubach and Williams 2015, Rachel and Smith 2015). Higher debt and asset prices can be regarded as natural equilibrating mechanisms to a move to a low interest rate environment. Yet it is possible to overshoot the new equilibrium, and any sudden correction would be disruptive. Because no one can know how such worries might materialize, regulatory policy needs to be prepared.

Keeping policy interest rates higher than warranted by macroeconomic conditions would not solve this quandary. This is because a prolonged period of subpar growth and high unemployment also creates financial stability risks. Such risks would be all the greater if prices are falling. The question whether a central bank should keep the policy rate higher than

---

9. This section draws on Turner (2017), which provides fuller details and references.

that needed on macroeconomic grounds to counter financial stability risks is not new. Dennis Robertson (1928/1966) answered this question with a clear "no" when he took the (young) Federal Reserve to task in 1928 for focusing its interest rate policy on limiting speculative lending of commercial banks. At that time, the Federal Reserve was guided by what it called the Principle of Productive Credit. Underlining the danger at that time of an undesirable fall in the general level of prices, Robertson proposed instead what he termed the Principle of Price Stabilization, "the stabilization of the price level as the sole and sufficient objective of (central) banking policy." The subsequent history surely vindicated his view. The Federal Reserve's acquiescence in the massive collapse of the money supply and a 25 percent decline in the price level after the 1929 crash turned an ordinary recession into the Great Depression.

As the head of economic research at the Reserve Bank of Australia (RBA) has documented, there is little historical evidence that low interest rate environments are inherently unstable—either in creating macroeconomic instability or in destabilizing the financial system (Simon 2015). The main common sense argument for not allowing financial stability worries to override the macroeconomic considerations driving monetary policy is that interest rates high enough to counter some potential financial threat would cripple the rest of the economy. In addition, expectations that determine asset prices or lending expansions are not as stable or predictable functions of policy variables as are macroeconomic variables (BIS 1998). The most general analysis of the issue to date shows that the marginal cost of keeping the policy rate high and accepting higher unemployment outweighs the marginal benefit from the lower probability of a crisis under a wide range of assumptions about the economy (Svensson 2016).

Recent history fully supports this conclusion. From mid-2004 to mid-2006, a substantial rise in policy rates worldwide, which bond markets expected to be sustained, went together with increased risk-taking in the global financial system on all the standard metrics (Turner 2017). In his press conferences as chairman of the bimonthly global economy meetings of central bank governors at the Bank for International Settlements (BIS), Jean-Claude Trichet repeatedly during 2006 and early 2007 underlined the concerns of the governors about overextended financial markets. He explained that central banks had prepared the ground by raising interest rates substantially as economies neared full employment and that the financial industry should prepare for a significant correction. But banks and markets remained entirely complacent.

One telling international comparison between the Bank of England and the Bank of Canada throws some useful light on what would have happened had short-term rates been kept higher before 2004. The Bank of England, worried about strong domestic demand as well as continued rises in house prices and expecting a return of core inflation to around 2 percent from a lower level, did not follow the sharp cuts in the US federal funds rate in 2001. By mid-2004, the bank rate had been raised to 4¾ percent—even though core inflation was below 1½ percent during almost all of 2003 and 2004. The bank was concerned about "financial imbalances creating problems beyond the two-year horizon of our inflation target." Yet tighter monetary policy did not prevent the buildup of financial imbalances in the United Kingdom. And this policy did contribute to an overvalued currency, which created its own financial risks.

The Bank of Canada, by contrast, cut interest rates aggressively. But lower rates did not induce Canadian banks to become overextended because of much stricter regulation (notably the existence of a leverage ratio and limits to banks' off-balance sheet exposures to securitized products) and because a less contestable domestic banking market allowed fatter margins. The major policy shortcomings that aggravated the 2008–09 financial crisis were not related to monetary policy. They were rather the failures of domestic supervisors to address the new risks that innovation in the financial industry had created (Ramaswamy 2017).

The BIS has challenged the Svensson (2016) analysis. In its *2016 Annual Report*, the BIS put forward an alternative path for the federal funds rate from 2002 (BIS 2016). The new policy rule guiding this path was a Taylor rule augmented by a financial cycle proxy. Had the Federal Reserve followed this rule, the BIS argues, the financial crisis would have been avoided and there would have been a gain of about 1 percent a year in real US GDP over a decade or so, or 12 percent cumulatively.

As Turner (2017) documents, however, the methodology underlying this calculation raises many questions. The federal funds rate implied by the financial cycle-augmented Taylor rule rises earlier but by much less than the actual funds rate over the 2003–06 period. As noted above, substantial rises in the Bank of England's policy rate and in the federal funds rate to over 5 percent failed to curb financial market risk-taking—much to the chagrin of Trichet and the other governors. Why then would a more modest rise started a little earlier have worked? It is implausible that a new monetary policy rule would have significantly reined in the housing bubble and added so much to US GDP. We are skeptical that a Taylor rule augmented by any financial cycle proxy would be a useful guide to policy. As Federal Reserve chair Janet Yellen put it shortly after the publication of the 2014 BIS *Annual Report*, which had urged central banks to more quickly return interest rates to normal levels because of financial stability worries, "there is no simple rule that can prescribe, even in a general sense, how monetary policy should adjust to shifts in the outlook for financial stability."[10]

The implication from this new rule for monetary policy that was underlined by the BIS in June 2017 was that central banks "may have to tolerate longer periods of inflation below target, and tighten monetary policy if demand is strong, even if inflation is weak, so as not to fall behind the curve with respect to the financial cycle."[11] Certainly, strong demand growth especially when the economy is near full employment justifies a tightening in monetary policy. But we would not agree that central banks should keep interest rates up in the face of prolonged periods of inflation below their targets. Such a policy would run counter to the inflation targeting mandates of many central banks and aggravate the risks of recession.

Almost everywhere, the postcrisis policy response focused primarily on tightening regulation and developing new macroprudential tools. Monetary policy was progressively eased to counter a deep and prolonged weakness in aggregate demand. Although such a recession was perhaps inevitable given the severity of the global financial crisis, its persistence was a surprise. Few (if any) expected interest rates to remain low for so long. The United States both tightened regulations (notably forcing the banks to recapitalize) more rigorously and uniformly and eased monetary policy more promptly than was the case in the euro area. This difference, as well as the fragmented policy response to the euro area's existential crisis, likely explains why the United States was more successful is ending its recession.

The implications of unusually low interest rates globally for the balance sheets of households, companies, and financial institutions are going to be much larger than in the past because rates have been low for so long (Hannoun and Dittus 2017). Those responsible for prudential regulation need to pay particular attention to two important classes of risk. The first is the risk associated with borrowers becoming more highly leveraged. The second is the interest rate risks on the balance sheets of financial intermediaries. Near-zero or negative interest rates on shorter maturities have induced banks and other investors to seek yield by lengthening the maturity of the bonds they hold as assets. The profitability of interest rate carry-trades for many years has led many financial firms to lengthen the maturity of their debt instruments, which has lowered long-term rates. Falling long-term interest rates for some years have given large capital gains to financial firms holding bonds on the asset side of their balance sheets.

---

10. Janet Yellen, "Monetary policy and financial stability," 2014 Michel Camdessus Central Banking Lecture, International Monetary Fund, Washington, DC, July 2, 2014.

11. "Central banks warned on inflation risk: BIS annual report focuses on danger of interest rates staying low for too long," *Financial Times*, June 26, 2017.

At the same time, this lengthening in duration has made the market value of portfolios of debt securities more sensitive to changes in benchmark long-term rates. Interest rate risk exposures have therefore risen. Even in normal times, regulatory and accounting rules do not treat interest rate risk well. Some recent regulations (e.g., the international banking rules of Basel 3 and the Solvency 2 regulations for European insurance companies) have inadvertently magnified interest rate exposures. When global interest rates are lower and more stable than they have been historically, those supervising banks and institutional investors need to look especially hard at how their current rules encourage greater interest rate risk exposures. And they need to redouble efforts to better manage such exposures.

Interest rate developments should also influence the design of macroprudential instruments. Consider the evolution of rules on household property mortgages. One way of protecting households from borrowing too much when interest rates are unusually low is to impose debt-to-income ratios. After successfully using loan-to-value (LTV) ratios, for example, the Reserve Bank of New Zealand (RBNZ) recently proposed that it be given powers to use debt-to-income ratios. It argues that such ratios would help to constrain the credit/asset price cycle in a manner most other macroprudential ratios would not (Reserve Bank of New Zealand 2017).

To those who argue that macroprudential tools are not perfect and occasionally may need to be reinforced by monetary policy, we counter that all policy tools are imperfect. It is better to develop new macroprudential tools—or improved techniques for existing tools—than to sacrifice the important objectives of monetary policy for a goal that it is ill suited to achieve. In many cases, the financial risks that cause most concern are sector-specific (e.g., increased mortgage debt in many Asian countries) and require a tailored policy response. A recent speech by the vice president of the ECB exemplified the approach we support.[12] QE has produced stronger growth, which has helped make banks in the euro area stronger. But he also reported ECB data on how very low interest rates were creating larger maturity mismatch risks in nonbank financial institutions and then explained the need to expand the macroprudential toolkit to address these new risks.

So our answer to the question of this section is: No, financial stability considerations should not in general constrain monetary policy. But prudential policies may need to be adapted to curb risks created by higher levels of debt and by the maturity mismatches/interest rate exposures associated with a long period of very low rates. A possible rejoinder is that this answer amounts to advocating that one arm of policy (regulation) undo

12. Vítor Constâncio, "The evolving risk landscape in the euro area," speech at a Banco do Portugal conference on financial stability, October 17, 2017.

the inevitable consequences of another arm of policy (monetary expansion). This rejoinder is not convincing. Expansionary monetary policy in a depressed economy can also improve financial stability (higher incomes from stronger growth lower debt-to-income ratios of many borrowers, lower interest charges help liquidity-constrained but viable debtors avoid default, encouraging investors to buy risky assets that are typically undervalued in a recession, and so on). It deserves emphasis that there is no logical presumption that monetary tightening needs to complement macroprudential tightening measures.

In many circumstances the central bank will want to ease monetary policy but tighten macroprudential policies. The recent policies of the RBNZ illustrate this well. As the governor noted, the introduction of macroprudential speed limits on high loan-to-value lending for mortgages "moderated excesses in the housing market, thereby enabling the Bank to delay the tightening of interest rates, and reducing the incentive for further capital inflows into the New Zealand dollar."[13]

Exchange Rate Policy

If Asian economies were suffering a loss of external demand, it might be argued that officials should seek a more competitive exchange rate by selling domestic currency for foreign currencies. However, in economies where the growth slowdown is most pronounced (Korea, Japan, Thailand, Hong Kong, Singapore, and Taiwan) the cause is domestic not external. These economies have current account surpluses, and in all but Hong Kong, these surpluses have been rising in recent years (see figure 13.9). Thus, the external sector has on net been supporting growth in most of the Asian economies experiencing slower growth. Among the large emerging Asian economies, only India and Indonesia have current account deficits, which in both cases are quite modest at around 2 percent of GDP.

Figure 13.10 shows that many Asian economies have piled up unprecedented levels of foreign exchange reserves and paid down official external debts in some cases. In many cases, official foreign assets far exceed reasonable precautionary needs (Bergsten and Gagnon 2017). Moreover, combatting currency mismatches in the private sector is much more important than accumulating reserves for preserving financial stability and preventing future balance of payments crises (Gagnon 2013). For instance, the currency mismatch data reported in Chui, Kuruc, and Turner (2016) show that foreign-currency debts in the corporate sector in some Asian economies grew too rapidly because foreign lenders took too much comfort from

---

13. Wheeler, "Reflections on 25 years of inflation targeting."

Figure 13.9   Current account balances in Asia, 1985–2016
(percent of GDP)

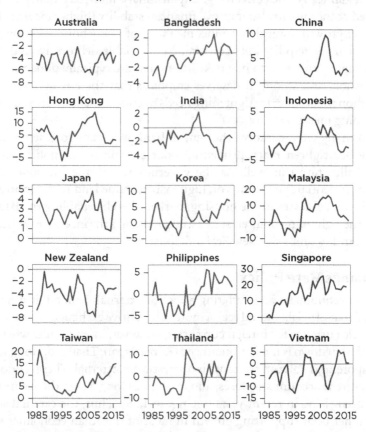

Source: IMF *World Economic Outlook* database.

very high levels of official foreign exchange reserves. In some cases, quasi-fixed exchange rate regimes encourage foreign-currency borrowing. Neither macroeconomic nor precautionary needs justify continued accumulation of foreign exchange reserves by most large Asian economies. The IMF estimates that the aggregate savings ratio of developing Asia has exceeded 40 percent of GDP for many years—far above that prevailing elsewhere. In such circumstances, and given the chronic shortfall of aggregate demand at the global level since the global financial crisis, excess reserve accumulation that supports a current account surplus exerts a powerful negative externality on the rest of the world.

In some cases, the stock of foreign exchange reserves may fall as officials seek to prevent unwanted currency depreciation. For example, China's reserves fell by roughly $1 trillion over the past three years. The central bank

Figure 13.10 Foreign exchange reserves and net official assets in Asia, 1985–2016 (percent of GDP)

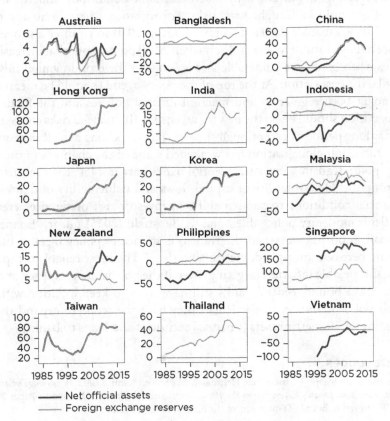

Net official assets
Foreign exchange reserves

Note: Net official assets are foreign exchange reserves plus other official assets (including sovereign wealth funds) minus official borrowing in foreign currencies.

Source: Bergsten and Gagnon (2017).

may want to prevent a credit-depressing shrinkage of its balance sheet. In the case of China, a rise in loans to domestic banks offsets the decline in foreign-currency assets on the central bank's balance sheet.

Conclusion

Growth in several Asian economies remains disappointing, and there are downside risks. With inflation declining to very low levels, central banks in Asia should be ready to use the policy tools at their disposal to sustain aggregate demand to meet medium-term inflation targets. Indeed, for Thailand at least, conditions already support further monetary ease.

Financial stability worries do not in general justify keeping the policy rate higher than warranted by macroeconomic conditions. Indeed, such a policy would be fraught with risks: For instance, when discussing the Swedish Riksbank's decision to raise rates in 2010 to counter a property price bubble, Brunnermeier and Schnabel (2016) pointed out that increasing rates when banks are vulnerable and leverage in the economy high might not be the best option. At the top of the policy agenda should be measures to adapt both regulatory and macroprudential policies and the focus of supervision should be on the new (or accentuated) financial risks created by a very long period of exceptionally low interest rates, long as well as short.

Although globalization has weakened some of the channels of monetary policy transmission, Asian central banks have not lost their monetary autonomy.[14] The volatility of capital flows and vulnerability of domestic financial conditions to sudden shifts in investor risk preferences create difficult monetary policy dilemmas. As Obstfeld (2015) put it, "financial globalization has worsened the trade-offs monetary policy faces in navigating between multiple domestic objectives." The most reliable compass remains flexible inflation targeting. Even if the policy rate gets stuck at the zero lower bound, central banks still have tools to keep inflation within their policy mandate. In particular, they have the scope to expand their holdings of domestic assets (financial securities and loans to banks).

References

Ahearne, Alan, Joseph Gagnon, Jane Haltmaier, and Steven Kamin. 2002. *Preventing Deflation: Lessons from Japan's Experience in the 1990s.* International Finance Discussion Paper 729. Washington: Board of Governors of the Federal Reserve System.

Akerlof, George, William Dickens, and George Perry. 1996. The Macroeconomics of Low Inflation. *Brookings Papers on Economic Activity* 1: 1–59. Washington: Brookings Institution.

Ball, Laurence, Joseph Gagnon, Patrick Honohan, and Signe Krogstrup. 2016. What Else Can Central Banks Do? *Geneva Reports on the World Economy* 18. Geneva: International Center for Monetary and Banking Studies.

Bank of Canada. 2013. *Backgrounders: Measurement Bias in the Canadian CPI.* Available at www.bankofcanada.ca/wp-content/uploads/2010/11/measurement_bias_canadian_cpi.pdf (accessed July 13, 2017).

Bank of England. 2014. *Inflation Report* (November). London.

Bayoumi, Tamim, and Joseph Gagnon. 2018. Unconventional Monetary Policy in the Asian Financial Crisis. *Pacific Economic Review* 23, no. 1: 80–94.

Benigno, P., and Luca Ricci. 2011. The Inflation-Output Tradeoff with Downward Wage Rigidities. *American Economic Review* 101, no. 4: 1436–66.

---

14. Veerathai Santiprabhob, panel remarks at the 2017 Andrew Crockett Lecture: Boom-Bust Cycles, Interest Rates and the Global Financial System, Bank for International Settlements, Basel, June 25, 2017.

Bergsten, C. Fred, and Joseph Gagnon. 2017. *Currency Conflict and Trade Policy: A New Strategy for the United States.* Washington: Peterson Institute for International Economics.

BIS (Bank for International Settlements). 1998. *The Role of Asset Prices in the Formulation of Monetary Policy.* BIS Conference Paper 5 (March). Basel.

BIS (Bank for International Settlements). 2009. *Capital Flows and Emerging Economies.* CGFS Paper 33 (January). Basel: BIS Committee on the Global Financial System.

BIS (Bank for International Settlements). 2016. *The Financial Cycle, the Natural Rate of Interest and Monetary Policy.* 86th Annual Report (June). Basel.

Brunnermeier, M. K., and I. Schnabel. 2016. Bubbles and Central Banks: Historical Perspectives. In *Central Banks at a Crossroads: What Can We Learn from History?* ed. Michael D. Bordo, Øyvind Eitrheim, Marc Flandreau, Jan F. Qvigstad. Cambridge: Cambridge University Press.

Campbell, Jeffrey, Charles Evans, Jonas Fisher, and Alejandro Justiniano. 2012. Macroeconomic Effects of Federal Reserve Forward Guidance. *Brookings Papers on Economics Activity* (Spring): 1–80. Washington: Brookings Institution.

Chui, Michael, Emese Kuruc, and Philip Turner. 2016. *A New Dimension to Currency Mismatches in the Emerging Markets: Non-Financial Companies.* BIS Working Paper 550 (March). Basel: Bank for International Settlements.

Dickens, W., L. Goette, E. Groshen, S. Holden, J. Messina, M. Schweitzer, J. Turunen, and M. Ward. 2007. How Wages Change: Micro Evidence from the International Wage Flexibility Project. *Journal of Economic Perspectives* 21, no. 2: 195–214.

Engen, Eric, Thomas Laubach, and David Reifschneider. 2015. *The Macroeconomic Effects of the Federal Reserve's Unconventional Monetary Policies.* Finance and Economics Discussion Series 2015-005. Washington: Board of Governors of the Federal Reserve System.

Fallick, Bruce, Michael Lettau, and William Wascher. 2016. *Downward Nominal Wage Rigidity in the United States during and after the Great Recession.* Finance and Economics Discussion Series 2016-001. Washington: Board of Governors of the Federal Reserve System.

Farmer, Roger. 2017. *Prosperity for All.* Oxford: Oxford University Press.

Friedman, B. M. 2014. *Has the Financial Crisis Permanently Changed the Practice of Monetary Policy? Has It Changed the Theory of Monetary Policy?* NBER Working Paper 20128 (May). Cambridge, MA: National Bureau of Economic Research.

Gagnon, Joseph. 2013. Currency and Maturity Mismatches in Asia. In *Asian Capital Market Development and Integration,* ed. Iwan Azis and Hyoung-Tae Kim. New Delhi: Oxford University Press.

Gagnon, Joseph E. 2016. *Quantitative Easing: An Underappreciated Success.* PIIE Policy Brief 16-4. Washington: Peterson Institute for International Economics.

Gertler, M., and P. Karadi. 2013. Monetary Policy Surprises, Credit Costs and Economic Activity. Paper presented at NBER conference on Lessons from the Crisis for Monetary Policy, October 18–19, Boston.

Hannoun, Hervé, and Peter Dittus. 2017. *Revolution Required: The Ticking Time Bombs of the G7 Model.* Kindle edition.

Holston, Kathryn, Tomas Laubach, and John Williams. 2016. *Measuring the Natural Rate of Interest: International Trends and Determinants.* Federal Reserve Bank of San Francisco Working Paper 2016-11. Federal Reserve Bank of San Francisco.

Hördahl, P., J. Sobrun, and P. Turner. 2016. *Low Long-Term Interest Rates as a Global Phenomenon.* BIS Working Paper 574 (August). Basel: Bank for International Settlements.

King, M., and D. Low. 2014. *Measuring the "World" Real Interest Rate.* NBER Working Paper 19887 (February). Cambridge, MA: National Bureau of Economic Research.

Laubach, T., and J. C. Williams. 2015. *Measuring the Natural Rate of Interest Redux.* Hutchins Center Working Paper 15. Washington: Hutchins Center of Fiscal and Monetary Policy at the Brookings Institution.

Lombardi, M., and F. Zhu. 2014. *A Shadow Policy Rate to Calibrate US Monetary Policy at the Zero Lower Bound.* BIS Working Paper 452 (June). Basel: Bank for International Settlements.

Mohanty, M. S. 2014. *The Transmission of Unconventional Monetary Policy to the Emerging Markets.* BIS Papers 78. Basel: Bank for International Settlements.

Nakaso. H. 2001. *The Financial Crisis in Japan during the 1990s: How the Bank of Japan Responded and the Lessons Learnt.* BIS Papers 6 (October). Basel: Bank for International Settlements.

Obstfeld, M. 2015. *Trilemmas and Tradeoffs: Living with Financial Globalisation.* BIS Working Paper 480 (February). Basel: Bank for International Settlements.

Posen, Adam S. 1998. *Restoring Japan's Economic Growth.* Washington: Institute for International Economics.

Rachel, L., and T. D. Smith. 2015. *Secular Drivers of the Global Real Interest Rate.* Bank of England Staff Working Paper 571 (December). London: Bank of England.

Ramaswamy, S. 2017. *Financial Crisis and Regulatory Reforms.* Basel: IngramSpark.

Reddy, Y. V. 2017. *Advice and Dissent: My Life in Public Service.* New York: HarperCollins.

Reifschneider, David, and John Williams. 2000. Three Lessons for Monetary Policy in a Low-Inflation Era. *Journal of Money, Credit, and Banking* 32: 936-78.

Reserve Bank of New Zealand. 2017. *Serviceability Restrictions as a Potential Macroprudential Tool in New Zealand.* RBNZ Consultation Paper (June). Wellington.

Robertson, D. H. 1928/1966. Theories of Banking Policy. Lecture at the London School of Economics, February 13, 1928. Reprinted in *Essays in Money and Interest* (1966, Collins, Fontana Library).

Shek, J., I. Shim, and H. S. Shin. 2015. *Investor Redemptions and Fund Manager Sales of Emerging Market Bonds: How Are They Related?* BIS Working Paper 509 (August). Basel: Bank for International Settlements.

Shirakawa, M. 2015. *Excessive Debt and the Monetary Policy Regime.* BIS Papers 80 (January). Basel: Bank for International Settlements.

Simon, J. 2015. Low Interest Rate Environments and Risk. Paper presented at the Paul Woolley Centre for the Study of Capital Market Dysfunctionality Conference, October 8, Sydney.

Svensson, L. E. O. 2016. *Cost-Benefit Analysis of Leaning Against the Wind: Are Costs Larger Also with Less Effective Macroprudential Policy?* IMF Working Paper WP/16/13 (January). Washington: International Monetary Fund.

Tobin, James. 1969. A General Equilibrium Approach to Monetary Theory. *Journal of Money, Credit, and Banking* 1: 15-29.

Turner, Philip. 2017. *Did Central Banks Cause the Last Crisis? Will They Cause the Next?* Special Paper 249 (November). London School of Economics, Financial Markets Group.

Williams, Rebecca. 2017. Characterizing the Current Economic Expansion: 2009 to Present Day. *Reserve Bank of New Zealand Bulletin* 80, no. 3: 3-22.

Wu, Cynthia, and Dora Xia. 2015. *Measuring the Macroeconomic Impact of Monetary Policy at the Zero Lower Bound.* Chicago Booth Research Paper 13-77. University of Chicago, Booth School of Business (revised 2015).

Wyplosz, Charles. 2001. Do We Know How Low Inflation Should Be? In *Why Price Stability? Proceedings of the First ECB Central Banking Conference,* ed. A. García-Herrero, V. Gaspar, L. Hoogduin, J. Morgan, and B. Winkler. Frankfurt: European Central Bank.

14

Monetary Policy in the New Mediocre

RANIA AL-MASHAT, KEVIN CLINTON, BENJAMIN HUNT,
ZOLTAN JAKAB, DOUGLAS LAXTON, HOU WANG, AND
JIAXIONG YAO

The global economy has been underperforming for several years. The performance of advanced economies has been lackluster since the 2008–09 global financial crisis. Strong expansion in emerging-market economies boosted global growth, but growth in these economies has also decelerated since 2011, largely because of weak commodity prices and the transition in China to a more balanced pattern of growth. Although global growth picked up in 2017, output gaps remain in many economies, and most countries' inflation rates were still below official central bank target rates. Interest rates have been historically low—but evidently not low enough to fuel a normal recovery and strong expansion. Fiscal policies have been inconsistent, with priorities switching between stimulus and consolidation, often without a long-term strategy, sometimes adding to cyclical instability. Political opposition has caused long delays to structural reforms that would raise trend growth.

With a still weak global economy and excess capacity, the possibility of further large negative shocks remains a concern. Financial vulnerabilities remain evident in various parts of the world. Credit-fueled booms have inflated real estate values in many cities. Corporate balance sheets have weak-

Rania Al-Mashat is an advisor at the Research Department of the International Monetary Fund (IMF) and former subgovernor for monetary policy at the Central Bank of Egypt. Kevin Clinton is a former research adviser at the Bank of Canada and a consultant to the IMF. Benjamin Hunt is assistant director at the Research Department of the IMF. Zoltan Jakab is a senior economist at the Research Department of the IMF. Douglas Laxton is the chief of the Economic Modeling Division of the Research Department of the IMF. Hou Wang is an economist at the Research Department of the IMF. Jiaxiong Yao is an economist at the Research Department of the IMF. The views expressed in this chapter are those of the authors and do not necessarily represent the views of the IMF, its Executive Board, or its management.

ened, with leverage rebounding to high levels. Restructuring in China could bring disruptive adjustments and financial stress. Governments have been raising trade barriers, and protectionist sentiment is on the rise.

In Asia demographics are another potential source of chronic demand shortfalls. Some analysis suggests that a decline in population growth could reduce aggregate demand, with few or no self-correcting forces. Several Asian economies, advanced and emerging alike, are in or will soon enter the phase of the demographic transition in which fertility declines and lower mortality results in rapidly aging populations and sharply lower population growth. This demographic change could mean that "the new mediocre" could become a problem in Asia—a concern that in part motivated this volume.

Gaspar et al. (2016) argue for assertive policy actions following persistent demand weakness. For countries with wide output gaps, low levels of employment, below-target rates of inflation, and extremely low long-term rates of interest, the argument in favor of such a response extends beyond regular cyclical stabilization. Assertive policy action is also called for to avoid risk, because a negative shock to the global economy could push several countries into a low-inflation trap, with central banks unable to respond strongly, as interest rates are already near their effective lower bound. Another recession could set off a downslide in expectations of inflation, even a deflation mentality, undermining the nominal anchor that central bank inflation targets are supposed to provide. The outcome would be a bad quasi-equilibrium (a "dark corner"): a low-inflation or deflation trap in which resources lie idle, with no end in sight.[1]

A comprehensive, consistent, and coordinated approach (which Gaspar et al. 2016 refer to as "the 3Cs") is needed across all macroeconomic instruments. This chapter focuses on monetary policy, with country case studies of Australia, India, and Japan.

Assertive monetary policy responses to negative output shocks may lead central banks to overshoot the official inflation target in the medium term; they can also cause it to undershoot the target, as in India, where the response to a jump in food prices may mean that a year of above-target headline inflation is followed by a short period below target. Central banks should not be averse to such outcomes when a bad equilibrium lies nearby. In these situations, the prudent policy is to get away from the bad equilibrium as quickly as possible. A prolonged period of below- or above-target inflation is more likely to destabilize the nominal anchor than a cycle that sees inflation on both sides of the target rate.

---

1. The term *low-inflation trap* refers to a situation in which inflation expectations are stuck significantly below the inflation target and there are significant risks of deflation.

In India the central bank is attempting to reduce long-term expectations of inflation. Shocks (e.g., to food prices) could unhinge inflation expectations on the upside (another dark corner). Prompt action is needed, especially in view of India's history of high and volatile inflation and therefore imperfect credibility.

This chapter is organized as follows. The first section discusses a risk-avoidance approach to monetary policy in a world with chronic underperformance and downside risks to growth. Section two illustrates the argument with country studies on Australia, India, and Japan. Section three describes the role of macroprudential policies, stressing the importance of sound banking systems and orderly markets for sustainable growth. The last section makes the case that risk avoidance may involve assertive policy actions when public confidence in policy objectives is low.

Risk Avoidance Strategy for Monetary Policy

From Inflation Targeting to Inflation-Forecast Targeting

In 1977 Kydland and Prescott reported that discretionary monetary policy has a bias toward inflation. Following the inflation of the 1970s, their finding made a strong impression on central banks and led to a search for a more robust framework for monetary stability. The solution proposed by Barro and Gordon (1983) was for the central bank to commit to a time-consistent price stability policy, in order to prevent policymakers from yielding to the temptation to give output a short-run boost through a surprise spurt of monetary stimulus.

During the 1980s, inflation in most economies was moderate but persistent. Some central bankers saw a parallel with the chronic inflation predicted for discretionary monetary policy by the time-consistency theory.

Early practitioners of inflation targeting saw hitting their targets, short run as well as long run, as important in establishing their commitment to price stability. The first country to adopt inflation targeting, New Zealand, started out with a fairly rigid approach. It produced a rapid decline in inflation to the long-run target, along with instrument instability.

During the 1990s, as inflation stabilized at low rates, in line with the announced objective, it became clearer that the key to establishing confidence in inflation targeting was not rigid adherence to targets but a transparent strategy to eliminate over time any deviations that arose or were expected to arise. Announcing an explicit numerical target was in itself a major step toward clarifying what monetary policy was aiming to achieve.

Following the introduction of inflation targeting, central banks took additional steps to improve their monetary policy communications, through regular monetary policy reports (sometimes called inflation reports), speeches by senior officials on strategy, media briefings after interest rate decision meetings, and so on. By the turn of the 21st century, one could argue that the transparent pursuit of a low-inflation objective by a politically accountable central bank provided a solution to the Kydland-Prescott time-consistency problem. Inflation targeting had put a constraint on discretion, removing the inflation bias.

Another interpretation of the evidence would be that the success of inflation targeting refuted the Kydland-Prescott theory. Central banks showed no sign of reneging on inflation control in pursuit of short-run output goals; in inflation-targeting countries, at least, the authorities did not display the short-sighted bias at the heart of the argument. On the contrary, governments left and right of center supported the low-inflation objective—by a formal instruction where the central bank does not have goal independence (e.g., the United Kingdom); by an endorsement where it does (e.g., the Czech Republic); or by a statement of agreement where the government and central bank jointly assume responsibility for the goal (e.g., Canada and New Zealand).

Under these arrangements, the central bank is typically accountable for the conduct of monetary policy, to government or parliament and implicitly to the general public. In large part because of the clear delegation of responsibility, implementation of inflation targeting has been accompanied by a vast increase in the transparency of the conduct of monetary policy.

During the 1990s, central bankers came to realize that the better their policies were understood, the more effective they were—a remarkable turnaround within one generation for a profession formerly known (not entirely fairly) for its secrecy. With respect to numerical variables, the debate has been about what to disclose above and beyond the target for the rate of inflation and the current setting of the policy rate—in particular, which elements of the quarterly macroeconomic forecast of the central bank should be released. Publishing the forecast for inflation and output has not been controversial, because policymakers had to show the public that they had a plan for keeping inflation on target and that the plan recognized the potential short-run implications for output. Svensson (1997) pointed out that the central bank's inflation forecast represents an ideal conditional intermediate target, because it takes into account all available information, including the preferences of policymakers and their view of how the economy works.

The flexible inflation targeting regime now in place at many central banks can be described as inflation-forecast targeting. It implies a balancing between the deviations of inflation from its target and the deviations of output from its potential. Under a flexible inflation-forecast targeting regime, the central bank has a dual mandate (either explicit or implicit): It recognizes that there is a short-run tradeoff between output and inflation.

The history of inflation targeting and the transition to full-fledged inflation-forecast targeting provides a line of openness, or accountability. Milestones along the way include the following:

- announcement of targets with a multiyear horizon (clarity of target),
- precision on policy interest rate setting (clarity of instrument),
- transparent communications on policy implementation,
- publication of a complete macro forecast (including inflation) (clarity of the intermediate target [inflation-forecast targeting]), and
- publication of a conditional forecast path, alternative scenarios, and confidence bands for the short-term interest rate (full-fledged inflation-forecast targeting).

Unlike pioneers, such as New Zealand, newcomers to inflation targeting do not have to reach each of these milestones. The road has already been tested, over a few decades.[2] Depending on its technical capacities, a central bank can take to the road at any point.

Numerous countries have built durable inflation targeting regimes from unpromising starting conditions, as the survey of central banks by Batini and Laxton (2007) shows. None had a reputation for stable low inflation. Many were emerging from a financial or exchange market crisis that had shaken confidence in the monetary authorities (e.g., the United Kingdom, Sweden, and the Czech Republic). Some were in the midst of economywide structural changes that would completely alter the transmission of monetary policy (e.g., New Zealand and the Czech Republic). Special problems enfeebled the monetary transmission mechanism in certain countries (e.g., dollarization in Peru and severe financial fragility in the Czech Republic).

Of the early adopters of inflation targeting, only the Bank of Canada had anything close to a forecasting and policy analysis system matched to the task. A common omission was the lack of an appropriate policy model. No country had the external communications program required to explain how the monetary policy objective was to be achieved and maintained. The list of prerequisites is not demanding; if a central bank can conduct monetary policy, it can engage in inflation targeting.

Central banks that adopted inflation targeting put in place suitable frameworks for making it effective. These frameworks are still evolving, as central banks learn by doing.

---

2. For a discussion of the timeline for several inflation-targeting countries, see Clinton et al. (2015).

Loss-Minimization Approach to Policy Formulation

The model or models used by central banks to conduct policy under inflation-forecast targeting should incorporate an endogenous interest rate. A model in which the interest rate is exogenous has no nominal anchor; the inflation rate drifts indeterminately following disturbances. For inflation targeting to be logically consistent, the interest rate must adjust to the requirements of the target. Many central banks incorporate this principle into their forecasting models and thus produce an endogenous path for the interest rate.[3]

Endogenous monetary policy in this type of model is often represented by a linear inflation forecast–based policy reaction function for the short-term interest rate, with equal weighting of marginal changes in deviations from target for any starting point. For inflation-forecast targeting, the current setting of the policy rate (i in the example below) takes into account the contemporaneous output gap (y), the model's forecast of year-on-year inflation ($\pi 4$), the equilibrium real interest rate ($\bar{r}$), the inflation target (π^*), and possible shocks to the policy rate (ε^i). In the example below, the forecast horizon is set at three quarters:

$$i_t = 0.7 i_{t-1} + (1 - 0.7)\left[\bar{r}_t + \pi 4_{t+3}^{Core} + 1.2\left(\pi 4_{t+3}^{Headline} - \pi^*\right) + 0.4 y_t\right] + \varepsilon_t^i$$

In contrast to the Taylor rule, in which the policy rate reacts to the contemporaneous output gap and inflation deviation from the target, the inflation forecast–based reaction function ignores inflation shocks that are expected to reverse within the three-quarter policy horizon. Although central banks should not care about small temporary deviations, they should care a lot about large, long-lasting deviations. A quadratic loss function, in which the marginal cost of deviations of inflation and output from desired values increases exponentially as they grow, better captures such preferences. It is particularly appropriate when a bad equilibrium threatens to take hold of the economy. Historically, two types of bad equilibrium (in both of which inflation expectations go adrift) have preoccupied central banks: a low-inflation trap and an inflation spiral. As a quadratic loss function would imply aggressive policy actions when confronted with a mate-

---

3. Indeed, policy modelers design these models to make it impossible to simulate with an exogenous path (constant or based on market expectations) for the policy rate. Sometimes these models are simulated by assuming that the interest rate is exogenous over some short-term horizon but that agents believe that at some point in the future the monetary authority will start to adjust its instruments sufficiently aggressively to anchor inflation and inflation expectations. In these forward-looking models, this assumption helps anchor inflation expectations in the short run. Policymakers should be skeptical of forecasts based on exogenous paths for the policy rate.

rial probability of such situations, it provides the basis for a risk-avoidance strategy.

An appropriate quadratic loss function for inflation-forecast targeting includes the discounted sum of squared expected deviations of headline inflation from the target, the squared expected output gap, and (with a smaller weight) the squared change in the policy rate. The central bank sets the path of the policy interest rate to minimize this loss function, which heavily penalizes large deviations of the target variables, output, and inflation from their preferred values. The discounting factor (β, a value between 0 and 1) means that a given deviation from target imposes a lower cost the farther it is in the future:

$$Loss_t = \sum_{i=0}^{\infty} \beta^i [(\pi 4_{t+i}^{Headline} - \pi^*)^2 + y_{t+i}^2 + 0.5(i_{t+i} - i_{t+i-1})^2]$$

The rationale for an aversion to large changes in the interest rate, which is not in itself a target variable, is to avoid overreacting to small transitory disturbances and the associated problem of instrument instability and to ensure that the central bank provides clear signals for the intent of its actions (Woodford 2005). In effect, inclusion of this term in the loss function smooths the response of the interest rate following shocks to the system. It has strong empirical support in the actual, incremental, rate-setting behavior of central banks.

A procedure that minimizes a loss function can best illustrate the principles of robust monetary policymaking under uncertainty. The principal arguments of the loss function are the deviation of inflation from its target and the deviation of output from potential (i.e., the output gap). Given the dual-mandate preferences of policymakers, central banks engaging in flexible inflation-forecast targeting in effect choose a policy rate path such that the forecasts for inflation and output "look good," where "looking good" means finding the best policy interest rate path to stabilize the inflation forecast around its target and output around its long-run sustainable path.

Linear reaction functions may give reasonable results in normal times, but they perform poorly in abnormal times. When policy interest rates are at or very near the effective lower bound, the loss-minimization approach produces better results, because its response to disinflationary conditions involves an extended commitment to keep the rate at the floor. As the effective lower bound approaches, the loss-minimization approach provides ever stronger policy reactions to contractionary shocks, to keep the economy away from the deflation dark corner. At the effective lower bound, this risk-avoidance principle is reflected in a commitment to hold the short-term interest rate low long enough that inflation will rise, perhaps above the long-run target rate for a while. The boost to inflation expectations reduces the real medium-term interest rate and depreciates the real exchange rate, even though the nominal short rate can go no lower.[4] Where there is very little risk of sustained inflationary pressure but a high risk of getting stuck in a low-inflation trap, such a policy reaction represents prudent policymaking.

Conventional Forward Guidance for Transparent Communications

The Bank of Canada, the US Federal Reserve, the Bank of England, the Bank of Japan, and other central banks provided forward guidance on the policy interest rate after the global financial crisis. Such guidance "talks down" the expected policy rate path and term premium, thereby reducing longer-term interest rates. In this respect, forward guidance succeeded (Charbonneau and Rennison 2015; Engen, Laubach, and Reifschneider 2015). This type of communication represents unconventional forward guidance, because it was introduced along with other unconventional measures as an ad hoc tool when the effective lower bound put constraints on reductions in the policy rate.

Another form of forward guidance is more robust. Conventional forward guidance, as practiced by the Czech National Bank and the Reserve Bank of New Zealand, is a systematic part of the policy framework. It involves the publication of a complete central bank macroeconomic forecast, with an endogenous interest rate path and confidence bands around key variables. The endogenous policy rate moves to achieve the announced inflation target over a medium-term horizon in a way that reflects policymakers' preferences with respect to the short-run tradeoffs between output, inflation, and interest rate variability. The policy rate path is clearly conditional on a range of assumptions and subject to a range of uncertainty, as indicated by the confidence bands around it.

Publication of the forecast policy rate path increases the effectiveness of the interest rate instrument in good times as well as bad. In and of itself, setting a short-term interest rate for the following six weeks (a typical interval between policy meetings) has no material impact on inflation or output. The policy rate has an effect only as far as it moves the longer-term interest rates at which households and firms borrow and invest. In effect, the central bank must ensure that public expectations of the future overnight rate move in line with the current setting. If market participants have similar forecasts as the central bank, longer-term interest rates, the exchange

---

4. See annex II of Clinton et al. (2015) for the analytics.

rate, and asset prices generally are likely to move in support of the objectives of monetary policy.[5]

That full disclosure helps lead expectations has long been accepted with respect to the inflation rate. Expected inflation and the actual nominal interest rate are the two components of the real interest rate. The published inflation rate forecast influences the expected real interest rate, generally in support of monetary policy. When nominal interest rates are, or are likely to be, constrained by the effective lower bound, disclosure is particularly important. A central bank fighting deflation risks might well envisage a strategy in which it temporarily overshoots the inflation target (as in policy simulations reported later in this chapter). Overshooting would reduce the real interest rate and help move the economy away from a deflation, or low-inflation, dark corner. With full publication of its forecast, the central bank can communicate the whole story underlying its strategy, allaying any risk to the credibility of the target that the planned overshoot might otherwise create.

Many Asian countries have the opportunity to leapfrog some of the countries that have well-established inflation-forecast targeting regimes by adopting full-fledged inflation-forecast targeting. Figure 14.1 shows the path of the Dincer-Eichengreen index of transparency for four Asian countries (Japan, Australia, Korea, and India); the United States; and the three most transparent central banks in the index (the Sveriges Riksbank, the Czech National Bank, and the Reserve Bank of New Zealand). All institutions improved over time, but there is a sizable gap between the top central banks and the rest.

The main objection to publication of the interest rate forecast is its conditionality. Monetary policy must allow the interest rate to vary to offset shocks. It cannot commit unconditionally to a forecast path for the rate. Central bankers have worried that their credibility might be impaired if it becomes necessary to deviate from a previous forecast. With effective communications, this issue need not arise: Markets have readily adjusted in countries where the central bank publishes its interest rate. Indeed, with a deeper understanding of the intentions of policymakers, markets are more likely to perform a strong buffering role against shocks. Model-derived confidence bands, and alternative forecasts based on shocks to the baseline forecast, are useful tools for communicating the conditionality of the projection and the implications of disturbances for which the probability is not calculable from historical data.

---

5. For a discussion of the Czech experience with publishing forecasts, see Clinton et al. (2017).

Figure 14.1   Central bank transparency index, 1998–2014

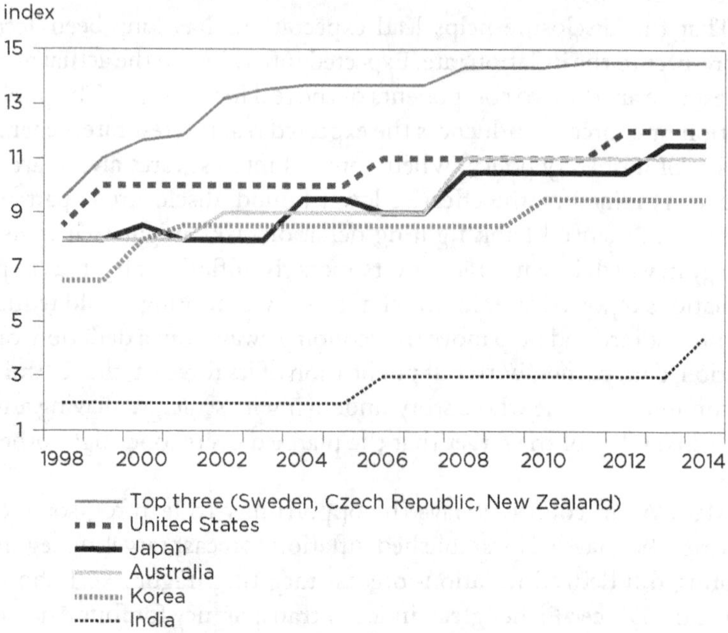

index

Legend:
- —— Top three (Sweden, Czech Republic, New Zealand)
- ∎ ∎ ∎ United States
- ▬▬ Japan
- ////// Australia
- |||||| Korea
- ········ India

Source: Dincer and Eichengreen (2014).

Country Examples

Three country examples illustrate how a risk-avoidance strategy for monetary policy can be implemented. Australia is a large commodity-exporting economy closely linked to the rest of the world. Its monetary policy faces several challenges going forward—challenges that are similar to those that central banks in other advanced economies have faced. With the completion of the institutional foundation of a flexible inflation-targeting regime, India has seen Consumer Price Index (CPI) inflation decline markedly, but it will take time to establish credibility in the new regime. After years of low growth and near deflation, Japan needs comprehensive policies to achieve a higher sustainable growth path and anchor inflation to the 2 percent target.

Australia: Managing Downside Risks and Avoiding a Deflation Trap

The Reserve Bank of Australia practices flexible inflation targeting, with a target range of 2–3 percent. As its mandate calls for the maintenance of full employment, its monetary policy must consider objectives for output as well as inflation. The inflation-forecast targeting model is squarely in line with this policy framework (see appendix 14A for a summary of the model).

Baseline Scenario with Alternative Policy Strategies

Figure 14.2 shows a baseline scenario for a hypothetical forecast for Australia for the period between the third quarter of 2016 and the fourth quarter of 2019. The assumptions are that the global economy gradually recovers and commodity prices rise smoothly. The policy rate is constrained by the effective lower bound, which is assumed to be 0.75 percent for the Reserve Bank of Australia.

The black line shows a forecast based on the linear inflation forecast-based reaction function. The policy rate declines a little in the short run and then rises toward its long-run equilibrium value as the output gap approaches zero and inflation approaches 2.5 percent, the midpoint of the target range. The process of adjustment gets an early boost from an increase in the exchange rate (a depreciation of the Australian dollar) of about 8 percent.

The light grey line shows results for the alternative, risk-avoidance, strategy. Here the central bank cuts the interest rate to the lower bound of 0.75 percent and holds it there for four quarters. The lower-for-longer interest rate implies a considerably greater depreciation in the exchange rate (of about 13 percent from the peak). These changes boost output, closing the gap more rapidly. Headline inflation quickly returns to the target range, by virtue of the pass-through to consumer prices from the depreciation of the Australian dollar. In all, the risk-avoidance strategy results in better outcomes than a strategy based on delaying rate cuts and "keeping the powder dry."

An early fiscal stimulus (the dotted line in figure 14.2) could further improve outcomes. With the direct addition to aggregate demand, the central bank keeps the interest rate at the floor for only one quarter. This policy experiment illustrates how fiscal policy can assist monetary policy in providing support to the economy when there are significant risks that monetary policy could be constrained by the effective lower bound.

Downside Scenario with Alternative Policy Strategies

The downside scenario includes a large and unexpected weakening of economic growth in China, such that the Chinese output gap is 3.5 percent wider than in the baseline case. Weakening in China has significant spillovers to the rest of the world. For Australia it reduces export incomes by a few percentage points and leads to about a 5 percent decline in the prices of Australian commodity exports. Both changes reduce output in Australia.

Figure 14.3 shows the simulated results from the model. In response to the shocks, the central bank cuts the interest rate in a series of steps, reaching the effective lower bound after about three quarters. Together with

Figure 14.2 Baseline scenario with alternative policy strategies for Australia

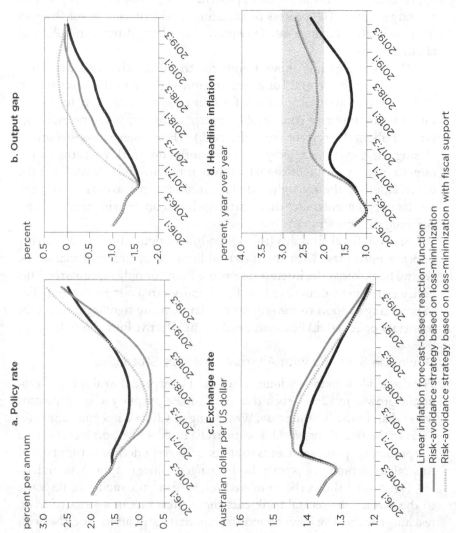

a. Policy rate

percent per annum

b. Output gap

percent

c. Exchange rate

Australian dollar per US dollar

d. Headline inflation

percent, year over year

Linear inflation forecast–based reaction function

Risk-avoidance strategy based on loss-minimization

Risk-avoidance strategy based on loss-minimization with fiscal support

Source: Helbling et al. (2017).

Figure 14.3 Alternative policy strategies for Australia following a negative external shock

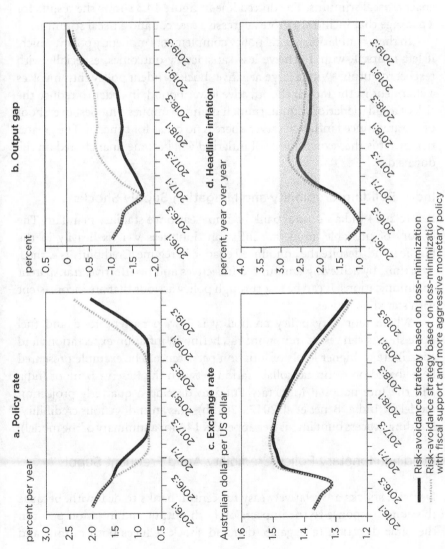

Source: Helbling et al. (2017).

the worsening in the terms of trade, the cut causes a jump in the exchange rate. As a result, despite the widening of the output gap, the inflation rate rises, reaching the center of the target range within a year. The gap in output performance remains below -1 percent for two years.

Given these results, one might question the appropriateness of the strategy. In view of the size and prominence of the shock, the rationale for smoothing the adjustment of the interest rate disappears. It would be more prudent to cut the policy rate quickly to the effective lower bound. In addition, as the effective lower bound becomes effective and constrains the amount of stimulus monetary policy can deliver, the government might enact a fiscal stimulus. The dotted line in figure 14.3 shows the results for a package that includes a more aggressive rate cut and a fiscal stimulus.

In these simulations, fiscal policy complements monetary policy, which, if left to itself, would achieve less satisfactory outcomes, especially with respect to output. With a large negative shock, prudent policy thus involves a sharp cut in the rate to the effective lower bound, in order to reduce the risk of a bad (deflation) equilibrium. If doing so implies a modest overshoot of the announced inflation target, there is no cause for concern. The greater risk by far is that expectations of inflation will become unanchored on the downside.

India: Building Credibility and Mitigating Supply Shocks

Before 2014 India's central bank had no clear price stability mandate. The history of unstable, moderate inflation doubtless weighs heavily in the public mind, despite the announced change in regime. Credibility is earned, over time, by achieving announced objectives and by effective, transparent communications. It can be lost through policy actions that are inconsistent with stated objectives.

Where monetary policy credibility is low, persistent food and fuel price shocks can result in upward ratcheting in inflation expectations and contribute to higher levels of inflation persistence. The example presented here—based on technical collaboration between the Reserve Bank of India and the International Monetary Fund to develop a quarterly projection model for India (Benes et al. 2017a, 2017b)—has an endogenous credibility-building process built into it (see appendix 14A for a summary of the model).

Building Monetary Policy Credibility Amid Frequent Supply Shocks

Demand shocks are relatively easy for central banks to deal with, because the policy response to the impacts on both output and inflation point in the same direction (a negative demand shock reduces both output and inflation, unambiguously calling for a cut in the policy rate). In contrast, supply shocks present a dilemma, because the effects on output (decrease) and inflation (increase) move in different directions.

The policy conflict is stark in the context of repeated supply shocks, such as a drought lasting several years, which would cause repeated upward shocks to the headline rate of inflation. Core inflation is also affected to some extent, through the pass-through of higher costs of intermediate agricultural goods. Although output is depressed at the same time as inflation is rising, the central bank must respond, at least in the short run, with an interest rate hike, because the primary objective of Indian monetary policy is to establish firm expectations that inflation will, over time, return to the announced target rate and the Reserve Bank of India is still in a phase in which it needs to bolster the credibility of the inflation target.

Figure 14.4 shows the results of simulations of the model. The simulated, loss-minimizing policy response is severe: a sharp rise in the interest rate that provokes a steep decline in the foreign exchange rate and widens the output gap. Even so, over the medium term, inflation increases and the short-run policy tradeoff looks bad ("stagflation"). Monetary policy credibility unavoidably takes a hit for a while, because of the nature of the shock, not because of any failure of policy. Under the risk management strategy, policy eventually restores inflation to 4 percent and prevents long-term inflation expectations from ratcheting upward. These simulations illustrate that, even with bad luck, a committed central bank can anchor long-term inflation expectations.

Importance of Prompt Action

In the previous experiment, prompt effective action helped reduce the losses of output and credibility in monetary policy that may follow supply shocks. The importance of timely policy can be shown with experiments in which policymakers wait before responding to a large, nasty supply shock. The eventual interest rate hike has to be much greater than in the baseline (no delay) case, and the cumulative output loss is much greater (figure 14.5). Inflation is also higher over the medium term, and it stays above 4 percent longer. Delay thus causes a substantial deterioration in the medium-term tradeoff between output and inflation, as well as long-lasting damage to the credibility of the 4 percent target.

Contrary to popular misunderstanding, the historical dominance of the food component in major cycles in the inflation rate is not a valid argument against an inflation target–based monetary policy. It underlines instead the major weakness in the old monetary policy regime, which did not provide a firm enough anchor to resist pass-through of food price shocks.

Figure 14.4 Sequence of adverse supply shocks in India

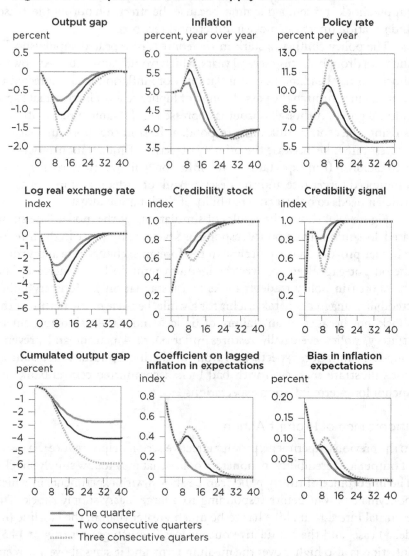

Source: Benes et al. (2017a).

Japan: Comprehensive Policies to Exit Deflation

Since the early 1990s, Japan has experienced weak nominal and real GDP growth and repeated deflationary episodes. The effective lower bound has constrained the Bank of Japan.

A 2013 policy package, which included fiscal stimulus, monetary easing, and structural reforms, aimed at reflating the economy. It helped narrow the wide output gap, reversed an appreciation of the yen, boosted corpo-

Figure 14.5 Delay of policy responses in India

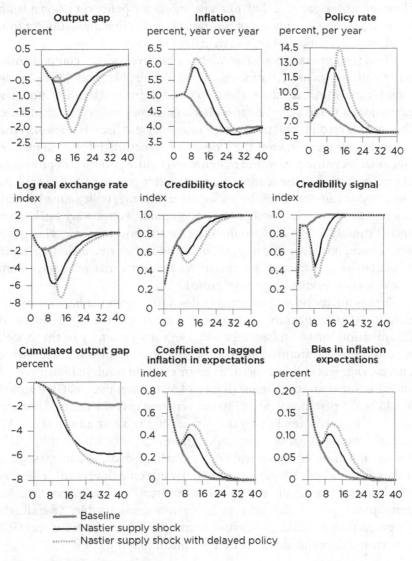

Source: Benes et al. (2017a).

rate profits, and lifted actual and expected inflation into positive territory. The economy reached close to full employment, and base wages increased modestly.

Despite this progress, the economy was still in a dark corner in early 2017, with interest rates at their floor and long-term inflation expectations well below 2 percent. Adoption of inflation-forecast targeting should have provided the basis for more consistent communications to explain how the Bank of Japan was adjusting its instruments to achieve its objectives. However, as Gaspar et al. (2016) argue, monetary policy on its own is unlikely to jolt the economy out of the trap it is in. It will require support from fiscal policy, incomes policy, and structural reforms.

This section examines what might be achieved with a comprehensive set of policies against deflation that Gaspar et al. (2016) call Three Arrows Plus (Prime Minister Abe's Three Arrows of fiscal stimulus, monetary expansion, and structural reform plus an incomes policy).[6] It emphasizes the need for credible and transparent monetary and fiscal frameworks that reinforce one another. Over the longer run, structural reforms to increase labor market participation and mobility and reduce government protection of certain sectors of the economy support faster growth of real output. An unorthodox component of the package is an incomes policy aimed directly at sluggish wage–price dynamics, through public sector wage settlements and a "comply or explain" requirement for the private sector. This policy would build on recent measures taken by the authorities, including higher minimum wage increases, tax incentives for firms that raise wages, and moral suasion to encourage wage growth.

The simulations are presented as deviations from the baseline projections for Japan included in the Staff Report for the 2016 Article IV Consultation for Japan (see appendix 14A for a summary of the model). According to the simulations, over the medium term the Three Arrows Plus package (excluding structural reforms) would result in higher growth and inflation than the baseline (figure 14.6). On average, real GDP growth would be 0.4 percentage point higher every year over the forecast horizon, and CPI inflation (excluding the effects of the value-added tax [VAT] increase) would overshoot the Bank of Japan target of 2 percent by 2019.[7] The combination of higher real GDP growth, gradual VAT increases, and inflation would put the net-debt-to-GDP ratio on a downward trajectory, which would marginally reduce the term premium, as financial market participants viewed the debt as being more sustainable. Overall, the proposed policy would end deflation and moderately improve real GDP growth and debt sustainability over the medium term.

---

6. This section is based largely on Arbatli et al. (2016) and Gaspar et al. (2016).

7. Monetary policy in the simulations targets inflation excluding the direct impact of the VAT increase. As a result, the relevant inflation comparison between the scenarios is the one excluding the direct impact of the VAT increase.

Figure 14.6   Japan's Three Arrows Plus policy package

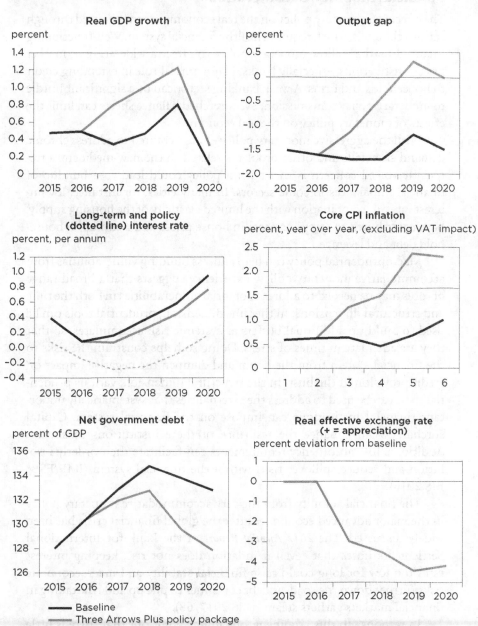

CPI = consumer price index; VAT = value added tax

Note: Baseline reflects the projections in the IMF Staff Report for the 2016 Article IV Consultation for Japan. In the baseline scenario, the direct VAT impact is 0.3 percentage point in 2019 and 1.0 percentage point in 2020. In the other scenario, the direct VAT impact is 0.4 percentage point in 2017 and 0.5 percentage point thereafter.

Source: Arbatli et al. (2016).

Financial Stability Considerations

The effects of monetary policy on the real economy are transmitted through various channels, which require a healthy financial system. Well-functioning financial markets allow monetary policy to affect a wide array of market prices. Institutions, especially banks, play a critical role in extending credit to households and firms. A weak banking sector can be a significant hurdle to monetary policy transmission; overstretched balance sheets can limit the effects of monetary policy on the real economy.

With the aggressive monetary policy easing required to address chronic demand shortfalls and other problems related to the new mediocre, a frequently voiced concern is that such a policy could lead to a buildup of financial imbalances in some sectors. In many cities, for instance, low interest rates, in combination with the limited elasticity of the housing supply, have contributed to steep increases in house prices and a run-up in household debt and leverage.

Macroprudential policy can help address building vulnerabilities from accommodative monetary policy. Experience suggests that a broad range of tools may be needed to address potential vulnerabilities in both the time and structural dimensions. In the time dimension, prudential tools can be used to build up additional buffers as systemic risk accumulates, so that they are adequate in times of stress. Doing so helps constrain the risks to the financial system from the boom and dampen the negative impact on credit provision in the bust. In the structural dimension, various prudential tools can be used to address the externalities that systematically important financial institutions can impose on the financial system. Capital surcharges can enhance the resilience of these institutions to shocks. Additional loss absorbency requirements can facilitate their orderly resolution and reduce spillover risks within the financial system (IMF/FSB/BIS 2016).

The financial stability from the very accommodative monetary policy in the major advanced economies after the global financial crisis has been widely discussed. The *2017 Annual Report* of the Bank for International Settlements notes that "even if inflation does not rise, keeping interest rates too low for long could raise financial stability and macroeconomic risks further down the road, as debt continues to pile up and risk-taking in financial markets gathers steam" (BIS 2017, 68).

In response to this argument, one might point out that there is little evidence that the very low interest rates of recent years weakened financial systems. Indeed, it is more likely that monetary ease reduced the risks of banking system loan portfolios, by boosting economic activity, which strengthened the incomes of households and firms, and raising the values of assets. After the global crisis, the United States, which applied monetary stimulus early and aggressively, also reestablished financial stability relatively quickly.

The greater risk is that low rates may lead central banks to hold back in their response to a negative output shock. When the economy is at risk of slipping into a dark corner, with expectations of inflation falling below target rates, and the policy rate is near the effective lower bound, prompt corrective action is a risk-avoiding strategy for the central bank. Delay would shake confidence in the nominal anchor and jeopardize financial stability.

Conclusion

The global economy has underperformed for a decade. There is strong evidence that the real equilibrium level of the interest rate—the rate consistent with the maintenance of full employment and stable inflation—may be close to zero. Bond yields have fallen to extremely low levels, and negative output gaps and below-target inflation rates persist, despite near-zero central bank policy rates. The effective lower bound on rates suggests that conventional monetary policy may not be able to put up strong resistance to a future economic downturn.

Current uncertainties suggest that policymakers should prepare for nasty surprises from a variety of sources, including structural rebalancing in China; financial sector vulnerabilities in several countries; weakened corporate balance sheets; an asymmetric tightening of monetary conditions; runaway real estate booms in cities, allied to high levels of household debt; a low but rising tide of protectionism; and the deleterious effects of demographics. The effect of a large shock from one or more of these sources could be worse than a short-lived global recession. It could push the world economy to the dark corner of a low-inflation or deflation trap, in which resources lie idle with no end in sight. The nominal anchor for the economy could become unhinged, as the public comes to expect that official inflation targets will not be met and large-scale unemployment becomes chronic. Weak growth in nominal incomes would worsen prospects for stabilizing the uptrend in government debt-to-GDP ratios.

Governments and central banks should have contingency plans for dealing with such dismal prospects. Despite widespread perception that monetary and fiscal policies have run out of ammunition, there is room for maneuver. Transparent, assertive policies must be conducted within a credible framework for long-term stability. A prudent approach to a recessionary shock from a weak starting point may be to take an aggressive stance, committing to holding the policy rate at the effective lower bound for an extended period. Such an approach may well lead to a short-run overshooting of the inflation rate—but under the circumstances, such overshooting would not be a cause for alarm. In countries in which there is a history of high and unstable inflation and the central bank is still in the middle of a credibility-building exercise, prompt reactions to shocks are the key to establishing credibility.

Appendix 14A Summary of Models

Open-Economy New Keynesian Model for Australia

The open-economy New Keynesian model for Australia bears many similarities to the models many central banks use for forecasting and policy analysis. It has a standard core structure, with equations for the output gap, core inflation, the policy interest rate, and the exchange rate. Expectations are forward looking, consistent with the projections of the model itself, but the behavioral equations also embody significant lags and rigidities. In addition, the model includes equations for headline, food, and energy inflation; commodity terms of trade; trade and financial linkages with the rest of the world; and bond yields of various maturities. It exhibits some nonlinearities, primarily as a result of the effective lower bound constraint on the policy interest rate and its implications for monetary policy.

The model is calibrated with reference to both historical data and the theoretical literature, to ensure that it plausibly replicates historical data and generates sensible projections. In practice, real-time forecasts also involve a substantial deal of judgment and data analysis, given the well-known problems with simple model-driven projections in the short term. That caveat notwithstanding, under given forecasts and preferences, the model simulations can demonstrate the key features of an optimal monetary policy strategy.

Model of Endogenous Policy Credibility for India

The model of endogenous policy credibility is a stripped-down version of the practical forecasting and policy analysis models many central banks use. The simple core structure allows nonlinearities in the policy reaction function, the Phillips curve, and a credibility-building process, along with other technical modifications, which enable the exploration of more complex problems and policy options than linear models can examine. The simple core structure includes equations for the output gap, core inflation, the policy interest rate, and the exchange rate. The Phillips curve contains a nonlinear output gap, which implies an increasing marginal effect on the inflation rate as the gap increases. At wide negative output gaps, the curve becomes quite flat.

In a context of low monetary policy credibility, persistent food and fuel price shocks can result in upward ratcheting in inflation expectations and contribute to higher levels of inflation persistence. Inflation expectations are modeled as a linear combination of backward-looking expectations (lags) and forward-looking, model-consistent expectations (leads). The weight on the former is decreasing with the stock of credibility. When central bank credibility is imperfect, inflation expectations are biased upward relative to the linear combination of backward-looking and forward-looking components. This property strengthens the propagation mechanism from supply shocks and therefore requires a more aggressive tightening in monetary conditions, to contain inflationary pressures and anchor long-term inflation expectations. Over time, an established inflation forecast–targeting regime provides an effective strategy for dealing with the second-round effects of supply shocks.

Credibility is earned, over time, by achieving announced objectives and by providing effective, transparent communications. It can be lost through policy actions that are inconsistent with stated objectives. Technically, the modeling is done by introducing a credibility signal that takes a higher value if policy outcome is closer to announced objectives. High values of the credibility signals increase the stock of credibility. However, because of the built-in high persistence in the credibility stock, it takes repeated good signals to improve credibility significantly.

Monetary policy minimizes a quadratic loss function, which penalizes squared deviations from output and inflation objectives as well as squared deviations of changes in the policy interest rate. This approach penalizes dark corners (deflation or high-inflation traps). For India the relevant dark corner could be a situation in which expectations of high inflation become so entrenched that their elimination would require huge costs in lost output and employment.

The International Monetary Fund's G20MOD Module of Flexible System of Global Models (FSGM)

G20MOD is an annual, forward-looking, multieconomy model of the global economy that combines both micro-founded and reduced-form formulations of economic sectors. This model contains individual blocks for the G-20 countries and five additional regions to cover the remaining countries in the world. The key features of a typical G20MOD country model are outlined below. More detailed description of the model can be found in Andrle et al. (2015).

Consumption and investment have microeconomic foundations. Consumption features overlapping-generations households, which can save and smooth consumption, and liquidity-constrained households, which must consume all of their current income every period. Firms' investment is determined by a Tobin's Q combined with the Bernanke-Gertler-Gilchrist model. Firms are net borrowers. Their risk premiums rise during periods of excess capacity, when the output gap is negative, and fall during booms, when the output gap is positive. This pattern mimics the effect of falling/rising real debt burdens.

Trade is modeled by reduced-form equations. They are a function of a competitiveness indicator and domestic or foreign demand. The competitiveness indicator improves one-for-one with domestic prices; there is no local market pricing.

Potential output is endogenous. It is modeled by a Cobb-Douglas production function with endogenous capital and labor. Total factor productivity (TFP) is also endogenous and affected by public investments and commodity prices.

Consumer price and wage inflation are modeled by reduced-form Phillips' curves. They include weights on both lagged and future inflation and on the output gap as well. Consumer price inflation also includes a weight on the real effective exchange rate and second-round effects from commodity prices.

Monetary policy is governed by an interest rate reaction function. For most countries, it is an inflation forecast–based rule that seeks to achieve a long-run inflation target through uncovered risk-adjusted interest rate parity.

Fiscal policy is governed by long-run fiscal policy targets that seek to maintain a stable debt level. Short-run fiscal policy can result in significant deviations away from this target; automatic stabilizers also operate. The model includes four types of expenditures: public consumption, public investments, targeted transfers, and general transfers. Public capital is productive and has an impact on potential output. Major taxes are consumption taxes, personal income taxes, and capital taxes.

Inclusion of three commodities (oil, metals, and food) allows for a distinction between headline and core consumer price inflation and provides richer analysis of the macroeconomic differences between commodity-exporting and commodity-importing regions. Demand for commodities is driven by world demand; it is relatively price inelastic in the short run, because of limited substitutability of the commodity classes considered. The supply of commodities is also price inelastic in the short run. Countries can trade in commodities, and households consume food and oil explicitly, allowing for the distinction between headline and core CPI inflation. The global output gap (a short-run effect), the overall level of global demand, and global production of the commodity in question determine global real prices.

Commodities can moderate business cycle fluctuations. In times of excess aggregate demand, upward pressure on commodity prices from sluggish adjustment in commodity supply relative to demand will put some downward pressure on demand. If there is excess supply, falling commodities prices will ameliorate the deterioration.

Countries are largely distinguished from one another in the G20MOD by their unique parameterizations. Each economy in the model is structurally identical (except for commodities) but has different key steady-state ratios and behavioral parameters.

References

Andrle, M., P. Blagrave, P. Espaillat, K. Honjo, B. Hunt, M. Kortelainen, R. Lalonde, D. Laxton, E. Mavroeidi, D. Muir, S. Mursula, and S. Snudden. 2015. *The Flexible System of Global Models: FSGM.* IMF Working Paper 15/64. Washington: International Monetary Fund.

Arbatli, E., D. Botman, K. Clinton, P. Cova, V. Gaspar, Z. Jakab, D. Laxton, C. Ngouana, J. Mongardini, and H. Wang. 2016. *Reflating Japan: Time to Get Unconventional?* IMF Working Paper 16/157. Washington: International Monetary Fund.

Barro, R., and D. Gordon. 1983. Rules, Discretion, and Reputation in a Model of Monetary Policy. *Journal of Monetary Economics* 12, no. 1: 101–21.

Batini, N., and D. Laxton. 2007. Under What Conditions Can Inflation Targeting Be Adopted? The Experience of Emerging Markets. In *Monetary Policy Under Inflation Targeting*, ed. F. S. Mishkin and K. Schmidt-Hebbel. Santiago: Banco Central de Chile.

Benes, J., K. Clinton, A. George, J. John, O. Kamenik, D. Laxton, P. Mitra, G.V. Nadhanael, H. Wang, and F. Zhang. 2017a. *Inflation-Forecast Targeting for India: An Outline of the Analytical Framework.* IMF Working Paper 17/32. Washington: International Monetary Fund.

Benes, J., K. Clinton, A. George, P. Gupta, J. John, O. Kamenik, D. Laxton, P. Mitra, G.V. Nadhanael, R. Portillo, H. Wang, and F. Zhang. 2017b. *Quarterly Projection Model for India: Key Elements and Properties.* IMF Working Paper 17/33. Washington: International Monetary Fund.

BIS (Bank for International Settlements). 2017. *87th Annual Report* (June). Basel.

Charbonneau, K., and L. Rennison. 2015. *Forward Guidance at the Effective Lower Bound: International Experience.* Bank of Canada Staff Discussion Paper 2015-15. Ottawa: Bank of Canada.

Clinton, K., C. Freedman, M. Juillard, O. Kamenik, D. Laxton, and H. Wang. 2015. *Inflation-Forecast Targeting: Applying the Principle of Transparency.* IMF Working Paper 15/132. Washington: International Monetary Fund.

Clinton, K., T. Hlédik, T. Holub, D. Laxton, and H. Wang. 2017. *Czech Magic: Implementing Inflation-Forecast Targeting at the CNB.* IMF Working Paper 17/21. Washington: International Monetary Fund.

Dincer, N., and B. Eichengreen. 2014. Central Bank Transparency and Independence: Updates and New Measures. *International Journal of Central Banking* 10, no. 1: 189–259.

Engen, E., T. Laubach, and D. Reifschneider. 2015. *The Macroeconomic Effects of the Federal Reserve's Unconventional Monetary Policies.* Finance and Economic Discussion Series 2015-005. Washington: Federal Reserve Board.

Gaspar, V., M. Obstfeld, R. Sahay, D. Laxton, D. Botman, K. Clinton, R. Duval, K. Ishi, Z. Jakab, L. Jaramillo Mayor, C. Lonkeng Ngouana, T. Mancini Griffoli, J. Mongardini, S. Mursula, E. Nier, Y. Ustyugova, H. Wang, and O. Wuensch. 2016. *Macroeconomic Management When Policy Space Is Constrained: A Comprehensive, Consistent and Coordinated Approach to Economic Policy.* IMF Staff Discussion Note 16/09. Washington: International Monetary Fund.

Helbling, T., P. Karam, O. Kamenik, D. Laxton, H. Wang, and H. Yao. 2017. *Inflation Targeting in Australia: Performance, Challenges, and Strategy Going Forward.* IMF Country Report 17/43. Washington: International Monetary Fund.

IMF/FSB/BIS (International Monetary Fund/Financial Stability Board/Bank for International Settlements). 2016. *Elements of Effective Macroprudential Policies: Lessons from International Experience* (August). Washington: International Monetary Fund.

Kydland, F., and E. Prescott. 1977. Rules Rather than Discretion: The Inconsistency of Optimal Plans. *Journal of Political Economy* 85, no. 3: 473–92.

Svensson, L. 1997. Inflation Forecast Targeting: Implementing and Monitoring Inflation Targets. *European Economic Review* 41, no. 6: 1111–46.

Woodford, M. 2005. Central-Bank Communication and Policy Effectiveness. Paper presented at the Federal Reserve Bank of Kansas City Symposium, Jackson Hole, WY, August 25–27.

15

Avoiding a New Mediocre in Asia: What Can Fiscal Policy Do?

ANA CORBACHO, DIRK MUIR, MASAHIRO NOZAKI, AND EDDA ZOLI

Several countries in Asia face the risk of settling into a new mediocre of lower growth. Rapid population aging and weak productivity are increasingly taking a toll on medium- to long-term economic potential. There is a lot fiscal policy can do to address the risk of a new mediocre. Investing in productive public infrastructure, lowering distortionary taxes, and reforming labor markets are prominent avenues through which fiscal policy can improve productivity and growth paths. These fiscal initiatives can be costly, however. Countries already experiencing symptoms of the new mediocre face the double challenge of absorbing higher levels of age-related spending and coping with low productivity growth.

This chapter analyzes the implications of the new mediocre for medium- to long-term fiscal sustainability and quantifies the potential of fiscal reforms to improve growth. It is organized as follows. The first section examines the effects of the new mediocre on long-term projections of public debt. The second section examines whether current public spending and revenue policies are aligned with the challenges of the new mediocre. The third section illustrates the growth payoff of fiscal reform packages in three areas: public infrastructure, tax rebalancing, and labor markets. The last

Ana Corbacho is division chief at the Intenational Monetary Fund (IMF). Dirk Muir, Masahiro Nozaki, and Edda Zoli are senior economists at the IMF. The authors thank Medha Madhu Nair for valuable research assistance; Francis Landicho for coordination of the editing and production; and Thomas Helbling, Kenneth Kang, Junghun Kim, Changyong Rhee, Markus Rodlauer, and IMF country teams for useful comments and feedback. The views expressed in this chapter are those of the authors and do not necessarily represent the views of the IMF, its Executive Board, or its management.

section discusses the design of fiscal institutions and key reforms to address the new mediocre and boost growth in Asia.

Public Debt Dynamics under the New Mediocre

Asia is expected to have generally favorable public debt dynamics in the near to medium term, for two reasons. First, public debt is lower than in other regions. In 2016 the median public debt-to-GDP ratio was 40 percent in advanced Asia and 42 percent in developing Asia—lower than in other advanced economies (66 percent), Latin America (50 percent), and emerging Europe (44 percent) (figure 15.1). Japan, with a debt ratio of 240 percent in 2016, is an outlier in Asia. Second, with a few exceptions (including China), public debt-to-GDP ratios in Asia are projected to decrease or remain stable over the medium term (figure 15.2).[1]

Population aging in the new mediocre can pose a challenge for public debt sustainability over the long term. The speed of aging in Asia is remarkably high compared with the historical experience of Europe and the United States. It took 26 years in Europe and more than 50 years in the United States for the old-age dependency ratio to increase from 15 to 20 percent; it will take China, Korea, and Thailand less than a decade to complete the same demographic transition (IMF 2017a). Moreover, several countries in Asia are likely to face the fiscal costs of aging at relatively low levels of income per capita. Age-related public spending on pensions and health care is thus projected to increase substantially in several Asian economies. If the spending increase is financed by borrowing, public debt will rise.

Prospects for age-related spending differ significantly across countries. Japan, which already has the oldest population in the world, spent 20 percent of GDP on pensions and health care in 2015 (figure 15.3). In China, Korea, and Thailand, age-related spending is projected to rise over the next several decades, approaching Japan's current level by 2050. India, Indonesia, and the Philippines will see their working-age populations grow substantially in coming decades. As they will continue to reap a demographic dividend, their age-related spending should remain contained over the long term.

Aside from the fiscal cost, aging will slow potential growth, through its negative impact on the labor force and on trend total factor productivity (TFP). The impact of aging on the labor force could reduce annual growth by about 0.5 to 0.75 percentage points in China, Korea, and Thailand. For the region as a whole, aging could slow annual trend TFP growth by 0.1 to 0.3 percentage point (IMF 2017a).

---

1. Projections are based on the *World Economic Outlook* of April 2017 (IMF 2017c).

Figure 15.1 Public debt as percent of GDP, by region, 2016

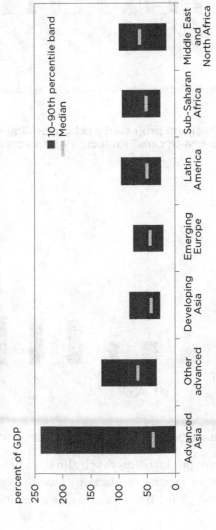

Sources: IMF, World Economic Outlook April 2017 database; IMF Staff calculations.

345

Figure 15.2   Actual and projected public debt in selected Asian economies

percent of GDP

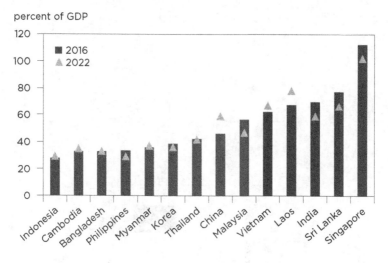

Sources: IMF, *World Economic Outlook* April 2017 database; IMF Staff calculations.

Figure 15.3   Actual and projected public spending on pensions and health care in selected Asian economies

percent of GDP

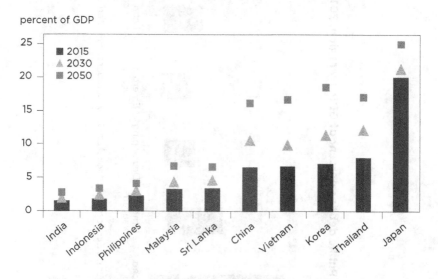

Sources: United Nations (2015); Amaglobeli and Shi (2016); IMF Staff calculations.

The slowdown in productivity growth also has a bearing on public debt dynamics. As in other regions, productivity growth in many parts of Asia has slowed since the global financial crisis, as a result of sluggish investment, little impetus from trade, weaker human capital formation, and the reallocation of resources to less productive sectors of the economy. The productivity slowdown has been most pronounced in the advanced economies of the region and China (IMF 2017b). The decline in real interest rates observed since the 1980s can be expected to reverse only moderately over the medium term (IMF 2014c).

This section presents long-term projections for public debt reflecting the impact of the new mediocre. The analysis covers 10 Asian economies (chosen based on data availability): Japan (Group 1); China, Korea, and Thailand (Group 2); and India, Indonesia, Malaysia, the Philippines, Sri Lanka, and Vietnam (Group 3). (See box 15.1.)

Methodology

The ratio of public debt to GDP(d_t) evolves as follows:

$$d_{t+1} = d_t + \frac{i_{t+1} - g_{t+1}}{1 + g_{t+1}} d_t - pb_{t+1},$$

where i_t, g_t, and pb_t denote the nominal interest rate on public debt (computed as interest payments divided by the previous year's debt outstanding), nominal GDP growth, and the primary balance as percent of GDP, respectively. The debt ratio increases at the rate of $\frac{i_{t+1}-g_{t+1}}{1+g_{t+1}}$ (the interest rate growth differential [IRGD] divided by $(1 + g_{t+1})$) and decreases with the primary surplus.

Four scenarios are considered, based on extrapolation of the projections in the IMF's *World Economic Outlook* April 2017 database (IMF 2017c) for 2022–50:[2]

- *Scenario 1: Status quo.* The primary balance, nominal GDP growth, and nominal interest rate for 2023–50 are assumed to remain at 2022 levels. The IRGD is negative for all countries. The primary balance is in surplus in Korea, Malaysia, and Sri Lanka and in deficit for the remaining countries (table 15.1).

- *Scenario 2: Historical primary balance.* The primary balance for 2023–50 is assumed to reflect its historical average over 2000–15. This scenario examines cases in which the projected primary balance for 2022 appears optimistic compared with the historical track.[3] GDP growth and the interest rate for 2023–50 are unchanged at their 2022 levels.

- *Scenario 3: Demographics.* The primary balance is assumed to worsen from the 2022 level by the projected increase in pension and healthcare spending.[4] GDP growth from Scenario 1 is adjusted by the impact of aging on the underlying labor force.[5] The interest rate is left unchanged at the 2022 level.

- *Scenario 4: Productivity and interest rates.* Productivity growth could continue to slow. Together with the demographic shift, it could cause the

---

2. These scenarios correspond to stylized simulations under certain assumptions for the key parameters that underlie the evolution of the public debt-to-GDP ratio and should not be considered the baseline projections of the IMF. For the latter, refer to the respective Article IV Staff Reports.

3. In some countries (e.g., India), the lower primary balance projected by 2022 is supported by structural reforms driving a decline in primary fiscal spending.

4. Pension and healthcare spending projections are based on United Nations (2015) and Amaglobeli and Shi (2016). These projections incorporate mainly the impact of demographics on age-related spending, holding constant the coverage as well as replacement ratios, except in countries with ongoing parametric reforms. Reforms that improve coverage or benefits would translate into higher spending. The IMF *Fiscal Monitor* (www.imf.org/en/publications/fm) publishes estimates of the net present value of the projected increase in pension and healthcare spending over 2015–50.

5. The labor force is assumed to grow at the rate of the working-age population, computed from United Nations (2015).

Table 15.1 Key parameters for long-term public debt projections in selected Asian economies

Country	Group	Projection for 2022				Historical average for 2000-15			
		Primary balance (percent of GDP)	Real GDP growth (percent)	Real interest rate on public debt (percent)	Interest rate growth differential (percent)	Primary balance (percent of GDP)	Real GDP growth (percent)	Real interest rate on public debt (percent)	Interest rate growth differential (percent)
Japan	1	-2.0	0.6	-0.6	-1.2	-5.8	0.9	1.9	1.0
China	2	-2.1	5.7	-0.3	-6.0	-0.8	9.6	-2.0	-11.6
Korea	2	1.7	3.1	1.9	-1.2	1.5	4.3	2.3	-2.0
Thailand	2	-0.6	3.0	1.7	-1.3	0.4	4.1	0.1	-4.0
India	3	-1.3	8.2	3.4	-4.8	-3.7	7.1	2.2	-4.8
Indonesia	3	-0.8	5.5	2.3	-3.2	1.1	5.4	-3.4	-8.8
Malaysia	3	0.9	4.8	2.2	-2.6	-2.5	5.1	2.0	-3.1
Philippines	3	-0.4	7.0	1.5	-5.5	2.2	5.1	3.7	-1.4
Vietnam	3	-2.2	6.2	-0.7	-6.9	-2.0	6.5	-6.7	-13.2
Sri Lanka	3	1.2	5.3	2.2	-3.1	-1.7	5.7	-1.5	-7.2

Sources: IMF *World Economic Outlook* April 2017 database; IMF Staff calculations.

natural interest rate to fall. The net effect on the IRGD for debt dynamics is ambiguous. Two scenarios are therefore considered, both of which assume the primary balance is as in Scenario 3. In Scenario 4a, the IRGD decreases gradually to 1 percentage point below the 2022 level by 2030, as interest rates charged on public debt fall by more than growth. In Scenario 4b, the IRGD rises gradually, reaching 2 percentage points above the 2022 level by 2030, as the sovereign risk premium increases with rising public debt and/or conditions underlying negative IRGDs (e.g., financial repression) reverse.

Some caveats are in order. First, Scenarios 3, 4a, and 4b assume that the increase in age-related spending will be fully financed by government borrowing. But governments would likely react by rationalizing spending, mobilizing revenue, or both. Second, an acceleration of problems in later years makes the response of governments even more uncertain and difficult to assess. Third, when considering the IRGD, whether sovereign risk premia can remain contained in countries with a rapid increase in public debt is questionable and can modify the results. Fourth, the methodology abstracts from the impact of exchange rate movements on the debt ratio or any fiscal risks.

Results

Countries' public debt-to-GDP ratios develop as follows under each scenario (figure 15.4):

- Under Scenario 1, the debt ratio decreases or stabilizes in all economies, driven by the negative IRGD. The debt ratio is contained well below 50 percent of GDP in the long term for all economies except Japan, where the debt ratio is projected to decrease but remain above 200 percent of GDP.

- Under Scenario 2, the debt ratio increases in Japan, India, and Malaysia and remains flat in Sri Lanka, where the historical primary deficit was substantially higher than the level projected for 2022.

- Under Scenario 3, pension and healthcare spending impose a significant fiscal burden on the rapidly aging Asian economies. In China, Japan, and Thailand, the debt ratio rises shortly after 2022. In China and Thailand it exceeds 100 percent by 2050. In Korea and Vietnam, the debt ratio hits its nadir around 2030 and then rises to 110 percent in Korea and 115 percent in Vietnam by 2050. The debt paths for Malaysia and Sri Lanka are well above those of Scenario 1. For India, Indonesia, and the Philippines—the youngest economies in the sample—the impact of aging on the debt path is much more muted, with the debt ratio for 2050 exceeding that in Scenario 1 by only about 15 percentage points.

Figure 15.4 Actual and projected public debt in selected Asian economies, 2000–50 (percent of GDP)

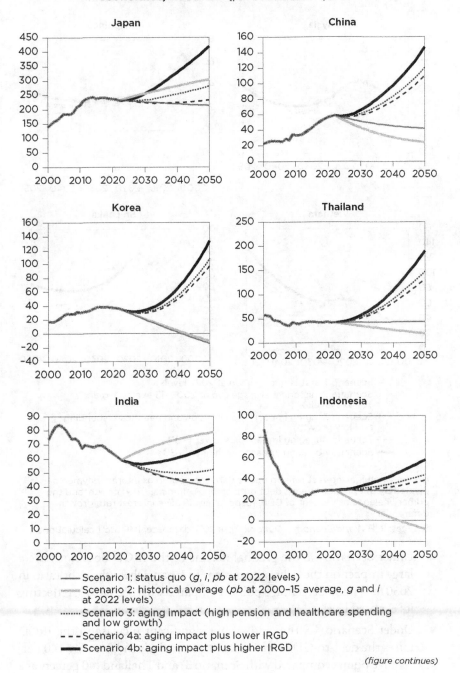

Scenario 1: status quo (*g*, *i*, *pb* at 2022 levels)

Scenario 2: historical average (*pb* at 2000–15 average, *g* and *i* at 2022 levels)

Scenario 3: aging impact (high pension and healthcare spending and low growth)

Scenario 4a: aging impact plus lower IRGD

Scenario 4b: aging impact plus higher IRGD

(figure continues)

Figure 15.4 Actual and projected public debt in selected Asian economies, 2000–50 (percent of GDP) *(continued)*

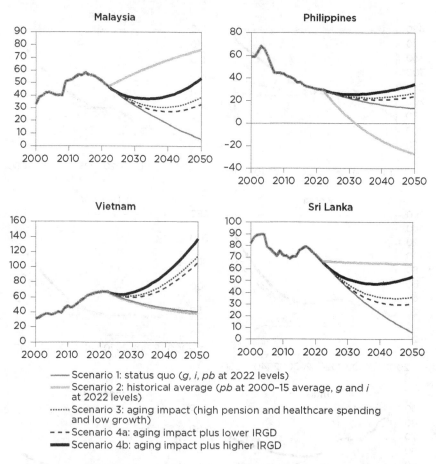

Scenario 1: status quo (*g, i, pb* at 2022 levels)
Scenario 2: historical average (*pb* at 2000–15 average, *g* and *i* at 2022 levels)
Scenario 3: aging impact (high pension and healthcare spending and low growth)
Scenario 4a: aging impact plus lower IRGD
Scenario 4b: aging impact plus higher IRGD

i, g, pb = nominal interest rate on public debt (computed as interest payments divided by the previous year's debt outstanding), nominal GDP growth, and the primary balance as percent of GDP, respectively; IRGD = interest rate growth differential

Sources: IMF *World Economic Outlook* April 2017 database; IMF Staff calculations.

- Under Scenario 4a, the gradual decline in the IRGD does not have a large impact on the debt path, except in Japan, where the debt ratio in 2050 falls by 50 percentage points compared with Scenario 3, reflecting its elevated level.

- Under Scenario 4b, the gradual but significant increase in the IRGD raises the debt-to-GDP ratio in 2050, particularly in Japan (by 140 percentage points compared with Scenario 3) and Thailand (40 percentage points). A potential reversal of the negative IRGD constitutes a significant upside risk for the debt path.[6]

Figure 15.5 decomposes the change in the debt ratio over 2022–50 under Scenario 4b into three factors: the status quo primary balance as of 2022, the increase in age-related spending, and the IRGD. In Japan, where the debt level is already very high, the stability of the debt path hinges on maintaining a favorable IRGD and a primary balance in the face of still rising age-related spending. China, Korea, and Thailand (Group 2) face significant fiscal pressures from aging in the long term, but Korea has kept its debt level low and will have more time to address rising age-related spending than China and Thailand. Group 3 countries are more diverse. Indonesia and the Philippines have built fiscal buffers, and demographic prospects do not appear to pose a threat to fiscal sustainability. Stabilizing debt paths in India, Malaysia, and Sri Lanka hinges on a negative IRGD (India) or a behavioral shift from the past to maintain a primary surplus over the long term (Malaysia and Sri Lanka). Vietnam's debt prospects look similar to China's, with demographics negatively affecting debt dynamics relatively early.

Are Public Spending and Revenue Policies Aligned with the Challenges of the New Mediocre?

Fiscal policy can play an important role in supporting sustained and inclusive growth (IMF 2014c, 2015a). Aside from its overarching role in ensuring macroeconomic stability, fiscal policy can boost potential growth through the following channels:

- physical capital accumulation, through efficient public investment, especially in infrastructure (Buffie et al. 2012; IMF 2014c, 2015b), and taxation of capital and other incentives;
- labor supply, through provision of social benefits for specific groups (e.g., public spending for child care and active labor market policies); taxation of labor income to encourage labor force participation (IMF 2014a); and spending on education and health care to boost human capital accumulation;
- trend TFP, through spending on research and development (R&D); tax incentives to encourage private R&D or new business ventures that spur

---

6. Theoretically, a negative IRGD implies that the economy is dynamically inefficient (i.e., reducing the saving rates would leave all generations better off). Mankiw (2015) argues that such a Pareto-improving opportunity is unlikely to be sustained. Escolano, Shabunina, and Woo (2017) attribute negative IRGDs in developing economies to real interest rates well below market equilibrium, reflecting financial repression and captive and distorted markets.

Figure 15.5 Decomposition of change in debt ratio under Scenario 4b

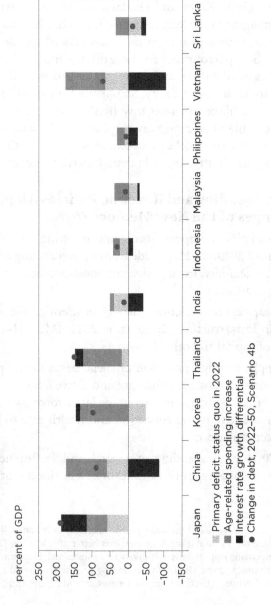

Sources: IMF, *World Economic Outlook* April 2017 database; IMF Staff calculations.

innovation (IMF 2016); and fiscal policies for labor and product market reforms that increase productivity (IMF 2014b, Banerji et al. 2017).

This section presents stylized facts on the level, composition, and efficiency of public spending and tax systems in Asian economies, benchmarked against countries from other regions at similar income levels.

Public Spending Level and Efficiency

Infrastructure. In many Asian economies, there is scope to increase the level and quality of infrastructure spending, through public investment and public-private partnerships (PPPs). In Japan (Group 1) and the advanced economies in Group 2, the quality of infrastructure exceeds that in peer economies. In some developing economies in Group 2 and Group 3, it has room to catch up to levels in emerging markets in Europe and Latin America (figure 15.6).[7] Most developing economies in Asia in Group 2 and Group 3 lie within the public investment efficiency frontier (figure 15.7).[8]

Health Care. Despite increases in per capita income since the early 2000s, public spending on healthcare remains modest in Asia (except in Japan) (figure 15.8), although private healthcare expenditure is broadly at similar levels.[9] Public health care spending in Hong Kong, Korea, and Singapore reached at most 4 percent of GDP—less than half the average of 8.5 percent of GDP in advanced economies outside of Asia. In most Asian developing countries, public healthcare spending is below the average in emerging Europe and Latin America.[10]

The efficiency of public healthcare spending is also low in parts of Asia: Group 3 countries fall well within the frontier (figure 15.9), indicating that better health outcomes could be achieved with the same level of healthcare spending.

Education. The level and efficiency of public spending on education is low in some parts of Asia (figure 15.10). Public spending on education in advanced economies in Group 2 is somewhat lower than in other countries

---

7. Emerging Europe includes countries belonging to the Commonwealth of Independent States.

8. The efficiency frontier is calculated using Data Envelopment Analysis techniques, which use linear programming methods. See appendix 15A.

9. In Group 2 and Group 3 countries, private healthcare spending amounted to 2.3 and 2.6 percent of GDP, respectively, in 2015, compared with 1.8 percent of GDP in advanced economies outside Asia and about 3 percent of GDP in emerging markets in other regions.

10. In Indonesia, Korea, and Thailand, the gap between actual and expected public spending on health care was 0.8–1.7 percentage points of GDP in 2015 (Phillips et al. 2013).

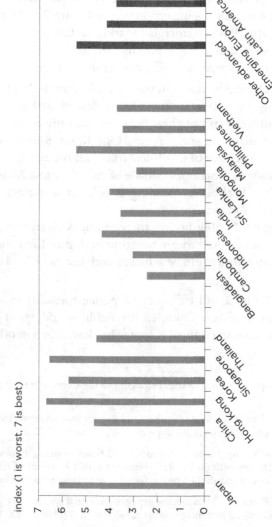

Figure 15.6 Index of quality of infrastructure

index (1 is worst, 7 is best)

Sources: IMF, *World Economic Outlook* April 2017 database; World Economic Forum; IMF Staff calculations.

Figure 15.7 Efficiency frontier of public investment

indicator of quality of infrastructure
(100 = average in advanced economies)

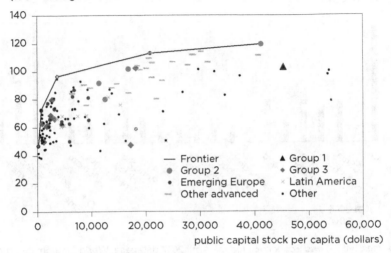

public capital stock per capita (dollars)

Note: The efficiency frontier is calculated using Data Envelopment Analysis (DEA) techniques (described in appendix 15A). The distance to the efficiency frontier Indicates the size of the loss in infrastructure quality as a result of inefficiencies in public investment (IMF 2015b).

Sources: IMF, *World Economic Outlook* April 2017 database; World Economic Forum; IMF Staff calculations.

at similar income levels. For developing countries in Group 2 and Group 3, public spending on education is generally lower than in peers in Latin America. Based on secondary school enrollment (figure 15.11, panel a) and PISA scores (figure 15.11, panel b), most Group 2 and 3 countries lie within the efficiency frontier (Korea is on the frontier for PISA scores).

R&D spending. Data on R&D spending are limited. They seem to indicate that Group 2 economies except Hong Kong are roughly comparable to their peers in other regions but that Group 3 countries (most notably Indonesia, the Philippines, and Sri Lanka) lag their peers (figure 15.12).

Some public R&D spending is not effective. In Korea, for instance, high R&D expenditure has not been accompanied by sustained gains in productivity because of weak links between government research institutes, universities, and industry that hinder technology transfers and commercialization (Jones and Kim 2014).

Figure 15.8 Public spending on health care as percent of GDP in selected economies, 2001 and 2014

percent of GDP

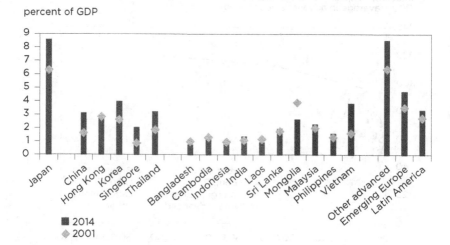

■ 2014
◆ 2001

Sources: IMF, *World Economic Outlook* April 2017 database; World Economic Forum; IMF Staff calculations.

Figure 15.9 Efficiency frontier of public spending on health care, 2015

healthy life expectancy (years)

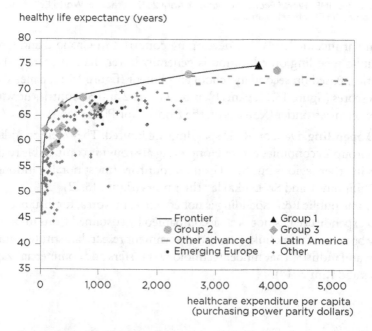

healthcare expenditure per capita
(purchasing power parity dollars)

Sources: IMF, *World Economic Outlook* April 2017 database; World Economic Forum; IMF Staff calculations.

Figure 15.10 Public spending on education as percent of GDP in selected economies, 2001 and 2014

percent of GDP

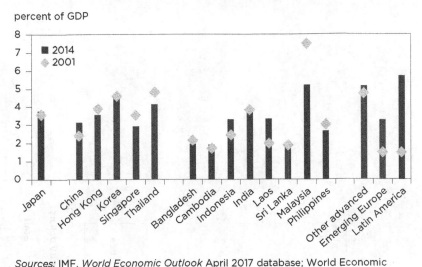

Sources: IMF, *World Economic Outlook* April 2017 database; World Economic Forum; IMF Staff calculations.

Revenue Collection and Composition

Group 2 economies will face increasing spending pressures from demographic trends, and Group 3 economies need to step up public spending on infrastructure, health care, and education. Is there scope to expand the revenue intake?

In several of these economies, general government revenue ratios are low compared with other economies at similar income levels (figure 15.13). In the advanced economies of Group 2, revenue-to-GDP ratios are almost 20 percentage points lower than in advanced economies in other regions. In emerging economies from Group 2 and Group 3, revenue-to-GDP ratios average 7 and 13 percentage points less than in peers from Latin America and Europe, respectively.

The relatively low revenue intake partly reflects an explicit policy choice in favor of a low tax environment. However, tax yields, which are indicators of the efficiency of the tax system, also tend to be low in several Asian economies. Figure 15.14 shows two measures of personal income tax (PIT) yields: PIT revenues as a percent of GDP divided by the middle and the maximum statutory PIT.

Three factors contribute to low tax yields: narrow tax bases, reflecting widespread exemptions, which are often inefficient (IMF 2012, World Bank 2012); lingering weaknesses in tax administration, despite reform efforts (Araki and Claus 2014); and extensive informality.

Figure 15.11 Efficiency frontier of public spending on education

a. Secondary school enrollment

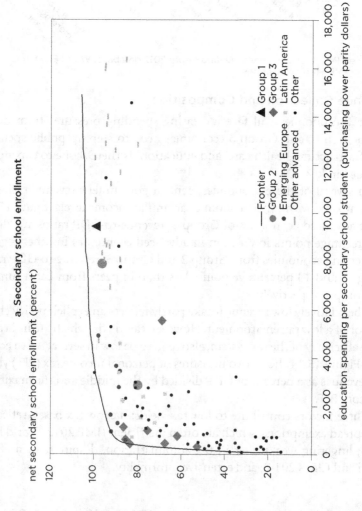

net secondary school enrollment (percent)

education spending per secondary school student (purchasing power parity dollars)

Frontier
Group 2
Emerging Europe
Other advanced

Group 1
Group 3
Latin America
Other

Sources: IMF, *World Economic Outlook* April 2017 database; World Economic Forum; IMF Staff calculations.

Figure 15.11 Efficiency frontier of public spending on education

b. PISA scores

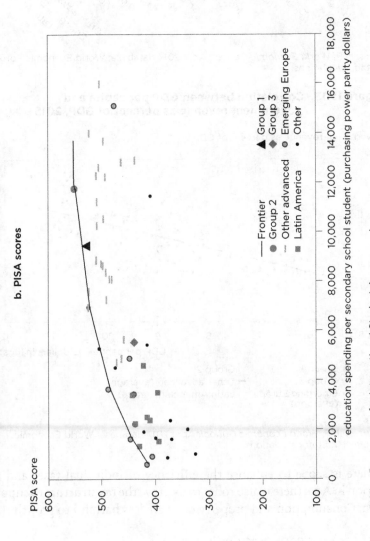

PISA = Programme for International Student Assessment

Sources: IMF, *World Economic Outlook* April 2017 database; World Economic Forum; IMF Staff calculations.

Figure 15.12 Spending on research and development in selected economies, 2015

percent of GDP

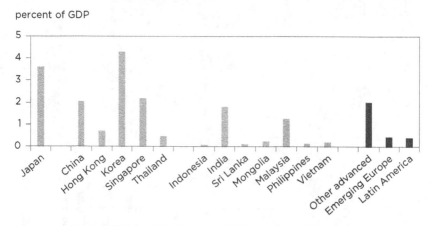

Sources: IMF, *World Economic Outlook* April 2017 database; World Economic Forum; IMF Staff calculations.

Figure 15.13 Correlation between GDP per capita and government revenue as percent of GDP, 2015

government revenue as percent of GDP

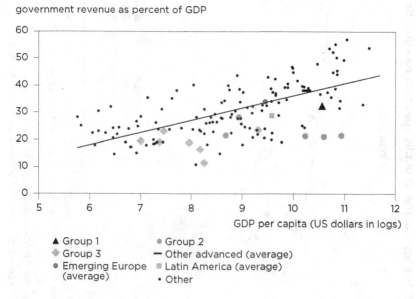

GDP per capita (US dollars in logs)

▲ Group 1 • Group 2
◆ Group 3 — Other advanced (average)
• Emerging Europe ▪ Latin America (average)
(average) • Other

Sources: IMF, *World Economic Outlook* April 2017 database; World Economic Forum; IMF Staff calculations.

There is scope to enhance the efficiency of individual taxes and tax collection in Asia; there is also room to improve the tax structure to support growth. Consumption and property taxes are less harmful to growth than

Figure 15.14　Yields from personal income tax (PIT) in selected economies, 2015

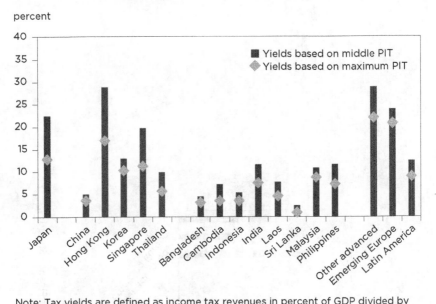

percent

Legend:
■ Yields based on middle PIT
◆ Yields based on maximum PIT

Categories: Japan, China, Hong Kong, Korea, Singapore, Thailand, Bangladesh, Cambodia, Indonesia, India, Laos, Sri Lanka, Malaysia, Philippines, Other advanced, Emerging Europe, Latin America

Note: Tax yields are defined as income tax revenues in percent of GDP divided by the middle and the maximum statutory tax rates.

Sources: IMF, *World Economic Outlook* April 2017 database; IMF, Government Finance Statistics; IMF Staff calculations.

taxes on factors of production, such as personal or corporate income tax (Arnold et al. 2011). A broad-based, single-rate VAT is regarded as relatively efficient, because it does not introduce large distortions in relative prices or saving decisions (Ebrill, Keen, and Summers 2001).

Relative to advanced and developing economies outside Asia, many Asian countries rely more on personal and corporate income tax than on general consumption taxes (figure 15.15). Tax rebalancing away from direct taxes on labor and capital toward indirect taxes on consumption could boost economic growth.

Quantifying the Payoff of Fiscal Policy Reforms

This section quantifies the growth payoff of fiscal reforms that reallocate expenditure and revenue composition toward growth- and productivity-enhancing items. The fiscal packages cover three areas: public infrastructure, tax rebalancing, and labor markets. The purpose of these packages is to raise long-term growth, through higher TFP, labor productivity, or labor force participation. A more flexible labor force, better infrastructure, and a more favorable tax environment should also allow economies to adjust more rapidly to shocks, increasing resilience and stability.

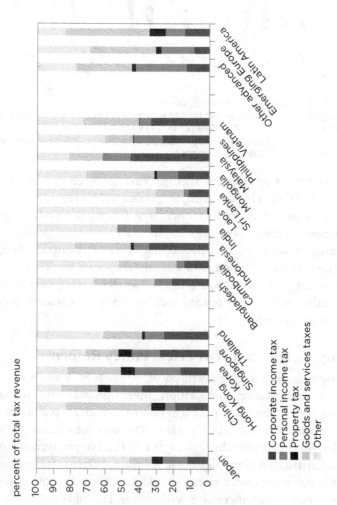

Figure 15.15 Sources of tax revenue in selected economies, 2015

Sources: IMF, *World Economic Outlook* April 2017 database; IMF, Government Finance Statistics; IMF Staff calculations.

The simulations are based on the IMF's APDMOD, a semi-structural model of the global economy that includes blocks for 16 Asian countries and 8 regions representing the rest of the world.[11] The model's fiscal sector includes spending on consumption; infrastructure; transfers; lump-sum taxation on households; and distortionary taxation on consumption, labor, and capital. Only some households ("saving" households) hold debt as a source of wealth, which allows them to smooth consumption in the face of shocks or policy changes. Other households cannot save effectively; these liquidity-constrained households live off their current income.[12] These non-Ricardian properties allow a powerful role for fiscal policy in both the short and long term. For most countries, monetary policy is assumed to follow an inflation-targeting regime.

By implementing fiscal policy reforms, Asian countries can achieve stronger growth and productivity, although some measures impose short-term costs on households and firms. These costs can be mitigated by addressing adverse effects on income equality and by phasing implementation over time. Better results may be achievable by taking advantage of synergies with monetary policy in countries facing low inflation.[13]

Illustrative Fiscal Reform Packages

Most of the simulations of the three packages are implemented in a budget-neutral manner. The size of the measures is illustrative and not necessarily optimal. Policies account for idiosyncratic country features and tackle the main gaps in the composition of tax and expenditure policies identified in the previous section. Measures are notionally carried out relative to a baseline scenario consistent with the IMF's *World Economic Outlook* (IMF 2017c). Appendix 15B provides details on the fiscal packages in each economy.

The three packages include the following:

1. *Public infrastructure push.* Infrastructure investment increases by 1 percent of GDP for five years in developing countries in Groups 2 and 3, driving

---

11. APDMOD is part of the Flexible System of Global Models (FSGM). See Andrle et al. (2015) for a complete treatment of the model.

12. APDMOD assumes that 60 percent of households in Asian countries are liquidity constrained, except in Hong Kong, Japan, Korea, and Singapore, where liquidity-constrained households represent just 35 percent of the population. Liquidity-constrained households account for 20 to 30 percent of total consumption in the advanced Asian economies and 45 to 55 percent in the others.

13. For a discussion of the concepts of coordination and comprehensiveness, particularly around the use of spending, tax, and labor measures, see Gaspar, Obstfeld, and Sahay (2016).

up the size of the public capital stock by 5 percentage points.[14] Investment then increases permanently by 0.2 percent of GDP to replace the loss from an annual depreciation rate of 4 percent. Economies near the frontier or in which spending is already high (the advanced economies and China) do not participate.

Financing varies across the region. In many of the economies analyzed, half of it is in the form of PPP, accounted for as private investment and debt and recouped by user fees.[15] The other half is traditional public investment, financed by a temporary reduction in general transfers. In two countries (Cambodia and the Philippines), the fiscal deficit is allowed to increase.

2. *Rebalancing toward indirect taxes.* VAT collection increases by 1.5 percent of GDP. It is offset by cuts of 0.75 percent of GDP to both the personal and the corporate income tax.[16] The increase excludes additional tax changes needed to finance labor sector reforms (see below). Some economies do not participate fully or at all, either because doing so would conflict with other goals (Japan and India, with baseline scenarios that already factor in VAT increases) or because direct taxes already represent a small share of tax revenues (Bangladesh, China, Hong Kong, and Sri Lanka).

For countries in Group 3, liquidity-constrained households receive a 0.5 percent of GDP rebate, to address the adverse impact of tax reform on income inequality. To achieve a net VAT increase of 1.5 percent of GDP, VAT collection is increased by 2 percent of GDP. In addition, the cut in personal income tax is progressive, benefiting only liquidity-constrained households.

3. *Labor sector reforms.* All countries participate in the following reforms:

- The retirement age is increased by two years. Average retirement ages are currently 57 in Asia, 61 in emerging-market economies in Europe, 62 in Latin America, and 64 years in advanced economies

---

14. The exception in Group 3 is India, which has limited scope to reallocate spending within the budget envelope.

15. The exception is Bangladesh, whose PPP framework needs further development, where the assumption is that 100 percent of infrastructure is built through public procurement and accounted for as public investment.

16. In APDMOD the personal income tax is combined with social security taxes. Simulations here consider only changes to the personal income tax.

outside Asia. The longer working life raises the labor force participation rate of people 55–64 (and hence the overall participation rate).[17]

- Childcare spending is permanently increased by 0.25 percent of GDP a year, leading to higher female labor force participation.[18]
- Active labor market policies permanently increase government spending by 0.25 percent of GDP a year, lowering long-term unemployment and consequently raising labor productivity.[19]

The financing of labor sector reforms varies across economies. It includes a slight increase in VAT in Bangladesh and Japan, an increase in the fiscal deficit in Cambodia and the Philippines, an increase in excise taxes in India (where the personal income tax base is small), and an increase in personal income tax elsewhere. In China, Thailand, and most Group 3 countries, the increase in personal income tax is progressive, exempting liquidity-constrained households.

Other avenues to improve productivity and long-term growth include public spending on R&D, education, and health care. The model does not capture these components directly, but some of their effects are implied. For example, some infrastructure investment, such as building high-tech facilities, is related to R&D; spending on schools and medical facilities supports human capital accumulation. Cuts in corporate income tax could be in the form of tax credits for innovation or R&D. Active labor market policies generally include adult education, which contributes to human capital accumulation.

Effects of the Reforms across Asia

If all countries in Asia implemented these fiscal reforms, growth in the region would be about 0.3 percentage point higher during the first three years and about 0.1 to 0.2 percentage point a year higher from then on once reforms were completed. In the short term, more than two-thirds of the increase in growth would come from labor sector reforms. In the long term, investment in infrastructure is the largest contributor to growth.

---

17. Figures are based on estimates in Bouis and Duval (2011), originally calculated for the OECD.

18. Figures are based on estimates in Bassanini and Duval (2006), originally calculated for the OECD.

19. Figures are based on estimates in Bouis and Duval (2011), originally calculated for the OECD.

Figure 15.16 Projected effects of fiscal measures on real GDP in selected Asian economies

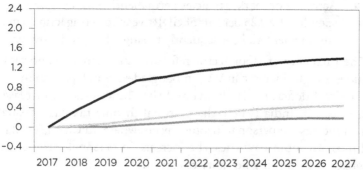

a. Asia

percentage point difference in
real GDP associated with fiscal measure

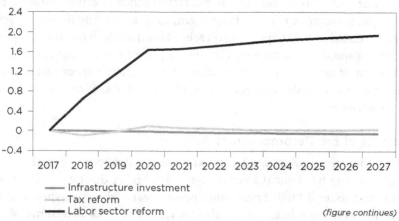

b. Group 1 (Japan)

percentage point difference in
real GDP associated with fiscal measure

——— Infrastructure investment
········· Tax reform
——— Labor sector reform

(figure continues)

Panel a of figure 15.16 shows the effects on real GDP. By the end of the first decade, labor reforms contribute about half of the increase in real GDP; infrastructure investment and tax reform each contribute about a quarter.

Infrastructure investment has the longest-lasting impact on growth, through higher productivity. The larger stock of infrastructure lowers transaction and transportation costs. Healthcare- and education-related infrastructure can also increase the quality and productivity of the labor force in the long term.

Rebalancing toward indirect taxes provides most of the benefits to growth in the short term. A hike in VAT discourages consumption, but a cut in personal and corporate income tax more than compensates by stim-

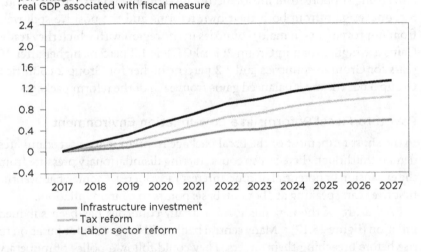

c. Group 2

percentage point difference in real GDP associated with fiscal measure

d. Group 3

percentage point difference in real GDP associated with fiscal measure

— Infrastructure investment
⋯ Tax reform
— Labor sector reform

Source: IMF Staff projections.

ulating investment and encouraging exports, so that real GDP is higher overall (the light grey line minus the dark grey line in figure 15.16). Cutting the personal income tax not only increases the labor supply, it can lower wage costs (the pre-tax wage) faced by firms. Therefore, all else equal, firms pay a higher post-tax wage to households. Similarly, a cut in the corporate income tax encourages investment and capital formation, expanding potential output, lowering the cost of consumer goods, and increasing firms' demand for labor to complement their new capital.

Labor reforms also have a long-term impact (the black line minus the light grey line in figure 15.16). Raising the retirement age shrinks the cohort that relies on government pensions and increases the labor supply. It allows governments to increase the size of pensions per capita without increasing overall spending, which may be crucial in countries where replacement ratios are too low. Provision of child care expands the labor supply by making it easier for women to work, which can be especially useful in countries facing downward labor supply pressures from demographics. Active labor market policies can help lower the long-term unemployment rate. All three measures expand the labor force and increase tax collection (especially personal income tax).

The effect of reforms varies across the three country groups. In Group 1 (Japan) benefits accrue only from increasing childcare spending, which would offset some of the significant impact of demographics; the remaining impacts are spillovers from other countries' measures. Group 2 countries benefit most strongly from labor sector reforms. Outside of China, there is also strong support from infrastructure investment and tax reform. Group 3 countries gain from both their own reforms and the positive spillovers from improvements in major countries in the region with which they trade. Gains are higher than in Group 2: Real GDP is 1.3 percent higher after 10 years for Group 3 countries and 1.2 percent higher for Group 2 countries. Group 3 has the most balanced gains from each of the reform packages.

Payoff to Fiscal Reforms in a Low-Inflation Environment

In the short term, most of the fiscal package is inflationary, as it stimulates demand, although there is also counteracting disinflationary pressure from the expansion of potential output. Interest rates increase somewhat over the first five years, peaking at about 50 basis points to contain inflation.

A feature of the new mediocre in many countries has been subdued inflation (figure 15.17).[20] Many central banks still have room for inflation to rise before breaching their targets. They could follow a policy of monetary accommodation in the short term, which would lead to lower real interest rates than if monetary policy worked to offset the inflationary impact. Such a strategy could be justified in countries facing persistently low inflation, allowing temporary inflation overshooting and convergence to the target from above.[21]

---

20. See Garcia Morales et al. (2018) for a discussion of the Association of Southeast Asian Nations (ASEAN) countries.

21. Similar results are obtained in a scenario in which, rather than adopting a standard linear Taylor rule, monetary policy follows a policy reaction function that minimizes a quadratic loss function of inflation and output gaps.

Figure 15.17 Average number of months inflation rate was below inflation target in selected Asian economies

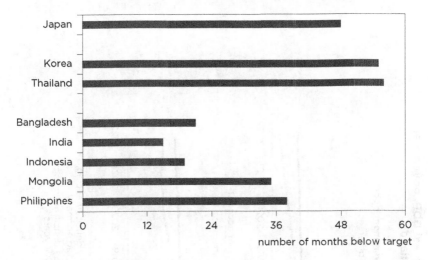

number of months below target

Note: Figure excludes effects of changes in indirect taxes on Consumer Price Index inflation. Data cover January 2013–December 2017.

Sources: IMF, *International Financial Statistics*; IMF Staff calculations.

Infrastructure spending in Thailand—which is financed by lowering general transfers, while the central bank conducts policy as usual—illustrates this point (figure 15.18). If instead the central bank chose to accommodate the stimulus for five years, real GDP would increase by 1.2 percentage points.

Fiscal policy reinforces this effect, provided that higher debt does not increase the sovereign risk premium. If the government were to use debt financing instead of cutting general transfers, it would achieve the same level of growth with the normal conduct of monetary policy, as consumption would be stronger (figure 15.18, solid light grey line minus solid dark grey line). Monetary accommodation with debt financing (figure 15.18, dashed light grey line) would lead to higher real GDP, for two reasons. First, the lower real interest rate provides more stimulus to private investment. Second, higher inflation would further increase nominal GDP, reducing the impact on the debt-to-GDP ratio to 0.8 percent of GDP. Overall, monetary accommodation with debt financing would lead to real GDP that would be 3.2 percent higher by the fifth year.

Need for Supporting Fiscal Institutions and Structural Reforms

Given the fiscal pressures exerted by rapid population aging in many countries, ensuring medium- to long-term sustainability calls for upgrading

Figure 15.18   Projected effect of accommodative monetary policy on real GDP, government debt, consumption, and current account balance in Thailand

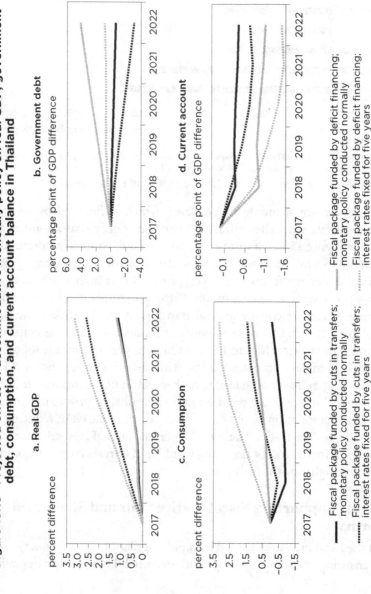

Source: Saenz et al. (2018); IMF Staff calculations.

fiscal institutions and delivering structural reforms. This section focuses on four issues:

- fiscal rules to provide a credible medium-term anchor,
- structural reforms to ensure the viability of pension and healthcare systems,
- efficient revenue mobilization and energy pricing reforms to create fiscal space for spending needs, and
- reforms to state-owned enterprises (SOEs) to unlock growth potential while managing fiscal risks.

Fiscal Rules

A fiscal rule imposes a long-lasting constraint on fiscal policy by setting numerical limits on budgetary aggregates, in order to establish a credible medium- and long-term anchor for fiscal sustainability while mitigating any resulting short-term economic volatility. There are four types of fiscal rules: debt rules, fiscal balance rules, expenditure rules, and revenue rules (Schaechter et al. 2012).

Figure 15.19 shows the share of countries with one of the four types of fiscal rules in each country group over the 30-year period between 1985 and 2015. Most advanced economies, including Japan and Singapore, adopted fiscal rules. In contrast, only about a quarter of Asia's developing economies (including Indonesia, Malaysia, Maldives, Mongolia, Sri Lanka, and Thailand) did so—a significantly smaller share than in emerging Europe, Latin America, or Sub-Saharan Africa.

The design of fiscal rules should be guided by the following principles and practices (Schaechter et al. 2012), while taking country circumstances into account:

- *Provide broad coverage and ensure strong legislative support.* Fiscal rules should also cover all revenue and expenditure items. Excluding public investment from a fiscal balance rule weakens the rule's link to public debt and can provide incentives for creative accounting. Rules enshrined in high-level legislation or the constitution can instill greater commitment and policy credibility.
- *Be neutral or countercyclical.* Rules governing the (unadjusted) fiscal balance can lead to procyclical fiscal policy. To prevent such an effect, rules can set limits on the cyclically adjusted or structural fiscal balance (although there are technical challenges in estimating these measures). An expenditure rule that limits expenditure growth to potential GDP growth is one way to reduce procyclicality.

Figure 15.19 Share of countries with fiscal rules, by region, 1985–2015

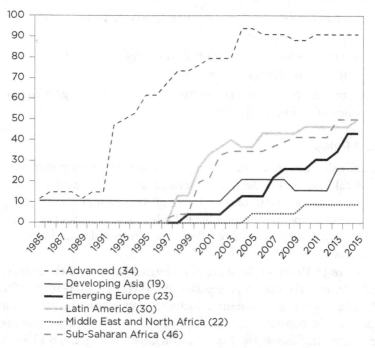

percent of all countries in region

- – – Advanced (34)
- —— Developing Asia (19)
- —— Emerging Europe (23)
- ～～ Latin America (30)
- ······· Middle East and North Africa (22)
- — – Sub-Saharan Africa (46)

Note: Figure excludes supranational rules for countries belonging to currency unions. The number of countries in each group is shown in parentheses in legend.

Source: IMF Fiscal Rules Dataset, www.imf.org/external/datamapper/fiscalrules/map/map.htm; IMF Staff calculations.

- *Allow flexibility in the face of large shocks.* An escape clause can provide flexibility in dealing with a rare but devastating shock (such as a natural disaster). A defined trigger and exit strategy should be articulated.

- *Create supportive arrangements.* Effective implementation of fiscal rules calls for sound public financial management institutions, including medium-term budget frameworks, procedural and transparency requirements for budget processes and fiscal authorities, and independent fiscal councils tasked with assessing compliance with fiscal rules (Corbacho and Ter-Minassian 2013).

Reform of Pension and Healthcare Systems

Rising age-related spending in aging Asian economies may result in unfunded liabilities over the long term. This risk can be mitigated by parametric reforms on pension systems and structural reforms in the healthcare sector.

Aging reduces the sustainability of defined-benefit pension systems. Pensions in China, Japan, Korea, Thailand, and Vietnam—where pension spending is projected to rise faster than in the rest of the region—are at least partially defined-benefit systems (Arbatli et al. 2016). A defined-benefit system with unfunded liabilities requires parametric reforms: raising retirement ages, cutting pension benefits, and/or increasing contribution rates. Among these options, raising retirement ages is generally perceived as preferable, given increases in life expectancy in recent decades and the positive effects of older workers on labor force participation (Clements, Eich, and Gupta 2014). Many Asian economies have scope to increase retirement ages (Arbatli et al. 2016). Reforms could accompany enhanced antipoverty programs for older people and a larger role for private retirement saving schemes to help offset the potential decline in lifetime retirement income (Clements et al. 2015).

Such reforms should start now and proceed gradually, in order to spread the burden across generations. They can be accompanied by automatic adjustment mechanisms that respond to demographic, macroeconomic, and financial developments in a predetermined fashion and without the need for additional policy intervention. Automatic adjustment mechanisms have been embedded in the pension systems of many advanced economies, including Japan, but not in the rest of Asia (Arbatli et al. 2016). Another option is to adopt a notional defined contribution pension scheme, in which contributions are accumulated in an individual account with a notional rate of return and the pension benefit is calculated by dividing the pension wealth by the life expectancy at retirement (Arbatli et al. 2016).

Healthcare costs tend to grow faster than GDP, because of population aging and technological improvements that result in better but less affordable services (Clements et al. 2015). The experience in advanced economies suggests that structural reforms to slow the increase in healthcare costs include promoting some degree of competition among insurers and service providers, supporting primary and preventive care, and improving provider payment systems (Clements et al. 2015).

Given population pressures, policymakers in developing Asia need to consider how to manage the process of expanding the coverage of pensions and healthcare systems. In economies with low labor market informality and efficient revenue administration, it is easier to expand a social insurance scheme. In economies with high labor informality, general taxes may need to finance such protection (Jenkner, Clements, and Shang 2012).

Efficient Revenue Mobilization and Energy Pricing Reforms

Many Asian economies will need to mobilize revenue mobilization to increase spending on physical and human capital, health care, and pensions.

Increasing efficiency calls for a larger role for indirect taxes. Closing VAT collection gaps arising from exemptions and low compliance can enhance the productivity of the tax without increasing rates. Raising excise taxes on alcohol, tobacco, and even sugar can be justified on health grounds (IMF 2015a). The regressive impact of higher indirect taxes can be compensated for by expanding programs that disproportionately benefit the poor. Rationalizing tax exemptions and preferential tax treatment could mobilize revenue and promote equity. Revenue administration should be improved through risk-based compliance strategies, proper segmentation of taxpayers, and simplification of laws and procedures (IMF 2015a).

Continuing to eliminate energy subsidies and introducing environmental taxes can create fiscal space efficiently and equitably. Energy subsidies distort consumption and production decisions and are often very poorly targeted (Coady, Flamini, and Sears 2015). Replacing these subsidies with targeted social assistance can free up resources for productive spending while enhancing the redistributive role of fiscal policies. Environmental taxes such as carbon taxes can create fiscal space while addressing negative environmental externalities.

Reform of State-Owned Enterprises

Reforming SOEs can boost productivity growth and create new jobs by increasing market orientation. SOEs have large footprints in emerging Asia. A composite measure of SOEs' share in sales, assets, and market values exceeds 50 percent in China, India, Indonesia, and Malaysia (Kowalski et al. 2013). Unlocking growth potential requires establishing a level playing field for SOEs and privately owned enterprises operating on a commercial basis (OECD 2015). It can be accomplished by increasing the share of SOEs' profits that go to the government budget, eliminating government subsidies, strengthening governance, and improving SOEs' commercial orientation. Ultimately, reform must also include greater tolerance of bankruptcy or exit of SOEs (Lipton 2016).

At the same time, contingent liabilities emanating from SOEs need to be managed prudently. Bailouts of troubled SOEs cost governments about 3 percent of GDP on average—15 percent of GDP in the most extreme cases—between 1990 and 2014 (Bova et al. 2016). Governments can reduce exposure to SOE-related fiscal risks by strengthening governance arrangements, holding SOE management accountable for performance against financial and operational targets, mandating financial reporting and audits based on International Financial Reporting Standards, and legislating explicit no-bailout clauses for SOEs (IMF 2016, Allen and Alves 2016).

Concluding Remarks

This chapter analyzed the implications of rapid population aging and weak productivity for medium- to long-term fiscal sustainability and quantified the potential of fiscal reforms to improve future growth paths.

Left unchecked, rapid population aging and the related increase in public pension and healthcare spending may threaten long-term fiscal sustainability in many Asian economies. The scenario analysis conducted in this chapter shows that the impact of demographics will drive public debt up over the long term, even under the benign assumption that interest rates remain low enough and growth high enough. A reversal of the favorable differential between interest rates and growth that helped keep debt ratios in check in recent times would put debt dynamics at further risk. In a highly uncertain global setting, higher sovereign risk premia or tighter financing conditions could trigger this risk, particularly for countries with weaker fundamentals.

Fiscal policy can, and must, address the long-term implications of the new mediocre. Many countries have scope to spur growth by redirecting budgets to infrastructure, human capital, and R&D and increasing the efficiency of spending and tax systems. Model-based simulations calibrated for Asia illustrate the growth payoff of fiscal reform packages that increase infrastructure spending, rebalance taxes toward VAT, and implement labor sector reforms. Even budget-neutral packages have the power to raise growth, in both the short and the long term. Dividends are higher when reforms exploit synergies, mitigate any adverse on impact inequality, and generate positive regional spillovers.

The time for action is now. After the global financial crisis, inflation and interest rates remained low by historical standards but are expected to rise over the medium term. In this environment, a case can be made for financing fiscal reforms through debt and for combining fiscal and monetary stimulus. In the example in the chapter, the impact on growth of an infrastructure stimulus financed with debt under monetary accommodation could be 2.5 times larger than the same budget-neutral reform without monetary accommodation. Critical to this result is that sovereign risk premia be contained. Given pressures from rapid aging in many countries, credible fiscal anchors and broader institutional and fiscal reforms should be immediate priorities to secure long-term fiscal sustainability and reap the growth benefits of fiscal stimulus.

Appendix 15A Public Spending Efficiency Frontiers

Data Envelopment Analysis (DEA) applies linear programming methods to build an efficiency frontier by connecting the bundles of units (countries) for which no other unit (country) produces the same or more output with a given amount of input. For each economy analyzed in this chapter, table 15A.1 shows the distance from the efficiency frontier, calculated as the percentage difference in the output variable (e.g., quality of infrastructure, secondary school enrollment, scores on the Programme for International Student Assessment (PISA), and healthy life expectancy relative to the frontier at the corresponding level of the input variables (public capital stock, public spending on education and health care).

Table 15A.1 Distance of selected Asian economies from public spending efficiency frontier (percent)

Group/ economy	Quality of infrastructure	Secondary school enrollment	PISA score	Healthy life expectancy
		Group 1		
Japan	−13.7	−2.1	−4.1	0
		Group 2		
Korea	−10.0	−5.2	−5.8	0
Singapore	0	n.a.	0	−1.0
China	−29.2	n.a.	−14.7	−4.7
Thailand	−18.9	−19.9	n.a.	−6.4
		Group 3		
Bangladesh	−31.0	−36.9	n.a.	−2.3
Cambodia	−13.3	n.a.	n.a.	−7.1
India	−30.4	−32.9	n.a.	−6.5
Indonesia	−31.4	−18.2	−4.7	−3.8
Laos	−28.8	n.a.	n.a.	−6.7
Malaysia	−9.6	−30.9	−9.6	−6.7
Mongolia	−58.1	−13.2	n.a.	−6.8
Philippines	−36.2	−19.1	n.a.	−7.5
Sri Lanka	−17.1	−7.2	n.a.	−1.8
Vietnam	−36.6	n.a.	n.a.	−2.2

n.a. = not available; PISA = Programme for International Student Assessment

Sources: Organization for Economic Cooperation and Development; World Economic Forum; World Health Organization.

Appendix 15B Composition and Cost of Fiscal Packages

Tables 15B.1 and 15B.2 show the composition and cost of the fiscal packages examined in this chapter. Spending and tax measures are permanent (annual) unless stated otherwise; spending measures are phased in over three years. For spending, a positive number indicates higher spending; for taxes, a positive number indicates higher collection. For the decomposition of the personal income tax household shares in table 15B.2, the share of liquidity-constrained households is approximate.

Table 15B.1   Composition of fiscal packages in selected Asian economies

Group/economy	Infrastructure spending	Tax reform (increase in VAT, cut in personal and corporate income tax)	Labor reforms (increase in retirement age, extension of child care, active labor market policies)
Group 1			
Japan	None	Personal income tax only (1 percent of GDP to liquidity-constrained households from saving households)	Yes, financed by higher VAT
Group 2			
China	None	None	Yes, financed by additional personal income tax (not imposed on liquidity-constrained households)
Hong Kong	None	Cut to taxes other than personal income tax	Yes, financed by additional personal income tax
Korea	None	Yes	Yes, financed by additional personal income tax
Singapore	None	Yes	Yes, financed by additional personal income tax
Thailand	Public-private partnership (PPP), financed by five-year cut in transfers	Liquidity-constrained households receive all of the personal income tax cut and a VAT rebate of 0.5 percent of GDP	Yes, financed by additional personal income tax (not imposed on liquidity-constrained households)
Group 3			
Bangladesh	Public only, financed by tax reform	VAT increase only (not imposed on liquidity-constrained households); no personal or corporate income tax	Yes, financed by tax reform
Cambodia	PPP, funded by deficit finance	Liquidity-constrained households receive all of the personal income tax cut and a VAT rebate of 0.5 percent of GDP	Yes, funded by deficit finance
India	None	None	Yes, financed by additional excise taxes

Group 3

Indonesia	PPP, financed by five-year cut in transfers	Liquidity-constrained households receive all of the personal income tax cut and a VAT rebate of 0.5 percent of GDP	Yes, financed by additional personal income tax (not imposed on liquidity-constrained households)
Malaysia	PPP, financed by five-year cut in transfers	Liquidity-constrained households receive all of the personal income tax cut and a VAT rebate of 0.5 percent of GDP	Yes, financed by additional personal income tax (not imposed on liquidity-constrained households)
Mongolia	PPP, financed by five-year cut in transfers	Liquidity-constrained households receive all of the personal income tax cut and a VAT rebate of 0.5 percent of GDP	Yes, financed by additional personal income tax (not imposed on liquidity-constrained households)
Philippines	PPP, financed by five-year cut in transfers	Liquidity-constrained households receive all of the personal income tax cut and a VAT rebate of 0.5 percent of GDP	Yes, deficit finance
Sri Lanka	PPP, financed by five-year additional VAT	None	Yes, financed by additional personal income tax (not imposed on liquidity-constrained households)
Vietnam	PPP, financed by five-year cut in transfers	Liquidity-constrained households receive all of the personal income tax cut and a VAT rebate of 0.5 percent of GDP	Yes, financed by additional personal income tax (not imposed on liquidity-constrained households)
Pacific Island countries	PPP, financed by five-year cut in transfers	Liquidity-constrained households receive all of the personal income tax cut and a VAT rebate of 0.5 percent of GDP	Yes, financed by additional personal income tax (not imposed on liquidity-constrained households)

VAT = value-added tax; PPP = purchasing power parity

Source: IMF Staff assumptions for illustrative purposes.

Table 15B.2 Cost of fiscal packages in selected Asian economies (percent of GDP change in fiscal instruments relative to baseline)

Group/economy	Government deficit	Government consumption	Share of public investment	General transfers	Transfers to liquidity-constrained households	Value-added tax	Personal income tax	Corporate income tax
Group 1								
Japan	None	0.25	None	0.25	None	0.5	-1.00 for liquidity-constrained households, +1.00 for saving households	None
Group 2								
China	None	0.25	None	0.25	None	None	+0.50 for saving households	None
Hong Kong	None	0.25	None	-0.25 for five years, +0.25 thereafter	None	1.5	-0.40 for liquidity-constrained households, +0.15 for saving households	-0.75
Korea	None	0.25	None	0.25	None	1.5	-0.40 for liquidity-constrained households, +0.15 for saving households	-0.75
Singapore	None	0.25	None	-0.25 for five years, +0.25 thereafter	None	1.5	-0.40 for liquidity-constrained households, +0.15 for saving households	-0.75
Thailand	None	0.25	+0.50 for five years	-0.25 for five years, +0.25 thereafter	0.5	2	-0.59 for liquidity-constrained households, +0.34 for saving households	-0.75

	Group 3							
Bangladesh	-0.80 after year five years	0.25	+1.00 for five years	+0.25	0.5	2	None	None
Cambodia	0.5	0.25	+0.50 for five years	+0.25	0.5	2	-0.75 for liquidity-constrained households	-0.75
India	None	0.25	None	0.25	None	None, but +0.5 on excise tax	None	None
Indonesia	None	0.25	+0.50 for five years	-0.25 for five years, +0.25 thereafter	0.5	2	-0.59 for liquidity-constrained households, +0.34 for saving households	-0.75
Malaysia	None	0.25	+0.50 for five years	-0.25 for five years, +0.25 thereafter	0.5	2	-0.59 for liquidity-constrained households, +0.34 for saving households	-0.75
Mongolia	None	0.25	+0.50 for five years	-0.25 for five years, +0.25 thereafter	0.5	2	-0.59 for liquidity-constrained households, +0.34 for saving households	-0.75
Philippines	0.5	0.25	+0.50 for five years	+0.25	0.5	2	-0.75 for liquidity-constrained households	-0.75
Sri Lanka	None	0.25	+0.50 for five years	+0.25	0.5	+0.5 five years only	+0.50 for saving households	None
Vietnam	None	0.25	+0.50 for five years	-0.25 for five years, +0.25 thereafter	+0.5	2	-0.59 for liquidity-constrained households, +0.34 for saving households	-0.75
Pacific Island Countries	None	0.25	+1.00 for five years	-0.25 for five years, +0.25 thereafter	0.5	2	-0.59 for liquidity-constrained households, +0.34 for saving households	-0.75

Source: IMF Staff assumptions for illustrative purposes.

References

Allen, R., and M. Alves. 2016. *How to Improve the Financial Oversight of Public Corporations*. IMF Fiscal Affairs Department How-to-Note 5/2016. Washington: International Monetary Fund.

Amaglobeli, D., and W. Shi. 2016. *How to Assess Fiscal Implications of Demographic Shifts: A Granular Approach*. IMF Fiscal Affairs Department How-to-Note 2/2016. Washington: International Monetary Fund.

Andrle, M., P. Blagrave, P. Espaillat, K. Honjo, B. Hunt, M. Kortelainen, R. Lalonde, D. Laxton, E. Mavroeidi, D. Muir, S. Mursula, and S. Snudden. 2015. *The Flexible System of Global Models (FSGM)*. IMF Working Paper 15/64. Washington: International Monetary Fund.

Araki, S., and I. Claus. 2014. *A Comparative Analysis of Tax Administration in Asia and the Pacific*. Manila: Asian Development Bank.

Arbatli, E., C. Feher, J. Ree, I. Saito, and M. Soto. 2016. *Automatic Adjustment Mechanisms in Asian Pension Systems?* IMF Working Paper 16/242. Washington: International Monetary Fund.

Arnold J., B. Brys, C. Heady, A. Johansson, C. Schwellnus, and L. Vartia. 2011. Tax Policy for Economic Recovery and Growth. *Economic Journal* 121: 1006–1036.

Banerji, A., V. Crispolti, E. Dabla-Norris, R. Duval, C. Ebeke, D. Furceri, T. Komatsuzaki, and T. Poghosyan. 2017. *Labor and Product Market Reforms in Advanced Economies: Fiscal Costs, Gains, and Support*. IMF Staff Discussion Note 17/03. Washington: International Monetary Fund.

Bassanini, A., and R. Duval. 2006. *Employment Patterns in OECD Countries: Reassessing the Role of Policies and Institutions*. OECD Economics Department Working Paper 486. Paris: OECD Publishing.

Bouis, R., and R. Duval. 2011. *Raising Potential Growth After the Crisis: A Quantitative Assessment of the Potential Gains from Various Structural Reforms in the OECD Area and Beyond*. OECD Economics Department Working Paper 835. Paris: OECD Publishing.

Bova, E., M. Ruiz-Arranz, F. Toscana, and H. Elif Ture. 2016. *The Fiscal Costs of Contingent Liabilities: A New Dataset*. IMF Working Paper WP/16/14. Washington: International Monetary Fund.

Buffie, E., A. Berg, C. Pattillo, R. Portillo, and L. Zanna. 2012. *Public Investment, Growth, and Debt Sustainability: Putting Together the Pieces*. IMF Working Paper WP/12/144. Washington: International Monetary Fund.

Clements, B., K. Dybczak, V. Gaspar, S. Gupta, and M. Soto. 2015. *The Fiscal Consequences of Shrinking Populations*. IMF Staff Discussion Note 15/21. Washington: International Monetary Fund.

Clements, B., F. Eich, and G. Gupta, eds. 2014. *Equitable and Sustainable Pensions: Challenges and Experience*. Washington: International Monetary Fund.

Coady, D., V. Flamini, and L. Sears. 2015. *The Unequal Benefits of Fuel Subsidies Revisited: Evidence for Developing Countries*. IMF Working Paper WP/15/250. Washington: International Monetary Fund.

Corbacho, A., and T. Ter-Minassian. 2013. Public Financial Management Requirements for Effective Implementation of Fiscal Rules. In *The International Handbook of Public Financial Management*, ed. R. Allen, R. Hemming, and B.H. Potter. London: Palgrave Macmillan.

Ebrill, L. P., M. Keen, V. P. Summers, eds. 2001. *The Modern VAT*. Washington: International Monetary Fund.

Escolano, J., A. Shabunina, and J. Woo. 2017. The Puzzle of Persistently Negative Interest-Rate-Growth Differentials: Financial Repression or Income Catch-Up? *Fiscal Studies* 38, no. 2: 179–217.

Garcia Morales, J.A. et al. 2018. Monetary Policy in the New Normal. In *The ASEAN Way: Sustaining Growth and Stability*, ed. A. Corbacho and S. J. Peiris. Washington: International Monetary Fund.

Gaspar, V., M. Obstfeld, and R. Sahay. 2016. *Macroeconomic Management When Policy Space Is Constrained: A Comprehensive, Consistent, and Coordinated Approach to Economic Policy*. IMF Staff Discussion Note 16/09. Washington: International Monetary Fund.

Global Infrastructure Hub and Oxford Economics. 2017. *Global Infrastructure Outlook: Infrastructure Investment Needs: 50 Countries, 7 Sectors to 2040*. https://www.gihub.org/.

IMF (International Monetary Fund). 2012. *Philippines: Technical Assistance Report on Road Map for pro-Growth and Equitable Tax System*. IMF Country Report 12/60. Washington

IMF (International Monetary Fund). 2014a. Can Fiscal Policy Do More for Jobs? *Fiscal Monitor*, October. Washington.

IMF (International Monetary Fund). 2014b. Is It Time for an Infrastructure Push? The Macroeconomic Effects of Public Investment. *World Economic Outlook*, October. Washington.

IMF (International Monetary Fund). 2014c. Perspectives on Global Real Interest Rates. *World Economic Outlook*, April. Washington.

IMF (International Monetary Fund). 2015a. *Fiscal Policy and Long-Term Growth*. IMF Policy Paper, June. Washington.

IMF (International Monetary Fund). 2015b. *Making Public Investment More Efficient*. IMF Policy Paper, June. Washington.

IMF (International Monetary Fund). 2016. *Analyzing and Managing Fiscal Risks: Best Practices*. IMF Policy Paper, May. Washington.

IMF (International Monetary Fund). 2017a. Asia: At Risk of Growing Old before Becoming Rich? In *Regional Economic Outlook: Asia and Pacific*, April. Washington.

IMF (International Monetary Fund). 2017b. The New Mediocre. and the Outlook for Productivity in Asia. In *Regional Economic Outlook: Asia and Pacific*, April. Washington.

IMF (International Monetary Fund). 2017c. *World Economic Outlook*, April. Washington.

Jenkner, E., B. Clements, and B. Shang. 2012. Health Reform Lessons from Experiences of Emerging Economies. In *The Economics of Public Health Care Reform in Advanced and Emerging Economies*, ed. B. Clements, D. Coady, and S. Gupta. Washington: International Monetary Fund.

Jones, R., and M. Kim. 2014. *Fostering a Creative Economy to Drive Korean Growth*. OECD Economics Department Working Paper 1152. Paris: OECD Publishing.

Kowalski, P., M. Büge, M. Sztajerowska, and M. Egeland. 2013. *State-Owned Enterprises: Trade Effects and Policy Implications*. OECD Working Paper of the Trade Committee, TAD/TC/WP(2012)10/FINAL. Paris: Organization for Economic Cooperation and Development.

Lipton, D. 2016. Preparing the Ground: China's Quest for Sustainable Growth Calls for Bold Fiscal Reforms. *Finance & Development*, March.

Mankiw, N. G. 2015. Yes, r > g. So What? *American Economic Review: Papers and Proceedings* 105, no. 5: 43–47.

OECD (Organization for Economic Cooperation and Development). 2015. *Guidelines on Corporate Governance of State-Owned Enterprises*. Paris.

Phillips, Steven T., Luis Catão, Luca A. Ricci, Rudolfs Bems, Mitali Das, Julian Di Giovanni, Filiz D. Unsal, Marola Castillo, Jungjin Lee, Jair Rodriguez, Mauricio Vargas. 2013. *The External Balance Assessment (EBA) Methodology*. IMF Working Paper 13/272. Washington: International Monetary Fund.

Saenz, M., A. Corbacho, I. Fukunaga, D. Muir, S.J. Peiris, and S. Rafiq. 2018. Macroeconomic Policy Synergies for Sustained Growth. In *The ASEAN Way: Sustaining Growth and Stability*, ed. A. Corbacho and S.J. Peiris. Washington: International Monetary Fund.

Schaechter, A., N. Budina, T. Kinda, and A. Weber. 2012. *Fiscal Rules in Response to the Crisis: Toward the "Next-Generation" Rules. A Dataset*. IMF Working Paper 12/187. Washington: International Monetary Fund.

United Nations. 2015. *World Population Prospects: The 2015 Revision*. New York: Population Division, Department of Economic and Social Affairs.

World Bank. 2012. *Creating Fiscal Space through Revenue Mobilization*. South Asia Economic Focus, June. Washington.

16

Global Imbalances and the Trade Slowdown: Implications for Asia

CAROLINE FREUND

The current global trade slowdown is unprecedented in recent history. Global trade volumes plummeted 13 percent in 2009, many times the 2 percent decline in real GDP growth experienced in the depths of the Great Recession. While the trade collapse shocked economists, the slowdown in trade growth since 2011 has been an even bigger surprise. Real trade grew more than twice as fast as real GDP from 1990 to 2007, and more than 1.5 times as fast even before 1990, but since 2011 trade has grown only slightly faster than GDP.

Researchers have explored a number of potential explanations for the recent change in the relationship between income growth and trade growth. Most research points to a decline in demand, especially for investment goods that weigh heavily in trade flows, as the main factor.

Overlooked in the debate is how greater capital mobility and widening global imbalances may have enhanced the effects of demand on trade in the 1990s and early 2000s. In the period when trade surged, global imbalances also ballooned. If the excess savings in some countries financed more consumption and investment in other countries, then trade and trade imbalances would logically move together. Put differently, the ability to borrow from abroad allowed deficit countries to import more than they would have if they had been constrained by their exports, thus stimulating trade growth.

Caroline Freund, senior fellow at the Peterson Institute for International Economics since May 2013, is on leave for public service as director of trade, competition and investment climate at the World Bank. She is grateful to Olivier Blanchard, Jérémie Cohen-Setton, Davin Chor, Joseph Gagnon, Thomas Helbling, Maurice Obstfeld, Adam Posen, and conference participants for discussions and comments on an earlier draft.

Figure 16.1 Global imbalances and global trade since 1982

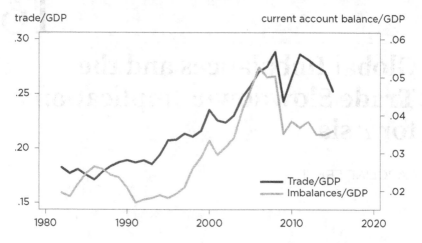

Note: Data are for a balanced sample of 76 countries, taken in US dollars.
Sources: World Bank, World Development Indicators; author's calculations.

Figure 16.1 shows global imbalances across 76 countries with data going back to 1982. Global imbalances are calculated as the sum of the absolute values of the countries' current account balances relative to the sum of their incomes. When savings and investment in the large countries are equal, global imbalances will be close to zero. When some countries, such as China, Japan, Korea, and the Gulf countries, expanded their surpluses, and others, like the United States and several Southern European countries, expanded their deficits, the measure of global imbalances grew.

The figure also shows the ratio of trade to GDP, measured as total imports to total GDP for the same group of countries. Since about 1995, as global imbalances surged, so too did trade growth. The correlation between the ratio of trade to GDP and the ratio of global imbalances to GDP since 1995 is 0.80; the correlation before 1995 was –0.61.

Figure 16.2 shows the relationship in growth rates. Again, the correlation expands over time. The correlation was zero prior to 1995 and is 0.66 after 1995.

Further evidence of the relationship between imbalances and trade is apparent when countries are split according to the magnitude of their current account balances. For countries with current account balances exceeding 2.5 percent of GDP, the correlation between trade growth and growth in global imbalances since 1995 is 0.67, while for the group with more balanced trade it is 0.25. The high correlation is not just a US and China effect. Excluding China and the United States, the correlation between global imbalances and trade growth for large-imbalance countries is 0.55 and the correlation for balanced-trade countries remains 0.25.

Figure 16.2 Growth in ratios of trade/GDP and imbalances/GDP

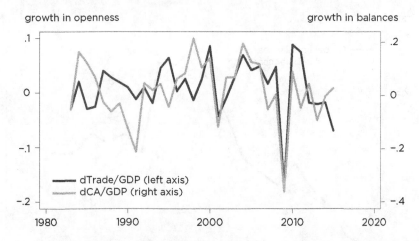

Note: Data are for a balanced sample of 76 countries, taken in US dollars.
Sources: World Bank, *World Development Indicators*; author's calculations.

Relationship between Imbalances and Trade

There is no reason that growing imbalances must be associated with rapid trade growth, but there is a potential mechanical relationship if trade grows faster than GDP. This section shows that rapid trade growth was not sufficient to explain widening trade balances in the late 1990s and 2000s.

Assume imports and exports both grow at a constant rate, higher than GDP growth. Starting from a position of unbalanced trade, imbalances as a share of income will expand over time as trade grows. However, in this case, global imbalances relative to global trade should remain constant. This is a conservative assumption in the sense that it implies that for deficit countries international borrowing expands faster than income as trade grows.

For example, assume exports and imports are growing twice as fast as GDP (as happened in the 1990s), but trade growth is constant across exports and imports, then we have:

Global imbalances/GDP at time

$$t+1 = t+1 = \frac{\sum_i |(1+2x)*X_i - (1+2x)*M_i|}{\sum_i (1+x)GDP_i} = \frac{(1+2x)}{(1+x)} * \frac{\sum_i |X_i - M_i|}{\sum_i GDP_i} \qquad (16.1)$$

Global imbalances/total trade at time

$$t+1 = t+1 = \frac{\sum_i |(1+2x)*X_i - (1+2x)*M_i|}{\sum_i (1+2x)(X_i + M_i)} = \frac{\sum_i |X_i - M_i|}{\sum_i (X_i + M_i)} \qquad (16.2)$$

where x denotes GDP growth and i is the index for individual countries.

As trade grows faster than income, imbalances as a share of GDP increase, but imbalances as a share of total trade do not. In fact, over the period

Figure 16.3 Global imbalances/GDP versus global imbalances/trade

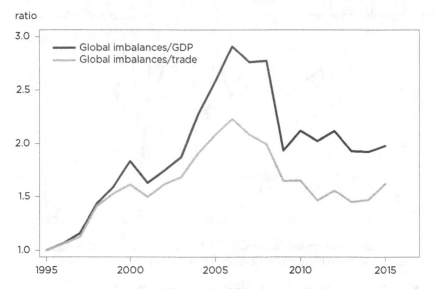

ratio

Note: Data are for a balanced sample of 76 countries, taken in US dollars.
Sources: World Bank, *World Development Indicators*; author's calculations.

in question both increased (figure 16.3), indicating that the growth in imbalances was associated with relatively high import growth in the importer/deficit countries and relatively high export growth in the exporter/surplus countries.

Decomposing Trade Growth

If trade imbalances boosted trade growth in the 1990s and 2000s, then exports from surplus countries and imports by deficit countries would be expected to drive a large share of global trade. In fact, this is exactly what happened.

Figure 16.4 divides countries into three groups: deficit countries (those with average deficit above 2.5 percent of GDP), surplus countries (those with average surplus above 2.5 percent of GDP), and countries with balanced trade. It shows each group's contribution to global real trade growth during the rapid growth period and during the slowdown. The period of rapid trade growth is 1998–2008 (1998 is the first year because data on real trade growth for China begin in this year). As shown in the left panel, during the period of rapid trade growth, strong import growth in deficit countries and strong export growth in surplus countries were important contributors to trade growth. In the recent slowdown (2012–15), trade growth has been both lower and more balanced.

Figure 16.4   Contribution to real trade growth, by type, before and after the financial crisis

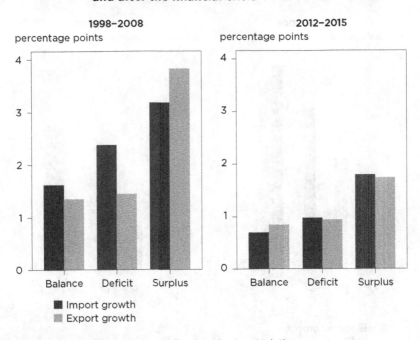

Sources: International Monetary Fund; author's calculations.

Figure 16.5 shows contributions by region. The rapid trade growth period was associated with rapid export growth in Asia and rapid import growth in the Americas. During the slowdown, trade in Europe also slowed markedly, but it was more balanced, linked to slowing growth associated with the euro crisis.

Figure 16.6 shows the contribution to trade growth by countries in East Asia and the United States, before and after the financial crisis. China recorded especially fast-growing exports and the United States recorded especially fast-growing imports in the rapid growth period. Both moderated in the slowdown period, the gaps between export and import growth closed, and in the case of China reversed. Among other East Asian countries, Japan and Korea also experienced widening trade imbalances in the early period, which have disappeared or reversed since 2011.

Imbalances and Trade Growth at the Country Level

If imbalances are associated with more trade, this link should be apparent at the country level as well, at least for the large countries driving aggregate trade and imbalances. This section examines whether trade grew faster than GDP in periods when imbalances were expanding, within countries

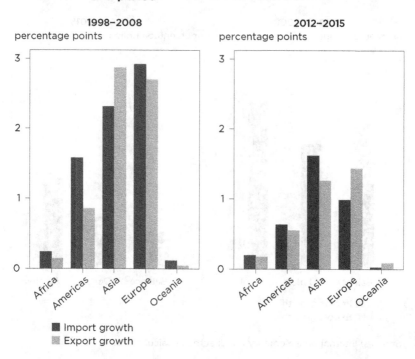

1998–2008

percentage points

2012–2015

percentage points

■ Import growth
▨ Export growth

Sources: International Monetary Fund; author's calculations.

over time, controlling for global growth. In the basic regression, the dependent variable is the change in the ratio of trade to GDP and the independent variable is the change in the absolute volume of imbalances to GDP. Year fixed effects are included in all regressions to pick up global trade growth.

One concern with this specification is that if exports and imports are growing at a constant rate, then trade imbalances could widen because of the mechanical relationship described earlier. To account for this possibility, the growth in absolute balance relative to trade is, conservatively, used as an alternative independent variable:

$$\frac{Trade_{it}}{GDP_{it}} - \frac{Trade_{it-1}}{GDP_{it-1}} = \gamma_t + \beta \left[\frac{AbsBalance_{it}}{Trade_{it}} - \frac{AbsBalance_{it-1}}{Trade_{it-1}} \right] + \varepsilon_{it}$$

The variable of interest, the growth in the absolute balance relative to trade, will increase only if imbalances expand faster than total trade. This regression tests whether periods when trade is growing faster than income are also periods when imbalances are growing faster than total trade. The year fixed effect, γ_t, controls for increasing openness over the period and

**Figure 16.6 Contribution to global real trade growth, by country
and period**

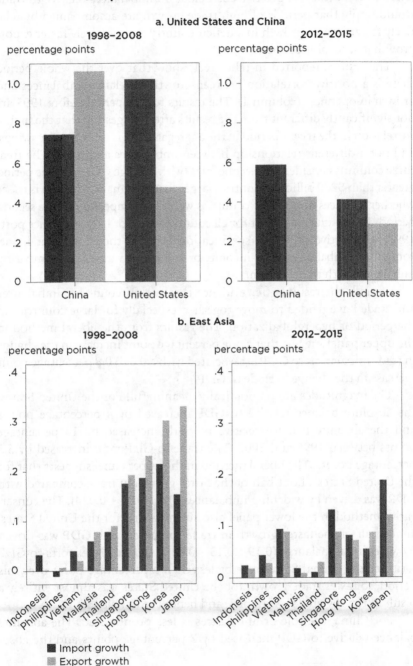

a. United States and China

1998–2008
percentage points

2012–2015
percentage points

b. East Asia

1998–2008
percentage points

2012–2015
percentage points

■ Import growth
■ Export growth

Sources: International Monetary Fund; author's calculations.

global shocks.[1] The variable of interest is the increase in the level of imbalances to total trade. A positive coefficient on imbalances relative to trade would imply that periods of high trade growth are accompanied by relatively faster import growth in a deficit country and relatively faster export growth in a surplus country.

The results, reported in table 16.1, show that over the whole period there is a positive correlation between growth in relative imbalances and growth in openness (column 1). The results for the period before 1995 are not significantly different from the results after, suggesting that the higher correlation in the recent period in the aggregate data is due to larger swings, and not a different relationship between imbalances and trade. The final three columns consider large economies (with average GDP over the period greater than $200 billion), countries larger than Denmark. The idea is to see whether balances in systemic countries were more important in the second period. The results are robust for all countries and for large countries post-1995, irrespective of which specification is used—the more liberal one, comparing imbalances with income, or the conservative one, comparing imbalances with trade (column 6).

Overall, the results offer evidence that within countries, imbalances and trade have tended to move together, especially for large countries in the period of hyperglobalization. The results from the liberal method in the upper panel suggest that a one percentage point increase in the change in trade imbalances to GDP is associated with a 0.6 to 0.8 percentage point increase in the change in trade to GDP.

The magnitudes are economically meaningful. For the United States, the absolute balance relative to GDP increased by 4 percentage points and the absolute balance relative to trade increased by 13 percentage points between 1995 and 2007. The trade-to-GDP ratio increased by 5.5 percentage points. The liberal method in the upper panel suggests that for the United States, about half of the faster growth in trade compared with GDP was driven by widening imbalances (0.6 * 0.04 = 0.024). The conservative method in the lower panel also suggests that for the United States, about half of the faster growth in trade compared with GDP was driven by widening imbalances (0.19 * 0.13 = 0.025). In fact, the exports-to-GDP ratio for the United States rose by less than a percentage point over this period, so faster trade growth for the United States was almost entirely a result of rapidly growing imports, and hence the imbalance.

For China, the role of imbalances is less pronounced. The absolute balance relative to GDP increased by 7 percentage points and the abso-

---

1. Results are almost identical if country fixed effects are included (not reported). Since the equation is in first differences, country effects control for constant growth in openness.

Table 16.1 Panel regressions on trade and absolute balance

Variable	Dependent variable: d(trade/GDP)					
	All (1)	Pre-1995 (2)	Post-1995 (3)	Large (4)	Pre-1995 large (5)	Post-1995 large (6)
d(absolute value of imbalance/GDP)	0.756*** (0.0550)	0.813*** (0.0654)	0.730*** (0.0765)	0.669*** (0.245)	0.829 (0.553)	0.560*** (0.163)
Observations	5,870	2,013	3,857	922	356	566
R-squared	0.317	0.281	0.337	0.270	0.175	0.356
d(absolute value of imbalance/trade)	0.123* (0.0641)	0.155** (0.0654)	0.1000 (0.0999)	0.0916 (0.0608)	0.0342 (0.0736)	0.194** (0.0913)
Observations	5,870	2,013	3,857	922	356	566
R-squared	0.065	0.034	0.082	0.203	0.082	0.316

Notes: All regressions include year fixed effects. Robust standard errors in parentheses. *** p<0.01, ** p<0.05, * p<0.1

Source: Author's calculations.

lute balance relative to trade increased by 9 percentage points between 1995 and 2007, implying that imbalances contributed to an expansion of openness in China of only 2 to 4 percentage points. For China, the trade-to-GDP ratio increased by 28 percentage points, mainly driven by the exports-to-GDP ratio, which increased by 18 percentage points. But import growth was also vibrant: The imports-to-GDP ratio was up 10 percentage points.

What Would Trade Growth Have Looked Like under More Balanced Global Trade?

An alternative way of investigating the potential effect of global imbalances on trade growth is to assume exports constrain current account deficits. The focus is on import constraint in deficit countries because global imbalances after the financial crisis contracted almost entirely because of a reduction in demand in deficit countries (IMF 2014). In addition, widening deficits—not surpluses—are a systemic risk.

For this exercise, nominal data are used because current accounts are measured in current dollars. The year 2015 is excluded because nominal trade declined sharply that year owing to the 50 percent drop in oil prices.

Two series are created: one restricts countries to trade balance and the second allows countries to run deficits similar to historical norms. Specifically, under the latter case, for each deficit country, imports are assumed to be constrained to ensure that the trade deficit to GDP does not exceed

1. 2.5 percent of GDP and

2. the average value plus 2 standard deviations, during the period 1980–95.

The first criterion ensures that the deficit is reasonably large. The second ensures that it is larger than its historical norm. The second condition is important because a number of small developing countries had large imbalances in the 1990s, and the rule allows them to maintain these imbalances.

For countries where the deficit reaches the limit, imports are assumed to decline to the level that would allow the current account deficit to be within one standard deviation of its historical value or to trade balance, whichever is larger. This case maintains global imbalances near an average of 2.5 percent of GDP.

For both specifications, feedback effects to surplus countries are incorporated because exports use imports in their production. The feedback

Figure 16.7 Trade/GDP ratio without growing imbalances

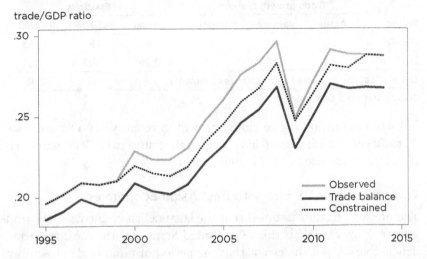

trade/GDP ratio

Sources: International Monetary Fund; Organization for Economic Cooperation and Development; author's calculations.

effect is based on the import content of exports in each year.[2] Specifically, for global trade to be balanced, exports above balance from surplus countries must decline by the same amount as the decline in excess imports by deficit countries. The export reduction is then translated to an import reduction in surplus countries, using the annual average import content of exports. No further feedback effects from the decline in imports by surplus countries are assumed.

Figure 16.7 shows observed exports and predicted exports assuming current account balances were restricted to be balanced or to prevent imbalances from exceeding historical norms. In both cases, the ramp-up in trade would have been somewhat slower than was realized. In the case where trade deficits are constrained, but not limited to balanced trade, the 2012–14 growth slowdown is less dramatic because the 2010–11 rebound in trade happens more gradually than actually occurred.

Table 16.2 records average trade growth for the periods 1995–2008 and 2012–14, for observed flows and the series where current account balances were restricted. It also shows average trade growth relative to average income growth. The evidence is consistent with growing imbalances contributing to more rapid trade growth during the first period and moderating trade

---

2. Data on exports, imports, GDP, and the import share of exports are available for 57 countries from the OECD Trade in Value Added (TiVA) database.

Table 16.2 Responsiveness of trade to income and global imbalances

Period	Trade growth (percent)			Elasticity		
	Actual	Balanced	Restricted	Actual	Balanced	Restricted
1995–2008	8.5	8.1	8.1	1.60	1.53	1.53
2012–2014	2.2	2.3	2.7	0.98	1.03	1.21
Share of decline explained by imbalances (percent)					19	48

Source: Author's calculations.

imbalances contributing to slower growth in recent years. Overall, about 20 to 50 percent of the drop in trade growth relative to GDP growth can be explained by the rise and fall in imbalances.

Transmission of US Shock to East Asian Economies

The previous section assumed that the large deficit countries drove trade growth. How feasible is this? The United States was the most important deficit country. To the extent that the period of rapid trade growth was driven by US demand fueling export growth in Asia, trade in the Asian economies would tend to move with US total imports. This section explores whether US imports are positively correlated with the total exports and imports of East Asian surplus countries.

Table 16.3 shows results from regressing real import and export growth in the East Asian countries on real US import growth. East Asian imports may also be correlated with US imports, because a high share of the imports are inputs used in exports. For example, in Japan the import share of exports is 20 percent, in China it is 30 percent, and in Korea it is 40 percent.

Table 16.3 shows that, for surplus Asian countries, both import growth and export growth are highly correlated with US import growth. In contrast, for the East Asian countries with roughly balanced trade or trade deficits, the correlations are much lower and not significant. While the surplus economies and the United States could be responding to global growth or other excluded variables, the fact that only the surplus countries show a strong correlation with US import growth is consistent with movements in imbalances enhancing the transmission from slow US growth to East Asian exports and imports.

Is This Explanation Consistent with the Existing Literature?

The main explanations put forward for the recent trade slowdown are (1) weak demand, especially for investment goods that are a big part of trade flows, (2) a slowdown in the development of global supply chains, and (3) protectionism.

Table 16.3 Trade growth in surplus Asian countries is highly correlated with US import growth

Variable	Deficit		Balance							Surplus			
	Laos	Cambodia	Vietnam	Indonesia	Philippines	Japan	Korea	China	Thailand	Hong Kong	Taiwan	Malaysia	Singapore
Dependent variable: Import growth													
US import growth	0.0223 (0.414)	0.66 (0.489)	-0.186 (0.418)	0.505 (0.523)	0.0767 (0.375)	0.636*** (0.174)	0.695 (0.400)	0.596* (0.282)	1.110** (0.417)	0.625** (0.234)	1.237*** (0.206)	1.173*** (0.323)	0.825*** (0.269)
Observations	18	18	18	18	18	18	18	18	18	18	18	18	18
R-squared	0.00	0.10	0.01	0.06	0.00	0.46	0.16	0.22	0.31	0.31	0.69	0.45	0.37
Average CA/GDP	-16.26	-5.82	-1.14	1.12	1.83	2.72	3.28	3.84	3.86	7.22	7.66	10.28	18.89
Dependent variable: Export growth													
US import growth	0.275 (0.343)	0.783* (0.381)	-0.108 (0.238)	0.133 (0.371)	0.434 (0.464)	1.189*** (0.241)	0.718*** (0.177)	1.051*** (0.364)	0.931*** (0.131)	0.720*** (0.222)	1.013*** (0.206)	0.918*** (0.206)	0.740*** (0.212)
Observations	18	18	18	18	18	18	18	18	18	18	18	18	18
R-squared	0.039	0.209	0.013	0.008	0.052	0.603	0.508	0.342	0.761	0.397	0.602	0.553	0.432
Average CA/GDP	-16.26	-5.82	-1.14	1.12	1.83	2.72	3.28	3.84	3.86	7.22	7.66	10.28	18.89

Notes: * indicates significance at the 10 percent level; ** 5 percent level, and *** 1 percent level. Data are real import and export growth from the International Monetary Fund.

Source: Author's calculations.

The IMF *World Economic Outlook* (2016) did the most extensive study to date and found that demand is largely to blame for the trade slowdown, accounting for 50 to 80 percent, with supply chains and protectionism each explaining at most 5 percent. The results are consistent with research showing that investment tends to drive trade movements (Bussière et al. 2013). While trade imbalances are, of course, related to demand, neither study considered whether increasing global imbalances in the mid-1990s may have affected the relationship between trade and growth.

A number of studies focus on the role of China in the trade slowdown. Constantinescu, Mattoo, and Ruta (2015) find that the deceleration in vertical integration, particularly in China, is important. Gaulier et al. (2015) focus on China's rise as a manufacturing center and its shift to domestic demand as important in explaining changes in global trade growth over time. Consideration of the role of widening global imbalances in fueling trade growth is complementary to these studies in that it helps to explain how China's exports could grow so rapidly and the timing of the shift to domestic demand-driven growth.

The importance of borrowing in the period of hyperglobalization before the financial crisis is also consistent with work by Shin (2011) and Borio, James, and Shin (2014) on the surge in credit in the period leading up to the financial crisis. A banking glut led to an expansion of gross and net capital flows in the United States. On the real side, that was reflected in an import surge in the United States and the credit expansion also fueled greater unbundling of production.

While there is no reason trade could not surge in an environment of more balanced trade (indeed, most trade models assume trade is balanced), the ability to have large trade imbalances could enhance trade growth because countries can import more when demand is strong. The growth in cross-border capital flows magnifies the effects of the existing explanations because budget constraints are no longer binding. In terms of demand as an explanation, the ease of borrowing from abroad means that demand can exceed supply for longer periods, without price increases. Similarly, in the presence of greater capital mobility, the buildup of supply chains was likely faster than it otherwise would have been.

The trade growth puzzle may therefore be the next of kin to one of the major paradoxes in macroeconomics from the 1980s, the high correlation between savings and investment across countries. Theory predicts that savings should flow to the best investment opportunities. Because the top investment prospects may not be in the domestic market, the correlation between savings and investment across countries should be low. Instead economists found it to be very high in the 1960s and 1970s. This paradox, known as the Feldstein-Horioka puzzle (Feldstein and Horioka 1980) for the economists who uncovered it, has unraveled in recent decades, as the cross-country correlation between savings and investment declined. The widening and then narrowing of global imbalances that resulted from greater capital mobility contributed to more volatile trade growth. If instead the gap between savings and investment had remained limited, trade growth would have very likely been more balanced over time as shown in figure 16.7.

Implications for Trade and Growth

The unprecedented trade growth that followed the rise of cross-border capital flows is linked to widening trade imbalances. Similarly, the recent period of slow trade growth is associated with a narrowing of global imbalances. From this perspective, the dramatic trade slowdown stems not just from weak global growth but also from weaker growth combined with a return to more balanced capital flows.

Going forward, even as global growth picks up, the new weaker relationship between trade and income may remain in place if global imbalances remain constrained. Overall, the dismantling of the Feldstein-Horioka puzzle may have ushered in a period when the relationship between global trade growth and global income growth is more volatile. In periods when demand is strong in large countries, their widening imbalances fuel trade growth to a greater extent than if they were constrained by their exports. Similarly, the eventual pressure to narrow trade deficits could eventually result in slower trade growth.

An alternative way of viewing the results is that the export-led growth policies in Asia, especially China, fueled strong trade growth in the late 1990s and early 2000s and widening imbalances. Those policies effectively shifted export growth from the future to that period, resulting in slower trade growth in recent years as pressure for more balanced trade increased. An important implication for the East Asian surplus countries is that they will now need to rely more on domestic reform and less on export-led growth. Over time, a new wave of global income and trade growth could result if the roles reversed and surplus East Asia absorbed a higher share of global capital flows.

References

Borio, Claudio, Harold James, and Hyun Song Shin. 2014. *The International Monetary and Financial System: A Capital Account Historical Perspective*. Working Paper 204. Dallas: Federal Reserve Bank of Dallas, Globalization and Monetary Policy Institute.

Bussière, Matthieu, Giovanni Callegari, Fabio Ghironi, Giulia Sestieri, and Norihiko Yamano. 2013. Estimating Trade Elasticities: Demand Composition and the Trade Collapse of 2008-2009. *American Economic Journal: Macroeconomics* 5, no. 3: 118-51.

Constantinescu, Cristina, Aaditya Mattoo, and Michele Ruta. 2015. *The Global Trade Slowdown: Cyclical or Structural?* IMF Working Paper 15/6. Washington: International Monetary Fund.

Feldstein, Martin, and Charles Horioka. 1980. Domestic Saving and International Capital Flows. *Economic Journal* 90, no. 358: 314–29.

Gaulier, Guillaume, Gianluca Santoni, Daria Taglioni, and Soledad Zignago. 2015. The Power of the Few in Determining Trade Accelerations and Slowdowns. In *The Global Trade Slowdown: A New Normal?*, ed. Bernard Hoekman. VoxEU.org eBook. London: Centre for Economic Policy Research. Available at http://voxeu.org/sites/default/files/file/Global%20Trade%20Slowdown_nocover.pdf.

IMF (International Monetary Fund). 2014. Are Global Imbalances at a Turning Point? In *World Economic Outlook.* Washington.

IMF (International Monetary Fund). 2016. Global Trade: What's Behind the Slowdown? In *World Economic Outlook.* Washington.

Shin, Hyun Song. 2011. Global Banking Glut and Loan Risk Premium. Mundell Fleming Lecture presented at the 12th Jacques Polak Annual Research Conference, November 10–11, Washington.

Comment
Davin Chor

Caroline Freund presents an original and thought-provoking hypothesis on a mechanism that could have contributed to the current global trade slowdown. Specifically, she links the steady unwinding of global imbalances over the past five to ten years to the decline in the growth rate of international trade flows. The logic behind this relationship is an intuitive one: For several decades, the ability to run persistent current account deficits has enabled countries such as the United States to sustain (and even increase) their imports from the rest of the world, well above levels that would have been possible if these imports had to be balanced in each period against the value of the countries' exports. But as these current account imbalances have shrunk in recent years, growth in trade relative to output has inevitably declined, which we are now seeing in the data.

The chapter marshals several key pieces of evidence in support of this hypothesis. First, it shows very clearly that since 1995, global imbalances and global trade have indeed become more tightly correlated; this is true regardless of whether one traces the evolution of these variables in levels (figure 16.1) or in their growth rates (figure 16.2). This correlation stands up to closer scrutiny in a series of panel regressions: Movements in current account imbalances tend to be positively associated with corresponding shifts in the trade-to-GDP ratio, particularly among large economies in the post-1995 period (table 16.1). Second, the chapter documents how the trade position of individual countries has shifted since the global financial crisis. Among countries that were running large current account deficits prior to the crisis—such as the United States—import growth has since moderated in tandem with narrowing global imbalances. On the other hand, in countries that were initially building up large current account surpluses—such as China—export growth has tapered off. These observed patterns (reported in figures 16.4 to 16.6) are entirely in line with how one would expect an unwinding of global imbalances to affect these countries' export and import positions.

Freund's argument thus carries some natural appeal. The economic mechanisms articulated here and the evidence that has been presented would strike a chord with observers familiar with the ongoing policy debates over the United States' large current account deficit and how best to address it. While economists have long been aware of the relationship between global imbalances and trade flows, credit is nevertheless due to the author

---

Davin Chor is professor in the Department of Economics at the National University of Singapore.

for making explicit in this chapter how this relationship could account for (at least some part of) the global trade slowdown. At the same time, it bears mentioning that the association between imbalances and trade flows is not simply a mechanical accounting identity, since trade in goods is only one component of a country's current account.

That said, the ideas that this chapter has seeded do raise questions for further research. As compelling as the descriptive evidence presented here is, it remains an open (and intensely interesting) question whether these correlations actually reflect a *causal* relationship running from narrowing global imbalances to a slowdown in global trade growth. To make the case that this effect is indeed causal, one would in principle like to be able to exploit instances of plausibly exogenous policy changes that were introduced with the express objective of reducing current account imbalances, yet at the same time did not seek to directly target exports and imports to meet this policy objective. This exercise, however, raises clear challenges from a research design perspective.

Consider, for example, a country running a current account deficit. To reduce such deficits in practice, expenditure-switching policies have often been adopted—via say an exchange rate depreciation or an import tariff—to encourage consumers to purchase domestic goods instead of imported ones. (Such thinking, in particular the threat of unilateral tariffs, has in fact pervaded the recent rhetoric of the Trump administration to address the large bilateral US deficits with key trading partners like Mexico and China.) If successful, such policies would shrink the country's external imbalance position, but they would also be doing so by directly reducing the demand for imports. One would then be hard-pressed to disentangle the effects of the policy to address imbalances from the effects of weak import demand. Put otherwise, the finding in recent studies that weak global demand has been the dominant factor in the global trade slowdown could indirectly also be capturing the effect of current account reductions by large deficit countries.

An alternative and possibly more promising research strategy might be to focus on surplus countries. To take a prominent example, China has widely been seen in recent years to be seeking to lower its burgeoning current account surplus and instead pursue a growth strategy that is driven more by domestic consumption rather than by a reliance on exports. There may well be interesting policy measures—such as restrictions on lending of surplus funds to foreign entities or a reduction in China's holdings of US treasuries—that could allow researchers to parse out the effect of a decrease in China's surplus on its and other countries' trade performance. Research along these lines would be extremely useful to more definitively resolve the direction of causality. Such an exercise would help to provide more reliable estimates from which to trace the effects of shifts in global imbalances on countries' subsequent trade positions.

In sum, this chapter has presented an intriguing hypothesis that clearly deserves to be investigated more extensively. I hope it will encourage further study of the links between developments in international macroeconomic policy and international trade flows, which all too often have been treated as disjoint subjects by academic researchers. The findings documented here also bear a key lesson for policymakers, namely that measures to reduce global imbalances can and should be expected to have effects that show up in a country's trade statistics, and these repercussions should not be ignored.

17

Toward a "New" Asian Model

SUBIR GOKARN

Two themes shaped the discussions during this conference. The first is that the "old" Asian model is obsolete and that countries in the region have to reorient their strategies for sustaining growth. The second is that an important element of any such reorientation must take into account the opportunities the region itself provides. This chapter explores both themes and draws some implications for a "new" Asian model.

The "Old" Asian Model

All of the countries referred to during the conference grew because there was demand for their products in the advanced economies, mainly the United States and Europe. The contribution of specific export-led strategies to growth performance varied across countries. Overall, the model delivered very successfully from the 1950s onward.

Many observers view the flying geese formation as an apt metaphor for the Asian model. It implies strategic replication over succeeding generations of countries. There are two aspects to this replication, both of which are important when considering the future of the model.

The first is what might be referred to as *leverage*. The growth process begins at the lowest end of the supply chain: garments, footwear, and other goods that directly satisfy consumer needs. Competitiveness in these

Subir Gokarn is executive director for Bangladesh, Bhutan, India, and Sri Lanka at the International Monetary Fund. The views expressed in this chapter are those of the author and do not necessarily represent the views of the IMF, its Executive Board, or its management.

sectors required combining low-cost labor, organized in efficient structures, with the lowest-cost intermediate and capital goods. Initially, the latter were sourced from abroad (for countries entering the formation later, possibly from predecessors who had developed these capabilities). The key to leverage was that even as countries began to integrate backward into upstream segments of the supply chain, preserving the competitiveness of the downstream remained paramount.

Leverage contributed to efficient backward integration, the basis of the second aspect of replication, which might be referred to as *succession*. Even as downstream competitiveness in earlier generations of countries eroded as labor costs rose, upstream competitiveness allowed the export-led growth process to sustain. Of course, as standards of living rose, domestic demand became increasingly significant in the growth process. However, the virtuous circle of efficiency and competitiveness moving upstream over the supply chain was a key contributor to the sustainability of exports. Downstream products shifted location and the export baskets of individual countries changed over time, but the importance of exports in the growth of the region remained.

Opportunities for a "New" Model

It is against this backdrop that the issue of obsolescence has to be viewed. Changing demand patterns in the advanced economies, perhaps induced by slower growth and demographic dynamics, suggest that these markets will become less and less important sources of demand for Asian products. This change was inevitable. But even as the role of the advanced economy markets in Asian growth declines, the key element of the Asian model—the promotion of efficiency and competitiveness up the supply chain—provides the basis for the "new" model.

The second theme of the conference was the significance of being in a particular neighborhood at a particular time. In his inaugural presentation, Adam Posen displayed the shares of different countries in the global economy over time, as laid out in Subramanian (2011). In the late 19th century, the two growth powerhouses, Great Britain and Germany, were neighbors. There was significant economic benefit to the entire region from having two large engines of growth located in it.

Asia is in a similar situation today, with China and India—whose shares of global GDP will rise to 18 and 6 percent, respectively, over the next decade—potentially providing significant growth momentum to the region. Of course, that potential will be realized only if the countries in the region implement appropriate policies. But with so many countries having developed competitive capabilities in a variety of downstream and upstream sectors, they should be able to take advantage of opportunities in the neighborhood.

The power of clusters and agglomeration is well understood. At the sectoral level—Silicon Valley, Seattle, Cambridge, and Bengaluru—or the country level, being in a dynamic and rapidly growing neighborhood provides all members of the cluster an opportunity to leverage their competencies. The tailwinds that can be generated by having two very large players in a neighborhood are significant and represent an opportunity that should not be missed by the smaller countries in the region.

Under the "new" Asian model, countries in the region move away from supplying the advanced-economy markets to meeting the needs of the growing markets in the region itself. There is a great deal of diversity and heterogeneity in the region, including a range of per capita income levels. But many of its markets are growing rapidly and, under a reasonable set of global and domestic conditions, will continue to do so for a long time. The region provides opportunities for producers in several countries to collaborate to exploit complementary competencies in a variety of sectors. Regional supply chains are already well established in several countries. The full potential across sectors and geographies is yet to be fully tapped.

Challenges of a "New" Model

Several challenges also need to be addressed. Aging and its implications for labor supply and public spending in the form of health and social security are going to be important considerations for all countries—for many, sooner rather than later. Most Asian countries will cross dependency thresholds at far lower levels of per capita income than the advanced economies of North America and Europe did.

Technology is another challenge. It will affect different countries in the region in different ways. In countries with abundant labor resources, the implications of automation are a cause of grave concern. In many Asian countries, low-skilled work is likely to be the predominant mode of employment for years to come. Transiting to a work situation in which relatively skilled people work collaboratively with robots is a distant prospect at the macro level. The fact that the labor-intensive manufacturing/services pathway to affluence is no longer open is very difficult to tell constituents. How do countries in this situation deal with a threat that may be imminent and against which they have no obvious buffer?

A third set of challenges relates to the nature of trade between countries that are similarly endowed. Classical trade theory posits that trade is most likely to take place and to generate the most benefits between countries with different endowments. The old Asian model was firmly rooted in this theoretical framework, with its emphasis on exporting labor-intensive products to relatively labor-scarce advanced economies. The new Asian model involves a pivot to the neighborhood, which means establishing significant trading relations with similarly endowed countries. How does it square with trade theory?

Fortunately, there are enough grounds to believe that the pivot is achievable. Gravity models indicate that geographical proximity is always conducive to trade. Evidence based on new trade theories emphasizes features such as intraindustry trade and the importance of cross-border supply chains in achieving efficiency and increasing trade volumes. Intra-Asian trade is already an established phenomenon, diluting concerns about similar endowments. Multiple trade agreements are in place within the region. And there are important historical precedents. Trade between advanced economies is significant. The European Union is a vivid example of the power of geographic contiguity in enlarging trade opportunities, even between countries that are similarly endowed. These trends bode well for the new Asian model.

The conditions necessary for the new model to work will not fall into place automatically. Various kinds of barriers will have to be addressed by countries, with a high level of coordination. Trade-facilitating infrastructure will have to be expanded or built to accommodate potential increases in volumes. To the extent that some of the increase in trade will be in services, rules, standards, and procedures will have to be framed and harmonized.

Encouraging the development and expansion of supply chains will require clarity and predictability in both domestic and cross-border procedures. Training and skills systems will have to be geared up in anticipation of the new opportunities that will arise as a result of the pivot. All of these issues will pose significant challenges to governments in the region, in that they reflect a significant departure from the old model, which was relatively simple in its focus on labor-intensive manufacturing.

Summary

Several key messages emerged from the conference. First, the changing landscape in advanced-economy markets is combining with structural changes in Asia to render the traditional export channels less and less significant for the region as a whole.

Second, the obsolescence of the old model should be a cause for concern only if there is nothing to succeed it. But the two elements of the old model—leverage and replicability—have created centers of efficiency across the region along the entire supply chain in many sectors. And decades of sustained growth in Asia have created a large market and set of opportunities for all countries in the region. The new model requires the pivoting of Asian economies away from advanced-economy markets toward the region. The fact that two large and fast-growing economies, China and India, are in the neighborhood will facilitate this process.

Third, although the opportunities for a successful pivot are well grounded in the historical experiences of other regions, several challenges exist. Automation requires a strategic response. Countries seeking to do more business with their neighbors will have to coordinate on many fronts, from building infrastructure to harmonizing rules and procedures. To a large extent, they are already doing so. But the issue gains some urgency when seen in the context of a paradigm shift in regional strategy.

Whether the new Asian model is a move toward mediocrity or renewed excellence depends on how effectively the countries in the region recognize and act on the opportunities and respond to the challenges.

Reference

Subramanian, Arvind. 2011. *Eclipse: Living in the Shadow of Chinese Economic Dominance.* Washington: Peterson Institute for International Economics.

Index

Abe, Shinzo, 130
Abenomics, 130, 131, 139, 141
academic and industry sectors, connections, 76*b*
academic salaries, in Japan, 78
adult education, contributing to human capital accumulation, 367
advanced economies
    behavior in Asia, 124
    demand patterns in, 5, 408
    external demand growth from, 6
    lowered interest rates after the crisis, 116
    policies following the financial crisis, 237
    productivity slowdown in, 347
    public debt as percent of GDP, 345*f*
    quality of infrastructure, 355, 356*f*
    secular stagnation transmitted to domestic output dynamics, 253
    slowdown perceived as durable, 237
    syndromes perpetuating stagnation, 135
    at the technological frontier, 107, 257
    weakness in demand leading to lower exchange rates abroad, 243
advanced economy group, imbalances within, 281
aerodynamics, evolution of, 17*n*
Africa, 19, 38
age of Enlightenment, 26

age profile, in Korea, 166, 168*f*
age-related spending, 344, 353
age-wage profile, in Japan, 144
aggregate capital accumulation, declining in Korea, 167–168
aggregate demand, exceeding aggregate supply, 20
aging
    creating a demographic "tax," 40
    as a disinflationary factor, 175*n*
    impact on investment, 49–50
    impact on labor force participation rates (LFPRs), 46–49
    impact on total factor productivity (TFP), 43–46, 48*f*
    implications for labor supply and public spending, 409
    of Korea's population, 169
    in the late- or post-dividend stages, 64
    lowering growth, 6
    low per capita income levels, 37, 67–68
    migration softening the impact of rapid, 43
    mitigating the economic effects of, 20, 134
    not leading to declining aggregate demand, 20
    pushing for deflation and protectionism, 136
    reducing aggregate demand and aggregate supply, 175*n*
    slowing potential growth, 344

aging speed
  associated with higher current account
    balances, 52
  change between 2020 and 2030, 58*f*
  creating a demographic tax on growth,
    3
  defined, 58*f*
  effects on interest rates, 58, 60
  rapid in Asia, 37, 66–67, 344
  resulting in lower investment, 51
  setting to create a demographic tax on
    growth, 67
airplane design, trial and error used in, 17*n*
"All 100 Million Playing an Active Role"
  (Ichi-Oku Sou-Katsuyaku), 141
Android platform, as Google's innovation,
  91
annual growth rates, in Korea and the
  global economy, 166, 167*f*
*Annual Report on Exchange Arrangements and
  Exchange Restrictions* (AREAER), 110,
  125
Anti-Monopoly Law, in Japan, 82
APDMOD semi-structural model of the
  global economy (IMF), 365, 365*n*,
  365*n*, 366*n*
arbitrage, between foreign and domestic
  bonds, 114
artificial intelligence (AI), replacing
  workers, 28
ASEAN (Association of Southeast Asian
  Nations), real GDP growth relative to,
  2000–16, 241*f*
ASEAN-4 (Malaysia, Thailand, and the
  Philippines), 244
ASEAN-9 (Cambodia, Indonesia, Laos,
  Malaysia, Myanmar, the Philippines,
  Singapore, Thailand, and Vietnam),
  249
Asia
  adopting full-fledged inflation-forecast
    targeting, 323
  China and India providing growth
    momentum, 408
  contribution to real trade growth, 392*f*
  countries crossing dependency
    thresholds, 409
  demographic impact on 10-year real
    interest rates, 61*f*
  demographic impact on current
    account, 53*f*
  demographic trends, 34–40
  growth leadership shifting from Japan
    to China, 270

  macroeconomic developments in,
    287–289, 287*f*
  projected effects of fiscal measures,
    368*f*
Asia-15 economies, inflation rates in,
  288–289, 288*f*
Asian crisis (1997–98), 269
Asian economies
  danger from secular stagnation, 1–2
  dominated by China and India, 116
  largest, 33*n*
  public debt, 346*f*
  public spending on pensions and
    health care, 346*f*
Asian model
  efficiency and competitiveness up the
    supply chain, 408
  as obsolete, 5
asset churning, 275
"asset market meltdown" hypothesis, 62
asset prices, 194, 304
asset returns, demographics and, 62–64,
  62*t*, 63*t*
atmospheric pressure, Torricelli's discovery
  of, 17
Australia
  alternative policy strategies, 326*f*, 327*f*
  change in 10-year government yield,
    55*f*
  demographic characteristics, 35*t*
  demographic impact on current
    account, 53*f*
  higher old-age dependency by 2020, 52
  immigration, 37
  impact of aging on TFP, 48*f*
  impact of continued immigration on
    the workforce, 43
  impact of demographics on 10-year
    real interest rates, 61*f*
  impact of demographic trends, 42*f*
  labor force participation rates, 48*f*, 49*f*
  as a large commodity-exporting
    economy, 324
  as a late-dividend economy, 35, 37
  lower speed of aging, 52
  maintained higher real interest rates,
    116
  managing downside risks and avoiding
    a deflation trap, 324–328
  old-age dependency ratio, 36*t*, 38*f*, 57*f*
  open-economy New Keynesian model,
    337
  per capita income level, 39*f*
  real neutral interest rates, 56*f*

share of older workers, 44f
share of workforce with productivity
rising or falling, 45f
youth dependency ratio, 57f
authoritarian regimes, rise of, 22
automatic adjustment mechanisms, in
pension systems, 375
automation, 409, 411

baby boomers, retiring and drawing down
savings, 62
backward integrating, leverage contributed
to, 408
backward-looking expectations (lags), 337
Bacon, Francis, 18
bad equilibrium, 316, 320
bad governance, 23
balanced trade countries, 390, 391f
balance-of-payments equation, 112
"balance sheeting working group," 190n
balance sheets
banks making greater use of, 297
central banks expanding, 286
crises in the twenty-first century, 278
overstretched limiting the effects of
monetary policy, 334
policies of central banks, 286
potential of policies, 4
vulnerabilities, 282–283
Baltic nations, scores on governance
indicators, 22
Bangladesh
CPI inflation rates, 288f
current account balances, 310f
direct taxes, 366
fertility rates, 19
fiscal packages, 380t, 383t
foreign exchange reserves and net
official assets, 311f
in Group 3, 347b
infrastructure, index of quality of, 356f
months inflation rate below inflation
target, 371f
personal income tax (PIT) yields, 363f
PPP framework needing further
development, 366n
public debt, actual and projected, 346f
public spending efficiency frontier,
378t
public spending on education, 359f
public spending on health care, 358f
real per capita GDP, growth rate of,
287f
real short-term interest rate, 293f

scope for quantitative easing,
December 2016, 303t
tax revenue sources, 364f
Bank for International Settlements (BIS)
alternative path for the federal funds
rate, 306
concerns about overextended financial
markets, 305
credit gap measures produced by, 119
credit-to-GDP gap statistics, 125
banking cartel, in Japan, 81
banking crisis, in Japan in 2003, 135
banking glut, in the United States, 400
banking problems, depressing Japanese
productivity growth, 107
bank lending, to zombies, 170
Bank of Canada, 306, 319
Bank of England, 306
Bank of Japan (BoJ), 131–132, 290, 290f,
291, 303
Bank of Korea, 2, 295
banks, Park nationalized Korea's, 85
Basic Survey on Wage Structure, 152
below-target inflation rates, persisting, 335
best practices, adopting in Japan, 164
Betzig, Eric, 24
Betzig-Hell microscope, 24
birth rates, not rising with income, 10–11
BIS. See Bank for International Settlements
(BIS)
bond markets
domestic influencing financial
conditions, 4
measure of integration, 125
more important in monetary policy
transmission, 286
risks from global, 297–298
worries about destabilizing, 304
bonds, 307, 335
booms, emergence of unsustainable, 124
borrowing
from abroad, 400
by local governments in China, 188
risks of highly leveraged, 307
Bragg, William Henry, 24
Bragg, William Lawrence, 24
Brent crude oil price, 1991–2017, 275f
budgetary aggregates, numerical limits on,
373
budget constraints, as no longer binding,
400
Bulgaria, 22, 117, 117n
"burden of knowledge," increasing, 26
Burke, Edward, 23

business cycle synchronization, 239*n*
business enterprise research and
    development (BERD), in Japan, 151*f*
business environment, in Indonesia, 242
business models, development in China of
    new, 185
business R&D and government support, in
    Japan, 151*f*
business regulation and taxation,
    simplifying in India, 222

Cambodia
    fiscal packages, 380*t*, 383*t*
    in Group 3, 347*b*
    infrastructure, index of quality of, 356*f*
    personal income tax (PIT) yields, 363*f*
    public debt, actual and projected, 346*f*
    public spending efficiency frontier,
        distance from, 378*t*
    public spending on education, 359*f*
    public spending on health care, 358*f*
    tax revenue sources, 364*f*
    trade growth in, 399*t*
capacity utilization gap, in the US,
    299–300, 299*t*
capital
    cost of, 124
    taxation of, 353
capital accumulation, in Indonesia,
    256–257
capital exporters and importers, 51, 53
capital flows
    across borders, 275, 276*f*
    demographic factors strengthening,
        52–53
    management of, 118
    opportunities for, 67
    spurred by unconventional monetary
        policy, 237
capital formation, in Japan, 143
capital gains, to financial firms holding
    bonds, 307
capital inflows, 114
capital mobility, 112, 387
capital openness index (CO), 58
capital stock, in Indonesia, 262, 262*f*
capital surcharges, enhancing resilience to
    shocks, 334
capital-to-effective-labor ratio, remaining
    constant, 41
capital-to-labor ratio, 50
capital-to-output ratio
    approaching ratios in advanced
        countries, 166, 168*f*

in Korea and selected countries,
    1970–2015, 168*f*
carbon prices, 183
Cartagena Protocol on Biosafety, 23
cartels, in Japan, 82
Ceauşescu, Nicolae, 22, 23
CEIC database, 224
Central Asian republics, governance
    indicators, 22
central bank(s)
    active use of balance sheets, 301–302,
        302*t*
    avoiding the traps of fiscal and
        financial dominance, 304
    balance sheets
        advancing objectives, 286
        keeping markets for local financial
            assets operating, 298
        policies, 4
    clear signals, providing, 321
    conducting QE through purchases of
        government bonds, 302
    deflation risks, fighting, 323
    easing monetary policy but tightening
        macroprudential policies, 309
    inflation, control of low, 298–304
    interest rate, publishing, 323
    interest rates, 125
    limited influence of in China, 187, 188
    monetary autonomy of, 312
    monetary policy
        in China, 189
        conduct of, 318
    nominal interest rate, determining,
        114
    official inflation targets of, 316
    policy interest rate, setting the path
        of, 321
    policy rates, reducing below zero, 300
    scope when inflation expectations
        settle at low levels, 286
    tolerating longer periods of inflation
        below target, 307
    world real interest rate, ready for
        external shocks to, 297
central bankers, managing inflation, 269
central bank transparency index, 323, 324*f*
Centre for Monitoring the Indian Economy
    (CMIE), 225
CGE model, showing China's annual GDP
    growth, 183
chaebols (Korea's industrial
    conglomerates), 86, 86*n*, 88
channels of spillover, for low productivity
    growth, 104

channels of transmission, from advanced economies to Indonesia, 242–244

chemicals, market share of exports over time, 212*f*

Chen Shui-bian administration, in Taiwan, 95

Chiang Kai-shek, authoritarian regime of, 91–92

child care, provision of, 370

childcare spending, permanently increasing, 367

child rearing, support for in Japan, 141

children, having higher-quality, 11

China
    absolute decline in, 38
    account balances and reserve purchases, 271*f*
    age-related spending, 344, 346*f*
    aging
        experiencing rapid until 2030, 52
        fiscal pressures from, 353
        impact on growth, 41
        impact on TFP, 48*f*
    aging speed change between 2020 and 2030, 58*f*
    capital control regime, 280*n*
    capital inflows, 122
    central government setting growth targets, 186
    CPI inflation rates, 288*f*
    current account balances, 274*f*, 310*f*
    debt ratio change under Scenario 4b, 354*f*
    deceleration pressures, 185–186
    demographic characteristics, 35*t*
    demographic impact on current account, 53*f*
    demographics, impact on 10-year real interest rates, 61*f*
    demographic trends, impact of, 42*f*
    development zones, 187, 189
    direct taxes, 366
    drag on growth, 41*n*
    engineering, 18
    environmental costs, 182–184
    expansion of credit, 119, 120
    export growth tapered off, 403
    export-led growth policies, 401
    export market, catching up with Korea in, 171
    exports, fast-growing, 391
    exposure to, affecting trade-related spillovers, 243
    fertility rates, 19

financial sector risks, prevention of, 181

fiscal packages, 380*t*, 382*t*

foreign capital, volatility of the supply of, 2000–15, 251*f*

foreign exchange reserves and net official assets, 311*f*

GDP growth targets, abandoning, 188

global exports share versus India, 198*f*

global real trade growth, 393*f*

governance indicators, improvements in, 22

in Group 2, 347*b*

growth
    deceleration, 182
    higher since the global financial crisis, 194
    a more balanced pattern of, 315
    slowdown as inevitable, 184–185
    strategy driven more by domestic consumption, 404

imbalances, role of, 394–396

import share of exports, 398

Indonesian exports to, 246*f*, 247*n*

Indonesian imports from, 246*f*, 247*n*

infrastructure, index of quality of, 356*f*

labor force aging, 344

labor force participation, 48*f*, 49*f*

loans to domestic banks offsetting the decline in foreign-currency assets, 311

long-term public debt projection, 349*t*

macroeconomic policy framework for, 181–191

macroeconomic stability screening mechanism, 189

median age, projected rise in, 20*n*

monetary policy independence, enhancing, 188

most-favored nation (MFN) applied tariff rates, 230*f*

natural rates remaining high, 54

net investment, 2002–17, 279*f*

nonfinancial credit-to-GDP ratio, 181

old-age dependency ratio, 36*t*, 38*f*, 57*f*, 344
    older workers, share of, 44*f*

overinvestment, aftereffects of, 165

patents, average quality of, 186

pensions, 375

per capita income level, 39*f*

personal income tax (PIT) yields, 363*f*

phone makers. market shares of increasing, 91*n*

polity not democratic and open, 22
as a post-dividend economy, 35
primary commodity exports from
    Indonesia, 243n
productivity, slowdown in, 347
public debt, actual and projected, 351f
public spending
    on education, 359f
    efficiency frontier, distance from,
        378t
    on health care, 358f
    on pensions and health care, 346f
quasi-fiscal debt of local governments,
    190
real GDP growth correlated to
    Indonesia's, 253t
real GDP volatility, 2000–16, 241f
real neutral interest rates, 56f
real per capita GDP, growth rate of,
    287f
real short-term interest rate, 293f
rebalancing from investment toward
    consumption, 243
research and development spending,
    362f
reserves fell over the past three years,
    310–311
restructuring in, 316
Scenario 3 and, 350
scope for quantitative easing,
    December 2016, 303t
services and manufacturing sectors as
    percent of GDP, 185f
shift in consumer preference from
    goods to services, 184
slowdown in economic growth, 3–4,
    191
SOEs in, 376
spillovers to the rest of the world, 325
State Council setting monetary growth
    targets, 187
tariff rates, 230
tax revenue sources, 364f
10-year government yield, 55f
trade growth in, 399t
trade slowdown, role in, 400
trade surpluses, expanded, 388
trade-to-GDP ratio driven by exports-
    to-GDP ratio, 396
WTO, accession to, 270
youth dependency ratio, 57f
Chinn-Ito index, 109–110, 118, 125
chonsei, rental system of Korea, 174n
city-states, set up city governments, 13

cloud technology, just getting started, 26
clusters and agglomeration, power of, 409
Cobb-Douglas production function, 339
Cœur, Jacques, 12n
commodities, 339
competition, in Japan, 82–83
competitiveness indicator, 339
Complete Dictionary of Arts and Sciences
    (Croker), 26n
composition effects, accounting for drag on
    wage growth in the US, 134
Comprehensive and Progressive Agreement for
    Trans-Pacific Partnership (CPTPP), 130
computer memory, decreasing cost of, 27n
computers, improvements in, 24–25
conditional forecast path, publication of,
    319
conditionality, communicating, 323
Condorcet, 1795 essay on human progress,
    16n
constant true prices, reflected by an
    inflation rate of 1 percent, 292
consumer and industrial goods, US market
    for, 76b
consumer preference, shifting from goods
    to services in China, 184
consumer price and wage inflation,
    modeled by reduced-form Phillips'
    curves, 339
consumer price inflation, domestic, 251
consumption, 267, 338
consumption tax, in Japan, 131, 132, 289n
contagion, channels of, 3, 108
contingent liabilities, emanating from
    SOEs, 376
conventional forward guidance, 322
convergence argument, 169n
core CPI inflation
    for Japan, 333f
    in Korea, 296f
    in Thailand, 296f
core inflation, keeping at or above 2
    percent, 285
Corporate Enterprise Annual Statistics, from
    the Ministry of Finance in Japan, 150
corporate income tax, effects of cutting, 369
correlations, reflecting a causal
    relationship, 404
corruption indices, 14
corrupt nations, interacting with nations
    with better institutions, 22
corrupt regimes, being deposed, 24
countercyclical fiscal rules, 373

countries
    with bigger current account deficits,
        278
    changing political structure, 22
    groups of in regard to trade, 390, 391f
    illustrating risk-avoidance strategy for
        monetary policy, 324–333
    trade positions shifting, 403
    unique parameterizations in the
        G20MOD, 340
country groupings, in Asia, 347b
coverage, for fiscal rules, 373
CPI inflation rates, in Asia, 288f
credibility, earning, 338
credit
    buildup of excessive, 119
    changes in reflecting demand
        rebalancing, 122
    surge in before the financial crisis, 400
credit and asset prices, excessive growth in
    domestic, 114
credit availability, as a driver of resource
    misallocation in India, 232
credit booms
    countries with seeing increases in net
        capital inflows, 121
    precipitating major growth slowdowns
        or financial crises, 123
    risk of unsustainable, 124
credit expansions, 119, 400
credit gap, 119–122, 120f, 122f
credit growth, in India, 231
creditor countries, deciding to spend more,
    278
creditors, seeking to ensure resources for
    the future, 278
credit-to-GDP gap, 119, 125
cross-border capital flows, growth in, 400
cross-border financial stability risks,
    addressing, 283
cross-border risk sharing, opportunities
    for, 67
cross-border supply chains, 410
cross-country differences, in interest rate
    transmission, 118
cross-country regressions, of the change in
    interest rate associated with the global
    financial crisis, 117–118
CTFP, measuring the productivity level
    across counties, 125
Cullen, William, 17
currency depreciation, seeking to prevent
    unwanted, 310
currency mismatches, 280, 309

current account(s)
    balances
        in Asia, 1985–2016, 310f
        correlated with credit, 120
        correlated with initial net foreign
            assets, 278
        measuring net capital outflows, 121
        1991–2017, 274f
        in 2015, 54f
    behavior leading net international
        investment positions, 281f
    deficits, 403, 404
    demographic impact on, 51t, 53f, 54f
    driving divergence in net foreign
        assets, 280, 282f
    imbalances, associated with shifts in
        the trade-to-GDP ratio, 388f, 389f,
        403
    surpluses, 309, 310f

Daewoo, 86n
dark corner, for India, 338
Data Envelopment Analysis (DEA), 357f,
    378
data mining, in artificial neural networks,
    25
data science, new era of, 25
debt financing, 188, 371, 372f
debt liabilities, declined in Indonesia, 249
debtors, going farther into debt, 278, 281f
debt ratio, change in under Scenario 4b,
    354f
debt ratios, under Scenario 1, 350
debt ratio under Scenario 4b, 353, 354f
debt rules, 373
debt-to-income ratios, imposing, 308
deceleration of demand, lowering import
    demand, 242
deceleration pressures, measures taken to
    offset in China, 185–186
de facto financial integration, as the ratio of
    foreign assets plus liabilities to GDP,
    118
de facto integration, having no impact on
    productivity growth, 110
deficit countries, 390, 391f
    countering macroeconomic forces with
        import barriers, 280
    demographic trends exerting
        downward pressure, 52
    facing the risk that lenders will
        withdraw, 282
    importing more by borrowing, 387
    reduction in demand, 396

deficits, as a systemic risk, 396
deficits (and surpluses), in slower-growing
 advanced debtors (and creditors), 280
defined-benefit pension system, 375
deflation
 Japan's policies to exit, 330–333
 response to in the early 1990s, 291
 threat of faded in most countries, 285
deflationary spiral, fear of, 291
demand
 boosting aggregate in the short term,
  267
 changes in domestic correlated with
  changes in domestic credit, 122
 China's shift to domestic, 400
 cyclical changes in, 108
 domestic in Indonesia, 239–240
 exceeding supply without price
  increases, 400
 trade slowdown and, 400, 404
demand elasticity, decline in, 229
demand rebalancing, planting seeds of
 secular stagnation, 123
demand shocks, central banks dealing with,
 328
demand-side issues, in Indonesia, 267
demand slump, countering, 237
demand stimulus, tradeoff with financial
 stability, 7
demand weakness, assertive policy actions
 following, 316
demographic changes
 baseline impact of, 41
 effects of, 176, 177f
demographic classification, of Asia, 35t
demographic dividend
 for early- and late-dividend countries,
  41
 ending for many Asian economies, 33
 harnessing for early-dividend
  countries, 64
 in Indonesia, 261
 reversing in many countries, 6
demographic model, on the effect of the
 two-child policy in China, 182
demographic negative feedback, 10
demographic projections, long-term, 43n
demographics
 in Asia, 316
 in Korea and Japan, 171f
 labor productivity and, 47t
 rapid decline in the labor force in
  China, 182

scenario for public debt projection,
 348
 taking as destiny, 134
demographic "tax," on growth, 40
demographic transitions, 6
demographic trends
 affecting savings, investment, and
  current account balance, 50
 in Asia, 34–40
 for Asian growth, 67
 baseline growth impact of, 42f
 global impact of, 42f
 implications of, 40–64
 policy implications of, 64–66
 for post-dividend countries, 41
 reducing growth in post-dividend
  countries, 50
demographic variables, 52n, 60n
demography, Korea's following Japan's, 170
deregulating, targeted sectors, 141
Desaguliers, John T., 18
developing Asia, public debt as percent of
 GDP, 345f
development zones, in China, 187, 189, 191
difference-in-difference methodology, 108n
diffusion of technologies, determining
 productivity growth, 107
diminishing returns to research, in
 individual sectors, 27
Dincer-Eichengreen index of transparency,
 for four Asian countries, 323, 324f
direct taxes, 366
discount, high rate of, 14
discretionary monetary policy, 317
distribution system, in Japan, 82
DNA molecule, 24
"doctrine of equivalents," 79
domestic and global factors, correlation
 to domestic real GDP growth in
 Indonesia, 253, 253t
domestic assets, expanding holdings of, 312
domestic factors, explaining deviation of
 Indonesia's growth, 253, 254f
domestic financial assets, buying, 302
domestic financial markets, 286. See also
 financial markets
domestic interest rate, 112, 113, 114
domestic supply linkages, strengthening in
 India, 230
dominant elites, extracting rents, 12
downside scenario, in China, 325
downward nominal wage rigidity, 292
DRAM chips, Korean production of, 89,
 89n

drugs and pharmaceuticals, market share of exports over time, 212f
"dual economy," in Japan, 150
dual labor market structure, in Korea, 169
dynamics of foreign assets equation, 112

early-dividend demographic characteristic, 35t
early-dividend economies, 37
ease of doing business, Indonesia ranking poorly on, 259
East Asia
    with balanced trade or trade deficits, 398
    contribution to trade growth, 391, 393f
    current account balances, 274f
    economies maintaining currencies at undervalued levels, 280
    imports correlating with US imports, 398
    more market-based flexible exchange rate systems, 101
    regressing real import and export growth, 398, 399t
    surplus countries needing to rely more on domestic reform, 401
    transmission of US shock to, 398, 399t
    as the world's fastest-aging region, 34
East Asia (other), net investment, 2002-17, 279f
EBA (external balance assessment) model, 50, 50n, 52, 56n
economic embargoes, 14
economic equilibrium, 292
economic growth, low, reorganized as the "new normal," 193
economic/high-tech development zones, in China, 186
economic integration, pursuing international, 8
economic nationalism, threat of, 15
economic structure, of Korea similar to that of Japan, 171
economic underperformance, not turning into public outcry in Japan, 136
economies
    before the Industrial Revolution, 12
    less advanced catching up to the frontier, 107
education
    efficiency frontier of public spending on, 360f-361f

moving to universities and vocational schools, 163
    policies to encourage in Japan, 164
    public spending as a percent of GDP, 359f
    public spending on, 355, 357, 359f
    South Korean compared to Japan's, 88
education-to-employment pipeline, in Japan, 164
effective lower bound, constrained the Bank of Japan, 330
efficiency frontier
    calculated using Data Envelopment Analysis techniques, 355n
    of public investment, 357f
    of public spending on education, 360f-361f
    of public spending on health care, 358f
Electronic Research and Service Organization (ERSO), 93
electronics-based industrial park, built by Taiwanese industrial planners, 94-95
electronics industry, in Taiwan, 93
EMDEs (emerging-market and developing economies)
    accumulation of foreign reserves by, 271f, 273
    higher net saving by, 272
    pervasive foreign currency denomination of foreign liabilities, 280
Emerging Asia, defined, 294f
emerging economies, 3, 237
Emerging Market Bond Index (EMBI) spread, 251
    in Indonesia, 252f, 253t
emerging-market capital growth, declining over the medium term, 262
emerging-market economies
    credit booms in, 124
    growth decelerated, 315
    having higher nominal interest rates, 117
    reduced policy interest rates, 116
emerging-market funds, 297
emerging markets
    deceleration in trend growth, 237
    fraction of the global economy, 236
    macroeconomic dynamics, 236
    TFP accounting for postcrisis decline in potential growth rate, 257
emigration, of working-age people, 37
empirical literature, on the link between exporting and productivity growth, 108

empirical models, data for, 224–228
employees by firm size, all industries, Japan
    and United States, 2001, 2006, 159*t*
employment
    gap, in the US, 299–300, 299*t*
    as the most important macroeconomic
        policy objective in China, 186, 191
    scenario analysis for Indonesia, 262*f*
    security, in Japan, 81
    system, in Japan, 146*n*
endogenous credibility-building process,
    328
endogenous interest rate, producing, 320
endogenous monetary policy, 320
endogenous policy credibility, model for
    India, 337–338
endogenous policy rate, 322
energy
    clean more expensive than dirty, 183
    pricing reforms, 376
    subsidies, 376
engineering goods, exporting from India,
    198
Enlightenment Europe, artisans and
    scientists, 18
enterprise creation and growth, Japan
    behind the United States, 163
entry barriers, in Korea, 170
environmental costs, in China, 182–184
environmental taxes, introducing, 376
epistemic base, in technology, 18
"equality before the law," 12
"equal work, equal pay" rule, in Japan, 141
equilibrium rates of interest, decline in,
    292, 294
equities, official purchases of, 302
equity and real estate price bubbles, in
    Japan, 289
equity prices, run-up in US, 272
equity purchases, as the most untapped
    channel for QE, 303
escape clauses, for fiscal rules, 374
EU-28, workforce with productivity rising
    or falling, 45*f*
EU-Japan trade agreements, 130
Euler, Leonhard, 17*n*
Europe, old-age dependency ratio, 38*f*, 57*f*
exchange rates
    changes not affecting exports, 229
    diminished passthrough not specific
        to Japan, 135
    effects of weaker, 243
    fixed keeping Japan's cost of
        production relatively low, 79–80

    impact larger with greater foreign
        currency exposure, 244
    Japan's real and nominal, 80
    movements not affecting exports in
        India, 202
    policies, 101, 309–311
    of the yen and the won in the mid-
        1980s, 89
excise taxes, raising, 376
exogenous path, for the policy rate, 320*n*
expected stock returns, 62*n*
expenditure on wages and salaries,
    strengthening the rupee, 205,
    218*t*–219*t*
expenditure rules, 373
expenditures, types of, 339
expenditure-switching policies, 404
export(s)
    changing composition of India's,
        198–199
    constraining current account deficits,
        396
    as a critical driver of India's slowdown,
        197, 197*f*
    decline of Indonesia's, 244
    elasticity of India's, 200–201
    elasticity of with respect to the
        exchange rate, 204, 206*t*–207*t*
    examining the drivers of India's, 229
    growing twice as fast as GDP, 389
    growth rates on for Indonesia, 244*n*
    increasing in sophistication and value
        addition from India, 198
    India increasing its share of global,
        197, 198*f*
    India's, 194*f*
    market share of by sectors in India,
        205, 211*f*
    measuring the elasticity of India's, 200
    observed and predicted, 397, 397*f*
    reduction translating to an import
        reduction in surplus countries, 397
    by region for Indonesia, 245, 246*f*, 247
    response to exchange rate movements,
        222
    role in India's growth slowdown, 196*f*,
        197*f*
    sensitivity of India's, 200–202
    share of India's in GDP, 195*f*
    supporting economic growth in
        Indonesia, 266
    from surplus countries, 390
export basket, composition of Indonesia's,
    241*n*

export diversification, reducing export volatility, 266

export elasticities, decline in, 229

export goods, Japan's expanding range of, 79

export industries, Japan's relocating production abroad, 149

exporting firms, reacting to exchange rate changes in India, 202, 204–221

export-led growth policies in Asia, fueled strong trade growth, 401

export-led strategies, contribution to growth performance, 407

export-oriented manufacturing industries, in Korea and Japan, 171, 172*f*

"export-oriented policy," effects of, 101

exports elasticity, post-2005 decline in, 232

exports-exchange rate equations, estimation of, 202

export side, measuring India's exposure on, 194–195, 195*f*

exports-to-GDP ratio, for the United States, 394

export volatility, 266

external assets, reflecting an increase in outward FDI and other investment, 249*n*

external balance assessment (EBA) model, 50, 50*n*, 52, 56*n*

external balances, implications for, 50–53

external balance sheet, foreign currency exposure of Indonesia's, 250*f*

external demand
in India, 229
in Indonesia, 241, 242

external factors, impacting Indonesia's growth, 251, 253, 253*t*, 255

external financing, cost of for Indonesia, 250, 252*f*

external liabilities, in Indonesia, 249, 250*f*

external sector
in Indonesia, 244, 245*f*
supporting growth, 309

External Sector Reports (IMF), 278, 280, 282

External Wealth of Nations dataset, 125

factors of trade, inefficient allocation of, 258

"fair" trade, 15

family circumstances, making regular employment compatible with, 148

famines, man-made in the 20th century, 11

FDI Regulatory Restrictiveness Index (OECD), 248–249

Federal Reserve, purchased long-term bonds, 303

feedback loops, negative, 6

Feldstein-Horioka puzzle, 400–401

female employment, potential of, 46

female labor force participation rates (LFPRs), 46*n*

female workers
better utilizing, 134
in Japan, 133, 141, 143, 143*f*, 146

fertility rates
in Asia, 34*f*
in Bangladesh, 19
in China, 182
control of by inexpensive means, 11
decline in encouraging more women in the labor force, 46
declining since the late 1960s, 34
effect of after 10 years, 176, 177*f*
in Japan, 148
in Korea, 166*n*
in Korea and select countries, 1980–2015, 168*f*
lower with richer nations or persons, 11
in the Philippines, 37
slowdown worldwide, 19
in the United States, 168*f*

fertilizers, from emergence of organic chemistry, 17

financial capital, provided to "insider" firms in Japan, 81

financial conditions, easy promoting leverage, 278

financial crisis, in Japan, 289*n*

financial cycle-augmented Taylor rule, federal funds rate implied by, 306

financial deregulation, in Japan proceeded slowly, 82

financial distortions, powering the US current account deficit, 275

financial exposure, stock and flow indicators of, 248–251

financial frictions, spilling over across countries, 107

financial globalization, 312

financial imbalances, buildup of, 334

financial integration, 66*n*, 110, 117

financial intermediaries, interest rate risks on the balance sheets of, 307

financial linkages, 243, 244

financial markets
allowing monetary policy to affect a wide array of market prices, 334

demographic trends for, 67
efficiency of in Korea, 170
expecting a permanent slowdown in
    advanced economies, 244
implications of demographic trends
    for, 53–64
improving access to in India, 222
in Japan, 81–82
financial openness
    Chinn-Ito index of, 109–110, 118, 125
    of Indonesia, 245, 245f
financial policies, in Indonesia, 242
financial risks, sector-specific, 308
financial sector, supervisory oversight in
    Indonesia, 242
financial side effects, risks during recovery
    phases, 7
financial stability
    from accommodative monetary policy,
        334
    considerations regarding, 334–335
    mitigating risks, 64
    risks to, 286, 304–309
    worries not justifying keeping the
        policy rate higher than warranted,
        312
financial vulnerabilities, in various parts of
    the world, 315
financing, of labor sector reforms, 367
finite resource, planet earth as, 21
firm-level data, results often difficult to
    translate to the aggregate level, 108
firms. See also large firms
    deferring compensation in Japan, 144
    early emergence of leading, 75b
    increasing part-time workers in Japan,
        146
    incumbent resisting rendering existing
        business models obsolete, 76b
    investment determined by a Tobin's
        Q combined with the Bernanke-
        Gertler-Gilchrist model, 338
    in job training contributing more to
        firm-size wage differences, 155
    as net borrowers, 338
    not adjusting investments in response
        to exchange rate fluctuations, 205,
        220t–221t
    paying a premium to part-time
        workers, 145
    productivity and wage gaps between
        large and small in Japan, 149–159
    reluctant to employ more regular
        employees in Japan, 162

response to demand shocks in Korea,
    169
firm-size differences, in labor quality and
    TFP, 158
firm-size wage differences, 149, 156
"the first 21st century crisis," 269
fiscal and quasi-fiscal expenditures,
    planning of, 186, 191
fiscal institutions, need for supporting, 371,
    373–376
fiscal measures, effects on real GDP in
    selected Asian economies, 368f–369f
fiscal packages
    composition and cost of, 379–383,
        380t–381t, 382t–383t
    covering public infrastructure, tax
        rebalancing, and labor markets, 363
fiscal policy
    addressing long-term implications of
        the new mediocre, 377
    addressing the risk of a new mediocre,
        343
    assisting monetary policy, 325
    complementing monetary policy, 328
    governed by long-run fiscal policy
        targets, 339
    political desire for wasteful procyclical,
        132–133
    supporting sustained and inclusive
        growth, 353, 355
fiscal reforms
    effects across Asia, 367–370
    financing through debt, 377
    illustrative packages, 365–367
    payoff in a low-inflation environment,
        370–371
    potential to improve growth, 343
    quantifying the payoff of, 363–371
fiscal room, determining available, 132
fiscal rules, 373–374, 374f
fiscal space
    in Indonesia, 242
    using, 7
fiscal stabilization, in Japan, 130, 133
fiscal stimulus
    in Abenomics, 139
    early improving outcomes in Australia,
        325
fiscal sustainability, 5
flexible inflation targeting, 318–319, 324
floating exchange rate era, 269
flow deficit, 278
flow indicators, 248
flying geese formation, 407

forecast, deviating from a previous, 323
foreign assets, 112, 309
foreign capital, volatility of, 251*f*
foreign currency
    debts in the corporate sector, 309–310
    exposure of liabilities, 250*n*
    liabilities, rapid decline in, 249
foreign direct investment (FDI)
    attracting, 267
    gross external positions representing, 275, 278
    regulatory environment impeding, 248
foreign exchange reserves
    accumulation of after the Asian financial crisis, 301–302
    continued accumulation not justified, 310
    in many Asian economies, 309–311, 311*f*
foreign exchange reserves and net official assets in Asia, 1985–2016, 311*f*
foreign interest rates, 113, 114
foreign investors, 297
foreign secular stagnation. *See also* secular stagnation
    developments representing, 111
    impact on the real exchange rate, 113
    leading initially to a boom in capital inflows, 114
    responses to, 112
foreign workers, 65, 65*n*
forward guidance, on the policy rate, 301, 322
forward-looking, model-consistent expectations (leads), 337
forward-looking models, anchoring inflation expectations in the short run, 320*n*
"frankenfoods," concerns about, 23
frontier firms, TFP differences with nonfrontier firms, 149*n*
fuel subsidies, lowering in Indonesia, 242
full disclosure, 323
full employment, mandated for in Australia, 324
Funding for Lending scheme, of the Bank of England, 302

G-7 economies, growth slowdown besetting, 1
G20MOD country model, 338–340
gaslighting, supported by pneumatic chemistry, 17
GDP. *See also* real GDP

data in current prices from the CEIC, 224–225
gap shrinking in Japan, 141
growth
    abandoning targets in China, 188
    higher real, 332
    impact of demographic trends, 42*f*
    in India, 197
    overemphasis on performance, 188
growth rate
    in China, 181
    in Korea and Japan, 173*f*
    imbalances to, 392
    per capita
        correlation with government revenue as percent of GDP, 2015, 362*f*
        impacted by demographic trends, 42*f*
    ratio of trade to, 388, 388*f*
GEMPACK software, 183*n*
gems and jewelry, as exports, 212*f*
gender inequality index, 49*n*
generalized method of moments (GMM) estimator, 204*n*
Germany, 20*n*, 39*f*, 55*f*, 136
"gig economy," 20*n*
global business cycles, export basket in India sensitive to, 199
global current account balances and reserve purchases, 271*f*
global current account imbalances, 270, 271*f*
global deflationary spiral, likelihood of, 237
global economy
    forward-looking, multieconomy model of, 338
    Indonesia's financial integration with, 248*f*
    profound changes, 239
    stagnation of, 166
    underperforming for several years, 315
global financial crisis
    background to, 273–278
    channels of contagion during, 105
    effects on different countries, 104
    as an important step in diffusion of secular stagnation, 104
    Indonesia not suffering from the recessionary impact of, 238
    interest rates before and after by country, 2000–16, 117*f*
    interest rates before and after by region, 115*f*
    as a "natural experiment," 123

natural rate of interest declining after, 54
of 2008–09, 270
global financial cycle, 121
global financial integration, across emerging markets, 249*f*
global financing shocks, 250
global gross financial flows, 276*f*
global growth, 194, 195, 199
global imbalances. *See also* imbalances
calculated, 388, 388*f*
correlated with global trade, 403
effects of shifts in on countries' subsequent trade positions, 405
in the emerging markets, 270
excess, 278, 282
and global trade since 1982, 366*f*
linking to the decline in the growth rate of international trade flows, 403
mono-causal explanations for excessive, 4
owing little to foreign exchange intervention by EMDEs, 281
policy implications, 282–283
relationship with trade, 5
relationship with trade flows, 403–404
relative to global trade remaining constant, 389
rise of, 270–273
risks from excess, 278–282
role in fueling trade growth, 400
twenty-five years of, 269–283
widening and narrowing of, 387, 397*f*, 401
global imbalances/GDP, versus global imbalances/trade, 390*f*
global implications, of Asia's demographic evolution, 38
global integration, India's, 194, 223
global investment liabilities stock, 277*f*
global liquidity trap, 105
globally integrated economy, channels of international transmission of secular stagnation, 103
global neutral real rate, settling at around 1 percent in the medium to long run, 293
global real prices, determining, 339
global real trade growth, contributions to, 390, 392*f*, 393*f*
global risks, India vulnerable to, 4
global supply chains. *See also* supply chains
development of explaining the recent trade slowdown, 398

India's growing participation in, 229
global trade
slowdown symptomatic of secular stagnation, 242
slowdown unprecedented in recent history, 387
world trade growth under more balanced global trade, 396–401
global value chains, India's limited role in, 230, 231*f*
Gourinchas-Rey effect, 280
government(s)
fiscal stimulus targeting the lower middle class in Indonesia, 267
policies encouraging entrepreneurship and global competitiveness in Japan, 164
publishing balance sheets in China, 190
purchases of bonds, 302
reducing exposure to SOE-related fiscal risks, 376
resisting higher bond yields, 304
revenue as percent of GDP, 362*f*
revenue ratios compared with other economies, 359, 362*f*
spending or taxation mattering more than debt levels, 132
supported the low-inflation objective, 318
gravity models, indicating geographical proximity conducive to trade, 410
"gray market" for capital, tolerated in Taiwan, 92
Great Depression, described, 305
Great Enrichment, 9, 18
Great Recession, 105, 111
Greece, governance indicators, 22
gross capital flows, 282–283
gross external positions, 275, 277*f*
Group 1 (Japan), 347*b*, 368*f*, 370
Group 2 countries
effect of fiscal reforms, 370
including China, Hong Kong, Korea, Singapore, and Thailand, 347*b*
increasing spending pressures from demographic trends, 359
projected effects of fiscal measures, 369*f*
Group 3 countries
gaining from reforms and positive spillovers, 370

including Bangladesh, Cambodia, India, Indonesia, Laos, Malaysia, Maldives, Mongolia, Myanmar, the Philippines, Sri Lanka, Vietnam, and the Pacific Island countries, 347*b*
needing to step up public spending, 359
projected effects of fiscal measures, 369*f*
growth
in absolute balance relative to trade, 392, 394
accounting
components of decelerated, 166, 167*f*
of Korea, 167*t*
results of, 166–169
deceleration, in China, 182–185
demographic trends, implications of, 40–50
in imbalances, 390
impact of demographic trends and higher labor force participation, 49*f*
as natural-resource-using or resource-saving, 21
normal in the 20th and 21st centuries, 10
outlines of a model for sustaining, 8
payoff of fiscal reforms, 363–371
promoting slower but higher-quality in China, 186
rate(s)
in Korea decreasing, 169
ratio of trade to GDP and the ratio of global imbalances to GDP, 388, 389*f*
of real per capita GDP, 287–288, 287*f*
in ratios of trade/GDP and imbalances/GDP, 389*f*
role of demographic and structural factors in, 133–135
role of exports in India's, 195, 196*f*, 197
slowdown in China, 184–185
"Smithian" in nature in the pre-Industrial Revolution era, 14
strategy
structural reforms in Abenomics, 139
targeting manufacturing in Indonesia, 267
guest worker programs, targeting specific skills, 65

Haber-Bosch nitrogen-fixing process, 12*n*
"handbooks," compiled by groups of experts, 26
Hansen, Alvin, 28
Hartz IV labor market reform, in Germany, 133
healthcare
efficiency frontier of public spending on, 358*f*
making available for older workers, 65
public spending on, 355, 358*f*
reform of, 374–375
heterogeneity, in external exposure, 245
high-tech startup incubators, in China, 185
historical primary balance scenario, for public debt projection, 348
Hong Kong
aging
change between 2020 and 2030, 58*f*
impact on growth, 41
impact on TFP, 48*f*
rapid until 2030, 52
contribution to real trade growth, 393*f*
CPI inflation rates, 288*f*
credit gaps, increases in, 119
current account balances, 1985–2016, 310*f*
demographic characteristics, 35*t*
demographic trends, impact of, 42*f*
fiscal packages, 380*t*, 382*t*
foreign exchange reserves and net official assets, 311*f*
in Group 2, 347*b*
immigration, 37, 43
infrastructure, index of quality of, 356*f*
interest rates
lowered after the crisis, 116
nominal fell close to zero, 124
real short-term, 293*f*
labor force participation, 48*f*, 49*f*
old-age dependency ratio, 36*t*, 38*f*, 52, 57, 57*f*
older workers, share of, 44*f*
personal income tax (PIT) yields, 363*f*
as a post-dividend economy, 35
public spending
on education, 359*f*
on health care, 355, 358*f*
R&D spending, 357
real per capita GDP, growth rate of, 287*f*
research and development spending, 362*f*

scope for quantitative easing, December 2016, 303*t*
tax revenues, direct taxes as a small share of, 366
tax revenue sources, 364*f*
trade growth in, 399*t*
workforce, share of, with productivity rising or falling, 45*f*
youth dependency ratio, 57*f*
Hong Kong Monetary Authority, 298
household deposits, lack of pass-through of negative rates, 300
household property mortgages, rules on, 308
households, types of in APDMOD, 365
housing bubble, 306
Hsinchu Science Park, 94–95
Huawei, 91, 91*n*
"human bridges," 76*b*
human capital
    concentrated in large firms in Japan, 81
    East Asian investment in, 78
    growth rate of slowing, 258
    in Japan, 77–78
    raising in India, 222
    upgrading, 65
human capital accumulation
    affecting TFP, 258
    boosting, 353
    economic loss by reducing, 162
    growth rate in Indonesia, 258
    high-skill in Indonesia, 258, 259*f*
    supporting, 367
hydrostatics, needed for ship design, 17*n*
hyperglobalization, 270, 400
Hyundai, 86*n*

ideas, 27, 28
imbalances. *See also* global imbalances
    enhancing transmission from slow US growth to East Asian exports and imports, 398
    expanding openness in China, 396
    moving together with trade within countries, 394
    relationship with trade, 388, 389–390
    and trade growth at the country level, 391–392, 394–396
IMF. *See* International Monetary Fund (IMF)
immigration
    effects on the workforce, 43, 43*n*

prolonging the demographic dividend, 65
softening the impact of aging, 67
impact theory, 17*n*
import constraint, in deficit countries, 396
imported intermediate inputs, in sectors with low domestic value, 205, 210*t*
imported intermediates, response to an appreciation of the rupee, 204, 208*t*–209*t*
imports
    by deficit countries, 390
    growth rates declining for Indonesia, 244*n*
    by region to Indonesia, 245, 246*f*, 247
    temporary trade restrictions on Indonesian, 258, 260*f*
imports-to-GDP ratio, for China, 396
income growth, relationship with trade growth, 387
income per capita, on a global scale as self-limiting, 21
incomes policy, aimed directly at sluggish wage-price dynamics, 332
India
    aging, impact on TFP, 48*f*
    aging speed change between 2020 and 2030, 58*f*
    banks' nonperforming and restructured assets, 232*f*
    central bank, attempting to reduce long-term expectations of inflation, 317
    central bank, transparency, 323, 324*f*
    Consumer Price Index (CPI) inflation declining, 324
    CPI inflation rates, 1985–2016, 288*f*
    credibility, building, 328–330
    current account balances, 1985–2016, 310*f*
    dark corner for, 338
    debt paths, stabilizing, 353
    debt ratio change under Scenario 4*b*, 354*f*
    demographic characteristics, 35*t*
    demographic impact on current account, 53*f*
    demographics, impact on 10-year real interest rates, 61*f*
    demographic trends, impact of, 42*f*
    as an early-dividend economy, 37
    endogenous policy credibility, model of, 337–338
    exchange rate appreciation, 231

exporting firms reacting to exchange
  rate changes, 202, 204–221
exports
  changes in, 193
  changing composition of, 198–199
  global share versus China, 198*f*
  of goods and services in current US
    dollars, 196*f*
  and imports, 194*f*
  pillars for increasing, 222
  reflecting the new normal, 193–223
  revelation, 4
  sensitivity to changes, 200–202
  as a share of GDP, 195, 195*f*, 196*f*
  weak relationship with exchange
    rates, 202
fertility rate, 37
financial integration with the rest of
  the world, 194
firm outcomes and exchange rates
  by domestic value added, 210*t*
  investment, 220*t*–221*t*
  profits, 217*t*
  salaries and wage expenses,
    218*t*–219*t*
  total expenses, 215*t*–216*t*
  total sales, 213*t*–214*t*
  value of exports, 206*t*–207*t*
  value of imported raw materials,
    208*t*–209*t*
fiscal packages, 380*t*, 383*t*
foreign capital, volatility of the supply
  of, 251*f*
foreign exchange reserves and net
  official assets, 1985–2016, 311*f*
GDP growth, 197
global value chains, limited role in,
  230, 231*f*
in Group 3, 347*b*
growth, continued to enjoy higher, 194
growth slowdown, role of experts in,
  196*f*, 197*f*
infrastructure, index of quality of, 356*f*
insulation from global growth and/or
  protectionist shocks, 194
internal trade barriers, 231
labor force participation, 48*f*, 49*f*
long-term public debt projection, 349*t*
manufacturing and services exports:
  check for nonlinearity, 227*t*–228*t*
manufacturing exports, sectoral
  change in, 2003–15, 199*f*
market share of exports over time,
  211*f*, 212*f*

merchandise and service exports,
  200–201, 201*t*, 203*t*
monetary policy, establishing
  expectations on inflation, 329
months inflation rate below inflation
  target, 371*f*
most-favored nation (MFN) applied
  tariff rates, 230*f*
old-age dependency ratio, 38*f*, 57*f*
older workers, share of, 44*f*
openness of the economy, 193–198,
  232–233
per capita income level, 39*f*
personal income tax (PIT) yields, 363*f*
policy responses, delay of, 331*f*
primary commodity exports, demand
  for from Indonesia, 243*n*
public debt, actual and projected, 346*f*,
  351*f*
public spending
  on education as percent of GDP,
    359*f*
  efficiency frontier, 378*t*
  on health care as percent of GDP,
    358*f*
  on pensions and health care, 346*f*
quarterly projection model for, 328
real per capita GDP, growth rate of,
  1985–2016, 287*f*
real short-term interest rate, 292
real short-term interest rate, 1985–
  2016, 293*f*
research and development spending,
  362*f*
resources, misallocation of, 232
Scenario 3 and, 350, 352
scope for quantitative easing,
  December 2016, 303*t*
scope limited to reallocate spending,
  366*n*
services in export basket (including
  oil), 199*f*
SOEs in, 376
structural rigidities, needing to
  address, 233
supply shocks, 328–330, 330*f*
tariff barriers, relatively high, 230, 230*f*
tax revenue sources, 364*f*
VAT increases, already factoring in,
  366
working age populations growing
  substantially, 344, 346*f*
youth dependency ratio, 57*f*
indirect taxes, 366, 368–369, 376

Indonesia
  aging, impact on TFP, 48f
  aging speed change between 2020 and
    2030, 58f
  average openness (exports + imports),
    2000–16, 245, 245f
  budget deficit legally limited, 266
  CPI inflation rates, 288f
  credit gaps, increases in, 119
  current account balances, 310f
  debt ratio change under Scenario 4b,
    354f
  demographic characteristics, 35t
  demographic impact on current
    account, 53f
  demographics, impact on 10-year real
    interest rates, 61f
  demographic trends, impact of, 42f
  domestic and external factors role in
    the deceleration of TFP growth in,
    258
  domestic demand, 239, 241
  domestic real GDP growth, correlation
    with domestic and global factors,
    253, 253t
  as an early-dividend economy, 37
  Emerging Market Bond Index (EMBI)
    spread, 252f
  energy and commodities, producer of,
    266
  export demand, insulated from weaker,
    247
  exports by region, 245, 246f, 247
  external balance sheet foreign currency
    exposure, 250f
  external demand from advanced
    economies, 247, 247f
  external financing, cost of, 250, 252f
  external sector, 244, 245f
  fertility rates, 19, 37
  financially integrated economies, one
    of the least, 249, 249f
  fiscal buffers, 353
  fiscal packages, 381t, 383t
  foreign exchange reserves and net
    official assets, 311f
  foreign participation, bans on, 249
  global developments, insulated from,
    263
  global economy, financial integration
    with, 248, 248f
  global economy, reduced financial
    integration with, 248f
  global financial integration, 249f

  in Group 3, 347b
  growth
    domestic and external contributions
      to, 251, 253–255
    higher since the global financial
      crisis, 194
    rate of real per capita GDP, 287f
    rate of the working-age population,
      261f
    sources of lower potential, 256
  health care, gap between actual and
    expected public spending on, 355n
  imports by region, 245, 246f, 247
  infrastructure, index of quality of, 356f
  labor, future paths for, 261
  labor force participation, impact of
    higher, 49f
  labor force participation rate, 48f,
    261–262, 261f
  long-term public debt projection, 349t
  medium-term potential growth
    increasing, 262
  months inflation rate below inflation
    target, 371f
  more exposed than other large
    economies, 245
  most-favored nation (MFN) applied
    tariff rates, 230f
  as a net debtor, 243n
  net emigration from, impact of, 43
  old-age dependency ratio, 36t, 38f, 57f
  older workers, share of, 44f
  output dynamics, 238–242, 255–257
  per capita income level, 39f
  personal income tax (PIT) yields, 363f
  population with tertiary education,
    259f
  potential growth rate, 256–257, 257f
  potential output growth rate, 255–256,
    256f
  protectionism, increase in, 258
  public debt, actual and projected, 346f,
    351f
  public spending
    on education as percent of GDP,
      359f
    efficiency frontier, distance from,
      378t
    on health care as percent of GDP,
      358f
    on pensions and health care, 346f
  R&D spending, 357
  real GDP growth, 239f, 240f, 241f, 247f
  real GDP volatility, 241f

real neutral interest rates, 56f
real output growth, low volatility of, 239, 241f
real short-term interest rate, 293f
real trade growth, 393f
regulatory environment impeding foreign direct investment (FDI), 248
regulatory quality, 1996–2015, 260f
research and development spending, 362f
Scenario 3 and, 350, 352
scenario analysis, 262f
scope for quantitative easing, December 2016, 303t
secular stagnation
    the age of, 235–263
    countering, 255–262
    exposure to in advanced economies, 244–251
SOEs in, 376
spillovers of secular stagnation, 238–255
students with higher education, 259f
tax revenue sources, 364f
temporary trade restrictions on imports, 258
temporary trade restrictions on imports, 1996–2015, 260f
10-year government yield, change in, 55f
trade and financial engagement, ongoing decline in, 238
trade-based exposure to secular stagnation, 244–248
trade growth in, 399t
turning inward, 4
volatility of the supply of foreign capital, 251f
working age populations growing, 344, 346f
youth dependency ratio, 57f
inductive method, in science, 25
Industrial Bank of Korea, rate for 3-year bonds issued by, 175f
industrial concentration, in Korea, 86
industrial research productivity, decline in Japanese, 83–85, 84f
Industrial Revolution, 15, 16
Industrial Technology Research Institute (ITRI), in Taiwan, 93
industry creation, science-based and closely connected to university research, 76b
inflation
    in Asia, 2

under a central bank's target, 67
correlation to Indonesia's real GDP growth, 253t
dangers of ultra-low, 289–298
deviation from targeted, 321
expectations, 321–322, 337
failing to increase as no longer Japan-specific, 130
keeping at or above 2 percent, 4
keeping within policy mandate, 312
lower expected accompanied by low nominal rates of interest, 292
overshooting target, 323
persistence, higher levels of, 328
secular downward pressure on, 294
inflationary pressures, containing for India, 338
inflation forecast-based reaction function, ignoring inflation shocks, 320
inflation forecasts, 318
inflation-forecast targeting, 319, 320, 324
inflation rate(s)
    in the Asia-15 economies, 288–289, 288f
    failure to raise in Japan, 130
    of at least 2 percent needed, 291–292
    low coupled with a low equilibrium real interest rate, 294
    measured by CPI in Japan, 290f
    number of months below inflation target in selected Asian economies, 371f
inflation spiral, 320
inflation surprises, 295, 300, 301f
inflation targeting, 285, 317–319
informality, contributing to low tax yields, 359
infrastructure
    building and improving in India, 222
    increasing spending, 355
    index of quality of, 356f
    investment, 353, 367
        in China, 187
        impact on growth, 368
        in physical and human in India, 222
innate ability, gap across workers in Japan, 155
innovation
    bad institutions supporting resistance to, 23
    determining productivity growth at the frontier, 107
    incremental, 90, 100

Japanese companies underinvested in, 163
Japanese style focused on relatively incremental invention, 79n
leadership in East Asia, 74
maintaining a high level of, 29
pro-incremental and pro-incumbent biases in East Asia, 96
rates of, 6
reform of Japan's system for, 84
shifting from radical experimentation to incremental improvements of existing designs, 75b
systems, 3, 75b
innovative activity, incremental, 75b
innovative firms, motivating employees in Japan, 85
innovators, output sustaining growth without increasing effort, 27
institutional changes, reorienting from external to domestic demand, 237
institutions
    extending credit to households and firms, 334
    quality of, key to adopting superior technologies, 259
insufficient final demand (excess saving problem), in Japan, 139
insularity, in Indonesia, 244n
insurers and service providers, competition among, 375
intellectual property protection, in Japan, 78-79
intellectual property rights, 6, 76b
intellectual property system, strengthened in Japan, 84
interest parity equation, 112
interest rate(s)
    adjusting to the target, 320
    adverse effects of low, 124
    before and after the global financial crisis, 115f, 117f
    aversion to large changes in, 321
    decline in (real) attributable to changes in real sector fundamentals, 176
    decline in long-term, 54, 55f
    declining in Asia, 2
    decreasing everywhere since the early 1990s, 123
    demographic trends, impact of, 54-62
    demographic variables, impact of, 56t
    domestic demographic factors, impact of, 59

exogenous having no nominal anchor, 320
exposures rising to risks, 308
financial stability risks, keeping too raising, 334
foreign secular stagnation, insulating from, 114
high enough to counter a potential financial threat as crippling, 305
levels before the global financial crisis and after, 115
low
    creating larger maturity mismatch risks, 308
    encouraging debtors to continue borrowing, 278
    having problematic side effects, 103
    leading central banks, 335
    transmitted across countries, 104
in the macroeconomic spillover data, 115
near their effective lower bound, 316
not responding to much higher public debt levels, 132
policy in Taiwan, 92
world real, 55f
interest rate growth differential. See IRGD (interest rate growth differential)
interest rates, low, reducing debt service burdens of borrowers, 304
interfirm alliances, in Japan, 82-83
international financial cooperation, need for, 283
international financial institutions, structural impediments in Indonesia, 259-260, 260f
international financial integration, measures of, 125
International Monetary Fund (IMF)
    Asia and Pacific Department of, 2
    on export performance of India, 229
    monitoring external excess imbalances annually, 282
    projecting a bigger US current account deficit in coming years, 281
    projections of growth prospects for advanced economies, 280
international monetary regime, period of adjustment to the new, 269
international spillovers, exposing lower-income economies to secular stagnation, 2
intra-Asian trade, as an established phenomenon, 410

inventions
  epistemic base of, 15
  as incremental, 75*b*
  land-augmenting, 12*n*
  recombining existing devices, 26
  temporary impact in the Middle Ages,
    15
inventors, 26
investment
  adjusting over time to the labor force,
    41*n*
  impact of aging on, 49–50
  impact of demographic variables, 51
  tending to drive trade movements, 400
  weak, accounted for three-quarters of
    the global trade slowdown, 229
  zero population growth changing the
    composition of, 20
inward-looking stance, of Indonesia, 238,
  263
inward migration, prolonging the
  demographic dividend, 43
iPhone, by Apple, 90
Iran, fertility rates, 19
Ireland, taking advantage of inventions
  made elsewhere, 28
IRGD (interest rate growth differential),
  348, 350, 353, 353*n*
Italy, per capita income level, 39*f*

James Webb Space Telescope, 24
Japan
  aging
    impact on growth, 41
    impact on TFP, 48*f*
    rapid until 2030, 52
    of the working-age population, 169*n*
  aging speed change between 2020 and
    2030, 58*f*
  banking system, subsidized lending
    to, 302
  business R&D and government
    support for business R&D, by firm
    size, 151*f*
  capital-to-output ratios, 168*f*
  central bank transparency, 323, 324*f*
  colonial rule markedly less harsh in
    Taiwan than in Korea, 91
  competition in, 82–83
  consumer price index (CPI), 174*f*
  CPI inflation rates, 288*f*
  current account balances, 274*f*, 310*f*
  debt path, stability of, 353
  debt ratio as an outlier in Asia, 344

  debt ratio change under Scenario 4b,
    354*f*
  deflation, policies to exit, 330–333
  deflation spirals, never fell into, 130
  deflation trap, struggling to escape
    from, 165
  demographic characteristics, 35*t*
  demographic impact on current
    account, 53*f*
  demographics in, 171*f*
  demographic trends, impact of, 42*f*
  early postwar era, novelty in, 77
  economic development of, 77–85
  economic integration, pursuing greater
    with the world, 130
  economy still in a dark corner in early
    2017, 331
  educational excellence in the postwar
    era, 77–78
  employees by firm size, all industries,
    159*t*
  exchange rate advantages and effects,
    79–80
  fertility rates in, 168*f*
  financial markets, 81–82
  firms
    filing a large number of patent
      applications, 79
    losing ground in the 1990s, 84
    outengineering Western rivals,
      73–74
  fiscal packages, 380*t*, 382*t*
  foreign exchange reserves and net
    official assets, 311*f*
  foreign technology purchases,
    government policy of limiting,
    93*n*–94*n*
  GDP, spent on pensions and health
    care, 344, 346*f*
  Government Pension Investment Fund
    reforms in, 66
  in Group 1, 347*b*
  growth
    drag on stable for, 41*n*
    driven by domestic sources of
      demand, 82
    policies to achieve higher
      sustainable, 324
  human capital development, 77–78
  import share of exports, 398
  industrial research productivity,
    decline in, 83–85, 84*f*
  inflation, 286, 289–291
  inflation rate measured by CPI, 290*f*

infrastructure, index of quality of, 356f
innovation system, 78, 83n
interest rates lowered after the crisis,
    116
Korea caught up with in the export
    market, 171
Korea's monetary policy compared
    with, 174n
labor, decline in the quality of, 163
labor force participation, impact of
    higher, 49f
labor force participation rate by age
    and employment status, 2013, 147f
labor force participation rates, 48f
labor market flexibility enhancing with
    human capital accumulation, 148
labor market institutions, 80–81
labor productivity, 140f, 150f
labor quality gap, 157f
labor supply, transformation of, 134
LFPRs increased the most in, 49
literacy proficiency, 142f, 143f
long-term public debt projection, 349t
lost decades, 3, 129
macroeconomic developments, 290f
monetary policy in the 1990s, 174n
months inflation rate below inflation
    target, 371f
natural interest rate around zero, 178n
natural interest rate below zero, 178
net investment, 279f
nominal GDP, growth rates, 290f
nominal GDP growth rates, 173f
nonmanufacturing sector wage and
    productivity differences by firm size,
    156f
nonregular employees, share of in total
    workers, by sector, 144f
nonregular employment problem,
    143–149
observed phenomena today occurring
    worldwide, 135
off-the-job training expenses by firm
    size, 158f
old-age dependency ratio, 35, 36t, 38f,
    52, 57f
older workers, share of, 44f
output gap, 1954Q1–2017Q1, 290f
patent system of Bismarck-era
    Germany, 78–79
pension system with automatic
    adjustment mechanisms, 375
per capita income level, 39f
personal income tax (PIT) yields, 363f

as a post-dividend economy, 35
productivity growth, 73
public debt, actual and projected, 351f
public spending
    on education as percent of GDP,
        359f
    efficiency frontier, distance from,
        378t
    on health care as percent of GDP,
        358f
    on pensions and health care, 346f
QE, currently engaged in, 302
quality of infrastructure, 355, 356f
R&D productivity, trends in, 84f
real 10-year bond yield, 272f
real estate market in a bubble in the
    1990s, 173–174
real estate prices and consumer price
    index, 174f
real neutral interest rates, 56f
real per capita GDP, growth rate of,
    287f
real short-term interest rate, 293f
real trade growth, 393f
research and development spending,
    362f
revealed comparative advantages of,
    172f
Scenario 3 and, 350
Scenario 4a and, 352
Scenario 4b and, 352
scope for quantitative easing,
    December 2016, 303t
secular stagnation, 2, 139
students, government subsidized study
    abroad for, 77
students, regularly outperform
    Americans, 87
tax revenue sources, 364f
10-year government yield, change in,
    55f
Three Arrows Plus policy package, 333f
total factor productivity, 96, 141f
trade growth, slowdown in, 194
trade growth in, 399t
trade imbalances, widening, 391
trade surpluses, expanded, 388
unemployment rate, 1954Q1–2017Q1,
    290f
universities underperforming in
    graduate education, 78
VAT increases, factoring in, 366
wage and productivity differences,
    153f, 154f, 155f

wage level, 145f
workforce, share of, 45f
working-age population, decline in, 38
youth dependency ratio, 57f
Japan Industrial Productivity (JIP)
    Database, 144–145, 163
Japanization, Korea at risk of, 170–175
job card system, in Japan, 148, 163
Jorgenson-Griliches-type labor quality
    indices, 152

keiretsu networks, in Japan, 82
Kircher, Athanasius, 26n
KLEMS-type data of the market economy,
    in Japan, 150
kleptocracies, 14
knowledge
    exponential growth of, 27
    making accessible, 26
    propositional and prescriptive, 18
    of underlying natural rules, 16
knowledge-based jobs, age making no
    difference in performance, 20n
knowledge-based technological change, 16n
knowledge transmission, improved
    methods of, 27
Korea (South Korea)
    age-related spending projected to rise,
        344, 346f
    aging
        fiscal pressures from, 353
        impact on growth, 41
        impact on TFP, 48f
        rapid until 2030, 52
    aging speed change between 2020 and
        2030, 58f
    capital-to-output ratios, 168f
    central bank transparency, 323, 324f
    commodity semiconductor products,
        producers of, 89
    consumer price index (CPI), 174f
    core CPI inflation, 296f
    core inflation, 295, 296f
    CPI inflation rates, 288f
    current account balances, 310f
    debt ratio change under Scenario 4b,
        354f
    deflation, not replicating Japan's, 173
    demographic characteristics, 35t
    demographic impact on current
        account, 53f
    demographic projections for, 166n
    demographics, 171f
    demographics, impact on 10-year real
        interest rates, 61f
    demographic trends, impact of, 42f
    economic development of, 85–91
    economic performance of, 165
    educational excellence in the postwar
        era, 77–78
    educational system expanded in reach
        and quality, 87
    fertility rates, 168f, 177f
    firms rarely the source of major
        product innovations, 90
    fiscal packages, 380t, 382t
    foreign exchange reserves and net
        official assets, 1985–2016, 311f
    fundamentals similar to those in Japan
        20 years ago, 170
    in Group 2, 347b
    growth, declining potential, 165–178
    growth accounting of, 167t
    growth rate of real per capita GDP,
        287f
    growth trend, 166–170
    health care, gap between actual and
        expected public spending on, 355n
    housing prices rising with general
        prices, 174, 174f
    human capital policy choices, 78
    import share of exports, 398
    with inflation below 1 percent in 2016,
        289
    infrastructure, index of quality of, 356f
    innovative strengths, 91
    interest rates, lowered after the crisis,
        116
    Japanese patent system, inherited by,
        88
    "Japanization," at risk of, 170–175
    in Japan's footsteps by the end of the
        1980s, 74
    labor force aging, impact of, 344
    labor force participation, impact of
        higher, 49f
    labor force participation rates, 48f
    labor productivity, 2014, 140f
    level of productivity remained the
        same over the past 20 years, 96
    literacy proficiency among 16–65-year-
        olds, 142f
    long-term public debt projection, 349t
    median age, projected rise in, 20n
    monetary policy compared with
        Japan's, 174n

monetary policy since the Asian
financial crisis, 296f
months inflation rate below inflation
target, 371f
mortality rate, 177f
natural interest rate, declining, and
monetary policy, 175–178, 175f,
176t, 177f
natural interest rate, estimating, 178n
negative shocks, preparing policy
measures for large, 178
nominal and real interest rates, 175f
nominal GDP growth rates, trends in,
173f
nominal interest rates, 124, 175
old-age dependency ratio, 36t, 57f, 344
expected to rise relatively quickly, 57
higher by 2030, 52
increasing from 15 to 20 percent,
38f
older workers, share of, 44f
pensions in as partially defined-benefit
systems, 375
per capita income level, 39f
per capita income trailing Japan's by
20 years, 172, 173f
personal income tax (PIT) yields, 363f
PISA scores, on the frontier for, 357,
361f
policies and pro-incremental bias in,
87–91
as a postdividend economy, 35
production sites squeezed by Chinese
manufacturing capabilities, 90
public debt, actual and projected, 346f,
351f
public health care spending, 355
public spending
on education as percent of GDP,
359f
efficiency frontier, distance from,
378t
on health care as percent of GDP,
358f
on pensions and health care, 346f
R&D expenditure, high, 357
R&D spending among, 88f
real estate prices and consumer price
index, 174f
real natural interest rates, effects of
changes in fundamental variables
on, 176t
real neutral interest rates, 56f, 177f
real short-term interest rate, 293f

real trade growth, 393f
recession, heading for a prolonged, 3
research and development spending,
362f
resource allocation, efficiency of,
169–170
revealed comparative advantages of,
172f
Scenario 3 and, 350
scope for quantitative easing,
December 2016, 303t
secular stagnation, exhibiting features
of, 2
short-term interest rates, 295, 296f
students regularly outperform
Japanese students, 87
tax revenue sources, 364f
10-year government yield, change in,
55f
total factor productivity, 177f
trade growth, 194, 399t
trade imbalances, widening, 391
trade surpluses, expanded, 388
trend growth in nominal GDP
deviating from that of Japan, 173
20-year lag, mimicking Japan, 3
underpriced Japanese rivals in the
1980s, 89
universities, limited research
capabilities of, 88
workforce, share of with productivity
rising or falling, 45f
working-age population, absolute
decline in, 38
youth dependency ratio, 57f
Korean Ministry of Strategy and Finance, 2
Kuwait, invasion of in August 1990, 21

labor
future paths in Indonesia, 261
increases in the supply of, 133–134
increasing supply through provision of
social benefits, 353
reforms having a long-term impact,
368f–369f, 370
reforms package, 366–367
labor force
declining in China, 184–185
impact of aging on, 344
impact on economic growth, 40–43
participation
in China, 183f
increasing, 65
participation rate

by age and employment status, in
Japan, 147f
ages 15-64 in, 48f
impact of aging on, 46-49
impact on growth for small changes
in, 49n
in Indonesia, 261-262
Indonesia vs. EU-28 and OECD,
261f
male, 46n
projections and assumptions about,
261
remaining unchanged, 41
shrinkage, postponement of in Japan,
134
significant decline in since 2013 in
China, 182, 183f
labor income, 62n, 353
labor input, in Japan, 150
labor-intensive manufacturing/services
pathway, 409
labor market
bias against workers over 50, 20n
changes in Japan, 133, 162
decrease in the number of workers
entering in Korea, 166
enhancing flexibility, 134
institutions in Japan, 80-81
issues key to Japan's revitalization, 142
policies increasing government
spending, 367
policies promoting active, 65
pro-incumbent bias of institutions in
Japan, 81
reforms in Japan, 130
reforms offsetting adverse growth
effects of aging, 65
reforms relieving Japan's two
structural problems, 143
rigidity of Japan's, 148
tightening in Japan, 141
labor mobility
across firms limited in Japan, 78, 155
importance of, 75b, 76b
in response to demand shocks in
Korea, 169
labor productivity
differences between small and large
firms by country, 150f
gap between Japan and the United
States widening, 162
growth declining reducing annual
economic growth, 184
in Japan, 149, 150f, 152, 162

in Japan and United States, 1947-
2012, 140f
in major OECD countries,2014, 140f
raising, 367
labor quality
as critical to Japan's worsening
productivity performance, 162
differences declining between large
and small firms, 152
differences in based on Jorgenson-
Griliches approach, 153, 157f
effects of improvement in in Japan,
145n
gap, 157f
implications for policy and companies,
163
labor unions, prioritizing job security in
Japan, 148
land and natural resources, diminishing
returns from, 11
land contamination, costs likely to rise, 183
Laos
actual and projected public debt, 346f
distance from public spending
efficiency frontier, 378t
in Group 3, 347b
personal income tax (PIT) yields, 363f
public spending on education as
percent of GDP, 359f
public spending on health care as
percent of GDP, 358f
tax revenue sources, 364f
trade growth in, 399t
large balance sheet effects, absence of not
specific to Japan, 135
large firms. See also firms
decline in technology spillovers from
in Japan, 149
labor quality based on the Jorgenson-
Griliches approach, 153-154, 157f
providing more job training to workers
in Japan, 155
lasers, 24-25
late-dividend demographic characteristic,
35t
late-dividend economies, 35, 37
Laue, Max von, 24
learning-by-exporting hypothesis, 107
Lee Jae-yong, 87
Lee Kuan Yew, 22
Lee Kun-hee, 87
Lee Myung-bak, 86
legal systems, biased, 12
legislative support, for fiscal rules, 373

Lehman Brothers, collapse of, 294f
leverage, relating to strategic replication, 407–408
LG, 86n
liberal democracy, in Italy and Germany after 1945, 23
life-cycle savings, positive effect of aging speed, 58
life expectancy
    in Asia, 34f
    increases in, 46
    linking changes in the retirement age (or benefits) to, 65–66
    rising, 34
lifetime employment system, 80–81, 148
life-work balance, in Japan, 141, 148
light radar (Lidar), 25
"limited regular employment," in Japan, 148
linear inflation forecast-based reaction function, for Australia, 325, 326f
linear reaction functions, performing poorly in abnormal times, 321
liquidity-constrained households, 365
liquidity constrained households, 365n
liquidity traps
    avoiding the danger of, 295
    emerging-market and developing economies at a safe distance from, 124
    falling into, 114
    global, 105
    international propagation of, 105n
    pushing economies into, 124
literacy proficiency, 142f, 143f
loan-to-value (LTV) ratios, compared to debt-to-income ratios, 308
local bond market liquidity, swings in affecting local financial conditions, 297
local governments (China)
    avoiding further expansion of debt, 189
    central government issuing mandates for, 186
    contingent and implicit liabilities of, 190
    debt surging, 187
    promotion of officials, 186
    topping up the national growth target, 188
longevity, impact on current account balances, 51–52

long-term and policy interest rate, for Japan, 333f
long-term bond yields: Emerging Asia and selected advanced economies, 294f
long-term inflation expectations
    for India, 338
    in Japan, 291
long-term interest rates
    declined since 2000, 292, 294f
    demographics and, 60t
    of emerging Asian economies, 292
    in Korea, 175, 175f
    lowered, 307
long-term output, estimating, 41
long-term public debt projections, 349t
long-time employment relationships
    declining in importance in Japan, 147f
    in Japan, 146
loss absorbency requirements, reducing spillover risks, 334
loss function, procedure minimizing, 321
loss-minimization approach, to policy formulation, 320–322
loss-minimizing policy response, simulated, 329, 330f
lost decade, in Japan, 129
lower-for-longer interest rate, 325
lower-income countries, tending to grow faster, 169n
low-inflation environment, payoff to fiscal reforms in, 370–371
low-inflation trap, 316, 316n, 320

M2 growth, in China, 181–182, 187
macroeconomic developments
    in Asia, 287–289, 287f
    in Japan, 290f
macroeconomic forecast, publication of, 322
macroeconomic frameworks, undertaking stabilizing stimulus, 8
macroeconomic leverage, 181, 184, 187
macroeconomic management framework, in China, 4, 181, 187, 191
macroeconomic policies, 7, 64, 68
macroeconomic policy frameworks, 7, 186–190
macroeconomic slowdown, in Japan, 84
macroeconomic spillovers, in the transmission of secular stagnation, 111
macroeconomic stability screening, setting a limit on total government borrowing, 189

macroeconomic theory, on spillovers in productivity growth, 104
macro forecast, publication of, 319
macroprudential instruments, design of, 308
macroprudential policies
  addressing vulnerabilities from accommodative monetary policy, 334
  on high loan-to-value lending for mortgages, 309
  intensity of, 120, 121f
  new tools, 287
  using, 114
Malaysia
  aging, impact on TFP, 48f
  aging speed change between 2020 and 2030, 58f
  CPI inflation rates, 288f
  credit gaps, increases in, 119
  current account balances, 310f
  debt paths, stabilizing, 353
  debt ratio change under Scenario 4b, 354f
  demographic characteristics, 35t
  demographic impact on current account, 53f
  demographics impact of on 10-year real interest rates, 61f
  demographic trends, impact of, 42f
  fiscal packages, 381t, 383t
  foreign capital, volatility of the supply of, 251f
  foreign exchange reserves and net official assets, 1985–2016, 311f
  government yield, change in 10-year, 55f
  in Group 3, 347b
  infrastructure, index of quality of, 356f
  labor force participation, 48f, 49f
  as a late-dividend economy, 35, 37
  long-term public debt projection, 349t
  most-favored nation (MFN) applied tariff rates, 230f
  old-age dependency ratio, 36t, 38f, 57f
  older workers, share of, 44f
  per capita income level, 39f
  personal income tax (PIT) yields, 363f
  public debt, actual and projected, 346f, 352f
  public spending
    on education as percent of GDP, 359f
    efficiency frontier, distance from, 378t
    on health care as percent of GDP, 358f
    on pensions and health care, 346f
  real GDP growth relative to ASEAN-4, 2000–16, 241f
  real GDP volatility, 2000–16, 241f
  real neutral interest rates, 56f
  real per capita GDP, growth rate of, 1985–2016, 287f
  real short-term interest rate, 1985–2016, 293f
  real trade growth, 1998–2008, 2012–2015, 393f
  regulatory quality, 1996–2015, 260f
  research and development spending, 362f
  Scenario 3 and, 350
  scope for quantitative easing, December 2016, 303t
  SOEs in, 376
  tax revenue sources, 364f
  trade growth in, 399t
  workforce, share of with productivity rising or falling, 45f
  youth dependency ratio, 57f
Maldives, in Group 3, 347b
Malthus, Thomas, 10
Malthusian checks, evidence for the existence of, 11n
Malthusian curse, 10–12, 19
manufacturing center, China's rise as, 400
manufacturing exports, 198, 199f
manufacturing firms, connections with commercial banks, 81
manufacturing sector
  differences in labor productivity and wages increased in Japan, 153, 154f, 155f
  variation in partner income elasticities across, 202, 203t
marginal productivity of capital, determining the (real) interest rate, 176n
market leaders, attracting talented pioneers, 75b
market liquidity, in bond markets, 297
markets, buffering role against shocks, 323
median age, in the United States increasing, 19n–20n
median public debt-to-GDP ratio, 344, 345f
medical care, crushing expenses of, 20

medieval economy, as dynamic in many areas, 15
Meiji Restoration of 1868, 77
mercantilist protectionist policies, 14
merchandise and service exports, determinants of India's, 200–201, 201t
merchandise exports, from India, 4, 222, 231f
microeconomic foundations, of consumption and investment, 338
microscopes, improvements to, 24
middle-income trap, idea of, 134
migration, 37, 41, 43
minimum pension guarantees, providing, 66
ministries, setting targets for sectoral growth, 186
Ministry of Finance, pilot programs in China, 190
model(s)
 deep learning, engaging in data mining, 25
 of endogenous policy credibility for India, 337–338
 of a small open economy responding to secular stagnation abroad, 111–114
 summary of, 337–340
 for sustaining growth for Asian economies, 8
 used by central banks to conduct policy, 320
model-based simulations, illustrating the growth payoff of fiscal reform packages, 377
Moerner, William, 24
monetary accommodation, with debt financing leading to higher real GDP, 371, 372f
monetary and exchange rate policies, for sustained growth in Asia, 285–312
monetary and fiscal frameworks, reinforcing one another, 332
monetary and fiscal policies, room for maneuver, 335
monetary ease, reduced the risks of banking system loan portfolios, 334–335
monetary expansion, natural bias toward excess in China, 188
monetary growth targets, setting in China, 187
monetary policy
 accommodative in Thailand, 372f

adjusting to the outlook for financial stability, 307
aggressive easing in Abenomics, 139
allowing the interest rate to vary, 323
avoiding prolonged underemployment of resources and to sustain investment, 288
buffer to counter negative shocks in Korea and Japan, 178
building credibility amid frequent supply shocks, 328–329
countering weakness in aggregate demand, 307
credibility of, 337
easy, encouraging risky behavior in financial markets, 286
effects on the real economy, 334
enhancing the independence of in China, 186, 188, 191
expansionary improving financial stability, 309
following an inflation-targeting regime in APDOMD, 365
governed by an interest rate reaction function, 339
impact on inflation, 286
implications of slower growth rates, 285
improving communications, 317
in Indonesia, 253t
interest rate by region 2000–16, 115f
in Korea since the Asian financial crisis, 296f
measures of the BOJ, 291
minimizing a quadratic loss function, 338
in the new mediocre, 315–340
not providing a firm enough anchor in India, 329
reacting promptly to negative shocks to growth, 285
regular reports, 317
responses to negative output shocks, 316
results from low credibility, 328
risk avoidance strategy for, 317–324
risks to financial stability constraining, 304–309
scope for unconventional, 300–304
slowdown in growth for, 4
in Thailand, 296f
unable to offset the impact of fiscal shocks in Japan, 131

unlikely to jolt an economy out of a
    trap, 332
monetary transmission, changing with
    aging, 64
money laundering, addressing, 283
Mongolia
    distance from public spending
        efficiency frontier, 378t
    fiscal packages, 381t, 383t
    in Group 3, 347b
    infrastructure, index of quality of, 356f
    months inflation rate below inflation
        target, 371f
    public spending on health care as
        percent of GDP, 358f
    research and development spending,
        362f
    tax revenue sources, 364f
mortality rates, 11, 11n
most-favored nation (MFN) applied tariff
    rates, 230f
Mubarak, overthrow of, 24
multilateral dispute resolution, 283
Myanmar
    actual and projected public debt, 346f
    in Group 3, 347b

national integration, promoting in India,
    230–231
natural phenomena and patterns, observing
    and analyzing, 24
natural philosophers, 16
natural rate of interest
    in advanced economies, 1990–2016,
        273f
    change in, 176t
    decline in, 54, 56f, 175, 178
    domestic falling by the same amount
        as foreign, 112
    drivers of the secular decline in,
        55n–56n
    estimating for Korea, 178n
    keeping close to the natural level, 111
    variables of the decline in Korea's, 176
natural resources, exported from Indonesia,
    243n
net capital inflow with an increase in
    domestic demand, 112
net debtor, lower NIIP, 243n
net-debt-to-GDP ratio, downward for
    Japan, 332
net export improvement, limited following
    a depreciation, 135
net government debt, for Japan, 333f

Netherlands, 14, 28. See also low countries
net international investment position
    (NIIP), 243n, 278, 279f
"new" Asian model, 408–410, 411
new mediocre
    avoiding in Asia with fiscal policy,
        343–383
    implications for medium- to long-term
        fiscal sustainability, 343
    as a problem in Asia, 316
    public debt dynamics under, 344–353
Newton, Isaac, theory on hydrostatics, 17n
New Zealand
    aging, lower speed of, 52
    aging impact on TFP, 48f
    demographic characteristics, 35t
    demographic dividend, 41, 43
    demographic impact on current
        account, 53f
    demographic trends, impact of, 42f
    higher old-age dependency by 2020, 52
    immigration, impact of on the
        workforce, 43
    immigration in, 37
    labor force participation, 48f, 49f
    as a late-dividend economy, 35, 37
    old-age dependency ratio, 36t, 38f, 57f
    older workers, share of, 44f
    per capita income level, 39f
    real interest rates, maintained higher,
        116
    youth dependency ratio, 57f
Nigeria, theft and corruption by ruling
    elites, 14
90 percent debt-to-GDP ratio, as a
    tipping point for government debt
    sustainability, 132
nitrogen-fixing process, 12n
nominal and real interest rates, in Korea,
    175f
nominal GDP
    growth rate in Japan, 290f
    growth rates in Korea and Japan, 173f
nominal interest rate
    close to zero in the future, 294
    constrained by the effective lower
        bound, 323
    equation for, 114
    hitting the zero lower bound, 123
    source for, 125
    zero bound on, 114
non-Asian advanced economies, comparing
    with emerging-market and developing
    economies, 115

non-Asian emerging-market economies, inflation was significantly higher, 116
nonfinancial corporate debt, low in India, 232
nonfrontier firms, TFP differences with frontier firms, 149*n*
nonmanufacturing sector, in Japan, 143–144, 144*f*, 153, 156*f*
nonmarket economy, in Japan, 143*n*
nonmonetary factors, having a major influence on inflation, 133
nonperforming loans, 232
nonregular employees
  defined, 162
  investing in the human capital of, 163
  in Japan, 143*n*, 154, 157*f*
  in total workers by sector, in Japan, 144*f*
  training for, 144
nonregular employment, in Japan, 143–149, 162
nonregular workers
  accumulating less human capital, 162
  employment adjustment in Korea, 169
  increase in rising, 146
  providing benefits to, 163
  wages rising in Japan, 148
nontraditional employment, in the nonmanufacturing market economy, 162
notional defined contribution pension scheme, 375
nuclear blackmail, by medium-sized but poor nations, 21
numerical target, clarifying monetary policy, 317

obsolescence, issue of, 408
off-the-job training expenses, by firm size, 1975–2010, in Japan, 158*f*
oil exporters
  current account, 275*f*
  with exchange rate pegs, 280*n*
oil imports, countries understanding the cost of, 273*n*
Okun's law, on an excess unemployment rate, 290–291
old-age dependency
  capital-to-labor ratio and, 51
  higher found to reduce interest rates, 59
  impact on interest rates, 57, 57*f*
  reducing current account balance, 51
old-age dependency ratio
  in Asia, 36*t*
  change between 2020 and 2030, 57*f*
  defined, 36*t*, 38*f*, 57*f*, 58*f*
  in East Asia, 34
  increasing from 15 to 20 percent in China, Korea, and Thailand, 344
  in Korea following that of Japan, 170, 171*f*
  rising globally, 19
  years to increase from 15 to 20 percent, 38*f*
"old" Asian model, 407–410
"old corruption," declined in Britain after 1750, 23
older people, 65, 375
older workers
  associated with reduction in labor productivity growth, 46, 47*t*
  male, as nonregular employees in Japan, 146
  positive effects on labor force participation, 375
  reducing annual growth, 46
  in working-age population in Asia, 44*f*
one-child policy, 182
"one county, one zone," as inappropriate in China, 189
one-year US Treasury bond rate, 251, 253*n*, 253*t*
open capital markets, 76*b*
open-economy New Keynesian model, for Australia, 337
openness and integration, in Asia, 136
Oppo, 91, 91*n*
Organization for Economic Cooperation and Development (OECD), Japan the first nonwestern nation to join, 77
"original sin," 250*n*
output, 321, 329
output dynamics
  in Indonesia, 238–242, 255–257
  Indonesia's output dynamics, 238
output gap
  alternative measures of, 299–300, 299*t*
  BOJ's estimate of, 290, 290*f*
  defined, 321
  for Japan, 333*f*
  negative persisting, 335
output growth, in Indonesia, 238
output growth rates, paths for potential, 260–262
"output of ideas," 28
outward-looking strategy, in Indonesia, 266

overlapping generations model, of Kwon for Korea, 176, 176*t*
overnight interbank call rate, in Korea, 178
overpopulation, risk of thoroughly discredited, 19
overshooting, of the inflation rate, 336

Pacific Island countries
    fiscal packages, 381*t*, 383*t*
    in Group 3, 347*b*
Parent, Antoine, 18
Park Chung-hee, 85–87
Park Gyeun-hye, 87
partial equilibrium analysis, 53
part-time workers, reliance of firms on, 146
passivity, reinforced in Japan, 136
"patent production function," regression of, 83
patents
    awarded to Taiwanese inventors, 94*f*
    in exporting firms in Korea, 89
    holders of bargaining with contract manufacturers and other business partners, 76*b*
    infringement in Japan, 79
    as a measure of output of R&D, 28
    one-stop services in China, 185
Paulson, Henry, 270
pensions, 20, 66, 375
pension systems
    generosity of, 53*n*
    reform of, 65–66, 374–375
per capita GDP growth, in Japan, 129
per capita income, relative to the United States, 37–38, 39*f*
performance-based wage system, 65
personal and corporate income tax
    relying more on, 363
    relying more on than on general consumption taxes, 364*f*
personal income tax (PIT)
    cut in as progressive, 366
    cutting increasing the labor supply and lowering wage costs, 369
    measures of yields, 359, 363*f*
    yields from in selected economies, 363*f*
Philippines
    aging impact on TFP, 48*f*
    aging speed change between 2020 and 2030, 58*f*
    CPI inflation rates, 1985–2016, 288*f*
    current account balances, 1985–2016, 310*f*

debt ratio change under Scenario 4b, 354*f*
demographic characteristics, 35*t*
demographic dividend, 41, 43
demographic impact on current account, 53*f*
demographics impact on 10-year real interest rates, 61*f*
demographic trends, impact of, 42*f*
as an early-dividend economy, 37
fertility rate, 37
fiscal buffers, 353
fiscal packages, 381*t*, 383*t*
foreign capital, volatility of the supply of, 2000–15, 251*f*
foreign exchange reserves and net official assets, 1985–2016, 311*f*
global financial integration across emerging markets, 249*f*
in Group 3, 347*b*
infrastructure, index of quality of, 356*f*
labor force participation, 48*f*, 49*f*
long-term public debt projection, 349*t*
months inflation rate below inflation target, 371*f*
most-favored nation (MFN) applied tariff rates, 230*f*
net emigration from, impact of, 43
old-age dependency ratio, 36*t*, 57*f*
old-age dependency ratio increasing from 15 to 20 percent, 38*f*
older workers, share of, 44*f*
per capita income level, 39*f*
personal income tax (PIT) yields, 363*f*
public debt, actual and projected, 346*f*, 352*f*
public spending
    on education as percent of GDP, 359*f*
    efficiency frontier, distance from, 378*t*
    on health care as percent of GDP, 358*f*
    on pensions and health care, 346*f*
R&D spending, 357
real GDP growth relative to ASEAN-4, 241*f*
real GDP volatility, 241*f*
real per capita GDP, growth rate of, 287*f*
real short-term interest rate, 293*f*
real trade growth, 393*f*
regulatory quality, 260*f*

research and development spending,
362f
Scenario 3 and, 350, 352
scope for quantitative easing,
December 2016, 303t
tax revenue sources, 364f
trade growth in, 399t
working-age people, emigration of, 37
working age populations growing
substantially, 344, 346f
youth dependency ratio, 57f
Phillips curve
containing a nonlinear output gap,
337
declining estimates of the slope of, 286
as dormant, 298–300
estimate of an expectations-
augmented, 298–299, 299t
regressions on US GDP deflator, 299t
physical capital accumulation, 353
Pitt, William, 23
Poland, governance indicators, 22n
policy
adapting to older population, 37
delay of responses in India, 331f
emerging markets making changes
to, 237
implications for global imbalances,
282–283
implications of demographic trends,
64–66
loss-minimization approach to
formulation, 320–322
need for a forward-looking, 5–8
preserving space as the wrong strategy
for an economy at risk of deflation,
295
strategies for Australia, 325–328, 326f,
327f
tools as imperfect, 308
policy interest rates
choosing, 321
as conditional, 322
keeping higher than warranted by
macroeconomic conditions, 304
against the same variable after the
crisis, 116–117, 117f
population
of Korea projected to decrease, 170
Malthusian responses to, 11
projections affecting output through
aggregate labor and capital, 41
population aging
effect on inflation, 175n

increasing rapidly, 34
as inflationary, 175n
and lower growth in Asia, 2
macroeconomic impact on saving and
investment, 51
negative effects of on TFP, 169n
posing a challenge for public debt
sustainability, 344
threatening long-term fiscal
sustainability, 377
population dynamics, holding back growth,
10
population growth. See also youth
dependency
in Asia, 34f
capital-to-labor ratio and, 51
changes expected to be relatively small
between 2020–2030, 52n
lower lowering growth, 6
rate for Asia, 34
triggering technological responses, 11
"positive checks," Malthusian, 11
positive supply shock, deflationary effect on
aggregate wages, 134
post-65 cohort, extended number of years
of productivity, 20
post-dividend demographic characteristic,
35t
post-dividend economies, 35
potential growth, considering the evolution
of, 260–262
potential growth rate
declined in emerging markets, 255
decomposition into the actual
capital growth rate and potential
employment growth rate, 256n
decomposition of Indonesia's,
2001–14, 256–257
in Indonesia, 257f, 262
potential output
declined in Indonesia as a result of
lower TFP growth, 263
as endogenous, 339
scenario analysis for Indonesia, 262f
potential output growth rate in Indonesia
actual and forecast, 256f
actual and forecast, 2000–22, 255–256
potential shocks, sources of, 335
practical knowledge, sense of contempt
for, 18
Prandtl, Ludwig, theory of aerodynamics,
17n
"precautionary principle," 23

predatory foreigners, attracted to riches of economic success, 14
predatory wars, likelihood of, 21
"premature deindustrialization," phenomenon of, 6
prescriptive knowledge, connection with propositional knowledge, 18
price stability policy, time-consistent, 317
primary and preventive care, supporting, 375
prime-age population, choice for examining savings-investment relationships, 50n
Principle of Price Stabilization, 305
Principle of Productive Credit, 305
private consumption, in Indonesia, 267
privateers, use of, 14
private investment, stimulating in targeted sectors in Japan, 141
private retirement saving schemes, 375
private sector R&D, changes in Japanese, 83–84
procyclical fiscal policy, reducing, 373
production function in China, labor share in, 182n
productivity
    determined by the efficiency of factor allocation, 108
    gap between part-time and regular employees in Japan, 145
    in the generation of ideas, 27
    impact of aging on, 44
    improving Japan's performance, 162
    Indonesia focusing on, 267
    spillovers, 106–111
productivity and interest rates scenario, for public debt projection, 348, 350
productivity-enhancing reforms, discussed in the IMF's Regional Economic Outlook (2017), 68
productivity-enhancing spillovers, limited diffusion to Indonesia, 263
productivity growth
    deceleration of in China, 184
    decreasing everywhere since the early 1990s, 123
    literature on the determinants of, 105–106
    lower transmitted across countries through financial channels, 107
    measuring in Japan and other East Asian economies, 100
    policies prioritizing to tackle country-specific factors impeding, 101

product market efficiency, declining in Korea, 170
Product Market Regulation Index of the OECD, Korea's ranking in 2013, 170n
product markets, Korea's among the most heavily regulated, 170
professional education system, reforming Japan's, 148
professions, impact of aging differing across, 44
proficiency, greater utilization of needed in Japan, 143
profits, no significant relationship with exchange rate movements, 205, 217t
Programme for International Student Assessment (PISA), scores, 361f, 378
"pro-incremental" bias, in innovation systems, 100
pro-incumbent bias, 87, 92, 100
projected purchasing power parity, per capita income growth rate, 39f
prompt corrective action, as a risk-avoiding strategy, 335
prompt effective action, following supply shocks, 329–330, 331f
propositional knowledge, connection with prescriptive knowledge, 18
protectionism, 258, 283, 398. See also "fair" trade
protectionist sentiment, on the rise, 316
provider payment systems, improving, 375
prowess database, collected by the CMIE, 225–226
prudential policies, adapting to curb risks, 308
Prussia, rent-seeking in, 23
public capital, impact on potential output, 339
public debt
    actual and projected in selected Asian economies, 346f, 351f–352f
    dynamics under the new mediocre, 344–353
    long-term projections for reflecting the impact of the new mediocre, 347–350
    lower in Asia, 344
    as percent of GDP, by region, 345f
    ratio to GDP, 347–348
public debt-to-GDP ratios, 344, 346f
public debt-to GDP ratios, 350, 352–353
public healthcare spending, 53n, 355, 358f
public infrastructure push package, 365–366

public investment efficiency frontier, 355,
357f
public pension funds, reforming the
management of, 66
public policy choices in East Asia, during
years of rapid growth, 74
public-private partnerships (PPPs), for
infrastructure spending, 355
public spending
challenges of the new mediocre and,
353–363
on education as percent of GDP, 359f
efficiency frontiers, 378, 378t
on health care as percent of GDP, 358f
level, composition, and efficiency of,
355–359
on pensions and health care, 346f
purchasing power, in Indonesia, 267
"pure imitator," transitioning to
"incremental innovator," 90

quadratic loss function, 320–321
quantitative easing (QE), scope for in the
Asia-15 economies, 302–304, 303t
quasi-equilibrium (a "dark corner"), of low-
inflation or deflation trap, 316
quasi-fiscal borrowing, 190, 191
quasi-fiscal expenditures, 189

R&D (research and development)
East Asian approach having both
strengths and weaknesses, 74
increased government expenditure on
in China, 185
investment, appropriating the returns
to in Japan, 79
labs, top corporate effectively led by
PhD recipients in the United States,
78
productivity
declined in the US, 100
declining in East Asia, 96
slowdown in growth, 3
trends in Japanese, 84f
sector, increasing the proportion of the
labor force engaged in, 28
spending
concentration of among South
Korean firms, 88f
concentration of in a single chaebol-
the Samsung Group, 86
productivity of Japan's corporate,
73n

public spending on, 357–359, 362f
spending on in selected economies,
2015, 362f
strategy, in Japan, 84
radical innovation, effects of, 100
rate of real exchange rate appreciation
versus the US dollar, 251
real 10-year bond yield, in advanced
economies, 1990–2018, 272f
real 10-year Treasury rates, after the Asian
crisis, 272, 272f
real depreciation, shifting domestic and
foreign spending, 112
real effective exchange rate
correlation to Indonesia's real GDP
growth, 253t
for Japan, 333f
real equilibrium level, of the interest rate as
close to zero, 335
real estate
markets in Japan and Korea, 173–174
prices and CPI in Korea and Japan,
174f
relationship with demographic
variables, 63–64
real exchange rate
constant in the long run, 113
defined, 112
depreciating less in the short run, 113
depreciating over time, 114
index for, 225
source of, 125
real GDP. See also GDP
effects of fiscal reforms, 368, 368f
growth rate of in Indonesia and in the
United States, 238–239, 240f
volatility for selected countries, 241f
real GDP growth
contribution of domestic and global
factors to Indonesia's, 254f
contributions to Indonesia's, 247f
for Japan, 333f
rates in Indonesia, 239f
rates in Indonesia and the United
States, 240f
relative to ASEAN-4, 241f
trends in Korea and the world, 167f
real growth rate, in China, 251
real interest rate(s)
change in, 118
components of, 323
computing, 175f
decreased, 54, 116, 123, 272
defined, 293f

depending on global growth, 280
higher, spelling trouble for advanced
  debtors, 280
impact of demographic variables on
  the 10-year, 58–61
insulating, 114
interpreted as the "natural" rate of
  interest, 111
by region, 115f
real long-term rate, declining for about 30
  years, 292
real natural interest rate, effects of changes
  in fundamental variables in Korea,
  177f
real neutral interest rates, in selected
  countries, 56f
real output growth rate, in Indonesia, 251
real short-term interest rate, 292, 293f
real trade growth, 391f
rebalancing
  economies from foreign to domestic
    demand, 119
  toward indirect taxes package, 366
recessionary impact, of tax hikes of 1997
  and 2014 in Japan, 131
reforms, effects across Asia, 367–370
regional integration, preventing domestic
  stagnation traps, 135–136
regional supply chains, 409
regular employees
  defined, 162
  increases in marginal productivity with
    age in Japan, 146
  in Japan, 143n
  training for, 144
regular workers
  excessive projections for in Korea, 169
  firms' decisions on wage rates
    depending on expectations of future
    inflation, 149
  very limited wage increases in Japan,
    148
regulation, undoing the consequences of
  monetary expansion, 308–309
regulatory capture, in Japan, 83
regulatory policies, preserving financial
  stability, 286–287
regulatory quality
  declining path of, 260
  in Indonesia, Malaysia, the Philippines,
    and Thailand, 260f
relative prices, adjusting, 291
religion, in the secular and humanistic
  West, 11

remediation costs, in China, 182–183
rental rate, not always moving together
  with housing prices, 64n
rental system of Korea, called chonsei, 174n
rent-seeking
  at historically low levels today, 14
  internal, 14, 21–22
  pairwise correlation coefficients of
    measures closest to, 15n
  pervasive in the age of mercantilism,
    12
  unlikely to stifle long-term economic
    growth worldwide, 23
repetitive work, productivity declining with
  age, 20n
repressing savings, trap of, 136
Republic of Samsung. See Samsung Group
research, questions for further, 404
research and development. See R&D
  (research and development)
reserve accumulation, excess exerting a
  powerful negative externality, 310
Reserve Bank of India, bolstering the
  credibility of the inflation target, 329
resource allocation, efficiency in Korea,
  169–170
resources, finiteness of nonreproducible, 12
restrictions on trade, in Indonesia, 258–259
retirement age
  average of 57 in Asia, 366
  increasing by two years, 366
  raising, 370, 375
retirement system reforms, 66
retrenchment, of Indonesia from the global
  economy, 238, 263
revealed comparative advantage, 172f
revenue
  collection and composition, 359–363
  efficient mobilization of, 375–376
revenue policies, challenges of the new
  mediocre and, 353–363
revenue rules, 373
Ridley, Matt, 26
risk
  assertive action called for to avoid, 316
  classes of, 307
risk-avoidance strategy
  based on loss-minimization for
    Australia, 326f, 327f, 328
  for monetary policy, 4–5, 317–324
  resulting in better outcomes in
    Australia, 325
risk management strategy, policy
  preventing long-term inflation, 329

robotization, replacing workers, 28

robots, skilled people working collaboratively with, 409

Romania, improved governance indicators, 22

Rome, technological progress not sustainable, 18

rule of bad law, 12

rupee, appreciation of, 204–205

rural labor migration, projected for 2028, 185n

Russia, theft and corruption by ruling elites, 14

"safe assets," increasing the availability of, 66

Samsung Electronics, R&D expenditure in 2010, 88f

Samsung Group
  high fraction of Korean exports, 86
  produced more DRAM chips, 89n
  prominence in the global smartphone industry, 90, 91
  share of global smartphone shipments, 91n
  value of, 86n

savers, maintaining faith in domestic assets, 133

saving behavior, impact of aging on, 50n

saving determinants, survey of, 50n

"saving" households, holding debt as a source of wealth, 365

savings
  aging-related, 52
  demographic trends affecting, 50
  excess in some countries, 105, 387
  and investment across countries, 400

Scandinavia, rent-seeking in by 1850, 23

Scenario 1: status quo
  debt ratio decreasing or stabilizing in all economies, 350
  for public debt projection, 348, 349t

Scenario 2: historical primary balance
  debt ratio increasing in Japan, and Malaysia and remaining flat in Sri Lanka, 350
  for public debt projection, 348

Scenario 3: demographics
  pensions and healthcare spending, 350
  for public debt projection, 348

Scenario 4: productivity and interest rates
  gradual decline in the IRGD, 352
  increase in the IRGD raising the debt-to-GDP ratio, 352–353

IRGD decreasing gradually to 1 percentage point below the 2022 level by 2030, 350

IRGD rising gradually reaching 2 percentage points above the 2022 level by 2030, 350

for public debt projection, 348, 350

scholars, contempt for practical knowledge, 18

science, advancing with better tools, 24

Science and Technology Basic Law, implemented in Japan, 84

scientific knowledge, access to the existing pool of, 25–26

scientific products, for commercial use in China, 185

scientific research, 27

scientists, 17, 18, 26

second 21st century crisis, 269

secondary school enrollment, spending on, 360f

sectors, increased market shares with the strengthening of the rupee, 205, 212f

secular stagnation
  in advanced economies as transmitted to Indonesia, 242–244, 255
  affected nominal or real interest rates, 118
  appropriate frequency to study, 121
  competing explanations for, 236
  contagion across countries, 103
  diffusing via international trade in goods and services, 107
  exposure of Indonesia to, 244–251
  foreign, 111, 112, 113, 114
  history and reality, 9–29
  Indonesia countering, 255–262
  Japan's steps to address, 130
  likelihood of in the foreseeable future, 19
  limited transmission of from advanced economies to Indonesia, 263
  literature on, 105–106
  as normal, 9
  reducing foreign interest rate and demand in the long run, 113
  results from a shortage of safe assets, 105
  risk of getting trapped in, 7
  as the rule rather than the exception until 1800, 3
  spillovers to output dynamics in Indonesia, 238–255
  structural causes of Japan's, 139

symptoms of, 2, 103, 123
as a syndrome, 103
threat to Asian economies, 1–2
transmitted through links to China,
243
transmitting from advanced to
emerging economies, 236
self-fulfilling crises, model of, 105
senior leadership roles, lack of women in
Japan, 163
serfdom, abolition of, 23
service economy, in Japan, 83
service exports, surge in from 2003 to 2007,
198
services
per capita consumption of in China,
184
share in India's export basket, 199f
services exports
in Indonesia, 267
plateaued over the last decade, 198,
199f
services sector, rise in the share of in China,
184, 185f
shadow federal funds rate, 303–304
shocks
effect of large, 335
flexibility of fiscal rules in the face of
large, 374
identification of, 253n
possibility of further large negative,
315
prompt reactions to establishing
credibility, 336
unhinging inflation expectations, 317
short-run fiscal policy, resulting in
significant deviations, 339
short-term interest rate
in Indonesia, 251
in Korea, 296f
in Thailand, 296f
short-term "natural" policy rates (r^*),
pattern for, 272, 273f
simulations, spawning entirely new
"computational" fields of research, 25
Singapore
aging
experiencing very rapid until 2030,
52
impact on growth, 41
impact on TFP, 48f
aging speed change between 2020 and
2030, 58f
CPI inflation rates, 1985–2016, 288f

credit gaps, increases in, 119
current account balances, 1985–2016,
310f
demographic characteristics, 35t
demographic trends, impact of, 42f
fiscal packages, 380t, 382t
foreign exchange reserves and net
official assets, 1985–2016, 311f
in Group 2, 347b
immigration, 37
immigration, impact on the workforce,
43
inflation below 1 percent in 2016, 289
infrastructure, index of quality of, 356f
interest rates lowered after the crisis,
116
labor force participation, 48f, 49f
as a late-dividend economy, 37
most-favored nation (MFN) applied
tariff rates, 230f
nominal interest rates fell close to zero,
124
old-age dependency, expected to rise
relatively quickly, 57
old-age dependency, higher by 2030,
52
old-age dependency ratio, 36t, 38f, 57f
older workers, share of, 44f
personal income tax (PIT) yields, 363f
projected to transition to post-
dividend status by 2030, 35
public debt, actual and projected, 346f
public health care spending, 355
public spending
on education as percent of GDP,
359f
efficiency frontier, distance from,
378t
on health care as percent of GDP,
358f
real per capita GDP, growth rate of,
287f
real short-term interest rate, 293f
real trade growth, 393f
research and development spending,
362f
scope for quantitative easing,
December 2016, 303t
tax revenue sources, 364f
10-year government yield, change in,
55f
trade growth in, 399t
workforce, share of, with productivity
rising or falling, 45f

youth dependency ratio, 57*f*
zero lower bound, currently at, 295
65–80 bracket, increased labor force
     participation by, 20
SK, 86*n*
small and medium enterprises (SMEs),
     R&D intensity of in Japan, 149, 151*f*
smaller firms, easier access to capital in
     Taiwan than in South Korea, 92
small firms, more prevalent in Japan than
     in the United States, 158
social knowledge, defining, 26
social security system, improving in Japan,
     141
"social skills" jobs, productivity rising with
     age, 20*n*
SOEs (state-owned enterprises), bailouts of
     troubled, 376
spillovers
     from advanced economies, 106, 109,
          109*t*
     complexity of to Indonesia, 255
Sri Lanka
     debt ratio change under Scenario 4*b*,
          354*f*
     direct taxes as a small share of tax
          revenues, 366
     fiscal packages, 381*t*, 383*t*
     in Group 3, 347*b*
     infrastructure, index of quality of, 356*f*
     long-term public debt projection, 349*t*
     personal income tax (PIT) yields, 363*f*
     public debt, actual and projected, 346*f*,
          352*f*
     public spending
          on education as percent of GDP,
               359*f*
          efficiency frontier, distance from,
               378*t*
          on health care as percent of GDP,
               358*f*
          on pensions and health care, 346*f*
     R&D spending, 357
     research and development spending,
          362*f*
     Scenario 3 and, 350, 352
     stabilizing debt paths in, 353
     tax revenue sources, 364*f*
stabilization policy, against negative
     shocks, 133
"stagflation," 329
stagnation
     in emerging markets, 236–237
     exceptions to the rule of, 9*n*

internal factors of, 105
standard economic models, naïve view of
     the inflation process, 133
Standard International Trade Classification
     (SITC) codes, 172*f*
startups and new entrants, limited in Japan,
     81
stasis, likelihood of reverting to a world
     of, 29
State Council in China, 188
state-owned enterprises (SOEs), reform of,
     376
status quo
     average annual growth impact relative
          to, 41
     primary balance as of 2022, 353
     scenario for public debt projection,
          348, 349*t*
steam engine, theory of thermodynamics
     and, 17
steel, discovery of the chemical composition
     of, 16
Stein-Hardenberg reforms, in Prussia after
     1806, 23
stimulus programs, temporary, 133
stock and bond markets, regulation of in
     Japan, 82
stock indicators, 248
stock returns, demographic trends
     affecting, 62, 63
storage-and-search techniques, 26
strategic replication, 407
stress tests, of the balance sheets of
     financial intermediaries, 287
structural break, in India around 2005, 222
structural reforms
     addressing challenges of aging, 68
     in Japan, 141, 332
     in Korea, 178
     as the main policy option, 288
     need for supporting, 371, 373–376
     offsetting adverse growth effects of
          aging, 65–66
     slowing the increase in healthcare
          costs, 375
     undertaking, 8
structural supply-side policies, in Indonesia,
     267
students
     with higher education in Indonesia,
          259*f*
     sending to the best universities in the
          world from Indonesia, 267

subdued inflation, in many countries, 370, 371*f*

sublicensing, practice of, 93, 93*n*

succession, as an aspect of replication, 408

supply, boosting in India as critical, 223

supply chains, 400, 410. *See also* global supply chains

supply shocks, 329, 330*f*

supply-side policies and interest rate cuts, not necessarily producing demand, 267

supportive arrangements, creating for fiscal rules, 374

surplus countries, 390, 391*f*
  demographic trends exerting upward pressure on current balances, 52
  facing little that would force them to adjust excess, 282
  feedback effects to, 396–397
  focusing research on, 404
  import growth and export growth highly correlated with US import growth, 398

Survey of Adult Skills (PIAAC), ranking Japan at the top, 142, 142*f*

sustained growth, experienced only in 3 percent of human history, 9

Switzerland, 23, 28

syndrome, defined, 103*n*

tailwinds, of very large players in a neighborhood, 409

Taiwan
  activity in sectors that no longer hold technological opportunities, 96
  committed to educational excellence in the postwar era, 77–78
  concentration of US patent rights in electronics hardware, 94, 94*f*
  CPI inflation rates, 288*f*
  current account balances, 310*f*
  economic development of, 91–96
  electronics firms attracted by China's low costs, 95
  entrepreneurial character of managers, 92–93
  exports and industrial structure concentrated in electronics and information technology (IT), 93
  foreign exchange reserves and net official assets, 311*f*
  government directing and subsidizing substantial international technology transfer, 93
  growth rate of real per capita GDP, 287*f*
  human capital policy choices effects, 78
  increasingly squeezed between Silicon Valley and China, 96
  in Japan's footsteps by the end of the 1980s, 74
  less diversified than Korea, 93
  level of industrial concentration much lower than in Korea, 92
  lowered interest rates after the crisis, 116
  nominal interest rates fell close to zero, 124
  pro-incremental bias in innovation system, 96
  real short-term interest rate, 293*f*
  scope for quantitative easing, December 2016, 303*t*
  small firms focused on implementing and refining technologies developed by others, 95
  trade flows to and from China, 95
  trade growth in, 399*t*
  at the zero lower bound, 295

Taiwan Semiconductor Manufacturing Corporation (TSMC), 93

Takenaka, Heizo, 135

talent sources, unlocking in Japan, 164

taper tantrum, in July 2013, 294*f*, 297–298

tax administration, weaknesses in, 359

tax bases, narrow, 359

taxes
  rebalancing toward indirect, 368–369, 376
  types of, 339

taxes and tax collection, efficiency of in Asia, 362

tax minimization strategies, addressing, 283

tax revenue, sources of in selected economies, 364*f*

tax structure, improving to support growth, 362

tax yields, 359, 363*f*

Taylor rule, 306

"technical compendia," compiled by groups of experts, 26

technical progress, negative feedback loops from demographics to, 6

technological advances, limited diffusion to Indonesia, 263

technological breakthroughs, fueled by
rapid entry of a large number of new
firms, 75*b*

technological followers, catching up by, 28

technological frontier, moving ahead to
avoid secular stagnation, 28

technological innovation
accounting for low growth in advanced
economies, 257
promotion of in China, 185

technologically dynamic sectors, risks and
rewards for talented young American
managers and engineers, 76*b*

technological paradigm, creating a new, 75*b*

technological progress
Chinese and pre-1700 Western as
experience-based, 16*n*
impact on economic well-being in the
Middle Ages, 15
land- and resource-augmenting, 12
most critical for East Asian economies,
101
resource-augmenting, 21

technological spillovers, found to raise TFP
and growth, 257

technology
acceleration of development, 186
adopting new in Japan, 164
allowing the elderly to cope with
handicaps of old age, 20*n*
as another challenge, 409
coevolving with science, 24
developing and improving, 24
gap narrowing in Korea, 169
gradual widening epistemic base of, 16
partially offsetting downward pressure
on economic growth in China, 186

telescopes, improvements to, 24

Temporary Trade Barriers database (World
Bank), 258

10-year government yield, change in, 55*f*

10-year real interest rates, 58–61, 61*f*

terms-of-trade growth, correlation to
Indonesia's real GDP growth, 253*t*

tertiary education, low levels of in
Indonesia, 258, 259*f*

TFP. *See* total factor productivity (TFP)

Thailand
age-related spending projected to rise,
344, 346*f*
aging
fiscal pressures from, 353
impact on growth, 41
impact on TFP, 48*f*

rapid until 2030, 52

aging speed change between 2020 and
2030, 58*f*

core CPI inflation, 296*f*

core inflation remaining well below 2
percent, 286

CPI inflation rates, 288*f*

credit gaps, increases in, 119

current account balances, 1985–2016,
310*f*

debt ratio change under Scenario 4*b*,
354*f*

demographic characteristics, 35*t*

demographic impact on current
account, 53*f*

demographics impact on 10-year real
interest rates, 61*f*

demographic trends, impact of, 42*f*

fiscal packages, 380*t*, 382*t*

foreign capital, volatility of the supply
of, 251*f*

foreign exchange reserves and net
official assets, 311*f*

gap between actual and expected
public spending on health care,
355*n*

global financial integration across
emerging markets, 249*f*

in Group 2, 347*b*

inflation below 1 percent in 2016, 289

infrastructure, 356*f*, 371, 372*f*

labor force aging, impact of, 344

labor force participation, 48*f*, 49*f*

long-term public debt projection, 349*t*

monetary ease, conditions supporting
further, 311

monetary policy, effects of
accommodative, 372*f*

monetary policy since the Asian
financial crisis, 296*f*

months inflation rate below inflation
target, 371*f*

old-age dependency ratio, 36*t*, 38*f*, 57*f*,
344

older workers, share of, 44*f*

pensions in a partially defined-benefit
systems, 375

per capita income level, 39*f*

personal income tax (PIT) yields, 363*f*

as a post-dividend economy, 35

public debt, actual and projected, 346*f*,
351*f*

public spending

on education as percent of GDP, 359*f*

efficiency frontier, distance from, 378*t*

on health care as percent of GDP, 358*f*

on pensions and health care, 346*f*

real GDP growth relative to ASEAN-4, 2000–16, 241*f*

real GDP volatility, 241*f*

real per capita GDP, growth rate of, 287*f*

real short-term interest rate, 293*f*

real trade growth, 393*f*

regulatory quality, 260*f*

research and development spending, 362*f*

Scenario 3 and, 350

Scenario 4b and, 353

scope for quantitative easing, December 2016, 303*t*

short-term interest rate, 296*f*

sustained deflation, risk of falling into, 295, 296*f*

tax revenue sources, 364*f*

10-year government yield, change in, 55*f*

trade growth in, 399*t*

workforce, share of with productivity rising or falling, 45*f*

working-age population, absolute decline in, 38

youth dependency ratio, 57*f*

thermodynamics, theory of, 17

Thirty Years' War, 13

Three Arrows Plus package, 332, 333*f*

"the 3Cs" approach, comprehensive, consistent, and coordinated, 316

time-consistency problem, solution to, 318

time dimension, prudential tools building up buffers, 334

total factor productivity (TFP)
accounting for factor utilization, 258*n*

aging, impact on, 43–46, 48*f*

at constant national prices (RTFPNA), 125

as endogenous, 339

factors boosting, 169

human capital component of declining during downturns, 258

impact on growth in Indonesia, 256–257

improving Japan's macro-level by improving quality of workers in SMEs, 158

increasing in Korea, 178

of Japan's macroeconomy, 141

large differences between large and small firms, 163

for older workers, 47*t*

from the Penn World Tables version 9.0, 125

scenario analysis for Indonesia, 262*f*

sources of changes in, 257–260

total factor productivity (TFP) growth
assumed to rise, 262

causes of slowing in Indonesia, 238

contributors to slowdown in Indonesia, 263

declining as a result of convergence to the technological frontier, 258

in the economy as a whole, 27–28

of emerging-market economies correlated with that of advanced economies, 106

in Japan, 139

as the only source of growth for Korea, 169

postcrisis relationship with measures of economic openness, 111

remaining unchanged, 40

results of three cross-country regressions, 109

in the United States, 186

total sales and costs, increased following an appreciation of the rupee, 205, 213*t*–214*t*, 215*t*–216*t*

tradable sector, growth of India's, 194, 194*f*

trade
and absolute balance, panel regressions on, 395*t*

balance, 112

barriers, internal in India, 231

deficits, eventual pressure to narrow, 401

and financial spillover, lower limiting the diffusion of technology, 257

flows, facilitating international knowledge spillovers, 107

growth
associated with rapid export growth in Asia and rapid import growth in the Americas, 391, 392*f*

decomposing, 390–391

implications for, 401

moderating imbalances associated
with slowing, 5
not sufficient to explain widening
trade balances, 389
period of rapid, 390, 391*f*
for the periods 1995–2008 and
2012–14, 397–398, 398*t*
periods of high accompanied by
relatively faster import and export
growth, 394
in surplus Asian countries
correlated with US import growth,
399*t*
imbalances, 400, 401
improvement in Indonesia, 266
integration
having a negative impact on TFP
growth, 110
in Japan, 130
measured by the ratio of exports to
GDP in 2007, 109
liberalization, encouraging firms to
reduce the number of products,
146*n*
linkages, as a direct source of
transmission of spillovers of secular
stagnation, 242
modeled by reduced-forms equations,
339
nature of between countries similarly
endowed, 409
relationship with imbalances, 389–390
responsiveness to income and global
imbalances, 398*t*
restrictions
doing little to alter global current
imbalances, 283
in Indonesia, 258–259
slowdown, explanations for, 398,
400–401
and specialization, growth from
vulnerable to political shocks, 14
tensions between the United States
and trading partners in Asia, 6
warfare, sparked global imbalances,
280
trade-facilitating infrastructure, expanding
or building, 410
trade/GDP ratio, without growing
imbalances, 397*f*
Trade in Value Added (TiVA) database
(OECD), 397*n*
trade-related exposure, of Indonesia to
secular stagnation, 244–248

trade-to-GDP ratio, increased, 394
training
differences in on-the-job and off-the-
job, 155, 158*f*
gearing up, 410
moving to universities and vocational
schools, 163
transformative innovations, requiring
incremental inventions, 75*b*
transgenic crops, opposition to, 23
Trans-Pacific Partnership (TPP), Japan
pushing for, 141
Transparency International, corruption
indices, 14
transparent communications, conventional
forward guidance for, 322–324
trend total factor productivity (TFP)
growth
boosting potential, 353, 355
impact of aging on, 344
Trump administration, rhetoric on bilateral
US deficits, 404
turning Japanese, risk of in the late 1990s
sense, 129

ultra-low inflation, dangers of, 289–298
undisbursed loans, steadily rising in
Indonesia, 267
unemployment, lowering long-term, 367
unemployment rate
in Japan, 290, 290*f*
lowering the long-term, 370
United Kingdom
change in 10-year government yield,
55*f*
per capita income level, 39*f*
United States
absolute balance relative to GDP and
to trade, 394
account balances and reserve
purchases, 271*f*
aging speed change between 2020 and
2030, 58*f*
business R&D and government
support for business R&D, by firm
size, 151*f*
capital-to-output ratios, 168*f*
central bank transparency, 323, 324*f*
current account balances, 1991–2017,
274*f*
deficit, growing after the mid-1990s,
270
demand, fueling export growth in Asia,
398

dollar, strengthening, 281
external deficit, widening of after the
    mid-1990s, 272, 274f
fertility rates, 168f
firm-size wage differences explained by
    labor characteristics, 154–155
global real trade growth, 393f
growth in trade, faster driven by
    widening imbalances, 394
growth rate in, 238–239, 238n, 240f
housing bubble, 274
import growth moderated, 403
imports, correlation with the total
    exports and imports of East Asian
    surplus countries, 398
inflation, 251
    correlation to Indonesia's real GDP
        growth, 253t
    and the output gap in, 298–300,
        299t
    shocks, affecting all variables other
        than US growth, 253n
    surprises, 300, 301f
labor productivity, 140f, 150f
lessons of real estate bubbles and
    banking crises, 289
literacy proficiencies, 142f, 143f
long-run equilibrium real rate of
    around 1 percent for, 293n
long-term bond yields, 294f
mortgage-related assets, surge in
    European purchases of, 275
as the most important trade deficit
    country, 398
natural rate of interest, 273f
net investment, 279f
number of employees by firm size, all
    industries, 159t
old-age dependency ratio, 38f, 57f
patent grants, 86, 94, 94f
per capita income level, 39f
Phillips curves for GDP inflation and
    employment gap, 301f
prevalence of small firms, 158
real 10-year bond yield, 1990–2018,
    272f
real GDP growth, 240f, 251, 253t
real neutral interest rates, 56f
reestablished financial stability after
    the global crisis, 335
revealed comparative advantages of,
    172f

10-year government yield, change in,
    55f
tightened regulations and eased
    monetary policy, 307
trade deficits, expanded, 388
trade frictions with the rest of the
    world, 281
trade growth before and after the
    financial crisis, 391, 393f
unexpected fall in net exports, 280
youth dependency ratio, 57f
zero bound constraining conventional
    monetary policy, 294
universities
    excelling in global science, 78
    graduates of top-ranked in Japan, 155
    Indonesia sending students to the best
        in the world, 267
    limited research capabilities of Korean,
        88
    moving education and training to, 163
    reformed in Japan, 85
    underperforming in graduate
        education, 78
upstream competitiveness, allowed export-
    led growth to sustain, 408
urbanization, slowing in China, 184

validation, becoming increasingly more
    costly, 27
valuation effects, moderating tendency for
    net international investment positions
    to diverge, 282f
VAT (value-added tax)
    collection
        closing gaps, 376
        increasing under rebalancing
            package, 366
    as efficient, 363
    increases
        direct impact of, 332n
        gradual, 332
vector auto-regression (VAR) analysis, 251,
    251n, 253, 253n
Venezuela, 14
venture capital market
    in Japan, 85
    in Taiwan, 92
vertical integration, deceleration in, 400
Vietnam
    aging, rapid until 2030, 52
    aging impact on TFP, 48f
    aging speed change between 2020 and
        2030, 58f

CPI inflation rates, 1985-2016, 288f
current account balances, 1985-2016, 310f
debt prospects similar to China's, 353
debt ratio change under Scenario 4b, 354f
demographic characteristics, 35t
demographic trends, impact of, 42f
emigration from, impact of net, 43
fiscal packages, 381t, 383t
foreign exchange reserves and net official assets, 1985-2016, 311f
in Group 3, 347b
infrastructure, index of quality of, 356f
labor force participation, 48f, 49f
long-term public debt projection, 349t
old-age dependency ratio, 36t, 38f, 57f
older workers, share of, 44f
pensions, 375
per capita income level, 39f
public debt, actual and projected, 346f, 352f
public spending
    efficiency frontier, distance from, 378t
    on health care as percent of GDP, 358f
    on pensions and health care, 346f
real per capita GDP, growth rate of, 1985-2016, 287f
real short-term interest rate, 292, 293f
real trade growth, 1998-2008, 2012-2015, 393f
research and development spending, 362f
Scenario 3 and, 350
scope for quantitative easing, December 2016, 303t
tax revenue sources, 364f
10-year government yield, change in, 55f
trade growth in, 399t
workforce, share of with productivity rising or falling, 45f
youth dependency ratio, 57f
virtual reality, as an educational tool, 27
Vivo, 91n
volatility
    defined, 241f
    of Indonesia's net nonofficial inflows compares favorably with regional peers, 250, 251f
    of the supply of foreign capital, 251f
voluntary saving, encouraging, 66

wage and labor productivity differences, between large and small firms, 152, 153f
wage gap
    between large and small firms in Japan, 162
    between nonregular and regular employees in Japan, 144, 145f, 162
    regulations reducing between regular and nonregular employees in Japan, 148
    between the two firm groups, 153f, 154
wage profile, relationship with marginal productivity of employees in Japan, 145
wages and prices, forcing down, 291
water pollution costs, likely to rise, 183
water power, improvement in, 16-17
Watt, James, 17
weak demand, explaining the recent trade slowdown, 398
wealth, of urban areas before the Enlightenment, 13
Wells, H. G., 10
women
    increasing labor force participation, 65
    retaining in the workforce, 133
"Womenomics," in Japan, 133
won
    depreciated sharply against the yen, 89
    strength of the Korean, 90
workers
    accumulating human capital, 144
    flow across firms and industries limited in Japan, 81
    LFPRs and, 46n
    not changing jobs because of deferred compensation in Japan, 149
    retraining, 65
    working hours in Japan, 133
workforce aging
    associated with higher capital per worker, 49
    estimated impact of projected on growth, 46, 48f
    estimating the effect on productivity, 44-45
    share with productivity rising or falling, 45f
workforce composition, changes in, 3
working-age population
    absolute changes for different demographic country groups in Asia, 38, 40f

change in in Asia and the rest of the world, 40*f*

changes in LFPRs for, 46, 48*f*, 49

declining in 2017, 166

defined, 40*f*, 44*f*, 50*n*

growth rate of in Indonesia, 261*f*

projected to decline, 34

shrinking of in Korea, 166

working life, longer, 367

World Bank, indices of, 14, 15*n*

World Development Indicators (World Bank), 225

World Economic Outlook, evidence of the Gourinchas-Rey effect for advanced economies, 280

world economy, rise in financial integration, 248

"world" interest rate, 292

world long-term rate, depressed, 297

world oil price and oil exporters' current account, 275*f*

World Population Prospects: 2015 Revision (United Nations), 34*n*

world real interest rates, decline in, 54, 55*f*

world real long-term interest rate, hovering around zero, 292–293

world trade growth, under more balanced global trade, 396–401

World Trade Organization (WTO), founding of, 269

Xiaomi, 91, 91*n*

x-ray crystallography, 24

Yanukovych, overthrow of, 23

yen, appreciated sharply against the US dollar, 89

Young, Thomas, 26*n*

youth dependency. *See also* population growth

impact of, 51, 56, 56*t*, 59

ratio defined, 57*f*

zero bound constraint, on nominal interest rate, 115–116

zero inflation, twenty years of in Japan, 291

zero or negative population growth, 19

zombie firms

in India, 232

in Korea, 170

Other Publications from the
PETERSON INSTITUTE FOR INTERNATIONAL ECONOMICS

WORKING PAPERS

94-1 APEC and Regional Trading Arrangements in the Pacific
Jeffrey A. Frankel with Shang-Jin Wei and Ernesto Stein

94-2 Towards an Asia Pacific Investment Code
Edward M. Graham

94-3 Merchandise Trade in the APEC Region: Is There Scope for Liberalization on an MFN Basis? Paul Wonnacott

94-4 The Automotive Industry in Southeast Asia: Can Protection Be Made Less Costly? Paul Wonnacott

94-5 Implications of Asian Economic Growth
Marcus Noland

95-1 APEC: The Bogor Declaration and the Path Ahead C. Fred Bergsten

95-2 From Bogor to Miami...and Beyond: Regionalism in the Asia Pacific and the Western Hemisphere Jeffrey J. Schott

95-3 Has Asian Export Performance Been Unique? Marcus Noland

95-4 Association of Southeast Asian Nations and ASEAN Free Trade Area: Chronology and Statistics Gautam Jaggi

95-5 The North Korean Economy
Marcus Noland

95-6 China and the International Economic System Marcus Noland

96-1 APEC after Osaka: Toward Free Trade by 2010/2020 C. Fred Bergsten

96-2 Public Policy, Private Preferences, and the Japanese Trade Pattern
Marcus Noland

96-3 German Lessons for Korea: The Economics of Unification Marcus Noland

96-4 Research and Development Activities and Trade Specialization in Japan
Marcus Noland

96-5 China's Economic Reforms: Chronology and Statistics Gautam Jaggi, Mary Rundle, Daniel H. Rosen, and Yuichi Takahashi

96-6 US-China Economic Relations
Marcus Noland

96-7 The Market Structure Benefits of Trade and Investment Liberalization
Raymond Atje and Gary Clyde Hufbauer

96-8 The Future of US-Korea Economic Relations Marcus Noland

96-9 Competition Policies in the Dynamic Industrializing Economies: The Case of China, Korea, and Chinese Taipei
Edward M. Graham

96-10 Modeling Economic Reform in North Korea Marcus Noland, Sherman Robinson, and Monica Scatasta

96-11 Trade, Investment, and Economic Conflict Between the United States and Asia Marcus Noland

96-12 APEC in 1996 and Beyond: The Subic Summit C. Fred Bergsten

96-13 Some Unpleasant Arithmetic Concerning Unification Marcus Noland

96-14 Restructuring Korea's Financial Sector for Greater Competitiveness
Marcus Noland

96-15 Competitive Liberalization and Global Free Trade: A Vision for the 21st Century C. Fred Bergsten

97-1 Chasing Phantoms: The Political Economy of USTR Marcus Noland

97-2 US-Japan Civil Aviation: Prospects for Progress Jacqueline McFadyen

97-3 Open Regionalism C. Fred Bergsten

97-4 Lessons from the Bundesbank on the Occasion of Its 40th (and Second to Last?) Birthday Adam S. Posen

97-5 The Economics of Korean Unification
Marcus Noland, Sherman Robinson, and Li-Gang Liu

98-1 The Costs and Benefits of Korean Unification Marcus Noland, Sherman Robinson, and Li-Gang Liu

98-2 Asian Competitive Devaluations
Li-Gang Liu, Marcus Noland, Sherman Robinson, and Zhi Wang

98-3 Fifty Years of the GATT/WTO: Lessons from the Past for Strategies or the Future
C. Fred Bergsten

98-4 NAFTA Supplemental Agreements: Four Year Review Jacqueline McFadyen

98-5 Local Government Spending: Solving the Mystery of Japanese Fiscal Packages
Hiroko Ishii and Erika Wada

98-6 The Global Economic Effects of the Japanese Crisis Marcus Noland, Sherman Robinson, and Zhi Wang

98-7 The Relationship Between Trade and Foreign Investment: Empirical Results for Taiwan and South Korea Li-Gang Liu, The World Bank, and Edward M. Graham

99-1 Rigorous Speculation: The Collapse and Revival of the North Korean Economy
Marcus Noland, Sherman Robinson, and Tao Wang

99-2 Famine in North Korea: Causes and Cures Marcus Noland, Sherman Robinson, and Tao Wang

99-3 Competition Policy and FDI: A Solution in Search of a Problem? Marcus Noland

99-4 The Continuing Asian Financial Crisis: Global Adjustment and Trade
Marcus Noland, Sherman Robinson, and Zhi Wang

99-5 Why EMU Is Irrelevant for the German Economy Adam S. Posen

99-6 The Global Trading System and the Developing Countries in 2000
C. Fred Bergsten

99-7 Modeling Korean Unification
Marcus Noland, Sherman Robinson, and Tao Wang

99-8 Sovereign Liquidity Crisis: The Strategic Case for a Payments Standstill
Marcus Miller and Lei Zhang

99-9 The Case for Joint Management of Exchange Rate Flexibility C. Fred Bergsten, Olivier Davanne, and Pierre Jacquet

99-10 Does Talk Matter After All? Inflation Targeting and Central Bank Behavior
Kenneth N. Kuttner and Adam S. Posen

99-11 Hazards and Precautions: Tales of International Finance Gary Clyde Hufbauer and Erika Wada

99-12 The Globalization of Services: What Has Happened? What Are the Implications?
Gary Clyde Hufbauer and Tony Warren

00-1 Regulatory Standards in the WTO
Keith Maskus

00-2 International Economic Agreements and the Constitution Richard M. Goodman and John M. Frost

00-3 Electronic Commerce in Developing Countries Catherine L. Mann

00-4 The New Asian Challenge C. Fred Bergsten

00-5 How the Sick Man Avoided Pneumonia: The Philippines in the Asian Financial Crisis Marcus Noland

00-6 Inflation, Monetary Transparency, and G-3 Exchange Rate Volatility
Kenneth N. Kuttner and Adam S. Posen

00-7 Transatlantic Issues in Electronic Commerce Catherine L. Mann

00-8 Strengthening the International Financial Architecture: Where Do We Stand? Morris Goldstein

00-9 On Currency Crises and Contagion
Marcel Fratzscher

01-1 Price Level Convergence and Inflation in Europe John H. Rogers, Gary Clyde Hufbauer, and Erika Wada

01-2 Subsidies, Market Closure, Cross-Border Investment, and Effects on Competition: The Case of FDI on the Telecommunications Sector
Edward M. Graham

01-3 Foreign Direct Investment in China: Effects on Growth and Economic Performance Edward M. Graham and Erika Wada

01-4 IMF Structural Conditionality: How Much Is Too Much? Morris Goldstein

01-5 Unchanging Innovation and Changing Economic Performance in Japan
Adam S. Posen

01-6 Rating Banks in Emerging Markets
Liliana Rojas-Suarez

01-7 Beyond Bipolar: A Three-Dimensional Assessment of Monetary Frameworks
Kenneth N. Kuttner and Adam S. Posen

01-8 Finance and Changing US-Japan Relations: Convergence Without Leverage—Until Now Adam S. Posen

01-9 Macroeconomic Implications of the New Economy Martin Neil Baily

01-10 Can International Capital Standards Strengthen Banks in Emerging Markets?
Liliana Rojas-Suarez

02-1 Moral Hazard and the US Stock Market: Analyzing the "Greenspan Put"?
Marcus Miller, Paul Weller, and Lei Zhang

02-2 Passive Savers and Fiscal Policy Effectiveness in Japan Kenneth N. Kuttner and Adam S. Posen

02-3 Home Bias, Transaction Costs, and Prospects for the Euro: A More Detailed Analysis Catherine L. Mann and Ellen E. Meade

02-4 Toward a Sustainable FTAA: Does Latin America Meet the Necessary Financial Preconditions? Liliana Rojas-Suarez

02-5 Assessing Globalization's Critics: "Talkers Are No Good Doers???"
Kimberly Ann Elliott, Debayani Kar, and J. David Richardson

02-6 Economic Issues Raised by Treatment of Takings under NAFTA Chapter 11
Edward M. Graham

03-1 Debt Sustainability, Brazil, and the IMF
Morris Goldstein

03-2 Is Germany Turning Japanese?
Adam S. Posen

03-3 Survival of the Best Fit: Exposure to Low-Wage Countries and the (Uneven) Growth of US Manufacturing Plants
Andrew B. Bernard, J. Bradford Jensen, and Peter K. Schott

03-4 Falling Trade Costs, Heterogeneous Firms, and Industry Dynamics
Andrew B. Bernard, J. Bradford Jensen, and Peter K. Schott

03-5 Famine and Reform in North Korea
Marcus Noland

03-6 Empirical Investigations in Inflation Targeting Yifan Hu

03-7 Labor Standards and the Free Trade Area of the Americas Kimberly Ann Elliott

03-8 Religion, Culture, and Economic Performance Marcus Noland

03-9 It Takes More than a Bubble to Become Japan Adam S. Posen

03-10 The Difficulty of Discerning What's Too Tight: Taylor Rules and Japanese Monetary Policy Adam S. Posen and Kenneth N. Kuttner

04-1 Adjusting China's Exchange Rate Policies
Morris Goldstein

04-2 Popular Attitudes, Globalization, and Risk Marcus Noland

04-3 Selective Intervention and Growth: The Case of Korea Marcus Noland

05-1 Outsourcing and Offshoring: Pushing the European Model Over the Hill, Rather Than Off the Cliff! Jacob Funk Kirkegaard

05-2 China's Role in the Revived Bretton Woods System: A Case of Mistaken Identity Morris Goldstein and Nicholas R. Lardy

05-3 Affinity and International Trade
Marcus Noland

05-4 South Korea's Experience with
International Capital Flows
Marcus Noland

05-5 Explaining Middle Eastern
Authoritarianism   Marcus Noland

05-6 Postponing Global Adjustment: An
Analysis of the Pending Adjustment of
Global Imbalances   Edwin M. Truman

05-7 What Might the Next Emerging Market
Financial Crisis Look Like?
Morris Goldstein, assisted by Anna Wong

05-8 Egypt after the Multi-Fiber Arrangement:
Global Approval and Textile Supply
Chains as a Route for Industrial
Upgrading   Dan Magder

05-9 Tradable Services: Understanding the
Scope and Impact of Services Offshoring
J. Bradford Jensen and Lori G. Kletzer

05-10 Importers, Exporters, and Multinationals:
A Portrait of Firms in the US that Trade
Goods   Andrew B. Bernard,
J. Bradford Jensen, and Peter K. Schott

05-11 The US Trade Deficit: A Disaggregated
Perspective   Catherine L. Mann and
Katharina Plück

05-12 Prospects for Regional Free Trade in Asia
Gary Clyde Hufbauer and Yee Wong

05-13 Predicting Trade Expansion under FTAs
and Multilateral Agreements
Dean A. DeRosa and John P. Gilbert

05-14 The East Asian Industrial Policy
Experience: Implications for the Middle
East   Marcus Noland and Howard Pack

05-15 Outsourcing and Skill Imports: Foreign
High-Skilled Workers on H-1B and L-1
Visas in the United States
Jacob Funk Kirkegaard

06-1 Why Central Banks Should Not Burst
Bubbles   Adam S. Posen

06-2 The Case for an International Reserve
Diversification Standard
Edwin M. Truman and Anna Wong

06-3 Offshoring in Europe—Evidence of a
Two-Way Street from Denmark
Peter Ørberg Jensen, Jacob Funk Kirkegaard,
and Nicolai Søndergaard Laugesen

06-4 The External Policy of the Euro Area:
Organizing for Foreign Exchange
Intervention   C. Randall Henning

06-5 The Eurasian Growth Paradox
Anders Åslund and Nazgul Jenish

06-6 Has EMU Had Any Impact on the Degree
of Wage Restraint?   Adam S. Posen and
Daniel Popov Gould

06-7 Firm Structure, Multinationals, and
Manufacturing Plant Deaths
Andrew B. Bernard and J. Bradford Jensen

07-1 The Trade Effects of Preferential
Arrangements: New Evidence from the
Australia Productivity Commission
Dean A. DeRosa

07-2 Offshoring, Outsourcing, and
Production Relocation Labor-Market
Effects in the OECD Countries and
Developing Asia   Jacob Funk Kirkegaard

07-3 Do Markets Care Who Chairs the Central
Bank?   Kenneth N. Kuttner and
Adam S. Posen

07-4 Industrial Policy, Innovative Policy,
and Japanese Competitiveness: Japan's
Pursuit of Competitive Advantage
Marcus Noland

07-5 A (Lack of) Progress Report on China's
Exchange Rate Policies   Morris Goldstein

07-6 Measurement and Inference in
International Reserve Diversification
Anna Wong

07-7 North Korea's External Economic
Relations   Stephan Haggard and
Marcus Noland

07-8 Congress, Treasury, and the
Accountability of Exchange Rate Policy:
How the 1988 Trade Act Should Be
Reformed   C. Randall Henning

07-9 Merry Sisterhood or Guarded
Watchfulness? Cooperation Between the
International Monetary Fund and the
World Bank   Michael Fabricius

08-1 Exit Polls: Refugee Assessments of North
Korea's Transitions   Yoonok Chang,
Stephan Haggard, and Marcus Noland

08-2 Currency Undervaluation and Sovereign
Wealth Funds: A New Role for the WTO
Aaditya Mattoo and Arvind Subramanian

08-3 Exchange Rate Economics
John Williamson

08-4 Migration Experiences of North Korean
Refugees: Survey Evidence from China
Yoonok Chang, Stephan Haggard, and
Marcus Noland

08-5 Korean Institutional Reform in
Comparative Perspective   Marcus Noland
and Erik Weeks

08-6 Estimating Consistent Fundamental
Equilibrium Exchange Rates
William R. Cline

08-7 Policy Liberalization and FDI Growth,
1982 to 2006   Matthew Adler and
Gary Clyde Hufbauer

08-8 Multilateralism Beyond Doha
Aaditya Mattoo and Arvind Subramanian

08-9 Famine in North Korea Redux?
Stephan Haggard and Marcus Noland

08-10 Recent Trade Patterns and Modes of
Supply in Computer and Information
Services in the United States and NAFTA
Partners   Jacob Funk Kirkegaard

08-11 On What Terms Is the IMF Worth
Funding?   Edwin M. Truman

08-12 The (Non) Impact of UN Sanctions on
North Korea   Marcus Noland

09-1 The GCC Monetary Union: Choice of
Exchange Rate Regime   Mohsin S. Khan

09-2 Policy Liberalization and US
Merchandise Trade Growth, 1980–2006
Gary Clyde Hufbauer and Matthew Adler

09-3 American Multinationals and American Economic Interests: New Dimensions to an Old Debate   Theodore H. Moran

09-4 Sanctioning North Korea: The Political Economy of Denuclearization and Proliferation   Stephan Haggard and Marcus Noland

09-5 Structural and Cyclical Trends in Net Employment over US Business Cycles, 1949–2009: Implications for the Next Recovery and Beyond   Jacob Funk Kirkegaard

09-6 What's on the Table? The Doha Round as of August 2009   Matthew Adler, Claire Brunel, Gary Clyde Hufbauer, and Jeffrey J. Schott

09-7 Criss-Crossing Globalization: Uphill Flows of Skill-Intensive Goods and Foreign Direct Investment   Aaditya Mattoo and Arvind Subramanian

09-8 Reform from Below: Behavioral and Institutional Change in North Korea   Stephan Haggard and Marcus Noland

09-9 The World Trade Organization and Climate Change: Challenges and Options   Gary Clyde Hufbauer and Jisun Kim

09-10 A Tractable Model of Precautionary Reserves, Net Foreign Assets, or Sovereign Wealth Funds   Christopher D. Carroll and Olivier Jeanne

09-11 The Impact of the Financial Crisis on Emerging Asia   Morris Goldstein and Daniel Xie

09-12 Capital Flows to Developing Countries: The Allocation Puzzle   Pierre-Olivier Gourinchas and Olivier Jeanne

09-13 Mortgage Loan Modifications: Program Incentives and Restructuring Design   Dan Magder

09-14 It Should Be a Breeze: Harnessing the Potential of Open Trade and Investment Flows in the Wind Energy Industry   Jacob Funk Kirkegaard, Thilo Hanemann, and Lutz Weischer

09-15 Reconciling Climate Change and Trade Policy   Aaditya Mattoo, Arvind Subramanian, Dominique van der Mensbrugghe, and Jianwu He

09-16 The International Monetary Fund and Regulatory Challenges   Edwin M. Truman

10-1 Estimation of De Facto Flexibility Parameter and Basket Weights in Evolving Exchange Rate Regimes   Jeffrey Frankel and Daniel Xie

10-2 Economic Crime and Punishment in North Korea   Stephan Haggard and Marcus Noland

10-3 Intra-Firm Trade and Product Contractibility   Andrew B. Bernard, J. Bradford Jensen, Stephen J. Redding, and Peter K. Schott

10-4 The Margins of US Trade   Andrew B. Bernard, J. Bradford Jensen, Stephen J. Redding, and Peter K. Schott

10-5 Excessive Volatility in Capital Flows: A Pigouvian Taxation Approach   Olivier Jeanne and Anton Korinek

10-6 Toward a Sunny Future? Global Integration in the Solar PV Industry   Jacob Funk Kirkegaard, Thilo Hanemann, Lutz Weischer, Matt Miller

10-7 The Realities and Relevance of Japan's Great Recession: Neither Ran nor Rashomon   Adam S. Posen

10-8 Do Developed and Developing Countries Compete Head to Head in High Tech?   Lawrence Edwards and Robert Z. Lawrence

10-9 US Trade and Wages: The Misleading Implications of Conventional Trade Theory   Lawrence Edwards and Robert Z. Lawrence

10-10 Wholesalers and Retailers in US Trade   Andrew B. Bernard, J. Bradford Jensen, Stephen J. Redding, and Peter K. Schott

10-11 The Design and Effects of Monetary Policy in Sub-Saharan African Countries   Mohsin S. Khan

10-12 Managing Credit Booms and Busts: A Pigouvian Taxation Approach   Olivier Jeanne and Anton Korinek

10-13 The G-20 and International Financial Institution Governance   Edwin M. Truman

10-14 Reform of the Global Financial Architecture   Garry J. Schinasi and Edwin M. Truman

10-15 A Role for the G-20 in Addressing Climate Change?   Trevor Houser

10-16 Exchange Rate Policy in Brazil   John Williamson

10-17 Trade Disputes Between China and the United States: Growing Pains so Far, Worse Ahead?   Gary Clyde Hufbauer and Jared C. Woollacott

10-18 Sovereign Bankruptcy in the European Union in the Comparative Perspective   Leszek Balcerowicz

11-1 Current Account Imbalances Coming Back   Joseph E. Gagnon

11-2 Too Big to Fail: The Transatlantic Debate   Morris Goldstein and Nicolas Véron

11-3 Foreign Direct Investment in Times of Crisis   Lauge Skovgaard Poulsen and Gary Clyde Hufbauer

11-4 A Generalized Fact and Model of Long-Run Economic Growth: Kaldor Fact as a Special Case   Daniel Danxia Xie

11-5 Integrating Reform of Financial Regulation with Reform of the International Monetary System   Morris Goldstein

11-6 Capital Account Liberalization and the Role of the RMB   Nicholas R. Lardy and Patrick Douglass

11-7 Capital Controls: Myth and Reality—A Portfolio Balance Approach   Nicolas E. Magud, Carmen M. Reinhart, and Kenneth S. Rogoff

11-8 Resource Management and Transition in Central Asia, Azerbaijan, and Mongolia Richard Pomfret

11-9 Coordinating Regional and Multilateral Financial Institutions C. Randall Henning

11-10 The Liquidation of Government Debt Carmen M. Reinhart and M. Belen Sbrancia

11-11 Foreign Manufacturing Multinationals and the Transformation of the Chinese Economy: New Measurements, New Perspectives Theodore H. Moran

11-12 Sovereign Wealth Funds: Is Asia Different? Edwin M. Truman

11-13 Integration in the Absence of Institutions: China-North Korea Cross-Border Exchange Stephan Haggard, Jennifer Lee, and Marcus Noland

11-14 Renminbi Rules: The Conditional Imminence of the Reserve Currency Transition Arvind Subramanian

11-15 How Flexible Can Inflation Targeting Be and Still Work? Kenneth N. Kuttner and Adam S. Posen

11-16 Asia and Global Financial Governance C. Randall Henning and Mohsin S. Khan

11-17 India's Growth in the 2000s: Four Facts Utsav Kumar and Arvind Subramanian

11-18 Applying Hubbert Curves and Linearization to Rock Phosphate Cullen S. Hendrix

11-19 Delivering on US Climate Finance Commitments Trevor Houser and Jason Selfe

11-20 Rent(s) Asunder: Sectoral Rent Extraction Possibilities and Bribery by Multinational Corporations Edmund Malesky, Nathan Jensen, and Dimitar Gueorguiev

11-21 Asian Regional Policy Coordination Edwin M. Truman

11-22 China and the World Trading System Aaditya Mattoo and Arvind Subramanian

12-1 Fiscal Federalism: US History for Architects of Europe's Fiscal Union C. Randall Henning and Martin Kessler

12-2 Financial Reform after the Crisis: An Early Assessment Nicolas Véron

12-3 Chinese Investment in Latin American Resources: The Good, the Bad, and the Ugly Barbara Kotschwar, Theodore H. Moran, and Julia Muir

12-4 Spillover Effects of Exchange Rates: A Study of the Renminbi Aaditya Mattoo, Prachi Mishra, and Arvind Subramanian

12-5 Global Imbalances and Foreign Asset Expansion by Developing-Economy Central Banks Joseph E. Gagnon

12-6 Transportation and Communication Infrastructure in Latin America: Lessons from Asia Barbara Kotschwar

12-7 Lessons from Reforms in Central and Eastern Europe in the Wake of the Global Financial Crisis Anders Åslund

12-8 Networks, Trust, and Trade: The Microeconomics of China-North Korea Integration Stephan Haggard and Marcus Noland

12-9 The Microeconomics of North-South Korean Cross-Border Integration Stephan Haggard and Marcus Noland

12-10 The Dollar and Its Discontents Olivier Jeanne

12-11 Gender in Transition: The Case of North Korea Stephan Haggard and Marcus Noland

12-12 Sovereign Debt Sustainability in Italy and Spain: A Probabilistic Approach William R. Cline

12-13 John Williamson and the Evolution of the International Monetary System Edwin M. Truman

12-14 Capital Account Policies and the Real Exchange Rate Olivier Jeanne

12-15 Choice and Coercion in East Asian Exchange Rate Regimes C. Randall Henning

12-16 Transactions: A New Look at Services Sector Foreign Direct Investment in Asia Jacob Funk Kirkegaard

12-17 Prospects for Services Trade Negotiations Jeffrey J. Schott, Minsoo Lee, and Julia Muir

12-18 Developing the Services Sector as Engine of Growth for Asia: An Overview Marcus Noland, Donghyun Park, and Gemma B. Estrada

12-19 The Renminbi Bloc Is Here: Asia Down, Rest of the World to Go? Revised Aug. 2013 Arvind Subramanian and Martin Kessler

12-20 Performance of the Services Sector in Korea: An Empirical Investigation Donghyun Park and Kwanho Shin

12-21 The Services Sector in Asia: Is It an Engine of Growth? Donghyun Park and Kwanho Shin

12-22 Assessing Potential Inflation Consequences of QE after Financial Crises Samuel Reynard

12-23 Overlooked Opportunity: Tradable Business Services, Developing Asia, and Growth J. Bradford Jensen

13-1 The Importance of Trade and Capital Imbalances in the European Debt Crisis Andrew Hughes Hallett and Juan Carlos Martinez Oliva

13-2 The Elephant Hiding in the Room: Currency Intervention and Trade Imbalances Joseph E. Gagnon

13-3 Does High Home-Ownership Impair the Labor Market? David G. Blanchflower and Andrew J. Oswald

13-4 The Rise of Emerging Asia: Regional Peace and Global Security Miles Kahler

13-5 Peers and Tiers and US High-Tech Export Controls: A New Approach to Estimating Export Shortfalls Asha Sundaram and J. David Richardson

13-6 The Hyperglobalization of Trade and Its Future Arvind Subramanian and Martin Kessler

13-7 How to Measure Underemployment? David N. F. Bell and David G. Blanchflower

13-8 The Greek Debt Restructuring: An Autopsy Jeromin Zettelmeyer, Christoph Trebesch, and Mitu Gulati

13-9 Asian and European Financial Crises Compared Edwin M. Truman

13-10 Why Growth in Emerging Economies Is Likely to Fall Anders Åslund

13-11 AGOA Rules: The Intended and Unintended Consequences of Special Fabric Provisions Lawrence Edwards and Robert Z. Lawrence

14-1 Regime Change, Democracy, and Growth Caroline Freund and Mélise Jaud

14-2 Labor Market Slack in the United Kingdom David N. F. Bell and David G. Blanchflower

14-3 Oil Prices and Interstate Conflict Behavior Cullen S. Hendrix

14-4 Demographic versus Cyclical Influences on US Labor Force Participation William R. Cline with Jared Nolan

14-5 The Federal Reserve Engages the World (1970–2000): An Insider's Narrative of the Transition to Managed Floating and Financial Turbulence Edwin M. Truman

14-6 Wages and Labor Market Slack: Making the Dual Mandate Operational David G. Blanchflower and Adam S. Posen

14-7 What Goes into a Medal: Women's Inclusion and Success at the Olympic Games Marcus Noland and Kevin Stahler

14-8 Official Financial Flows, Capital Mobility, and Global Imbalances Tamim Bayoumi, Joseph Gagnon, and Christian Saborowski

14-9 Sustainability of Public Debt in the United States and Japan William R. Cline

14-10 Versailles Redux? Eurozone Competitiveness in a Dynamic Balassa-Samuelson-Penn Framework Kevin Stahler and Arvind Subramanian

14-11 Understanding Differences in Growth Performance in Latin America and Developing Countries between the Asian and Global Financial Crises Roberto Alvarez and José De Gregorio

14-12 Foreign Investment and Supply Chains in Emerging Markets: Recurring Problems and Demonstrated Solutions Theodore H. Moran

15-1 The Economic Scope and Future of US-India Labor Migration Issues Jacob Funk Kirkegaard

15-2 Myanmar: Cross-Cutting Governance Challenges Cullen S. Hendrix and Marcus Noland

15-3 Financing Asia's Growth Gemma B. Estrada, Marcus Noland, Donghyun Park, and Arief Ramayandi

15-4 Maintaining Financial Stability in the People's Republic of China during Financial Liberalization Nicholas Borst and Nicholas Lardy

15-5 The Financial Sector and Growth in Emerging Asian Economies William R. Cline

15-6 Financing Productivity- and Innovation-Led Growth in Developing Asia: International Lessons and Policy Issues Ajai Chopra

15-7 The Future of Worldwide Income Distribution Tomáš Hellebrandt and Paolo Mauro

15-8 Testing the Modigliani-Miller Theorem of Capital Structure Irrelevance for Banks William R. Cline

15-9 An Old Boys' Club No More: Pluralism in Participation and Performance at the Olympic Games Marcus Noland and Kevin Stahler

15-10 Recent Declines in Labor's Share in US Income: A Preliminary Neoclassical Account Robert Z. Lawrence

15-11 The Resilient Trade Surplus, the Pharmaceutical Sector, and Exchange Rate Assessments in Switzerland Philip Sauré

15-12 The Tradability of Services: Geographic Concentration and Trade Costs Antoine Gervais and J. Bradford Jensen

15-13 Enhancing Financial Stability in Developing Asia Adam S. Posen and Nicolas Véron

15-14 The OECD's "Action Plan" to Raise Taxes on Multinational Corporations Gary Hufbauer, Euijin Jung, Tyler Moran, and Martin Vieiro

15-15 The Influence of Foreign Direct Investment, Intrafirm Trading, and Currency Undervaluation on US Firm Trade Disputes J. Bradford Jensen, Dennis P. Quinn, and Stephen Weymouth

15-16 Further Statistical Debate on "Too Much Finance" William R. Cline

15-17 Are Capital Inflows Expansionary or Contractionary? Theory, Policy Implications, and Some Evidence Olivier Blanchard, Jonathan D. Ostry, Atish R. Ghosh, and Marcos Chamon

15-18 Can Foreign Exchange Intervention Stem Exchange Rate Pressures from Global Capital Flow Shocks? Olivier Blanchard, Gustavo Adler, and Irineu de Carvalho Filho

15-19 Inflation and Activity: Two Explorations and Their Monetary Policy Implications Olivier Blanchard, Eugenio Cerutti, and Lawrence Summers

16-1 The Origins of the Superrich: The Billionaire Characteristics Database Caroline Freund and Sarah Oliver

16-2 The Economic Effects of the Trans-Pacific Partnership: New Estimates Peter A. Petri and Michael G. Plummer

16-3 Is Gender Diversity Profitable? Evidence from a Global Survey Marcus Noland, Tyler Moran, and Barbara Kotschwar

16-4 Russian Doping in Sports Marcus Noland

16-5 Adjustment and Income Distribution Impacts of the Trans-Pacific Partnership Robert Z. Lawrence and Tyler Moran

16-6 Benefits and Costs of Higher Capital Requirements for Banks William R. Cline

16-7 A Portfolio Model of Quantitative Easing Jens H. E. Christensen and Signe Krogstrup

16-8 Large Depreciations: Recent Experience in Historical Perspective José De Gregorio

16-9 Currency Wars, Coordination, and Capital Controls Olivier Blanchard

16-10 The Divergent Postcommunist Paths to Democracy and Economic Freedom Simeon Djankov with Owen Hauck

16-11 The Origins and Dynamics of Export Superstars Caroline Freund and Martha Denisse Pierola

16-12 Preferential Liberalization, Antidumping, and Safeguards: "Stumbling Block" Evidence from Mercosur Chad P. Bown and Patricia Tovar

16-13 US–COOL Retaliation: The WTO's Article 22.6 Arbitration Chad P. Bown and Rachel Brewster

16-14 Foot-and-Mouth Disease and Argentina's Beef Exports: The WTO's US–Animals Dispute Chad P. Bown and Jennifer A. Hillman

17-1 Multinational Investors as Export Superstars: How Emerging-Market Governments Can Reshape Comparative Advantage Caroline Freund and Theodore H. Moran

17-2 Kicking a Crude Habit: Diversifying Away from Oil and Gas in the 21st Century Cullen S. Hendrix

17-3 Global Competition and the Rise of China Caroline Freund and Dario Sidhu

17-4 Supply-Side Policies in the Depression: Evidence from France Jérémie Cohen-Setton, Joshua K. Hausman, and Johannes F. Wieland

17-5 Effects of Consumption Taxes on Real Exchange Rates and Trade Balances Caroline Freund and Joseph E. Gagnon

17-6 Does Greece Need More Official Debt Relief? If So, How Much? Jeromin Zettelmeyer, Eike Kreplin, and Ugo Panizza

17-7 Manufacturing and the 2016 Election: An Analysis of US Presidential Election Data Caroline Freund and Dario Sidhu

17-8 Boom, Slump, Sudden Stops, Recovery, and Policy Options: Portugal and the Euro Olivier Blanchard and Pedro Portugal

17-9 Trade and Fiscal Deficits, Tax Reform, and the Dollar: General Equilibrium Impact Estimates William R. Cline

17-10 Going It Alone in the Asia-Pacific: Regional Trade Agreements Without the United States Peter A. Petri, Michael G. Plummer, Shujiro Urata, and Fan Zhai

17-11 The End of the Bretton Woods International Monetary System Edwin M. Truman

17-12 Recent US Manufacturing Employment: The Exception that Proves the Rule Robert Z. Lawrence

17-13 A New Index of External Debt Sustainability Olivier Blanchard and Mitali Das

17-14 Should We Reject the Natural Rate Hypothesis? Olivier Blanchard

17-15 Do Governments Drive Global Trade Imbalances? Joseph E. Gagnon

18-1 ECB Interventions in Distressed Sovereign Debt Markets: The Case of Greek Bonds Christoph Trebesch and Jeromin Zettelmeyer

18-2 Global Imbalances and the Trade Slowdown Caroline Freund

18-3 The Search for a Euro Area Safe Asset Alvaro Leandro and Jeromin Zettelmeyer

18-4 Slower Productivity and Higher Inequality: Are They Related? Jason Furman and Peter Orszag

18-5 Productivity and Pay: Is the Link Broken? Anna Stansbury and Lawrence H. Summers

18-6 EU Financial Services Policy since 2007: Crisis, Responses, and Prospects Nicolas Véron

18-7 Growth-indexed Bonds and Debt Distribution: Theoretical Benefits and Practical Limits Julien Acalin

18-8 Real and Imagined Constraints on Euro Area Monetary Policy Patrick Honohan

18-9 Effects of Low Productivity Growth on Fiscal Sustainability in the United States Louise Sheiner

18-10 Living with Lower Productivity Growth: Impact on Exports Filippo di Mauro, Bernardo Mottironi, Gianmarco Ottaviano, and Alessandro Zona-Mattioli

18-11 Implications of Lower Trend Productivity Growth for Tax Policy Karen Dynan

18-12 Productivity in Emerging-Market Economies: Slowdown or Stagnation? José De Gregorio

18-13 Trade Policy toward Supply Chains after the Great Recession Chad P. Bown

POLICY BRIEFS

98-1 The Asian Financial Crisis Morris Goldstein

98-2 The New Agenda with China C. Fred Bergsten

98-3 Exchange Rates for the Dollar, Yen, and Euro Simon Wren-Lewis

98-4 Sanctions-Happy USA Gary Clyde Hufbauer

98-5   The Depressing News from Asia
        Marcus Noland, Sherman Robinson, and
        Zhi Wang
98-6   The Transatlantic Economic Partnership
        Ellen L. Frost
98-7   A New Strategy for the Global Crisis
        C. Fred Bergsten
98-8   Reviving the "Asian Monetary Fund"
        C. Fred Bergsten
99-1   Implementing Japanese Recovery
        Adam S. Posen
99-2   A Radical but Workable Restructuring
        Plan for South Korea   Edward M. Graham
99-3   Crawling Bands or Monitoring Bands:
        How to Manage Exchange Rates in a
        World of Capital Mobility
        John Williamson
99-4   Market Mechanisms to Reduce the Need
        for IMF Bailouts   Catherine L. Mann
99-5   Steel Quotas: A Rigged Lottery
        Gary Clyde Hufbauer and Erika Wada
99-6   China and the World Trade
        Organization: An Economic Balance
        Sheet   Daniel H. Rosen
99-7   Trade and Income Distribution: The
        Debate and New Evidence   William R.
        Cline
99-8   Preserve the Exchange Stabilization Fund
        C. Randall Henning
99-9   Nothing to Fear but Fear (of Inflation)
        Itself   Adam S. Posen
99-10   World Trade after Seattle: Implications
        for the United States   Gary Clyde Hufbauer
00-1   The Next Trade Policy Battle
        C. Fred Bergsten
00-2   Decision-Making in the WTO
        Jeffrey J. Schott and Jayashree Watal
00-3   American Access to China's Market:
        The Congressional Vote on PNTR
        Gary Clyde Hufbauer and Daniel H. Rosen
00-4   Third Oil Shock: Real or Imaginary?
        Consequences and Policy Alternatives
        Philip K. Verleger, Jr.
00-5   The Role of the IMF: A Guide to the
        Reports   John Williamson
00-6   The ILO and Enforcement of Core Labor
        Standards   Kimberly Ann Elliott
00-7   "No" to Foreign Telecoms Equals "No"
        to the New Economy!
        Gary Clyde Hufbauer and Edward M.
        Graham
01-1   Brunei: A Turning Point for APEC?
        C. Fred Bergsten
01-2   A Prescription to Relieve Worker Anxiety
        Lori G. Kletzer and Robert E. Litan
01-3   The US Export-Import Bank: Time for an
        Overhaul   Gary Clyde Hufbauer
01-4   Japan 2001—Decisive Action or Financial
        Panic   Adam S. Posen
01-5   Fin(d)ing Our Way on Trade and Labor
        Standards?   Kimberly Ann Elliott
01-6   Prospects for Transatlantic Competition
        Policy   Mario Monti
01-7   The International Implications of Paying
        Down the Debt   Edwin M. Truman

01-8   Dealing with Labor and Environment
        Issues in Trade Promotion Legislation
        Kimberly Ann Elliott
01-9   Steel: Big Problems, Better Solutions
        Gary Clyde Hufbauer and Ben Goodrich
01-10   Economic Policy Following the Terrorist
        Attacks   Martin Neil Baily
01-11   Using Sanctions to Fight Terrorism
        Gary Clyde Hufbauer, Jeffrey J. Schott, and
        Barbara Oegg
02-1   Time for a Grand Bargain in Steel?
        Gary Clyde Hufbauer and Ben Goodrich
02-2   Prospects for the World Economy: From
        Global Recession to Global Recovery
        Michael Mussa
02-3   Sovereign Debt Restructuring: New
        Articles, New Contracts—or No Change?
        Marcus Miller
02-4   Support the Ex-Im Bank: It Has Work to
        Do!   Gary Clyde Hufbauer and
        Ben Goodrich
02-5   The Looming Japanese Crisis
        Adam S. Posen
02-6   Capital-Market Access: New Frontier in
        the Sanctions Debate   Gary Clyde Hufbauer
        and Barbara Oegg
02-7   Is Brazil Next?   John Williamson
02-8   Further Financial Services Liberalization
        in the Doha Round?   Wendy Dobson
02-9   Global Economic Prospects
        Michael Mussa
02-10   The Foreign Sales Corporation: Reaching
        the Last Act?   Gary Clyde Hufbauer
03-1   Steel Policy: The Good, the Bad, and the
        Ugly   Gary Clyde Hufbauer and
        Ben Goodrich
03-2   Global Economic Prospects: Through the
        Fog of Uncertainty   Michael Mussa
03-3   Economic Leverage and the North
        Korean Nuclear Crisis
        Kimberly Ann Elliott
03-4   The Impact of Economic Sanctions on US
        Trade: Andrew Rose's Gravity Model
        Gary Clyde Hufbauer and Barbara Oegg
03-5   Reforming OPIC for the 21st Century
        Theodore H. Moran and C. Fred Bergsten
03-6   The Strategic Importance of US-Korea
        Economic Relations   Marcus Noland
03-7   Rules Against Earnings Stripping: Wrong
        Answer to Corporate Inversions
        Gary Clyde Hufbauer and Ariel Assa
03-8   More Pain, More Gain: Politics and
        Economics of Eliminating Tariffs
        Gary Clyde Hufbauer and Ben Goodrich
03-9   EU Accession and the Euro: Close
        Together or Far Apart?   Peter B. Kenen and
        Ellen E. Meade
03-10   Next Move in Steel: Revocation or
        Retaliation?   Gary Clyde Hufbauer and
        Ben Goodrich
03-11   Globalization of IT Services and
        White Collar Jobs: The Next Wave of
        Productivity Growth   Catherine L. Mann

04-1 This Far and No Farther? Nudging Agricultural Reform Forward
Tim Josling and Dale Hathaway

04-2 Labor Standards, Development, and CAFTA Kimberly Ann Elliott

04-3 Senator Kerry on Corporate Tax Reform: Right Diagnosis, Wrong Prescription
Gary Clyde Hufbauer and Paul Grieco

04-4 Islam, Globalization, and Economic Performance in the Middle East
Marcus Noland and Howard Pack

04-5 China Bashing 2004 Gary Clyde Hufbauer and Yee Wong

04-6 What Went Right in Japan Adam S. Posen

04-7 What Kind of Landing for the Chinese Economy? Morris Goldstein and Nicholas R. Lardy

05-1 A Currency Basket for East Asia, Not Just China John Williamson

05-2 After Argentina Anna Gelpern

05-3 Living with Global Imbalances: A Contrarian View Richard N. Cooper

05-4 The Case for a New Plaza Agreement
William R. Cline

06-1 The United States Needs German Economic Leadership Adam S. Posen

06-2 The Doha Round after Hong Kong
Gary Clyde Hufbauer and Jeffrey J. Schott

06-3 Russia's Challenges as Chair of the G-8
Anders Åslund

06-4 Negotiating the Korea–United States Free Trade Agreement Jeffrey J. Schott, Scott C. Bradford, and Thomas Moll

06-5 Can Doha Still Deliver on the Development Agenda?
Kimberly Ann Elliott

06-6 China: Toward a Consumption Driven Growth Path Nicholas R. Lardy

06-7 Completing the Doha Round
Jeffrey J. Schott

06-8 Choosing Monetary Arrangements for the 21st Century: Problems of a Small Economy John Williamson

06-9 Can America Still Compete or Does It Need a New Trade Paradigm?
Martin Neil Baily and Robert Z. Lawrence

07-1 The IMF Quota Formula: Linchpin of Fund Reform Richard N. Cooper and Edwin M. Truman

07-2 Toward a Free Trade Area of the Asia Pacific C. Fred Bergsten

07-3 China and Economic Integration in East Asia: Implications for the United States
C. Fred Bergsten

07-4 Global Imbalances: Time for Action
Alan Ahearne, William R. Cline, Kyung Tae Lee, Yung Chul Park, Jean Pisani-Ferry, and John Williamson

07-5 American Trade Politics in 2007: Building Bipartisan Compromise
I. M. Destler

07-6 Sovereign Wealth Funds: The Need for Greater Transparency and Accountability
Edwin M. Truman

07-7 The Korea-US Free Trade Agreement: A Summary Assessment Jeffrey J. Schott

07-8 The Case for Exchange Rate Flexibility in Oil-Exporting Economies Brad Setser

08-1 "Fear" and Offshoring: The Scope and Potential Impact of Imports and Exports of Services J. Bradford Jensen and Lori G. Kletzer

08-2 Strengthening Trade Adjustment Assistance Howard F. Rosen

08-3 A Blueprint for Sovereign Wealth Fund Best Practices Edwin M. Truman

08-4 A Security and Peace Mechanism for Northeast Asia: The Economic Dimension Stephan Haggard and Marcus Noland

08-5 World Trade at Risk C. Fred Bergsten

08-6 North Korea on the Precipice of Famine
Stephan Haggard, Marcus Noland, and Erik Weeks

08-7 New Estimates of Fundamental Equilibrium Exchange Rates
William R. Cline and John Williamson

08-8 Financial Repression in China
Nicholas R. Lardy

09-1 Did Reagan Rule In Vain? A Closer Look at True Expenditure Levels in the United States and Europe Jacob Funk Kirkegaard

09-2 Buy American: Bad for Jobs, Worse for Reputation Gary Clyde Hufbauer and Jeffrey J. Schott

09-3 A Green Global Recovery? Assessing US Economic Stimulus and the Prospects for International Coordination
Trevor Houser, Shashank Mohan, and Robert Heilmayr

09-4 Money for the Auto Industry: Consistent with WTO Rules? Claire Brunel and Gary Clyde Hufbauer

09-5 The Future of the Chiang Mai Initiative: An Asian Monetary Fund?
C. Randall Henning

09-6 Pressing the "Reset Button" on US-Russia Relations Anders Åslund and Andrew Kuchins

09-7 US Taxation of Multinational Corporations: What Makes Sense, What Doesn't Gary Clyde Hufbauer and Jisun Kim

09-8 Energy Efficiency in Buildings: A Global Economic Perspective Trevor Houser

09-9 The Alien Tort Statute of 1789: Time for a Fresh Look Gary Clyde Hufbauer

09-10 2009 Estimates of Fundamental Equilibrium Exchange Rates
William R. Cline and John Williamson

09-11 Understanding Special Drawing Rights (SDRs) John Williamson

09-12 US Interests and the International Monetary Fund C. Randall Henning

09-13 A Solution for Europe's Banking Problem Adam S. Posen and Nicolas Véron

09-14 China's Changing Outbound Foreign
Direct Investment Profile: Drivers and
Policy Implication   Daniel H. Rosen and
Thilo Hanemann

09-15 India-Pakistan Trade: A Roadmap for
Enhancing Economic Relations
Mohsin S. Khan

09-16 Pacific Asia and the Asia Pacific: The
Choices for APEC   C. Fred Bergsten

09-17 The Economics of Energy Efficiency in
Buildings   Trevor Houser

09-18 Setting the NAFTA Agenda on Climate
Change Jeffrey J. Schott and Meera Fickling

09-19 The 2008 Oil Price "Bubble"
Mohsin S. Khan

09-20 Why SDRs Could Rival the Dollar
John Williamson

09-21 The Future of the Dollar
Richard N. Cooper

09-22 The World Needs Further Monetary Ease,
Not an Early Exit   Joseph E. Gagnon

10-1 The Winter of Their Discontent:
Pyongyang Attacks the Market
Stephan Haggard and Marcus Noland

10-2 Notes on Equilibrium Exchange Rates:
William R. Cline and John Williamson

10-3 Confronting Asset Bubbles, Too Big to
Fail, and Beggar-thy-Neighbor Exchange
Rate Policies   Morris Goldstein

10-4 After the Flop in Copenhagen
Gary Clyde Hufbauer and Jisun Kim

10-5 Copenhagen, the Accord, and the Way
Forward   Trevor Houser

10-6 The Substitution Account as a First Step
Toward Reform of the International
Monetary System   Peter B. Kenen

10-7 The Sustainability of China's Recovery
from the Global Recession
Nicholas R. Lardy

10-8 New PPP-Based Estimates of Renminbi
Undervaluation and Policy Implications
Arvind Subramanian

10-9 Protection by Stealth: Using the Tax
Law to Discriminate against Foreign
Insurance Companies
Gary Clyde Hufbauer

10-10 Higher Taxes on US-Based
Multinationals Would Hurt US Workers
and Exports   Gary Clyde Hufbauer and
Theodore H. Moran

10-11 A Trade Agenda for the G-20
Jeffrey J. Schott

10-12 Assessing the American Power Act:
The Economic, Employment, Energy
Security and Environmental Impact of
Senator Kerry and Senator Lieberman's
Discussion Draft   Trevor Houser,
Shashank Mohan, and Ian Hoffman

10-13 Hobbling Exports and Destroying Jobs
Gary Clyde Hufbauer and Theodore H.
Moran

10-14 In Defense of Europe's Grand Bargain
Jacob Funk Kirkegaard

10-15 Estimates of Fundamental Equilibrium
Exchange Rates, May 2010
William R. Cline and John Williamson

10-16 Deepening China-Taiwan Relations
through the Economic Cooperation
Framework Agreement   Daniel H. Rosen
and Zhi Wang

10-17 Turning Back the Clock: Japan's
Misguided Postal Law is Back on the
Table Gary Clyde Hufbauer and Julia Muir

10-18 Dealing with Volatile Capital Flows
Olivier Jeanne

10-19 Revisiting the NAFTA Agenda on Climate
Change Jeffrey J. Schott and Meera Fickling

10-20 Renminbi Undervaluation, China's
Surplus, and the US Trade Deficit
William R. Cline

10-21 The Road to a Climate Change Agreement
Runs Through Montreal Richard J. Smith

10-22 Not All Financial Regulation Is Global
Stéphane Rottier and Nicolas Véron

10-23 Prospects for Implementing the Korea
US Free Trade Agreement Jeffrey J. Schott

10-24 The Central Banker's Case for Doing
More   Adam S. Posen

10-25 Will It Be Brussels, Berlin, or Financial
Markets that Check Moral Hazard in
Europe's Bailout Union? Most Likely the
Latter!   Jacob Funk Kirkegaard

10-26 Currency Wars?   William R. Cline and
John Williamson

10-27 How Europe Can Muddle Through Its
Crisis   Jacob Funk Kirkegaard

10-28 KORUS FTA 2.0: Assessing the Changes
Jeffrey J. Schott

10-29 Strengthening IMF Surveillance: A
Comprehensive Proposal
Edwin M. Truman

10-30 An Update on EU Financial Reforms
Nicolas Véron

11-1 Getting Surplus Countries to Adjust
John Williamson

11-2 Corporate Tax Reform for a New Century
Gary Clyde Hufbauer and Woan Foong
Wong

11-3 The Elephant in the "Green Room":
China and the Doha Round
Aaditya Mattoo, Francis Ng, and Arvind
Subramanian

11-4 The Outlook for International Monetary
System Reform in 2011: A Preliminary
Report Card   Edwin M. Truman

11-5 Estimates of Fundamental Equilibrium
Exchange Rates, May 2011
William R. Cline and John Williamson

11-6 Revitalizing the Export-Import Bank
Gary Clyde Hufbauer, Meera Fickling, and
Woan Foong Wong

11-7 Logistics Reform for Low-Value
Shipments   Gary Clyde Hufbauer and
Yee Wong

11-8 What Should the United States Do about
Doha?   Jeffrey J. Schott

11-9 Lessons from the East European Financial Crisis, 2008–10 Anders Åslund

11-10 America's Energy Security Options Trevor Houser and Shashank Mohan

11-11 Keeping the Promise of Global Accounting Standards Nicolas Véron

11-12 Markets vs. Malthus: Food Security and the Global Economy Cullen S. Hendrix

11-13 Europe on the Brink Peter Boone and Simon Johnson

11-14 IFSWF Report on Compliance with the Santiago Principles: Admirable but Flawed Transparency Sarah Bagnall and Edwin M. Truman

11-15 Sustainability of Greek Public Debt William R. Cline

11-16 US Tax Discrimination Against Large Corporations Should Be Discarded Gary Clyde Hufbauer and Martin Vieiro

11-17 Debt Relief for Egypt? John Williamson and Mohsin Khan

11-18 The Current Currency Situation William R. Cline and John Williamson

11-19 G-20 Reforms of the International Monetary System: An Evaluation Edwin M. Truman

11-20 The United States Should Establish Normal Trade Relations with Russia Anders Åslund and Gary Clyde Hufbauer

11-21 What Can and Cannot Be Done about Rating Agencies Nicolas Véron

11-22 Oil Exporters to the Euro's Rescue? Philip K. Verleger

12-1 The Coming Resolution of the European Crisis C. Fred Bergsten and Jacob Funk Kirkegaard

12-2 Japan Post: Retreat or Advance? Gary Clyde Hufbauer and Julia Muir

12-3 Another Shot at Protection by Stealth: Using the Tax Law to Penalize Foreign Insurance Companies Gary Clyde Hufbauer

12-4 The European Crisis Deepens Peter Boone and Simon Johnson

12-5 Interest Rate Shock and Sustainability of Italy's Sovereign Debt William R. Cline

12-6 Using US Strategic Reserves to Moderate Potential Oil Price Increases from Sanctions on Iran Philip K. Verleger, Jr.

12-7 Projecting China's Current Account Surplus William R. Cline

12-8 Does Monetary Cooperation or Confrontation Lead to Successful Fiscal Consolidation? Tomáš Hellebrandt, Adam S. Posen, and Marilyne Tolle

12-9 US Tire Tariffs: Saving Few Jobs at High Cost Gary Clyde Hufbauer and Sean Lowry

12-10 Framework for the International Services Agreement Gary Clyde Hufbauer, J. Bradford Jensen, and Sherry Stephenson. Assisted by Julia Muir and Martin Vieiro

12-11 Will the World Trade Organization Enjoy a Bright Future? Gary Clyde Hufbauer and Jeffrey J. Schott

12-12 Japan Post: Anti-Reform Law Clouds Japan's Entry to the Trans-Pacific Partnership Gary Clyde Hufbauer and Julia Muir

12-13 Right Idea, Wrong Direction: Obama's Corporate Tax Reform Proposals Gary Clyde Hufbauer and Martin Vieiro

12-14 Estimates of Fundamental Equilibrium Exchange Rates, May 2012 William R. Cline and John Williamson

12-15 Restoring Fiscal Equilibrium in the United States William R. Cline

12-16 The Trans-Pacific Partnership and Asia-Pacific Integration: Policy Implications Peter A. Petri and Michael G. Plummer

12-17 Southern Europe Ignores Lessons from Latvia at Its Peril Anders Åslund

12-18 The Coming Resolution of the European Crisis: An Update C. Fred Bergsten and Jacob Funk Kirkegaard

12-19 Combating Widespread Currency Manipulation Joseph E. Gagnon

12-20 Why a Breakup of the Euro Area Must Be Avoided: Lessons from Previous Breakups Anders Åslund

12-21 How Can Trade Policy Help America Compete? Robert Z. Lawrence

12-22 Hyperinflations Are Rare, but a Breakup of the Euro Area Could Prompt One Anders Åslund

12-23 Updated Estimates of Fundamental Equilibrium Exchange Rates William R. Cline and John Williamson

12-24 Europe's Single Supervisory Mechanism and the Long Journey Towards Banking Union Nicolas Véron

12-25 Currency Manipulation, the US Economy, and the Global Economic Order C. Fred Bergsten and Joseph E. Gagnon

13-1 The World Needs a Multilateral Investment Agreement Anders Åslund

13-2 A Blueprint for Rebalancing the Chinese Economy Nicholas R. Lardy and Nicholas Borst

13-3 Debt Restructuring and Economic Prospects in Greece William R. Cline

13-4 Reengineering EMU for an Uncertain World Ángel Ubide

13-5 From Supervision to Resolution: Next Steps on the Road to European Banking Union Nicolas Véron and Guntram B. Wolff

13-6 Liquefied Natural Gas Exports: An Opportunity for America Gary Clyde Hufbauer, Allie E. Bagnall, and Julia Muir

13-7 The Congress Should Support IMF Governance Reform to Help Stabilize the World Economy Edwin M. Truman

13-8 Crafting a Transatlantic Trade and Investment Partnership: What Can Be Done Jeffrey J. Schott and Cathleen Cimino

13-9 Corporate Taxation and US MNCs: Ensuring a Competitive Economy Gary Clyde Hufbauer and Martin Vieiro

13-10 Four Changes to Trade Rules to Facilitate Climate Change Action   Aaditya Mattoo and Arvind Subramanian

13-11 Dealing with Cybersecurity Threats Posed by Globalized Information Technology Suppliers   Theodore H. Moran

13-12 Sovereign Damage Control   Anna Gelpern

13-13 Sizing Up US Export Disincentives for a New Generation of National-Security Export Controls   J. David Richardson and Asha Sundaram

13-14 Shadow Deposits as a Source of Financial Instability: Lessons from the American Experience for China   Nicholas Borst

13-15 Estimates of Fundamental Equilibrium Exchange Rates, May 2013   William R. Cline

13-16 Preserving the Open Global Economic System: A Strategic Blueprint for China and the United States   Arvind Subramanian

13-17 A Realistic Bridge Towards European Banking Union   Nicolas Véron

13-18 Avoiding the "Resource Curse" in Mongolia   Theodore H. Moran

13-19 Progress on Sovereign Wealth Fund Transparency and Accountability: An Updated SWF Scoreboard   Allie E. Bagnall and Edwin M. Truman

13-20 Role of Apprenticeships in Combating Youth Unemployment in Europe and the United States   Natalia Aivazova

13-21 Lehman Died, Bagehot Lives: Why Did the Fed and Treasury Let a Major Wall Street Bank Fail?   William R. Cline and Joseph E. Gagnon

13-22 Ukraine's Choice: European Association Agreement or Eurasian Union?   Anders Åslund

13-23 How to Form a More Perfect European Banking Union   Ángel Ubide

13-24 China's Credit Boom: New Risks Require New Reforms   Nicholas Borst

13-25 Governing the Federal Reserve System after the Dodd-Frank Act   Peter Conti-Brown and Simon Johnson

13-26 Financial Services in the Transatlantic Trade and Investment Partnership   Simon Johnson and Jeffrey J. Schott

13-27 US Employment Deindustrialization: Insights from History and the International Experience   Robert Z. Lawrence and Lawrence Edwards

13-28 Stabilizing Properties of Flexible Exchange Rates: Evidence from the Global Financial Crisis   Joseph E. Gagnon

13-29 Estimates of Fundamental Equilibrium Exchange Rates, November 2013   William R. Cline

13-30 Five Challenges for Janet Yellen at the Federal Reserve   David J. Stockton

14-1 Making Labor Market Reforms Work for Everyone: Lessons from Germany   Jacob Funk Kirkegaard

14-2 Addressing Currency Manipulation Through Trade Agreements   C. Fred Bergsten

14-3 Income Inequality Developments in the Great Recession   Tomáš Hellebrandt

14-4 Monetary Policy with Abundant Liquidity: A New Operating Framework for the Federal Reserve   Joseph E. Gagnon and Brian Sack

14-5 Is the European Central Bank Failing Its Price Stability Mandate?   Ángel Ubide

14-6 A Proposed Code to Discipline Local Content Requirements   Cathleen Cimino, Gary Clyde Hufbauer, and Jeffrey J. Schott

14-7 Rethinking the National Export Initiative   Caroline Freund

14-8 Women, Sports, and Development: Does It Pay to Let Girls Play?   Barbara Kotschwar

14-9 IMF Reform Is Waiting on the United States   Edwin M. Truman

14-10 Wages and Labor Market Slack: Making the Dual Mandate Operational   David G. Blanchflower and Adam S. Posen

14-11 Managing Myanmar's Resource Boom to Lock in Reforms   Cullen S. Hendrix and Marcus Noland

14-12 Going Beyond Economic Engagement: Why South Korea Should Press the North on Labor Standards and Practices   Marcus Noland

14-13 NAFTA at 20: Misleading Charges and Positive Achievements   Gary Clyde Hufbauer, Cathleen Cimino, and Tyler Moran

14-14 What Should Surplus Germany Do?   Jacob Funk Kirkegaard

14-15 Internationalization of the Renminbi: The Role of Trade Settlement   Joseph E. Gagnon and Kent Troutman

14-16 Estimates of Fundamental Equilibrium Exchange Rates, May 2014   William R. Cline

14-17 Alternatives to Currency Manipulation: What Switzerland, Singapore, and Hong Kong Can Do   Joseph E. Gagnon

14-18 The US Manufacturing Base: Four Signs of Strength   Theodore H. Moran and Lindsay Oldenski

14-19 US Policies toward Liquefied Natural Gas and Oil Exports: An Update   Cathleen Cimino and Gary Clyde Hufbauer

14-20 Debt Sanctions Can Help Ukraine and Fill a Gap in the International Financial System   Anna Gelpern

14-21 Is China's Property Market Heading toward Collapse?   Li-Gang Liu

14-22 Should Korea Join the Trans-Pacific Partnership?   Jeffrey J. Schott and Cathleen Cimino

14-23 Why Bail-In Securities Are Fool's Gold   Avinash D. Persaud

14-24 An Economic Strategy to Save Ukraine   Anders Åslund

14-25 Estimates of Fundamental Equilibrium Exchange Rates, November 2014 William R. Cline

14-26 Rapid Growth in Emerging Markets and Developing Economies: Now and Forever? Giang Ho and Paolo Mauro

15-1 What Next for the IMF? Edwin M. Truman

15-2 Service Sector Reform in China Ryan Rutkowski

15-3 Japanese Investment in the United States: Superior Performance, Increasing Integration Theodore H. Moran and Lindsay Oldenski

15-4 The True Levels of Government and Social Expenditures in Advanced Economies Jacob Funk Kirkegaard

15-5 How Not to Regulate Insurance Markets: The Risks and Dangers of Solvency II Avinash Persaud

15-6 From Rapid Recovery to Slowdown: Why Recent Economic Growth in Latin America Has Been Slow José De Gregorio

15-7 Quantity Theory of Money Redux? Will Inflation Be the Legacy of Quantitative Easing? William R. Cline

15-8 Estimates of Fundamental Equilibrium Exchange Rates, May 2015 William R. Cline

15-9 Too Much Finance, or Statistical Illusion? William R. Cline

15-10 Gains from Harmonizing US and EU Auto Regulations under the Transatlantic Trade and Investment Partnership Caroline Freund and Sarah Oliver

15-11 Hungary under Orbán: Can Central Planning Revive Its Economy? Simeon Djankov

15-12 From Populist Destabilization to Reform and Possible Debt Relief in Greece William R. Cline

15-13 Korea and the TPP: The Inevitable Partnership Jeffrey J. Schott

15-14 Reshoring by US Firms: What Do the Data Say? Lindsay Oldenski

15-15 Fiscal Tightening and Economic Growth: Exploring Cross-Country Correlations Paolo Mauro and Jan Zilinsky

15-16 Do Public Development Banks Hurt Growth? Evidence from Brazil Monica de Bolle

15-17 Chinese Investment and CFIUS: Time for an Updated (and Revised) Perspective Theodore H. Moran

15-18 Russia's Economy under Putin: From Crony Capitalism to State Capitalism Simeon Djankov

15-19 Stability Bonds for the Euro Area Ángel Ubide

15-20 Estimates of Fundamental Equilibrium Exchange Rates, November 2015 William R. Cline

15-21 World on the Move: The Changing Global Income Distribution and Its Implications for Consumption Patterns and Public Policies Tomáš Hellebrandt and Paolo Mauro

15-22 Pitching a Level Playing Field: Women and Leadership in Sports Barbara Kotschwar and Tyler Moran

15-23 Toward a European Migration and Mobility Union Jacob Funk Kirkegaard

15-24 An Assessment of the Korea-China Free Trade Agreement Jeffrey J. Schott, Euijin Jung, and Cathleen Cimino-Isaacs

16-1 The US Phillips Curve: Back to the 60s? Olivier Blanchard

16-2 The Case for Growth-Indexed Bonds in Advanced Economies Today Olivier Blanchard, Paolo Mauro, and Julien Acalin

16-3 Breaking the Link between Housing Cycles, Banking Crises, and Recession Avinash Persaud

16-4 Quantitative Easing: An Underappreciated Success Joseph E. Gagnon

16-5 How Offshoring and Global Supply Chains Enhance the US Economy Theodore H. Moran and Lindsay Oldenski

16-6 Estimates of Fundamental Equilibrium Exchange Rates, May 2016 William R. Cline

16-7 Enhancing Export Opportunities for Small and Medium-Sized Enterprises Caroline Freund, Gary Clyde Hufbauer, and Euijin Jung

16-8 Implications of the Trans-Pacific Partnership for the World Trading System Jeffrey J. Schott, Cathleen Cimino-Isaacs, and Euijin Jung

16-9 Converging on the Medal Stand: Rio 2016 Olympic Forecasts Marcus Noland

16-10 Reducing Government Debt Ratios in an Era of Low Growth Paolo Mauro and Jan Zilinsky

16-11 Do DSGE Models Have a Future? Olivier Blanchard

16-12 The US-EU Privacy Shield Pact: A Work in Progress Gary Clyde Hufbauer and Euijin Jung

16-13 The IMF and Euro Area Crises: Review of a Report from the Independent Evaluation Office Edwin M. Truman

16-14 The State of Advanced Economies and Related Policy Debates: A Fall 2016 Assessment Olivier Blanchard

16-15 Increased Trade: A Key to Improving Productivity Gary Clyde Hufbauer and Zhiyao (Lucy) Lu

16-16 Apple's Tax Dispute With Europe and the Need for Reform Gary Clyde Hufbauer and Zhiyao (Lucy) Lu

16-17 What Does Measured FDI Actually Measure? Olivier Blanchard and Julien Acalin

16-18 Uneven Progress on Sovereign Wealth Fund Transparency and Accountability Sarah E. Stone and Edwin M. Truman

16-19 Systemic Implications of Problems at a Major European Bank William R. Cline

16-20 Protectionism in the 2016 Election: Causes and Consequences, Truths and Fictions Cullen S. Hendrix

16-21 Making US Trade and Investment Policies Work for Global Development Robert Z. Lawrence and Terra Lawson-Remer

16-22 Estimates of Fundamental Equilibrium Exchange Rates, November 2016 William R. Cline

16-23 The US Export-Import Bank Stimulates Exports Caroline Freund

16-24 Should the United States Recognize China as a Market Economy? Chad P. Bown

17-1 Management and Resolution of Banking Crises: Lessons from Recent European Experience Patrick Honohan

17-2 Lessons for US Business Tax Reform from International Tax Rates Gary Clyde Hufbauer and Zhiyao (Lucy) Lu

17-3 Border Tax Adjustments: Assessing Risks and Rewards Gary Clyde Hufbauer and Zhiyao (Lucy) Lu

17-4 The Ryan-Brady Cash Flow Tax: Disguised Protection, Exaggerated Revenue, and Increased Inequality William R. Cline

17-5 Against the Wind: China's Struggle to Integrate Wind Energy into Its National Grid Long Lam, Lee Branstetter, and Inês M. L. Azevedo

17-6 Short-Run Effects of Lower Productivity Growth: A Twist on the Secular Stagnation Hypothesis Olivier Blanchard, Guido Lorenzoni, and Jean Paul L'Huillier

17-7 US Trade Policy Options in the Pacific Basin: Bigger Is Better Jeffrey J. Schott

17-8 Making the Best of Brexit for the EU-27 Financial System André Sapir, Dirk Schoenmaker, and Nicolas Véron

17-9 The City of London after Brexit Simeon Djankov

17-10 International Financial Cooperation Benefits the United States Edwin M. Truman

17-11 Will the Proposed US Border Tax Provoke WTO Retaliation from Trading Partners? Chad P. Bown

17-12 Race to the Top: The Case for the Financial Stability Board Nathan Sheets

17-13 Do Digital Currencies Pose a Threat to Sovereign Currencies and Central Banks? Daniel Heller

17-14 Corporate Tax Cuts: Examining the Record in Other Countries Simeon Djankov

17-15 G-7 Economic Cooperation in the Trump Era C. Fred Bergsten, Edwin M. Truman, and Jeromin Zettelmeyer

17-16 The Payoff to America from Globalization: A Fresh Look with a Focus on Costs to Workers Gary Clyde Hufbauer and Zhiyao (Lucy) Lu

17-17 How to Make Immigration the Bridge to an Orderly and Timely Brexit Jacob Funk Kirkegaard

17-18 Governance and Ownership of Significant Euro Area Banks Nicolas Véron

17-19 Estimates of Fundamental Equilibrium Exchange Rates, May 2017 William R. Cline

17-20 The Financial Stability Oversight Council: An Essential Role for the Evolving US Financial System Simon Johnson and Antonio Weiss

17-21 Steel, Aluminum, Lumber, Solar: Trump's Stealth Trade Protection Chad P. Bown

17-22 NAFTA Renegotiation: US Offensive and Defensive Interests vis-à-vis Canada Gary Clyde Hufbauer and Euijin Jung

17-23 Trade Balances and the NAFTA Renegotiation C. Fred Bergsten

17-24 Agriculture in the NAFTA Renegotiation Cullen S. Hendrix

17-25 Streamlining Rules of Origin in NAFTA Caroline Freund

17-26 The Case for an American Productivity Revival Lee Branstetter and Daniel Sichel

17-27 Will Rising Interest Rates Lead to Fiscal Crises? Olivier J. Blanchard and Jeromin Zettelmeyer

17-28 Tax Overhaul Risks Making the US Tax and Transfer System (Even) More Regressive Jacob Funk Kirkegaard

17-29 United States Is Outlier in Tax Trends in Advanced and Large Emerging Economies Simeon Djankov

17-30 Will Corporate Tax Cuts Cause a Large Increase in Wages? William R. Cline

17-31 Estimates of Fundamental Equilibrium Exchange Rates, November 2017 William R. Cline

18-1 China Needs Better Credit Data to Help Consumers Martin Chorzempa

18-2 Earmarked Revenues: How the European Union Can Learn from US Budgeting Experience Jacob Funk Kirkegaard

18-3 The New Tax Law's Impact on Inequality: Minor but Worse if Accompanied by Regressive Spending Cuts William R. Cline

18-4 Why Has the Stock Market Risen So Much Since the US Presidential Election? Olivier Blanchard, Christopher G. Collins, Mohammad R. Jahan-Parvar, Thomas Pellet, and Beth Anne Wilson

18-5 The Dispute Settlement Crisis in the World Trade Organization: Causes and Cures Tetyana Payosova, Gary Clyde Hufbauer, and Jeffrey J. Schott

18-6 Five Reasons Why the Focus on Trade Deficits Is Misleading Robert Z. Lawrence

18-7 Can a Country Save Too Much? The Case of Norway Joseph E. Gagnon

18-8 The Case for Raising *de minimis*
Thresholds in NAFTA 2.0
Gary Clyde Hufbauer, Euijin Jung, and
Zhiyao (Lucy) Lu

18-9 IMF Quota and Governance Reform
Once Again   Edwin M. Truman

18-10 How to Solve the Greek Debt Problem
Jeromin Zettelmeyer, Emilios Avgouleas,
Barry Eichengreen, Miguel Poiares Maduro,
Ugo Panizza, Richard Portes, Beatrice Weder
di Mauro, and Charles Wyplosz

18-11 NAFTA Termination: Legal Process in
Canada and Mexico   Tetyana Payosova,
Gary Clyde Hufbauer, and Euijin Jung

18-12 Trump Tariffs Primarily Hit
Multinational Supply Chains, Harm US
Technology Competitiveness
Mary E. Lovely and Yang Liang

18-13 China's Forced Technology Transfer
Problem—And What to Do About It
Lee G. Branstetter

18-14 China's Social Credit System: A Mark of
Progress or a Threat to Privacy?
Martin Chorzempa, Paul Triolo, and
Samm Sacks

18-15 The European Union's Proposed Digital
Services Tax: A De Facto Tariff
Gary Clyde Hufbauer and Zhiyao (Lucy) Lu

18-16 Vehicular Assault: Proposed Auto Tariffs
Will Hit American Car Buyers' Wallets
Mary E. Lovely, Jérémie Cohen-Setton, and
Euijin Jung

18-17 How the United States Should Confront
China Without Threatening the Global
Trading System   Robert Z. Lawrence

18-18 Sector Gains Are Uneven Under the 2017
Tax Act   Thomas Pellet

18-19 QE: A User's Guide Joseph E. Gagnon and
Brian Sack

POLICY ANALYSES IN INTERNATIONAL ECONOMICS SERIES

* = out of print

1 The Lending Policies of the International
Monetary Fund*   John Williamson
August 1982   ISBN 0-88132-000-5

2 "Reciprocity": A New Approach to World
Trade Policy?*   William R. Cline
September 1982   ISBN 0-88132-001-3

3 Trade Policy in the 1980s* C. Fred Bergsten
and William R. Cline
November 1982   ISBN 0-88132-002-1

4 International Debt and the Stability of the
World Economy*   William R. Cline
September 1983   ISBN 0-88132-010-2

5 The Exchange Rate System,* 2d ed.
John Williamson
Sept. 1983, rev. June 1985   ISBN 0-88132-034-X

6 Economic Sanctions in Support of Foreign
Policy Goals*   Gary Clyde Hufbauer and
Jeffrey J. Schott
October 1983   ISBN 0-88132-014-5

7 A New SDR Allocation?*   John Williamson
March 1984   ISBN 0-88132-028-5

8 An International Standard for Monetary
Stabilization*   Ronald L. McKinnon
March 1984   ISBN 0-88132-018-8

9 The Yen/Dollar Agreement: Liberalizing
Japanese Capital Markets*   Jeffrey Frankel
December 1984   ISBN 0-88132-035-8

10 Bank Lending to Developing Countries: The
Policy Alternatives*   C. Fred Bergsten,
William R. Cline, and John Williamson
April 1985   ISBN 0-88132-032-3

11 Trading for Growth: The Next Round of
Trade Negotiations*   Gary Clyde Hufbauer
and Jeffrey J. Schott
September 1985   ISBN 0-88132-033-1

12 Financial Intermediation Beyond the Debt
Crisis*   Donald R. Lessard and
John Williamson
September 1985   ISBN 0-88132-021-8

13 The United States-Japan Economic
Problem*   C. Fred Bergsten and
William R. Cline   *Oct. 1985, 2d ed. January 1987*
                ISBN 0-88132-060-9

14 Deficits and the Dollar: The World Economy at Risk*   Stephen Marris
Dec. 1985, 2d ed. November 1987
                ISBN 0-88132-067-6

15 Trade Policy for Troubled Industries*
Gary Clyde Hufbauer and Howard F. Rosen
March 1986   ISBN 0-88132-020-X

16 The United States and Canada: The Quest
for Free Trade*   Paul Wonnacott, with an
appendix by John Williamson
March 1987   ISBN 0-88132-056-0

17 Adjusting to Success: Balance of Payments
Policy in the East Asian NICs*   Bela Balassa
and John Williamson
June 1987, rev. April 1990   ISBN 0-88132-101-X

18 Mobilizing Bank Lending to Debtor
Countries*   William R. Cline
June 1987   ISBN 0-88132-062-5

19 Auction Quotas and United States Trade
Policy* C. Fred Bergsten, Kimberly Ann
Elliott, Jeffrey J. Schott, and Wendy E. Takacs
September 1987   ISBN 0-88132-050-1

20 Agriculture and the GATT: Rewriting the
Rules*   Dale E. Hathaway
September 1987   ISBN 0-88132-052-8

21 Anti-Protection: Changing Forces in United
States Trade Politics*   I. M. Destler and
John S. Odell
September 1987   ISBN 0-88132-043-9

22 Targets and Indicators: A Blueprint for the
International Coordination of Economic
Policy*   John Williamson and Marcus Miller
September 1987   ISBN 0-88132-051-X

23 Capital Flight: The Problem and Policy
Responses*   Donald R. Lessard and
John Williamson
December 1987   ISBN 0-88132-059-5

24 United States-Canada Free Trade: An Evaluation of the Agreement*   Jeffrey J. Schott
April 1988   ISBN 0-88132-072-2

25 Voluntary Approaches to Debt Relief*
John Williamson
Sept. 1988, rev. May 1989   ISBN 0-88132-098-6
26 American Trade Adjustment: The Global
Impact*   William R. Cline
March 1989   ISBN 0-88132-095-1
27 More Free Trade Areas?*   Jeffrey J. Schott
May 1989   ISBN 0-88132-085-4
28 The Progress of Policy Reform in Latin
America*   John Williamson
January 1990   ISBN 0-88132-100-1
29 The Global Trade Negotiations: What Can
Be Achieved?*   Jeffrey J. Schott
September 1990   ISBN 0-88132-137-0
30 Economic Policy Coordination: Requiem
for Prologue?*   Wendy Dobson
April 1991   ISBN 0-88132-102-8
31 The Economic Opening of Eastern Europe*
John Williamson
May 1991   ISBN 0-88132-186-9
32 Eastern Europe and the Soviet Union in the
World Economy*   Susan Collins and
Dani Rodrik
May 1991   ISBN 0-88132-157-5
33 African Economic Reform: The External
Dimension*   Carol Lancaster
June 1991   ISBN 0-88132-096-X
34 Has the Adjustment Process Worked?*
Paul R. Krugman
October 1991   ISBN 0-88132-116-8
35 From Soviet disUnion to Eastern Economic
Community?*   Oleh Havrylyshyn and
John Williamson
October 1991   ISBN 0-88132-192-3
36 Global Warming: The Economic Stakes*
William R. Cline
May 1992   ISBN 0-88132-172-9
37 Trade and Payments after Soviet Disintegra-
tion*   John Williamson
June 1992   ISBN 0-88132-173-7
38 Trade and Migration: NAFTA and Agricul-
ture*   Philip L. Martin
October 1993   ISBN 0-88132-201-6
39 The Exchange Rate System and the IMF: A
Modest Agenda   Morris Goldstein
June 1995   ISBN 0-88132-219-9
40 What Role for Currency Boards?
John Williamson
September 1995   ISBN 0-88132-222-9
41 Predicting External Imbalances for the
United States and Japan   William R. Cline
September 1995   ISBN 0-88132-220-2
42 Standards and APEC: An Action Agenda*
John S. Wilson
October 1995   ISBN 0-88132-223-7
43 Fundamental Tax Reform and Border Tax
Adjustments*   Gary Clyde Hufbauer
January 1996   ISBN 0-88132-225-3
44 Global Telecom Talks: A Trillion Dollar
Deal*   Ben A. Petrazzini
June 1996   ISBN 0-88132-230-X
45 WTO 2000: Setting the Course for World
Trade   Jeffrey J. Schott
September 1996   ISBN 0-88132-234-2

46 The National Economic Council: A Work in
Progress   I. M. Destler
November 1996   ISBN 0-88132-239-3
47 The Case for an International Banking
Standard   Morris Goldstein
April 1997   ISBN 0-88132-244-X
48 Transatlantic Trade: A Strategic Agenda*
Ellen L. Frost
May 1997   ISBN 0-88132-228-8
49 Cooperating with Europe's Monetary
Union   C. Randall Henning
May 1997   ISBN 0-88132-245-8
50 Renewing Fast Track Legislation*
I. M. Destler
September 1997   ISBN 0-88132-252-0
51 Competition Policies for the Global
Economy   Edward M. Graham and
J. David Richardson
November 1997   ISBN 0-88132-249-0
52 Improving Trade Policy Reviews in the
World Trade Organization   Donald Keesing
April 1998   ISBN 0-88132-251-2
53 Agricultural Trade Policy: Completing the
Reform   Timothy Josling
April 1998   ISBN 0-88132-256-3
54 Real Exchange Rates for the Year 2000
Simon Wren Lewis and Rebecca Driver
April 1998   ISBN 0-88132-253-9
55 The Asian Financial Crisis: Causes, Cures,
and Systemic Implications Morris Goldstein
June 1998   ISBN 0-88132-261-X
56 Global Economic Effects of the Asian
Currency Devaluations   Marcus Noland,
LiGang Liu, Sherman Robinson, and Zhi Wang
July 1998   ISBN 0-88132-260-1
57 The Exchange Stabilization Fund: Slush
Money or War Chest?   C. Randall Henning
May 1999   ISBN 0-88132-271-7
58 The New Politics of American Trade: Trade,
Labor, and the Environment I. M. Destler
and Peter J. Balint
October 1999   ISBN 0-88132-269-5
59 Congressional Trade Votes: From NAFTA
Approval to Fast Track Defeat
Robert E. Baldwin and Christopher S. Magee
February 2000   ISBN 0-88132-267-9
60 Exchange Rate Regimes for Emerging
Markets: Reviving the Intermediate Option
John Williamson
September 2000   ISBN 0-88132-293-8
61 NAFTA and the Environment: Seven Years
Later   Gary Clyde Hufbauer, Daniel Esty,
Diana Orejas, Luis Rubio, and Jeffrey J. Schott
October 2000   ISBN 0-88132-299-7
62 Free Trade between Korea and the United
States?   Inbom Choi and Jeffrey J. Schott
April 2001   ISBN 0-88132-311-X
63 New Regional Trading Arrangements in the
Asia Pacific?   Robert Scollay and
John P. Gilbert
May 2001   ISBN 0-88132-302-0
64 Parental Supervision: The New Paradigm
for Foreign Direct Investment and
Development   Theodore H. Moran
August 2001   ISBN 0-88132-313-6

65 The Benefits of Price Convergence: Speculative Calculations
Gary Clyde Hufbauer, Erika Wada, and Tony Warren
December 2001   ISBN 0-88132-333-0

66 Managed Floating Plus   Morris Goldstein
March 2002   ISBN 0-88132-336-5

67 Argentina and the Fund: From Triumph to Tragedy*   Michael Mussa
July 2002   ISBN 0-88132-339-X

68 East Asian Financial Cooperation
C. Randall Henning
September 2002   ISBN 0-88132-338-1

69 Reforming OPIC for the 21st Century
Theodore H. Moran
May 2003   ISBN 0-88132-342-X

70 Awakening Monster: The Alien Tort Statute of 1789   Gary Clyde Hufbauer and Nicholas Mitrokostas
July 2003   ISBN 0-88132-366-7

71 Korea after Kim Jong-il   Marcus Noland
January 2004   ISBN 0-88132-373-X

72 Roots of Competitiveness: China's Evolving Agriculture Interests   Daniel H. Rosen, Scott Rozelle, and Jikun Huang
July 2004   ISBN 0-88132-376-4

73 Prospects for a US-Taiwan FTA
Nicholas R. Lardy and Daniel H. Rosen
December 2004   ISBN 0-88132-367-5

74 Anchoring Reform with a US-Egypt Free Trade Agreement   Ahmed Galal and Robert Z. Lawrence
April 2005   ISBN 0-88132-368-3

75 Curbing the Boom-Bust Cycle: Stabilizing Capital Flows to Emerging Markets
John Williamson
July 2005   ISBN 0-88132-330-6

76 The Shape of a Swiss-US Free Trade Agreement   Gary Clyde Hufbauer and Richard E. Baldwin
February 2006   ISBN 978-0-88132-385-6

77 A Strategy for IMF Reform
Edwin M. Truman
February 2006   ISBN 978-0-88132-398-6

78 US-China Trade Disputes: Rising Tide, Rising Stakes   Gary Clyde Hufbauer, Yee Wong, and Ketki Sheth
August 2006   ISBN 978-0-88132-394-8

79 Trade Relations Between Colombia and the United States   Jeffrey J. Schott, ed.
August 2006   ISBN 978-0-88132-389-4

80 Sustaining Reform with a US-Pakistan Free Trade Agreement   Gary Clyde Hufbauer and Shahid Javed Burki
November 2006   ISBN 978-0-88132-395-5

81 A US–Middle East Trade Agreement: A Circle of Opportunity?   Robert Z. Lawrence
November 2006   ISBN 978-0-88132-396-2

82 Reference Rates and the International Monetary System   John Williamson
January 2007   ISBN 978-0-88132-401-3

83 Toward a US-Indonesia Free Trade Agreement   Gary Clyde Hufbauer and Sjamsu Rahardja
June 2007   ISBN 978-0-88132-402-0

84 The Accelerating Decline in America's High-Skilled Workforce   Jacob F. Kirkegaard
December 2007   ISBN 978-0-88132-413-6

85 Blue-Collar Blues: Is Trade to Blame for Rising US Income Inequality?
Robert Z. Lawrence
January 2008   ISBN 978-0-88132-414-3

86 Maghreb Regional and Global Integration: A Dream to Be Fulfilled   Gary Clyde Hufbauer and Claire Brunel, eds.
October 2008   ISBN 978-0-88132-426-6

87 The Future of China's Exchange Rate Policy
Morris Goldstein and Nicholas R. Lardy
July 2009   ISBN 978-0-88132-416-7

88 Capitalizing on the Morocco-US Free Trade Agreement: A Road Map for Success
Gary Clyde Hufbauer and Claire Brunel, eds.
September 2009   ISBN 978-0-88132-433-4

89 Three Threats: An Analytical Framework for the CFIUS Process   Theodore H. Moran
August 2009   ISBN 978-0-88132-429-7

90 Reengaging Egypt: Options for US-Egypt Economic Relations   Barbara Kotschwar and Jeffrey J. Schott
January 2010   ISBN 978-088132-439-6

91 Figuring Out the Doha Round
Gary Clyde Hufbauer, Jeffrey J. Schott, and Woan Foong Wong
June 2010   ISBN 978-088132-503-4

92 China's Strategy to Secure Natural Resources: Risks, Dangers, and Opportunities   Theodore H. Moran
June 2010   ISBN 978-088132-512-6

93 The Implications of China-Taiwan Economic Liberalization   Daniel H. Rosen and Zhi Wang
January 2011   ISBN 978-0-88132-501-0

94 The Global Outlook for Government Debt over the Next 25 Years: Implications for the Economy and Public Policy
Joseph E. Gagnon with Marc Hinterschweiger
June 2011   ISBN 978-0-88132-621-5

95 A Decade of Debt   Carmen M. Reinhart and Kenneth S. Rogoff
September 2011   ISBN 978-0-88132-622-2

96 Carbon Abatement Costs and Climate Change Finance   William R. Cline
July 2011   ISBN 978-0-88132-607-9

97 The United States Should Establish Permanent Normal Trade Relations with Russia   Anders Åslund and Gary Clyde Hufbauer
April 2012   ISBN 978-0-88132-620-8

98 The Trans-Pacific Partnership and Asia-Pacific Integration: A Quantitative Assessment   Peter A. Petri, Michael G. Plummer, and Fan Zhai
November 2012   ISBN 978-0-88132-664-2

99 Understanding the Trans-Pacific Partnership   Jeffrey J. Schott, Barbara Kotschwar, and Julia Muir
January 2013   ISBN 978-0-88132-672-7

100 Foreign Direct Investment in the United States: Benefits, Suspicions, and Risks with Special Attention to FDI from China Theodore H. Moran and Lindsay Oldenski
August 2013   ISBN 978-0-88132-660-4

101 Outward Foreign Direct Investment and US Exports, Jobs, and R&D: Implications for US Policy   Gary Clyde Hufbauer, Theodore H. Moran, and Lindsay Oldenski, Assisted by Martin Vieiro
August 2013   ISBN 978-0-88132-668-0

102 Local Content Requirements: A Global Problem   Gary Clyde Hufbauer, Jeffrey J. Schott, Cathleen Cimino, Martin Vieiro, and Erika Wada
September 2013   ISBN 978-0-88132-680-2

103 Economic Normalization with Cuba: A Roadmap for US Policymakers Gary Clyde Hufbauer, Barbara Kotschwar, assisted by Cathleen Cimino and Julia Muir
April 2014   ISBN 978-0-88132-682-6

104 Trans-Pacific Partnership: An Assessment Cathleen Cimino-Isaacs and Jeffrey J. Schott, eds.
July 2016   ISBN 978-0-88132-713-7

105 World on the Move: Consumption Patterns in a More Equal Global Economy Tomáš Hellebrandt and Paolo Mauro
December 2016   ISBN 978-0-88132-716-8

106 Banking's Final Exam: Stress Testing and Bank-Capital Reform   Morris Goldstein
May 2017   ISBN 978-0-88132-705-2

107 The Right Balance for Banks: Theory and Evidence on Optimal Capital Requirements William Cline
June 2017   ISBN 978-0-88132-721-2

108 The Paradox of Risk: Leaving the Monetary Policy Comfort Zone   Ángel Ubide
September 2017   ISBN 978-0-88132-719-9

BOOKS

* = out of print

IMF Conditionality*   John Williamson, ed.
1983   ISBN 0-88132-006-4

Trade Policy in the 1980s*   William R. Cline, ed.
1983   ISBN 0-88132-031-2

Subsidies in International Trade*
Gary Clyde Hufbauer and Joanna Shelton Erb
1984   ISBN 0-88132-004-8

International Debt: Systemic Risk and Policy Response*   William R. Cline
1984   ISBN 0-88132-015-3

Second-Best Responses to Currency Misalignments*   Stephen Marris
1984   ISBN 978-0-88132-019-0

Toward Cartelization of World Steel Trade?*
William R. Cline
1984   ISBN 978-0-88132-023-7

New International Arrangements for Foreign Direct Investment*   C. Fred Bergsten and Jeffrey J. Schott
1984   ISBN 978-0-88132-024-4

Trade Protection in the United States: 31 Case Studies*   Gary Clyde Hufbauer, Diane E. Berliner, and Kimberly Ann Elliott
1986   ISBN 0-88132-040-4

Toward Renewed Economic Growth in Latin America*   Bela Balassa, Gerardo M. Bueno, Pedro Pablo Kuczynski, and Mario Henrique Simonsen
1986   ISBN 0-88132-045-5

Capital Flight and Third World Debt*
Donald R. Lessard and John Williamson, eds.
1987   ISBN 0-88132-053-6

The Canada-United States Free Trade Agreement: The Global Impact*   Jeffrey J. Schott and Murray G. Smith, eds.
1988   ISBN 0-88132-073-0

World Agricultural Trade: Building a Consensus*
William M. Miner and Dale E. Hathaway, eds.
1988   ISBN 0-88132-071-3

Japan in the World Economy*   Bela Balassa and Marcus Noland
1988   ISBN 0-88132-041-2

America in the World Economy: A Strategy for the 1990s*   C. Fred Bergsten
1988   ISBN 0-88132-089-7

Managing the Dollar: From the Plaza to the Louvre*   Yoichi Funabashi
1988, 2d ed. 1989   ISBN 0-88132-097-8

United States External Adjustment and the World Economy*   William R. Cline
May 1989   ISBN 0-88132-048-X

Free Trade Areas and U.S. Trade Policy*
Jeffrey J. Schott, ed.
May 1989   ISBN 0-88132-094-3

Dollar Politics: Exchange Rate Policymaking in the United States*   I. M. Destler and C. Randall Henning
September 1989   ISBN 0-88132-079-X

Latin American Adjustment: How Much Has Happened?*   John Williamson, ed.
April 1990   ISBN 0-88132-125-7

The Future of World Trade in Textiles and Apparel*   William R. Cline
1987, 2d ed. June 1999   ISBN 0-88132-110-9

Completing the Uruguay Round: A Results-Oriented Approach to the GATT Trade Negotiations*   Jeffrey J. Schott, ed.
September 1990   ISBN 0-88132-130-3

Economic Sanctions Reconsidered (2 volumes)
Economic Sanctions Reconsidered: Supplemental Case Histories*   Gary Clyde Hufbauer, Jeffrey J. Schott, and Kimberly Ann Elliott
1985, 2d ed. Dec. 1990   ISBN cloth 0-88132-115-X/ paper 0-88132-105-2

Economic Sanctions Reconsidered: History and Current Policy*   Gary Clyde Hufbauer, Jeffrey J. Schott, and Kimberly Ann Elliott
December 1990   ISBN cloth 0-88132-140-0
ISBN paper 0-88132-136-2

Pacific Basin Developing Countries: Prospects for the Future*   Marcus Noland
January 1991   ISBN cloth 0-88132-141-9
ISBN paper 0-88132-081-1

Currency Convertibility in Eastern Europe
John Williamson, ed.
October 1991 ISBN 0-88132-128-1

Foreign Direct Investment in the United States, 2d ed.* Edward M. Graham and Paul R. Krugman
January 1991 ISBN 0-88132-139-7

International Adjustment and Financing: The Lessons of 1985–1991* C. Fred Bergsten, ed.
January 1992 ISBN 0-88132-112-5

North American Free Trade: Issues and Recommendations* Gary Clyde Hufbauer and Jeffrey J. Schott
April 1992 ISBN 0-88132-120-6

Narrowing the U.S. Current Account Deficit*
Alan J. Lenz
June 1992 ISBN 0-88132-103-6

The Economics of Global Warming
William R. Cline
June 1992 ISBN 0-88132-132-X

US Taxation of International Income: Blueprint for Reform* Gary Clyde Hufbauer, assisted by Joanna M. van Rooij
October 1992 ISBN 0-88132-134-6

Who's Bashing Whom? Trade Conflict in High-Technology Industries Laura D'Andrea Tyson
November 1992 ISBN 0-88132-106-0

Korea in the World Economy* Il SaKong
January 1993 ISBN 0-88132-183-4

Pacific Dynamism and the International Economic System* C. Fred Bergsten and Marcus Noland, eds.
May 1993 ISBN 0-88132-196-6

Economic Consequences of Soviet Disintegration* John Williamson, ed.
May 1993 ISBN 0-88132-190-7

Reconcilable Differences? United States-Japan Economic Conflict* C. Fred Bergsten and Marcus Noland
June 1993 ISBN 0-88132-129-X

Does Foreign Exchange Intervention Work?
Kathryn M. Dominguez and Jeffrey A. Frankel
September 1993 ISBN 0-88132-104-4

Sizing Up U.S. Export Disincentives*
J. David Richardson
September 1993 ISBN 0-88132-107-9

NAFTA: An Assessment* Gary Clyde Hufbauer and Jeffrey J. Schott, *rev. ed.*
October 1993 ISBN 0-88132-199-0

Adjusting to Volatile Energy Prices
Philip K. Verleger, Jr.
November 1993 ISBN 0-88132-069-2

The Political Economy of Policy Reform
John Williamson, ed.
January 1994 ISBN 0-88132-195-8

Measuring the Costs of Protection in the United States Gary Clyde Hufbauer and Kimberly Ann Elliott
January 1994 ISBN 0-88132-108-7

The Dynamics of Korean Economic Development Cho Soon
March 1994 ISBN 0-88132-162-1

Reviving the European Union*
C. Randall Henning, Eduard Hochreiter, and Gary Clyde Hufbauer, eds.
April 1994 ISBN 0-88132-208-3

China in the World Economy Nicholas R. Lardy
April 1994 ISBN 0-88132-200-8

Greening the GATT: Trade, Environment, and the Future Daniel C. Esty
July 1994 ISBN 0-88132-205-9

Western Hemisphere Economic Integration*
Gary Clyde Hufbauer and Jeffrey J. Schott
July 1994 ISBN 0-88132-159-1

Currencies and Politics in the United States, Germany, and Japan C. Randall Henning
September 1994 ISBN 0-88132-127-3

Estimating Equilibrium Exchange Rates
John Williamson, ed.
September 1994 ISBN 0-88132-076-5

Managing the World Economy: Fifty Years after Bretton Woods Peter B. Kenen, ed.
September 1994 ISBN 0-88132-212-1

Trade Liberalization and International Institutions* Jeffrey J. Schott
September 1994 ISBN 978-0-88132-3

Reciprocity and Retaliation in U.S. Trade Policy*
Thomas O. Bayard and Kimberly Ann Elliott
September 1994 ISBN 0-88132-084-6

The Uruguay Round: An Assessment*
Jeffrey J. Schott, assisted by Johanna Buurman
November 1994 ISBN 0-88132-206-7

Measuring the Costs of Protection in Japan*
Yoko Sazanami, Shujiro Urata, and Hiroki Kawai
January 1995 ISBN 0-88132-211-3

Foreign Direct Investment in the United States, 3d ed. Edward M. Graham and Paul R. Krugman
January 1995 ISBN 0-88132-204-0

The Political Economy of Korea-United States Cooperation* C. Fred Bergsten and Il SaKong, eds.
February 1995 ISBN 0-88132-213-X

International Debt Reexamined* William R. Cline
February 1995 ISBN 0-88132-083-8

American Trade Politics, 3d ed.* I. M. Destler
April 1995 ISBN 0-88132-215-6

Managing Official Export Credits: The Quest for a Global Regime* John E. Ray
July 1995 ISBN 0-88132-207-5

Asia Pacific Fusion: Japan's Role in APEC
Yoichi Funabashi
October 1995 ISBN 0-88132-224-5

Korea-United States Cooperation in the New World Order* C. Fred Bergsten and Il SaKong, eds.
February 1996 ISBN 0-88132-226-1

Why Exports Really Matter!*ISBN 0-88132-221-0
Why Exports Matter More!* ISBN 0-88132-229-6
J. David Richardson and Karin Rindal
July 1995; February 1996

Global Corporations and National Governments
Edward M. Graham
May 1996 ISBN 0-88132-111-7

Global Economic Leadership and the Group of Seven C. Fred Bergsten and C. Randall Henning
May 1996 ISBN 0-88132-218-0

The Trading System after the Uruguay Round*
John Whalley and Colleen Hamilton
July 1996 ISBN 0-88132-131-1

Private Capital Flows to Emerging Markets after the Mexican Crisis* Guillermo A. Calvo, Morris Goldstein, and Eduard Hochreiter
September 1996 ISBN 0-88132-232-6

The Crawling Band as an Exchange Rate Regime: Lessons from Chile, Colombia, and Israel
John Williamson
September 1996 ISBN 0-88132-231-8

Flying High: Liberalizing Civil Aviation in the Asia Pacific* Gary Clyde Hufbauer and Christopher Findlay
November 1996 ISBN 0-88132-227-X

Measuring the Costs of Visible Protection in Korea* Namdoo Kim
November 1996 ISBN 0-88132-236-9

The World Trading System: Challenges Ahead
Jeffrey J. Schott
December 1996 ISBN 0-88132-235-0

Has Globalization Gone Too Far? Dani Rodrik
March 1997 ISBN paper 0-88132-241-5

Korea-United States Economic Relationship*
C. Fred Bergsten and Il SaKong, eds.
March 1997 ISBN 0-88132-240-7

Summitry in the Americas: A Progress Report*
Richard E. Feinberg
April 1997 ISBN 0-88132-242-3

Corruption and the Global Economy
Kimberly Ann Elliott
June 1997 ISBN 0-88132-233-4

Regional Trading Blocs in the World Economic System Jeffrey A. Frankel
October 1997 ISBN 0-88132-202-4

Sustaining the Asia Pacific Miracle: Environmental Protection and Economic Integration Andre Dua and Daniel C. Esty
October 1997 ISBN 0-88132-250-4

Trade and Income Distribution
William R. Cline
November 1997 ISBN 0-88132-216-4

Global Competition Policy Edward M. Graham and J. David Richardson
December 1997 ISBN 0-88132-166-4

Unfinished Business: Telecommunications after the Uruguay Round Gary Clyde Hufbauer and Erika Wada
December 1997 ISBN 0-88132-257-1

Financial Services Liberalization in the WTO
Wendy Dobson and Pierre Jacquet
June 1998 ISBN 0-88132-254-7

Restoring Japan's Economic Growth
Adam S. Posen
September 1998 ISBN 0-88132-262-8

Measuring the Costs of Protection in China
Zhang Shuguang, Zhang Yansheng, and Wan Zhongxin
November 1998 ISBN 0-88132-247-4

Foreign Direct Investment and Development: The New Policy Agenda for Developing Countries and Economies in Transition
Theodore H. Moran
December 1998 ISBN 0-88132-258-X

Behind the Open Door: Foreign Enterprises in the Chinese Marketplace Daniel H. Rosen
January 1999 ISBN 0-88132-263-6

Toward A New International Financial Architecture: A Practical Post-Asia Agenda
Barry Eichengreen
February 1999 ISBN 0-88132-270-9

Is the U.S. Trade Deficit Sustainable?
Catherine L. Mann
September 1999 ISBN 0-88132-265-2

Safeguarding Prosperity in a Global Financial System: The Future International Financial Architecture, Independent Task Force Report Sponsored by the Council on Foreign Relations
Morris Goldstein, Project Director
October 1999 ISBN 0-88132-287-3

Avoiding the Apocalypse: The Future of the Two Koreas Marcus Noland
June 2000 ISBN 0-88132-278-4

Assessing Financial Vulnerability: An Early Warning System for Emerging Markets
Morris Goldstein, Graciela Kaminsky, and Carmen Reinhart
June 2000 ISBN 0-88132-237-7

Global Electronic Commerce: A Policy Primer
Catherine L. Mann, Sue E. Eckert, and Sarah Cleeland Knight
July 2000 ISBN 0-88132-274-1

The WTO after Seattle Jeffrey J. Schott, ed.
July 2000 ISBN 0-88132-290-3

Intellectual Property Rights in the Global Economy Keith E. Maskus
August 2000 ISBN 0-88132-282-2

The Political Economy of the Asian Financial Crisis Stephan Haggard
August 2000 ISBN 0-88132-283-0

Transforming Foreign Aid: United States Assistance in the 21st Century* Carol Lancaster
August 2000 ISBN 0-88132-291-1

Fighting the Wrong Enemy: Antiglobal Activists and Multinational Enterprises
Edward M. Graham
September 2000 ISBN 0-88132-272-5

Globalization and the Perceptions of American Workers Kenneth Scheve and Matthew J. Slaughter
March 2001 ISBN 0-88132-295-4

World Capital Markets: Challenge to the G-10
Wendy Dobson and Gary Clyde Hufbauer, assisted by Hyun Koo Cho
May 2001 ISBN 0-88132-301-2

Prospects for Free Trade in the Americas
Jeffrey J. Schott
August 2001 ISBN 0-88132-275-X

Toward a North American Community: Lessons from the Old World for the New Robert A. Pastor
August 2001 ISBN 0-88132-328-4

Measuring the Costs of Protection in Europe: European Commercial Policy in the 2000s
Patrick A. Messerlin
September 2001 ISBN 0-88132-273-3

Job Loss from Imports: Measuring the Costs
Lori G. Kletzer
September 2001 ISBN 0-88132-296-2

No More Bashing: Building a New Japan–United States Economic Relationship C. Fred Bergsten, Takatoshi Ito, and Marcus Noland
October 2001 ISBN 0-88132-286-5

Why Global Commitment Really Matters!
Howard Lewis III and J. David Richardson
October 2001 ISBN 0-88132-298-9

Leadership Selection in the Major Multilaterals
Miles Kahler
November 2001   ISBN 0-88132-335-7

The International Financial Architecture:
What's New? What's Missing?   Peter B. Kenen
November 2001   ISBN 0-88132-297-0

Delivering on Debt Relief: From IMF Gold to a
New Aid Architecture   John Williamson and
Nancy Birdsall, with Brian Deese
April 2002   ISBN 0-88132-331-4

Imagine There's No Country: Poverty,
Inequality, and Growth in the Era of
Globalization   Surjit S. Bhalla
September 2002   ISBN 0-88132-348-9

Reforming Korea's Industrial Conglomerates
Edward M. Graham
January 2003   ISBN 0-88132-337-3

Industrial Policy in an Era of Globalization:
Lessons from Asia   Marcus Noland and
Howard Pack
March 2003   ISBN 0-88132-350-0

Reintegrating India with the World Economy
T. N. Srinivasan and Suresh D. Tendulkar
March 2003   ISBN 0-88132-280-6

After the Washington Consensus: Restarting
Growth and Reform in Latin America
Pedro-Pablo Kuczynski and John Williamson, eds.
March 2003   ISBN 0-88132-347-0

The Decline of US Labor Unions and the Role of
Trade   Robert E. Baldwin
June 2003   ISBN 0-88132-341-1

Can Labor Standards Improve under
Globalization?   Kimberly Ann Elliott and
Richard B. Freeman
June 2003   ISBN 0-88132-332-2

Crimes and Punishments? Retaliation under the
WTO   Robert Z. Lawrence
October 2003   ISBN 0-88132-359-4

Inflation Targeting in the World Economy
Edwin M. Truman
October 2003   ISBN 0-88132-345-4

Foreign Direct Investment and Tax Competition
John H. Mutti
November 2003   ISBN 0-88132-352-7

Has Globalization Gone Far Enough? The Costs
of Fragmented Markets   Scott C. Bradford and
Robert Z. Lawrence
February 2004   ISBN 0-88132-349-7

Food Regulation and Trade: Toward a Safe and
Open Global System   Tim Josling, Donna Roberts,
and David Orden
March 2004   ISBN 0-88132-346-2

Controlling Currency Mismatches in Emerging
Markets   Morris Goldstein and Philip Turner
April 2004   ISBN 0-88132-360-8

Free Trade Agreements: US Strategies and
Priorities   Jeffrey J. Schott, ed.
April 2004   ISBN 0-88132-361-6

Trade Policy and Global Poverty
William R. Cline
June 2004   ISBN 0-88132-365-9

Bailouts or Bail-ins? Responding to Financial
Crises in Emerging Economies   Nouriel Roubini
and Brad Setser
August 2004   ISBN 0-88132-371-3

Transforming the European Economy
Martin Neil Baily and Jacob Funk Kirkegaard
September 2004   ISBN 0-88132-343-8

Getting Aid To Work: Politics, Policies and
Incentives For Poor Countries*
Nicolas Van De Walle
September 2004   ISBN 0-88132-379-9

Chasing Dirty Money: The Fight Against Money
Laundering   Peter Reuter and Edwin M. Truman
November 2004   ISBN 0-88132-370-5

The United States and the World Economy:
Foreign Economic Policy for the Next Decade
C. Fred Bergsten
January 2005   ISBN 0-88132-380-2

Does Foreign Direct Investment Promote
Development?   Theodore H. Moran,
Edward M. Graham, and Magnus Blomström, eds.
April 2005   ISBN 0-88132-381-0

American Trade Politics, 4th ed.   I. M. Destler
June 2005   ISBN 0-88132-382-9

Shell Global Scenarios to 2025: The Future
Business Environment: Trends, Trade-offs and
Choices*
June 2005   ISBN 0-88132-383-7

Why Does Immigration Divide America? Public
Finance and Political Opposition to Open
Borders   Gordon H. Hanson
August 2005   ISBN 0-88132-400-0

Reforming the US Corporate Tax
Gary Clyde Hufbauer and Paul L. E. Grieco
September 2005   ISBN 0-88132-384-5

The United States as a Debtor Nation
William R. Cline
September 2005   ISBN 0-88132-399-3

NAFTA Revisited: Achievements and Challenges
Gary Clyde Hufbauer and Jeffrey J. Schott, assisted
by Paul L. E. Grieco and Yee Wong
October 2005   ISBN 0-88132-334-9

US National Security and Foreign Direct
Investment   Edward M. Graham and
David M. Marchick
May 2006   ISBN 978-0-88132-391-7

Accelerating the Globalization of America: The
Role for Information Technology
Catherine L. Mann, assisted by Jacob Funk
Kirkegaard
June 2006   ISBN 978-0-88132-390-0

China: The Balance Sheet: What the
World Needs to Know about the Emerging
Superpower*
Center for Strategic and International Studies and
Institute for International Economics
2006   ISBN 978-1-58648-464-4

Delivering on Doha: Farm Trade and the Poor
Kimberly Ann Elliott
July 2006   ISBN 978-0-88132-392-4

Case Studies in US Trade Negotiation, Vol. 1:
Making the Rules   Charan Devereaux,
Robert Z. Lawrence, and Michael Watkins
September 2006   ISBN 978-0-88132-362-7

Case Studies in US Trade Negotiation, Vol. 2:
Resolving Disputes   Charan Devereaux,
Robert Z. Lawrence, and Michael Watkins
September 2006   ISBN 978-0-88132-363-2

C. Fred Bergsten and the World Economy
Michael Mussa, ed.
December 2006   ISBN 978-0-88132-397-9
Working Papers, Volume I   Peterson Institute
December 2006   ISBN 978-0-88132-388-7
The Arab Economies in a Changing World
Marcus Noland and Howard Pack
April 2007   ISBN 978-0-88132-393-1
Working Papers, Volume II Peterson Institute
April 2007   ISBN 978-0-88132-404-4
**Global Warming and Agriculture: Impact
Estimates by Country**   William R. Cline
July 2007   ISBN 978-0-88132-403-7
US Taxation of Foreign Income
Gary Clyde Hufbauer and Ariel Assa
October 2007   ISBN 978-0-88132-405-1
**Russia's Capitalist Revolution: Why Market
Reform Succeeded and Democracy Failed**
Anders Åslund
October 2007   ISBN 978-0-88132-409-9
Economic Sanctions Reconsidered, 3d ed.
Gary Clyde Hufbauer, Jeffrey J. Schott, Kimberly
Ann Elliott, and Barbara Oegg
November 2007
          ISBN hardcover 978-0-88132-407-5
     ISBN hardcover/CD-ROM 978-0-88132-408-2
Debating China's Exchange Rate Policy
Morris Goldstein and Nicholas R. Lardy, eds.
April 2008   ISBN 978-0-88132-415-0
**Leveling the Carbon Playing Field: International
Competition and US Climate Policy Design**
Trevor Houser, Rob Bradley, Britt Childs, Jacob
Werksman, and Robert Heilmayr
May 2008   ISBN 978-0-88132-420-4
**Accountability and Oversight of US Exchange
Rate Policy**   C. Randall Henning
June 2008   ISBN 978-0-88132-419-8
**Challenges of Globalization: Imbalances and
Growth** Anders Åslund and Marek Dabrowski, eds.
July 2008   ISBN 978-0-88132-418-1
China's Rise: Challenges and Opportunities
C. Fred Bergsten, Charles Freeman, Nicholas R.
Lardy, and Derek J. Mitchell
September 2008   ISBN 978-0-88132-417-4
**Banking on Basel: The Future of International
Financial Regulation**   Daniel K. Tarullo
September 2008   ISBN 978-0-88132-423-5
**US Pension Reform: Lessons from Other
Countries**   Martin Neil Baily and
Jacob Funk Kirkegaard
February 2009   ISBN 978-0-88132-425-9
**How Ukraine Became a Market Economy and
Democracy**   Anders Åslund
March 2009   ISBN 978-0-88132-427-3
Global Warming and the World Trading System
Gary Clyde Hufbauer, Steve Charnovitz, and Jisun
Kim
March 2009   ISBN 978-0-88132-428-0
The Russia Balance Sheet   Anders Åslund and
Andrew Kuchins
March 2009   ISBN 978-0-88132-424-2
The Euro at Ten: The Next Global Currency?
Jean Pisani-Ferry and Adam S. Posen, eds.
July 2009   ISBN 978-0-88132-430-3

**Financial Globalization, Economic Growth, and
the Crisis of 2007–09**   William R. Cline
May 2010   ISBN 978-0-88132-499-0
Russia after the Global Economic Crisis
Anders Åslund, Sergei Guriev, and Andrew Kuchins,
eds.
June 2010   ISBN 978-0-88132-497-6
Sovereign Wealth Funds: Threat or Salvation?
Edwin M. Truman
September 2010   ISBN 978-0-88132-498-3
**The Last Shall Be the First: The East European
Financial Crisis, 2008–10**   Anders Åslund
October 2010   ISBN 978-0-88132-521-8
**Witness to Transformation: Refugee Insights
into North Korea**   Stephan Haggard and
Marcus Noland
January 2011   ISBN 978-0-88132-438-9
**Foreign Direct Investment and Development:
Launching a Second Generation of Policy
Research, Avoiding the Mistakes of the First,
Reevaluating Policies for Developed and
Developing Countries**   Theodore H. Moran
April 2011   ISBN 978-0-88132-600-0
How Latvia Came through the Financial Crisis
Anders Åslund and Valdis Dombrovskis
May 2011   ISBN 978-0-88132-602-4
**Global Trade in Services: Fear, Facts, and
Offshoring**   J. Bradford Jensen
August 2011   ISBN 978-0-88132-601-7
NAFTA and Climate Change Meera Fickling and
Jeffrey J. Schott
September 2011   ISBN 978-0-88132-436-5
**Eclipse: Living in the Shadow of China's
Economic Dominance**   Arvind Subramanian
September 2011   ISBN 978-0-88132-606-2
**Flexible Exchange Rates for a Stable World
Economy**   Joseph E. Gagnon with
Marc Hinterschweiger
September 2011   ISBN 978-0-88132-627-7
**The Arab Economies in a Changing World,
2d ed.**   Marcus Noland and Howard Pack
November 2011   ISBN 978-0-88132-628-4
**Sustaining China's Economic Growth After the
Global Financial Crisis**   Nicholas R. Lardy
January 2012   ISBN 978-0-88132-626-0
Who Needs to Open the Capital Account?
Olivier Jeanne, Arvind Subramanian, and John
Williamson
April 2012   ISBN 978-0-88132-511-9
**Devaluing to Prosperity: Misaligned Currencies
and Their Growth Consequences** Surjit S. Bhalla
August 2012   ISBN 978-0-88132-623-9
**Private Rights and Public Problems: The Global
Economics of Intellectual Property in the 21st
Century**   Keith E. Maskus
September 2012   ISBN 978-0-88132-507-2
**Global Economics in Extraordinary Times:
Essays in Honor of John Williamson**
C. Fred Bergsten and C. Randall Henning, eds.
November 2012   ISBN 978-0-88132-662-8
**Rising Tide: Is Growth in Emerging Economies
Good for the United States?**   Lawrence Edwards
and Robert Z. Lawrence
February 2013   ISBN 978-0-88132-500-3

Responding to Financial Crisis: Lessons from Asia Then, the United States and Europe Now
Changyong Rhee and Adam S. Posen, eds.
October 2013 ISBN 978-0-88132-674-1
Fueling Up: The Economic Implications of America's Oil and Gas Boom Trevor Houser and Shashank Mohan
January 2014 ISBN 978-0-88132-656-7
How Latin America Weathered the Global Financial Crisis José De Gregorio
January 2014 ISBN 978-0-88132-678-9
Confronting the Curse: The Economics and Geopolitics of Natural Resource Governance
Cullen S. Hendrix and Marcus Noland
May 2014 ISBN 978-0-88132-676-5
Inside the Euro Crisis: An Eyewitness Account
Simeon Djankov
June 2014 ISBN 978-0-88132-685-7
Managing the Euro Area Debt Crisis
William R. Cline
June 2014 ISBN 978-0-88132-687-1
Markets over Mao: The Rise of Private Business in China Nicholas R. Lardy
September 2014 ISBN 978-0-88132-693-2
Bridging the Pacific: Toward Free Trade and Investment between China and the United States
C. Fred Bergsten, Gary Clyde Hufbauer, and Sean Miner. Assisted by Tyler Moran
October 2014 ISBN 978-0-88132-691-8
The Great Rebirth: Lessons from the Victory of Capitalism over Communism
Anders Åslund and Simeon Djankov, eds.
November 2014 ISBN 978-0-88132-697-0
Ukraine: What Went Wrong and How to Fix It
Anders Åslund
April 2015 ISBN 978-0-88132-701-4
From Stress to Growth: Strengthening Asia's Financial Systems in a Post-Crisis World
Marcus Noland; Donghyun Park, eds.
October 2015 ISBN 978-0-88132-699-4
The Great Tradeoff: Confronting Moral Conflicts in the Era of Globalization
Steven R. Weisman
January 2016 ISBN 978-0-88132-695-6
Rich People, Poor Countries: The Rise of Emerging-Market Tycoons and their Mega Firms Caroline Freund, assisted by Sarah Oliver
January 2016 ISBN 978-0-88132-703-8
International Monetary Cooperation: Lessons from the Plaza Accord After Thirty Years
C. Fred Bergsten and Russell A. Green, eds.
April 2016 ISBN 978-0-88132-711-3
Currency Conflict and Trade Policy: A New Strategy for the United States C. Fred Bergsten and Joseph E. Gagnon
June 2017 ISBN 978-0-88132-711-3
Sustaining Economic Growth in Asia
Jérémie Cohen-Setton, Thomas Helbling, Adam S. Posen, and Changyong Rhee, eds.
December 2018 ISBN 978-0-88132-733-5

SPECIAL REPORTS

1   Promoting World Recovery: A Statement on Global Economic Strategy* by Twenty-six Economists from Fourteen Countries
December 1982 ISBN 0-88132-013-7
2   Prospects for Adjustment in Argentina, Brazil, and Mexico: Responding to the Debt Crisis* John Williamson, ed.
June 1983 ISBN 0-88132-016-1
3   Inflation and Indexation: Argentina, Brazil, and Israel* John Williamson, ed.
March 1985 ISBN 0-88132-037-4
4   Global Economic Imbalances*
C. Fred Bergsten, ed.
March 1986 ISBN 0-88132-042-0
5   African Debt and Financing* Carol Lancaster and John Williamson, eds.
May 1986 ISBN 0-88132-044-7
6   Resolving the Global Economic Crisis: After Wall Street* by Thirty-three Economists from Thirteen Countries
December 1987 ISBN 0-88132-070-6
7   World Economic Problems*
Kimberly Ann Elliott and John Williamson, eds.
April 1988 ISBN 0-88132-055-2
Reforming World Agricultural Trade*
by Twenty-nine Professionals from Seventeen Countries
1988 ISBN 0-88132-088-9
8   Economic Relations Between the United States and Korea: Conflict or Cooperation?*
Thomas O. Bayard and Soogil Young, eds.
January 1989 ISBN 0-88132-068-4
9   Whither APEC? The Progress to Date and Agenda for the Future* C. Fred Bergsten, ed.
October 1997 ISBN 0-88132-248-2
10 Economic Integration of the Korean Peninsula Marcus Noland, ed.
January 1998 ISBN 0-88132-255-5
11 Restarting Fast Track* Jeffrey J. Schott, ed.
April 1998 ISBN 0-88132-259-8
12 Launching New Global Trade Talks: An Action Agenda Jeffrey J. Schott, ed.
September 1998 ISBN 0-88132-266-0
13 Japan's Financial Crisis and Its Parallels to US Experience Ryoichi Mikitani and Adam S. Posen, eds.
September 2000 ISBN 0-88132-289-X
14 The Ex-Im Bank in the 21st Century: A New Approach Gary Clyde Hufbauer and Rita M. Rodriguez, eds.
January 2001 ISBN 0-88132-300-4
15 The Korean Diaspora in the World Economy C. Fred Bergsten and Inbom Choi, eds.
January 2003 ISBN 0-88132-358-6
16 Dollar Overvaluation and the World Economy C. Fred Bergsten and John Williamson, eds.
February 2003 ISBN 0-88132-351-9

17 Dollar Adjustment: How Far? Against
    What? C. Fred Bergsten and John Williamson,
    eds.
    November 2004   ISBN 0-88132-378-0
18 The Euro at Five: Ready for a Global Role?
    Adam S. Posen, ed.
    April 2005   ISBN 0-88132-380-2
19 Reforming the IMF for the 21st Century
    Edwin M. Truman, ed.
    April 2006   ISBN 978-0-88132-387-0
20 The Long-Term International Economic
    Position of the United States
    C. Fred Bergsten, ed.
    May 2009   ISBN 978-0-88132-432-7
21 Resolving the European Debt Crisis
    William R. Cline and Guntram B. Wolff, eds.
    February 2012   ISBN 978-0-88132-642-0
22 Transatlantic Economic Challenges in an
    Era of Growing Multipolarity
    Jacob Funk Kirkegaard, Nicolas Véron, and
    Guntram B. Wolff, eds.
    June 2012   ISBN 978-0-88132-645-1

PIIE BRIEFINGS

14-1 Flirting With Default: Issues Raised by
      Debt Confrontations in the United States
      February 2014
14-2 The US-China-Europe Economic
      Reform Agenda. Papers presented at a
      Symposium in Beijing   *May 2014*
14-3 NAFTA: 20 Years Later   *November 2014*
14-4 Lessons from Decades Lost: Economic
      Challenges and Opportunities Facing
      Japan and the United States (with
      Sasakawa Peace Foundation USA)
      December 2014
14-5 Rebuilding Europe's Common Future:
      Combining Growth and Reform in the
      Euro Area   *December 2014*
15-1 Toward a US-China Investment Treaty
      February 2015   ISBN 978-0-88132-707-6
15-2 Raising Lower-Level Wages: When and
      Why It Makes Economic Sense
      April 2015   ISBN 978-0-88132-709-3
15-3 China's Economic Transformation:
      Lessons, Impact, and the Path Forward
      September 2015   ISBN 978-0-88132-709-0

15-4 India's Rise: A Strategy for Trade-Led
      Growth   C. Fred Bergsten
      September 2015   ISBN 978-0-88132-710-6
16-1 Assessing the Trans-Pacific Partnership,
      volume 1: Market Access and Sectoral
      Issues   *February 2016*
16-2 China's Belt and Road Initiative: Motives,
      Scope, and Challenges
      Simeon Djankov and Sean Miner, eds. *March
      2016*
16-3 Reality Check for the Global Economy
      Olivier Blanchard and Adam S. Posen, eds.
      March 2016   ISBN 978-0-88132-718-2
16-4 Assessing the Trans-Pacific Partnership,
      volume 2: Innovations in Trading Rules
      Jeffrey J. Schott and
      Cathleen Cimino-Isaacs, eds.   *March 2016*
16-5 China's New Economic Frontier:
      Overcoming Obstacles to Continued
      Growth   Sean Miner, ed.
16-6 Assessing Trade Agendas in the US
      Presidential Campaign   Marcus Noland,
      Gary Clyde Hufbauer, Sherman Robinson,
      and Tyler Moran
16-7 Prospects for Taiwan's Participation in
      the Trans-Pacific Partnership
      Jeffrey J. Schott, Cathleen Cimino-Isaacs,
      Zhiyao (Lucy) Lu, and Sean Miner
17-1 US-China Cooperation in a Changing
      Global Economy   Adam S. Posen and
      Jiming Ha, eds.   *June 2017*
17-2 A Path Forward for NAFTA
      C. Fred Bergsten and Monica de Bolle, eds.
      July 2017   eISBN 978-0-88132-730-4
18-1 Part I. US-China Economic Relations:
      From Conflict to Solutions Ha Jiming and
      Adam S. Posen, editors   *June 2018*

BOOKS IN PROGRESS

Facing Up to Low Productivity Growth
Adam S. Posen and Jeromin Zettelmeyer, eds.
The State Strikes Back: The End of Economic
Reform in China?   Nicholas R. Lardy
China, the United States, and the
Transformation of the Global Economic Order
C. Fred Bergsten